The Celtic Seers' Source Book

Vision and Magic in the Druid Tradition

EDITED AND SELECTED BY
JOHN MATTHEWS

Foreword by Caitlín Matthews

BLANDFORD

To all who follow the druid path

First published in the United Kingdom in 1999 by Blandford

Compilation and original texts copyright © 1999 John Matthews

Foreword copyright © 1999 Caitlín Matthews

Design and layout copyright © Blandford 1999

Distributed in the United States of America by Sterling Publishing Co., Inc. 387 Park Avenue South, New York, NY 10016–8810

A CIP catalogue record for this book is available from the British Library

ISBN 0–7137–2780–2

Typeset by Ben Cracknell Studios

Printed and bound in Great Britain by MPG Books Ltd, Bodmin, Cornwall

Blandford
Illustrated Division
The Orion Publishing Group
Wellington House
125 Strand
London WC2R 0BB

Contents

RESOURCES

Hallowquest Newsletter
John and Caitlín Matthews produce a quarterly newsletter that includes information on new and forthcoming books, workshops and lectures and other news. For a sample issue please send a stamped addressed envelope and eight first-class stamps (UK) or US$5.00 (worldwide) to BCM Hallowquest, London WC1N 3XX. See their web site: www.hallowquest.org.uk

Order of Bards, Ovates and Druids
For information about and details of correspondence courses, please send a stamped addressed envelope to PO Box 1333, Lewes, Sussex BN7 37G.

ACKNOWLEDGEMENTS

I am more than usually indebted to my wife, Caitlín, for the considerable input and help she gave me in the preparation of this book. Not only did she provide me with a wonderful Foreword but also with an extraordinary chapter on the Spells of Women. In addition to this, she allowed me to pillage her notes on augury and inspiration, to the point where I almost feel her name should be on the introduction rather than mine. For all this, and much more, I am eternally grateful to her, as well as to all the poets, visionaries, translators and writers whose work has gone into making what is, I hope, an exciting collection.

J.M.

FOREWORD

Readings from Rocks, Teachings from Trees

The Living Druidic Oral Tradition

MANY PEOPLE SHARE A CONCERN that our past was a long time ago and that our oral tradition is largely lost: that the fragments that are left do not give us a sufficient body of evidence to support our practice. I do not believe that this is true. The oral traditions of this land do not die just because there are not enough people to carry them forwards; they remain in the rocks, trees and waters, in the interwoven spirals of the elements, in the ground beneath our feet, in the animals and creatures and plants that surround us – they are in the very cells of our bodies.

There are many stories from our tradition that tell how forgetfulness became an issue for our ancestors, and in this connection the story of Mabon's finding comes to mind. The story plainly reveals the subtle ladder of living connection between human loss and animal wisdom: the vatic interpreter of tongues speaks to the animals and is led, by way of a series of animal encounters and referrals, to the prison of Mabon. Similarly, there is a time when the story of the *Taín Bó Cuailgnè* ('The Cattle Raid of Cooley') has been imperfectly remembered – the storytellers just haven't been doing their job – and the spirit of an ancestral storyteller has to be summoned from the otherworlds to fill them in. The message from these and other stories is clear: if you don't know something, ask!

But whom do we ask? First, we have to return to a primal state of connection in which we attune to the weaving of All That Is. This means standing soul to soul with the vast yet intimate threads of connection that link us – through cell, soul and knowledge -- with every particle of life. It also entails living *now*, not in the disappointments of the past nor in the expectations of the future. This is achievable in meditation, in silence, in literally singing a path of connection between ourselves and All That Is. After that, we need to ask and listen.

One of the oldest druidic teaching methods is that of the question. We find it used in many dialogues, extant in Wales and Ireland, to elicit wondrous answers. The more radical, the more *needful* the question, the more helpful and healing is the answer. Silly or inconsequential questions do not serve here, nor do questions whose answers we readily know. We need total darkness in order most to appreciate the light. The question might be about something deeply personal – 'Please show me how peace can be restored between myself and X, with whom I've quarrelled' – or it might be a universal question – 'How lies the land here and now?' 'What help is available for its needs?'

Having formulated a good question, we need to take ourselves outside into nature and make an augury of what is around us, letting our steps be led until we find the right place. Then, with our eyes closed, we ask our question, spin around, stop and see what lies about us on all sides. This method is a traditional *frith* (pron. free) or augury of the elements. Seeing what lies on all sides of us, and above and below us, we can observe the universe in many ways: seeing the trees, animals, clouds, plants and so on with our physical sight, but also looking at these with our subtle sight. Seeing with the *dha shealladh* (second sight; literally 'the two seeings'), we use both physical and subtle sight to read the universe around us. The 'answers' won't necessarily be in words. We may receive impressions, remembrances, tautly drawn connections of information that fire our synapses, strong physiological surgings in our body, tears, laughter, songs. All these are experienced when we take ourselves and our question out into nature and read the answers that are there for us to observe with *all* our senses.

What might look like a robin if we had been taking an ordinary walk, suddenly leaps into prominence as an individual, ensouled being with an intelligent knowing of our question. The answer comes immediately: the piece of stone jutting out of the wall reminds us of obligations left undone; the sway of a hazel branch becomes a blessing; the cry of rooks becomes an urgent warning; the ripple of a rill becomes an encouraging friend. Their messages and answers stream into our consciousness without check and 'hit' the question on the nail with an exactitude and resonance that is uncanny.

This is a very humbling experience and one that restores us to a right relationship with the universe. Although we may not intellectually comprehend every detail of the answer or answers, our body does.

The method is one that we do not utilize in every part and every time. It is one that is best tried when we have spent a period fasting from unnecessary print, radio and television, so that our senses are in good shape and not dulled by the passive reception of media output. It does not work unless it is properly motivated by a good question. The augury of nature is but one method of restoring our oral tradition to us, for this is what members of our druidic spiritual lineage did, and their ancestors before them, back to the first peoples. They read the signs of the universe with a divining eye and a heart full of questions: they read the eternal *now* in which our world meets the otherworld.

This experience is not in the past, nor is it in the future. The answers, the healing, the knowledge are all about us – but not in a finite sense. The tree that yesterday answered my question about healing may give other kinds of information another day when I ask a different kind of question. In this way, we develop the subtle senses whereby we can recognize not only the spiritual and physical forms of vatic allies but can also learn true respect for every living being as the repository of the knowledge of All That Is – a book bigger than anything currently on CD-ROM or any retrieval system that our descendants may yet invent.

I can well understand that it may be hard to accept all that I have written above. Our society has become one that invests authority in written sources and has begun to forget how to read the rocks and to be taught by the trees and animals. We similarly distrust information that comes by subtle means. For some people this sacred work brings them face to face with a frightening lack of control: if it isn't in their heads and brains, then it isn't – it can't be – real. I encourage students to suspend their disbelief for a period, to receive information and to test it for helpfulness and accuracy. If the fruit is good, we can confidently eat of the tree.

Although I have done much research into original source texts of our tradition and have translated many of them, I have always used forms of vatic augury to ask questions about them and about other aspects of spiritual traditions, asking nature, the ancestors and the gods to

6

guide my steps and reveal the way to me. I rarely write about the deep Celtic traditions from a practical perspective out of respect for the way in which I receive *fíos* (pron. fee'us), the oral esoteric knowledge that is found in the universe, rather than *sois* (pron. so'as), the received knowledge of books. Instead, I teach students orally so that they receive immediate and experiential help to foster and encourage their own oral explorations.

The beauty of this way of knowledge is one I would recommend to all students. The books and articles we read are only a half of a much greater body of knowledge, which lies ready and waiting to be recovered from the winds and waters, from the sunlight and the dear earth, from all our kindred who live in the universe, so that we may be once more part of All That Is. The wisdom found in collections like the one you are holding, combined with the natural wisdom of the universe, can bring us back to that deep ancestral place where *all* knowledge becomes accessible.

Caitlín Matthews

INTRODUCTION

Seeing the Truth, Speaking the Truth

The Vatic Tradition among the Celts

*Among the early Celtic peoples the inculcation of poetic
inspiration and the entire mantic art were developed and elaborated to a
degree for which we know of no parallel.*

Nora K. Chadwick, *Poetry and Prophecy*

THE TRADITION OF SEERSHIP and vision among the Celts is among the most highly developed of any early culture. Those who could divine or tell the future were accorded a unique status: they literally kept the life of the tribe in their hands. Among the druids, a separate order, the ovates (from the Latin *vates* or seers), had the task of recording the inner history of the people and of seeking the answers to questions posed both by individuals and the community. This makes them close kin to the shamans of both Celtic and other ancient cultures, whose tasks were identical in most instances, as well as including the offices of doctor and priest. But it is the ability to see beyond the immediate, to travel in the realms of the otherworld and to return with information that made the task of the seer of such extreme importance. Without this gift of insight and knowledge, how were the people to conduct their lives as the gods wished?

References occur throughout the literature and oral traditions of the Celts to a number of methods used in telling the future. These include divination by throwing ogham sticks (this will be dealt with in more detail in Part Two of the present collection); *nealdoracht* (cloud reading); and several kinds of incubatory sleep, in which precognitive dreams were studied and interpreted. E. Ettlinger's essay, included below, deals with this at some length, while Nora K. Chadwick's brilliant chapter on *imbas forosnai* details many others.

The Oracular Seer

Within the context of Celtic culture both ancient and modern, vaticination involves the (frequently oracular) inspiration of the individual by otherworldly beings – spirits, gods, ancestors – and most often includes the voyage of the individual's soul into regions of the Celtic otherworlds.

It is often argued by those who like to pigeonhole history that several centuries separate us from living Celtic tradition. This is not so. Despite the many comings and goings of peoples to these islands at the edge of northwestern Europe, ancient practice and custom have become deeply embedded in the lives of the people and the land. Even the institution of Christianity upon Britain and Ireland has enshrined many Celtic practices – the beating of the boundaries, the maintenance of holy wells and the sunwise circulation and prayer around holy sites to name but a few.[1]

Just because a people live under a regime that does not acknowledge the magical or supernatural areas of life (except within its own narrow theological definitions) does not mean that those people do not require someone to mediate for them in magical or supernatural ways nor does it mean that people with the gift of otherworldly mediation cease to practise. Historically, we see in northwestern Europe, beneath the official Christian culture and its clergy, the creation of a two-tier stratum, consisting of a set of professional augurs, shamans and seers (of varying titles) and a diffusion of increasingly folkloric or superstitious practices, which become the people's own divinatory answer-systems.[2]

Survivals of vatic methods in Britain and Ireland are legion. The most commonly attested method is that found in certain family lines, namely *an dha shealladh* (the second sight). This skill is manifestly inheritable and recurs down the generations. Its reception by family members is often tinged with dismay, for the gift is widely regarded as unfortunate for the individual possessing it. We may speculate whether it is a genetic trait or a gift that descends to members of a family whose ancestor formed the first alliance with the spirit inspiring prophecy. This is certainly the conclusion of the living seer Eilidh Watt from Skye, who has her own *co-imimeadh* (co-walker), a spirit or presence that accompanies her. She believes that her father may have had the gift transferred to him by the hand-clasp of her uncle, a second-sighted seer, who drew her father off the road to let a phantom funeral pass. On the touch of his uncle, her father also shared the grisly apparition and was afterwards able to predict events that came to pass.[3]

Those with the second sight have been formally and professionally employed for their skills, including the freers (augurs), who were retained as seers by the kings of Scotland. The family name, Freer, derives from the Gaelic word *frith* (augury).

On reading the Rev. Robert Kirk's account of Gaelic people's seership and spiritual relationship with the faery folk in the mid-seventeenth century, Samuel Pepys, Charles II's master of espionage, investigated the possibility of employing such seers as spies for his royal master's wars – a Cold War preoccupation of both American and Russian governments.[4]

Those gifted with the second sight see what all people see – the manifest appearance of things – but with its otherworldly appearance superimposed. This is experienced in various ways: the subject may become aware of disjected souls of the living (as when a distant relative is thinking about them) or of the dead (as when someone has recently died) or they will see the foreshadowing of things not yet enacted.

The term 'vatic' derives from the Latin *vates* (prophet), a word that was probably borrowed from the Gauls by the Romans. It originates from the proto-Indo-European term **uat* (to be inspired or possessed).[5] The term *ovateis* is given by the Greek historian Strabo in his description of the different intellectual classes of the Celtic peoples. He defines them as diviners and natural philosophers, assigning bards to the poetic task of praise and druids to the task of moral philosophy.[6] These rather rigid definitions of bard, ovate and druid are not entirely substantiated by the insular Celtic literary traditions of Britain and Ireland, where we find methods of vatic practice occurring in both *filidh* (the oracular or seer poet, whose duties passed beyond poetry into magic) and the druid.

9

In Ireland male seers or diviners were called *fáith* (pl. *fáithi*) – the female equivalent was *ban fáith* – and there is also mention of a *fáthliaig* (divining-doctor), Fingen, who could diagnose the nature of a person's illness before entering the house solely from observing the direction of the smoke from the smoke-hole and from hearing the sighs of the sick. In Britain a seer was known as *offydd* (pl. *offyddion*), but there is little documentation about the role of such people. The function may well have been partially inherited by the Welsh *awenyddion* (see below).

In Britain all aspects of druidry were officially outlawed by the Romans after the Boudiccan revolt of AD64, and all but the bardic tradition seemed to fail. After the institution of Christianity in Ireland we see the assumption of druidic status by certain saints and clerics, leaving the practice of poetry and prophecy to the *filidh* or oracular poets. The role of seer alone found no formal acknowledgement within Christian society, since an oracular seer requires the assistance of spirits in order to function. Seership did not die, however; nor did the vatic tradition. In Ireland today seers, healers and those who use vatic methods are accepted with a respect and seriousness that is not found in England, where such people are mostly ridiculed as fraudulent or deluded. A more cautious respect is accorded seers in modern Scotland and Wales, countries that have, significantly, been overlaid with Protestant, Presbyterian, Methodist and Calvinistic beliefs.

The Three Illuminations

The training of the *filidh* included not only the staples of the poetic life – the verse-forms, the nuts and bolts of poetry – but also the study of 'the three illuminations', a set of prophetic, divinatory methods that were regarded as the achievement and preserve of great poets. Each of these vatic and oracular skills is concerned with accessing the otherworlds by means of the poetic art. It is subtly nearer to prophecy and inspired song than it is to the poetry we understand today.

The bardic or poetic method of vaticination is firmly based on the support of long and arduous training in poetics – not only rhyme, assonance, metrication and so forth, but also in the more radical skills of metaphor, wherein they swim like good swimmers in a strong current. In addition, such long training gave the *filidh* the linguistic dexterity of a lexicographer, enabling them to draw forth from the world-hoard shades and gradations of allusive meaning and to arrange them in a complex marquetry of word-placement and double-meaning.

By immersing him- or herself in a welter of images and metaphors, the poet swims strongly to find the required answer to the querent. Rather like the intelligence of a computer racing down the super-highways of data to draw out the required information, the poet returns triumphantly with the result. Sometimes this process is quite short – the length of time it takes to recite a stanza or two. Sometimes it is a longer process, requiring incubation. To attain this information, the *filidh* engaged in a shamanic process of making an offering to his spirits and then immersing his awareness in the question or problem and allowing his oracular connection to provide the answer.

Draí .i. dorua aí	*Draí* (i.e., inspiration) will arrive
i. aircetal	a poem,
as is tria dán	for it is by poetry
dognisium a brechta.	he makes his spells.[7]

10

Here is a ninth-century description of the practice of *imbas forosnai* or 'the inspiration of tradition' by Cormac mac Cuilleanáin (831–905), the abbot-king of Cashel:

> The poet discovers through it whatever he likes or desires to reveal. This is the way in which it is done: the poet chews a bit of the flesh of a red pig, or of a dog, and he conveys it afterwards to the flag(stone) behind the door and pronounces an incantation on it, and offers it to idol gods, and then invokes his idols; and if he obtains not his desire on the day following, he pronounces incantations over both his palms, and invokes again unto him his idol gods, in order that his sleep may not be interrupted; and he lays his two palms on his two cheeks, and falls asleep; and he is watched, in order that no one may interrupt or disturb him, until every thing about which he is engages in revealed to him viz. in a minute or two or three, or as long as he was supposed to be at the offering.[8] (See also Chapter 3.)

Cormac is describing a practice that had been clerically forbidden in his day and on some points shows hesitation about procedure, yet he clearly tells us about the sharing of meat with the spirits and the subsequent incubation of the question in an invigilated sleep or entranced state. The laying of the palms over the cheeks ensures that the fingers are shielding the eyes from light – a primary requisite for both sleep and the shamanic spirit-voyage. It is possible that such a process was preceded by fasting.

The sacred consumption of the food of the land in order to gain answers is enacted by the druid Bicne:

> And to his successor he passed on this duty, that whenever he could not decide on some dark-meaning question which the men of Ireland posed him he should consume some of its fruit, corn, fish, milk or chestnuts.[9]

Food-offerings remained the chief method of 'sacrifice to spirits' throughout Europe after the spread of Christianity. The slaughter of large animals, like oxen, which yielded meat to feed a whole community, was usually performed in a manner reminiscent of ancient sacrificial rites in which both people and spirits partook of the meat. Throughout Europe such communal festivities continued with full pagan fervour, only marginally allowed and sometimes Christianized by the unofficial canonization of the feast's spirit to saintly status.[10]

The *tarbh feis* (bull-feast), an important communal event in pre-Christian Ireland, was a shamanic method employed to discover the rightful ruler. It involved the sacrifice and skinning of a bull. The druid would eat the flesh and drink the broth of the bull and then lie down for a shamanic, incubatory sleep wrapped in the bull's bloody hide. Four druids would sing incantations over the skin-wrapped druid, while his soul voyaged in search of the answer. On waking, he would tell his spirit-voyage, which would reveal the identity of the ruler.[11]

The second of the three illuminations is the practice of *tenm laida* (cracking open by poetry). It may be aptly described by the poet Cruitíne:

> *is mithid a hiarcháil*
> *no a thoiscél do theinnid.*
>
> One must crack open
> Its additional quality or its secret narrative.[12]

11

The secret narrative or subtext is not about literary meaning but about the hidden or otherworldly appearance of a subject. The Irish hero Fionn mac Cumhail has frequent recourse to this method of oracular divination. He uses it to discover the reasons for a nocturnal attack, as well as to learn the identity of a headless body. Putting his thumb into his mouth, he speaks through the power of *tenm laida*:

> He has not been killed by people –
> He has not been killed by the people of Laighné –
> He has not been killed by a wild boar –
> He has not been killed by a fall –
> He has not died on his bed – Lomna![13]

He further goes on to discover the murderer of Lomna, his fool. We see here that poetic and oracular skill is used to crack the conundrum and that the 'magical thumb' of Fionn is employed. According to a variety of stories, his thumb is imbued with otherworldly wisdom since he touched the Salmon of Wisdom (also known as the Salmon of Knowledge) with it or, alternatively, had it trapped in the door of a faery hill.

The fingers or thumb seem to figure prominently in the lore of seers (as we shall see in Chapter 4), and it is not surprising to find that the last of the three illuminations uses them in a specific way. *Dichetal do chennaib* (invocation from the finger-ends) is described thus: 'When the poet sees the person of thing before him, he makes a verse at once with the ends of his fingers, or in his mind without studying, and he composes and repeats at the same time.'[14] However, before St Patrick brought the New Testament to Ireland, there was another method:

> The poet placed his staff upon the person's body or upon his head, and found out his name, and the name of his father and mother, and discovered every unknown thing that was proposed to him, in a minute or two or three, and this is *tenm laida*.

Dichetal do chennaib was the only authorized method of divination allowed by St Patrick, because: 'he did not leave them after this, any rite in which offering should be made to the devil.' The Christianized rite does not allow for touching the subject nor for invocation of spirits; invocation from the finger-ends is thus robbed of its tactile and spiritually inspired method. In Cormac's *Glossary* we read that the blind *file*, Lugaid, was asked to identify a tiny skull thrown up on a beach. Touching it with his staff, he announces that it is the head of a dog belonging to a man called Brecan, but that he and his family drowned in the sea.[15]

It is interesting to note that in Irish the whorls on the ends of the fingers are called *suil méire*, 'the eyes of the fingers'. 'Seeing with the fingers' is a good description of vatic touch, a kind of psychometric sensing that yields information.

What becomes clear from a study of the three illuminations is that they stem from ancient oracular practices. After the introduction of Christianity to Ireland, these methods were frowned upon by clerics, since two – *imbas forosnai* and *tenm laida* – involved the invocation of pagan gods and spirits. Significantly, the three illuminations are listed in the 'fourteen streams' or qualities expected of an *ollamh* (doctor of poetry):

> Honesty and dignity,
> daily work, genealogy,
> *imbas forosnai* and *dichetal*,

anamain and judgement,
tenm laida and ocean of song,
purity of hand and of marriage,
purity of lips and of study.[16]

(*Anamain* means inspirational verse-form.)

It is notable that, of the fourteen streams that 'flow through' a master poet, three concern *oracular* (the three illuminations) and four *oral* integrity (*anamain*, judgement, song and purity of lips). In total, half of the streams concern vocal skills.

These vatic methods did not endure in their original formats, but the incubatory aspects of the *imbas forosnai* were still in use by the bardic schools of Ireland and Scotland as late as the eighteenth century. Bardic students were given poetic subjects for composition and then secluded in 'houses of darkness'; herein, they would lie, totally covered by a blanket, often with a stone on their chests to prevent drowsiness, to pursue their metaphors in the close darkness. This method of poetic incubation recalls aspects of the *imbas forosnai* and the *tarbh feis*. In the houses of darkness, the answer sought is a poem, its metaphors relentlessly pursued down the pathways of song to the regions of the otherworld.

The Spirit of Inspiration

The Celtic vatic tradition is primarily fuelled by the search for inspiration. Stories about finding *imbas* (in Irish) or *awen* (in Welsh) – both words for inspiration – are at the heart of the vatic tradition. *Imbas* resides in the Salmon of Wisdom, which swims elusively through the training of the *filidh*; *awen* is sought in the inspirational draught of many British cauldrons, from the initiatory cauldron belonging to the goddess, Ceridwen, to the regenerative cup of the Grail.[17]

Inspiration is treated as a spirit that is sought by the practitioner, courted under a variety of bewildering metaphors as a fish, a swiftly rushing river, hazelnuts, a spiral tower, a net of stars, a faery woman – to name but a few. The results of the union between inspiration and the practitioner are described in metaphors of abundance, overwhelming waters, vigorous energy, vortices of penetrative light and so on.

The text of *The Three Cauldrons*, a teaching intended for poetic students, provides a typical example in its description of the poetic reception of inspiration. The journey to the spirit of inspiration is rarely described in so detailed a manner:

joy at the approach of *imbas*
amassed by the nine hazels of fair fruitfulness
in Segais of the *sidhe*,
which hurtles upstream along the Boyne
in a ram's-head bore,
swifter than a three-year-old at the race-track,
in the middle of June each seventh year.[18]

If we turn to the British tradition, we find the art of the *awenydd* (inspired one; pl. *awenyddion*) is also concerned about oracular vision and inspiration. This account is related by the twelfth-century chronicler, Gerald of Wales:

When you consult them about some problem, they immediately go into a trance and lose control of their senses, as if they are possessed. They do not answer the question put to them in any logical way. Words stream from their mouths, incoherently and apparently meaningless and without any sense at all, but all the same well expressed; and if you listen carefully to what they say you will receive the solution to your problem. When it is all over, they will recover from their trance, as if they were ordinary people waking from a heavy sleep, but you have to give them a good shake before they regain control of themselves. ... They seem to receive this gift of divination through visions which they see in their dreams.[19]

Gerald goes on to cite biblical examples of prophecy, then concludes:

You will object that the prophets were not possessed when they prophesied, whereas we read that when Merlin Silvester made his prophecies he was in a frenzy, and in the same way the other soothsayers about whom I have written ... seem to be possessed.[20]

The British *awenyddion* are literally filled with *awen* or inspiration just as the Irish *filidh* are filled with *imbas*. Both are possessed by the spirit of inspiration. The poet pours himself into the augury, journeying through the channels provided by the unfolding metaphor, like a salmon thrashing upstream in order to spawn. This metaphor itself is often used by poets to describe this process, and there are myths about two of the major exponents of the poetic tradition, the British poet, Taliesin, and the Irish poet and hero, Fionn mac Cumhail, in which they are closely associated with the salmon. The possession of the Salmon of Wisdom is the possession of knowledge in the ancient Celtic world.[21]

The image of water is all-important to the Celtic vatic tradition, pervading everything from origination myths of inundation to the great cauldrons that purvey the food of heroes and confer immortality and regeneration. The use of water as the medium of shamanic voyage is paramount. The *immrama* stories of Irish tradition, which describe the wonder voyages to the Blessed Islands of the western otherworld, may themselves constitute a form of map, analogous to a 'Celtic Book of the Dead', in plotting the unfolding states of otherworldly wisdom available to the voyaging soul.[22]

The Ancestral Traditions

As we have seen from the testimony of Eilidh Watt, the transmission of such methods involves the physical touching of the subject by a seer. The Rev. Robert Kirk speaks of 'the investing of a man with the privileges of the whole mystery of the second sight':

He must run a tedder of hair (which bound a corpse to a bier) in a helix about his middle from end to end, and then bow his head downwards, and look back through his legs until he see a funeral advance, till the people cross two Marches; or he may look thus backwards through a hole where there was a knot of fir (in a fir-tree).[23]

It would seem that ancestral contact is an important part of the transmission of both seership and oracular skills. There is an important point to this: the dead have seen the otherworld, and so they may be the transmitters of vatic or inspired vision. In Celtic tradition there are numerous instances of the dead returning and being silenced, possibly for this reason. The

British dead, who are placed in the Cauldron of Rebirth for revival after the raid on Ireland by Bran the Blessed, are brought alive out of the cauldron but are unable to speak. In the foundation hagiography of Iona, St Columba's monastery will not be built until he has performed a very pagan foundation-burial of one of his monks. St Odhran volunteers to be buried alive in order that the monastic settlement may proceed. However, when Columba unearths him in a fit of unease after twenty days, Odhran cheerfully pipes up: 'Hell is not as it has been reported.' Columba orders the earth to be shovelled into the grave immediately, lest Odhran blab out any more unsettling revelations.[24]

The questioning of the ancestors as an oracle stands as a buffer zone between pagan and Christian traditions in Ireland. Many saints consult the spirits of long-dead beings about precedents, stories and customs in order to understand the land in which they are now living. We may even look to the Celtic tradition of head-hunting and veneration in the light of this concept, for the head was considered to be the seat of the soul and the mouthpiece of oracular ancestral wisdom.

Among the pre-Christian Celts and well into the Christian era, the consultation of the ancestors by their descendants has been simply to sit upon a tomb and to ask for the transmission of skills or for revelations and insights into problems. This accords with the practice, common in northwestern Europe, of 'sitting-out', usually on an ancestral site, tomb or sacred hill, in order to obtain answers to problems or for general divinatory purposes. This tradition is not one 'copied' from Native American customs but is a tradition indigenous to Europe, which has precedents in historical documentation.[25]

In more recent times this has devolved into 'the night-watch', whereby individuals spend a night in a graveyard in order to have a revelatory vision concerning future events, most often the identity of a future spouse.[26]

The Land as Resonator

Domestic and daily methods of augury remain embedded in the culture of Britain and Ireland, where the more professional vatic methods have retreated into certain family lines, local traditions and particular individuals. They are also accessible through close contact with the land itself. The indigenous traditions of Britain and Ireland are like an ancient instrument that can still produce music. Any musician taking up this instrument would automatically already know something about its playing; the rest would be learned over the years from the way the instrument itself played. Every instrumentalist knows that each instrument innately possesses melodies, patterns and certain dynamic responses. When the player discovers these, the instrument becomes strangely resonant and seems almost to meld with the player's body. Such moments, if pursued sensitively, lead the player to the instrument's secret heart; eventually the player becomes a devotee or servant of the music of that instrument. In the Celtic traditions, the musician does not 'master' the medium of music, but rather becomes a 'co-resonator' of the music.

This continuum is not always available to those born outside northwestern Europe. Although they may retain the ancestral blood-links, exiles and emigrants will forge new relationships with the lands in which they now live. This creates a different dynamic, for the music of the native tradition is being played on an instrument that is tuned to a different cultural continuum. The success of the transfer of a diasporic tradition depends largely on the maturity and adaptability of the transplanted individual.

That such adaptation is possible can be seen in the vigour of spiritual Afro-Caribbean traditions. For many people living in a different land in search of their Celtic spiritual roots, that quest begins with great humility and sensitivity, with pain and yearning. It is a genuine search, which should not be despised by those who feel secure in 'unchanging' or 'authentic' traditions. It is true that many of the spiritual traditions of northwestern Europe have been lost and overlaid, not least our sacred etiquette around land. It is often painful, not to say embarrassing, to see how some visitors to Britain and Ireland behave – often with great presumption – performing grandiose ceremonies to 'heal the land' and implanting crystals at sacred sites are but two of the practices that rankle with those who maintain a quiet, under-stated guardianship of our land's traditions. If we came from Britain to sacred tribal lands in, say, New Mexico and did either of these things, we would be rightly shunned and violently warned off by the native peoples whose sacred land we were violating.

The lack of respect for or the failure to understand the lands of Britain and Ireland is incomprehensible. This is not to say all visitors behave this way. The guardian of the *fougou* (Celtic underground stone chamber, probably used for sacred incubation) at Rosmerron in Cornwall related the story of a visitor to the site from Southeast Asia. The man would not approach the site without first sitting for two hours at the end of the long drive leading to it and 'tuning into' the hedgerows and the earth. This kind of behaviour is the most appropriate for understanding any sacred place whose culture you do not share daily.

The messages and abiding wisdom of the land well up with an ancestral and symbiotic resonance that is hard to ignore in Britain and Ireland. The vatic tradition springs up from the natural features of the land, from ancestral residues, from the memory of connection, from daily practice and from honouring the connections of our symbiotic life upon the land. These are our 'memory-resident' inspirations, and they send forth their spirits when we touch them with intention.

The subtle, undramatic methods of vatic tradition in these islands are available to those who live within the spiritual continuum of the land. The ancient role of the *filidh* was not merely fuelled by clairvoyance or poetic sensibility but by resonance, touch and connection. The ability to root into any object, place or person and discover identity, quality and answers to questions concerning these is part of this symbiotic continuum. This ability is fuelled by a proximity and familiarity with the spirits, which embody all living beings and things.

Chief of the skills that were anciently enacted was the ability to preserve the land from scathe and harm. The triple druidic task seems primarily rooted in this preservation: druids to maintain justice and peace, ovates or seers to perceive and divine spiritual need, bards to maintain harmony. British bardic tradition speaks of the 'perpetual choirs of song' that hold the land in unity and spiritual health. By the enchantment of dedicated people the land is made safe and blessedly preserved.

The Literature of Prophecy

In addition to the accounts of the methods of divination and seership, there also exists a vast collection of actual prophetic literature, which, although offering little in the way of clues to the methods involved in obtaining inner knowledge, does reflect the state of mind and situation of the people who sought it. In the third part of this collection we have included several examples of this kind of literature, dating from the earliest times to the comparatively recent period of the eighteenth century. Thus you will find the extraordinary poetic visions of the poet Suibhne (Sweeney the Mad), whose dialogues with a circle of unseen figures reflect the innermost journeys of the shaman seers. There is also a new translation, specially made for this collection, of the *Armes Prydein* ('Prophecy of Britain'), attributed to Myrddin (Merlin). Along with these are extracts from the medieval 'Prophecies of Merlin', compiled by Geoffrey of Monmouth in the eleventh century, and extracts from the prophetic utterances of Coinneach Odhar, the Brahan Seer, whose prophetic curse against the family responsible for his murder is among the most remarkable instances of extreme prophetic accuracy.

The tradition of seership among the Celts has thus continued, to a certain degree without interruption. When the coming of Christianity forced the old poets and seers to go into hiding, they took the traditions of seership with them. There it became part of the folklore of a conquered people. But as we have seen, it never really ceased to be practised, and when this was not openly admitted the number of people possessing 'the sight' continued undiminished, especially among the Highlands and Islands, the out-of-the-way places within the Celtic lands. Thus it has continued to the present, when a new generation of seers, mostly unknown outside their own immediate families, are keeping the traditions of seership alive. At the other end of the spectrum, in the revival of interest and the practice of druidry, the ancient vatic arts are as important as ever. While it is difficult when examining the old records to separate the skills of the druid, the bard and the ovate, each is a reflection of a total world view which remains at the heart of the Celtic races. I am glad that I have been able to complete the 'trilogy' of source books which have dealt with each of the three disciplines, and to emphasize the importance and vitality of the tradition that gave them birth and that, to the joy of many hearts, continues to flourish at the dark end of this century.

John Matthews
Oxford
September 1998

Notes

1 For a wider look at survivals see Prudence Jones and Nigel Pennick, *A History of Pagan Europe* (Routledge, London, 1995) and Anton Wessels, *Europe: Was it Ever Really Christian* (SCM Press Ltd, London, 1994).
2 We may see parallels here between the *santería* cults of Brazil, which fuse Catholic and African elements, or with the shamanic and oracular practice of both laity and Buddhist clergy in Ladakh.
3 H.R. Ellis Davidson, *The Seer in Celtic and Other Traditions* (John Donald Publishers Ltd, Edinburgh, 1989).
4 R.J. Stewart, *Robert Kirk: Walker Between Worlds* (Element Books, Shaftesbury, 1990).
5 Françoise Le Roux and Christian-J. Guyonvarc'h', *Les Druides* (Rennes, Ouest France, 1986).
6 Strabo, *Geographia* iv:4:7. As in Brazil, the Catholicism of Ireland is a more tolerant bedfellow of the older and native belief systems.
7 John Minahane *The Christian Druids* (Sanas Press, Dublin, 1993).
8 *Senchus Mor: The Ancient Laws of Ireland*, vol. 1 (Alexander Thom, Dublin, 1865).
9 Minahane, *op. cit.*
10 Ronald Hutton *The Pagan Religions of the Ancient British Isles* (Blackwell, Oxford, 1991).
11 Le Roux, *op. cit.*
12 Minahane, *op. cit.*
13 Caitlín Matthews, *The Celtic Tradition* (Element Books, Shaftesbury, 1995).
14 *Senchus Mor, op. cit.*
15 Le Roux, *op. cit.*
16 *Ibid.*, our translation.

17 For more about the interface of Celtic poetic and shamanic traditions see John Matthews, *Taliesin: Shamanism and the Bardic Mysteries in Britain and Ireland* (HarperCollins, London, 1991).

18 Trans. by Caitlín Matthews; from *The Encyclopedia of Celtic Wisdom: A Celtic Shaman's Sourcebook* by Caitlín and John Matthews (Element Books, Shaftesbury, 1994).

19 Gerald of Wales, *The Journey Through Wales/ The Description of Wales*, trans. by Lewis Thorpe (Penguin Books, Harmondsworth, 1978).

20 *Ibid.*

21 How tragically ironic is the modern practice of salmon farming whereby the wild salmon are imprisoned in deep-sea net-cages, forever unable to return to their ancestral spawning waters in the inland rivers. The *filidh* would have regarded this is a metaphor for the state of our tradition today, tamed and disempowered!

22 Caitlín Matthews, *The Celtic Book of the Dead* (Thorsons, Wellingborough, 1991).

23 Stewart, *op. cit.*

24 Matthews and Matthews, 1994, *op. cit.*

25 H.R. Ellis Davidson, *Myths and Symbols in Pagan Europe* (Manchester University Press, Manchester, 1988).

26 Davidson, 1989, *op. cit.*

PART ONE

VISION AND SEERSHIP: THE DRUIDS AND THE BARDS

T HE METHODS BY WHICH VISIONS were experienced among the Celts are well attested within both literature and tradition. Three methods in particular are known – the enigmatically titled *imbas forosnai, tenm laida* and *dichetal do chennaib* – and these are discussed in detail below by Nora K. Chadwick. There are references to these three disciplines throughout Irish mythology, but for a definition of sorts we have to turn to the vast collection of texts, compiled in the early Middle Ages and known as *The Ancient Laws of Ireland*.[1] Here we find listed the three things required of the *ollamh*-poet:

> *Teinm laegda,* that is to say, *teinm* means shining and *teinm* means to understand …
> through his poem ['laid'] the things which he wishes to say. … *Imus forosnad,* i.e., the
> abundant knowledge of the learning *given* by the tutor to the pupil. … *Dichedal do*
> *chennaib,* i.e., there goes at once from the head of his art the common headship.

This is all fairly obscure, though it can be explicated somewhat. *Tenm laida* appears to mean that the poet understands or receives meaning through his poem – or, to put it simply, that he experiences inspiration. *Imbas forosnai* is described as wisdom imbibed directly from master to pupil, as it were 'by word of mouth'. *Dichetal do chennaib* concerns 'headship', the acquiring of wisdom directly and without contemplation – that is, in an inspired manner. All three, then, have to do with inspired knowledge or teaching.

Another source, Cormac's *Glossary,*[2] adds further details to the effect that the person seeking enlightenment on any subject he wishes through *imbas forosnai* first chews a piece of raw meat, then places it on a doorstep and invokes the gods. He then puts his hands over his face and sleeps for two, three or nine days. During this time he is watched over to see that he does not turn over in his sleep and is not disturbed by anyone. There is also reference to the placing of the two palms over the cheeks, which seems to suggest that the eyes are covered. This seems like a reference to the darkened chamber in which poets were said to seek inspiration – or indeed to a meditational habit in which the outer world is excluded as far as possible.

The mention of chewing raw meat draws our attention to the appearances of *imbas forosnai* in the literature relating to the Irish hero Fionn mac Cumhail, who is often referred to as both a poet and a magician – indeed, he could be said to be more correctly described in these terms than as a hero, despite his prodigious feats of strength and warlike demeanour. Fionn indeed, like his Welsh counterpart Taliesin, imbibed his wisdom through eating a sacred substance, in this case the flesh of the Salmon of Wisdom, just as Taliesin drank from the Cauldron of Inspiration. Unlike Taliesin, whose received knowledge remained with him, Fionn had ever after to revive his memory by chewing his thumb. In the collection of tales known as the *Fiannagecht*[3] occurs the often-repeated phrase: 'Fionn put his thumb into his mouth; when he took it out again, his *imbas* enlightened him.' This suggests that *imbas* was akin to the *awen* received by Taliesin and recalls the chewing of raw flesh in the above account. If Fionn at one time did the same it would account for the later addition of the 'thumb of wisdom' theme and, because chewing suggests teeth, of the still later development in which he acquired a 'tooth of wisdom'. (This whole subject is considered in depth in Chapter 4 of the present collection.)

Yet another form of divinatory sleep, known as *tarbh feis* (bull-feast), carries the aspect of imbibing wisdom through consuming flesh. In this a bull, preferably white, is slaughtered and then cooked. The man desiring illumination eats of the flesh and broth and goes to sleep. Four druids then chant *or firindi* (true speech) over him, and he sees a vision that answers his question. Nor should we forget that in the Welsh story 'The Dream of Rhonabwy', part of the great collection of early myth assembled under the title of *The Mabinogion,*[4] the hero falls asleep on a yellow cow's hide and dreams a long and complex dream of the heroic Arthur. Both these examples may be compared with the procedure of the Yakut shamans of northern Siberia, who lay on a white mare's skin before beginning their visionary voyage to the otherworld.

The *Ancient Laws*, referring again to *tenm laida*, offers further explanation:

> The chief poet, i.e., the learned poet who explains or exhibits the great extent of his knowledge by composing a quatrain without thinking … . At this day it is by the ends of his bones he effects it … . And the way in which it is done is this: When the poet sees the person or thing before him he makes a verse at once with the ends of his fingers, or in his mind without studying, and he composes and repeats at the same time … but this is not the way it was done before Patrick's time … [then] the poet placed his staff upon the person's body or upon his head, and found out his name, and the name of his father and mother, and discovered every unknown thing that was proposed to him, in a minute or two or three; and this is Teinm Laegha, or Imus Forosna, for the same thing used to be revealed by means of them; but they were performed after a different manner, i.e., a different kind of offering was made at each.[5]

Despite the fact that the author here confuses *tenm laida* with *imbas forosnai*, what he says is, of itself, interesting. The introduction of the poet's staff at this juncture leads us into a completely different area. *Imbas forosnai* itself is a wholly interior act, but according to this definition *tenm laida* requires a wand or staff of power. Two stories, both from Cormac's *Glossary*,[6] illustrate this. The first concerns the blind poet, Lugaid, who arrived one day in Bangor, was shown a skull and asked whose head it was. Lugaid told them to put the end of the poet's wand upon it, whereupon he said:

> The tempestuous water, the waters the whirlpool destroyed Breccan. This is the head of Breccan's dog; and … Breccan was drowned with his people in that whirlpool.

Curiously enough, the second story also concerns the skull of a dog, which had been discovered by Connlae and taken to the poet Moen.

> Then the poet solved it by *tenm laido* [sic] 'illumination of song' and said … 'Dear indeed you were in this house … This,' says he, 'is the head of Mugh-eme, the first lapdog that was brought into Ireland.'

In the first story the method (the use of the poet's wand) is described, but in the second the process is named but not described. This may lead us to suppose that the same method was used in both cases and to deduce that *tenm laida* was, in fact, divination by wand. Other references to this staff suggest that it was carved with ogham characters and that it was regarded as a channel of the poet's power. Certainly, the following quotation, from the seventeenth-century *A Description of the Western Isles of Scotland* by M. Martin, seems to bear out the reality of conveying visionary insights by touch alone.

> All those who have the second sight do not always see these visions at once, though they be together at the time. But if one who has this faculty designedly touch his fellow-seer

at the instant of the vision's appearing then the second sees it as well as the first; and this is sometimes discerned by those that are near them on such occasions.[7]

In addition to the theme of touch, both *imbas forosnai* and *tenm laida* are associated with the presence of both light and fire – perhaps the fire of illumination itself. Both the words *forosnai* and *tenm* contain an element of burning, heat and brightness, suggesting that the definition of *imbas forosnai* as 'wisdom that illumines' refers to a literal illumination, such as the brilliant light that, in Irish tradition, is said to blast the eyes of all who drink from Nechtan's Well. Patrick K. Ford, who has dealt with this material at length, points to similar instances from Iranian and Indian mythology of a brilliant light that illuminates at the same time as it blinds.[8] It may be that here we have the seed from which sprang the later tradition that bards who had been blind from birth were the best, a tradition that was still prevalent as late as the eighteenth century with the famous Irish harper O'Carolan. Such men were believed to have a special insight into the otherworld since they could not see the world in which they lived, and it is possible to believe that part of the initiation process that resulted in an ability to prophesy included a ritual assumption of blindness.

It is notable that the seeker after knowledge in Cormac's *Glossary* is able to deliver his oracular speech after sleeping in a darkened cave. To this example we may add the fact that Taliesin himself is said to have uttered his first song after he was released from within the confines of a dark bag and that his brow was so bright that he received his name, which meant 'radiant brow'.

A further story from the *Echtra Cormaic* seems to bear this out. Here we are told of the poet Morann, who later became recognized as a great sage. Morann was born with a caul over his head, which was removed only when he was immersed in the sea and the ninth wave (traditionally associated with poetic insight) washed it off. He at once delivered a song, which began:

Worship, O mortals,
The God of this beautiful world![9]

What we may well be seeing here is a confused memory of a rite in which the bardic or shamanic seer sought illumination by first entering a darkened place or by covering his eyes with his hands and then, after a time, being brought forth into a brightly lit place – either fire or sunlight – at which point he gave forth his inspired utterance to all who were present. As is repeatedly the case in shamanic traditions, the physical manifestation of the inner experience assisted in the acquisition of the mantic fit. To this day, in modern magical practice, ritual and meditation perform the same function, externalizing the mysteries so that they are confirmed both in the operants and those who are looking on. Even the singing heads, of which there are sufficient within Celtic mythology to warrant a separate study, seem to bear out this theory. They are, after all, dead – at least nominally – and are able to return with messages after their shamanic ritual death, unlike the cauldron-born warriors who are brought back to life in 'The Story of Branwen' from *The Mabinogion* but are unable to speak of their experience.

The ethnologist Knud Rasmussen thus reported of Eskimo shamans that they often experience a mysterious light:

The shaman suddenly feels in his body, inside his head, within the brain, an inexplicable searchlight, a luminous fire, which enables him to see in the dark, both literally and metaphorically speaking, for he can now, even with closed eyes, see through darkness and perceive things and coming events which are hidden from others.[10]

A good deal of argument has raged over the exact meaning of *dichetal do chennaib*, the third of the divinatory practices, although it is, indeed, closely aligned with both the others. Some would translate it as 'extempore recital', others as 'extempore or inspired incantation', while others prefer 'incantation from the ends (of the fingers)' or even 'the ends of the bones', a description that is also applied to *imbas forosnai* by the author of Cormac's *Glossary*. It is evident that another kind of inspired utterance is being referred to here, and the actual meaning of the Irish word *dichetal* is probably 'spells'. So we have, 'inspired spells'. The fact that these are, somehow, conveyed from the ends of the fingers or bones poses a deeper problem. Does it mean that the poet made 'passes' with his hands, in the manner of a stage magician, or that he literally 'spelled out' words in ogham to constitute the spell?

In the light of the evidence it seems probable that a kind of hypnotic mantra of power-words might be inferred, which could either enable the poet to enter an immediate trance or to cause some change in events. This is in line with shamanic practice, which is full of instances of self-induced trance brought about through chanting or drumming.

The fact that, alone of the methods of divination mentioned in Cormac's *Glossary*, *dichetal do chennaib* is allowed to be practised even after St Patrick has placed the other two disciplines under interdict, indicates that it was seen as a less primitive and therefore less 'dangerous' practice than the rest. It is possible that St Patrick was convinced of this by some deliberate confusion. There seems little doubt that *dichetal* is every bit as powerful a method of divination as the others and that it was used primarily by poets seeking inspiration, when it enabled them to compose and deliver their songs with astonishing readiness.

The variety of translations possible for each one of these disciplines has continued to confuse the issue. Quite clearly, the early commentators on *dichetal do chennaib*, as well as *imbas forosnai* and *tenm laida*, frequently confused the methods. However, 'mediation by finger ends', with its accompanying sense of 'the cracking open of the nut', makes it clear that *dichetal* consisted of somehow imbibing the fruit of the hazel nut.

Several commentators have suggested that *tenm laida* meant, literally, 'the chewing (or breaking open) of the pith'. Some assume that this refers to Fionn's thumb, which he is said to chew 'from the skin to the flesh, from the flesh to the bone, from the bone to the marrow, from the marrow to the juice'.[11] Yet in the context of the stories it would seem that what is actually being referred to is the eating of a nut, the sense of the word *tenm* being 'to crack open, or husk, (a nut)'. In this instance we may infer that the nut in question is one of the Nine Hazels of (Poetic) Wisdom, referred to in various texts. The story of the origin of the River Shannon, contained in *The Dindsenchas*, a vast compilation of lore connected to physical sites in Ireland, tells us how:

> Sinend daughter of Lodan Lucharglan ... went to Connla's Well, which is under the sea, to behold it. That is a well at which are the hazels and inspirations of wisdom, that is the hazels of science and poetry, and in the same hour their fruit, and their blossoms and their foliage break forth, and these fall on the well in the same shower, which raises on the water a royal surge of purple. Then the salmon chew the fruit, and the juice of the nuts is in their bellies. And seven streams of wisdom spring forth and turn there again.[12]

Another text, a poetic tract on the subject of the getting of wisdom, says:

23

Into this spring [Segais] fell these nuts first of all, then out of the well every seven years or every year into the Boyne river, so that they – filled with *imus* (magical poetic quality) – come to certain persons. These drank the *imus* out of them, so that they then became master poets.[13]

The River Boyne, we may note, which is under the protection of the goddess Boann, is considered to be the source of inspiration in Irish poetic tradition in much the same way that those who are reborn of Ceridwen's cauldron are likewise full of knowledge in British tradition. Not only Fionn went there, for as it is said elsewhere: 'the poets thought that the place where poetry was revealed always was on the brink of water.'[14]

Thus the fruits of the tree of wisdom are carried downstream to rise again in Nechtan's Well or to be eaten by those in search of wisdom, like Fionn, in the flesh of the salmon. Here we come as near as we can to a definition of *dichetal do chennaib*: the gaining of wisdom through the cracking open and eating of the fruit of the sacred wisdom-nuts, the hazels from the otherworldly Well of Segais, which rises in the inner realms but sends forth its messages to the poets who seek to know.

A fourth divinatory method, of which almost nothing is known, is mentioned in the unpublished text of *Bretha Nemed*.[15] This is *anamain cetharreach* (*anamain* of the four intervals). According to Calvert Watkins, this is the name of an archaic metre, but it also contains the sense of both inspiration and breath. We have already seen the links between *awen* and breathing; this further evidence suggests an even stronger link, pointing to the imbibing of wisdom from the element of air itself. Alternatively, there is a further sense of 'soul', **ana-monn* in the word *anamain*, from which we may draw our own conclusions. Alexei Kondratiev also recently pointed out in his brilliant book *The Apple Branch*[16] that:

> what had come out of the visions in a torrent of words could be more easily remembered when patterned by metre and alliteration. So the craft of verse-making became intimately associated with magical practice and otherworld power.

One final method of divination requires our attention. This is *neladoracht* (divination by clouds). An example from MS Mat. 285 in Dublin refers to a certain king of Ireland named Dathi who happened to be at his residence on Croc-na-Druad (Druid's Hill) one Samhain Eve. He demanded that his druid forecast the events of the next year.

> The druid went to the top of the hill, where he remained the night, returning at sunrise. He then addressed the king with these words: 'Are you asleep, O King of Erin and Alban [Scotland]?' 'Why the addition to my title?' asked the King, 'I am not king of Alban.' To which the druid answered: 'I have consulted the clouds of the men of Erin, and have discovered that you shall make a conquest of Alban, Britain and Gaul'. Which accordingly he did soon afterwards.

Most of the above examples of the vatic arts come from Irish traditions, which are better preserved than those of Britain, but we can be assured that identical or similar methods to those discussed above were practised in Wales and Scotland and the south. That these have not been preserved is due to no small extent to the repeated conquests of Celtic tribal lands, which made it difficult to maintain the same continuity as we find in Ireland, which has, to some extent, remained inviolate. At least one British text, the *Itinerarium Cambriae* ('The Journey Through

Wales') of Giraldus Cambrensis (Gerald of Wales), although late in comparison with the Irish material, does more than merely suggest that parallel traditions existed in Britain. In Book I, Chapter 16 of his discourse, Gerald writes of the 'soothsayers' of the nation:

> There are certain persons in Cambria ... called Awenyddion, or people inspired; when consulted upon any doubtful event, they roar out violently, are rendered beside themselves, and become, as it were, possessed by a spirit. They do not deliver the answer to what is required in a coherent manner; but the person who skilfully observes them will find, after many preambles ... the desired explanation conveyed in some turn of a word: they are then roused from their ecstasy, as from a deep sleep, and, as it were, by violence compelled to return to their proper senses. After having answered the questions, they do not recover till violently shaken by other people; nor can they remember the replies they have given. ... These gifts are usually conferred upon them in dreams: some seem to have sweet milk or honey poured on their lips; others fancy that a written schedule is applied to their lips, and on awakening they publicly declare that they have received this gift.[17]

Surely these *awenyddion* – the word means 'inspired ones' and contains the root *awen*, which we have encountered before – are not so very different from the Irish shaman-poets who had to be shaken before they would awake and who immediately delivered themselves of prophecies that were often hard to understand?

In this first part of the collection we deal primarily with the methods of seership and divination, with the exception of the ogham methods, which are discussed in Part Two. E. Ettlinger's fascinating account of precognitive dreams in Celtic tradition is followed by two fragmentary accounts from early Irish literature of prognostication by ravens and wrens, both birds held to be the representative of the otherworld by the Celtic peoples. In this instance I have omitted the original Irish text and included only R.I. Best's translation. Those wishing to explore the text for themselves are recommended to read the original essay in the journal *Ériu*.

Having established some of the basic ground rules for vision seeking, we then move on to a fascinating essay by the renowned Celtic scholar Nora K. Chadwick. Her exploration of the three extraordinary methods of divination discussed above remains essential reading for all seeking to understand the subject of seership.

From here we move onward to Robert Scott's excellent exploration of the theme of the 'thumb of wisdom', an essential theme within the stories of the Welsh seer-poet Taliesin and the Irish Fionn mac Cumhail, who, while better known as a warrior and the leader of the heroic Fianna, was also a poet and visionary, whose ability to see into the otherworldly reality stood him in good stead when dealing with many adversaries.

This is followed by 'The Voice of the Stone of Destiny' by the great folklorist Ernest Hartland. Here he traces the long-debated themes of the stone's origin and purpose and in the process takes us on a wide-ranging journey through traditions of many other lands as well as demonstrating a more deeply nationalistic approach to the subject of vaticination.

John G. Campbell's chapter on 'Augury, Dream and Prophecy' begins our exploration of the continuing traditions relating to seership. Campbell was minister of Tiree and collected much of his material from oral sources, thus making him a valuable repository of the folklore traditions surrounding augury and vision work in the times long after the passing of the great heroic ages recorded in Celtic literature.

We have seen that there was a close connection between the roles of the poet and the seer. Poets were traditionally announced by the shaking of a branch decorated with silver or bronze bells, which were rung to tell everyone that a poet was about to speak. Eleanor Hull's study of the traditions surrounding this usage and of its association with the magical and otherworldly summoners adds another dimension to the subject of visionary encounters.

The parallels between the written and oral traditions of vaticination are profound and make for fascinating reading. The chapter on 'Illumination' by George Henderson, which follows here, continues the exploration of the continuity of these traditions by focusing on the ways in which the ancient methods of vision and divination have been developed and adapted through the ages by generations of practitioners.

Finally in this section we have Caitlín Matthews's powerful and illuminating examination of the role of human and otherworldly women in the traditions of augury and inspiration. Caitlín, who teaches the ancient art of augury to modern practitioners, draws not only on the background of Celtic literature but also (and fittingly in this context) on her own practical knowledge of the subject.

Notes

1 *Senchus Mor: The Ancient Laws of Ireland* (Alexander Thom, Dublin, 1865).

2 Cormac's *Glossary*, ed. by J. O'Donovan (Irish Archaeological and Celtic Society, Calcutta, 1868).

3 *Fianaigecht*, ed. by K. Meyer (Hodges, Figgis & Co., Dublin, 1910).

4 *The Mabinogion*, trans. by J. Gantz (Penguin Books, Harmondsworth, 1976).

5 *Senchus Mor, op. cit.*

6 Cormac's *Glossary, op. cit.*

7 M. Martin, *A Description of the Western Isles of Scotland* (D. Stirling, Edinburgh, 1934).

8 Patrick K. Ford, 'The Well of Nechtan and "La Gloire Luminesse"' in *Myth in Indo-European Antiquity* ed. by G.J. Larson (University of California Press, Berkeley, 1974).

9 'Echtra Cormaic' in *Ancient Irish Tales* by T.P. Cross and C.H. Slover (Hodges, Figgis & Co., Dublin, 1936).

10 Knud Rasmussen, quoted in R. Heinberg, *Memories and Visions of Paradise* (Aquarian Press, Wellingbrough, 1990).

11 J. Curtin, *Hero Tales of Ireland* (Macmillan, London, 1894).

12 E. Gwynn, *The Metrical Dindsenchas* (Hodges, Figgis & Co., Dublin, 1903–35).

13 Ford, *op. cit.*

14 'Immacallun in da Thuarad' quoted in P.K. Ford, *The Poetry of Llwyarch Hen* (University of California Press, Berkeley, 1974).

15 C. Watkins, 'Indo-European Metrics and Archaic Irish Verse' in *Celtica*, VI, 1963.

16 Alexei Kondratiev, *The Apple Branch* (The Collins Press, Cork, 1998).

17 Gerald of Wales, *The Journey Through Wales/ The Description of Wales*, trans. by Lewis Thorpe (Penguin Books, Harmondsworth, 1978).

CHAPTER ONE

Precognitive Dreams in Celtic Legend

E. Ettlinger

from *Folklore*

*When the body is awake the soul is its servant, and is never her own mistress.
... But when the body is at rest, the soul, being set in motion and awake ...
has cognizance of all things – sees what is visible, hears what is audible,
walks, touches, feels pain, ponders.*

Hippocrates, *Dreams*[1]

IN THIS PAPER WE SHALL DEAL rather with the Celtic attitude towards dreams than with the dreams themselves. Preference has been given to dreams which concern the entire community by leading to the election of a king, announcing his approaching death, referring to political events or to the issue of warfare. The material at our disposal has been divided into three groups: (1) unsolicited dreams; (2) dreams which were expected; (3) induced dreams. Related subjects, e.g., incubation for the purpose of healing, visions and divination, have been taken into account in order to substantiate or supplement certain statements. The words 'vision' and 'dream' will be used in accordance with Professor A. Guillaume's definitions: a vision 'is seen in a state other than sleep', while 'a dream that one knows to be a dream is not a vision'.[2]

The strikingly close resemblance between omens and dreams, which led to the assumption that dreams have greatly contributed to the belief in omens, is clearly revealed in the following episode taken from Irish legend:

On the arrival of the Tuatha De Danann in Ireland, a vision was revealed in a dream to Eochaid, son of Erc, high king of Ireland. He pondered over it with much anxiety, being filled with wonder and perplexity. He told his wizard, Cesard ... 'I saw a great flock of black birds ... coming from the depths of the Ocean. They settled over all of us, and fought with the people of Ireland. They brought confusion on us, and destroyed us. One of us, methought, struck the noblest of the birds and cut off one of its wings. And now, Cesard, employ your skill and knowledge, and tell us the meaning of the vision.' Cesard did so, and by means of ritual and the use of his science the meaning of the king's vision was revealed to him; and he said:

'I have tidings for you: warriors are coming across the sea, a thousand heroes covering the ocean; speckled ships will press in upon us; all kinds of death they announce, a people skilled in every art, a magic spell; an evil spirit will come upon you, signs to lead you astray (?); ... they will be victorious in every stress.' [3]

Four features of this narrative coincide with records of Celtic omens:[4] (1) the large flock of black birds; (2) its appearance at an anxious moment; (3) the king instantly considered the dream to convey a warning; (4) the magician connected the dream with imminent events. There is, however, one essential difference; while in Celtic literature bird-omens were intelligible to everybody, the dream-appearance of birds required a professional interpreter. This incident shows that although the Celts differentiated between objective facts and dream-perceptions, they 'did not find it unreasonable to seek illumination for the problems of the (waking) world in the phenomena of the (sleeping) world'.[5] There is no doubt that the colour of the birds – black is a universal symbol for misfortune and death – influenced the ill-foreboding prediction. Details of the ritual which preceded Cesard's revelation are missing, but the consultation of a magician, corresponding to the greater part of the legendary evidence,[6] permits us to assume that the ceremony was rather elaborate. Dreams were only in exceptional cases interpreted by a poet or a cleric.

It was when Dermot was of a night, and he sees two draw near him: the one man, as he deems, wears a cleric's semblance; the other one a layman's. They come up to him, take off his king's diadem, make of it a diadem apiece (either man of them having one half, for so they divide it between them), and with that depart from him. Dermot starts out of his sleep then, and tells his vision. 'Just so,' said Beg mac Dé and said Cairidh son of Finnchaemh (his mother) that was Dermot's poet: 'thy dream's interpretation we have for thee: Thy kingdom is determined, of thy reign there is an end, and for the future thy princely grasp of Ireland is cast off: division between Church and Lay namely, that is what shall subsist now; and that which thy royal diadem's partition forbodes is even such another apportioning of Ireland's sovereignty betwixt Church and State.' ...[7]

One night as Domhnall slept in this house, he had a vision and a dream: he saw a greyhound whelp, Fearglonn by name, which had been reared by himself, go forth from him, even from his knee, with rage and fury, gathering the dogs of Erin, Alba, Saxonland and Britain; and they gave the king and the men of Erin around him seven battles during the seven days of the week, and a slaughter of heads was made between them each day, but on the seventh day the dogs were worsted, and in the last battle the king's own hound, as he thought, was killed. The king then awoke from his sleep, and he sprang affrighted from his bed, so that he was naked on the floor of the house. ...

(The queen quieted him and) requested him to relate to her what he had seen in the vision. 'I will not tell it to thee, O queen ... nor to any one else, until I reach the place where Maelcobha, the cleric, my brother, is, for he is the best interpreter of dreams in Erin.'

(A month later) the king proceeded with a hundred chariots to Druim Dilair; where Maelcobha was dwelling. ... Domhnall fully revealed his dream to Maelcobha ... (who) grew red on hearing the dream, and said, 'It is long since the events shown in that dream were predicted. ... A greyhound whelp in a dream ... is the same as a king's son: thou hast two foster-sons, O king. ... Either of these will rise up against thee, O king, and will bring the plunderers and the doers of evil of Alba, France, Saxonland and

Britain with him to Erin, who will give seven battles to thee and the men of Erin, so that great slaughter shall be made between you both, and in the seventh battle ... thy foster-son shall fall. ...'

'Now it is proper for thee, O king ... to prepare a banquet, and to invite to it the men of Erin, and to obtain the hostages of every province in Erin, and also to detain in fetters, to the end of a year, these two foster-sons of thine ... because the venom goes out of every dream within the year'[8] (i.e., 'its fulfilment need not be dreaded after the lapse of that time').[9]

Two details disclose the great significance which the king attributed to his dream: (1) he concealed its content even to his queen; presumably in order to prevent any enemy learning about it and using his knowledge to the king's own detriment. An Irish gnome says: 'Do not tell your secret to women. The secret of a woman is not well kept.'[10] (2) The king's travelling with a hundred chariots gives to Maelcobha's consultation the nature of a state proceeding. The number seven is of little importance in Celtic legend. It is mainly found 'in works which were composed in their present form long after Christianity had worked upon the Celts'.[11] The cleric's favourable interpretation is based upon the Christian notion which associates the number seven with final victory if one is threatened and resurrection.

Geoffrey's account of King Arthur's dream is well known:

Arthyr and his hosts went to the port of Northhamtwn; and when he got a fair wind he sailed for ffraink. And when he had reached the middle of the ocean, a sleep as of the dead held him much of the night, and he saw a dream. He saw flying from the south a sort of monster, with a terrible voice, alighting on the shore of ffraink; and he saw a dragon coming from the west, and by the glare of its eyes the sea was lighted up. And he saw the dragon and the Bear (Arth) engaging; and when they had fought for a long time, he saw the dragon spitting out gleaming flames of fire upon the Bear, and burning him up completely. And perplexing was the dream to Arthyr. And then he awoke and told his comrades of the vision; and thus did they make interpretation: 'Thou, Lord, shalt fight some monster of a giant and conquer him, for the dragon signifies thyself.' But Arthyr put no trust in this, for he believed that it should be between the emperor and himself.[12]

The conventional setting of this dream belongs certainly to that type which caused Dr John Layard to write: 'they have clearly been selected by a process of elimination of the more personal elements so as to present a picture readily understandable by the general community.'[13]

In Geoffrey's story there is nothing remarkable with regard to our present subject apart from the fact that the king communicated his dream to 'his comrades'. I think we may deduce from the doubts which he expressed about their interpretation that there was no professional dream-reader among the king's attendants.

Celtic literature reflects the belief that supernatural agencies were confined to selected natural places. 'On the bank of the stream called "cas" or "the crooked" the Elements meted out death to (the perjurer) Laeghaire.'[14] Does this passage purport that of all the elements water was most intimately associated with death? There is an entire group of death-foreboding dreams and visions occurring on river-banks which may well confirm such a surmise.

'Cormac slept for a little space at the end of the ford, and an awful vision was shewn to (the doomed king). Thereafter Cormac awoke.'[15]

When the sons of Usnech 'went forward to Finncharn of the Watching, on Sliab Fuait,

Deirdre remained behind them in the glen, and her sleep fell upon her there,' (a dream appeared to her there). 'I beheld each (of the sons of Usnech) without a head, and Illann the Fair without a head.'[16]

The king Mes-gegra stayed behind the host alone with his charioteer (at a ford) at the Path of Clane. 'I will sleep at present,' saith the charioteer to Mes-gegra, 'and thou shalt sleep then.' 'I deem it well,' said the king. Now while Mes-gegra was looking at the water he saw a wonderful nut floating along the river towards him. Larger than a man's head was the nut. And he himself went down, and brought it to him, and cleft it with his skene, and left half the kernel for the gillie. And he saw that the gillie was lifted up in his sleep from the ground; and after that the gillie awoke from his sleep. 'How is it with thee, my lad?' saith the king. 'I have seen an evil vision,' saith the gillie. Both died immediately afterwards.

This unique case of levitation may be ascribed to the influence of Christian legend perceptible throughout the story of 'The Siege of Howth'.[17]

It was also at a ford that the war-goddess Badb announced approaching death to doomed heroes by appearing in the shape of a woman washing their blood-stained armour.[18] The relation between the Celtic Washer-at-the-Ford and the superhuman woman who predicted Drusus' death at the River Albis[19] has been remarked upon. The question arises – but can unfortunately not be answered – whether these prophetesses are reminiscences of priestesses living at sacred fords similar to those women who were in charge of certain wells.[20] However this may be, the stories of heroes dreaming of their approaching death or seeing visions which convey to them that death is imminent are probably based upon the ancient notion that doomed men are prescient. (North Britons denote the uncanny prophetic power of men whose death is close at hand with the word 'fey'.)[21]

The main difference between fortuitous, unsolicited dreams and those which were expected can be seen in the meditation and preparation preceding the latter. It is a universal belief that those who seek contact with supernatural powers are in great danger if they approach the spirits without being in a state of purity. In order to remain unharmed the suppliant has to undergo lustration, to submit to an ordeal or to make a sacrifice before calling upon the spirits for supreme guidance. After the purification-rite the consulter lay down in the dwelling-place of the spirit or on the hide of the sacrificed animal and fell asleep. The most detailed record of preliminaries to incubation, including the sacrifice of a bull, the consumption of sacred food, and a druidical ceremony, can be met with in the Irish legend 'The Sickbed of Cuchulainn'.

Seven years after the death of Conaire there was at Tara a meeting of the four great provinces of Erinn

to see if they could find a person whom they would select, to whom they would give the sovereignty of Erinn. ... There was then prepared a bull-feast ... in order that (the kings who were in that meeting) should discover out of it to whom they would give the sovereignty. Thus was that bull-feast prepared, namely: a white bull was killed, and one man ate enough of his flesh, and of his broth; and he slept under that meal; and a charm of truth was pronounced on him by four druids; and he saw in a dream the shape of the man who should be made king there, and his form, and his description, and the sort of work that he was engaged in. The man screamed out of his sleep and described what he saw to the kings, namely, a young, noble, strong man, with two red streaks around him, and he sitting over the pillow of a man in a decline in Emain Macha.[22]

This story is absolutely credible. Bull-sacrifices have been repeatedly recorded from the various parts of the British Isles up to the seventeenth century.[23] Pliny's statement (*H.N.*, XVI, 44) about the Gaulish sacrifices of white bulls may also be recalled. In the sagas as well as in Ptolemy (II, 2, 7) there are references to white cattle, which is even believed to survive in the white 'park-cattle' herd at Chillingham.[24] The choice of a white bull points either to the careful selection of a sacrifice without any blemish or to its dedication to some divinity of light to whom chiefly light-coloured offerings were due.[25]

The participation of the druids deserves particular consideration. Since the dreamer communicated his revelation to the assembled kings (probably because it was their privilege and duty to elect Conaire's successor), it seems as if the druids left the sleeper after having pronounced the charm of truth.[26] Assemblies of exactly four assistants in magical rites can be found in other legends.[27] The reason why just four men were required becomes apparent in the following passage:

> A day that Conn was in Tara, he went up at early morn upon the royal rath, and with him his three druids. Every day he went up there with that number to view all the points of the heavens that the 'sid' men should not rest on Ireland unperceived by him.[28]

When Aengus appeared to Cuchulainn[29] four people were placed at the four cardinal points around his sickbed, possibly with the intention of forming a magic circle for his protection.

Windisch has stated that the dreamer at Tara slept upon 'a bull-hide',[30] while in the bull-feast scene in 'The Destruction of Dá Derga's Hostel' 'a spell of truth was chanted over (the sleeper) in his bed'. The remark is added that he 'would perish if he uttered a falsehood (literally): his lips would perish'.[31] (After a vision Finn consulted the poet Fergus 'True-Lips'!)[32] Classical passages illuminate the meaning of the phrase: the sleeper's lips would perish if he uttered a falsehood. Pausanias (VII, 25, 13) and Tibullus (II, V, 63) leave no doubt that prophets were subject to an ordeal by partaking of sacred food, which was believed either to inspire the truth-speaking prophet or to poison the deceitful one.[33] It is not surprising to find that the supernatural power believed to bestow inspiration was also expected to silence lying lips. From the foregoing statements it becomes evident that, although this is not expressed, the dreamer at Tara submitted to an ordeal by partaking of the meat and broth of the sacrificed bull. It is highly probable that the next two quotations allude to similar ordeals by means of sacred food.

When the juggler Tulchinne had recognized that disaster was approaching he asked the man of the wood Fer Caille to sacrifice his pig and to 'find out who is in front of the house to injure the men of the Hostel'. Fer Caille enumerates the names of five men. 'They have announced a deed which is not feeble, the annihilation of Conaire.'[34]

Imbas forosnai ('knowledge that enlightens'):

> i.e., it discovers everything which the poet likes and which he desires to manifest. Thus it is done. The poet chews a piece of (the) flesh of a red pig, or of a dog or cat, and puts it afterwards on the flag behind the door, and pronounces an incantation on it, and offers it to idol-gods, and afterwards calls his idols to him and then finds them not on the morrow, and pronounces incantations on his two palms, and calls again unto him his idol-gods that his sleep may not be disturbed; and he lays his two palms on his two cheeks and (in this manner) he falls asleep; and he is watched in order that no one may interrupt (?) nor disturb him till everything about which he is engaged is revealed to him, (which may be) a minute or two or three, or as long as he was supposed to be at the offering.[35]

Thurneysen regards the description of *imbas forosnai* as the fantastic creation of a Christian etymologist's imagination.[36] As nearly all the details mentioned by Cormac reoccur in related ceremonies, I am inclined to see in the gloss traces of various actual divinatory rites, which have, however, been mistakenly pieced together. Not the palms but the right fist was used in the poet's incantation 'Cétnad' for finding out a theft: he sings it 'through the right fist, and goes to sleep upon it, and in (his) sleep the man (who has stolen the beast) is clearly shown and made known'.[37] (Before Marvan put the eye of Seanchan back into its own place 'he said his Pater in his right hand'!)[38]

A cat-sacrifice is referred to in Martin's description of the Gaelic rite the Taghairm (which is said to signify an Echo):[39]

> A party of men, who first retired to solitary places, remote from any house, and there they singled out one of their number, and wrap'd him in a big cow's hide, which they folded about him, his whole body was covered with it except his head, and so left in this posture all night until his invisible friends reliev'd him, by giving a proper answer to the question in hand, which he received, as he fancied, from several persons that he found about him all that time, his consorts return'd to him at break of day, and then he communicated his news to them. ...
>
> The same company who put the man into the hide, took a live cat and put him on a spit; one of the number was employed to turn the spit, and one of his consorts enquired at him, what are you doing? He answered, I roast this cat, until his friends answer the question, which must be the same that was proposed by the man shut up in the hide, and afterwards a very big cat comes attended by a number of lesser cats, desiring to relieve the cat turned upon the spit, and then answers the question: If this answer prove the same that was given to the man in the hide, then it was taken as a confirmation of the other which in this case was believed infallible.
>
> Mr Alexander Cooper present minister of North Uist, told me that one John Erach, in the Isle of Lewis, assured him it was his fate to have been led by his curiosity with some who consulted this oracle, and that he was a night within the hide as above mentioned, during which time he felt and heard such terrible things that he could not express them, the impression it made on him was such as could never go off, and he said that for a thousand worlds he would never again be concern'd in the like performance, for this had disordered him to a high degree; he confessed it ingenuously and with an air of great remorse, and seem'd to be very penitent under a just sense of so great a crime, he declared this about five years since, and is still living in the Lewis, for anything I know.[40]

We are neither informed about a sacrifice nor whether the consulter was awake or asleep. MacCulloch conjectured that in earlier times the animal, which provided the hide, was sacrificed and that the person clothed in the skin of a sacrificial animal 'is brought into contact with it and hence with the divinity to which it is offered ... (and that) in this Celtic usage, contact with divinity through the hide would be expected to produce enlightenment'.[41]

It seems possible, by examining the places of revelation, to determine more fully the nature of the power to which the sacrifice was made, and from which spiritual enlightenment was sought. Dalyell has recorded that in the rite 'the Taghairm' the querent was 'carried by assistants to a solitary spot, or left under the arch formed by the projected waters of a cataract'.[42] Retirement to a solitary place for meditation and visionary impressions is a worldwide practice. The reference to the cataract reminds us of Pythagoras who 'after being cleansed by the Idaean

Dactyls, slept by a river on the skin of a black lamb'.[43] In the 'Táin' there is a well-hidden allusion to such a form of incubation.

Before his fatal fight with Cuchulainn, Ferdiad asked at the ford of combat his gilla to

unharness the horses and spread for me the cushions and skins of my chariot under me here, so that I sleep off my heavy fit of sleep and slumber here ... The gilla ... spread beneath him the chariot-cloths. (Ferdiad) slept off the heavy fit of sleep that was on him. The gilla remained on watch and guard for him.[44]

Since river-worship is obviously reflected in incubation on river-banks, the inference may be drawn that those animals, which provided the hide for the Celtic dreamer to lie upon, were offered to the river-spirit (like the bulls in the *Iliad*, XI, 727; XXI, 131 f.) from whom supreme knowledge was craved. The dreams and visions of other doomed heroes, cited above, make us wonder if it was not self-understood that the *genius loci* foretold also Ferdiad's death.

In less remote parts of the British Isles than the Western Islands incubation on hides had faded from memory much earlier. Therefore we find the compiler of 'Rhonabwy's Dream' trying to explain somewhat circumstantially why Rhonabwy went to sleep on the yellow heifer-skin; but, nevertheless, his dream still retains the authority of a revelation.[45] It would be interesting to know why, in spite of Geoffrey's imitation of Virgil, his Bryttys 'laid himself down on the pelt of a white hind' and did not rest on the strewed fleeces of 'a hundred sheep' as Virgil's *Latinus* (*A.*, VII, 93).[46]

It should be observed that a glen is the scene of Finn's most unpleasant adventures with the Phantoms.[47] This fact as well as other stories about dreamers who were similarly flagellated suggest that Finn's adventures were happenings in a dream-world. The reason given for Finn's scourging is vengeance. While voluntary flagellation as a means to lustration and to bring on ecstasy is of great antiquity, the idea of flagellation as a punishment may, perhaps, be traced back to clerical influences.[48]

When Laurentius, St Augustine's successor as Archbishop of Canterbury, was about to leave England, St Peter appeared to him in a dream, rebuked him sharply for abandoning his post, and scourged him 'flagellis artioribus'.[49]

In 'The Sickbed' Cuchulainn 'put his back to a rock, where sleep soon fell upon him', and two women beat him badly. The cause for the beating remains obscure; but it may be inferred from the legend 'Tochmare Emire' that it was meant as a punishment for Cuchulainn's hitting two birds which were a transformation of the two women.[50]

In the *Mabinogion*

Pwyll arose to go for a walk, and he went to the top of a mound that was above the court, called Gorsedd Arberth. 'Lord,' said one of the court, 'it is the peculiarity of the mound that whatever noble sits upon it cannot go thence, without one of two things, either receiving wounds or blows or else seeing a wonder.' (The 'gorsedd', mound or tumulus, has throughout Welsh story been always associated with magic. The belief persisted well into the nineteenth century and is, indeed, far from dead yet.)[51]

According to legend, the full version of the 'Táin' having been lost, Murgan the Filé sang an incantation over the grave of Fergus mac Roig. A cloud hid him for three days, and during that time the dead man appeared and recited the saga to him.[52]

'A late Welsh predictive poem (Red Book of Hergest II) claims to be an utterance of

Myrddin from his grave. At the conclusion of this poem the speaker says that he has received information from certain "mountain spirits" (Wylyon mynyd).'[53]

These episodes agree well with Tertullian (*De Anima*, 57) who handed down to us Nicander's assurance that the Celts pass the night at the tombs of their heroes in order to obtain special oracles. While no evidence in support of mantic dreams acquired by incubation on grave-mounds is forthcoming in Celtic literature, incubation for the purpose of healing may possibly be hinted at in the 'Táin':

> When Lug came to help Cuchulainn, the latter said: 'Yea, heavy are the bloody wounds upon me; let thy healing be speedy.' 'Sleep then awhile, O Cuchulainn … thy heavy fit of sleep by Ferta in Lerga ("the Grave-mound on the Slopes") till the end of three days and three nights' … (Lug) examined each wound so that it became clean. Then he sang him the 'men's low strain' till Cuchulainn fell asleep withal … and recovered during his sleep without ever perceiving it.[54]

There is no information as to whether Lug came to Cuchulainn's assistance as a benevolent god or as his deified ancestor, his father in a metaphorical sense. Men sought from the manes as well as from the gods 'special help in special needs (and they) were too near and dear to the inmost heart of pre-Christian Europe to be done away with without substitutes'.[55] And so we find miraculous cures during sleep ascribed to Christian saints and incubation at their tombs surviving until comparatively recent times.[56]

Taking the evidence of expected dreams as a whole, two characteristics emerge: (1) pre-meditation had so much facilitated the dream-interpretation that expert dream-readers were no more required;[57] (2) the enquirer's frame of mind was in a normal condition. Before proceeding with induced dreams, when a marked contrast will be noticeable, I should like to quote Professor Plummer who dealt with the primitive belief that:

> the souls of men go forth from their bodies in sleep and visit distant scenes; … hence comes the idea that it is dangerous to wake a sleeping man suddenly, not only lest the soul's travels and acquisition of knowledge should be interrupted, but also lest the absent soul should be unable to find its way back to the body. … Restlessness in sleep showed that the soul was undergoing special experiences.[58]

A remarkable description of the soul's departure in sleep has been preserved in a Christian legend. Laisrén fasted thrice three days while purifying the church Cluain Chain which is in the territory of Connaught.

> At the end of the third three days' fast, sleep overpowered him in the oratory, and in his sleep he heard a voice saying to him: 'Arise!' The first time he did not move. When for the second time he heard the voice he raised his head and made the sign of the cross over his face. Then he saw the church in which he was, all alight, and yet there was still a part of the night. And between the chancel and the altar he saw a shining figure. Said the figure to him, 'Come towards me!' At that voice the cleric's whole body from crown to sole shook. Then all at once he beheld his soul (hovering) over the crown of his head, and knew not which way she had come out of the body. And he saw the church open above towards heaven, and two angels taking the soul between them and rising into the air.[59]

When the Ultonians wanted to awake Cuchulainn, who moved in his sleep, Fergus restrained them with these words: 'do not disturb him, he is seeing a vision.'[60] Noteworthy in this connection is the story of St Brendan:

[Il] alla retirer de l'enfer l'âme de sa mère. Son âme (de Brendan) eut à se battre continuellement avec les démons, jusqu'à ce qu'il retira sa mère des mains des démons. Pendant ce temps, l'évêque Mainenn gardait son corps. L'esprit de Brendan revint dans son corps tout affligé; et il poussa un soupir. L'évêque Mainenn l'interrogea alors.[61]

These two instances disclose that the following passage from Cormac's gloss to *imbas forosnai* is no more fantastic than those referred to above: the dreamer is watched 'in order that no one may interrupt nor disturb him till everything about which he is engaged is revealed to him'. Possibly, we should also take Lug's promise to keep watch while Cuchulainn recovered from his wounds, not in the sense of Lug's fighting against Cuchulainn's enemies,[62] but as guarding his body during his sleep. A similar idea may be contained in the stories of Ferdiad and Mes-gegra and their charioteers.

More grounds for the necessity of keeping a dreamer under observation can be deduced from Giraldus' description of the Welsh *awenydhyon* because the latter uttered the desired prophecy while rapt in ecstasy or being fast asleep and forgot the revelation when being roused or on awaking.

There are certain persons in Cambria, whom you will find nowhere else, called Awenydhyon, or people inspired; when consulted upon any doubtful event, they roar out violently, are rendered beside themselves, and become, as it were, possessed by a spirit. They do not deliver the answer to what is required in a connected manner; but the person who skilfully observes them, will find, after many preambles, and many nugatory and incoherent, though ornamented speeches, the desired explanation conveyed in some turn of a word: they are then roused from their ecstasy, as from a deep sleep, and, as it were, by violence compelled to return to their proper senses. After having answered the questions, they do not recover till violently shaken by other people; nor can they remember the replies they have given. If consulted a second or third time upon the same point, they will make use of expressions totally different; perhaps they speak by the means of fanatic and ignorant spirits. These gifts are usually conferred upon them in dreams.[63]

Apart from some means by which the 'skilful' observer reconstructed the *awenydhyon*'s revelation there is no further indication either about the observer or about his relation to the prophet. Giraldus' assertion, that the latter did not remember his impressions, is in 'The Battle of Crinna' apparently expressed by the phrase 'he passed his hand over his face'.

Just before the Battle of Crinna:

a great obnubilation was conjured up for (Teigue), so that he slept a heavy sleep and that things magic-begotten were shewn to him to enunciate, and power was lent him to declare that which was in store for him. But Cormac, free of sleep, listened to him, et dixit Teigue – 'Much valour, much incitement'. ... After the singing of that lay Teigue awoke; he passed his hand over his face, and said: 'it is time for us to go up to fight the battle.' 'Time it is indeed,' Cormac replied, and chanted a lay: 'The revelations, oh the revelations, that Teigue makes before Crinna's battle.'[64]

How was the great obnubilation conjured up for Teigue? Through 'illumination by rhymes', as MacCulloch supposes? By hypnotical influence of which the druids were certainly aware? Or by intoxicating drinks?[65] Two jars full of wine and food brought from the lands of Gaul caused the prophetic inspiration by which Dil, the Druid of the Ossory, betrayed his own tribe thus leading to its defeat at Inneoin.[66] These features are not necessarily incredible, as the actual wine-trade between West Gaul and Ireland has been extensively documented by H. Zimmer.[67] Manx customs as well as practices of the modern Greeks suggest that 'the food of Gaul' consisted of some thirst-giving salty ingredient. Besides its leading to the consumption of an undue quantity of wine, salt retained its ancient purifying character and continued to play a part in preliminaries to divination.[68] Beer was brought to druids engaged upon divination. When St Berach's miracles were reported:

> Aedan said to his druids: 'Find out who has done these mighty deeds and miracles.' And the druids went on to their hurdles of rowan, and new beer was brought to them. Four was the number of the druids(!) ... Keating ... says that this was the most potent form of druidic divination, and was only resorted to when everything else had failed. ... This is what they would do, namely, make round hurdles of rowan, and spread over them the hides of sacrificed bulls with the fleshy (or inner) side uppermost, and so proceed to summon the demons to extract information from them. And hence, adds Keating, it became a proverb to say of any one who has done his utmost to obtain information ... that he has gone on to his hurdles of knowledge.[69]

As the round hurdles combine the evil-averting virtue residing in the rowan-tree with that of the fortress-like magic circle, they were certainly meant as a powerful protection for the druids, who were believed to be exposed to great danger while 'conjuring' spirits.

Whatever may be the explanation for the cause of Teigue's revelation, 'adventitious aids were introduced to distract the mind from its preoccupation and to allow it to escape into that state of receptiveness in which revelation ... can come with the flash of illumination' ... because 'prophecy in its lower forms is not always at a man's command'.[70]

Of great interest for our immediate purpose is Teigue's relation to Cormac. Since communication through the senses was established between them, as well as between the Welsh *awenydhyon* and his observer, we are not entitled to speak of telepathy. Nevertheless, it seems that no words would better characterize their different roles than the terms used by modern science in relation to telepathy, namely 'sender' or 'agent' and 'receiver' or 'recipient'[71] There is only one indication which could help us to form a conviction as to what may have qualified Teigue for a 'sender' of prophecy: Teigue is the son of Cormac's sister and his heir. Sir John Rhys concluded from the frequently mentioned social arrangement, that the sister's son becomes the successor: the 'community appears to have recognized no paternity; but to have reckoned descent by birth alone; it is possible, however, that at a previous stage in its history the family was constituted on strictly matriarchal lines'.[72]

There are two instances for the understanding of which it is essential to bear in mind the almost mystic communion which existed between a king and his nephew: In the 'Táin' there is a short reference to the lad Cuchulainn's being appointed to sit between the two feet of Conchobar (his mother's brother), after having performed certain initiation-rites.[73]

Geoffrey recorded:

At the end of two years, Edwin asked permission of Kadwallon to make himself a crown, which he could wear when he did reverence on the festivals of the saints beyond the hymyr, according to the right of kings before them. And a conference was appointed for the wise men of the district to meet on the banks of the River named Dylas to consider the matter. And there Kadwallon put his head on the knee of Braint, son of Nefyn, his nephew. And Braint hir (the tall) wept until the tears fell on Kadwallon's face so that he awoke thinking that there was rain. And then the king asked Braint why he wept. Then said he: 'Cause of weeping will the bryttaniait have from this day on; for thou hast given up that which was of highest dignity for thyself and thy nation … in giving permission to these saesson, deceivers, traitors, faith-breaking pagans, themselves to make a king; and then they will combine together and by their deceit and craft will conquer the whole of ynys brydain. And for this reason it had been better to thee to oppress rather than favour them.' … And when Braint ended speaking, Kadwallon sent messengers to Edwin to tell him that the council would not permit that there should be any crown in ynys brydain except the crown of Llundain.[74]

It is certainly not accidental that this scene took place on the banks of a river. Braint's psychic activity, occurring in ideas rather than in pictures, should, according to Schleiermacher, be regarded as a characteristic part of the waking state.[75] The complicated nature of the contact by which Kadwallon's will-power was so strengthened that he resisted Edwin's demands, points, perhaps, to Geoffrey's not rightly understanding the older texts from which he drew. Or did he remember St Augustine who concluded a story about the spirit's departure in sleep with these words: 'And thus, that was exhibited to one by phantastic image while waking, which the other saw in dream?'[76]

According to the Irish legend 'The Destruction', king Conaire was capable of foreseeing the future after having slept in a most unusual position. At first sight it seems as if the king was so fortified by his rest that he could understand and interpret the ominous howl of his dog. But in the light of our studies it is more conceivable that the king describes pictures just seen in a dream.

Just before the attack by Ingcél and his band of pirates on Dá Derga's Hostel, Conaire was in the midst between his two fosterers, Dris and Snithe:

both of them, fair, with their hair and eyelashes; and they are as bright as snow. A very lovely blush on the cheek of each of the twain. … The tender warrior was asleep, with his feet in the lap of one of the two men and his head in the lap of the other. Then he awoke out of his sleep, and arose, and chanted this lay: 'The howl of Ossar (Conaire's lapdog) … cry of warriors on the summit of Tol Géisse; a cold wind over edges perilous: a night to destroy a king is this night.'

He slept again, and awoke thereout, and sang this rhetoric:

The howl of Ossar … a battle he announced: enslavement of a people: sack of the Hostel: mournful are the champions: men wounded: wind of terror: hurling of javelins: trouble of unfair fight: wreck of houses: Tara waste: a foreign heritage: like (is) lamenting Conaire: destruction of corn: feast of arms: cry of screams: destruction of Erin's king:

chariots a-tottering: oppression of the king of Tara: lamentations will overcome laughter: Ossar's howl.

He said the third time:

> Trouble hath been shewn to me: a multitude of elves: a host supine: foes' prostration: a conflict of men on the Dodder: oppression of Tara's king: in youth he was destroyed: lamentations will overcome laughter: Ossar's howl.[77]

The position of the sleeping king should not be dismissed as poetical imagination, since in the *Ancient Laws and Institutes of Wales* a foot-holder is enumerated among the members of a king's attendants: 'He is to hold the King's feet in his lap, from the time he shall begin to sit at the banquet, until he goes to sleep … and during that space of time, he is to guard the King against every mischance.'[78]

A faded memory of this custom can be found in *The Mabinogion*. Math, the son of Mathonwy, the lord over Gwynedd, 'could not live save while his two feet were in the hollow of a maiden's abdomen, except only when the strife of war prevented him'.[79]

Another version of 'The Destruction' is noteworthy because Conaire's position is depicted in a different way:

> I beheld a couch there, and fairer was its covering (?) than (that of) the other couches of the house, that is, three beautiful quilts and three blankets over them: a bolster at its head, another at the wall. I beheld a wondrous warrior on the couch; and many marvellous coverings, and with him on the couch a pair, the outer pair. White were the twain, with heads of hair and mantles, and bright as snow was the beautiful flush on the cheek of each of them. The wondrous warrior on the couch, never saw I human form that was like to him. … Pillows of gold were placed all around him.[80]

The white mantles of Conaire's fosterers, similar to the white robes of the druids, were probably worn in order that the colour of purity might protect them when dealing with supernatural beings.[81] The 'many marvellous coverings' are rather striking but too vaguely described to allow inferences. A bed was also mentioned in one version of the bull-feast at Tara. Do both these references go back to Pausanias' remark about the couch which stood in the temple of Aesculapius at Tithorea and was used for incubation?[82] And were they inserted in order to replace more primitive and crude customs?

But wherever the dreamer may have been resting, he was certainly isolated from the ground, just as the king sitting with his feet in the foot-holder's lap and as the men who were wrapped in a hide or lying upon one. (The neutralizing power of a hide was used for isolating the evil forces of a 'paricida' in the days of Cicero.)[83] A similar endeavour may also underlie the custom of resting between two pillar-stones while touching them simultaneously with head and feet. The evidence for this usage is extremely scanty.

Condla Coel Corrbacc was on the island, leaning his head against a pillar-stone in the western part of the island and the feet against a pillar-stone in its eastern part.[84]

> When [Cuchulainn] was a gilla, he slept not in Emain Macha till morning. 'Tell me,' Conchobar said to him, 'why sleepest thou not in Emain Macha, Cuchulainn?' 'I sleep not, unless it be equally high at my head and my feet.' Then Conchobar had a pillar-

stone set up at his head and another at his feet, and between them a bed apart was made for him. ... The broil of war arose between Ulster and Eogan son of Durthacht. The Ulstermen go forth to the war. The lad (Cuchulainn) is left behind asleep. The men of Ulster are beaten. ... Their groans awaken the lad. Thereat he stretches himself, so that the two stones are snapped that are near him.[85]

Can these incidents be linked up with the erecting of two pillar-stones on a grave? Conchobar's grave is on the brink of the ford of Daire Dá Báeth, 'where he fell, and a pillar-stone at his head, and another at his feet'.[86]

Before concluding this investigation the notion deserves our attention that spiritual capacities can be miraculously enhanced by physical contact; either by bringing one's head into contact with another person's lap (as Conaire did), or through implanting one's feet upon the feet of a person credited with superior insight.

Waldron has described the game 'Cutting off the Fiddler's Head' as follows:

On Twelfth-day the Fiddler lays his head in some one of the wenches' laps, and a third person asks who such a maid or such a maid shall marry, naming the girls then present one after another, to which he answers according to his own whim, or agreeable to the intimacies he has taken notice of during this time of merriment. But whatever he says is as absolutely depended on as an oracle.[87]

A charming anecdote reflects how a Celtic saint attempted with fine feeling to modify pagan conceptions. When a little boy appealed to St Aengus to help him to learn the Psalms by heart, the saint advised him: '"Put thy head on my knee, and go to sleep." The boy did so, and afterwards rose up ... and was not only word-perfect, but repeated more than the lesson set.'[88]

Are we not reminded of the well-known experiences of Caedmon, St Dunstan and Coleridge?[89] And, perhaps, also of our own school-days when the school-book under the pillow helped us to face the demands of the next morning with a much easier mind. Not very different is the 'external objective sensory stimulus' in the girls' habit of placing on Hallowe'en a particular briar-thorn under the pillow, 'and the dream to follow will be of the future husband'.[90]

Of great interest is the following record (the bulls were presumably originally sacrificed to the well-spirit which was succeeded, as so often, by a Christian saint):

According to the Presbytery Records of Applecross, dated Sept. 5, 1656, an inquiry was made into a bitter complaint by the parish minister, of certain superstitious practices prevalent on the island of St Mhaolrubh. The worthy cleric reported that the people were accustomed to sacrifice bulls on the 25th day of August, the day dedicated to the Saint. After the sacrifice of the animal there were frequent approaches to the chapel ruins and circulating round them. ... (Those) desirous of knowing their future or good fortune in travels, after depositing an offering in the (Holy) Well tried to force their head into a hole in a round stone. If successful all was well, but misfortune was sure to follow if the attempt failed.[91]

Some instances may be given of how visions were revealed to those who stood on the feet of some supernatural being or some person endowed with second sight. Two examples, though not Celtic in origin, are contained in 'Nova Legenda Anglie'. Sir John Rhys told the story of a farmer from Deunant, who, by standing on a fairy's foot, could get a glimpse of the fairy world. Somewhat different is the legend how Aengus mac Nadfraich, by laying his face on Enda's feet, was enabled to see the Isle of Aran, though many miles away.[92]

From a Welsh manuscript of the earlier part of the sixteenth century we learn that second sight might be imparted from one to another. In the Isle of Man 'there oft by daye tyme, men of that islonde seen men that bey dede to forehonde, byheded or hole, and what dethe they deyde. Alyens setten theyr feet upon feet of the men of that londe, for to see such syghtes as the men of that londe doon'.[93]

The implanting of the foot is a symbol of subjection; the basic idea of this action lies in the widespread belief that the various faculties of the subjected person can be transferred to the dominating one.[94]

Notes

1 Trans. by W.H.S. Jones (London, 1931), vol. iv, p. 421.

2 *Prophecy and Divination* (London, 1938), p. 217.

3 'The First Battle of Moytura', trans. by J. Fraser in *Ériu*, viii (Dublin, 1915), p. 19.

4 E. Ettlinger, 'Omens and Celtic Warfare' in *Man*, xliii (London, 1943), No. 4.

5 Havelock Ellis, *The World of Dreams* (London, 1922), p. 266.

6 *Irische Texte*, trans. by Whitley Stokes and E. Windisch, vol. iv, Heft I (Leipzig, 1900), p. 302; *Revue celtique*, xxiv (Paris, 1903), pp. 174–5.

7 St H. O'Grady, *Silva Gadelica* (London, 1892), vol. ii, p. 84; for a saint as a dream-reader see *Vita Sancti Lasriani*, § 32.

8 *The Banquet of Dun Na N-gedh*, trans. by J. O'Donovan (Dublin, 1842), pp. 9–13.

9 C. Plummer, *Vitae Sanctorum Hiberniae* (Oxford, 1910), vol. i, p. clx, note 5.

10 H.M. and N.K. Chadwick, *The Growth of Literature* (Cambridge, 1932), vol. i, p. 380, quoted from 'Mac Datho's Pig', cap. 3.

11 A.B. Keith, 'Numbers' in Hastings, *Encyclopaedia of Religion and Ethics*, vol. ix, p. 411a.

12 *The Historia Regum Britanniae of Geoffrey of Monmouth*, trans. by Acton Griscom, (London, 1929), pp. 468–9.

13 *Man*, vol. xxxviii (London, 1938), No. 158.

14 O'Grady, *op. cit.*, vol. ii, p. 407.

15 'Da Choka's Hostel', trans. by Whitley Stokes, *Revue celtique*, xxi (Paris, 1900), p. 159.

16 'The Death of the Sons of Usnech', *Irische Texte*, *op. cit.*, vol. ii, Heft II (Leipzig, 1887), p. 161.

17 Trans. by Whitley Stokes, *Revue celtique*, viii (Paris, 1887), pp. 57–9; R. Thurneysen, *Die Irische Helden- und Königsage* (Halle, 1921), p. 507, note 2.

18 'Da Choka's Hostel', *op. cit.*, pp. 157–9; E. Hull, *The Cuchullin Saga* (London, 1898), p. 247; T. Gwynn Jones, *Welsh Folklore and Folk-Custom* (London, 1930), p. 107.

19 Dio's *Roman History*, lv, I.

20 Sir John Rhys, *Celtic Folklore* (Oxford, 1901), vol. i, pp. 396–7.

21 W.R. Halliday, *Greek Divination* (London, 1913), p. 203 and note 2.

22 Trans. by Eugen Curry, *Atlantis*, i (London, 1858), p. 385.

23 A. Mitchell, *The Past in the Present* (Edinburgh, 1880), pp. 148–9, 275; J.A. MacCulloch, *The Religion of the Ancient Celts* (Edinburgh, 1911), p. 243.

24 Cormac's *Glossary*, trans. by J. O'Donovan, ed. by Whitley Stokes (Calcutta, 1868), pp. 71, 72, 134; O'Grady, *op. cit.*, vol. ii, p. 131; Sacheverell Sitwell, *Primitive Scenes and Festivals* (London, 1942), pp. 44–5.

25 Mengis, 'Weiss', *Handwörterbuch des Deutschen Aberglaubens*, vol. ix (Berlin, 1938), p. 344.

26 D'Arbois de Jubainville, *Littérature celtique* (Paris, 1883), vol. i, p. 152.

27 'The Second Battle of Moytura', trans. by Whitley Stokes, *Revue celtique*, xii (Paris, 1891), pp. 59, 95.

28 A. Nutt, *The Voyage of Bran* (London, 1895), vol. i, p. 187.

29 'The Sickbed', *op. cit.*, pp. 377–9.

30 *Das Keltische Brittanien, Abhandlungen der Philologisch-Historischen Klasse der Kgl. Sächsischen Gesellschaft der Wissenschaften*, vol. xxix (Leipzig, 1912), p. 132.

31 Trans. by Whitley Stokes, *Revue celtique*, xxii (Paris, 1901), p. 23, note 2.

32 O'Grady, *op. cit.*, vol. ii, p. 183.

33 Pausanias, *Description of Greece*, trans. by Sir J.G. Frazer (London, 1898), vol. iv, p. 175; see A. Guillaume, *op. cit.*, p. 281.

34 'The Destruction', *op. cit.*, p. 287.

35 Cormac's *Glossary, op. cit.*, pp. 94–5.

36 'Imbas For. Osndai', *Zeitschrift für Celtische Philologie*, xix (Halle, 1933), pp. 163–4.

37 D. Hyde, *A Literary History of Ireland* (London, 1899), pp. 241–2.

38 'The Proceedings of the Great Bardic Institution', trans. by Professor Connellan, *Trans. Ossianic Society*, v (Dublin, 1860), p. 101.

39 J.G. Dalyell, *The Darker Superstitions of Scotland* (Edinburgh, 1834), p. 495.

40 *A Description of the Western Islands* (London, 1703), pp. 111–13.

41 *Op. cit.*, p. 250.

42 *Op. cit.*, p. 495.

43 Halliday, *op. cit.*, p. 132, quoted from Porphyry, *Vit. Pythag.* 17.

44 *The Ancient Irish Epic Tale Táin Bó Cuailgnè*, trans. by J. Dunn (London, 1914) pp. 233–4.

45 *The Mabinogion*, trans. by T.P. Ellis and J. Lloyd (Oxford, 1929), vol. ii, pp. 6–7; Windisch, *Das Keltische Brittanien, op. cit.*, p. 153.

46 *Op. cit.*, p. 239; C. Bailey, *Religion in Virgil* (Oxford, 1935), p. 44.

47 'Finn and the Phantoms', trans. by Whitley Stokes, *Reveue celtique*, vii (Paris, 1886), pp. 297, 303.

48 Sir E.B. Tylor, *Primitive Culture*, 4th ed. (London, 1903), vol. ii, p. 419; 'Flagellants', *Encyclopaedia Brittanica*, 11th ed.

49 Quoted from Bede's *Historia Ecclesiastica*, ii, 6, by G.L. Kittredge in *Witchcraft in Old and New England* (Cambridge, Mass., 1929), p. 222.

50 *Op. cit.*, p. 377; Thurneysen, *op. cit.*, p. 393.

51 *Op. cit.*, vol. i, pp. 16–17 and note 47.

52 Thurneysen, *op. cit.*, p. 252.

53 Chadwick, *op. cit.*, vol. i, p. 650.

54 *Op. cit.*, pp. 182–3.

55 Sir E.B. Tylor, *op. cit.*, vol. ii, p. 120.

56 See Kittredge, *op. cit.*, pp. 221–2; *Archaeologia Cambrensis*, xii, 6th Series (London, 1912), p. 234; Dr Richard Pococke, *The Travels through England*, ed. by J.J. Cartwright (Camden Society, 1889), vol. ii, p. 175.

57 A. Bouché-Leclercq, *Histoire de la Divination* (Paris, 1879), vol. i, p. 289.

58 *Op. cit.*, vol. i, p. clxxii and note 3.

59 'The Vision of Laisrén', trans. by K. Meyer, *Otia Merseiana*, i (Liverpool, 1899), p. 116.

60 Quoted by Plummer, *op. cit.*, vol. i, p. clxxii, note 3, from *Irische Texte*, vol. i, p. 208.

61 'Trois Historiettes Irlandaises', J. Vendryes, *Revue celtique*, xxxi (Paris, 1910), p. 310.

62 'Táin', *op. cit.*, p. 182; R. Thurneysen, *Zu Irischen Handschriften* (Berlin, 1912), pp. 54–5.

63 *Description of Wales*, trans. by Thomas Wright (London, 1863), pp. 501–2.

64 O'Grady, *op. cit.*, vol. ii, p. 362.

65 *Op. cit.*, pp. 249, 324; R.A. St Macalister, *The Latin and Irish Lives of Ciaran* (London, 1921), pp. 149–50; *Irische Texte, op. cit.*, vol. iv, Heft I, p. 333; Sir John Rhys, *Celtic Heathendom* (London, 1888), pp. 359–60.

66 'The Expulsion of the Dessi', trans. by K. Meyer, *Y Cymmrodor*, xiv (London, 1901), pp. 119–21.

67 *Ueber direkte Handelsverbindungen Westgalliens mit Irland im Alterium and frühen Mittelalter, Sitzungsberichte der Kgl. Preussischen Akademie der Wissen-schaften*, xv (Berlin, 1909).

68 A.W. Moore, *The Folklore of the Isle of Man* (London, 1891), p. 125; J.C. Lawson, *Modern Greek Folklore and Ancient Greek Religion* (Cambridge, 1910), p. 303; Pauly Wissowa, *Real-Encyclopädie*, 2. *Reihe*, vol. i (Stuttgart, 1920), 'Salz', pp. 2093–4.

69 Plummer, *Lives of Irish Saints* (Oxford, 1922), vol. ii, p. 33 ('Life of Berach'); Plummer, *Vitae Sanctorum Hiberniae, op. cit.*, vol. i, p. cliv, note 5, quoted from *Keating*, ii, pp. 348–50.

70 Guillaume, *op. cit.*, p. 210.

71 J.B. Rhine, *New Frontiers of the Mind* (London, 1938), pp. 177–8.

72 Sir John Rhys and D. Brynmor-Jones, *The Welsh People* (London, 1900), p. 54.

73 *Op. cit.*, pp. 67, 78.

74 *Op. cit.*, pp. 513–15.

75 *Psychologie*, ed. by L. George (Berlin, 1862), p. 351, quoted by S. Freud, *The Interpretation of Dreams*, trans. by A.A. Brill, 3rd ed. (London, 1913), p. 40.

76 *De Civitate Dei*, xviii, 18, quoted by Sir E.B. Tylor, *op. cit.*, vol. i, p. 441.

77 *Op. cit.*, pp. 202, 208.

78 Trans. by Aneurin Owen (London, 1841), p. 29.

79 *Op. cit.*, vol. i, p. 100.

80 Trans. by Whitley Stokes, *Revue celtique*, xxii, p. 397.

81 Pliny, *H.N.*, xvi, 44; *The Tripartite Life of Patrick*, ed. by Whitley Stokes (London, 1887), vol. ii, pp. 325–6; Mengis, *op. cit.*, p. 342.

82 (x, 32, 12), *op. cit.*, vol. v, p. 549; L.F.A. Maury, *La Magie et l'Astrologie*, 3rd ed. (Paris, 1864), p. 240.

83 H.J. Rose, *Primitive Culture in Italy* (London, 1926), pp. 183–4.

84 *Irische Texte, op. cit.*, vol. ii, Heft I (Leipzig, 1884), p. 200.

85 'Táin', *op. cit.*, pp. 50–1.

86 K. Meyer, 'The Death-Tales of the Ulster Heroes', *Todd Lecture Series*, xiv (Dublin, 1906), p. 7.

87 Quoted by Moore, *op. cit.*, p. 104.

88 Quoted by G. Hartwell Jones, 'Primitive Magic in the Lives of the Celtic Saints' in *Trans. Soc. Cymmrodorian*, Session 1936 (London, 1937), p. 86.

89 Kittredge, *op. cit.*, pp. 221–2, quoted from *Memorials of St Dunstan*, ed. by Stubbs, pp. 40–2, cf. 48–9.

90 Leland L. Duncan, 'Notes from County Leitrim' in *Folklore*, v (London, 1894), p. 196.

91 Quoted by A.D. Lacaille, 'The Bull in Scottish Folklore' in *Folklore*, xli (London, 1930), p. 228.

92 Ed. by C. Horstman (Oxford, 1901), vol. i, p. 101; vol. ii, p. 413; *Celtic Folkore, op. cit.*, vol. i, p. 230; Plummer, *Vitae Sanctorum Hiberniae, op. cit.*, p. clxxi, note 9, quoted from *Vita Sancti Endei*, § 13.

93 Dalyell, *op. cit.*, p. 481.

94 Goldmann, 'Fusstreten' in *Handwörterbuch des Deutschen Aberglaubens*, vol. iii (Berlin, 1930–31), p. 243.

CHAPTER TWO

Prognostication from the Raven and the Wren

R.I. Best

THE FOLLOWING TWO SCRAPS of early Irish folklore, relating to the raven and the wren, are written by a late scribe into blank spaces left in the well-known codex *H*.3.17, preserved in the Library of Trinity College. The first, *Fiachairecht*, on col. 803 f., the second, *Dreanacht*, on col 831, where the *Tochmarc Ailbi* ends. These short tracts were first referred to by O'Donovan, in an interesting note to his edition of the so-called Lorica attributed to Columcille,[1] in which the practice of seeking omens from birds, sneezing, clapping of hands etc, is deprecated:

Ní adraim do gothaib én,
na sreód na sén for bith che,
ná mac ná mana ná mnai.
Is é mo draí Críst mac Dé.

'I adore not the voices of birds, nor sneezing nor lots in this world nor a boy nor omens nor woman. My druid is Christ the Son of God.'[2] It is from the Picts, six of whom settled in Magh Breagh, that the Irish are said to have derived 'every spell, every charm, every augury by sneezing, voices of birds, and every omen'.[3]

O'Curry in his lecture on druids and druidism (*Manners and Customs*, II. 223 f.) again mentions our two tracts, which, he shrewdly remarks, show that the Irish must have domesticated these birds for the purpose of divination. He translates part of the first on Raven lore, omitting unfortunately those passages where his aid would have been useful.

In a tract so inconsequent it is difficult, without the support of a second manuscript, to feel at all sure of one's rendering, and some of these prognostications are decidedly ambiguous. In several instances Dr Bergin has happily suggested the more likely meaning.

Some interesting lore about these birds, usually of ill-omen, will be found in Forbes's *Gaelic Names of Beasts and Birds etc*, pp. 324–8, 347–9, Edinburgh, 1905, and for Irish omens from birds in general, in Wood-Martin's *Traces of the Elder Faiths of Ireland*, II. 141 ff. Similar prognostications from the howling of dogs occur in Laud 615, whence they have been edited and translated by O'Grady (*Mélusine* v. 85–6, 1890), and the prognostications of the first day of January in Egerton 1782, edited with translation by Meyer (ibid. X. 113, 1900).

The language of the tracts is Middle-Irish; note the neuter *tormach mbidh*, the red. fut. with inf. rel. *d.*, *nodbébhus* (for Old-Irish *nodbeba*), the subj. form *dodeocha*.

Raven Lore

If the raven call from above an enclosed bed in the midst of the house, it is a distinguished grey-haired guest or clerics that are coming to thee, but there is a difference between them: if it be a lay cleric (?) the raven says *bacach*; if it be a man in orders it calls *gradh gradh*, and twice in the day it calls. If it be warrior guests or satirists that are coming it is *gracc gracc* it calls, or *grob grob*, and it calls in the quarter behind thee, and it is thence that the guests are coming. If it call *gracc gracc* the warriors are oppressed (?) to whom it calls. If women are coming it calls long. If it call from the northeast end of the house, robbers are about to steal the horses. If it call from the house door, strangers or soldiers are coming. If it call from above the door, satirists or guests from a king's retinue are coming. If it call from above the goodman's bed, the place where his weapons will be, and he going on a journey he will not come back safe; but if not, he will come back sound. If it is the woman who is about to die, it is from the pillow it calls. If it call from the foot of the man's bed, his son or his brother or his son-in-law will come to the house. If it call from the edge of the storehouse where the food is kept, there will be increase of food from the quarter it calls, that is, flesh-meat or first milking of kine. If its face be between the storehouse and the fire, agreeable (?) guests are coming to the house. If it be near to the woman of the house, where her seat is, the guests are for her, namely, a son-in-law or a friend. If it call from the south of the storehouse, fosterage or guests from afar are coming to the house. If it speak with a small voice, that is *err err* or *úr úr*, sickness will fall on some one in the house or on some of the cattle. If wolves are coming among the sheep, it is from the sheep-fold it calls, or from over against the good woman, and what it says is *carna carna* (flesh), *grob grob, coin coin* (wolves). If it call from the roof-tree of the house when people are eating, they throw away that food. If it call from a stone, it is death-tidings of an *aithech*.[4] If it call from a high tree, then it is death-tidings of a young lord. If from the top of the tree, death-tidings of a king or a youth of noble lineage. If it go with thee on a journey or in front of thee, and if it be joyful, thy journey will prosper and fresh meat will be given to thee. If thou come left-hand-wise and it calls before thee, he is a doomed man on whom it calls thus, or it is the wounding of some one of the company. If it be before thee when going to an assembly, there will be an uprising therein. If it be left-hand-wise it has come, some one is slain in that uprising. If it call from the corner where the horses are, robbers are about to attack them. If it turn on its back thereat and says *grob grob*, some of the horses will be stolen and they will not be recovered, and so on.

Wren Lore

If the little white-headed one call to thee from the east, pious men are journeying towards thee, with discourtesy for thee (?). If the wren call from the southeast, it is proud jesters that are coming. If from the southwest, ex-freemen (?) are coming to you. If it call from the northeast, folk with a bedfellow or women are coming. If it be from the north, dear to thee is he that is coming. If it come from the northwest, pious folk are on the way. If it call from the south side of thee, provided it be not between thee and the sun, a fond visitation is coming to you. If it be between thee and the sun, it is the slaying of a man that is dear to thee, or a horn on thyself. If it be at thy left ear, union with a young man from afar, or sleeping with a young woman. If it call from behind thee, importuning of thy wife by another man in despite of thee. If it be on the ground behind thee, thy wife will be taken from thee by force. If the wren call from the east, poets are coming towards thee, or tidings from them. If it call behind thee from the south, thou wilt see the heads of good clergy, or hear death-tidings of noble ex-laymen. If it call from the southwest, robbers and evil rustics and bad women are coming towards thee. If it be from the west, wicked kinsmen are coming. If it call from the northwest, a noble hero of good lineage and noble hospitallers and good women are coming. If it call from the north, bad people are coming, whether warriors or clerics or bad women, and wicked youths are on the way. If it call from the south, sickness or wolves among thy herds. If it be from the ground or from a stone or from a cross it calls, death-tidings of a great man it relates to thee. If it call from many crosses, it is a slaughter of men, and the number of times it alights on the ground is the number of dead it announces, and the quarter towards which its face is, from thence are the dead it announces.

Notes

1 *Miscellany of the Irish Arch. Soc.*, 1. p. 12 f. Cf. also the version of Laud 615, ZCP. vii. 303.
2 Cf. Todd's *St Patrick*, p. 122, and his *Irish Version of Nennius*, p. 144 note.
3 *Irish Version of Nennius*, ed. by Todd, p. 124 f.; cf. also p. 144.
4 *Aithech*, a class-name somewhat analogous to plebeian (Atkinson, Laws), also a 'peasant, boor, clown'.

CHAPTER THREE

Imbas Forosnai

Nora K. Chadwick

from *Scottish Gaelic Studies*

I MBAS FOROSNAI is the subject of an entry in Cormac's *Glossary*. This entry is of special interest for two reasons. In the first place, it purports to give us a recipe of the means employed by the ancient Irish poets (*filidh*) to obtain inspiration. In the second place, in an interesting colophon,[1] it claims to tell us something specific of St Patrick's attitude to the *filidh* and to poetry. This attitude is represented as highly judicial. Certain elements in the *file*'s art and practice are commended, others are condemned. In the following brief study an attempt is made to interpret this interesting entry in the light of some allusions to similar mantic practices contained in other early Irish texts. It is hoped that it may be possible by this method to come to a clearer understanding of the sources or the milieu from which the author of the entry derives his material. In saying this, however, I am well aware that I cannot hope to solve more than a modicum of the obscurities of the entry by this method. But where so much is veiled perhaps any effort to penetrate the obscurity may be not wholly unwelcome.

It need hardly be stated at the outset that the entry is both difficult and obscure. Indeed, the following translation by Stokes is offered rather as a basis to work from – a kind of schedule of our terms of reference – than an authoritative interpretation of the text. The concluding portions of the passage in particular are obscure in the extreme, and it is chiefly in the hopes of approximating more closely to an understanding of them that I have put together these brief notes on certain aspects of Irish mantic tradition. In doing so I am aware that any results which we may obtain can have only a partial value since I am not qualified to deal with the philological evidence, and must therefore leave this to others. In the following brief study it is proposed, first of all, to note some of the occurrences of these same difficult phrases in other contexts, more especially in the Irish technical treatises on learned and mantic literature published by Professor Thurneysen, and to refer to one or two actual examples of the types of poetry which are cited under these names in such treatises. We will then turn to the sagas to see how Irish tradition represents the mantic practice in actual operation. And, finally, we will consider the results of this examination in relation to some parallel evidence relating to similar phenomena in Celtic Britain.

The passage on *imbas forosnai* in Cormac's *Glossary* (*Sanas Cormaic*) was edited and translated by the late Whitley Stokes several times. First we may mention the text and translation of Laud 610, fol. 79A, in his edition and translation of the *Tripartite Life of St Patrick*,

46

Part II (Rolls Series, 1887), p. 568f. Before this he had given a translation of the first part of the passage from the *Lebor Brecc* and the Book of Leinster in his introduction to *Three Irish Glossaries* (London, 1862), p. xxxvi. Finally, in 1894, he published the text and translation of the fragment of Cormac's *Glossary* in the Bodleian Library at Oxford in the *Transactions of the Philological Society* (1891–4). The translation of our passage occurs on p. 156f. As this series is not easily accessible to the general reader, I will give Stokes's rendering of our passage from the Bodleian fragment in full.

> *Imbas forosna*, 'Manifestation that enlightens': (it) discovers what thing soever the poet likes and which he desires to reveal.[2] Thus then is that done. The poet chews a piece of the red flesh of a pig, or a dog, or a cat, and puts it then on a flagstone behind the door-valve, and chants an incantation over it, and offers it to idol gods, and calls them to him, and leaves them not on the morrow, and then chants over his two palms, and calls again idol gods to him, that his sleep may not be disturbed. Then he puts his two palms on his two cheeks and sleeps. And men are watching him that he may not turn over and that no one may disturb him. And then is revealed to him that for which he was (engaged) till the end of a *nómad* (three days and nights), or two or three for the long or the short (time?) that he may judge himself (to be) at the offering. And therefore it is called *Imm-bas*, to wit, a palm (*bas*) on this side and a palm on that around his head. Patrick banished that and the Tenm láida 'illumination of song,' and declared that no one who shall do that shall belong to heaven or earth, for it is a denial of baptism.
>
> *Dichetal do chennaib*, extempore incantation, however, that was left, in right of art, for it is science that causes it, and no offering to devils is necessary, but a declaration from the ends of his bones at once.

A translation of the first part of the entry was also made by K. Meyer, and published in the *Archaeological Review*, vol. I, 1888, p. 303, footnote.[3] As this translation differs in some details from Stokes's, and as it is also somewhat inaccessible, I quote it below for purposes of comparison.

> The *Imbas Forosnai* sets forth whatever seems good to the seer (*file*) and what he desires to make known. It is done thus. The seer chews a piece of the red flesh of a pig, or a dog, or a cat, and then places it on a flagstone behind the door. He sings an incantation over it, offers it to the false gods, and then calls them to him. And he leaves them not on the next day, and chants then on his two hands, and again calls his false gods to him, lest they should disturb his sleep. And he puts his two hands over his two cheeks till he falls asleep. And they watch by him lest no one overturn him and disturb him till everything he wants to know is revealed to him, to the end of nine days, or of twice or thrice that time, or, however long he was judged at the offering.

Stokes's rendering of the latter part of our passage is not altogether happy, and, indeed, Stokes himself remarked … in a note on the entry, 'my translation of this difficult article is merely tentative'. Meyer does not venture to translate this latter portion. In regard to the main portion of the entry, however, Stokes and Meyer appear to be in substantial agreement, the only important differences being (1) that the passage in which, according to Stokes's translation of the Bodleian text, the seer 'calls the idol gods to him that his sleep may not be disturbed' (i.e., presumably by others) is rendered by Meyer, 'he calls his false gods to him lest they should disturb his sleep' (i.e., presumably the gods themselves); and (2) that according to Stokes's translation of the Bodleian text the seer is watched in order to prevent him from turning over (i.e., by his own volition); whereas Meyer's translation seems to imply that it is the false gods who watch by him lest someone overturn him. Minor divergences between the various texts also occur; but the general sense of the passage appears to remain fairly constant.

Starting, then, with these renderings by Stokes and Meyer as a basis, we may ask: What is the nature of the *imbas* which St Patrick is said to have condemned, and what is the difference between the *imbas* and the *sous*? The latter seems generally to have reference to scientific, overt art and knowledge, as opposed to the occult art of manticism. *Sous* is acquired by legitimate means, generally by Christian learning, but Christian revelation is not excluded. *Imbas* is clearly opposed to *sous*, and seems to have reference, if we may judge from the text before us, to occult art and knowledge, acquired through mantic revelation.

The etymology of the words has been discussed recently by Professor Thurneysen,[4] who cites an early gloss in the Introduction to the *Senchus Mor*, where it is stated that the word *imbas* is a compositional form with *fius(s)*, 'knowledge,' or with the neuter *fess*, just as *so-us*, *so-as*, literally, 'good knowledge,' often with reference to poetry. The words of the gloss are as follows:

.i. *in sui fili dafursannand no dafaillsigend imad a sofesa* (.i. *dofuarascaib a soas*).[5]

In this derivation – Thurneysen points out – the glossator is right, *imbas* being derived from *imb-fiuss or *imb-fess. The gloss is interesting, so Thurneysen holds,[6] in that it is quite independent of the influence of the passage in Cormac's *Glossary*, cf. however below.

Thurneysen emphasizes the absurdity of the derivation of the term *imbas* in the passage in Cormac, and in a later gloss to the Introduction to the *Senchus Mor*, reference to which will be made later. He argues further that the whole entry in the *Glossary* is a fabric of the author's imagination, built up on this spurious etymology, and points to several instances in which the expression *imbas forosnai* occurs in sagas without an accompanying description of the mantic technique. He casts doubt on the value of the reference to St Patrick, regarding the statement that the saint banished certain mantic practices as a conjecture of the author of Cormac's *Glossary*, who was, perhaps, influenced by the fact that the examples of *imbas forosnai* and *tenm laida* cited in the sagas all relate to pre-Christian times.

Of the absurdity of the derivation of *imbas* as given in Cormac's *Glossary* there can be no doubt, though it is not impossible that it may have been suggested to the author by the habit of the *filidh* or sages – as described in the sagas – of covering their faces or otherwise seeking darkness and privacy before giving mantic utterances. We shall see later that there is some ground for suspecting that such was the traditional practice. There can be no doubt, also, that Thurneysen is right in regarding the prohibition ascribed to St Patrick as a conjecture or deduction on the part of the author of the *Glossary*. We may be equally certain that Thurneysen is right in supposing that in no part of the entry is the author drawing on his own experience or his personal knowledge of contemporary practice. On the other hand, it is difficult to accept Thurneysen's conclusion that the picture which the author of the entry gives us of the practice of the *fili* is wholly imaginary, or based entirely on a spurious etymology. The evidence which leads Thurneysen to this conclusion appears to be largely negative in character. He points out that in the instances which he cites from the sagas where reference is made to *imbas forosnai*, no reference is made to mantic sleep, or to elaborate technique, such as that described in our entry. In addition he refers to the nuts of *imbas* (*Cuill Crimaind*) which occur in certain texts, and which suggest quite a different process for the acquisition of *imbas*.

Yet when we consider the amount of variation existing between one version of an Irish saga and another, and the summary form in which much of the narrative has been committed to writing, we may well ask the question: Can one safely assume that any of the texts give us a full description of the procedure of Fedelm and Scathach? Had the redactor of the passages in which they figure given us an account of their technique, and had this technique differed from that described by the author of our entry, Thurneysen's argument would have been greatly strengthened; but this is not the case. It is true that when Finn's finger or thumb has been trapped in the door of the *sid*-mound, and he proceeds to suck it, his *imbas* enlightens him. But is it clear exactly how this comes about? We shall see presently that the saga in which this incident occurs is a difficult and obscure one, notwithstanding the fact that we possess several versions of it. We shall also see that several possible explanations offer themselves as to how Finn's enlightenment comes about by this action. I do not think that these alternative explanations are all at variance with the entry in Cormac's *Glossary*. It is true that the nuts of *imbas*, e.g., the *Cuill Crimaind* cited by Professor Thurneysen, suggest quite a different procedure by which *imbas* is acquired. This will be referred to later.

Turning now to the text of the entry in the *Glossary* itself, we may note that several of the phrases occurring in the difficult portion of our entry have the appearance of technical terms. *Imbas forosnai* and *tenm laida* are well known to be such. But what are *dichetal di chennaib* and *aisneis di chennaib (a) chnaime*? To determine more fully the nature of these technical terms, it may be of interest to notice some occurrences of identical and similar terms in the metrical tractates preserved in the Book of Ballymote and elsewhere, and also preserved in certain other technical treatises of a similar character. Here we find these technical terms figuring largely in the course of education prescribed for the *filidh*. In a gloss to a passage on the seven poetical grades contained in the *Uraicecht Becc*,[7] or 'Small Primer', we are told that there are three things required of the *ollam*-poet, viz., the *teinm laegda*, and the *imus forosnad* and *dichetal do chennaib*, as the Nemed-Judgements say: 'three things which dignify the dignities of a poet, *tenm laegda, imus forosnad, dichedul do cennaib*.'[8]

According to the second of the Metrical Tractates published by Thurneysen from the Book of Ballymote, the Book of Leinster etc, the *fili* had to learn in the eighth year of his training, among other things, three songs, viz., *imbas forosnai, tenm laida* and *dichetal do chennaib na tuaithe*.[9] In the same tractate we are told that in the twelfth year of his training a *fili* is expected to know twelve *rochetla*, of which nine are enumerated, the second being *cetal do chennaib*, with which Thurneysen associates *dichetal do chennaib na tuaithe* of the eighth year.[10] In the third of the Metrical Tractates published by Thurneysen we again find in close association the *tenm laida*, the *imbas forosnai*, and the *dichetal*,[11] and in a passage in LL. (30d) we find it stated that *tenm laida* belongs to the fourteen streams of poetry (*srotha eicsi*).[12] There can be no doubt, therefore, that *imbas forosnai, tenm laida* and *dichetal do chennaib* are three technical terms, which are closely and constantly associated together in relation to the art of the *filidh*. It may be added here that the three expressions, *tenm laida, imbas forosnai* and *dichetal di chennaib*, translated by Meyer as 'illumination of song', 'knowledge which illuminates' and 'extempore incantation' respectively, are associated together also in the *Macgnimartha Find*, § 19, to which fuller reference will be made below.

With these is associated in Cormac's *Glossary* what appears to be a fourth technical spell term, the *aisneis di chennaib a chname*. This close association is found also in the second of the Metrical Tractates,[13] where in the examples of various metres cited, No. 123 is *cetal do*[14] *chennaib*, while No. 125 is *cetal na haisense*. It is possibly worth noting that in the example immediately following the *cetal na haisnese*[15] the words *mo carusa cnaimine*[16] are found in all three texts. We have already seen that Thurneysen associates this *cetal do chendaib* characteristic of the twelfth year of training with the *dichetal do chennaib na tuaithe* of the eighth. We may therefore compare the construction of the *aisneis do chennaib a chnamae* with *dichetal do chennaib na tuaithe*, and with *imbass forosndi dia foirciunn* which occurs in several manuscripts of the account of the *Verba Scathaige*, and to which further reference will be made later.

These expressions are all obscure. They appear to represent something in the nature of rubrics,[17] i.e., phrases extracted from texts of spells or of mantic processes; but it is clear that they have now come to serve in many cases, as titles of the spells themselves. The variation in the number of words given, e.g., in *dichetal di chennaib* etc, rather suggests this. If this surmise is correct, it is manifest that it would be absurd to attempt to translate them in any syntactical relation to the rest of our text, though we may still hope to interpret them. Meyer and others translate *do (di) chennaib* as 'extempore,' though O'Davoran glossed it 'continuo.' The meaning 'extempore' hardly fits the context in the Preface to the *Amra Choluimb Chille*, in which the saint is represented as reproving Dallan Forgall for reciting a poem to him during his life which was only suitable for a dead man, '*7 is do chennaib dano do trial Dallán a dudin do denam.*' The expression *dia foirciunn*, to which we have referred above, is translated by Thurneysen as 'um ihn zu vollenden'.[18]

With the expression *dichetal do chennaib* we may compare *do cendaib colla* (? for *collan*) in the gloss to the Introduction to the *Senchus Mor*;[19] *dicetal di cennaib coll* in Laud 610, 57b; and *dicetul do chollaib cend* in Rawl. B. 512, 114b.[20] If we accept Thurneysen's translation the word *cenn* in these expressions would be translated in the sense of 'the future', and *dichetal do chennaib* in the sense of 'to chant in prophetic strains', and this must, I think, be the sense which it has come to bear in many of the passages where it is found, though there can be little doubt that it was originally used in another and more literal sense, as we shall see later. The phrase cited from Rawl. B. 512, 114b may then mean 'chanting by means of the hazels of prophecy'. To the hazels of prophecy also we shall return later. We may, however, compare a passage in the gloss in the 'Small Primer', which enumerates the privileges of poets, *dichedul dichendaib .i. dul do a cend adana focoir in cenda i act am adb asnedat gumradud.*[21] We may refer also to the phrase *dicetal do ceandaibh cnoc no cnatarbarc* which occurs as a part of a gloss[22] to the poem ascribed in the *Leabhar na Gabhala* to the *fili* Amargin as he landed in Ireland, and which is translated by Macalister and MacNeill: 'incantation from the tops of mountains or of ships.'

We are fortunate in possessing examples of the art of the *filidh* which bear as their titles all the rubrics or technical terms which occur in the closing lines of the passage from Cormac's *Glossary* which we have been considering. One of the fullest examples of a verse sung 'through *imbas forosnai*' (*triasa n-imbas forosnai*) is the poem attributed to Finn when he tracks Ferchess and avenges on him the death of Mac Con. The text will be found in the story of *Ailill Aulom, Mac Con and Find Ua Baiscne*,[23] to which fuller reference will be made below. A tentative translation is given by Meyer as follows:

> Here is the abode of Ferchess, at Ess Mage ... swiftly after great deeds; a great heroic champion has fallen swiftly after great deeds. To my lordly god I swear the oath of every one in the world a ... deed will be avenged. Mac Con was slain here.[24]

Another example of a poem (*dicetal*) chanted through *imbas forosnai* occurs in the story of *Finn and the Man in the Tree*.[25] Here we are told that when Finn finds his servant disguised in the tree he puts his thumb into his mouth, and when he takes it out again his *imbas* illumines him (*forlnosna a imbus*) and he chants the following rhetorics:

Con fri lon leth cno contethain cotith indithraib Dercc Corra comol fri hich ni ba filliud fobaill a uball fin mblais cona fricarbaith mac ui co dedail Daigre.

Whereupon he recognizes his servant and declares his identity.

As a further example of *imbas forosnai* (here, *imus forosnudk*) we may refer to the following brief passage which is quoted in Tractate III (No. 187) of the Metrical Tractates.

Fegaid uaib sair fothuaid inmuir muad milach adba ron rebach rán rogab lan linad.

The same passage is quoted also in Tractate II (No. 24), where in the text from the Book of Leinster, the poem is attributed to Finn.

An example of the *tenm laida* (here, *tedmleoda*) is given in Tractate III. immediately before the passage just cited relating to *imbas forosnai*. The passage is as follows:

Amhairbthene mongthigi mhinchuile asalchide
    sinnchaidhe salachluim
imarith galaidhe imcleacaire abrataire
    inbecuidhe ingataile
    incetaile rigataile
    nichetaile inlataile
    indleacaile apaidhe acaite anachlaim

As an example of *cetal do chennaib*, reference may be made to the poem contained in the first of the Metrical Tractates (No. 123), published by Thurneysen. Here it is actually cited as an example of *cetal do chendaib*; but the same poem is also quoted in the *Leabhar na Gabhala*, where it is attributed to the *fili* Amargin, and where it is said to have been recited by him when he first set foot on Irish soil.

The poem is too long to quote here in full, and a few lines will suffice to give an idea of its form and content:

Amm goeth i muir
Am tonn trethain,
Am fuaim mara
Am dam setir ...
Coiche notglen clochar slebe?
Cia du i luidh fuinedh greiniu?
Cia seacht siecht sith gan eccla?
Cis [*sic*] non dogar eassa uiscci?
Cia ber a buar o tigh Teathra? ...
Cainte gaeth.

which Macalister and MacNeill translate[26] as follows:

I am wind on the sea.
I am a wave of the ocean,
I am the roar of the sea.
I am a powerful ox ...

Who clears the stone-place of the mountain?
What the place in which the setting of the sun lies?
Who has sought peace without fear seven times?
Who names the waterfalls?
Who brings his cattle from the house of Tethra? …
A wise satirist.

In the second of the Metrical Tractates, where examples of various metres are cited, the following passage is given as an example of *cetal na haisnese*:

Adruid adoini dia huas domun dindnisnech ruithre adaitfrifebru fuilged forta bith lalaile ifailsid lasuba lam dia dilgedach rodaelb imniulu nemthech.[27]

This text, as has been pointed out by Stokes, is identical with a *laid* or song which occurs in the story of Morann contained in the *Echtra Cormaic* etc ('The Irish Ordeals and Cormac's Adventures in the Land of Promise').'[28] Here we are told that when Morann was born, a membrane covered his head, which was subsequently removed by immersion in the sea. As the ninth wave washed over him the membrane separated, releasing his head, whereupon he sang the *laid* which Stokes translates as follows:

Worship, ye mortals,
God over the beautiful world!
…
… wherein is a festival with joyance
With my forgiving God,
Who formed about clouds a heavenly house.[29]

Morann, whose *laid* is identical with the example of *cetal na haisnese* in the Metrical Tractates, afterwards became a great sage.[30] It is interesting to note that in this particular text of the Metrical Tractates, the example of *cetal na haisnese* occurs as No. 125 of the examples of metres cited. The example of the metre cited as No. 123 is *cetal do chendaib*. The *aisneis*, or *cetal na haisnese*, and the *cetal do chendaib* are therefore closely associated together in the traditional repertoire of the *filid*, and may be presumed to be connected in some way with one another.

Why, then, is the *dichetal di chennaib* allowed to remain 'in the order of art', and what is its association with the *aisneis dichennaib a chname*? The example of the *aisneis* just referred to appears to be, in its present form, a Christian hymn. If this interpretation given by Stokes is correct, it is easy to see why St Patrick is said to have permitted it to remain in the 'order of art', since it served as a declaration or testification to the Christian faith. In other words, it has been transformed from a heathen spell to a Christian hymn – a process for which analogies may be traced in Anglo-Saxon poetry. From the context in which it occurs, and from its close association with *dichetal di chennaib* it is possible that the latter form of incantation may have undergone a similar transformation.

It is not necessary, however, to assume such a transformation for the latter in order to account for St Patrick's tolerance. The primary meaning of the words *cetal* and *dicetal* is simply 'chanting'. Because the chanting of the *filid* was believed to be potent the words came to be used commonly with the sense of 'incantation', as in the *dicetul in druad* in the *Tripartite Life* of St Patrick.[31] That its use was not restricted to magical songs is proved, however, by the use of the word *cetal* in the curriculum of the *filid* in Text II of the Metrical Tractates ... where among the *rochetal*, we read of the '*cetal na haisnese*', a poetical summons to the adoration of God ... , and two *cetal* of the 'glorification' (*noud*) including *Fiac's Hymn to St Patrick* and *Broccan's Hymn to St Bridget.*

From the examples cited it is clear that the rubrics or technical terms which we are considering are associated especially with the *filid* and other mantic persons. Moreover, they all appear to be closely bound up with the art of poetry. It would seem, indeed, from the Metrical Tractates that they are here treated as titles of distinctive poetical forms or metres, though we may suspect that this development is due in some measure to the schematization of Christian antiquarian learning. It is probably due to their inclusion in the list of metres and in the curriculum of the *filid* that the terms have sometimes been spoken of by scholars as if they were themselves the titles of actual charms. It would seem, indeed, in certain cases that our terms were so used. But that this was not so in every case is clear from the text in Cormac's *Glossary* under discussion, where *imbas forosnai* is described, not as a charm, but as a process of revelation brought on by a mantic sleep. That the other terms which occur at the close of the text also had originally a practical bearing, and relate to various phases of the mantic experience, would seem to be indicated by the prose sagas in which they occur, and which we will consider as briefly as possible.

We will first take examples of *imbas forosnai*. One of the most interesting and important occurs in *Taín Bó Cuailgnè*, in connection with Fedelm the *banfaid* of Connacht. According to LU and YBL, Fedelm[32] tells Medb that she has been in Alba learning *filidecht*. Medb asks her if she has learnt *imbas forosnai*, and on hearing that she has, asks her to 'look' (*deca*) how her own (Medb's) undertaking will prosper. Fedelm 'looks', and then proceeds to chant in strophic form and at considerable length the result of her vision.[33]

In the account of Seathach's prophecies to Cuchulainn,[34] which is found in LU. fo. 125b9, and which almost certainly comes from the Book of Druim Suechta and was written down as early as the eighth century,[35] we read:

> Asbert iarom Scathach friss iar sin ani arid bói dia forciund ocus arcáchain dó tria imbas forosnai.[36]

which Thurneysen translates 'um ihn zu Vollenden'.[37]

According to the earliest texts of the *Wooing of Emer*, Scathach dwelt among the 'Alps' (*Alpi*), which appears in the latest version as *Albu* (Albion, Scotland, or perhaps Britain).[38] From this story, therefore, and from the passage in the *Taín* already cited, it would seem that according to Irish tradition the *imbas forosnai* was introduced into Ireland from outside, doubtless from Britain,[39] and that in the milieu represented in the Cuchulainn Cycle it was the special métier of women. The early period to which the origin and the personnel of the Cuchulainn Cycle are generally ascribed invests these references with considerable interest.

Turning next to the Finn Cycle, we find that in the story of *Finn and the Man in the Tree*,[40] which is believed to date from the late eighth or early ninth century,[41] the *imbas forosnai* is practised by Finn on two occasions. The story is given in the version of the *Senchus Mor* contained in *H.3.18*, where it is quoted as an example of the practice of *imbas forosnai*. According to this story, when the *fían* are on the brink of the Suir, Cúldub comes out of a *sid* or 'elf-mound', and steals their food three times in succession as it is being cooked. On the third occasion Finn ua Baiscne gives chase and catches up with him, and lays hold of him as he goes into the *sid*. At this point a woman seems to meet him as she is coming out of the *sid*, with a dripping vessel in her hand, having just distributed drink, and she jams the door against the *sid*! Finn squeezes his finger (*mer*) between the door of the *sid* and the post, and then sticks it into his mouth. When he takes it out again he begins to chant (*dicetal*). The *imbas* enlightens him (*fortnosmen an imbas*) and he recites a series of rhetorics.

Later in the same story, when he finds a man hiding in a tree, he and his followers fail to recognize him as his fugitive servant till 'Finn puts his thumb into his mouth. When he takes it out again, his *imbas* illumines him and he chants an incantation and says: (rhetorics follow, cf. above)'. (Is de dobert Finn a hordain ina beolo. Addonich as eisib afrithisi fortnosna a imbus 7 dichan dichetal co neipert.)[42]

A variant version of the story of the death of Cúldub, dating, as is believed, from the ninth century,[43] is also published and translated by Meyer with the title, 'How Finn obtained Knowledge, and the Slaying of Cul Dub'.[44] The concluding lines of the story relate that after Finn had trapped his thumb (*ordain*) in the door he could hear and understand the language of the *Side* or *Sid*-folk. It is clear that in this way he acquired his supernatural knowledge – his *imbas* – and was enabled to chant his poem, which is here referred to as *dichetal*. It appears that yet another version of this story is contained in MS. *H*.3.18, a summary of which is given by O'Curry.[45]

Reference may be made to a story[46] which is believed also to date from the ninth century, and which relates to Finn, Ailill Aulom and Mac Con. In this story Finn appears as a member of Lugaid Mac Con's *fian*. During the hostilities between Ailill and Mac Con, Ailill sends Ferchess, an old *fian* warrior and an aged member of his household, on the track of Mac Con's wandering host for the purpose of slaying Mac Con himself. As Ferchess comes on the track, Finn says, using the incantation called *imbas forosnai* (*triasa n-imbas forosnai*): 'A man on the track.' Mac Con replies that they will be the more delighted by the addition to their number. 'A man on the track,' Finn repeats: 'One man is always good sport,' says Mac Con. Meanwhile, however, Ferchess chants a spell upon his spear, saying, ' *Rincne*' etc, and casts it at Mac Con and slays him. Ultimately Ferchess is slain by Finn in vengeance for Mac Con. Finn again recites ' *triasa n-imbas forosnai*', the poem already cited. The incident suggests that it is by means of this incantation that he has succeeded in tracking Ferchess to his abode. In this story it is clear that *imbas forosnai* gives to Finn the power of supernatural vision, and enables him to see the spirit world.[47] A brief summary of the same story is given also in Cormac's *Glossary s.v. Rincne*. Stokes translates from the text of the Bodleian fragment as follows:

> *Rincne*, quasi *quinque*. Hence said Ferches, son of Mo Sechess, when Finn, grandson of Baiscne, was counting every five in turn of the host of Lugaid, the son of Mac-neit, to seek the champion Ferches. With that Ferches gave … past Finn, and cast the spear on Lugaid and killed him, and said thereat, *Rincne cairincne ris* (leg. *rus*?) *rig*, for that is what Finn used to say when he was numbering, every pentad in turn, *Rincne, quasi quinque*.[48]

It will be seen that the words *triasa n-imbas forosnai*, which are found in the version of the story referred to above, are absent from this version; but it is interesting to note that the words which Stokes has not translated are *tren foachnamai*, (cf. '*Imbas forosnai*'), which are found also in the text from Y.B.L. 280a[49] and elsewhere.[50] The reason why Stokes does not translate them is obvious: they do not stand in any syntactical relation to the sentence in which they occur. They are, in fact, a rubric or title of the charm recited by Ferchess over his spear before he casts it at Mac Con.

From the two versions of the story of Finn and Cúldub it is clear that Finn obtained his *imbas forosnai* by means of uncooked or partially cooked food which became the property of the *side*, and by some part of his person (thumb or finger) entering the *sid*-mound, and after its withdrawal being placed by Finn in his mouth. The text of the story from the *Senchus Mor* suggests that the reason why Finn put his finger (*mer*) into his mouth was because some of the liquid from the dripping vessel had been spilt on to it. But it is not clear whether it was because he tasted this (presumably) *sid* liquid, or because his finger had been in the *sid*-mound, or because his finger was grazed and he sucked it (i.e., as raw-red-flesh) that he acquired his revelation. It is, however, clear from this story and from the slaying of Ferchess that it was by his *imbas forosnai* that Finn was enabled not only to see what was invisible to physical vision – i.e., he obtained second sight – but also to hear and understand the spirits as they conversed with one another.

It will be seen that many of the elements contained in these sagas, and more especially the *Slaying of Cúldub*, correspond to features of the *imbas forosnai* as set forth for us in Cormac's *Glossary*. In both the uncooked or partially cooked flesh of a pig or some other animal is passed from the possession of the owner through (i.e., behind) some door (*comla*). It is a curious fact that in the passage in Cormac's *Glossary* the *fili* chews a *mir*,[51] while in the sagas Finn chews a *mer*, or in later versions, *ordain*. *Mir* seems to mean a piece or morsel, but I know of no parallel in Irish literature for the eating of the flesh of cat or dog,[52] and the passage is unconvincing. Again, it is curious that in both our passages and the stories of Finn, some object (*mir, mer*) is inserted in the doorway. Both Cormac's *fili* and Finn then proceed to chant incantations (*díchetal*), and the phrase in Cormac – 'chanted on his two palms' – is not remote from Finn chanting over his finger or thumb. In both our passage and the stories of Finn these motifs precede a revelation of occult knowledge. These resemblances may lead one to suspect that the 'gods of the idols' referred to in Cormac are the *side* (*sid*-folk), and that the phrase *at opair do deib idol* means 'take it to (from) the *side*', with reference to Finn's retrieving his meat. This is mere conjecture, however, and in any case the resemblance ends there. The sagas which we have considered tell us nothing of the mantic sleep, or of those who watch over him lest he should turn over or be disturbed.

Several of these elements of the *imbas forosnai* in Cormac's *Glossary* which are not found in the sagas already considered are to be found in the story of *Finn and the Phantoms*,[53] which, perhaps, also dates from the ninth century.[54] Here Finn and his companions arrive at night at a house inhabited by misshapen phantom beings with a giant at their head. The giant slays Finn's horse, and makes pretence of cooking its flesh, which he then offers to Finn and Cailte. It is emphatically stated, both here and elsewhere in the story, that the flesh was not cooked at all – quite raw. For this reason Finn indignantly refused it. The later poem[55] on the same subject contained in the Book of Leinster, and believed to date from the eleventh century,[56] is more explicit:

> Strophe 165
> Take away thy food, O giant!
> For I have never devoured raw food.
> I will never eat it from today till Doom.
> (Beir lett, a athig, do béad,
> uair né dúadus biad om riam,
> ni chathiub ondiu co bráth.)

Then a curious thing happens. According to Stern's translation of the prose version:

Alors, tout d'un coup tous partirent. Aussitôt le feu cessa de brûler; Finn seul fut serré dans un coin pour être secoué et battu (par les fantômes). Comme des autres ne se séparaient pas de Finn, ils étaient dans cette situation toute la nuit en jetant des cris. Enfin, ils tombèrent et restèrent faibles en défaillance complète. C'est ainsi qu'ils étaient comme des cadavres jusqu'au matin.

L'orsqu'ils se levèrent le lendemain de leur assouppissement, ils ne voyaient ni maison ni gens dans la plate campagne autour d'eux. Finn s'éveilla et trouva son cheval attaché à la houssine sans tache sans défaut et sans dégât. Ils tinrent conseil ensuite pour savoir qui leur aurait fait cet outrage. Finn chanta un *teinm laida* et mit son pouce sur sa dent de savoir, alors le chose lui fut révélée. 'Vraiment,' dit-il, 'les trois fantômes de Hibarglend (la vallée des ifs) sont tombés sur nous; ce sont eux qui nous ont fait cet outrage pour se venger sur nous de leur soeur Cuichlend au museau large que nous avons tuée.'

At the close of the prose version of *Finn and the Phantoms* we are told that Finn had a vision:

Il vit un massacre d'hommes vilandois sur la colline à droite, mais il ne vit ni bataille ni ordre de bataille y rangé. Puis, il apercut une flamme de feu descendant du ciel jusqu'à la terre. Enfin, il y vit une foule en costume inconnu … Alors Finn se réveilla du sommeil et raconta son songe à ses druides, Morna Mungairit et Ercoil Sainarma. Puis il mit son pouce sur sa dent de savoir et chant un *teinm laida*, et la chose lui fut découverte. 'Vraiment,' dit-il 'le fils de la Vie viendra ici, duquel l'Irlande sera pleine.' Finn s'énonca ensuite en ces termes, en prédisant l'arrivée de Saint Ciaron, fils de Charpentier.

From this it would seem that, as in folktales commonly, (1) the food of the *side* is uncooked; (2) to eat the food of the *sid* involves permanent detention among them. Finn's phantoms and their house leave him because he has not eaten the raw flesh. We may, perhaps, suppose, therefore, that in Cormac's *Glossary*, when the *fili* eats the raw flesh (of pig, dog or cat), the implication is that this is an unhallowed diet which immediately puts him into touch with heathen spirits. It may be added that this version of *Finn and the Phantoms* is late and considerably affected by Christianity. At the close of the story Finn has a Christian *aislinge* (vision). We may suspect that in the original version of the story Finn's vision was quite different, and, in view of other stories in which Finn is represented as tasting the food of the *side*, we may also suspect that in the original version of *Finn and the Phantoms* Finn did not refuse the meat.

The story throws yet further light on a passage in Cormac's entry. In *Finn and the Phantoms* the scene is laid in the *sid*. Finn refuses to eat the raw (horse) flesh of the *side*. In the first of the two paragraphs just quoted there is an obscure sentence to the effect that Finn is hustled into a corner to be shaken and beaten. Stern adds the words, 'by the phantoms' by way of explanation; but these words are not in the text, and I am not sure that the shaking and beating is not done on Finn by his own followers to bring him out of his trance. We shall see later that there is evidence for such a practice in Welsh tradition. In any case, if I am right in thinking that the passage in Cormac has a direct relation to some version of this story, the words, however we interpret them, may well have a bearing on the obscure phrase which Stokes translates as 'people are watching over him in order that he may not turn over and in order that no one may disturb him'.[57] We may note, also, that, like the *fili*, Finn (and, perhaps, also his followers) are plunged in a deep sleep or trance. It is, perhaps, worth noting that it is after this trance or sleep in the house of the 'phantoms' that Finn in enabled to chant a *tenm laida*, and to place his thumb on his 'tooth of knowledge' and obtain revelation of the occult.

An example of the *tenm laida* is also quoted in another story relating to Finn hua Baiscne, which is found in Cormac's *Glossary s.v. orc treith*. Here we are told that during Finn's absence his fool (*druth*), Lomna[58] the Coward by name, is slain at the instigation of Finn's wife, and his head is taken away, while his body is left. When Finn and his followers return they are unable to identify the body, and Finn is asked to make known who the dead man is. 'Then Finn put his thumb into his mouth, and he chants by *tenm laido*, illumination of song,' and he says: 'not ... from Lomna's head. This is Lomna's body,' says Finn. 'His enemies have taken the head from him.'[59]

A further example of the *tenm laida* is found also in Cormac's *Glossary s.v. mugh-éme*. In this story Connla, son of Tadg, son of Cian, son of Ailill Aulom, finds the skull of the first lap-dog which has come to Ireland, and takes it to the *fili* Moen, son of Etna, to be identified. The *fili* identifies the head *tre tenm laido*, 'by the *tenm laida*'. It is curious that in both these instances the *tenm laida* is used as a means of identifying a head – absent in the first story, present in the second. It is no doubt this circumstance which led O'Curry to regard the *tenm laida* as a 'rite for the identification of dead persons'.[60] Its occurrence in the story of Finn and the Phantoms is against this; but its association in these two entries in Cormac's *Glossary* and elsewhere with severed heads, and its constant association with Finn, are worth noting.

Finally, reference may be made to the story known as the *Macginamartha Find*,[61] which is assigned by Meyer to the twelfth century.[62] Here we are told that Finn cooked and ate the salmon of Fec's pool in the Boyne, which are manifestly the Salmon of Wisdom associated with the Boyne in the *Dindsenchas* of Boand. 'It is that which gave knowledge to Finn, to wit, whenever he put his thumb into his mouth and sang through *tenm laida*, then whatever he had been ignorant of would be revealed to him. He learnt three things that constitute a poet, to wit, *tenm laida* (which Meyer translates 'illumination (?) of song'), and *imbas forosna* ('knowledge which illumines,' Meyer), and *dichetal dichennaib* ('extempore incantation,' Meyer). It is interesting to note that the song which Finn composed 'to prove his poetry' is the 'Song of Summer', beginning 'May-day, season surpassing',[63] which belongs to a class of poetry on the seasons of which Irish literature offers several examples.

This brief survey of some of the instances in which *imbas forosnai* and *tenm laida* figure in the sagas may serve to give some idea of the circumstances under which the art was practised. When we seek for a third rubric – *dichetal di chennaib, aisneis di chennaib a chname* – we meet with disappointment. It has, however, been possible to gather certain data which may be briefly recapitulated here. We have seen that in the *Leabhar na Gabhala* the *fili* Amargin is represented as singing a *cetal do chennaib* – a series of mantic verses – as he lands in Ireland. We have also seen that the sage Morann sang a *laid* – which is elsewhere described as *cetal na haisnese* – as soon as his head was released from its covering. It has also been mentioned that in the *Macgnimartha Find*, the youthful Finn is said to have learned *dichetal di chennaib* along with *imbas forosnai* and *tenm laida* as a part of his training in the art of poetry and mantic lore.

He is further shown to us chanting (*dican*) his *dicetal* in order to be able to identify his fugitive servant in the story of *Finn and the Man in the Tree*. We have also seen Ferchess chanting *tren foachnamai* over his spear before casting it at Lugaid.

Referring once more to the chanting of Morann's head after it has been uncovered, and to the two instances just cited in which the *tenm laida* is chanted in connection with severed heads, we may suspect that such heads are sometimes associated with magical practices, and, perhaps, with the charms with which we are primarily concerned here. It may be worth while, therefore, to recall one or two stories in which severed heads play a prominent role.

The first which naturally occurs to us is the story related in Cormac's *Glossary s.v. orc treith*, to which we have just referred. We have seen that Finn identifies the dismembered body of his 'fool' (*druth*) Lomna by chanting through *tenm laida*. We next hear in the same version of the story that Finn goes to seek the missing head, and finds the murderer Cairpre, in an empty house, cooking fish on a gridiron, and distributing it, and Lomna's head on a spit beside the fire. The head is reported to have been speaking rhetorics, and the storyteller specially notes the fact that no food is offered to the head, as if the omission were something unusual. The story is told more fully in one of the extracts from the laws recently published (with translations) by Myles Dillon,[64] where the actual words spoken by the head are quoted. These words[65] make it quite clear that the severed head has the right to expect its share of the feast, and protests against its deprivation of its *mír*.

The story is very much like the fate of Finn's own head, as related in a fragment of an *Aided Finn* story, believed by Meyer to date from the tenth century.[66] Here we are told that Finn is killed while trying to leap across the Boyne, and his body is found by four fishermen, viz., the three sons of Urgriu and Aiclech, the son of Dubriu. Aiclech cuts off his head; but the sons of Urgriu slay Aiclech, and take Finn's head to an empty house, and place it before the fire, and then proceed to cut and divide their fish. A black, evil-jesting man (*fer dubh docluiche*) bids them give a bite (*dantmir*) of fish to the head. It is not explained who the black man is, but the description suggests that he is a *bachlach*. The sons of Urgriu, however, divide the fish into two portions only. But as often as they divide the fish into two portions, three portions are found, and the head beside the fire explains to them that it is in order that it may have its portion (*mír*) itself that the fish have been divided into three portions.[67]

The association of these talking heads with the cooking of food is curious. And it is interesting to find the persistence with which a head is said to have its right to a *mír*, or portion. The head is evidently habitually placed beside the fire, perhaps for the purpose of smoking and drying it for preservation. Can its proximity to the fire have anything to do with the term *tenm loida*, which is usually given to the songs chanted by such heads? The word *tenm* is generally regarded as derived from a root, *tep-*, 'heat'. Is it possible that in the first instance a *tenm loida* was the chant of a severed head beside the fire at a feast?

It is, of course, possible that the stories of the severed heads of Lomna and of Finn are not independent of one another. It is more probable, however, that the two stories are only single instances of a whole series of such stories associated with the severed heads of mantic persons which were preserved for purposes of divination. In this connection we may refer to other stories in which reference is clearly made to the presence of such heads at feasts. One of these again has reference to Finn himself and is known as the *Bruden Atha*.[68] In this story we are told that after Finn has made peace with Fothad Canainne, with whom he has been at feud, he invites him to an ale-feast. Fothad, however, replies that it is '*geis* to him to drink ale without dead heads in his presence' (*Fa geis immorro do Fothad Canainne ól corma cin chinn marbu ina fhiadnaise*).

The most interesting instance of a talking head occurs in the story of the *Battle of Allen*,[69] which is found in Y.B.L. and elsewhere. The story relates to a battle which took place during a raid made by Fergal, son of Maelduin, high-King of Ireland, against Murchad Mac Briain, King of Leinster. In this battle was slain DonnBo, an excellent reciter of poetry and saga (*as uadh budh ferr ra(i)nn espa ocus rigscela for an domhon.*) It may be suspected that DonnBo possesses second sight, and is aware of the impending disaster to Fergal's party, for though the story emphasizes the excellence of his skill and of his repertoire, and the extent to which Fergal's men depend on him to amuse and distract their thoughts, yet when Fergal asks him to make minstrelsy for them on the night before the battle, he replies that he is unable to utter a word on this night, and someone else must amuse them – tomorrow evening he will make minstrelsy. In the battle which follows both Fergal and DonnBo are killed. In the feast which the victorious Leinstermen hold that night, one of their party is told to go the battlefield to fetch a man's head. Baethgalach, a valiant Munsterman, volunteers, and as he comes near to where Fergal's body lies, he hears a voice and sweet music (apparently resembling that of an orchestra). He learns that a head in a clump of rushes is addressing him. 'I am DonnBo,' says the head; 'I have been pledged to make music tonight for Fergal.' The head consents to allow itself to be taken on condition that it is afterwards brought back to its body. Baethgalach promises, and returns to the feast with the head, which is then placed on a pillar in their midst. Baethgalach orders the head to make music for them, as it has been wont to for Fergal. But DonnBo 'turns his face to the wall of the house, so that it might be dark to him;'[70] and he sings a sweet melody, but so plaintive that the Leinstermen weep bitter tears, and presently the same warrior takes back the head of DonnBo to his body, and fits it to its trunk.

At a later stage in the same story we are told that the Leinstermen also carry Fergal's head to Cathal mac Findguini, king of Munster, as a trophy. Cathal has it washed, and plaited, and combed smooth, and a cloth of velvet put round it, and a great feast brought and placed before it (*ar belaib cind Fergail*).[71] The men of Munster then 'see red' round about the head, which opens its eyes to render thanks to God for the honour and respect which has been shown to it. Then Cathal distributes the food to the poor and the neighbouring churches. The phrase *ro himdergad iarsin imon ceand a feadnaisi fer Muman uili*, which I understand to mean that the men of Munster see red round about the head, is translated by Stokes: 'The head blushed in the presence of all the men of Munster.' The expression *derg* or *forderg* is, however, commonly used of mantic visions, and it is to be suspected that *himdergad* has a similar significance here also – 'Red was revealed,' i.e., a mantic vision was revealed to the men of Munster by means of the head. For the association of *derg* with such visions we may refer to the phrase *atciu forderg* used by Fedelm of her mantic vision in the *Táin*, when, through *imbas forosnai*, she looks (*deca*) by Medb's request, and reports her mantic vision of the future of the host. Again, in the *Togail Bruidne Da Derga* Conaire Mor has a supernatural vision of three beings in the form of three horsemen in red riding before him.

The presence of the two talking heads at the two feasts is a striking picture.[72] The head of DonnBo, like those of Lomna in *Orc Treith*, and of Finn in the fragment cited above, is manifestly the head of a mantic person. Lomna is called a *druth*.[73] DonnBo is a person of not very dissimilar character himself, for when he refuses to amuse Fergal's host on the night before the battle, he suggests that Hua-Maiglinni, the *rig-druth Erenn*, 'the chief *druth* of Ireland', should amuse them in his stead.[74] DunnBo, Hua-Maiglinni, Finn and Lomna all appear to practise an art which the author of our passage in the *Glossary* would have included *i corus cherddae*, 'under the heading of art'.

With the incident of the replacing of the severed head on its trunk, and the mournful strain chanted by the head itself, we may compare the closing lines of the story introducing the *Reicne Fothaid Canainne*,[75] attributed by Meyer to the close of the ninth, or the beginning of the tenth century. The poem (*reicne*), which is quoted at length, is said to be chanted by the severed head of Fothad Canainne to the wife of Ailill Flann Bee mac Eogain, with whom he has made a tryst, and by whose husband he has been killed; and the mournful lay is said to be chanted to the woman as she comes to fulfil her tryst in death, carrying the head to the grave where the body lies. Reference may also be made to the lament chanted by the severed head of Sualtam, Cuchulainn's father, in the *Táin Bó Cuailgnè*.[76]

All these people, then, are represented as performing after death an artistic feat which may be described as 'singing from the head'.[77] This art, however, is not confined *in the stories as we have them* to heathen mantic sages. The head of Fergal, when taken from its covering at a feast (exactly like the one at which DonnBo chants his dirge) performs a Christian *dicetal* or *asneis*. The head of the sage Morann is said to have performed a Christian *dicetal* or *asneis* when its covering falls off. It is not stated that his head was severed. The whole story is, indeed, very obscure; but it is clear that the sage was virtually headless so long as his head was covered with its 'hood' (con-aices rop aen pait uili o dib guaillibh suas, 7 'ni facas bel fair no sineistri etir).[78]

We may suspect that it is because these utterances from heads were clearly capable of transformation into Christian hymns and testifyings (*dicetal, asneis*) at the hands of Christian redactors that they are said by the author of Cormac's *Glossary* to be left *i corus cherddae* – though whether he intends to ascribe this tolerant attitude to St Patrick, or whether the statement is an afterthought, a kind of colophon of his own, is not clear. That the old mantic art was sometimes well known to Christian clerics we have clear testimony. The title Mac da Cherddae ('Boy of two arts'), borne by the famous cleric and scholar of Armagh, who is mentioned in Cormac's *Glossary s.v. ana* and elsewhere,[79] appears to have reference to his proficiency in both mantic (*imbas?*) and Christian (i.e., Latin) learning (*sous?*). The author of the *Aislinge meic Conglinne*, albeit his devoutness has been questioned, was clearly himself a man of both arts, and it is curious to observe that he is represented as a contemporary of Cathal mac Findguini, whose men brought DonnBo's head to their feast, and who himself treats in a similar manner the head of Fergal, though a Christian colouring has been given to this narrative.

It is tempting to pursue our enquiry into *imbas* further, and to examine the relationship of 'nuts' or 'hazels' of *imbas*, to which reference was made in the first part of this paper, and which are associated with the Springs of Shannon and Boyne in the *Dindsenchas* and elsewhere, to the *imbas* and the *tennlaida*[80] of the stories which we have already considered. In regard to Finn, the *imbas* derived from eating salmon fed on the hazel nuts of the spring at the source of the Boyne appears to represent a variant tradition from that which associates his *imbas* with the slaying of Cúldub. But the nuts of *imbas* are a curious and interesting subject deserving of a fuller treatment than space permits of here, and I hope to make them the subject of a separate study.

From the evidence before us it would seem, on the whole, that the practice described under *imbas forosnai* in Cormac's *Glossary* is most fully represented in the Finn stories, and that the technique ascribed here and elsewhere to the *fili* is most clearly exemplified in Finn himself. An attentive reading of the earliest stratum of Finn stories shows us Finn enacting, at one time or another – possibly all in close juxtaposition – the principal items of the procedure set forth by the author of the *Glossary*. Moreover, if we read the passage in the *Glossary* in the light of these Finn stories, though much still remains obscure to us, yet there is no doubt that many of the original obscurities become clearer – the raw meat, the 'chewing,' the association with the 'stone' and the 'doorway,' the 'heathen gods', or 'idol gods' (which we may presume to be the form of diction in which the Christian author refers to the *side*), the mantic sleep, the people watching over him and the reference to the shaking or turning of the sleeper. It almost looks as if the Christian antiquarian author of the passage in the *Glossary* has been pursuing a line of study not very dissimilar to our own, and searching the heathen traditions for accounts of mantic practices. If so we must suppose that the picture of the practice of the *fili* given in the *Glossary* is a synthesis based, not on observation, but on deduction from literary sources, perhaps not always very clearly understood. This would be fully in accord with what we know of his practice in other passages. If this conclusion is correct, we must suppose, either that the redactor has been drawing his material from a series of traditional stories of Finn, such as those which we have been considering, or else that the passages in the *Glossary* and the Finn Cycle are based on a common and widespread practice of which, nevertheless, we have no satisfactory traces elsewhere. Even if we suppose that the name of Finn has been inserted into some of these stories at a comparatively late date … , we need not suppose that the character of the stories has been substantially modified. The consistency of their general character would, indeed, be against such a supposition.

For many reasons the second of the alternatives suggested above is improbable. Considering the great wealth of Irish literary evidence, it is surprising that if the stories of *imbas forosnai* and *tenm laida* were commonly associated with other known heroes or *filid* besides Finn so few references to them should have been preserved. Nor have we anything in the Annals or the stories of the kings to suggest that such mantic practices were common. We have seen that the terms are found frequently in the metrical tractates and schedules for the education of the *filid*. But these entries contain nothing which suggests the widespread practice of the process under discussion. On the contrary, these references rather suggest, on the whole, that they are, like the entry in the *Glossary*, the result of antiquarian speculation on metres and poems to which the names *imbas forosnai, tenm laida* etc, have become attached after the terms had lost their original significance. And in several cases we have seen that the examples cited are identical with others which we have found in the sagas, from which there can be little doubt they are themselves derived.

Against this it may be urged that references to the actual practice of *imbas forosnai* and *tenm laida* are to be found in the ancient Irish laws. Thus there occurs in the Commentary on the Introduction to the *Senchus Mor*,[81] a reference to the means employed in order to discover a name. The passage opens with the words, *Indiu is do cendaib colla tall*; but the passage which follows is strongly reminiscent of our own and other passages in Cormac's *Glossary*,[82] to which it appears to me to bear direct and close verbal relationship. The passage in the *Senchus Mor* tells us that when the *fili* sees a person or thing before him he recites an extempore verse (*comrac*) *do focetair do cendaib a cnama*.

> But this is (only) since the Conversion; before St Patrick's time it was performed differently. At that time the *fili* placed his staff on the person's body or head (*fors in colainn no fors in cend*)[83] and found his name … and discovered every unknown thing which was put to him *co de* (? for *cend*) *nomaide do dala no tri*; and this is *tenm laida* or *imbas forosnai*, for the same thing used to be revealed through them; they, however, were performed after a different manner, for a different kind of offering was made at each of them (*ar is inand ni do foillsigtea treota; ocus ba sain imorro amail do gnitea cectar de, .i. sain cinel nudbairt do gnitea oc cectar de*).
>
> … But Patrick abolished those three things from among the poets, because they were heathen rites (*anidan*), for neither *tenm laida* nor *imbas forosnai* could be performed without the accompaniment of heathen offerings (*gin udbairt do deib idal ocaib*).

Again, in one of the 'Stories from the Law Tracts', recently edited and translated by Myles Dillon, the nobles of Ireland are represented as referring to the *filid*, 'so that they should try the revelation of *imas* as to what state Angus (i.e., an ancient King of Leinster) was in after death on account of the judgement, false through carelessness, which he had given.' The story goes on to tell that the *filid* 'tried the revelation of true *imas*, and he was shown to them condemned to half punishment' etc[84] (*ocus gu ndernsatsum faillsiugudh in fhirimais, ocus is amlaid ro faillsiged doib he iar tabairt leth-indechda*). There can be no doubt, however, that these references in the Laws are merely literary allusions, and cannot be used as evidence of historical practice.

The absence of satisfactory corroborative evidence in early Irish literature or of traces in early Irish history of the actual practice of the type of *imbas forosnai* described in the *Glossary* and the Finn stories is rather surprising, even making allowance for its notoriously heathen character. Indeed, we may suspect that literary men of antiquarian interests had themselves observed and been struck by the absence of such evidence, and had for this reason surmised that the rite had been banished by St Patrick at the outset. It is, moreover, surprising that the poetry generally cited as recited by Finn or other *filid* when they sing through *imbas forosnai* or *tenm laida* appears to be for the most part absolutely untranslatable.

We have seen that the *fili* Amargin is also represented in the *Leabhar na Gabhala* as reciting a set of rhetorics immediately on landing in Ireland. Presumably, therefore, he had acquired them elsewhere. The authority is too late to have independent value, but the rhetorics themselves resemble those ascribed to the Welsh poet, Taliesin, and those contained in the dialogue between Ferchertne and Nede in the *Immacaldam in da Thuarad*,[85] which is ascribed to the tenth century. In the latter work we are told that the youthful sage Nede, who is represented as defeated by the elderly sage, Ferchertne, in *filidecht*, has just returned from Britain, where he has been acquiring *imbas*. We have seen also that in the Cuchulainn Cycle *imbas forosnai* is said to have been learnt by the *banfaid* Fedelm in Britain, and to have been practised by Scathach also in Britain. It was long ago suggested by Sir John Rhys[86] that Welsh tradition has also preserved traces of communities resembling those of Scathach and Aoife in the Cuchulainn Cycle. In particular he pointed to the Nine Witches of Gloucester, who appear to be endowed not only with skill in arms, but also with the gift of prophecy, and who are also responsible for the training of the hero, Peredur. A careful scrutiny of this and other medieval Welsh stories – notably that of the Cave of the Addanc, also in Peredur – would doubtless bring other instances to light. Rhys regarded both the Welsh and Irish stories of female communities where instruction was given in military and mantic art as derived from a common origin,[87] but he sought this origin in a 'Goidelic' community settled in the southwest of England. If he were right in this, and if the arts were pre-eminently Irish, we may, indeed, ask why the prophetess Fedelm, and many heroes, notably the popular hero Cuchulainn himself, should be obliged to come over to this country to learn them?

We have seen, however, that the chief exponent in Irish legend of both the *imbas forosnai* and the *tenm laida* is Finn mac Cumaill, or, more correctly, Finn mac Umaill, who is represented in Irish tradition as having acquired all his magic arts in Ireland, though these traditions vary considerably among themselves as to the exact manner in which he acquired these arts. Finn is, perhaps, the most gifted magician of all Irish legend. He is, in fact, more of a magician than a hero. His character and mantic experiences have more in common with those of Conn Cétchathach and his line than with those of Cuchulainn, on the one hand, or the more authentic historical traditions of later kings on the other. These experiences, however, are never identical with those of Conn's line. We search the *baile* literature in vain for traces of mantic experiences analogous to those of the passage in Cormac's *Glossary* under *imbas forosnai*, or to those in the stories of Finn.

How are we to account for these individualities of Finn? And where do his closest affinities lie?

The nearest analogies of the stories associated with Finn which we have been considering are contained, not in Irish tradition,[88] but in Welsh legend. These stories of Finn are analogous especially to those of Pwyll Prince of Dyved, who, like Finn, visits Annwn or the heathen spirit world. We may refer also to Rhonabwy who lies down to sleep on a yellow calf-skin, and has a mantic sleep and dream. One would like to know the relationship between Finn and Gwyn (the Welsh phonetic equivalent of Finn) ap Nudd, to whom, according to a passage in *Kulhwch and Olwen*,[89] 'God gave control over the devils in Annwn' – the Welsh equivalent of the *side* of Irish saga, and of the 'idol gods' of Cormac's entry.[90]

Giraldus Cambrensis (*c*.1147–*c*.1223) mentions in his *Description of Wales* a class of people whom he calls *awenithion*, and who appear to practise an art closely resembling that described by Cormac as *imbas forosnai*.

Sunt et in hoc Kambriae populo quod alibi non reperies, viri nonnulli, quos Awennithion vocant, quasi mente ductos. Hi super aliquo consulti ambiguo statim frementes spiritu quasi extra se rapiuntur, et tanquam arrepti fiunt. Nec incontinenti tamen quod desideratur edisserunt: sed per ambages multas, inter varios quibus effluunt sermones nugatorios magis et vanos quam sibi coherentes, sed omnes tamen ornatos, in aliquo demum verbi diverticulo qui responsum solerter, observat quod petit accipiet enucleatum. Et sic denique de hac extasi tanquam a somno gravi ab aliis excitantur, et quasi per violentiam quandam ad se reverti compelluntur. Ubi et duo notanda reperies; quia post responsum, nisi violenter excitati et revocati, ab hujuscemodi quasi furore reverti non solent, et quod in se reversi, nihil horum omnium, qua ab his interim prolata sunt, ad memoriam revocabunt. (Unde et, si forte super hoc iterum vel alio consulti dicere debeant, aliis omnino verbis et alienis enantiabunt:)[91] forsan sicut per phanaticos et emergumenos spiritus interdum loquuntur, quanquam ignaros. Solent autem eis haec dona plerumque in somnis per visiones infundi. Quibusdam enim videtur, quod eis vel lac dulce, vel mel in ore infundatur: aliis autem, quod eis schedula inscripta ori imponatur. Et statim a somno erecti et canori effecti, se gratiam hanc suscepisse publice profitentur.[92]

It will be seen that the phenomenon of the *awenithion* (or, more properly, *awenyddion*) resembles that of the *imbas forosnai* as described for us in the *Glossary*, and as illustrated by the stories of Finn. The name is derived from the word *awen* or poetic (mantic) inspiration and is generally conferred on a person in a mantic sleep. These people become rapt in an ecstasy (cf. *imbas forosnai*), in which they deliver themselves of speech which is not easily intelligible because the utterances are veiled (cf. the Irish rhetorics), and apparently contradictory and highly figurative. Often such people have to be shaken violently before they can recover their normal condition. We do not know the exact source of Giraldus' account. It may have been based on contemporary custom, as he himself avers; or it may, as I suspect, be derived from literary (oral) tradition, like the entry in the *Glossary*. But whatever the source, there can be little doubt that in the time of Giraldus a practice similar to that of *imbas forosnai* was known in Wales, either as a living practice or a literary motif.

Talhaern, a poet of the Britons who is mentioned in the *Historia Brittonum*, as living in the time of Maelgwn, King of Gwynedd (548), is said to have been called Tataguen,[93] i.e., 'father of *awen* or poetic (mantic) inspiration,' and to have been a contemporary of the poet Taliesin, who almost certainly lived in the middle of the sixth century. The similarity of the poetry traditionally ascribed to Taliesin, to that ascribed – also by tradition – to the poet Nede and to the *fili* Amargin has already been commented on. There can, indeed, be little doubt that early traditions in this country imply the existence at an early date of a phenomenon similar to *imbas forosnai*. We have seen that Irish tradition suggests that the art was in a more advanced condition in this country, since it was from this country that, according to the same tradition, the earliest exponents known to Irish legend derived their art.

The result of our study suggests the following conclusions. The passage on *imbas forosnai* in Cormac's *Glossary* is a piece of antiquarian learning, based on literary evidence. It contains several technical terms, derived ultimately from mantic texts, but now extra-syntactical, and therefore not intended to be understood literally. The author of the passage was a Christian with no direct acquaintance with the phenomenon which he is describing, and which he apprehends imperfectly, whether through ignorance of the details of the traditions which he is following, or from the difficulty of reconciling variant versions. He gives us to believe that the *imbas forosnai* and the *tenm laida* are no longer practised, while certain other mantic phenomena, originally heathen, have been transmogrified under Christian influence. In this he appears to be right.

The phenomenon of *imbas forosnai* itself is well known in Irish tradition, alongside other mantic phenomena, some of which are also commented on in the *Glossary*. The *imbas forosnai*, in particular, is known to the earliest cycle of Irish saga, where we find an example of the mantic poetry associated with it. In these, the earliest cited examples, *imbas forosnai* appears to be a specifically female accomplishment, though later it is especially ascribed to Finn, and the male *filid*. The earliest Irish traditions represent it as acquired in this country. British tradition also knows the art in this country, apparently at an early date. On the whole, it would seem to be not improbable that Britain was a centre of prophetic poetry in the early centuries of our era, and we may suspect that it was in this country that the early Irish mantic poets acquired their *imbas*.

I am well aware that I have not succeeded in ascertaining the exact milieu to which the author of the colophon refers in his remarks on *dicetal* and *aisneis di chennaib*. It is impossible to avoid a suspicion that these expressions somehow contain a veiled allusion to the *baile* literature, such as the *Baile in scail* and the *Echtra Cormaic*, though so far as I am aware, 'heads' are not actually mentioned as playing a part in these stories. The redactor of the *Echtra Cormaic* is at pains in his colophon to bring the *baile* literature, and these two stories in particular, into the circle of Christian orthodoxy, and he tells us, in words which sound like an echo of the colophon to *imbas forosnai*, that these experiences were brought about by divine means, and were not connected with 'demons'.

We need not suppose that the author of the colophon to *imbas forosnai* is necessarily the same person as the author of the main entry. Indeed, the change of tense in itself would render it improbable that such was the case. The use of the present tense in the main entry is striking and unusual, most of the entries which embody individual stories being in the narrative (past) tense. The use of the present tense in our entry tends to confirm my suggestion that the entry itself has been composed as a synthesis. It is, however, by no means impossible that it represents a single version of a lost saga. If so, we must suppose that such a saga would have much in common with the stories of Finn referred to above. But whatever its precise origin, there can, I think, be little doubt that the material contained in the main portion of the entry is derived neither from contemporary custom nor from etymological speculation, but from oral narrative saga.

Notes

1 The striking similarity of this colophon to the one found at the conclusion of the *Echtra Cormaic* (ed. and trans. by Whitley Stokes, *Irische Texte*, Series III, p. 185 ff.) deserves careful consideration and can hardly be accidental.

2 *Do foillsiugud*, the words generally used of the revealing of knowledge to the druids and the *filid.* See the 'Adventures of Art, Son of Conn', ed. and trans. by R.I. Best (*Ériu*, vol. III, p. 155, § 8); cf. also 'Stories from the Law Tracts', ed. and trans. by Myles Dillon (*ibid.*, vol. XI, p. 46).

3 In 1912 Meyer also edited the text of the *Sanas Cormaic*, contained in the *Yellow Book of Lecan*, and published it in *Anecdota from Irish Manuscripts*, vol. IV (Halle, 1912).

4 *Zeit. f. celt. Philol.*, vol. XIX (1932), p. 164.

5 *Ancient Laws and Institutes of Ireland*, vol. I, ed. and trans. by W. Neilson Hancock (Dublin, 1865), p. 42.

6 *Zeit. f. celt. Philol.*, vol. XVI (1929), p. 186.

7 Ed. and trans by R. Atkinson, in the *Ancient Laws of Ireland*, vol. V (Dublin, 1901), p. 56 ff.

8 'Tredi dlegar dun ollamain filead .i. tenm loedga ocus imus forosnad, ocus dicedal do cennaib, amail adbeir breta nemed, "a tri nemtigter nemtusa filed, tenm laegda, imus forosnad, dicedul du cennaib."'

9 *Mittelirische Verslehren, Irische Texte* III, p. 117 (*tenmlaida, immas forosnai, dichetal do chennaib na tuaithe*).

10 *Ibid.*, p. 119.

11 *Ibid.*, p. 102 (*tedmleodu, Imus forosnudh, Delinlaide la dicetal*).

12 See L.C. Stern, *Revue celtique*, XIII, p. 16, footnote 2.

13 *Ed. cit.*, p. 61.

14 In this and several parallel phrases obviously used for *di.* (See K. Meyer, *Contributions to Irish Lexicography s.v. do*).

15 *Ed. cit.*, p. 63.

16 Is it worth mentioning that Cend-Cnáma is a proper name? Meyer, *Contrib.*

17 We may, perhaps, compare the expression, *co cnamaib cind,* Thurneysen, *Metr. Tr.*, p. 102, no. 192, words which, curiously enough, are lacking from the parallel text from LL and BB *ibid.*, p. 49, no. 89. Can they be a rubric which has been incorporated into the text? Cf. p. 99, rubric to no. 167.

18 *Irische Heldensage* (Halle, 1921), p. 377.

19 Ed. by W.N. Hancock, *Ancient Laws and Institutes of Ireland*, vol. I (London, 1865), p. 44.

20 See Meyer, *Contrib. s.v. Coll* (2); Meyer glosses as 'head'; but should it not rather come under his *coll* (1), 'hazel'?

21 BB 341. b. 34; cf. *Ancient Laws and Institutes of Ireland*, vol. V, p. 58.

22 *The Book of the Conquests of Ireland*, ed. and trans. by Macalister and Macneill (Dublin, 1916), p. 264.

23 *Fianaigecht*, ed. and trans. by K. Meyer (Dublin, 1910), p. 28 ff.

24 *Ibid.*, p. 39.

25 Ed. and trans. by K. Meyer, *Revue celtique*, vol. XXV, p. 345 ff; see especially, p. 347.

26 *Leabhar Gabhala, The Book of the Conquests of Ireland*, p. 262 f.

27 *Ed. cit.*, p. 63.

28 See Thurneysen's note in *Irische Texte*, Series III, p. 169.

29 *Ibid.*, pp. 189, 207.

30 *Ibid.*, p. 206 f.

31 Ed. and trans. by Whitley Stokes (Rolls Series, 1887), vol. I, p. 56, 1.11.

32 According to the text contained in LU, Fedelm is a mortal, but according to the text in YBL she is a supernatural being.

33 *Ériu* I, Pt. II, Suppl. p. 4.

34 Trans. by K. Meyer, *Archaeolog. Rev.* I (1888), No. 1–4; *Revue celtique* XI (1890), p. 433.

35 See Thurneysen, *Irische Heldensage*, p. 388.

36 Thurneysen, *Ir. Held.*, p. 377. Cf. *Zeit. f. celt. Philol.*, vol. IX, p. 487.

37 Thurneysen, *loc. cit.*

38 See Thurneysen, *Ir. Held.*, p. 388, footnote 1.

39 It is to be suspected that here, as elsewhere – as against Thurneysen's view (*Ir. Held.*, p. 376 f.) – the name *Alpi*, 'Alps,' has been substituted for *Alba*, through learned or ecclesiastical influence.

40 Ed. and trans. by K. Meyer, *Revue celtique*, vol. XXV (1904), p. 344 ff.

41 K. Meyer, *Fianaigecht*, p. xviii.

42 *Ibid.*, p. 348.

43 *Ibid.*, p. xix.

44 *Revue celtique*, vol. XIV (1893), p. 246 ff. For yet other versions of the slaying of Cúldub, see *Revue celtique*, XV (1894), p. 305; LL fo. 191a; E. Gwynn, *Metrical Dindsenchas*, Part II (Dublin, 1906), p. 64.

45 *Lectures on the Manuscript Materials of Ancient Irish History* (Dublin, 1878), p. 396 f.

46 Ed. and trans. by K. Meyer, *Fianaigecht*, p. 29 ff. Cf. also *ibid.*, p. xxi.

47 See Zimmer *Kelt. Beitr.* III. *Zeit. f.d. Alt.*, vol. 35, p. 115. Both Zimmer and Meyer held that there was probably no mention of Finn in the earlier version of this story. (See Meyer, *Fianaigecht*, p. xxi.) The incident and the words spoken recall the *Echtra Nerai* (ed. and trans. by K. Meyer), *Revue celtique*, vol. X, p. 212 ff.

48 On the Bodleian Fragment of Cormac's *Glossary*, *Transactions of the Philological Society*, 1891, p. 187.

49 See K. Meyer, *Fianaigecht*, p. xx f.

50 See Stokes, *Three Irish Glossaries* (Sanas Cormaic), *s.v. rincne*, p. 38 f.

51 We may refer to the *dantmir, mir, lit.* 'tooth-morsel' or 'bite', demanded by Finn's severed head from the fishermen as they cooked their fish after slaying the hero. See Meyer's translation of the 'Death of Finn mac Cumaill' in *Zeit. f. celt. Philol.* I, p. 465.

52 It is said to be *geis* to Cuchulainn to eat dog's flesh.

53 Ed. and trans. by L.C. Stern, *Revue celtique*, vol. XIII, p. 5 ff.

54 See Meyer, *Fianaigecht*, p. xxiii.

55 Ed. and trans. by Stokes *Revue celtique*, vol. VII, p. 289 ff.

56 Meyer, *Fianaigecht*, p. xxv.

57 See also Meyer's translation of the passage above.

58 He is generally identified with Lomna mac Duinn Desa, who plays a prominent role in the *Destruction of Da Derga's Hostel*, and who is mentioned also in the *Dindsenchas* and elsewhere. See Thurneysen, *Ir. Held.*, index and references there cited.

59 Whitley Stokes, 'On the Bodleian Fragment of Cormac's glossary' in *Transactions of the Philological Society*, 1891–4, p. 176 f.

60 *Manners and Customs*, vol. II, p. 208.

61 Ed. by Kuno Meyer, *Revue celtique*, vol. V, p. 195. ff.; cf. *Archiv. f. celt Lexicographie*, vol. I, p. 482; trans. by Meyer, *Ériu*, vol. I, p. 181 ff.

62 *Fianaigecht*, p. xxviii.

63 Trans. by K. Meyer, *loc. cit.*; also in *Four Songs of Summer and Winter* (London, 1903); and in *Ancient Irish Poetry* (London, 1913), p. 54 f.

64 *Ériu*, vol. XI, p. 58 ff.

65 '*Bid a drochmir dodngarba, bid lev a sealba.*'

66 *Zeitschr. f. celt. Philol.*, vol. I, p. 462 f.

67 A variant version of this story of the *Aided Finn* is published and trans. by O'Grady, *Silva Gadelica*, vols. I, p. 89 ff; II, p. 96 ff. The text is also published by K. Meyer, *The Battle of Ventry*, p. 72 ff. This version relates that Alclech cut off Finn's head, but omits its subsequent fate, and differs also in some other details. Finn is here presented as killed in battle.

68 Ed. and trans. by K. Meyer, *Revue celtique*, vol. XXIV, p. 41 ff.

69 Ed. and trans. by Whitley Stokes, *Revue celtique*, vol. XXIV, p. 41 ff.

70 We may compare the action of Mac Datho in the poem (str. 2) contained in ch. 3 of the *Scel Mucci Mic Datho* when he is taking council with himself as to how he ought to act in his dilemma. It is possible that the action of the *fili* in covering his face with the palms of his hands in *imbas forosnai*

is due to a desire for darkness. We may perhaps note also that the sage Morann chanted his *laid* as soon as his head was freed from its covering, and that the Welsh poet Taliesin is stated – in a late tradition – to have recited poetry as soon as he was taken out of the bag in which he had been found. Other instances might be cited. See Chadwick, *Growth of Literature*, vol. I, p. 658 ff.

71 We may refer to the manner in which the ancient Gauls are said to have treated the heads of their enemies. See Strabo, IV, 4, 5; cf. Diodorus, V, 2, 9. See especially the interesting account of the Boii, Livy, XXIII, 24.

72 Reference may be made to the head of Bendigeid Vran in the *Mabinogi* of Branwen, where the severed head of Bran is always present at the feasting of its convoy during their stay in Harlech and at Gwales in Penvro, and ensures their happiness and good cheer.

73 In the version from the Law-tracts he is called a *druí*, 'druid' (Dillon).

74 Mac-Con's *druth* Dadera was probably a similar person. See the verse quoted in the story of *Ailill Aulom, Mac-Con, and Finn Ua Baiscne, Meyer, Fianaigecht*, p. 35.

75 Ed. and trans. by K. Meyer, *Fianaigecht*, p. 1 ff.

76 Windisch, *ed. cit.*, p. 676.

77 With these talking (severed) heads of sages we may compare the early Norse story of Mimir's head in the *Ynglinga Saga*, ch. 4. Mimir, we are told, was the wisest of the Norse gods (Aesir). and was sent by them as a hostage to their enemies, the *Vanir*. The Vanir, however, cut off Mimir's head and sent it back to the Aesir. Othin smeared it with herbs to preserve it, and chanted spells over it, and bewitched it so that it spoke with him, and told him many hidden things.

78 *The Irish Ordeals*, etc, ed. and trans. by Whitley Stokes, *Irische Texte*, vol. III, p. 180.

79 See the description of him as *ardfili* and *oinmit* in *Comrac Liadaine ocus Cuirithir*, ed. and trans. by K. Meyer (London, 1902), p. 12. See also Thurneysen, *Ir. Held.*, p. 71; K. Meyer, *Aislinge Meic Conglinne*, pp. 7, 131; Whitley Stokes, *Three Irish Glossaries*, pp. 6, 36, LIII.

80 Is not the expression a *teinm 7 a tomoilt* used with reference to the nuts of Segais sent by Maer to Finn in the *Dindsenchas* of Rath Cnamrossa (*Revue celtique*, XV, p. 333) to be taken in connection with the *tenm laida*?

81 *Ancient Laws and Institutes of Ireland*, vol. I, p. 44.

82 For a discussion of the date and relationship of this passage in the laws, and for the date and relationship of the passage relating to the *sui filid* and *imbas*, already cited above, see Thurneysen, *Zeit. f. c. Philol.*, vol. XVI, p. 186.

83 See Cormac's *Glossary, s.v. Coire Brecain*, where the blind poet, Lugald Dall, discovers the name of Brecan's lapdog by asking his attendants to place the end of his wand on the dog's skull, and then reciting a verse over it in which he reveals the name and fate of the dog's owner.

84 *Ériu*, vol. XI, p. 56.

85 Ed. and trans. by Whitley Stokes, *Revue celtique*, vol. XXVI (1905), p. 4 ff.

86 'The Nine Witches of Gloucester' in *Anthropological Essays presented to Edward Burnett Tylor* (Oxford, 1907), p. 285 ff.

87 *Loc. cit.*, p. 288, footnote 1.

88 There is, of course, a certain amount in common between the adventures of Finn and those of the Irish hero Nera; but this does not carry us very far.

89 Loth, *Les Mabinogion*, vol. I, p. 314 f.

90 There is a passage in one of the Mongan stories which seems to suggest that Finn came to Ireland from 'Alba'. See Meyer, *Voyage of Bran*, vol. I, p. 48; cf. *Fianaigecht*, p. xxii.

91 *Unde ... enantiabunt* not in MS. D.

92 Giraldus Cambrensis, *Descriptio Cambriae*, ed. by J.F. Dimock (Rolls Series, Giraldi Cambrensis Opera vol. VI, 868), p. 194 f.

93 The same term is applied to at least one other person. See Chadwick, *Growth of Literature* (Cambridge, 1932). vol. I, pp. 637, 664.

CHAPTER FOUR

The Thumb of Knowledge

Robert D. Scott

O N THE BASIS OF SUCH EVIDENCE as may be obtained from available Irish texts, an attempt to ascertain how far the ideas of Finn's power of divination were current in Irish tradition previous to the tenth century appears almost hopeless. There is, however, ample evidence to prove that the idea was current, at least in some degree. This evidence, for convenience in treatment, may be separated into two classes. The evidence which makes up the first class consists of certain statements found in very ancient texts and relating only to the nature of Finn's miraculous power and the means by which it is put into action. The most noteworthy stories in which such statements appear may be cited as follows.

Stories Earlier than the Tenth Century Containing Statements which Bear upon the Nature of Finn's Power

The Death of Lomna

In this story, preserved in Cormac's *Glossary* (late ninth or early tenth century),[1] Finn is depicted as using his divining power in the identification of a headless corpse. A brief summary of the tale follows:[2]

> Lomna, Finn's fool, having discovered that one of Finn's wives or concubines was unfaithful, informed Finn of the fact. The woman in retaliation incited Coirpre, her lover, to kill Lomna. After the murder, Coirpre decapitated the corpse and carried the head away with him. Finn, returning to the hunting-bothy, found the body.
>
> 'A body here without a head!' says Finn. 'Make known to us,' say the Fiann, 'whose is the body.' Then Finn put his thumb into his mouth, and he chanted by *tenm láido* 'illumination of song,' and he said: 'Not … from Lomna's bed. This is Lomna's body,' says Finn. 'His enemies have taken the head from him.'

The remainder of this story has no bearing upon the tradition of the thumb of knowledge.

Finn and the Phantoms

In another text, which with considerable confidence may be assigned to the ninth century,[3] the divining power ascribed to Finn is somewhat different in character.

Finn and his companions once met a terrible giant. Having entered the giant's house, they were held prisoners and were mistreated in various ways by the giant and his supernatural associates. After the night's adventures, however, to the astonishment of Finn and his companions, both the house and the malign beings had disappeared. Furthermore, Finn's horse, which Finn and his companions had seen killed during the night, stood before them unharmed and tethered as they had left him. They held counsel among themselves in order to know who had perpetrated the outrage. Finn chanted through *tenm (la) edhae* and put his thumb under his *dhed-fis* (knowledge tooth). Then the thing was revealed to him. 'Truly,' said he, 'the three phantoms of Hibar-glend have done this in revenge for the death of their sister, Cuillend, whom we have killed.'

In the first of the foregoing tales it will be noted that Finn, in order to identify the headless body, put his thumb into his mouth and chanted a *tenm láido*. Thereupon follow several lines made up of words which, though translatable in most cases, are on the whole unintelligible. These lines, as in similar cases to be noted later, are suggestive of an incantation or a supernaturally induced utterance on the part of Finn, whose knowledge of the unknown seems to come from a conscious realization of what he has unconsciously uttered. According to the second story, Finn chanted a *tenm (la) edhae* and put his thumb under his tooth of knowledge. In this case there is nothing suggestive of an incantation in connection with the operation. The tooth of knowledge is, however, a feature lacking in the tale of the death of Lomna.

Stories Earlier than the Tenth Century which Purport to Explain the Origin of Finn's Power

In addition to the stories treated above, there are certain tales, likewise found in very ancient texts, which not only show the nature of Finn's power and the means by which it is put into action, but also provide explanations for its origin. Several of these concern Finn's killing of a fairy man, Cúldub, but, since they are obviously only variants of the same tale, each version, for purposes of treatment, may be designated by the title of the manuscript in which it is preserved.

The Death of Cúldub

The earliest reference, as far as is known, to Finn's power of divination occurs in a text (*H*.3.18) which in all probability may be dated as early as the ninth century, and which, indeed, may have been a product of the eighth.[4] The story in which this reference is found not only professes to explain the source of Finn's power, but is used as an example to explain the magical incantation *imbas forosna*.[5] A part of the tale, as translated by Meyer, may be quoted as follows:[6]

As did Finn ua Baiscne. When the fian were at Badamair on the brink of the Suir, Cúldub the son of Ua Birgge came out of the fairy-knoll on the plain of Femen (ut Scotti dicunt) and carried off their cooking from them. For three nights he did thus to them. The third time however Finn knew and went before him to the fairy-knoll on Femen. Finn laid hold of him as he went into the knoll, so that he fell yonder. When he withdrew his hand, a woman met him (?) coming out of the knoll with a dripping vessel in her hand, having just distributed drink, and she jammed the door against the knoll, and Finn squeezed his finger between the door and the post. Then he put his finger into his mouth. When he took it out again he began to chant, the *imbas* illumines him and he said [Here follows an untranslatable 'rhetoric'].[7]

This quotation constitutes about a third of the text edited by Meyer. The remainder of the text, apparently another story, concerns Finn's employment of his divining power in the identification of an enemy, a man in a tree. That portion of this second tale which bears upon the divining operation follows:[8]

Then his followers asked of Finn who he in the tree was, for they did not recognize him on account of the hood of disguise which he wore.

Then Finn put his thumb into his mouth. When he took it out again, his *imbas* illumines him and he chanted an incantation and said: [Here follows a 'rhetoric' which Meyer does not translate] "Tis Derg Corra son of Ua Daigre', said he, 'that is in the tree'.

The Death of Cúldub

This hitherto inedited text is preserved in the Yellow Book of Lecan (YBL), a manuscript of the late fourteenth or early fifteenth century. Another copy of the text is found in Stowe 992 (now *RIA, D.IV.2*),[9] a manuscript which may also be dated as early as the late fourteenth century.[10] The Stowe text, according to Meyer, may be considered a product of the ninth century.[11] An examination of the two versions, however, makes it appear highly probable that the Stowe text is either copied from the YBL text or is a less faithful reproduction of a common original.[12] Both may, therefore, be considered as old as the ninth century. They may be of even greater antiquity. The story preserved in YBL follows:

Another time Finn was at Cind Cuirrig. It is there he was accustomed to be. A man was charged every morning with the cooking of a pig for his day's food. One time now Oisin was charged with its cooking. When he thought it time (i.e., it was done), it lay upon the litter beside him on the prongs of the fork in the hand of his companion. It is there that he had placed it. It makes off. He ran after it, across the Suir, that is, over Ath Nemthen, across Ord, across the Maing (?), over Fan hua Faelan into the summit of the fairy-knoll of Fer Femin. The door was shut after it had gone into the fairy-knoll. Oisin was left [outside]. When the *fian* awoke, he came [back]. 'Where [is] the pig?' said Finn. 'A braver man has taken it,' said Oisin. Cailte undertakes it the next day. It was taken from him in the same way. He came [back] then. 'Where [is] the pig?' said Finn. 'I am not braver than he from whom it was taken yesterday,' said Cailte. 'Though I go myself to cook it,' said Finn, 'the young thorn is always sharper.' He went himself to cook it, his spear-hafts in his left hand, the other hand turning the pig. On the prongs, moreover, of the fork he had fixed it.[13] Finn gave a blow upon him, but the point of his spear only reached his back. However, he left the belly in the Plains of the Belly, the shoulder blade (?) in Cill [chtair, the breadth of the side] in Toib Muicce. Seven times it jumped over the Suir. 'Open,' said he before him in the top of the hill. 'Open,' said he, [as he raced] along the length of the mountain. '[Take] this from me,' said Finn. He gave it a blow as it was going into the fairy-knoll, so that he broke its back. He leaned his hand upon the door-post, so that the door was closed upon his thumb.[14] He put [it] into his mouth. Others say, therefore, that it was from this that there was knowledge to Finn, because as much of his finger as entered the *sid*, this it was that he put into his mouth. There was heard a wail. 'What is that?' said everyone. 'Cúldub has been killed,' said they. 'Who killed him?' [said one]. 'Finn hua Baiscne,' [said another]. They all wail. It is then he said: 'Bind bind berlai bind bec nimgnae buiruid tairb coi coistecht fri Femen furlae. Mai muiced sond ar femen fugiath sirchrand sirluth laitho Find fri ulaid Cúldub.' He thereupon carries his pig in his bosom and showed it to his people. *Finit.*

The versions in *H*.3.18 and YBL

Although an intimate connection between these two stories is at once apparent, an attempt to determine the exact relationship between them presents a number of vexing problems. It will at once be noted that the scene of the *H*.3.18 story (*H*) is Badamair, and that the action in the YBL version (*Y*)[15] takes place at 'Cind Curraig'. There is reason to believe, however, that the names 'Badamair' and 'Cind Curraig' were in early Irish tradition merely different names for the same place.[16] It then appears that, except for the episode relating to the woman in *H* and the speeches which immediately follow Finn's putting of his thumb into his mouth in *Y*, the two stories are fundamentally the same. It will be noted further that the fragment of 'rhetoric' preserved at the end of *H* agrees almost word for word with a portion of that given at the end of *Y*, and that both 'rhetorics' concern the killing of Cúldub. In the light of these facts it seems safe to assume that *H* is a condensed version – containing, however, an additional feature, viz., the episode relating to the woman – of the story preserved in *Y*.

Several questions at once suggest themselves: (1) Did the scribe of *H* make a condensed version of the *Y* text, introducing on his own initiative the episode concerning the woman? The presence of Cúldub's full name, *ua Birgge*, which occurs in *H* but not in *Y*, makes it difficult to believe that *Y* was the sole source of the *H* text. (2) Did the composer of *Y* make an elaborated version of *H*, omitting, however, the feature which concerned the woman? The fact that neither the allusion to *imbas forosna* nor the episode relating to the woman, the most important feature of *H*, appears in *Y*, lays the validity of such a conclusion open to serious doubt.[17] The logical inference seems to be that both versions had a common source in an earlier tale which concerned the killing of Cúldub and which may be designated **X*.

The presence in *H*, however, of the episode concerning the fairy woman suggests at once a question as to whether this incident was included in **X*. Some light may be thrown upon the matter through the examination of a tale printed by O'Curry and also incorporated in Sir Samuel Ferguson's poem 'The Death of Dermid'.[18]

A short summary of O'Curry's story follows:

Once upon a time Finn was hunting near *Sliabh na m-Ban* in the present County of Tipperary. As he was standing at a spring-well a strange woman suddenly appeared, filled a silver tankard at the spring, and walked away with it. Finn followed her until she came to the side of the hill. There a concealed door opened suddenly and she walked in. Finn attempted to followed her, but the door was slammed on his thumb. He put his thumb into his mouth to ease the pain and found himself possessed of the gift of foreseeing future events. This gift, however, was not, 'we are told', always present, but only when 'he bruised or chewed the thumb between his teeth'.

Unless O'Curry has practically reconstructed the story, his source must be something other than the *H* version, cited above. The statements concerning *Sliabh na m-Ban*, the spring-well, and the bruising or chewing of the thumb are not present in *H*. It will also be noted that in O'Curry's story Finn's 'thumb' is smashed in the door, while in the *H* text a 'finger' is the injured member. It furthermore seems quite unlikely that O'Curry would have omitted reference to that part of the tale which concerns the killing of Cúldub, had the source of his tale been the *H* text. Yet, even though it might be proved that the story printed by O'Curry is one which he reconstructed from the *H* text, there still remains the possibility that there had been in existence a tradition which did not concern Cúldub, but did attribute Finn's smashed thumb to an adventure with a fairy woman, and that a portion of this story had been inserted in *H*.

Further examination of the *H* and *Y* texts reveals other significant facts. Although the *Y* version contains a number of details which are not preserved in *H*, the stories through Finn's killing of Cúldub are practically identical in the two versions. From this point to the end, however, they not only show a wide divergence, but both present irregularities and appear hurried and inconsistent. As has been indicated above, *H* may have had its source in an earlier story, *X*, which concerns the slaying of Cúldub, and which in all probability was either directly or indirectly the source of *Y*. Three explanations for the two differing versions may then be considered. First, *X* was a story which concerned the slaying of Cúldub. It contained the episode relating to the fairy woman and resembled *H* in fundamental details. The composer of *Y* omitted the episode which concerned the fairy woman and arranged the details respecting Cúldub in such a way as to account for the origin of the magic thumb. Second, *X* did not contain the episode relating to the fairy woman but was, in general details, similar to *Y*. The composer of *H*, following the general outline of *X*, inserted the episode concerning the fairy woman, a part of another story bearing upon the origin of Finn's magic thumb, in place of the thumb-smashing incident as it is recorded in *Y*. Third, *X* resembled neither *H* nor *Y* in that it contained no allusion to the tradition of the thumb of knowledge or the thumb-smashing incident. It ended in a 'rhetoric' which concerned the death of Cúldub and which probably followed a statement regarding the wails, similar to that preserved in *Y*. The two different versions of the thumb-smashing incident were then later insertions in *H* and *Y* respectively.

An attempt to establish with any degree of certainty the relationship between these stories seems more or less futile. There are, however, preserved in Irish texts a number of ancient tales which are very similar to the foregoing legends of Finn and which contain elements practically identical with those found in *H* and *Y*. The similarity of basic details in these stories not only suggests that the tales which form the group, including *H* and *Y*, are intimately related, but this suggested relationship within the group furnishes a tentative explanation for the development of *H* and *Y*.[19] One of these tales appears as an episode in the *Macgnímartha Finn*, an extensive framework story, which in its present form may date from the twelfth century. There can be little doubt, however, that many of the tales incorporated in the *Macgnímartha Finn* may be assigned to a much earlier date.[20] A summary of the episode relating to Finn and the goblin follows:[21]

21. Finn had gone to Cethern, the son of Fintan, further to learn poetry with him. At that time there was a very beautiful maiden in the fairy-knoll of Bri Ele, and the men of Ireland were at feud about her. One man after another went to woo her. Every year at Hallowe'en the wooing used to take place, for at the time of Hallowe'en the fairy-knolls of Ireland were always open. Each man, however, who went to woo this maiden suffered a great injury, viz., one of his people was slain by an unknown assassin.

22. Now, Cethern, the poet, went to woo the maiden. His people went with him.

As they approached the fairy-knoll, one of Cethern's followers, Oircbel, was slain, and it was not known who slew him.

23. Thereafter, Finn went to dwell with the champion, Fiacail mac Conchinn. To Fiacail, Finn made his complaint and told him how the man had been slain among them at the fairy-knoll. Fiacail told Finn to go and sit down between the two strongholds which are between the two Paps of Anu.[22]

24. On Hallowe'en night Finn took a position at the place designated. The two fairy-knolls were opened around him, and he saw a great fire in each of the two strongholds. A voice from one of the fairy-knolls said: 'Is your sweet food good?' 'Good, indeed!' said a voice in the other fairy-knoll. 'A question. Shall anything be taken from us to you?' 'If that be given to us, something will be given to you in return.' A man thereupon came out of one of the fairy-knolls carrying a kneading-trough in his hand. On the kneading-trough there was food, which consisted of a pig, a cooked calf, and a bunch of wild garlic. As the man came past him, Finn made a cast with the spear of Fiacail mac Conchinn, saying: 'If the spear should reach any one of us, may he escape(?) alive from it! I think this was a revenge for my comrade.'

25. Soon afterward Finn heard a great lament and a great wail, saying:

On the Barrow, by a sharp-pointed spear,
Aed, Fidga's son, has fallen:
By the spear of Fiacail, Codna's son,
Finn has slain him … .

Then Fiacail came and asked Finn whom he had slain. Finn replied that he did not know, but that he had made a cast with the spear and believed that it had reached someone. He further told Fiacail that he had heard a great wailing in the fairy-knoll, saying:

Venom is this spear,
And venomous he whose it is,
Venomous whoever threw it,
Venom for him whom it laid low.

26. Outside the fairy-knoll of Cruachan Brig Ele, Finn seized a woman in pledge for his spear. The woman promised that she would return the spear on condition that Finn release her. This Finn did, and the woman went into the knoll. As she entered the knoll, however, she said:

Venom the spear,
And venom the hand that threw it!
If it is not cast out of the knoll,
A murrain will seize the land.

Thereupon the spear is thrown out, and Finn takes it with him to Fiacail. 'Well,' said Fiacail, 'keep the spear with which thou hast done the famous deed.'

27. After this Fiacail and Finn set out for Inver Colptha. Fiacail, fearing that Finn might not be able to keep pace with him, carried twelve balls of lead around his neck in order to restrain his vigour and swiftness. As they proceeded, Fiacail cast one ball

73

after another from him. These balls Finn picked up and carried with him, and yet Fiacail's running was no swifter than Finn's.

28. That night they were at Inver Colptha, and Finn kept watch during the night. While he was watching, he heard a cry from the north, and, without waking the warrior, he went alone in the direction of the cry to Slieve Slanga. While Finn was there, among the men of Ulster, at the hour of midnight, he overtook three women before him, at a green mound, with horns (?) of fairy-women. As they were wailing on that mound, they would all put their hands on the mound. Then the women flee into the fairy-mound before Finn. Finn caught one of the women as she was going into the fairy-knoll of Slanga, and snatched her brooch out of her cloak. The woman went after him, and besought Finn to give her back the brooch of her cloak, and said it was not fit for her to go into the fairy-knoll with a blemish, and she promises a reward.

The *Macgnimartha Finn* breaks off at this point. Another story, preserved in the oldest part of the *Acallam na Senórach*,[23] concerns Finn's slaying of a fairy man as the latter is entering the door of a fairy-knoll.

A summary of this tale, which relates to Finn's killing of the fairy man, Aillén mac Midhna, follows:[24]

Every year on Hallowe'en, the goblin, Aillén mac Midhna, came to the stronghold of Tara and, after putting everyone to sleep through the music of his *timpán*, emitted from his mouth a blast of fire which burned the stronghold. On the day of Hallowe'en, Conn, the King of Ireland, asked that some of the men of Ireland volunteer to protect Tara against the ravages of Aillén. After the others had refused, Finn accepted the commission. Fiacha mac Congha, a friend of Finn's father, thereupon supplied the youthful Finn with a deadly spear 'with which no devious cast was ever made'.

Finn then went out to defend the city. Soon he heard a plaintive strain of music, and he held the flat of the spear-head and its point to his forehead. After Aillén had put every one except Finn to sleep, he discharged from his mouth his blast of fire. Finn, however, warded off the blast with a fourfold mantle which he had been wearing, and thus saved the city.

Aillén thereupon returned to the fairy-knoll on the summit of *Sliabh Fuaid*. Finn followed him and, as Aillén passed in at the door of the knoll, delivered a cast of the spear that drove the goblin's heart out through his mouth. Finn then beheaded Aillén and carried his head back to Tara. Aillén's mother thereupon appeared outside the knoll and, calling upon the 'she-leech of Amartha', raised a great lamentation, saying: 'by Fiacha mac Congha's spear – by the fatal mantle and by the pointed javelin – Aillén mac Midhna is slain! Ochone! Aillén is fallen.'

An examination of certain passages included in a poem preserved in the well-known Book of Leinster makes it clear at once that versions of the foregoing stories concerning Finn's slaying of Aillén and Finn's slaying of Aed were known before the middle of the twelfth century. These passages from the poem ascribed to Gilla in Chomded may be quoted as follows:[25]

5

In the eighth year of his life when he was visiting Dathi's Tara, he slew [Aillén] whose hand was full with candle, ... with *timpán*

6

'A *timpán* for sleep!' said all, the practice at each Hallowe'en, a customary deed; every year, … the candle was burning brightly.

8

For fear of sword-fierce Conn Finn went to learn noble poetry: Cethern Fintan's son, he was his tutor in poetic composition.

9

After a feast the *fiana* bring Finn to avenge the poet Orcbél; the fairy-woman from Slieve Slánga had achieved the fierce bold deed.

10

When he had joined the *fian* with worth, this was his journey on that night: … from Bri Éle, …

13

In revenge of the poet Orcbél Finn slew Ua Fidga at a feast in the west at the Paps, … with the spear of Fiaclach, Conchenn's son.

14

Two staves Finn heard at the mound of the Paps above him: 'Stalwarth Ua Fidga has been slain' was the exact beginning of the first stave.

15

'Venom is the spear' was the powerful beginning of the second stave – I know it not; thereafter the deed of valour on bright All-hallowe'en he heard them.

16

Seven deer by Slieve Bloom was Finn's first chase, … at the end of seven years crowned with honour, at the famous Apple tree of the *fiana*.

17

A vessel full of gold, of glorious silver, the woman out of Slieve Slánga gave to him; we know for certain that this was the first fair treasure which he took to the *fian* for noble distribution.

It is practically certain that Strophes 5 and 6 of Gilla in Chomded's twelfth-century poem are based on some version of the story concerning Finn and Aillén preserved in the *Acallam*. It appears equally certain that Strophes 8, 9, 13, 14 and 15 of the same poem are in like manner based on some recension of the tale respecting Finn and Aed contained in the *Macgnímartha Finn*. It will be noted that the episode preserved in the *Macgnímartha Finn* which concerns Finn's capture of the fairy woman and the return of his spear does not appear in Gilla in Chomded's poem. This fact, however, does not supply evidence sufficient to establish a conclusion that such an episode was not present in Gilla in Chomded's source. Altogether, it appears not unlikely that the story as preserved in the *Macgnímartha Finn* was in existence at least as early as the twelfth century.

Further evidence concerning the early existence of tales relating to Finn's employment of Fiacail's spear in the slaying of fairy men is supplied by a passage which, like Gilla in Chomded's poem, is contained in the twelfth-century Book of Leinster. This passage, which Meyer assigns to the tenth century, has been translated by him as follows:[26]

Aed MacFidaig fell by the hand of Find,
From the spear of Fiacail Mac Conchenn,
For the love he gave to the maiden of Brí Eile.
By the same spear Find killed
Cúldub Mac Fidga Forfind.[27]

The allusion to the maiden of Bri Éile makes it clear that the first three lines of this passage refer to the incident preserved in the *Macgnímartha Finn*.[28] The identity of 'Cúldub Mac Fidga' is not clear.

In addition to the foregoing stories relating to Finn, another tale, *Móin Gai Glaiss*, which may be as old as the twelfth century, or possibly an earlier date, demands attention.[29] A translation by Stokes, *RC*, XV (1894), 305 ff., may be quoted as follows:

Gae Glas son of Luinde son of Lug Liamna was Fiacha Srabtine's champion. 'Tis for him that the smith made the intractable spear. From the south Cúldub son of Dían went on the day of *samain* (Nov. 1) to seek to slay some one, and he slew Fidrad son of Dam Dub, from whom *Ard Fidraid* is called. Then Gae Glas went a-following him and hurled at him the lance which the smith had made for him by magic, and it passed through Cúldub into the bog, and that lance was never found afterwards save once, when Mael-Odrán son of Dimma Cron, after he [leg. it ?] had been a year in the ground, found it and slew therewith Aithechdae king of Húi Máil. Whereof he sang this stave: *Imlech Ech* etc. 'This lance was the *Carr* of Belach Duirgen: 'tis it that would slay the thirty bands. Thus it was, with a fork under its neck, and none save the Devil would move it. So long as the lance is with its point southwards the strength of Conn's Half (the North of Ireland) will not be broken by Leinster.'

As Brown has pointed out, there are a number of details, common to this story of Gae Glas and to the stories of Finn cited above, which deserve consideration. First, Gae Glas slew Cúldub son of Dían with the cast of a spear in revenge for a wrong, just as Finn slew Cúldub in the tales previously cited. Again, in the story of Gae Glas and in the story of Finn and Aillén the spear is a magic weapon. It may further be noted that in the tale of Finn and Aed, as well as in the incident reflected in the passage quoted from the anonymous tenth-century poem relating to Fionn's slaying of 'Cúldub Mac Fidga', the spear is apparently the same magic weapon with which Aillén mac Midhna was slain. Furthermore, in the story concerning Gae Glas, as well as in those relating to Aillén and to Aed, the deed was done on Hallowe'en. Finally, in the tale of Gae Glas, a personage called Fiacha Srabtine appears as the patron of the hero, while in the story of Aillén and in that of Aed, a character by the name of Fiacha mac Congha or Fiacail mac Conchinn (Conchenn) plays a similar part. In his discussion of these details, Brown holds that the similarity of names and roles played in these stories 'can hardly be fortuitous', and concludes that the tale of Gae Glas is a variant of 'Finn and the Goblin', the essential elements of which are the slaying of a supernatural foe and the accomplishment of this deed through the use of a magic spear.

An examination of the details preserved in the foregoing stories not only justifies with reasonable certainty an assertion that the tales are closely related, but hints at what may have been the nature of certain relationships existing between them. In all of the stories a goblin has in some way inflicted injury upon the hero or upon the friends of the hero. In all of these stories the hero slays this goblin through the cast of a spear. In all of the stories except the *H* and *Y* versions of those relating to Finn and Cúldub, the spear which Finn casts is a magic weapon. It will further be noted that in all of the stories except that which concerns Gae Glas, Finn is definitely named as the hero. In this latter tale the presence of the name Fiacha, which also occurs in the story of Aed and in that of Aillén, and the appearance of the name Cúldub, which is also found in the several tales of Finn and this goblin, lend support to Brown's suggestion that the tale relating to Gae Glas is a variant of a primary story of 'Finn and the Goblin', according to which Finn by means of a magic spear slays a supernatural foe. There seems to be a possibility, however, that this basic story, 'Finn and the Goblin', was in turn a development from an earlier tale, the fundamental elements of which concerned the death of a goblin through the medium of a magic spear hurled by some hero. This hero may have been some one other than Finn; and we may then suppose that such an hypothetical basic tale relating to the death of a goblin at the hands of a hero, which tale may be designated *A, was the source of the story in which Gae Glas was named as the hero, as well as of another development, the primary tale of 'Finn and the Goblin', in which Finn takes the hero's role.

In the stories of Finn and Aillén, Finn and Aed, and Finn and Cúldub, all of which may be developments from the primary 'Finn and the Goblin', the occurrence of certain similar details furnishes ground for further conjecture concerning their relationships. In each of these Finn kills a goblin who has in some way injured either him or his friends. In each of the tales the slaying takes place at the door of a fairy-knoll. In the story relating to Aillén and in that relating to Aed the slaying is done with a magic weapon, the spear of Fiacha mac Congha or Fiacail mac Conchinn. In each of the tales a lament uttered by a fairy or by several fairies follows the killing, and, in each of the stories except the *Y* version of the tale respecting Finn and Cúldub, a fairy woman appears. These facts suggest a conclusion, indicated above, that all the foregoing tales relating to Finn are developments from a primary story, hereinafter designated *B^2, the essential details of which would seem to have been as follows:

> A goblin has injured either Finn or Finn's friends. On Hallowe'en, Finn, by means of a spear, perhaps the magic weapon of Fiacha mac Congha (Fiacail mac Conchinn), slays the goblin as the latter is entering the door of a fairy-knoll. A lament is uttered by the fairies, and a fairy woman appears with whom Finn does or does not have a meeting.

From such an hypothetical tale (*B^2) the stories of Finn and Aillén (C^1), Finn and Aed, Finn and Cúldub, as well as the story of Gae Glas (B^1), may be developments.

The tale of Finn and Aed and those of Finn and Cúldub, however, have further points in common. According to the stories of Finn and Cúldub, the goblin has stolen a pig which members of the *fian* were cooking. In the tale of Finn and Aed, although Finn is seeking to revenge the death of the poet Oircbel, the goblin whom Finn slew was engaged in carrying food, which included a cooked pig, at the time of the slaying. Again, in the story of Finn and Aed and in the *Y* version of Finn and Cúldub, after the slaying of Cúldub loud wails interspersed with cries concerning the name of the slayer arise within the *sidh*. Furthermore, in the story of Finn and Aed and in the *H* version of Finn and Cúldub, a fairy woman appears with whom Finn has a meeting. The presence of these details, common to the stories of Finn and Aed and of Finn and Cúldub, points toward an earlier tale ($*C^2$), in which the story of Finn and Aed and those of Finn and Cúldub had a common source. Such a tale, apparently a development from the primary $*B^2$, may not then be considered the source of the story relating to Finn and Aillén. This hypothetical story ($*C^2$) may be outlined as follows:

A goblin which had heretofore injured Finn or Finn's friends stole a pig which members of the *fian* were cooking. Finn followed the goblin and with the cast of a spear, perhaps a magic weapon, killed him as the goblin was entering the door of a fairy-knoll. Wails interspersed with cries concerning the name of the slayer arose within the *sidh*. A fairy woman thereupon appeared with whom Finn had a meeting.

If the existence of such an hypothetical tale as this ($*C^2$) may be assumed, a possible explanation of the story relating to Finn and Aed (D^1) appears, viz., that it is a literary treatment of some tale developed from the hypothetical $*C^2$. The assumption of such an hypothetical story ($*C^2$) also furnishes a possible explanation for the origin and nature of the H and Y versions of the tale which concerns Finn and Cúldub.

As has been pointed out above, there are reasons which make it appear that H is not a development from Y, and that, although Y may possibly have been evolved from H, both H and Y have their origins in a common source, $*X$. In H, it will be recalled, Finn's finger is smashed as a result of a meeting with a fairy woman. In Y the fairy woman does not appear. The fact, however, that the episode of the smashed thumb or finger appears in both H and Y prompts the inference that this feature was present in $*X$, the common source of H and Y. But what of the detail relating to Finn's pursuit of the fairy woman, which is found in H, but not in Y? Was this incident a part of $*X$?

That the stories concerning Gae Glas, Finn and Aillén, Finn and Aed, and Finn and Cúldub are intimately related, there can be no doubt. The similarity of names and features included in them is too close to make plausible any other conclusion. In the story of Finn and Aillén, in that of Finn and Aed, and in the H version of the tale concerning Finn and Cúldub, however, a fairy woman appears. Unless it might be assumed that the tale of Finn and Aed and that of Finn and Aillén are developments from H – an assumption which would necessitate an explanation for the omission of the thumb-smashing incident from these two stories, as well as for the presence in them of the allusions to the magic spear of Fiacail mac Conchinn – it appears safe to conjecture that an episode relating to a fairy woman was present in the common source of the stories respecting Finn and Aed, Finn and Aillén, and Finn and Cúldub, and that an incident relating to a fairy woman was also present in $*X$. Upon the basis of these assumptions, $*X$ may then be explained as a direct development from the hypothetical tale $*C^2$. In the development of $*X$, however, it appears that the composer, ignoring that part of his source which concerned a previous enmity between Finn and Cúldub, and possibly omitting an allusion to the spear of Fiacail mac Conchinn, began his narrative with the stealing of the pig and the killing of the goblin. Having followed his source through the slaying of Cúldub and the lamentation of the fairies, he modified the episode concerning the fairy woman which existed in his source by substituting the incident relating to the fairy woman and the smashed thumb or finger – a creation of his own designed to account for the tradition respecting Finn's power of divination. In keeping with this idea of explaining Finn's power, he blended certain parts of the fairies' lamentation with certain phrases of his own invention and made the whole an utterance on the part of Finn designed to serve as an incantation. Then H might be considered a condensed version of $*X$ in which the composer, desiring to explain *imbas forosna* – a term which he knew to be the name of a form of divination in some way connected with Finn's act – had incorporated the allusion to this magic practice. It, furthermore, appears not improbable that the composer of *H* was none other than the commentator on the version of the *Ancient Laws* in *H*.3.18. Accordingly, *Y* may be explained as a modified form of *X* in which the composer, having greatly elaborated certain features of his source, omitted the detail concerning the fairy woman. In conformity with the foregoing explanation, the story outlined by O'Curry may be explained as a comparatively late tale developed with certain modifications from that portion of *X* or of *H* which follows the slaying of Cúldub.

Based on the preceding facts and conjectures, a tentative explanation of the relationships between these tales of Finn may be presented in the following outline:

*A

A goblin has in some way injured a hero or the friends of a hero. The hero through the cast of a magic spear kills the goblin.

B^1
(*Móin Gai Glaiss*)

On Hallowe'en, Cúldub went forth and slew Fidrad. Gae Glas, the champion of Fiacha Srabtine, pursued Cúldub and with the cast of a magic spear killed him.[30]

*B^2

A goblin has injured Finn or Finn's friends. On Hallowe'en, as the goblin is entering the door of a fairy-knoll, Finn slays him through the cast of a magic spear, perhaps the spear of Fiacail mac Conchinn. A lament on the part of the fairies arises, and a fairy woman appears with whom Finn may or may not have a meeting.

C^1
(*Finn and Aillén*)

Aillén mac Midhna had burned Tara a number of times. One Hallowe'en, Finn not only frustrated Aillén's attempt to burn the city but, with a cast of Fiacail mac Conchinn's spear, killed the goblin as the latter was entering the fairy-knoll. Aillén's mother thereupon appeared and gave voice to great lamentations.

*C^2

A goblin had injured Finn or Finn's friends. On Hallowe'en, the goblin stole a pig which members of the *fian* were cooking. Finn pursued the goblin and with the cast of a spear, perhaps the magic weapon of Fiacail mac Conchinn, slew the goblin as the latter was entering a fairy-knoll. A great lamentation interspersed with cries concerning the name of the slayer arose within the knoll. A fairy woman thereupon appeared with whom Finn had a meeting.

D^1

(Finn and Aed)

On Hallowe'en, Finn went to the fairy-knoll in order to avenge the death of Oircbel, the poet, who had been slain by the fairy people. During the night, Aed mac Fidaig, a fairy man, appeared between the two knolls carrying food, which included a cooked pig. Finn with the magic spear of Fiacail mac Conchinn slew Aed as the latter was entering one of the knolls. A loud lamentation interspersed with cries concerning the name of the slayer arose within the knoll. A woman thereupon appeared. Finn captured this woman but later released her upon her promise to return the spear.

*X

(Possible Source of H and Y)

Once upon a time the members of the *fian* were engaged in cooking a pig. Cúldub ua Birgge stole the pig. Finn pursued and killed Cúldub with a spear (apparently not the magic weapon of Fiacail) while the goblin was entering a fairy-knoll. Lamentations interspersed with cries regarding the name of the slayer arose within the knoll. A fairy woman thereupon appeared carrying a dripping vessel in her hand. Finn followed the woman and *extended his hand so that it entered the doorway of the knoll. The woman immediately slammed the door upon Finn's thumb. Finn, in order to ease the pain, inserted his thumb in his mouth and repeated an incantation* [made up in part of words belonging to the lamentation of the fairies].

Z

(O'Curry's Story)

(A comparatively modern and elaborated rendering of that part of *X or H which follows the slaying of Cúldub.)

H

(Finn and Cúldub)

(Practically identical with *X except that the lamentation of the fairies is omitted, and the composer has inserted the allusion to *imbas forosna* as the name of Finn's divining power.)

Y

(Finn and Cúldub)

(An elaborated version of *X in which the detail regarding the fairy woman has been omitted. The composer, however, retained the episode of the smashed thumb as a detail in connection with the pursuit of Cúldub. The extensive 'rhetoric' of this version may have been present in *X. In such a case it may be assumed that part of it was omitted by the composer of H. On the other hand, it is possible that those parts of the 'rhetoric' which appear in this version and which are not preserved in H are creations by the composer of Y.)

Although this tentative explanation of the relationships between the foregoing tales of Finn seems to have a more or less logical foundation in the known facts, certain considerations in connection with the stories cited tend to cast some doubt upon the validity of the hypothesis. First, the presence of the names Cúldub and Fiacha in the story of Gae Glas (B^1) raises a question as to whether this tale did not have its origin in some source other than that indicated in the outline. Again, the fact that in neither version of the tale relating to Finn and Cúldub is there any allusion to a magic spear or to the illustrious Fiacail or Fiacha, calls forth a doubt regarding the postulated relationship of these stories concerning Cúldub to those of Finn and Aed and of Finn and Aillén, as presented in the foregoing explanation. Furthermore, the story of Finn and Cúldub, built up as it is about the episode relating to the goblin's stealing of a cooked pig, seems to be constructed of matter more primitive than that included in the tale of Finn and Aillén or that of Finn and Aed. In other words, there seems to be a possibility that the tale of Finn and Aillén and that of Finn and Aed are literary works of composers who, having a knowledge of much primitive lore that included the story of Finn and Cúldub, not only created new features, but in the composition of their works drew upon and fitted together various details from the mass of stories which they knew. Finally, the existence of such a tale as that printed by O'Curry, when added to the fact that the detail regarding the fairy woman is not preserved in *Y*, suggests that a story which concerned Finn's smashing his thumb or finger as the result of a meeting with a fairy woman may have existed as an independent tale, later blended with the story relating to Finn's killing of Cúldub.

On the basis of these considerations, a second hypothesis regarding the relationships between the stories cited above may be proposed. According to this theory it may be assumed that in very early times there was in existence a story (*A) the fundamental elements of which concerned a hero's killing of a goblin through the medium of a magic spear. As Brown has suggested, this motif may be in some way related to the story regarding Perceval and the bleeding lance. From this tale (*A) it may further be assumed that there developed a story in which Finn was named as the hero and Cúldub was given as the name for the goblin. This tale, which will be designated *B, may be outlined as follows:

> Once when certain members of the *fían* were at Cind Cuirrig, they were engaged in cooking a pig. Cúldub ua Birgge stole the pig from them. Finn pursued Cúldub and slew him as the goblin was entering the door of a fairy-knoll on the plain of Femen. A great lamentation interspersed with cries concerning the name of the slayer as well as the name of Cúldub arose within the knoll. Finn, thereupon, took the pig, which the goblin had dropped at the door of the knoll, and returned to his people.

As will be noted, this hypothetical story does not retain the detail regarding the magic spear postulated as one of the elements in the legend from which this tale is a development, nor does it contain any allusion to the fairy woman who appears in *H* or to the thumb-smashing incident preserved in both *H* and *Y*.

This second hypothesis further assumes the existence of a very early story (*O), similar to that published by O'Curry, according to which a fairy woman whom Finn attempts to capture slams the door of the fairy-knoll upon his finger or thumb. This tale, according to the hypothesis, may be regarded as existing wholly independent of the Cúldub story and as being an attempt on the part of some composer to explain the origin of an existing tradition relating to Finn's magic thumb or finger.

With the assumed existence of *O and *B, an explanation for the origin of *X, the source of *H* and *Y*, at once appears. It has previously been noted that both *H* and *Y* contain the incident concerning the smashed thumb, but that the fairy woman, though present in *H*, does not appear in *Y*. Since the thumb-smashing incident is preserved in both *H* and *Y*, it seems safe to assume that this incident was also present in *X, their common source. Yet there appears to be some ground for a conjecture that the fairy woman was not presented as a character in *X. This conjecture is based on the fact that it is difficult to explain why, had the fairy woman been present in *X, so conspicuous a detail should have been omitted by the composer of Y.

In accord with these considerations it would appear that the composer of *X followed the tale *B through the slaying of Cúldub. He then, knowing the story *O, borrowed from that tale the incident concerning the smashed thumb or finger and, without taking over the detail regarding the fairy woman, blended the borrowed incident into his tale of Finn and Cúldub at a point followed the slaying of the latter and preceding the wails of the fairy people. In conformity with the borrowed detail relating to the origin of Finn's magic thumb or finger, he put into Finn's mouth a 'rhetoric'. A part of this 'rhetoric' he may have adapted from the lamentations of the fairy people as they appeared in *B. The remainder of the 'rhetoric' he may have invented. Therefore, *X may be outlined as follows:

Once when certain members of the *fian* were at Cind Cuirrig, they were engaged in cooking a pig. Cúldub ua Birgge stole the pig from them. Finn pursued Cúldub and with the cast of a spear struck down the goblin as the latter was entering the door of a fairy-knoll on the plain of Femen. *Finn attempted to enter the knoll, but the door was slammed upon his thumb (or finger). In order to ease the pain he inserted his thumb (or finger) in his mouth.* He thereupon heard the lament which was interspersed with cries relating to the name of the slayer as well as to the name of the slain goblin. Finn then uttered the 'rhetoric' *Bind, bind* etc and, picking up the pig, which the goblin had dropped, carried it back to his people.

If it may be assumed that such a tale represented the hypothetical *X, then Y may be considered as an elaborated rendering of this tale in which the composer inserted details of his own creation. These details may have included certain portions of the 'rhetoric' preserved in Y.

An explanation of the origin of H, however, still presents a problem. Since, in accordance with this second hypothesis, it is to be assumed that both the story which concerns Finn and Aed and that respecting Finn and Aillén are developments from the tale of Finn and Cúldub, it follows that the story of Finn and Aillén and that of Finn and Aed must trace their origins to versions of the Cúldub tale in which a fairy woman plays a part. The difficulty presented by these considerations at once disappears if it may be imagined that, serving as an intermediate step between *X and H, there was a story which might be taken as the source of the tale relating to Finn and Aed.

This intermediate step, which will be designated *XX, may then be explained as a development from *X in which the composer, knowing some form of the story outlined by O'Curry and realizing that this tale contained not only the incident of the smashed thumb or finger but also an episode concerning a fairy woman, incorporated the latter episode in his composition. Accordingly, H may be explained as a condensed rendering of *XX in which the composer inserted the allusion to *imbas forosna*, a term believed by him to be the name of the magic practice attributed to Finn. The story of Finn and Aed, as has been indicated above, may in like manner be explained as a literary composition based in part upon *XX, but greatly modified in pursuance of the whims of the composer. The tale of Finn and Aillén may similarly be considered in some degree a reflection of either *XX or H, while that of Gae Glas may be a story developed under the influence of *A, *B and *X. O'Curry's printed tale, Z, might then be regarded as a version of the original *O, a part of which had been inserted in *X, and a further part in *XX. This second hypothesis presented in outline form appears as follows:

*A

A goblin has injured a hero or a hero's friends. The hero kills the goblin through the medium of a magic spear.

(*Perceval*)

*B

Once when members of the *fian* were at Cind Cuirrig, they were engaged in cooking a pig. Cúldub ua Birgge stole this pig. Finn pursued Cúldub and killed him with the cast of a spear as the goblin was entering the door of a fairy-knoll on the plain of Femen. A great lamentation intersperesed with cries concerning the name of the slayer arose within the fairy-knoll. Finn took the pig, which the goblin had dropped at the door of the knoll, and carried it back to his people.

(*Gae Glas*)
(A development reflecting details from *A, *B and, perhaps, *X.)

*O

Once Finn was standing near a spring-well in the vicinity of *Sliabh na m-Ban*. A fairy woman appeared with a dripping vessel in her hand. Finn pursued her, but she escaped into the fairy-knoll. *As Finn extended his hand, the door of the fairy-knoll was closed, catching Finn's thumb (or finger) between the door and the post. Finn inserted his thumb (or finger) in his mouth.* At once he acquired the power of divination. Thereafter when he wished to know anything, he put his thumb (or finger) into his mouth.

*X

Once when members of the *fian* were at Cind Cuirrig, they were engaged in cooking a pig. Cúldub ua Birgge stole the pig. Finn pursued Cúldub and slew him as the latter was entering the door of the fairy-knoll on the plain of Femen. *As Finn extended his hand, the door of the knoll was slammed upon his thumb. In order to ease the pain, Finn put his thumb into his mouth.* Thereupon he heard a great lamentation which arose within the knoll. Finn uttered an incantation as follows: '*Bind, bind ... friulaid Cúldub.*' He then took the pig back to his people.

*XX
(Practically the same as *X, except that the composer has included details regarding the fairy woman, a further borrowing from *O.)

Y
(An elaborated rendering of *X.)

H
(A condensed version of *XX in which the composer has omitted certain parts of the 'rhetoric' but has inserted an allusion to *imbus forosna*.)

(*Finn and Aed*)
(A literary composition based in part upon *XX.)

(*Finn and Aillén*)
(A literary composition reflecting certain details from *XX or H.)

Z
(O'Curry's Story. A modern version of *O.)

Two additional explanations, which, however, are very similar to the first of the hypotheses outlined above, may also be presented. The first of these (Hypothesis III) differs from Hypothesis I, above, in a number of details: (1) according to this explanation, one assumes – as in Hypothesis II, above – that a story, $*O$, similar to that outlined by O'Curry, entirely unrelated to the legend of Cúldub and containing the episode of Finn's pursuit of the fairy woman and the smashed thumb, was extant in very early times; (2) it is assumed that the composer of $*X$, instead of inventing the thumb-smashing detail – as is postulated in Hypothesis I – borrowed the incident relating to the pursuit of the fairy woman and the smashed thumb from $*O$, substituting it for the detail regarding the fairy woman in his source, $*C^2$; (3) it is assumed that H and Y are developments from $*X$ – the author of Y, however, ignoring the detail regarding the fairy woman present in $*X$ – and that O'Curry's version (Z) had its origin in $*O$.

The second of these hypotheses (Hypothesis IV) differs from Hypothesis I, above, in the following particulars: (1) in this explanation the early existence of $*O$ is assumed as in Hypothesis III; (2) it is assumed that the author of $*X$, ignoring the allusion to the fairy woman which was present in his source, $*C^2$, as well as that which appeared in $*O$, borrowed from $*O$ merely the detail regarding the smashed finger; (3) it is assumed that O'Curry's story, Z, is a direct development from $*O$, that Y is traceable to $*X$, but that the author of H – basing his story upon $*X$ – drew upon $*O$ for the details concerning the fairy woman, which had not been taken over in the previous borrowing from $*O$ by the composer of $*X$.

As has been indicated, an attempt to establish with any great degree of probability the exact relationships between these stories concerning Finn appears more or less futile. That the tales are intimately related, there can be no doubt. That there were many stories now lost which served as intermediate steps in the development of the tales still extant, seems to be a safe conjecture. It also appears not improbable that had such stories been preserved, conclusions which now seem plausible might be untenable.

Although there are certain weaknesses in the tentative explanations which have been suggested, on the whole the hypotheses seem to be relatively logical deductions from the facts at hand. According to the second hypothesis, a story of Finn and Cúldub is set forth as a basis for the tale of Finn and Aed as well as for that of Finn and Aillén. The scene of this story of Finn and Cúldub is laid at Cind Cuirrig and on the plain of Femen. In support of this second hypothesis, it may be pointed out that, as far as can be determined, the oldest stratum of the Finn-cycle is composed in large measure of tales which are localized in this same territory. An attempt to justify the second hypothesis, in accordance with which the tale of Finn and Aillén and that of Finn and Aed are developments from $*XX$, demands, however, an explanation to account for the omission of the incident relating to the smashed thumb or finger from the stories of Finn and Aillén and Finn and Aed.

Altogether, of the several hypotheses the fourth appears to be the most plausible. Whether or not any of them supplies a valid analysis of the relationships between these stories, it is relatively certain that prior to the tenth century traditions concerning Finn's magic thumb or finger were current in Ireland. It is also relatively certain that one or more stories purporting to explain the origin of this magic thumb or finger were in existence in Ireland at an equally early date.

Notes

1 The text of Cormac's *Glossary*, either in complete or fragmentary form, is found in a number of different manuscripts. Concerning these manuscripts, their relationships, various editions and translations of the texts etc, see Thurneysen. *Festschrift Ernst Windisch* (Leipzig, 1914), pp. 8 ff. For further information concerning editions, as well as for the probable date of Cormac's *Glossary*, see Thurneysen, *Königsage*, pp. 19 ff., and notes. See also Vendryes, *RC*, XXXVII (1917–19), pp. 368 ff., and Meyer, *ZCP*, VIII (1912), pp. 178.

2 The summary, including the quotation, is taken from Whitley Stokes's edition and translation of the Bodleian fragment of Cormac's *Glossary* in *Phil. Soc. Trans.*, 1891–4, pp. 149 ff., *s.v.* 'Orc tréith'.

3 This tale, which, according to the late Kuno Meyer, *Fianaigecht*, p. xxiii, may be as old as the ninth century, is preserved in MS *Is. Vossii cod. lat. quart.* No. 7 of the University of Leiden. It has been edited and translated by Stern, *RC*, XIII (1892), pp. 1 ff., from which this summary is made. The story recounted in this prose version is also the subject of a poem, preserved in the twelfth-century Book of Leinster, p. 206b, ed. and trans. by Stokes, *RC*, VII (1886), pp. 289 ff. For that portion of the Irish text which relates to Finn's power, see *RC*, XIII, p. 7.

It might also be noted that in this same manuscript (*op cit.*, p. 11) Finn, through putting his thumb under his *ded-fis* (knowledge tooth) and chanting a *teinm laoga*, is said to have prophesied the coming of the Son of Life to Ireland.

4 For the Irish text and translation of this story, see Meyer, *RC*, XXV (1904), pp. 344 ff. The tale is incorporated in a version of the *Senchus Mor* found in the sixteenth-century vellum manuscript, *H.3.18*, Trinity College, Dublin. Meyer states, *loc. cit.*, that, so far as he knows, the story has not been preserved elsewhere. For the probable date of the text, see Meyer. *Fianaigecht*, p. xviii. On the date of the manuscript, see D'Arbois, *Essai*, p. lxxii.

5 This term, which is spelled in various ways, *imbas forosnai, imbass forosna, imbass for-ossna* etc, will here be written *imbas forosna* throughout.

6 *RC*, XXV (1904), pp. 345 ff.

7 The Irish text of this 'rhetoric' (Meyer's edition, *loc. cit.*) runs thus: 'Tair Femen fuigial formuig meis mui muic cetson sirchrand sirlúath laith find sra [leg. fri] aulad Cúlduib chanmae.'

8 Meyer, *RC*, XXV (1904), p. 349. It may be stated that in the 'rhetoric' which forms the end of this tale and which Meyer does not translate, the name 'Dercc Corra' is mentioned. From this fact it would appear that Finn gained his conscious knowledge of the man's name through the incantation.

9 See Best, *Bibl.*, p. 104, and Thurneysen, *Königsage*, p. 50.

10 For the date of the Yellow Book of Lecan, see O'Curry, *Materials*, p. 190. Cf. *The Yellow Book of Lecan, RIA Facs.*, Introduction. For the date of Stowe 992, see Meyer, *RC*, VI (1883–5), p. 173. Cf. D'Arbois, *Essai*, p. xciii, who holds that Stowe 992 is a manuscript of the fifteenth or sixteenth century. Thurneysen, *Königsage*, pp. 50 ff., assigns *RIA, D.IV.2* (Stowe 992) to an earlier date. There is reason to believe, however, that the manuscript is not older than the end of the fourteenth century.

11 *Fianaigecht*, p. xix.

12 The Stowe text has been edited and translated by Meyer, *RC*, XIV (1893), pp. 245 ff. The YBL text, as edited below, is not only more exact but contains several sentences not found in Stowe. A casual examination of the two reveals the probable relationship between them. Although the spellings frequently disagree, the word order in the two texts, except for the sentences omitted in Stowe, is practically identical. One of these omitted sentences seems to be an error in copying. In two consecutive lines of the YBL text the expression *ina beolu* (in his mouth) occurs. Stowe agrees almost word for word with YBL through the first *ina beolu*. It omits, however, what in the YBL text lies between the two occurrences of the expression, and is again in exact accord after the second occurrence. Compare the YBL text below (lines 24 and 25) with the Stowe text, *loc. cit.* The Stowe scribe, at the end of his text, remarks: '*Isam scithach*' ('I am tired'). Apparently, in copying, he wrote to the first *ina beolu*, then, glancing at his original, misread the second occurrence of the expression for the first and, unconscious of his omission, copied on. Statements regarding the personal mood

or feeling of the hard-working scribe, as in this case in Stowe, are not infrequent in Irish manuscripts. See the article by J.L. Gerig, *Modern Language Notes*, XXIII (1908), p. 264, and the note by Whitley Stokes, *Review celtique*, IX (1888), pp. 99–100.

The agreement of the word order in the two texts indicates that one was copied from the other, or that both were copied either from a common original, or from copies that go back to a common original. Although the YBL scribe may have copied the Stowe text, inserting the additional sentence on his own initiative, it appears more likely that the missing sentence in Stowe resulted from a copyist's blunder on the part of the tired Stowe scribe. It thus seems safe to assume that the Stowe text is either a copy of the YBL text, or, more probably, that they both come, either directly or indirectly, from a common original.

An edition of the YBL text follows [Brackets indicate parts of the text which have been supplied from Meyer's edition of Stowe, *loc. cit.* These parts are either illegible in YBL or are missing because of a hole in the manuscript]:

YELLOW BOOK OF LECAN, 212b, 3

[1] Feacht n-aile d[o Fi]nd a cind curraig. Isinti ba gn[athach som]. Rohearga (leg. roerbad?) fer cacha maidni do fuine mu[icci dia cuit] lai do som. Fecht and didiu roerbad Oisine [dia fuine. Intan] ba mithig leis dos [5] rala forsan esair secha im belaib na gabla illaim acheli. Is and arosiuir. Imsai ass. Soithi ass na di aid dar Siuir .i. fer ath nenithen. Dar Ord dar í muí dar fan .h. Faela[i]n i mullach sith fer Femin. Iadthar in cóm la iarna hesi iar teacht san sith. Fonacaib Oisne [imoig]. Intan [10] ron[d]uisig ind fiand isand ranic. Caidi in muc or Find. Rosfuc fer as calmu or Oisine. Gaibthe Cailte iarnamarach berar uad fon indus cetna. Ric side didiu. Caide in muc or Find. Nidam calmu innass o rucad ané or Cailte. Cia thi[a]sarsa dia fuine or Find as aithe cach [15] n-delg ass ou. Luid side fesin dia fuine a crundu na laim cli ind laim ele oc impud na muici im belaib im na gabla arosisir. Dobeir Find forgum fair ni roacht acht fograinde in gai didiu for a druim forfacaib in tairr didiu i maigib tarra in lethe i cill ichtair lethet intoib itoib muicce. Co ba secht [20] roling darsin Siuir. Oslaic or se reme im mullach int sleibe. Oslaic or se tar fot int [s]lebe. Uinsi uaim ar Find. Dobeir forgom fair oc teacht isin sid coraimid a druim trid. Aroisir a laim fris an ersaind corodruid in comla ara ordain cotard ina beolu. Asherat didiu alaile isde sin robai fis ac Find ar a [25] ndechaid da mer is an sid ised nogebed ina beolu. Coclos an gol. Cid sin or cach. Cúldub romarbad. Cia rosmarb. Find hua Baiscne. Guilid uili. Isand asbert som. Bind bind berlai bind bec nimgnae buiruid tairb coi cois techt fri Femen furlae. Mai muiced sond ar femen [30] fugiath sirchrand sirluth laitho Find fri ulaid Cúldub. Berid a muic na ucht co d-a-raisseilb dia muintir. Fi[nit].

The word *Oslaic* of line 20, which is written above the line in YBL, and the words *Oslaic or se tar fot int slebe Uinsi* of line 21, as well as the sentence beginning *Asberat didiu* and ending with *ina beolu*, lines 24–25, are not found in Stowe.

13 Something evidently omitted at this point.

14 In the Stowe text Finn is specifically named in this sentence.

15 As has been shown above, note 12, the text in Stowe 992 is probably either a copy of that in YBL, or both Stowe and YBL are copies of a common original of which YBL is the more faithful reproduction. The letter *Y* may thus stand for the YBL version, as well as for its textual source.

16 According to a very ancient Irish story, ed. and trans. by Meyer, *RC*, XIV (1893), pp. 241 ff., the warrior Currech Lifi killed Finn's paramour, Badamair. Finn, in revenge, cut off Currech's head and took it to the west, hence the place-name 'Cind (or Cenn) Currig'. In the *Acallam na Senórach. 2* (*Irische Texte*, IV, i, line 7926), Cailte states that he brought Currech's head to the hill above 'Badhamair'. See also O'Grady, *Silva Gadelica*, II (1892), p. 262. From these statements it appears that Badamair was understood to be a strand, perhaps on the brink of the Suir River, and that 'Cind Curraig' was a hill immediately above it. The teller of the tale probably knew that the names were associated in locality as they were in story.

'Badamair' is a name now lost. It was originally the name of a place near Cahir, County Tipperary. Dún Iascaig, a place mentioned in a part of the *H.*3.18 text not here quoted (*RC*, XXV [1904], pp. 346 ff.), is now Cahir, County Tipperary. Sidh Fer Femen, the fairy-knoll mentioned in *H*, was supposed to be located in the plain of Femen, near Cahir. See Hogan, *Onomasticon Goedelicum* Dublin. 1910, *s.v.* 'Badamair', 'Cenn cuirrig', 'Sid femin', 'Sid fer feimin' etc.

These three tales, together with a number of other very ancient legends concerning Finn, are all localized about this neighborhood. The significance of this fact will be discussed in my volume on the early Ossianic Cycle now near completion.

17 It will likewise be noted that the 'rhetoric' of *Y*, although identical in part, is much more extensive than that of *H*. Unless one may assume that the composer of *Y* created this additional 'rhetoric' on his own initiative, the source of *Y* must be considered something other than the text of *H*.

18 O'Curry, *Materials*, Re-issue 1878, p. 396. In presenting the summary of this story O'Curry states that the tale is preserved in the manuscript *H*.3.18, Trinity College, Dublin. Since he failed to give a more exact citation concerning the source of his story, it is impossible to state, without a minute examination of the manuscript, that his original was not the tale designated *H*, above. It is also impossible to determine whether O'Curry, with respect to details of the story and of the divining operation, followed the original text, whatever it might have been, or whether he supplied these details from modern tradition.

For Sir Samuel Ferguson's poem, see his *Lays of the Western Gael*, London, 1897, pp. 116 ff. Sir Samuel cites S.H. O'Grady's edition of *Toruigheacht Dhiarmuda agus Ghrainne*, OS, III (1855), as a translation of his source for the matter of the poem. Although the *Toruigheacht* may have been in a general way the basis of the poem, it does not contain this story about Finn's thumb; see O'Grady, *op. cit.*, p. 185. The origin of Sir Samuel's version of this episode is therefore apparently unknown. He may have borrowed the matter for this incident from O'Curry's summary, noted above. On the other hand, he may have taken it directly either from ancient manuscripts or from late oral tradition. At all events, it is not possible to state that Sir Samuel's episode regarding Finn and the fairy woman did not have its origin in the version of the Cúldub story in *H*.3.18.

19 This group of tales has been collected and studied by A.C.L. Brown, *Modern Philology*, XVIII (1920–21), pp. 201 ff., pp. 661 ff., who holds that the tales comprising the group are developments from a very ancient story, the basic elements of which concerned the death of a goblin at the hands of a hero. Brown also suggests the original goblin story as a possible source of the tradition relating to Perceval and the bleeding lance.

20 The *Macgnímartha Finn* is preserved in the Bodleian Codex, Laud 610. Part of it was edited and translated by O'Donovan, *OS*, IV (1856), pp. 281 ff., and again by David Comyn, *The Youthful Exploits of Finn*, (Dublin, 1881). Concerning these two editions, see a letter by Meyer, *Academy*, XX (1881), p. 122. The complete text from Laud 610 has been edited in *RC*, V (1881–3), pp. 195 ff., and translated in *Ériu*, I (1904), pp. 180 ff., by Meyer. See *AfcL*, I (1900), p. 482, for Meyer's corrections. For the probable date of this text, see Meyer, *Fianaigecht*, p. xxviii.

21 This summary is made from Meyer's translation, *Ériu*, I (1904), pp. 187 ff.

22 Two mountains in County Kerry.

23 The *Acallam na Senórach* is preserved in no manuscript older than the fifteenth century. There is reason to believe, however, that the tale in its present form was in existence in the early part of the thirteenth century. It has been edited in part and translated by S.H. O'Grady, *Silva Gadelica*, I (1892), pp. 94 ff., and II (1892), pp. 101 ff. See also the complete edition by Whitley Stokes, *Irische Texte*, IV, i (1900), pp. 1 ff., and notes, pp. 272 ff. On the date of the story, see Thurneysen, *Königsage*, p. 48; Meyer, *Fianaigecht*, pp. xxviii and 47; Brown, *Modern Philology*, XVIII (1920–21), p. 205.

24 This summary of the tale respecting Finn and Aillén is made from O'Grady's translation, *Silva Gadelica*, II (1892), pp. 142 ff., revised according to Stokes, *Irische Texte*, IV, i (1900), pp. 287 ff. A more complete outline of the legend appears in Brown's study, *Modern Philology*, XVIII (1920–21), pp. 205 ff. In order to make clear certain arguments which follow, however, it seems well to include a somewhat condensed summary of the story in this investigation.

25 Meyer's edition and translation, *Fianaigecht*, pp. 46 ff. This poem is preserved only in a single copy, *LL* 143a–145a. Meyer assigns it to the twelfth century, *op. cit.*, p. xxviii.

26 D. MacInnes and A. Nutt, *Folk and Hero Tales* (London, 1890), p. 405. Cf. Brown, *Modern*

Philology, XVIII (1920–21), p. 203, note 2; Meyer, *RC,* XIV (1893), p. 249. On the date and for the Irish text, see Meyer, *Fianaigecht,* p. xxiii.

27 According to the *LL* text the place-name is *Breg Éile.* In *RC,* XIV (1893), p. 249, Meyer translates the last line quoted above thus: 'Cúldub the son of Fidga the very fair.'

28 Allusions to Aed mac Fidaig also appear in the *Acallam na Senórach* (Stokes, *Irische Texte,* IV, i, lines 1047 and 3116) and in Broccán Cráibdech's tenth-centuiry poem (*LL* 43b, 28), where he is cited as a famous hero. See Meyer, *Fianaigecht,* p. xxiii, note 1, and *Ériu,* I (1904), p. 188, note 4.

29 This tale, entitled *Móin Gai Glaiss* (*Moin Gai Glais*), is recounted in both the prose and verse *Dindsenchas.* The prose version has been edited and translated by Stokes, *RC,* XV (1894), pp. 305 ff., and the verse version, by Edward Gwynn, *The Metrical Dindsenchas,* Part II, *RIA, TLS,* IX (1906), pp. 64 ff. On the date, see Thurneysen, *Königsage,* pp. 36 ff.; Stokes, *RC,* XV (1894), p. 272; Brown, *Modern Philology,* XVIII (1920–21). p. 203.

30 As has been indicated above, the presence of the names Cúldub and Fiacha makes any attempt to explain the origin of this tale, B^1, extremely hazardous. It may even be a development from *A which has been influenced by tales similar to $C^1 D^1$ or *X.

CHAPTER FIVE

The Voice of the Stone of Destiny

Ernest S. Hartland

T HE FAMOUS CORONATION STONE has an authentic history of six hundred years. At the time of the conquest of Scotland by Edward I, it was the stone on which the kings of the Scots were, according to immemorial custom, installed. Regarded by the Scots as sacred, it was therefore removed by Edward's order from Scone, where it stood, to Westminster, and was inclosed in what is now, and has been ever since, the Coronation Chair. Its earlier history, as distinguished from conjecture and legend, goes no farther back than the middle of the thirteenth century, or something less than half a century before its removal to Westminster, when it is recorded by Fordun that Alexander III was solemnly placed upon it and hallowed to king by the Bishop of St Andrews (1249). But what is wanting in authentic history has been abundantly made up in legend. The tale, of which there are two versions, is the creation of a literary age. The Irish version brings it, with the Tuatha Dé Danann, from Lochlann, or Scandinavia, to Ireland. The Scottish version traces it on the other hand from Egypt, whence it was carried by the Milesians. This was improved upon, to the extent of identifying the stone with that used by Jacob as a pillow on his journey from Beersheba to Haran. The attempt was thus made, by connecting the ruling race in Scotland with the legends of the Hebrew patriarchs, to confer upon the stone the united sanctity of religion, of antiquity, and of patriotism.

In the course of its wanderings the stone is said to have reached Tara; and it is declared to be the famous *Lia Fáil*, or Stone of Destiny, one of the two wonders of Tara celebrated in Irish sagas. We are indebted to the *Book of Lismore*, a fifteenth-century manuscript, for an enumeration of the wonderful properties of the *Lia Fáil*. The Colloquy with the Ancients, which is comprised in this precious manuscript, records a number of Irish traditions, some of which would else in all probability have perished beyond recovery. There we learn – the account is put into the mouth of no less a personage than Ossian himself – that:

Any one of all Ireland on whom an *ex parte* imputation rested was set upon that stone: then if the truth were in him he would turn pink and white; but if otherwise, it was a black spot that in some conspicuous place would appear on him. Farther, when Ireland's monarch stepped on to it the stone would cry out under him, and her three archwaves would boom in answer: as the wave of Cleena, the wave of Ballintoy, and the wave of

Loch Rury; when a provincial king went on to it the flag would rumble under him; when a barren woman trod on it, it was a dew of dusky blood that broke out on it; when one that would bear children tried it, it was a 'nursing drop'.

That is, says Mr Standish O'Grady, from whose translation I quote, semblance of milk – 'that it sweated'.[1] The Colloquy is imperfect, the legible portion of the manuscript ceasing a line or two further on, just as we are about to be told how it was that the stone left Ireland.[2] Its subsequent adventures are related by Keating, who says that it was sent to Feargus the Great, 'to sit upon, for the purpose of being proclaimed king of Scotland'. However, it is not to the adventures of the stone, but to its properties that I wish now to direct attention. With regard to the former, all that I need add is that the legend has been subjected by Skene, and more recently by Mr P.J. O'Reilly, to an exhaustive analysis, which renders it clear that there is no trustworthy evidence that the stone of Tara is the Coronation Stone. The antecedent improbability is great; and even if it were indisputable that the stone in question was no longer at Tara in the eleventh century, the chasm between that period and Fergus, whose very existence only rests on legend, would still have to be bridged, and the variants of the story would need to be reconciled.[3]

The properties of the stone of Tara were oracular; and the stone itself was one of a large class of stones endowed in popular opinion with divining powers, and actually resorted to for the purpose of inquiry. When the reputation of an oracle is once established, it is consulted for many purposes. Not only political, but juridical and domestic purposes are enumerated by the author of the Colloquy in regard to the *Lia Fáil*. Among these functions is the recognition of the monarch. The phrase used in the Colloquy is ambiguous. It is not stated why, or on what occasion, the stone was expected to make its voice heard. In practice the only object of obtaining such a recognition would be that of determining the succession to the throne. Keating supplies the missing explanation. 'It was a stone,' he says, 'on which were enchantments, for it used to roar under the person who had the best right to obtain the sovereignty of Ireland at the time of the men of Ireland being in assembly at Tara to choose a king over them.'[4] Whether as a matter of fact the stone ever was consulted with this object is another question. It is enough at present to know that Irish tradition asserted this use of the oracle. In a semi-civilized community a disputed succession is of frequent occurrence. To prevent a dispute, and to settle it when it arises, various means are adopted. The usual Irish plan seems to have been the custom of Tanistry. 'During the lifetime of a chief,' Sullivan tells us, 'his successor was elected under the name of *Tanaiste*; and on the death of the former the latter succeeded him. The *Tanaiste* was not necessarily the son of the chief: he might be his brother or nephew; but he should belong to his *Fine*, or family.[5]

That this mode of election was not always successful we may easily believe. That it was the gradual outcome of the experience of a long series of generations is probable. Where for one cause or another it failed, how would the succession be determined? The most obvious means would be either conflict or divination. According to the legends, divination was sometimes actually used to determine the appointment of king. On one occasion in the days of Conchobar, the famous King of Ulster, the monarchy of Ireland had been vacant for seven years. This state of things being found intolerable, a general assembly was held at Tara to choose a king. The royal houses of Connaught, South Munster, North Munster and Leinster were there, but the Ulstermen were absent; for there was bitter feud between Ulster and the rest of Ireland, and they would not hold kingly counsel together. The mode of election adopted was divination by means of a dream induced by certain ceremonies. The ceremonies began with a bull-feast. A bull was killed, and a man was gorged with its flesh and broth. We are told 'he slept under that meal'. It is not incredible. Then 'a true oration', which I understand to mean an incantation, was pronounced over him by four druids. He dreamed, and screamed out of his sleep, and related to the assembled kings that he had seen in his dream 'a soft youth, noble, and powerfully made, with two red stripes on his skin around his body, and he standing at the pillow of a man who was lying in a decline at Emain Macha', the royal palace of Ulster. Messengers were accordingly sent thither, and the description was found to correspond with that of Lugaidh Reo-derg, the pupil of Cuchulainn, who was then lying ill. Lugaidh was brought to Tara, recognized as the subject of the vision and proclaimed as monarch of Ireland.[6]

This is not the only instance in Irish legend of election to the throne by *incubatio*, or divination by means of a dream. Conaire, whose tale is filled with incidents explicable only by the comparative studies of ethnologists, was thus elected. Though really begotten by a supernatural bird-man, he was regarded as the son of his predecessor, Eterscéle. But this does not seem to have given him any title to succeed. A bull-feast was accordingly given; and the bull-feaster in his sleep at the end of the night beheld a man stark-naked, passing along the road of Tara with a stone in his sling. Warned and counselled by his bird-relatives, Conaire fulfilled these requirements. He found three kings (doubtless of the under-kings of Ireland) awaiting him, with royal raiment to clothe his nakedness, and a chariot to convey him to Tara. It was a disappointment to the folk of Tara to find that their bull-feast and their spell of truth chanted over the feaster had resulted in the selection of a beardless lad. But he convinced them that he was the true successor, and was admitted to the kingship.[7]

A traditional story is not a record of fact. It is a record only of what is believed. Probably both Lugaidh Reo-derg and Conaire are mythical personages, but their stories certainly embody what was thought to be possible. The description of the election by divination is substantially the same in both. It may therefore be taken, if not as approximately correct, at least as showing that election by divination was regarded among the ancient Irish as in the last resort a reasonable and proper manner of ascertaining and appointing a king. In this the Irish were by no means singular. The traditions of other nations point to the same result, and the customs in various parts of the world confirm it. The incident of election by divination is so picturesque and so suitable for the purposes of a storyteller that it is to be expected far more often in a tale than in real life. But that the story-incident is based on actual practice, I think there is sufficient ground for believing.

We will first shortly review a few stories of election by divination. The Saxons of Transylvania tell of a peasant who had three sons, of whom the youngest was despised by the others because he was weak and small while they were tall and strong. In that kingdom God himself chose the king from time to time. The mode of ascertaining the divine will was to call a general assembly of the people on the king's meadow in the largest commune of the country, and there to lay the crown at a certain hour on a hillock or mound. All the bells in the town pealed forth together; and the crown slowly raised itself in the air, floated round over the heads of the assembly, and finally alighted on that of the destined sovereign. The two elder brothers made ready to attend the ceremony, but bade the youngest remain at home in the ashes, where his place was. However, he slipped out after them, and, for fear they would see him, crept into a pigsty that stood at the end of the town abutting on the meadow. The crown, passing over all the people present, sank down upon the pigsty. Surprised and curious to know what this strange proceeding meant, the people ran to the pigsty, there found the trembling boy, and drawing him forth bowed the knee and saluted him as the new king, called by God to occupy the throne.[8]

In this Transylvanian *Märchen* the crown is the instrument of divination. Going next to the dim and distant East we find other emblems of royalty thus represented. In the *Jataka*, the great book of Buddhist Birth-stories, the supposititious child of a merchant's wife of Maghada is the hero of a similar adventure. He is, however, no ordinary child but the Bodhisatta, the future Buddha in an earlier birth. He was called Banyan, from having been found under a banyan tree, where his own mother had forsaken him at his birth. Travelling with two faithful companions who had been born on the same day as himself, he came to Benares, and entering the royal park lay down upon a slab of stone with his two companions beside it. The previous night they had slept in the city under a tree at a temple. One of the youths had awakened at dawn and heard some cocks quarrelling in the branches. He listened, and learnt that whoever killed a certain one of these birds and ate of his fat would become king that very day, he who ate the middle flesh would become commander-in-chief, and he who ate the flesh about the bones would become treasurer. He killed the bird, gave the fat to Banyan, the middle flesh to his other friend, and gnawed the bones himself. Now the king of Benares was dead, and that day the festal car was going forth with the five symbols of royalty, the sword, the parasol, the diadem, the slippers, and the fan, within it, to choose the king's successor. As the three youths lay in the royal park, the ceremonial chariot rolled up and stopped before them. The chaplain (presumably a Brahman) followed. Removing the cloth from Banyan's feet he examined the marks upon them. 'Why!' he exclaimed 'he is destined to be king of all India, let alone Benares!' and he ordered the gongs and the cymbals to strike up. This awoke Banyan, who sat up. The chaplain fell down before him, saying: 'Divine being, the kingdom is thine.' 'So be it,' quietly answered the youth; the chaplain placed him upon the heap of precious jewels and sprinkled him to be king.[9]

In a Calmuck tale the instrument of divination is not one of the royal insignia, but a sacrificial cake. An assembly of the people is held to choose a new khan; and it is decided to appeal to the judgement of heaven by throwing a sacrificial cake, called *Baling*, apparently a figure of dough, into the air, at the time of the sacrifice (*Streuopfer*). On whosesoever head the cake fell, he should be khan.[10]

A tale of the Teleut Tartars tells of a father who was enraged with his son because he interpreted the cry of some birds, declaring that they foretold that he himself would become emperor, and his father would drink his urine. The father, in his anger, struck off his son's head. He then killed his horse, skinned it, rolled his son's body in the hide and flung it into the sea. The waves carried the package to a village, where an old woman found it. She opened the leather, and the youth came out alive. The prince of that land had died, leaving no son. His subjects took two golden posts, and fastened on their tops two tapers. They then set up the posts in the middle of the village. Every one was required to jump through them, and the tapers would fall on him who was to be the prince. But they obstinately remained standing until the destined youth came, when they both fell on his neck and burst into flame. If he had not become an emperor, at least he was now a prince: and with that variation, the whole of the bird's prophecy was in due course fulfilled.[11] But we need not follow it further. The hero of a Balochi tale likewise falls under his father's displeasure. His father was a king, and the son took advantage of his royalty to break the crockery of his father's subjects. When the people complained, his father drove him away. In the course of his wanderings, he came to a town where the king had just died. The palace door was shut, and upon it was written: 'He whose hand shall open this door, shall be king of this city.' The wandering prince, reading this, said: 'Bismillah.' He pushed the door: it opened. He entered, seated himself on the throne and became king.[12]

The *Kah-gyur,* a sacred work of Tibetan Buddhism dating back to the eleventh century or thereabouts, contains a story of king Ánanda. The name Ánanda is famous in the literature of Buddhism as that of a favourite disciple of the master; but it is here used in the indiscriminate way in which the medieval friars used the names of Pompey, Titus, Pliny and other famous Romans, in the *Gesta Romanorum.* This king had five sons, of whom the youngest was endowed with qualities better suited to a ruler than the others, and to whom accordingly he desired to leave the kingdom. But he feared that if he invested his youngest son with sovereign power, his kinsmen would reproach him for having passed over his elder sons. As a way of escape from the difficulty he decreed that after his death his sons should be tested, and that he should be made king whom the jewel-shoes should fit, under whom the throne should remain steadfast, and on whose head the diadem should rest unshaken, whom the women should recognize, and who should guess six objects to be divined by insight.[13] There is a triple test here – divination by the royal insignia, the choice of the harem, and the solution of a riddle. I shall return to the two former tests. But before passing to another type of story I may note that in the *Bakhtyár-Náma,* a Persian romance translated by Sir William Ouseley, who brought it from the East in the early part of the last century, there is a story in which the succession to the throne is made to depend upon the solution of three riddles. The king having died without issue, it was resolved to go to the prison and propound three questions to the criminals confined there. He who answered best was recognized as king.[14] Riddles are regarded in certain stages of civilization as a test of more than ordinary wisdom. Their position in the evolution of thought and custom is well worth investigation. It is too large a subject for discussion here.

Occasionally the instrument of divination is wholly wanting, and the first man met with is taken for king. Among a tribe in Morocco is told a tale of which the hero is made king, because he is the first man found outside the city-gate when it is opened in the morning.[15] Another of these stories is that of Ali Shar and Zumurrud in the *Arabian Nights.* Ali Shar was a prodigal, and Zumurrud was his favourite female slave. By a series of diverting adventures which do not concern us, they are separated. After much suffering, Zumurrud contrives to possess herself of a man's clothes, horse and sword. In the course of her wanderings she draws nigh to a city-gate, where she finds the emirs and nobles with the troops drawn up and waiting, as Conaire found the three kings waiting on the way to Tara. The soldiery, on seeing her, dash forward. They dismount and prostrate themselves before her, saluting her as lord and sultan. On enquiry she learns that the sultan of the city is dead; and on such occasions it is the custom that the troops sally forth to the suburbs, there to sojourn for three days. Whoever comes during that time from the quarter whence she has come is made king. Being a lady of resource, she accepts the position, administers the kingdom with efficiency, and ultimately finds means to avenge herself on her enemies and to be reunited with her master, Ali Shar.[16] An Indian folktale relates that in a certain city 'it was the custom that when the rajah died the nobles of the kingdom used to take their seats at the gate of the city, and the first man who appeared before them they made their rajah.'[17]

The same tale is told by the Taranchi Tartars, an agricultural people who are now settled in the valley of the Ili, a large river flowing into Lake Balkash, in Central Asia. But it is told with this difference. When the hero draws nigh to the gate of the city, all the people cry out 'Cuckoo, cuckoo!' On enquiring why they do this, they reply: 'Our ruler has been dead for three days. He had a magical bird, which has been let fly, and on whosesoever head the bird settles, him we raise to be our prince.' Here the augury is drawn from a bird.[18]

In another Tartar *Märchen,* this time from the west of Siberia, the ruler of the town has grown old and is desirous of retiring. He has a bird which is let fly and chooses a woman. She is immediately accepted as prince and installed in the place of the old man.[19] In a Kurdish *Märchen* a special bird called 'the bird of dominion' is fetched, it is not said whence, for the purpose of the divination.[20]

An animal of some kind is, in fact, the agent in most of these tales. A Buddhist tale from Cambodia tells us that, the royal family having become extinct, it was the custom to ask the royal family of another kingdom to furnish a king. The council of mandarins determined to take this course. Under the advice of an old astrologer horses were harnessed to the carriage – we must understand, no doubt, the royal carriage – and then allowed to go in any direction they pleased, without a driver. This is described as consulting the horses. The first day the horses re-entered the palace. The next day they drew the carriage in the direction of a neighbouring kingdom. Twice, thrice the carriage was turned back; but the horses persisted in drawing it again in the same direction. It was accordingly decided to demand a prince from that kingdom.[21]

In the East, however, as might be expected, it is usually the royal animal, the elephant, which thus confers the kingdom. I have already cited one great collection of Indian tales. There is another, only second to the *Jataka* in extent, the *Kathá Sarit Ságara*, or Ocean of the Streams of Story, translated a few years ago by Dr Tawney. It contains a *Märchen*, perhaps derived from that older and more famous collection, the *Panchatantra*, of a man who retired with his wife to the forest, to practise austerities. While there he rescued from the river a wretch whose hands and feet had been cut off, and who had been thrown by his enemies into the stream to die. His wife, probably sick of austerities, falls in love with the cripple thus rescued, and plots her husband's death. She succeeds in precipitating him into the river; but instead of being drowned he is thrown on the bank near a city. 'Now it happened that at that time the king of that city had just died, and in that country there was an immemorial custom, that an auspicious elephant was driven about by the citizens, and any man that he took up with his trunk and placed on his back, was anointed king.' The hero of the story, who is 'an incarnation of a portion of a Bodhisattva', is of course chosen; and when he gets the chance he inflicts condign punishment on his wife.[22] The elephant is here described as 'an auspicious elephant'. Sometimes he is called the 'crown-elephant', the special property and symbol of royalty. So in a Tamil story we learn that the king of a certain city dying childless, on his death bed called his ministers together and directed them 'to send his crown-elephant with a flower-wreath in his trunk, and to choose him on whom the elephant throws the garland, as his successor'.[23] In a folktale from the far north of India it is 'the sacred elephant' before whom all the inhabitants are required to pass in file, and the animal is expected to elect one of them to the vacant throne 'by kneeling down and saluting the favoured individual as he passed by, for in this manner kings were elected in that country'.[24] In a story which appears to come from Gujerat, the king dies without an heir, and the astrologers prophesy that his heir would be the first who entered the gates of the city on the morrow of the king's decease, and around whose neck the sacred elephant would throw a garland of flowers.[25]

At other times the elephant alone does not make the choice. With him is conjoined some other animal or symbol of royalty. A tale from Kashmir speaks of a land where, when the king died, his elephant 'was driven all over the country and his hawk was made to fly here, there, and everywhere in search of a successor; and it came to pass that before whomsoever the elephant bowed and on whosoever hand the hawk alighted, he was supposed to be the divinely chosen one'.[26] In the *Kathákoça*, a collection of stories illustrating the tenets and practice of Jainism, five ordeals, as they are expressly called, are invoked.

The mighty elephant came into the garden outside the city. There the elephant sprinkled Prince Amaradatta [we have already heard of sprinkling as a means of hallowing to kingship], and put him on its back. Then the horse neighed. The two chowries fanned the prince. An umbrella was held over his head. A divine voice was heard in the air: 'Long live King Amaradatta.'[27]

In most of these cases the decision is clearly regarded as the judgement of Heaven; and in every case the judgement of Heaven may at least be inferred. The incident is hardly less a favourite in the West than in the East. In the West, too, it is an appeal to the judgement of Heaven. All the European stories, however, in which it occurs have been recorded within the last century; consequently the incident in question appears only in a very late form. Now an appeal to the judgement of Heaven in the selection of a ruler is familiar to the peasant mind of the continent in one solitary instance – that of the choice of a pope. Accordingly this is the favourite, if not the only form of the story as it is told in France, Italy and Switzerland. The charming collection by the late M. Luzel of religious and quasi-religious tales of Lower Brittany contains one entitled 'Pope Innocent'. The hero is a son of the King of France cast off by his parents, who attempt to put him to death. He sets out for Rome to be present at the election of a new pope. On the way he falls in with two Capuchin monks. The elder of them is gentle to him, the other suspicious and hostile. The youth is a bit of a prig. Perhaps this is not to be wondered at, seeing that he is endowed with supernatural knowledge and power. These qualities make his conduct throughout the journey enigmatical to the point of excusing, if not justifying, the attitude of his unfriendly companion. Everyone takes him for a sorcerer; and the younger monk says in so many words to the other, that they will be lucky if he do not bring them to the gallows or the stake before reaching Rome. As they draw near the holy city, the boy hears some birds in a hedge foretell that one of the three will be made pope, just as the cocks were overheard in the story I cited a few minutes ago from the *Jataka*. There upon he enquires of each of his companions what office he will give him if he (the monk) attain this dignity. The elder monk promises to make him his first cardinal, the younger contemptuously says he will make him beadle in his cathedral. Arrived at Rome, they find that the choice of a pope proceeds in this way: There are to be three days' processions. Every pilgrim has to carry a candle, not lighted, in his hand; and he whose candle lights of itself is the person designated by God to the office of pope. The youth, however, has no money to buy candles. So he carries merely a white wand which he has cut in the hedge where the birds sang; and people, seeing him, shrug their shoulders and exclaim: 'Look at that poor innocent!' It is, however, not the candle of an archbishop, or bishop, or of any great dignitary of the church; it is not that of an abbot, or a monk, or even of a simple priest, which lights; it is the boy Innocent's white wand. The omen is refused on the first day; nor is it accepted until it has been repeated on the second and third days of the ceremony. At last the premier cardinal kneels before him, acknowledges him as pope and asks for his benediction. Thus Innocent becomes pope at Rome, by the will of God.[28]

The story of Pope Innocent belongs to the cycle of the Outcast Child, a well-known group of folktales, of which the examples most familiar to us are the story of King Lear and that of Joseph and his brethren. The hero (or heroine) of these tales is cast off by his relatives for reasons at the least excusable. Sometimes, as in the Teleut tale already mentioned, his life is attempted. But in the end he attains a place and dignity which enable him to compel recognition of his wrongs, and, after the infliction of retributive humiliation, to pardon the offenders. In these *Märchen* the pope is not always chosen by the burning of a taper. In the Italian variants the favourite method is by a dove which alights on the hero's head. In a Swiss story from the Upper Valais two snow-white doves settle on his shoulders. In a Basque story, as the travellers approach Rome the bells begin to ring of themselves. In a story from Upper Brittany the will of Heaven is declared by a bell, which rings of itself when the destined pope passes beneath it. In a story from Normandy the new pope is indicated by 'a portion of Heaven stooping upon him whom Jesus would choose to govern his church'. The collector, while faithfully recording this singular phrase, is puzzled by it, and suggests that it must mean a cloud resting on him.[29] In all cases it is quite clear that the falling of the lot, however it may be accomplished, is regarded as a direct expression of the divine will. The sacred character of the papacy, and the names of historical popes, as Innocent and Gregory, given to the heroes, raise the suspicion that these tales are something more than *Märchen*, and lead directly to the enquiry, not whether such prodigies have in fact been the means of determining the succession to the popedom, but whether they have been believed to have occurred.

Now it happens that this very event was reported in connection with the election of the great Pope Innocent III, in the year 1198. Three doves, it was said, flew about the church during the proceedings, and at last one of them, a white one, came and perched on his right side, which was held to be a favourable omen.[30] In the atmosphere of the Middle Ages an occurrence of the kind, if it happened, could not fail to make a great impression on the popular mind. The dove would be regarded as no less than the embodiment of the Holy Spirit. Long before Innocent's day – indeed before the Middle Ages began – something like this would seem to have happened. It is recorded by Eusebius that in the reign of the Emperor Gordian, who ruled from AD 238 to 244, when all the brethren were assembled in the church for the purpose of electing a successor to Anteros, Bishop of Rome, suddenly a dove flew down from on high and sat on the head of Fabian. Thereupon the assembly with one voice acclaimed him bishop and seated him on the episcopal throne.[31]

Nor were popes alone thus honoured. Dr Conyers Middleton, in his once famous *Letter from Rome*, records that 'in the cathedral church of Ravenna I saw, in mosaic work, the pictures of those archbishops of the place who, as all their historians affirm, were chosen for several ages successively by the special designation of the Holy Ghost, who in a full assembly of the clergy and people, used to descend visibly on the person elect in the shape of a dove'.[32] Among the apocryphal stories in *The Book of Sir John Maundeville* we are told that in the convent on Mount Sinai are many lamps burning. The author, whoever he may have been, writes rather a muddled account of the election of 'prelate of the abbey'. I gather from it that each monk has a lamp, and that when a prelate is chosen his lamp will light of itself, if he be a good man and worthy of the office; if otherwise, the lamp, though lighted, will go out. An inconsistent tradition ran that the priest who sang mass for the deceased dignitary found written upon the altar the name of him who was to be chosen in his place. But though the miracle-monger who writes under the name of Sir John Maundeville professes to have been at the monastery and questioned the monks, he admits that he could not induce them to tell him the facts.[33]

The marvels reported of the election of Christian bishops are told with little variation of the election of other rulers. Paulus Diaconus relates that when Liutprand, king of the Lombards, a contemporary of Charles Martel, was thought to be dying, his subjects met outside the walls of his capital, Pavia, at the church of St Mary ad Perticas, to choose a successor. Their choice fell on the king's nephew, Hildeprand, in whose hand they formally placed the royal spear. Immediately a cuckoo flew down and settled on the point of the spear, as it will be remembered a cuckoo in the Tartar story settled on the kalender's head. This, however, was reckoned by Lombard wiseacres as an evil omen. Their augury was so far justified, that King Liutprand did not die after all, but recovered from his sickness and was not well pleased that his subjects had been in such a hurry to find a successor. Yet he did not refuse to recognize his nephew as co-ruler; and when he at last died, Hildeprand succeeded him.[34] Of another king of the Lombards, Desiderius, a contemporary of Charles the Great, the story is told that the Lombard nobles were meeting to choose a king at Pavia, and Desiderius, a pious man of noble lineage who dwelt at Brescia, journeyed thither to be present, accompanied by a serving man. At Leno, between Brescia and Cremona, being weary, he lay down under a tree to sleep. As he slept his servant beheld a snake crawl forth and wind itself round his head like a crown. The servant was afraid to move, lest the snake might injure his master; but after a while it uncoiled and crept away. Desiderius, meanwhile had dreamt that the crown of the Lombards was placed on his head. When he reached Pavia, the dream was fulfilled.[35]

Everyone is familiar with the story told by Herodotus concerning the election of a successor to Smerdis the Magian, usurper of the throne of Persia, how it was agreed that the successful conspirators should meet at sunrise, and that he whose horse first neighed should be king. According to Herodotus, Darius won by a trick of his groom. That may or may not have been. What interests us in the story is that it was believed that the succession on this occasion to the throne of Persia was determined by an augury drawn from horses, and that the neighing of Darius' horse was instantly followed by the further manifestation of the will of Heaven in thunder and lightning from a clear sky.[36] The elephant, the horse and the divine voice of Indian *Märchen* here find their counterpart, if not in actual fact, at least in the serious belief of the venerable historian, and the people whose tradition he reports. In this connection it must not be forgotten that among many people, horses were sacred animals. They were sacrificed to the gods; they were looked upon as in the counsels of the gods; their neighing was a favourable omen. It is therefore not at all improbable that Herodotus is here recording the mode of choice actually adopted.[37]

Similarly in the annals of Keddah, a portion of the Malay Peninsula, there is a story of a rajah who was dethroned and fled. His nobles and queen sent to the King of Siam for a new ruler. He, having consulted his astrologers, was advised that the true heir to the throne could only be discovered by a supernaturally intelligent elephant, named Kamala Jauhari, which was wandering about on the confines of Kedda and Patani. When the envoys brought back the message to the Kedda chiefs, they decked the palace for a fête.

Then, all the people held a fast for seven days and nights. ... On the night of the seventh day the *dupa* and incense were burned, and all sorts of perfumes were diffused around, and at the same time the name of the super-intelligent elephant was invoked to attend upon the four *mantris* [nobles]. Immediately almost there was a sound, like the rushing of a coming tempest, from the East, with earthquakes, agitations and terrific sounds. In the midst of all this uproar the terrified spectators were delighted to see Kamala Jauhari standing at the hall, and thrusting up her trunk into it. The four *mantris* instantly rubbed her with cosmetics and sweet-smelling oils, rubbing these over its whole body. Then a meal was served up to it, and put into its mouth. The state howdah was now placed on its back, along with all its appurtenances, curtains and hanging. Then one of the *mantris* read the King of Siam's letter close to the ear of Kamala Jauhari, acquainting her that she was expected to assist in finding out a rajah for Kedda by all means. When Jauhari heard all this, she bowed her head and played her trunk, and then set forth in the direction of the East, followed and attended by from three to four hundred men, having banners and flags streaming in the wind, and being supplied with all necessaries, and armed with various kinds of spears, held in hand.

It is needless to say that the expedition thus pompously described was successful in discovering the boy. The elephant caught him up in her trunk, and placing him on her back in the howdah, carried him off in triumph to the palace, where he was forthwith clad in royal robes and crowned.[38]

In Indian belief it is not only super-intelligent elephants which can discover the future occupant of a throne. The elephant is the possession and symbol of royalty. But in the stories, other royal properties are also instruments of divination for that purpose. That these stories were founded on current superstitions is shown by the fact that among the ornaments of the throne of the famous Tippoo, conquered by the British at the end of the eighteenth century, was a bird of paradise made of gold and covered with diamonds, rubies and emeralds, and represented in the act of fluttering. Of this bird it was believed that every head it overshadowed would, in time, wear a crown. When Tippoo was defeated and slain, the Marquis Wellesley, at that time governor-general, sent it home to the Court of Directors of the East India Company.[39] It is now, I believe, at Windsor.

Coming back to Europe, we find the succession to the throne of one of the Scythian tribes determined by the possession of a certain stone. The author of the work on the names of rivers and mountains attributed to Plutarch relates that in the river Tanais a stone like a crystal grows. It resembles in shape a man wearing a crown. When the king dies, whosoever finds it, and can produce it in the assembly held on the banks of the river to elect a new sovereign, is recognized as the rightful successor.[40] For this statement Ctesiphon on Plants and Aristobulus on Stones are cited, authors whose works are lost and who are unknown by any other citations. It is, therefore, impossible for us to judge how far they are likely to have known, or with what accuracy they may have presented, the practice of the barbarous tribe referred to. There can, however, be no doubt that election by divination has been resorted to by peoples in many parts of the world. The succession of Grand Lamas of Lhasa supplies examples of both story and custom. The custom used to be to write on slips of paper the names of all likely male children born under miraculous portents (of which anon) just after the death of the preceding Lama, to put these slips into a golden urn and thus ballot for his successor (or, as it is believed, his new incarnation) amid constant prayer. But the Chinese court, which has a considerable stake in the decision, was thought to influence the selection. The state-oracle has therefore predicted disaster by the appearance of a monster as the Dalai or Grand Lama, if the ancient practice were continued; and on the last vacancy, in 1876, he foretold the discovery, by a pious monk, of the present Grand Lama, announcing that his discovery would be accompanied by horse-neighings. He sent this monk to Chukorgye, where he dreamed that he was to look in a certain lake for the future Dalai. There, pictured in the bosom of the lake, the monk saw the child with his parents in the house where he was born, and at the same instant his horse neighed. In due course the child himself was found, and successfully encountered the usual test, by recognizing the articles which had belonged to him in his previous life. Every child who is a candidate has to pass this test. He is confronted with a duplicate collection of various sacred objects, and he is required to point out among them the genuine possessions of the Dalai Lama. The Dalai Lama is not the only Grand Lama. The head of every lamasery, or convent of lamas, bears this title. When the Grand Lama of such a lamasery dies, his successor, or new incarnation, is sought first of all by divination. A diviner is called in, who, after consulting his books, directs the lamas where to look for the boy. When they have found him, he has to pass a similar test to that just described. In addition he has to submit to cross-examination on the name and situation of the lamasery, and how many lamas reside there, and on the habits of the deceased Grand Lama, and the manner of his death.

The portents at the birth of a Dalai Lama are magnificent. It is not irrelevant to mention them here, as they may be regarded as part of the auguries which decide the succession. An official report from the Chinese Commissioner to the Emperor, on such an occasion in the year 1839, declares among other things, that it was ascertained that on the night before the boy was born, a brilliant radiance of many colours was manifested in the air, and the water in the well of the temple courtyard changed to a milk-white colour. Seven days later a flame appeared on the rock behind the post-station. When the rock was examined, no trace of fire remained, but a sacred image and characters were found, together with the print of footsteps. Moreover, on the night when the child was born, the sound of music was heard, and milk dropped upon the pillars of the house.[41]

The Buddhists are not the only sect in the Chinese Empire which has a supreme head appointed by religious divination. The arch-abbot of Taoism dwells in a princely residence on the Dragon and Tiger Mountains, in the province of Kiang-si. 'The power of this dignitary,' we are told, 'is immense, and is acknowledged by all the priests of his sect throughout the empire.' The office has been confined for centuries to one family or clan. When the arch-abbot dies, all the male members of his clan are cited to appear at the official residence. The name of each one is engraved on a separate piece of lead and deposited in a large earthenware vase filled with water. Standing round this vase are priests who invoke the three persons of the Taoist Trinity to cause the piece of lead bearing the name of the person on whom the choice of the gods has fallen, to come to the surface of the water.[42]

The Taoist dignitary seems to possess only spiritual power, except probably in his own monastery. The Dalai Lama, on the other hand, retains some portion of civil rule. In both cases the person of the ruler is looked upon as sacred. Among savage and barbarous nations the office of priest or medicine-man is often not clearly distinguished from that of temporal ruler. The instances in which the chief or king is looked upon as divine, in which he is responsible for the weather, in which he causes the crops to grow, and performs other superhuman functions, are too numerous, and too well known to be mentioned here. Since the publication of *The Golden Bough* they have been among the common-places of folklore. I need only remind you that 'the divinity that doth hedge a king' is not confined to savagery and barbarism. It has lasted far into civilization, and been sedulously cultivated for political purposes by royalty in every age. A Roman Emperor was Divus Augustus. When the dignity of king becomes hereditary, the monarch is held to be at least descended from the gods. The Mikado traces his descent from the Sun-goddess. King Edward VII traces his from Woden, the war-god of the Anglo-Saxon tribes which colonized Britain in the fifth and sixth centuries. It is true that this genealogy, at one time seriously credited, is now treated as fable, but even yet the coronation ceremonies of 'His Sacred Majesty', though not directly of pagan origin, witness to the mysterious sanctity that surrounds him.

A view of kingship thus exalted renders it easy to understand why, when circumstances compelled the choice of a king, the divine will must have been most anxiously consulted. It was not merely that the qualities of a leader in battle, a wise judge and administrator, and a prudent politician were needed. Luck and the favour of the gods were more than these, to say nothing of the marks of god-head, which in many cases it was necessary to discover in his person, conduct or knowledge. Hence the choice of the people, or rather the recognition by the people, would depend upon the auguries, or upon more direct indications of the decision of heaven. When Dagara, the King of Karague, on the western shore of Lake Victoria Nyanza, died, he left behind him three sons, any of whom was eligible to the throne. The officers of state put before them a small mystic drum. It was of trifling weight, but being loaded with charms, no one could lift it, save he to whom the ancestral spirits were inclined as the successor. Nor was this enough. The victor in this contest was required to undergo a further trial of his right. He was made to sit, as he himself informed Captain Speke, on the ground at a certain spot where the land would gradually rise up under him, like a telescope, until it reached the skies. The aspirant who was approved by the spirits was then gradually lowered in safety; whereas, if not approved, the elastic hill would suddenly collapse, and he would be dashed to pieces. It is needless to add, that Rumanika, Captain Speke's informant, claimed to have gone through the ordeal with success.[43]

These are barbarous auguries. But all auguries and oracles are barbarous. We do not know how Melchizedek was appointed King of Salem. The writer of the Epistle to the Hebrews refers to him as 'without father, without mother, without genealogy,' as if there were something peculiar in the omission of his pedigree, though in this respect he did not differ from the other kings mentioned in the narrative. However, the discovery at Tel-el-Amarna of letters from Ebed-tob, King of Salem in the fifteenth century BC, to his suzerain the King of Egypt, has rendered it possible to suppose that Melchizedek did not come to the throne by inheritance, and consequently that his parentage was unimportant. Ebed-tob, protesting his loyalty as an ally and a tributary of the King of Egypt, says: 'Neither my father, nor my mother, (but) the oracle of the mighty king, established (me) in the house of (my) father.' In other words he states, as Professor Sayce interprets the expression, 'that his authority was not based on the right of inheritance; he had been called to exercise it by a divine voice'.[44] We must beware of drawing too large an inference from a single phrase. Assuming that 'the mighty king' is the god 'Shalim, and not the suzerain whom he is addressing, there remains the question what is meant by 'the house of his father'. Evidently it is the royal office; but is it not the royal office previously filled by his ancestors? The correct view would seem to be that the kingship was, like that of Karague, descendible to any scion of the royal house, subject to the decision of the oracle. The pedigree then would be important, but not all-important. The god would decide among the candidates. Some such arrangement would seem to have been recognized in the heroic age of Greece, if we may trust the somewhat obscure expressions of the *Odyssey*. There are examples in the Homeric poems of kings who have succeeded to the inheritance of their sires. Agamemnon is one. On the other hand, the position of Ulysses is enigmatical. It is enigmatical in regard to Laertes, his father, who was still alive; while, if Ulysses were dead, it would seem that Telemachus, his son, would only have the first, but by no means an indefeasible, claim. As Mr Crooke has pointed out, it results from the interview between Telemachus and the wooers in the first book of the *Odyssey*, that some kind of divine nomination should appoint the king, and that the choice might fall, not on Telemachus, but on another of the Achaeans in sea-girt Ithaca.[45] It is dangerous to read into the poem what is not expressed. The poet is describing an age already mythical, though no doubt he has embodied considerable fragments of actual custom in the representation. He does not detail the process of appointment of king. Consequently, all we can safely say (and that on the assumption that here we have one of the fragments of actual custom) is that the manners and whole atmosphere of the poem correspond with a stage of culture in which the will of the gods would be ascertained by augury. In this connection it may not be irrelevant to refer to the early traditions of Rome. The quarrel between Romulus and Remus concerned not merely the site of the city, but also the founder after whose name it should be called – in other words, the royal dignity. It was settled by an augury taken from the flight of vultures. Numa, the successor of Romulus, though elected, took care to assure himself by auguries that the gods approved of the choice. It must be remembered that the legends, as we have them, took shape under the republic when the ordinary human process of election had been long established. The habit thus formed probably affected them; and I think we are warranted in suspecting that if we could recover them at a prior stage, we should find the appointment of king resting on the will of the gods and ascertained by divination.

No argument is needed to show that the form of tradition is affected, even where the substance remains, by external changes. Customs referred to in a legend may become obsolete and consequently unintelligible; and the reference to them must of necessity be modified into something which is understood, or it will be dropped into oblivion. The tradition of the *Lia Fáil*, with which I started, is an example. To step on the stone was to put one's claim to sovereignty to proof. As Keating relates, doubtless from some older author, on it 'were enchantments, for it used to roar under the person who had the best right to obtain the sovereignty of Ireland'. But this is the latest form of the tradition. We can, however, reconstruct the earlier form by comparison with custom and tradition elsewhere. They render it clear that the stone was once held to declare the divine will as to the succession. Further back still, it may have been regarded as itself endowed with power of choice.[46] Strictly speaking, this is not augury, for augury is the ascertainment and declaration of a higher will. But some such animistic belief may have been the seedplot out of which augury grew as gods properly so called were evolved. At the stage at which the tradition reaches us the *Lia Fáil* no longer either chooses on its own account or makes known the choice of heaven. At this stage, not only is it enchanted, consequently diabolic rather than divine in the source of its power, but also it merely points out him who has 'the best right'. The principle of heredity is now firmly established; its application alone is uncertain. When the principle is established and the application certain, it is not necessary to consult an oracle.

The changes I thus venture to postulate are steps in the disintegration of the myth. A Welsh tale now to be cited has taken a further step in that it simply credits the instrument of divination with the diagnosis of blood royal, the practical purpose of determining the succession to the kingdom having disappeared. According to Giraldus Cambrensis it happened that in the time of Henry I Gruffydd ap Rhys ap Tudor, who, although he only held of the king one commote, namely, a fourth part of the cantref of Caio, yet was reputed as lord in Deheubarth, was returning from court by way of Llangorse Lake, in Brecknockshire, with Milo, Earl of Hereford and Lord of Brecknock, and Payn FitzJohn, who then held Ewyas, two of the king's secretaries and privy councillors. It was winter, and the lake was covered with water-fowl of various kinds. Seeing them, Milo, partly in joke, said to Gruffydd: 'It is an old saying in Wales that if the natural prince of Wales, coming to this lake, command the birds upon it to sing, they will all immediately sing.' Gruffydd replied: 'Do you, therefore, who now bear sway in this country, command them first.' Both Milo and Payn having made the attempt in vain, Gruffydd dismounted from his horse, fell on his knees with his face to the East, and after devout prayers to God, stood up, and making the sign of the cross on his forehead and face, cried aloud: 'Almighty and all-knowing God, Lord Jesus Christ, show forth here today thy power! If thou hast made me lineally to descend from the natural princes of Wales, I command these birds in thy name to declare it.' Forthwith all the birds, according to their kind, beating the water with outstretched wings, began altogether to sing and proclaim it. No wonder that all who were present were amazed and confounded, and that Milo and Payn reported it to the king, who is said to have taken it philosophically enough. 'By the death of Christ!' (his customary oath), he replied, 'it is not so much to be wondered at. For although by our great power we may impose injustice and violence upon those people, yet they are none the less known to have the hereditary right to the country.'[47]

In the same manner, in India snakes are supposed to be specially gifted with the faculty of distinguishing persons of royal race or born to rule.[48] One example will be enough. The Gandharbs of Benares, a caste of singers and prostitutes, ascribe their origin to Doman Deo, the second Raghubansi Rajput king of Chandrâvati. He had a groom named Shîru, who one day went into the jungle to cut grass, and fell asleep. While he slept, a cobra raised its hood over his head, and a wagtail kept flying above him. In that condition his master saw him, and afterwards asked him what he would do for him if he became king. Shîru promised to make him his prime minister. Going subsequently to Delhi, the throne of which was vacant, Shîru was chosen emperor, in the manner with which we are already acquainted, by an elephant laying a garland on his neck; and he redeemed his word by making Doman Deo his wazîr.[49] In Further India a saga of the Chams relates that Klong Garay, who plays a great part in their legendary history, was found by a companion of his wanderings, after a temporary absence, sleeping and watched by two dragons, which were licking his body. Then he knew, we are told, that Klong Garay was of royal race.[50] The child of a King of Siam by a Naga, or divine snake, being exposed, was found and adopted by a hunter. The king's subjects were compelled by law to work in turn for the king. The hunter, when summoned, took with him his adopted child and laid it in the shadow of the palace, to protect it from the rays of the sun while he performed his task. But the spire of the palace inclined before the child, and the shadow appeared to fly. This prodigy put the king upon enquiry, and he identified his son by means of the ring and mantle which he had given to the lady, and which had been found with the child.[51] In the old English metrical romance of *Havelok the Dane*, the hero is identified by means of a royal mark, 'a croiz ful gent', shining brighter than gold on his right shoulder.

> It sparkede, and ful brith shon,
> So doth the gode charbucle ston,
> That men mouthe se by the lith
> A peni chesen, so was it brith.[52]

The romance in which the incident is found is a literary version of the local tradition of Grimsby, still commemorated in the seal of the corporation. The poem dates from the end of the thirteenth century. There are two French versions which I have not seen. Professor Skeat has epitomized the longer in the preface to his edition of the English romance. In it a flame issues from Havelok's mouth when he sleeps. This is a personal peculiarity, also found in the English lay. His heirship to the throne of Denmark is determined by his ability to blow a horn which none but the true heir could sound. Thus we are brought back to the succession by divination from which we started, and of which the simple diagnosis of royal descent is a corruption and a weakening. It is preserved here, we know not by what cause, after its true meaning had been forgotten. Adopted first of all into tradition from living custom, when the custom was superseded by other means of determining the succession it survived as a tradition until, its true intent being gradually lost, while the hereditary principle was strengthened and fenced about with sanctity, the incident faded into a merely picturesque presentation, in some places of prophecy, in other places of the claims of birth.

The study of folktales is often despised as mere trifling. But traditional narratives must always occupy an important place in the study of the past. Rightly used they have much to tell us of human history, of human thought and the evolution of human institutions. It may safely be said that of all the incidents that compose them there is none which is not a concrete presentation either of human institutions or of human belief. They are all thus in a sense the outcome of actual human experiences. The stories of election by augury are not wilder than the authentic facts. The telescopic mountain of Karague, which Rumanika averred himself to have experienced, is at least as wonderful as the groaning of the *Lia Fáil*, or the lighting of a dry twig. In one of the stories we found the dying monarch laying down among the conditions to be fulfilled by his successor, that the women of the royal household should recognize him. Secret intrigues of the harem are believed to determine the devolution of many an eastern crown. But that the formal and ceremonial choice of the heir should be made by the wives of the deceased ruler seems too grotesque to be known outside a fairy tale. Yet this was the law a hundred years ago in the kingdom of Quiteve, on the southeastern coast of Africa. When a king died the queens (that is to say, his legitimate wives) named the person who was to accompany his body to the burial-place, and the person thus named became the successor.[53] In an adjoining kingdom a similar law prevailed. It was forbidden to any prince to enter the palace where the women were, or to take possession of the kingdom without their consent, and whoever entered by violence and took possession against their will, lost his right of succession. The Portuguese friar, to whom we are indebted for the information, records a case which happened while he was in Sofala, and in which the claimant entered and formally seated himself in the royal hall with the royal widows. They, however, were unwilling to acknowledge him as their king and husband. Accordingly they secretly summoned another member of the royal family, seated him with them in the public place, and sent officers through the town to proclaim the new sovereign and call his subjects to do homage. The pretender fled. This instance is the more remarkable because the unsuccessful claimant had in his favour the nomination of the previous monarch. Though this constituted not an indefeasible title, it afforded at least a strong presumption in his favour. Yet it was defeated, in accordance with established and publicly acknowledged custom, by the choice of the harem.[54]

Notes

1 Standish H. O'Grady, *Silva Gadelica* (2 vols., London, 1892), vol. ii, p. 264.

2 There are other manuscripts of the Colloquy, but none of them contain the sequel of the adventures of the *Lia Fáil*. See the preface to Stokes's edition, *Irische Texte*, 4th ser. (Leipzig, 1900).

3 Skene's paper is in the *Proceedings of the Society of Antiquaries of Scotland*, vol. viii, p. 68; Mr O'Reilly's in *The Journal of the Royal Society of Antiquaries of Ireland*, vol. xxxii, p. 77. The stone now called the *Lia Fáil* at Tara is clearly not the stone of tradition.

4 Keating, *The History of Ireland* (ed. and trans. by David Comyn, London, 1902), vol. i, p. 101. See also pp. 207, 209. On the latter page 'a poem from a certain book of invasion' is quoted at length. It contains an enumeration of the four jewels of the Tuatha Dé Danann, among them the Lia Fáil, 'which used to roar under the king of Ireland'. In the *Baile au Scail* ('The Champion's Ecstasy') Conna of the Hundred Fights steps on the stone accidentally, and is told by the druid who accompanies him: 'Fál has screamed under thy feet. The number of its screams is the number of kings that shall come of thy seed for ever; but I may not name them.' In this passage the stone is said to have come from the Island of Foal to abide for ever in the land of Tailtin. Nutt, *The Voyage of Bran*, vol. i (1895), p. 187, summarizing O'Curry's translation.

5 O'Curry, *On the Manners and Customs of the Ancient Irish* (3 vols., London, 1873), vol. i (Sullivan's Introduction), p. clxxxiii. Spencer, *View of the State of Ireland*, says that the Tanist is 'the eldest of

the kinne'. *Ancient Irish Histories* (Dublin, Hibernia Press, 1809), vol. i, p. 12.

6 O'Curry, vol. ii, p. 199. From a reference in an Irish text translated by Professor Windisch from the *Lebor na hUidre* it seems that the bull was required to be white. *Irische Texte*, ser. i, p. 200.

7 *Revue celtique*, vol. xxii, p. 22, in the story of the Sack of Dá Derga's Hostel, translated by Whitley Stokes.

8 Haltrich, *Deutsche Volksmärchen aus dem Sachsenlande in Siebenbürgen* (4th ed., Vienna, 1885), p. 195.

9 *The Jataka, or Stories of the Buddha's former Births*, vol. iv (Cambridge, 1901), p. 23. Story no. 445.

10 Jülg, *Die Märchen des Siddhi-kür* (Leipzig, 1866), p. 60, Story no. 2. The version in Miss Busk's *Sagas from the Far East* is, as usual, not to be depended on.

11 Radloff, *Proben der Volkslitteratur der Türkischen Stämme Süd-Sibiriens*, vol. i (St Petersburg, 1866), p. 208.

12 *Folklore*, vol. iv, p. 202.

13 Ralston, *Tibetan Tales from Indian Sources* (London, 1882), p. 29.

14 Sir William Ouseley, *The Bakhtyár Náma* (ed. by W.A. Clouston, 1883), p. 51.

15 Stumme, *Märchen der Schluh von Tázervalt* (Leipzig, 1895), p. 123, Story no. 15.

16 Burton, iv. *Arabian Nights*, p. 210; Lane, ii. *Arabian Nights* (London, 1883), p. 406.

17 *North Indian Notes and Queries*, vol. iv, p. 66. Similarly in a story from Mirzapur, the first man met in the forest is made king. *Ibid.*, vol. ii, p. 81. In another story from Mirzapur a trained elephant is let loose to choose the king's bride. *Ibid.*, vol. iii, p. 103.

18 Radloff, *Proben der Volkslitteratur der Nördlichen Türkischen Stämme*, vol. vi (St Petersburg, 1886), p. 157.

19 *Ibid.*, vol. iv (1872), p. 143.

20 Prym und Socin, *Kurdische Sammlungen*, Erste Abteil (St Petersburg, 1887); übersetz., p. 143.

21 Leclère, *Cambodge, Contes et Légendes* (Paris, 1895), p. 16. 'Tous ceux qui étaient presents à ce conseil … decidèrent qu'on consulterait immédiatement les chevaux.'

22 *Kathá Sarit Ságara*, vol. ii (Calcutta, 1884), p. 102.

23 Pandit S.M. Natesa Sastri, *The Dravidian Nights Entertainments, being a translation of Madana-kâmarâjankadai* (Madras, 1886), p. 126.

24 F.A. Steel and R.C. Temple, *Wide-Awake Stories. A collection of tales told by little children, between sunset and sunrise, in the Panjab and Kashmir* (Bombay, 1884), p. 140. In other stories from Kashmir, it is 'an elephant'. Knowles, *Folk-tales of Kashmir* (London, 1888), pp. 169, 309.

25 *Revue des Traditions Populaires*, vol. iv, p. 442.

26 Knowles, *op. cit.*, p. 158. Other stories, *Ibid.*, pp. 17, 309; *The Bakhtyár Náma*, p. 169 (notes by the editor); Lal Behari Day, *Folk-tales of Bengal* (London, 1883), p. 99, Story no. 5.

27 *The Kathákoça: or Treasury of Stories*. Translated from Sanskrit manuscripts by C.H. Tawney, M.A. (London, 1895), p. 155.

28 Luzel, *Légendes Chrétienues de la Basse Bretagne*, vol. i (Paris, 1881), p. 282 (part iii, Story no. 11); a variant, *Mélusine*, vol. i, col. 300.

29 *Folk-Lore Journal*, vol. iv, p. 338, *sqq.*, including the references at foot of p. 348.

30 Friedrich von Raumer, *Geschichte der Hohenstaufen und ihrer Zeit*, vol. iii (Leipzig, 1824), p. 74.

31 Eusebius, *Eccles. Hist.*, Book vi, c. 29.

32 Middleton, *Works*, vol. v (2nd. ed. London, 1755), p. 153, citing 'Hist. Raven., &c. Aring [hus], Rom[a] Subt[erranea], 1. vi, c. 48.'

33 *Early Travels in Palestine*, ed. by Thomas Wright (London, 1848), p. 158.

34 Paulus Diaconus, *Gesta Longobard.*, 1. vi, c. 55. See also Soldan, *Sagen und Geschichten der Langobarden* (Halle-am-Saale, 1888), pp. 145, 148. Hildeprand did not reign long. He was deprived of the throne a few months later by Ratchis, who reigned for five years, 744–749.

35 Soldan, *op cit.*, p. 150.

36 Herodotus, 1, iii, cc. 84, *sqq.*

37 Grimm has collected instances, *Teutonic Mythology*, trans. by Stallybrass, vol. i, p. 47, vol. ii, p. 658, vol. iv, pp. 1301, 1481. Also von Negelein, in *Zeitschrift des Vereins für Volkskunde*, vol. x, pp. 408, *sqq.*

38 *Journal of the Indian Archipelago*, vol. iii, p. 316.

39 *Oriental Memoirs*, by James Forbes, F.R.S. (London, 1813), vol. iv, p. 191.

40 Plutarch, *De Fluv.*, xiv.

41 Huc, *Souvenirs d'un Voyage dans la Tartarie, le Thibet et la Chine* (2 vols., Paris, 1850), vol. ii, p. 343; vol. i, p. 278. *The Buddhism of Tibet* by L. Austine Waddell, M.B. (London, 1895), pp. 245, *sqq.*

42 *China, a History of the Laws, Manners, and Customs of the People*, by John Henry Gray, M.A., I.L.D., vol. i (London, 1878), p. 103.

43 *Journal of the Discovery of the Source of the Nile* by John Hanning Speke (Edinburgh, 1863), p. 221.

44 *Records of the Past*, 2nd series, vol. v. (London, N.D.), [1891], pp. 68, 62.

45 *Folklore*, vol. ix, p. 13. Mr Crooke does not refer to the speech of Eurymachus immediately following that of Telemachus, which confirms what has been said on this subject by Antinous and Telemachus.

46 I am indebted to Miss Burne for suggesting that something like this is the true interpretation of the use alike of the *Lia Fáil* and of the various regal paraphernalia employed in the stories. As she puts it, they would know their rightful owner. This, however, is to assume the principle of heredity as already established. The animistic belief involved in the interpretation suggested was perhaps applied even before then.

47 Giraldus Cambriensis, *Itinerarium cambriae*, l. i, c. 2.

48 W. Crooke, *The Popular Religion and Folklore of Northern India*, vol. ii (London, 1896), p. 142.

49 Crooke, *The Tribes and Castes of the Northwestern Provinces and Oudh*, vol. ii (Calcutta, 1896), p. 380. Cf. the Legend of Dhatu Sena, king of Ceylon. Tennent, *Ceylon*, vol. i (London, 1859), p. 389.

50 A. Landes, *Contes Tjames* (Saigon, 1887), p. 104.

51 *Journal of the Indian Archipelago*, vol. iii, p. 571.

52 *The Lay of Havelok the Dane* (E.E.T.S.), ll. 602 *sqq.*; 2139, *sqq.*

53 Owen, *Narrative of Voyages to explore the shores of Africa, Arabia and Madagascar* (2 vols., London, 1833), vol. ii, p. 418, translating a manuscript of Signor Ferão, a Portuguese governor of the coast. This translation is reprinted by Theal, *Records of Southeastern Africa*, vol. vii, pp. 371, *sqq.*

54 Theal, *Records*, vol. vii, pp. 191, *sqq.*

CHAPTER SIX

Augury, Dream and Prophecy

John G. Campbell

Augury[1]

THE ANXIETY OF MEN to know the future, the issue of their labours and the destinies awaiting them, makes them ready listeners to the suggestions of fancy and an easy prey to deception. The mind eagerly lays hold on anything that professes to throw light on the subject of its anxiety, and men are willing victims to their own hopes and fears. Where all is dark and inscrutable, deception and delusion are easy, and hence augury of all kinds, omens, premonitions, divinations, have ever exercised a noticeable power over the human mind.

The ordinary manner which superstition takes to forecast the future is to look upon chance natural appearances under certain circumstances as indications of the character, favourable or unfavourable, of the event about which the mind is anxious. Any appearance in nature, animate or inanimate, can thus be made an omen of, and an inference be drawn from it of impending good or bad fortune. If it be gloomy, forbidding, awkward or unpleasant, it is an unlucky omen, and the subsequent event, with which the mind associates it, will be unfavourable, but if pleasant, then it is a good omen and prognosticates pleasant occurrences.

Omens which proceed upon a similarity of character between the prognostic and its fulfilment are easy of interpretation. There are other omens which have no connection, natural, possible or conceivable, with the impending event, and of which consequently the meaning is occult, known only to people of skill instructed in their interpretation. These probably had their origin in one or two accidental coincidences. For instance, if the appearance of a fox is to be taken as an omen, it will naturally be taken as a bad sign, the stinking brute can indicate nothing favourable; but no amount of sagacity will teach a person that an itching in the point of his nose prognosticates the receipt of important news, or the cuckoo calling on the house-top the death of one of the inmates within the year. His utmost acuteness will fail to find in a shoulder blade any indication of destiny, or any prophetic meaning in the sediment of a cup of tea. The meaning of these is a mystery to the uninitiated, and it is easy to see how they might be reduced to a system and lead to the wildest delusions of fortune-telling.

Everything a Highlander of the old school set about, from the most trifling to the most important, was under the influence of omens. When he went to fish, to catch his horse in the hill, to sell or buy at the market, to ask a loan from his neighbour, or whatever else he left home to do, he looked about for a sign of the success of his undertaking, and, if the omen were unpropitious, returned home. He knew his journey would be of no avail. He consulted mystagogues as to his fate, and at the proper seasons looked anxiously for the signs of his luck. Like the rest of mankind, he was, by means of these, pleased or depressed in anticipation of events that were never to occur. Hence the saying, 'Take a good omen as your omen, and you will be happy.'

Probably the Greek μαντεία, prediction by an oracle, is cognate to the Gaelic *manadh*, a foretoken, anything from which a prediction can be drawn. Both among Greeks and Celts a great number of omens were taken from birds.

As already mentioned, it is a bad sign of a person's luck during the day that he should rise from bed on his left hand, wash himself with water in which eggs have been boiled, or the cakes for his breakfast should frequently break in the baking, or fall backwards. The coming evil can be averted in the latter case by giving plenty of 'butter without asking' (*im gun iarraidh*) with the cakes. Indeed, 'butter unasked for' is of sovereign value as an omen of luck. A cake spread with it, given to fishermen, secures a good day's fishing. It is reckoned good in diseases, particularly measles, and a most excellent omen for people going on a journey. Its not being given to Hugh of the Little Head, on the morning of his last battle, was followed by his losing the battle and his life.

Omens are particularly to be looked for at the outset of a journey. If the first animal seen by the traveller have its back towards him, or he meet a sheep or a pig, or any unclean animal, or hear the shrill cry of the curlew, or see a heron, or he himself fall backward, or his walking-stick fall on the road, or he have to turn back for anything he has forgot, he may as well stay at home that day; his journey will not prosper. A serpent, a rat, or a mouse is unlucky unless killed, but if killed becomes a good omen. If the face of the animal be towards one, even in the case of unlucky animals, the omen becomes less inauspicious.

It is of great importance what person is first met. Women are unlucky, and some men are the most unfortunate omen that can be encountered. These are called *droch còmhalaichean*, i.e., bad people to meet, and it was told of a man in Skye, that to avoid the mischance of encountering one of them when setting out on a journey, he sent one of his own family to meet him. If he met any other he returned home. In a village in Ayrshire there are three persons noted for being inauspicious to meet, and fishermen (upon whom as a class this superstition has a strong hold) are much dissatisfied at meeting any of them. One of them is not so bad if he puts his hand to his face in a manner peculiar to him. It is inauspicious to meet a person from the same village as oneself, or a man with his head bare, or a man going to pay rent. Old people going to pay rent, therefore, took care to go away unobserved. A plain-soled person is unlucky, but the evil omen in his case is averted by rolling up the tongue against the roof of the mouth. The Stewarts were said to have insteps; water flowed below their foot; it was, therefore, fortunate to meet any of them. All risk of a stranger proving a bad *còmhalaiche* is avoided by his returning a few steps with the traveller.

A hare crossing one's path is unlucky, and old people, when they saw one before them, made considerable detours to avoid such a calamity. The disfavour with which this harmless animal and the pig were regarded no doubt arose from their being unclean under the Levitical Law. The hare chews the cud, but divides not the hoof; the pig divides the hoof, but does not chew the cud.

The fox is unlucky to meet, a superstition that prevails also in East Africa. The King of Karague told Captain Speke that 'if a fox barked when he was leading an army to battle, he would retire at once, knowing that this prognosticated evil' (*Journal*, p. 241).

It is unlucky to look back after setting out. Old people, if they had to turn to a person coming after them, covered their face. This superstition probably had its origin in the story of Lot's wife. Fin MacCoul, according to a popular tale, never looked back after setting out on a journey. When he went on the expedition that terminated in his being 'in the house of the Yellow Forehead without liberty to sit down or power to stand up', he laid spells on his companions, that no man born in Ireland should follow him. Fergus, who was born in Scotland, followed, and Fin, hearing footsteps behind him, called out without turning his head, in a phrase now obsolete, *Co sid a propadh mo cheaplaich?* i.e., it is supposed, 'Who is that following my footsteps?'

To be called after is a sure omen that a person will not get what he is going in search of. This belief gave great powers of annoyance to people of a waggish humour. When everything prognosticated success, and the fishing boat had left the shore, or the old man, staff in hand, had set out on his journey, some onlooker cried out, 'There is the fox before you and after you'; or, 'Have you got the fish-hooks?' or, 'Have you taken the Bait-stone?'[2] Immediately a damp was thrown on the expedition, a return home was made for that day, and the wag might be glad if the party called after did not make him rue his impertinence.

Of omens referring to other events in the life of man than the success of particular expeditions may be mentioned the following:

A golden plover (*Feadag*, Charadrius pluvialis), heard at night, portends the near approach of death or other evil. The cry of the bird is a melancholy wailing note. A pied wagtail (*Breac an t-sìl*, Motaeilla alba), seen between them and the house, was a sign of being turned out of the house that year and 'losing the site' (*call na làraich*). The mole burrowing below a house is a sign the tenants will not stay long on that site. If the cuckoo calls on the house-top, or on the chimney (*luidheir*), death will occur in the house that year.

In spring and early summer the omens of happiness and prosperity, or misery and adversity for the year, are particularly looked for. It is most unfortunate if the first foal or lamb seen that season have its tail toward the beholder, or the first snail (some say stonechat) be seen on the road or on a bare stone, and a most unmistakable sign of misfortune to hear the cuckoo for the first time before tasting food in the morning, 'on the first appetite' (*air a chiad lomaidh*), as it is called. In the latter case, the cuckoo is said 'to soil upon a person' (*chac a chuthag air*), and, to avoid such an indignity, people have been known, at the time of the cuckoo's visit, to put a piece of bread below their pillow to be eaten the first thing in the morning.

Cock-crowing before midnight is an indication of coming news. Old people said the bird had 'a tale' to tell; and, when they heard it, went to see if its legs were cold or not. If cold, the tale will be one of death; if hot, a good tale. The direction in which the bird's head is turned indicates the direction in which the tale is to come.

In visiting the sick, it is a sign of the termination of the illness whether it be the right or the left foot that touches the threshold first.

Women pretended to know when they laid their hand on a sick person whether he would recover.

It is a good sign if the face of the chimney-crook (*aghaidh na slabhraidh*) be toward the visitor, but an evil omen if its back be toward him.

Premonitions

These are bodily sensations by which future events may be foreknown. An itching in the nose foretells that a letter is coming, and this in olden times was a matter of no small consequence.

There is an itching of the mouth that indicates a kiss, and another indicating a dram. A singing or tingling in the ears denotes death, a friend at the moment of its occurrence has expired and news of his death will be heard before long; an itching of the cheek or eyes, weeping; itching of the left hand, money; of the right, that one is soon to meet a stranger with whom he will shake hands; of the elbow, that he will soon change beds or sleep with a stranger; of the brow, that some person will make you angry before long.

Hot ears denote that some person is speaking about your character. If the heat be in the right ear, he is supporting or praising you; if in the left, he is speaking ill of you (*Chluas dheas gam thoirt a nuas; 's a chluas chli gam shìor-chàineadh*). In the latter case persons of a vindictive nature repeated the following words:

He who speaks of me,
If it be not to my advantage,
May he be tossed
On sharp grey knives,
May he sleep in an ant-hill,
And may it be no healthy sleep to him,
But a furious woman between him and the door
And I between him and his property and sleep.[3]

The evil wish went on, that 'an iron harrow might scrape his guts', and something about 'a dead old woman' that my informant could not remember.

Trial (*Deuchainn*)

The *deuchainn* al. *diachuinn*, sometimes called *frìdh*, omen, was a 'cast' or trial made by lots or other appeal to chance to find out the issue of undertakings – whether an absent friend was on his way home or would arrive safe; whether a sick man will recover; whether good or bad fortune awaits one during the year; what the future husband or wife is to be; the road stolen goods have taken etc. This cast may be either for oneself or for another, 'for him and for his luck' (*air a shon 's air a shealbhaich*). On New-Year day people are more disposed to wonder and speculate as to their fortunes during the year upon which they have entered than to reflect upon the occurrences of the past. Hence these 'casts' were most frequently made on that day. Another favourite time was Hallowmas night. Most of them might be made at any time of the year, and the difficulty was not in making them but in interpreting them.

In making a 'cast' for one's future partner, the approved plan is for him to go at night to the top of a cairn or other eminence where no four-footed beast can go, and whatever animal is thence seen or met on the way home is an omen of the future husband or wife. It requires great shrewdness to read the omen aright.

Another way is to shut the eyes, make one's way to the end of the house, and then, and not till then, open the eyes and look around. Whatever is then seen is an indication of fortune during the year. It is unlucky to see a woman, particularly an old woman bent with age and hobbling past. A man is lucky, particularly a young man riding gaily on a mettlesome horse. A man delving or turning up the earth forebodes death; he is making your grave, and you may as well prepare. A duck or a hen with its head below its wing is just as bad, and the more that are seen in that attitude the speedier or more certain the death. A man who had the second sight once made a 'trial' for a sick person at the request of an anxious friend. He went out next morning to the end of the house in the approved manner. He saw six ducks with their

109

heads under their wings, and the sick man was dead in less than two days.

Other seers, who made 'trials' for reward, made the person who consulted them burn straw in front of a sieve and then look through to see 'what they should see'. From the objects seen the seer foretold what was to befall.

When a trial was made to ascertain whether an absent friend would return, if on going out to the end of the house a man is seen coming, or a duck running towards the seer, his safe arrival will soon be; but if the object be moving away, the indication is unfavourable. By this trial it may also be known whether the absent one will return empty-handed or not.

Another mode of *deuchainn*, for the same purpose, is to take a chance stick and measure it in thumb-breadths, beginning at its thick or lower end, and saying, when the thumb is laid on the stick, no or yes as the opinion of the person consulting the oracle may incline, and repeating yes, no, alternately till the other end is reached. According to the position of the last thumb will the answer be affirmative or negative or doubtful.

When a young woman wants to ascertain whether a young man in whom she feels an interest loves her, let her look between her fingers at him and say the following charm. If his first motion is to raise his right arm she is secure of his affections.

> I have a trial upon you,
> I have a looking at you,
> Between the five ribs of Christ's body;
> If it be fated or permitted you
> To make use of me,
> Lift your right hand,
> And let it not quickly down.[4]

In the detection of theft the diviner's utmost skill could only determine the direction the stolen goods had taken.

Divination

Divination (*Fiosachd*)

The same causes which in other countries led to oracles, astrology, necromancy, card-reading, and other forms of divination, in the Scottish Highlands led to the reading of shoulder blades and tea-cups, palmistry, and the artless spinning of tee-totums (*dòduman*). In a simple state of society mummeries and ceremonies, dark caves, darkened rooms, and other aids to mystification are not required to bring custom to the soothsayer. The desire of mankind, particularly the young, to have pleasant anticipations of the future, supply all deficiencies in his artifices. One or two shrewd guesses establish a reputation, and ordinarily there is no scepticism or inquiry as to the sources of information. It is noticeable that the chief articles from which the Highland soothsayer drew his predictions, supplied him with a luxury.

Shoulder Blade Reading (*Slinneineachd*)

This mode of divination was practised, like the augury of the ancients, as a profession or trade. It consisted in foretelling important events in the life of the owner of a slaughtered animal from the marks on the shoulder blade, speal or blade-bone. Professors of this difficult art deemed the right speal-bone of a black sheep or a black pig the best for this purpose. This was to be boiled thoroughly, so that the flesh might be stripped clean from it, untouched by nail or knife or tooth. The slightest scratch destroyed its value. The bone being duly prepared was divided into upper and lower parts, corresponding to the natural features of the district in which the divination was made. Certain marks indicated a crowd of people, met, according to the skill of the diviner, at a funeral, fight, sale etc. The largest hole or indentation was the grave of the beast's owner (*úaigh an t-sealbhaduir*), and from its position his living or dying that year was prognosticated. When to the side of the bone, it presaged death; when in its centre, much worldly prosperity (*gum biodh an saoghal aige*).

Mac-a-Chreachaire, a native of Barra, was a celebrated shoulder blade reader in his day. According to popular tradition he was present at the festivities held on the occasion of the castle at *Bàgh Chiòsamul* (the seat of the MacNeills, then chiefs of the island) being finished. A shoulder blade was handed to him, and he was pressed again and again to divine from it the fate of the castle. He was very reluctant, but at last, on being promised that no harm would be done him, he said the castle would become a cairn for thrushes (*càrn dhruideachun*), and this would happen when the Rattle stone (*Clach-a-Ghlagain*) was found, when people worked at sea-weed in *Baile na Creige* (Rock town, a village far from the sea), and when deer swam across from Uist, and were to be found on every dunghill in Barra. All this has happened, and the castle is now in ruins. Others say the omens were the arrival of a ship with blue wool, a blind man coming ashore unaided, and that when a ground officer with big fingers (*maor na miar mòra*) came, Barra would be measured with an iron string. A ship laden with blue cloth was wrecked on the island, and a blind man miraculously escaped; every finger of the ground officer proved to be as big as a bottle (!), and Barra was surveyed and sold.

When Murdoch the Short (*Murchadh Gearr*), heir to the Lordship of Lochbuy in the Island of Mull, *c*.AD1400, was sent in his childhood for protection from the ambitious designs of his uncle, the Laird of Dowart, to Ireland, he remained there till eighteen years of age. In the meantime his sister (or half-sister) became widowed, and, dependent on the charity and hospitality of others, wandered about the Ross of Mull from house to house with her family. It was always 'in the prophecy' (*san tairgneachd*) that Murdoch would return. One evening, in a house to which his sister came, a wedder sheep was killed. After the meal was over, her oldest boy asked the farmer for the shoulder blade. He examined it intently for some time in silence, and then, exclaiming that Murdoch was on the soil of Mull (*air grunnd Mhuile*), rushed out of the house and made for Lochbuy, to find his uncle in possession of his rightful inheritance.

On the night of the massacre of Glencoe, a party of the ill-fated clansmen were poring over the shoulder blade of an animal slain for the hospitable entertainment of the soldiers. One of them said, 'There is a shedding of blood in the glen' (*tha dòrtadh fuil sa ghleann*). Another said there was only the stream at the end of the house between them and it. The whole party rushed to the door, and were among the few that escaped the butchery of that dreadful night.

It is a common story that a shoulder blade seer once saved the lives of a company, of whom he himself was one, who had 'lifted' a cattle spoil (*creach*), by divining that there was only the stream at the end of the house between them and their pursuers.

A shoulder blade sage in Tiree sat down to a substantial feast, to which he had been specially invited, that he might divine whether a certain friend was on his way home or not. He examined the shoulder-bone of the wedder killed on the occasion critically, unable to make up his mind. 'Perhaps', he said, 'he will come, perhaps he will not.' A boy, who had hid himself on the top of a bed in the room, that he might see the fun, could not help exclaiming, 'They cannot find you untrue.' The bed broke, and the diviner and his companions, thinking the voice came from the skies, fled. When the boy recovered he got the dinner all to himself.

Palmistry (*Dearnadaireachd*)

Of this mode of divination, as practised in the Highlands, nothing seems now to be known beyond the name. Probably from the first the knowledge of it was confined to gipsies and such like stray characters.

Divination by Tea or Cup-reading (*Leughadh chupaichean*)

When tea was a luxury, dear and difficult to get, the 'spaeing' of fortunes from tea-cups was in great repute. Even yet young women resort in numbers to fortune-tellers of the class, who for the reward of the tea spell out of them most excellent matches.

After drinking the tea, the person for whom the cup is to be read, turning the cup *deiseal*, or with the right-hand turn, is to make a small drop, left in it, wash its sides all round, and then pour it out. The fortune is then read from the arrangement of the sediments or tea-leaves left in the cup. A large quantity of black tea grounds (*smùrach du*) denotes substance and worldly gear. The person consulting the oracle is a stray leaf standing to the one side of it. If the face of the leaf is towards the grounds, that person is to come to a great fortune; if very positively its back, then farewell even to the hope 'that keeps alive despair'. A small speck by itself is a letter, and other specks are envious people struggling to get to the top, followers etc. Good diviners can even tell to their youthful and confiding friends when the letter is likely to arrive, what trade their admirer follows, the colour of his hair etc.

Dreams and Prophecies

Dreams (*bruadar*) have everywhere been laid hold of by superstition as indications of what is passing at a distance or of what is to occur, and, considering the vast numbers of dreams there are, it would be matter of surprise, if a sufficient number did not prove so like some remote or subsequent event, interesting to the dreamer, as to keep the belief alive. On a low calculation, a fourth of the population dream every night, and in the course of a year, the number of dreams in a district must be incredible. They are generally about things that have been, or are, causes of anxiety, or otherwise occupied men's waking thoughts. 'A dream cometh through the multitude of business,' Solomon says, and a Gaelic proverb says with equal truth 'An old wife's dream is according to her inclination' (*Aisling caillich mas a dùrachd*). Its character can sometimes be traced directly to the health or position of the body, but in other cases, it seems to depend on the uncontrolled association of ideas. Out of the numberless phantasies that arise there must surely be many that the imagination can without violence convert into forebodings and premonitions.

To dream of raw meat indicates impending trouble; eggs mean gossip and scandal; herring snow; meal, earth; a grey horse, the sea. To dream of women is unlucky; and of the dead, that they are not at rest. In the Hebrides, a horse is supposed to have reference to the Clan Mac Leod. The surname of horses is Mac Leod, as the Coll bard said to the Skye bard:

Often rode I with my bridle,
The race you and your wife belong to.[5]

In some districts horses meant the Macgnanean, and a white horse, a letter.

Prophecies (*Fàisneachd*)

In Argyllshire and Perthshire, the celebrated Thomas the Rhymer (*Tòmas Reuvair, T. Réim*) is as well known as in the Lowlands of Scotland. He is commonly called 'the son of the dead woman' (*mac na mna mairbh*), but the accounts vary as to the cause of this name. One account says, he was, like Julius Caesar, taken out through his mother's side, immediately after her death; another, that the cry of the child was heard in the mother's tomb after her burial, and on the grave being opened Thomas was found in the coffin. A third account says, that a woman, whose husband had been cut in four pieces, engaged a tailor, at the price of the surrender of her person, to sew the pieces together again. He did so in two hours time. Some time after the woman died and was buried. Subsequently, she met the tailor at night, and leading him to her tomb, the child was found there. Both the Highland and Lowland accounts agree that Thomas's gift of prophecy was given him by a Fairy sweetheart, that he is at present among the Fairies, and will yet come back.

The Highland tradition is, that Thomas is in Dunbuck hill (*Dùn buic*) near Dunbarton. The last person that entered that hill found him resting on his elbow, with his hand below his head. He asked, 'Is it time?' and the man fled. In the outer Hebrides he is said to be in Tom-na-heurich hill[6] hear Inverness. Hence MacCodrum, the Uist bard, says:

When the hosts of Tomnaheurich come,
Who should rise first but Thomas?[7]

He attends every market on the look-out for suitable horses, as the Fairies in the north of Ireland attend to steal linen and other goods, exposed for sale. It is only horses with certain characteristics that he will take. At present he wants but two, some say only one, a yellow foal with a white forehead (*searrach blàr buidhe*). The other is to be a white horse that has got 'three March, three May, and three August months of its mother's milk' (*trì Màirt, trì Màigh, agus trì Iuchara 'bhainne mhàthar*); and in Mull they say, one of the horses is to be from the meadow of Kengharair in that island. When his complement is made up he will become visible, and a great battle will be fought on the Clyde.

When Thomas comes with his horses,
The day of spoils will be on the Clyde,
Nine thousand good men will be slain,
And a new king will be set on the throne.[8]

You may walk across the Clyde, the prophecy goes on to relate, on men's bodies, and the miller of Partick Mill (*Muilionn Phearaig*), who is to be a man with seven fingers, will grind for two hours with blood instead of water. After that, sixteen ladies will follow after one lame tailor,[9] a prophecy copied from Isaiah iv.i. A stone in the Clyde was pointed out as one, on which a bird (*bigein*) would perch and drink its full of blood, without bending its head, but the River Trustees have blasted it out of the way that the prophecy may not come true. The same prophecy, with slight variation, has been transferred to Blair Athole in Perthshire. 'When the white cows come to Blair, the wheel of Blair Mill will turn round seven times with people's blood.'[10] The writer was told that the Duke of Athole brought white cattle to Blair more than fifteen years ago, but nothing extraordinary happened.

Other prophecies, ascribed to the Rhymer, are, 'the sheep's skull will make the plough useless', 'the south sea will come upon the north sea' and 'Scotland will be in white bands, and a lump of gold will be at the bottom of every glen'.[11] The former has received its fulfilment in the desolation caused by the extension of sheep farms, the second in the making of the Caledonian canal, and the last in the increase of highroads and houses.

113

In the north Highlands, prophecies of this kind are ascribed to *Coinneach Odhar* (i.e. Dun Kenneth), a native of Ross-shire, whose name is hardly known in Argyllshire. He acquired his prophetic gift from the possession of a stone, which he found in a raven's nest. He first found a raven's nest with eggs in it. These he took home and boiled. He then took them back to the nest, with a view to finding out how long the bird would sit before it despaired of hatching them. He found a stone in the nest before him, and its possession was the secret of his oracular gifts. When this became known an attempt was made to take the stone from him, but he threw it out in a loch, where it still lies.

He prophesied that 'the raven will drink its fill of men's blood from off the ground, on the top of the High Stone in Uig',[12] a place in Skye. The High Stone is on a mountain's brow, and it is ominous of the fulfilment of the prophecy, that it has fallen on its side. Of the Well of Ta, at *Cill-a-chrò* in Strath, in the same island, he said:

Thou well of Ta, and well of Ta,
Well where battle shall be fought,
And the bones of growing men,
   Will strew the white beach of Laoras;
And Lachlan of the three Lachlans be slain
Early, early,
   At the well of Ta.[13]

In Harris a cock will crow on the very day on which it is hatched, and a white calf, without a single black hair, will be born, both which remarkable events have, it is said, occurred. A certain large stone will roll up the hill, turning over three times, and the marks of it having done so, and the proof of the prophecy, are still to be seen. On the top of a high stone in Scaristavor parks,[14] the raven will drink its fill of men's blood, and the tide of battle will be turned back by Norman of the three Normans (*Tormod nan trì Tormoidean*) at the Steps of Tarbert (*Càthaichean an Tairbeart*).[15]

The Lady of Lawers

Of similar fame for her prophetic gifts was the Lady of Lawers (*Bantighearna Lathuir*), one of the Breadalbane family, married to Campbell of Lawers. Her prophecies relate to the house and lands of Breadalbane, and are written, it is believed, in a book shaped like a barrel, and secured with twelve iron hoops or clasps in the charter room of Taymouth Castle. This book is called 'The Red Book of Balloch'.

An old white horse will yet take the lineal heirs of Taymouth (or, according to another version, the last Breadalbane Campbells) across Tyndrum Cairn. When she said this there were thirty sons in the family, but soon after twenty-five of them were slain in the battle at *Sron-a-chlachair* near Killin (*Cill-Fhinn*).

If the top stone were ever put on Lawers Church no word uttered by her would ever come true, and when the red cairn on Ben Lawers fell the church would split. In the same year that the cairn, built by the sappers and miners on Ben Lawers, fell, the Disruption in the Church of Scotland took place.

A mill will be on every streamlet,
A plough in every boy's hand,
The two sides of Loch Tay in kail gardens;

The sheep's skull will make the plough useless,
And the goose's feathers drive their memories from men.

This was to happen in the time of 'John of the three Johns, the worst John that ever was, and there will be no good till Duncan comes'.
A stone called the 'Boar Stone' (*Clach an Tuirc*),

Bi muilionn air gach sruthan,
Crann an laìmh gach giullain,
Da thaobh Loch Tatha na ghàracha-càil,
Cuiridh claigionn na caorach an crann o fheum,
'S cuiridh ite gèoidh an cuimhn' a duine.

a boulder of some two or three hundred tons in a meadow near Loch Tay, will topple over when a strange heir comes to Taymouth, and the house will be at its height of honour when the face of a certain rock is concealed by wood.

Notes

1 *Manadaireachd.*
2 The Bait-stone (*Clach shuill*) was a stone on which to break shell-fish, potatoes etc, to be thrown into the water to attract fish. The broken bait was called *soll, faoire.*
3 A neach tha gam iomradh,
Mar h-ann air mo leas e,
Esan bhi ga iomluain
Air sgeanabh geura glasa,
Cadal an tom seangain da,
'S na na cadal fallain da;
Ach baobh eadar e 's an dorus,
'S mis' eadar e 's a chuid 's a chadal.
Cliath-chliat iarruinn a sgrìobadh a mhionaich,
… Cailleach nharbh … .
4 Tha deuchainn agam dhuit,
Tha sealltuinn agam ort,
Eadar còig aisnean cléibh Chriosd;
Ma tha 'n dàn no 'n ceadachadh dhuit,
Feum dheanadh dhiom,
Tog do làmh dheas a suas,
'S na luaith i nìos.
5 Is tric a mharcaich mi le 'm shréin
An dream gam bheil the fhéin 's do bhean.
6 *Tom-na-h-iubhraich*, the Boat Mound, probably derives its name from its resemblance to a boat, bottom upwards. Another popular account makes it the abode of the Feinné, or Fin Mac Coul and his men. There is a huge chain suspended from the roof, and if any mortal has the courage to strike it three times with his fist, the heroes will rise again. A person struck it twice, and was so terrified by the howling of the big dogs (*donnal na con mòra*) that he fled. A voice called after him, 'Wretched mischief-making man, that worse hast left than found' (*Dhuine dhon a dhòlaich, 's miosa dh'fhàg na fhuair*).

7 Dar thigedh sluagh Tom na h-iubhraich,
Co dh' eireadh air tùs ach Tòmas?

8 Nuair thig Tòmas le chuid each,
Bi latha nan creach air Cluaidh,
Millear naoi mìle fear maith,
'S theid righ òg air a chrùn.

9 'Bi sia baintighearnun diag as deigh an aon tàilleir chrùbaich.'

10 'Meair thig an cro bàn do Bhlàr, cuirear seachd cuir de chulbhle mhuilinn Bhlàir le fuil sluaigh.'

11 'Cuiridh claigionn na caorach an crann s fheum, no an crann araidh air an fharadh;
Thig a mhuir deas air a mhuir tuath;
Bi Albainn na criosun geala,
'S meall òir ann am bun gach glinne.'

12 'Olaidh am fitheach a shàth, bhar an làir, air mullach clach àrd an Uig.'

13 Tobar Tàth sin, 's tobar Tàth,
Tobar aig an cuirear blàr,
'S bi cnaimhean nam fear fàs
Air tràigh bhàn Laorais
'S marbhar Lachunn nan trì Lachunn
Gu moch, moch, aig tobar Tàth.
Al. Torcuil nan trì Torcuil.

14 This stone is about ten feet high, and is one of the three fragments into which a larger stone, used by an old woman of former days as a hammer to knock limpets off the rocks (*òrd bhàirneach*), was broken. Of the other two, one is in *Uigh an du tuath*, and one in Tarnsa Islet. At a spot from which these three fragments can be seen, there is hidden an urn of silver and an urn of gold (*croggan òir's cr. airgid*). It is easy to find a place whence one can see two, but when about to see the third, one of the first two disappears. Five or six yards make all the difference. A herdsman once found the spot, but when digging for the treasure he happened to see a heifer that had fallen on its back in a stream. He ran to its rescue, and never could find the place again.

15 *Càth*, probably a step path in a rock.

CHAPTER SEVEN

The Silver Bough in Irish Legend

Eleanor Hull

In the early chapters of Mr Frazer's *Golden Bough* the author, following the Commentary of Servius, connects the rites performed at Nemi with the allusion of Virgil to the bough plucked by command of the Sibyl and carried by Aeneas into the underworld. So far as the present writer is aware, there is no other and no better ground for the connection than this one passage from Servius. The references given by the author to Pausanias, Strabo and Suetonius, do indeed bear upon the legend and the rites of the Grove of Aricia, but none of them suggest any further tradition connecting the bough broken off by the runaway slave within the sanctuary of Nemi, with the Golden Bough plucked near the entrance to Avernus from the wondrous tree sacred to 'Infernal Juno' (i.e., Proserpine), without which none might enter the realm of Pluto. Is there, in fact, any likelihood that such a connection really existed?

Without unduly emphasizing the fact that Servius lived nearly 400 years later than Virgil, we would remind the reader that Servius is a voluminous writer, who drags in every possible and impossible allusion collected in the course of a laborious life, however remotely bearing upon the matter in hand, which can by any means be used to illustrate his subject. He is quite devoid of the power of discrimination, and his work is rather to be regarded as a repository of legends, many of which might otherwise have been lost, than as a trustworthy guide to the origin of any particular tradition. Nothing indeed could better illustrate his system of gathering together and setting down every allusion occurring to his well-stocked mind, which bore in the most distant way upon the subject in hand, than his treatment of this very point. Here is the passage:

> Licet de hoc ramo hi qui de sacris Proserpinae scripsisse dicuntur, quiddam esse mysticum affirment; publica tamen opinio hoc habet. Orestes post occisum regem Thoantem in regione Taurica cum sorore Iphigenia.

(Here begins the story of the flight of Orestes with Iphigenia and of the carrying off of the statue of Diana, as related by Mr Frazer.)

> Nunc ergo istum inde sumpsit colorem. Ramus enim necesse erat ut et unius causa esset interitus unde et statim mortem subiungit Miseni: et ad sacra Proserpinae accedere, nisi sublato ramo, non poterat. Inferos autem subire hoc dicit sacra celebrare Proserpinae.
> (Servius, Aen., vi, 136 sqq.)

After which, Servius wanders into a discussion of the doctrine of Pythagoras that life is like the letter Y, in which he finds again the symbol of the branch in the dividing ways of good and evil.

We may read the passage in English as follows:

Although such as are said to have written on the rites of Proserpine assert of this branch that there is something mystic in it, the current view is as follows. Orestes, after the slaying of king Thoas in the Tauric district, fled with his sister Iphigenia. ... Now therefore he (i.e., the poet) has coloured his story from this source. The branch had to be the cause of one death; wherefore he adds at once the death of Misenus: and he could not join the rites of Proserpine without having the branch to hold up. And by 'going to the shades' he (the poet) means celebrating the rites of Proserpine.[1]

It will be seen that Servius endeavours to rationalize the story by connecting it with the Orestes legend and the death of Misenus, adding that he derives the former connection from a current tradition, popular in his day. That there was some such confused popular tradition is likely enough, but it seems to have had as little foundation in the thought of Virgil as had the further suggestion that the bough represented to Virgil the diverging paths of virtuous and evil living, represented by the letter Y of Pythagoras. As explanations of the bough of Aeneas, both seem to be equally far-fetched ideas.[2]

The point in no way touches Mr Frazer's main line of argument, derived from a consideration of the rites of Nemi, and it might not have been worth while to call attention to it, but that it would seem a pity that a modern scholar should give prominence to a far-fetched theory of post-classical origin, to explain an episode so full of beautiful and mystic meaning as the plucking of the bough before entering the underworld. It certainly had no such cut-and-dry rationalistic meaning in the mind of the poet. Even Servius recognizes an older meaning, though it had become faded and obscured in his day, when he says: 'Such as have written on the rites of Proserpine assert of this branch that there is something mystic in it.' And again, 'He could not take part in the rites of Proserpine without having the branch to hold up, and by "going to the shades" he means celebrating the rites of Proserpine;' that is to say, the well-known and constantly recurring Mysteries of Eleusis, in which the disappearance of the Maiden into Hades was continually re-enacted. Here Servius endeavours to explain away the supernatural element in the history of Aeneas, and to that end credits Virgil with an allegorical method of relating history. Again, the branch could not have caused the death of Misenus, as Misenus was dead before the bough was plucked. This seems a wholly gratuitous addition on the part of Servius to support his theory. Nor can it be said that the branch had a connection with the burial, for the surprise of Charon at the sight of the Bough, 'so rarely seen' in Hades, shows that it was only those who entered the realms of the dead during life who presented the branch to Proserpine. She herself was a native of the upper world, dwelling in the shades, but able to return to earth at intervals. Hence, no doubt, the need that the living man who would enter Hades and return, should appear there in the character of her votary. The connection with the death of Misenus was simply that the truth of the Sibyl's announcement with regard to Misenus strengthened the belief of Aeneas in the righteousness of her further command to pluck the bough.

The idea of the poet is wholly different from that of his commentator. In Virgil, the Golden Bough, which grew concealed in the shades of gloomy woods, and could only be gathered 'the fates permitting', was dedicated to Proserpine. It was to be presented to her as her peculiar gift. It could never come to an end, because no sooner was one bough broken off than another succeeded it. It was this shining bough, plucked by Aeneas, and carried by the Sibyl, that gained them admission into Hades. When Charon withstood their passage, refusing to ferry living beings across the Stygian lake, the Sibyl 'showed the shining bough, concealed within her breast'.

> Nor more was needful; for the gloomy god
> Stood mute in awe to see the golden rod;
> Admired the destined offering to his queen,
> A venerable gift, so rarely seen.
>   (translated by John Dryden)

With limbs and body cleansed with water, Aeneas later approaches the gate of Pluto's palace, and 'fixes the fatal bough required by his queen above the porch'. The Golden Bough was thus plainly a talisman, empowering the bearer to enter in safety during his lifetime the underworld. It was the property of the queen of the unseen abode.[3]

Now it is interesting to find the same idea running through a number of very early pagan legends derived from Gaelic or Irish sources. We propose to throw together a few of these examples, gathered out of that large storehouse of visions regarding the unseen world which Irish literature provides us with. Probably these surviving visions or voyages are only the remains of a body of legend originally extending far beyond Ireland, though some of the conceptions which we find in them seem special to the Western Gael. The bough in Irish legend was not intended to avert the anger of the gods of the underworld, who are always represented as craving for the presence of the chosen being; it is rather the gift of the queen or presiding genius of the Land of the Ever Living and Ever Young, to draw to her domain the favoured mortal on whose companionship her heart is set. For the mortal generally enters by invitation, and the branch is held out as a clue binding the desired one to enter her abode. It acts the double part of a link to the unseen world and of a means of sustenance while there. Often also it produces sweet and soothing music, which both allures the mortal, and wiles into forgetfulness the bereaved who are left behind. The Irish conception of the unseen differs so entirely from the classical, that it is only to be expected that the functions of the bough should differ slightly also. The idea of torture, pain or expiation for sin never enters into the Celtic future. His Elysium is wholly happy; the Plain of Flowers, the Land of Youth, the Country of the Ever-living, the Plain of Honey, these are his names for it. It is only after the introduction of Christianity that these joyous ideas become overshadowed by gloom, and the conception of guilt and expiation fills the canvas.

Let us take first a vision which in its structure and substance retains, with very little infusion of Christian elements, its pagan form and feeling. The *Voyage of Bran, Son of Febal,* describes the visit of Bran to the Elysium of the pagan Celt. It begins thus:

It was fifty quatrains that the woman from the unknown land sang on the floor of the house to Bran, son of Febal, when the royal house was full of kings; they knew not whence the woman had come, for the ramparts were closed. This is the beginning of the story. One day in the neighbourhood of his stronghold Bran went about alone, when he heard music behind him. As often as he looked back it was still behind him the music was. At last he fell asleep at the sound of the music, such was its sweetness. When he awoke from his sleep he saw close by him a branch of silver with white blossoms, so that it was not easy to distinguish the blossoms from the branch. Then Bran took the branch in his hand to the royal house. When the hosts were in the royal house, they saw a woman in strange raiment on the floor of the house. 'Twas then she sang the fifty quatrains to Bran, the host listening, and all beholding the woman. And she sang:

> A branch of the apple-tree from Emain
> I bring, like those we know;
> Twigs of white silver are on it
> Crystal brows with blossoms, &c.

Thereupon the woman went from them and they knew not whither she went. And she took her branch with her. The branch sprang from Bran's hand into the hand of the woman, nor was there strength in Bran's hand to hold the branch.[4]

We would note, in passing, that the branch is always said to be the bough of an apple-tree, and we shall see in future extracts that the apples of the branch served for meat and drink in the Land of Promise. They tasted of every sort of delicious flavour, and their sustenance lasted during the whole sojourn of the visitor to the invisible world. The tree is described in the *Sickbed of Cuchulainn* as growing in Magh Mell, 'the Plain of Honey', another name for the Irish Elysium.

> There is a tree at the door of the Court,
> It cannot be matched in harmony,
> A tree of silver upon which the sun shines,
> Like unto gold is its splendid lustre.

> There are at the eastern door
> Three stately trees of crimson hue,
> From which the birds of perpetual bloom
> Sing to the youth from the kingly rath.

Mr Frazer takes it for granted that the Golden Bough of Virgil, and also that cut by the fugitive at Nemi, which in his view were the same, but to our mind were probably unconnected, was the mistletoe.[5] This is possible, but it is worth remark that this plant, though we learn from Latin authors that it played a part in the religious ceremonies of the pagan Celts of Britain and Gaul, is seldom if ever mentioned in Irish literature. The ceremonial cutting of the mistletoe bough either belonged to a later system of things than that described in Irish Gaelic literature, or it was confined to the more easterly branches of the Celtic race.[6] The yew was the tree from which the Irish druid's wand of divination was made, and it is the apple-tree that plays the greatest part in his romance. In the *Voyage of Bran* the talisman given by the unknown woman to Bran, is said to be 'a branch of the apple-tree from Emain', i.e., the kingly residence of the Kings of Ulster, the earthen ramparts of which still exist not far from Armagh. Now the three halls or forts of this ancient palace were called the Royal Branch (*Craebh Ruadh*), the Red Branch (*Craebh Derg*), and the Speckled House (*Teiti Brec*); while the bodyguard or knights of the king were styled Champions of the Royal Branch. It was only by special proficiency in the arts of combat that admittance into this order was gained. So far as is known to the writer, the origin of these names is lost;

120

could we regain their significance, some light would probably be thrown upon the choice of the 'apple-tree of Emain' as the magic talisman insuring safety and nourishment in the invisible world. But to turn to another story. We meet the silver branch again in a tale entitled *Cormac's Adventure in the Land of Promise.*[7] The youth who acts the hero of this tale was one of the most famous kings of early Ireland. The portion of the tale bearing upon this point runs as follows:

> One day at dawn in May-time, Cormac, grandson of Conn, was alone on Mur Tea in Tara. He saw coming towards him a sedate, grey-headed warrior. A branch of silver with three golden apples on his shoulder. Delight and amusement to the full was it to listen to the music of that branch, for men sore wounded, or women in child-bed, or folk in sickness, would fall asleep at the melody which was made when that branch was shaken.

The warrior tells Cormac that he comes from a land wherein is naught but truth; where is neither age nor decay, nor gloom, nor sadness, envy nor jealousy, hatred nor haughtiness. Cormac begs the warrior to give him the branch. This the unknown consents to, on condition that he receives in return any three boons that he shall ask. On getting Cormac's promise, he gives the branch to the young prince, and disappears, Cormac knows not whither. Cormac returns to his palace. He shakes the branch and deep slumber falls on all. But at the end of a year the warrior returns and demands in succession the three boons promised him by Cormac. They are Cormac's daughter Ailbe; his son, Cairpre Lifechair; and finally Cormac's wife, Ethne the Tall. Twice Cormac uses the magic bough to sooth the grief of the survivors, but the third time he follows the messenger into the invisible land, where he finds his wife, and sups with her and his children in a country of wonderful happiness. He finds that it was Manannan mac Lir who drew away his wife, the same god who interferes between Cuchulainn and Fand in *The Sickbed of Cuchulainn,* and who probably was conceived of as the ruler of the unseen world. In the latter story it is a cloak that he shakes between the seen and unseen to hide the invisible world from Cuchulainn. The cloak seems here to have for some reason replaced the branch. The close of the story of Cormac's adventure in the Land of Promise is that Cormac gets the cup of truth and the branch of music and joy, and returns home.

The branch performs the double function of sustaining life by providing nourishment and of producing sounds of entrancing harmony. There may be a connection, conscious or unconscious, between this latter power possessed by the branch and the symbolic branch carried by the bards as a sign of their profession. The purpose of the branch (*Craebh Ciuil*) was exactly the same as that described above; it was used to bring about peace and order in moments of excitement, and its authority seems never to have been questioned. The shaking of the bardic wand, which seems to have been a little spike or crescent, with gently tinkling bells upon it, quieted the most turbulent assembly. For instance, in the piece called *Mesca Ulad,* in the midst of a bloody fray, the chief poet of Ulster, Sencha, arose 'and waved the peaceful branch of Sencha, and all the men of Ulster were silent, quiet'; while in another passage in the same piece, he is described as 'bearing a bronze branch at the summit of his shoulder'. His title of 'pacificator of the hosts of Ulad' probably comes from this. In another piece entitled *Agallamh an dá Shuadh* or the Dialogue of the Two Sages, the symbol is thus described: 'Neidhe' (a youthful bard who aspired to succeed his father as chief poet of Ulster) 'made his journey with a silver branch over him. The *Anradhs,* or poets of the second order, carried a silver branch, but the *Ollamhs,* or chief poets, carried a branch of gold; all other poets bore a branch of bronze.' The King of Ulster also had in his palace, at the right hand of his seat at table, a bronze post, which he struck with his wand or sceptre of silver, and which had the same instantaneous effect of pacifying feuds between his followers. In the tales of the Irish Elysium, there may be some remembrance of these well-known kingly and bardic boughs of peace.

In the story of *Conla Ruadh*, the maiden who calls him away uses a single apple as a bait to draw him to fairyland. He is the son of a famous monarch of early Ireland, Conn, the fighter of a hundred (Cet-da-thach) and the story seems to have been told to explain why his brother Art, the succeeding king, should have been named 'the Solitary'. Conn and his son Conla were seated together one day on the hill of Usnech in Meath, when Conla perceives a beautiful maiden, visible only to himself, who speaks to him and invites him to join her in *Magh-Mell* (viz. the 'Plain of Honey', one of the Irish names for Elysium).

The king is startled at the abstraction into which the vision has thrown Conla, and frightened at hearing him converse with an invisible being. He hastily sends for his druids to exorcize his son and chant their incantation against the invisible siren, who disappears.

But when the chant of the druids was driving her away, she threw an apple to Conla. For a full month Conla ate nothing but this apple; no bit nor drink beside it passed his mouth, for he deemed all other food poor and unworthy beside that apple. Yet, however much he ate of it, nothing was gone from the apple; it was still quite whole.

At the end of a month the lady appears again, beseeching him to come and reign as King over the Ever-living Ones, the people of Tethra, Ocean King. Conla is grieved and perplexed between his duty to his kingdom and his strong desire to go; and seeing him wavering, the lady breaks out into song, describing in terms so ravishing the joys and glories of the Land of the Living, that he gives one spring into her 'very strong, well-balanced, gleaming curach' and disappears. 'And it is not known whither they went.'[8]

In the next story that attracts our attention, however, we learn 'whither they went'. In it the same hero plays a part. We meet Conla again in the semi-Christian tale of *Teigue, Son of Cian*. It is, like so many of the Irish stories of the unseen world, thrown into the form of a voyage. The invisible world is conceived of sometimes as being beneath the hills, and entered through the tumuli that in several places in Ireland mark the burial places of early heroes or gods; or as being far over the seas, and approachable either by boat or by means of a magic horse which rides across the waves, and which carries the chosen hero to the land of happiness. There is quite a large literature, full of imagination and romance, dealing with these voyages; a literature that is exceptionally interesting as showing the gradual modification of thought brought about by the infusion of Christian ideas. The two most important points regarding the pagan conception, unadulterated by Christianity, are (1) that the Irish unseen world was a land of absolute delight, unclouded by any idea of pain or expiation for sin; (2) that it was not attained through death: but generally at the call or invitation of an inhabitant of the invisible world, often a woman who sets her love upon some human being and entices him away. The passage from the story of *Teigue, Son of Cian*, bearing on our point is as follows:

Now for all they had suffered of cold, of strain on their endurance, of foul weather, and of tempest, yet after reaching the coast on which they were thus landed, they felt no craving at all for fire or for meat; the perfume of that region's fragrant crimsoned branches being meat and satisfying nourishment for them. Through the nearest part of the forest they take their way, and come by-and-by upon an orchard full of red-laden apple-trees, with leafy oaks too in it, and hazels yellow with nuts in their clusters. They quit this spot and happen on a wood; great was the excellence of its scent and perfume; round purple berries hung on it, and every one of them bigger than a man's head. Birds beautiful and brilliant feasted on these grapes; they were fowls of unwonted kind: white, with scarlet heads and golden beaks. As they fed, they warbled music and minstrelsy exquisitely melodious, to which the sick of every kind and the many times wounded would have fallen asleep, and Teigue hearing, chanted this melody: 'Sweet to my fancy, as I consider them, the strains of this melody to which I listen.'[9]

They advance over a plain, clad in flowering clover all bedewed with honey, and enter a fort with a silver rampart in the 'Earth's Fourth Paradise', where they find a charming youthful couple, with torques of gold about their necks.

Now the youth held in his hand a fragrant apple having the hue of gold; a third part of it he would eat, and still, for all he consumed, never a whit would it be diminished. This fruit it was that supported the pair of them, and when once they had partaken of it, nor age nor dimness could affect them.

The youth explains that he is Conla and that he has been drawn away by the girl of many charms who sits beside him. Then as they wander round the splendid mansion, now empty, but reserved 'for the righteous kings who after acceptance of the Faith shall rule Ireland', Teigue looks away across the capacious palace and 'marks a thickly furnished wide-spreading apple tree that bore both blossoms and ripe fruit at once. "What is that apple tree yonder?" he asked, and she made answer: "That apple tree's fruit it is that shall serve for meat for all who come to this mansion, and a single apple of it was that which coaxed away Conla to me."'

The pagan idea of the apple-branch as a talisman is, in such semi-Christian visions as the above, evidently becoming confused with the idea derived from biblical sources of the tree in the midst of the Christian Paradise; yet its original meaning is not entirely lost. In the visions in which the Christian idea is paramount, such as the *Vision* ascribed to Adamnán, or the piece entitled the *Two Sorrows of Heaven's Kingdom*, the notion of the talisman is altogether lost, while the idea of the tree of nourishment, which is pagan and Christian alike, remains. The birds of pagan legend inhabiting its boughs become in the later visions the souls of the righteous in the form of birds. In the *Voyage of Brendan* we find, amid many details inspired by Christian tradition, a confused remembrance of the fair maiden of the pagan tales, in the monstrous maiden, 'smooth, full-grown, yellow-haired, whiter than snow or the foam of the wave' who is found floating dead upon the ocean, and is brought to life by Brendan in order that she may be baptized and receive the Sacrament, 'before going at once to Heaven'.

In the Ossianic tale of *Oisin in Tir-na-nog*, the wanderers, Oisín (Ossian) and the beautiful maiden who entices him away, meet, twice in their voyage 'a lovely young maiden riding the waves on a brown steed, with a golden apple in her hand, followed by a young warrior on a white steed, who closely pursued her'. In the *Voyage of Maelduin* a similar idea is latent in the rod plucked by the voyager from the wood as they were passing, which sprouted on the third day with a cluster of three apples, and each of these apples sufficed them for forty nights.

Putting together all these examples, which no doubt might be added to from other sources, may we not ask, is not the Gaelic Apple-Bough of entrance into the unseen world nearer in idea to the conception of Virgil than the legend of the bloody sacrifice within the groves of Nemi, or the story of the flight of Orestes from which this is supposed to have had its origin? In both, the mortal entered alive into the unseen world, guided by the bough; in both, the bough, though in classic tradition it grew above Avernus, while in Irish tradition it grew in the invisible land itself, was the special property of the presiding goddess of that world. It would be curious if a folk-belief, once perhaps widely-spread, had been retained only in the verse of Virgil, and the folk-tradition of Ireland.

Notes

1   I am indebted to the kindness of Mr W.H.D. Rouse for the above translation. With reference to the phrase 'non poterat', Mr Rouse adds: 'I think *poterat* is used loosely, as if Aeneas had been meant, when the writer should have said "a man". Aeneas was to pluck the bough because he could not join, &c., to imply that none could. Not Misenus, certainly, is meant; grammatically, the poet; by intent, Aeneas; by implication, anyone.' Miss Burne suggests that Servius must have seen in his own lifetime the last days, perhaps the final extinction, of the 'Rites of Proserpine', i.e., the famous Eleusinian Mysteries. This throws an interesting light on his use of the imperfect, *poterat.*

2   Since writing the above, my attention has been drawn to the passage in Mr Andrew Lang's book *Magic and Religion*, pp. 207–9. In the main his view of Servius' methods agrees with the above, but he does not appear to be aware of the Irish folklore belief. It is far more likely that Virgil took his legend from prevalent tradition than that he 'invented' it. I can see no connection between the Golden Bough and the drawing of Arthur's sword, which belongs to a different set of legends, viz. the hero-test series.

3   In *G.B.*, iii, 455, n. 5, Mr Frazer seems suddenly to revert to this idea, though the whole of his previous argument hangs upon the bough bearing a different signification.

4   Ed. by Dr Kuno Meyer in Mr Nutt's *Voyage of Bran*, vol. i.

5   It is nowhere stated that the bough of Aeneas was the mistletoe. Virgil *compares* it to the mistletoe, which, as Mr A. Lang remarks, argues to the contrary.

6   I believe the mistletoe was rare in Ireland.

7   Ed. by Dr Whitley Stokes, *Irische Texte*, vol. iii, pp. 183–229.

8   Ed. by O'Beirne Crowe, *Kilkenny Archaeological Journal,* 1874–5, p. 118 etc.

9   Ed. by Dr Standish Hayes O'Grady, *Silva Gadelica*, pp. 342–59.

CHAPTER EIGHT

Illumination

George Henderson

ILLUMINATION EMBRACES EVERY FORM of vision and of magic knowledge. From being adepts in the magic arts, the wise man of old received the name of druid, *i.e.*, *dru-vid*, 'very knowing, very wise.'[1] This species of attempted knowledge ranges from the premonition (*meanmuin*) to various kinds of omens (*manadh, tuar, glaim*) and the arts of divination (*fiosachd, fàistneachd, tairngireachd, fàth-fìth*). The terms *fàth-fìth* or *fìth-fàth* was 'applied to the occult power which rendered a person invisible to mortal eyes and which transformed one object into another'.[2] Dr Joyce[3] has equated this with the *fáed-fíada* associated with St Patrick when he and his companions were transformed into deer on their way to Tara.

Vision in folk-belief may embrace the seeing of the semblance or form (*riochd*) of the departed by one who cannot recognize them, not having known them when alive. One of the instances in point is connected with the old manse of Lairg. That this house was haunted was long believed by the people in the parish to my own knowledge; nor is the belief yet dead. The Rev. Thomas Mackay, minister of Lairg, died in 1803. A son of a successor, the late Rev. A.G. MacGillivray, a most excellent man whom I warmly remember, tells the story in a lecture appended to William Mackay's *Narrative of the Shipwreck of the 'Juno'*,[4] of which Byron says it is one of the narratives in which poetry must be content to yield the palm to prose. MacGillivray, with whose father's[5] family the incident is connected, writes:

> It was firmly believed in our parish that Mr Thomas Mackay was once seen, twenty-three years after his death, in the old manse. Of course the story must have some satisfactory explanation, but it was not explained in my time. On a fine summer day, in 1826, two young girls were sitting in the manse dining-room; they heard a step advancing to the door, the door opened, and there stood a thin venerable old man, dressed in black, with knee breeches and buckles, black silk stockings, and shoes with buckles. He looked closely all round the room, at them, and then walked out. One of the girls ran upstairs and told the minister then in the manse that a very old minister had come in and was looking for him. The minister hurried down and looked for his visitor, but in vain; he could nowhere be found. The manse is so placed that every object can be seen for a quarter of a mile around, but not a trace of the visitor was visible. The old people who heard the girls describe the old man they had seen, declared that they

recognized Mr Thomas Mackay from their description. Ten or twelve years thereafter granddaughters of Mr Mackay came to reside in the parish. One of the young girls, by that time grown a woman, said to one of these ladies, 'Oh! how like you are to your grandfather'; to which the other replied, 'So the old people tell me, but how can you know that, for he died before you were born?' The other coloured and got confused, and could give no reply. She had recognized the lady's resemblance to the old minister who had appeared to her in the manse.

> I cannot say how the truth may be,
> I say the tale as 'twas told to me.

When it is the evil eye that has fallen on a creature, the person who makes the *snàithlean*, or magic 'thread,' for its cure is seized with a fit of yawning. It is by the *frìth* that those who cure the evil eye tell whether it be the eye of a male or female that has done the harm[6] (Benbecula). The longer the evil eye has lain on a creature unobserved, the longer it takes to be cured, and the sicker the person, becomes who makes the *snàithlein*.

In making the *frìth* some enjoin the reciting of the formula *through the hand loosely closed*. A formula used in Benbecula is: *Mise dol a mach orra* (= air do) *shlighe-sa, Dhé! Dia romham, Dia 'm dheaghaidh's Dia luirg! An t-eolas rinn Moire dha 'mac, shéid Brighd 'romh bas* (*glaic*). *Fios fìrinne gun fhios bréige; mar a fhuair ise gum faic mise samhladh air an rud a tha mi fhéin ag ìarraidh*, i.e., 'I am going out on thy path, O God! God be before me, God be behind me, God be in my footsteps. The charm which Mary (the Virgin) made for her Son, Brigit blew through her palms – knowledge of truth and no lie. As she found, may I see the likeness of what I myself am seeking.' The use of the *frìth* or horoscope is not at all extinct, as declared by a young woman who was present, and who actually asked the *frìth* to be made so that information might be got as to the state of health of a person at some distance who was ill. The woman who made the *frìth* said after making it that she would rather say the woman was dead. The woman was actually dead at the time, so my authority was informed.

It is not right for a woman to try and kindle the fire by fanning it with the skirt of her dress. The reason is that when Our Lord was going to be nailed to the Cross, and the nails were being got ready, that the smith's bellows refused to work, and the smith's daughter fanned the fire with her skirt.

The Omen (*Manadh*) forms the transition to what it is felt proper to do, and is thus the initial and rudimentary stage of illumination. It is a subjective sort of oracle. Early Irish *mana*, 'omen', is cognate with Latin *meneo*, Old English *manian*, 'warn'. Examples are: 'When one hears piping in the ears it is recommended to say a prayer for the dead.' Others say: 'May it be well for us and our friends; if thou it be who didst hear it, it will not be thou who wilt weep.'[7] For this piping is a sign of somebody dying at the time.

It was an omen of ill-luck to hear the cuckoo on its first return without having broken one's fast,[8] or to see a lamb with its back towards one if it were seen for the first time for the season.

If a cat mewed for flesh meat it was an omen of the death of a cow, and to avert the prediction one said: 'With your wanting (the meat of an animal), misfortune take thee! May it be thine own hide that will be the first hide to go on the roof-spar.'[9]

In the rite of 'averting', water is taken from a boundary stream and put into a vessel in which is a silver coin. The water is thrown over the beast. If the coin adheres to the bottom of the vessel it is taken as an omen that the evil eye was at work.

Another word for omen is *tuar*, used in that sense by Keating, and surviving in the

Highland proverb: *Cha do chuir gual chuige mach do chuir tuar thairis*, i.e., none ever set shoulder to that did not overcome foreboding. It is thus specially something foreboding of evil. Among such may be put the cry of a cuckoo heard from a house-top or chimney, as a presage of death to one of the inmates within the year. Mr Forbes notes for some district in Ireland that a cuckoo always appears to a certain family before a death in that family. He quotes the late Rev. Dr Stewart of Nether Lochaber as to a euphemistic way of speaking of the cuckoo as the 'grey bird of May-tide' (*ian glas a Chéitein*), it being discreet not to speak of it by its proper name. 'In the popular imagination so connected with fairyland was the cuckoo that the very name was in a sense taboo.'[10] The howling of the house dog at night is usually held to be an omen of a funeral that will soon pass by. In Breadalbane a moving ball of fire or a moving light (*gealbhan*) is a precursor of a funeral.[11] This corresponds to the *dreag, driug* of other parts. In Lochbroom a cat washing its face is an omen of its soon getting either fish or flesh: as there is a danger of its fulfilment being brought about through the death by mishap of cattle or sheep, the cat is given a cuff to stop it and avert the evil.[12] To be suddenly seized by peculiar sensations of horror at certain places may be an omen of one having drowned one's self there.[13] A white bird flapping its wings towards a burying ground is a precursor of a corpse and an omen of death.[14] An omen of calamity is known as *glaim*,[15] a peculiar sound in the ear, a howling; it has been taken as cognate with the German *klagen*, 'weep, complain': the root idea is 'make moan'. If a particle of food get into the wind-pipe it is polite to say: *Deiseal*, i.e., 'sun-ways or right! it is not grudging it that I am to thee.'[16]

When going from home with a mare at early morning it is a good omen if one put the right foot over and around the beast's head in name of the Father, and then make the sign of the Cross on one's self, which ensures that no witch or evil spirit can come nigh. It was said of a country carrier who did so: R.M. never went from home without putting his left foot over his mare's head in the name of the Father, and making the sign of the Cross of Christ on himself, and then no wizard nor any evil spirit could come nigh him.[17]

Prognostications were made from the 'first-foot':[18] to meet a woman with red hair was unlucky; a beast, man or thing unexpectedly encountered on stepping out of doors or on setting out on a journey betokened weal or woe. On entering a new abode it was unlucky to find a dead crow before one on the hearthstone. Out of ill-will it has been known to have been put in the pulpit of a vacant parish.

Some stones or crystals have associations with curative magical agencies: such are the Ardvoirlich Charm, Barbreck's Stone, the Loch Mo Nair Stone, and the varieties of 'witch' stones one has known of; others are associated with clairvoyance and divination, such as Coinneach Odhar's Stone; a few may be specially remarkable as having been *omens* of success: the merits imputed to such have influenced human lives, and their story belongs to local history. An instance of a stone of good omen is that of *Clach Na Brataich*, i.e., the Banner Stone of the Clan Robertson. Its story as told by Mr D. Robertson[19] is as follows:

In joining the muster of St Ninians under King Robert Bruce, previous to the Battle of Bannockburn, Donnachadh Reamhar encamped with his men on their march to the rendezvous. On pulling up the standard pole out of the ground one morning before marching off, the chief observed something glittering in a clod of earth which adhered to the end of the staff. He immediately plucked it out, and there being something apparently fateful in such an incident occurring under such circumstances, he retained it in his own possession after holding it up to his followers, as a happy omen of success in the fortunes of their expedition.

It became associated with the glorious victory of Bannockburn, and thenceforth was accepted by the clan as its Stone of Destiny or Palladium. It has always been carried by the chief on his person when the clan mustered for war or foray, and its various changes of hue were consulted as to the result of the coming strife.

It was carried by 'The Tutor' when in command of Clan Donnachaidh under the great Montrose, and the Poet Chief carried it gallantly at the head of 500 of his men at Sheriffmuir. On this occasion he, as his ancestors had done before him, consulted the oracle, and observed for the first time an extensive flaw or crack in it. This was accepted as an adverse omen, inasmuch as the Stuart cause was for the time crushed, and from this time, it has been held, dates the decline of the power and influence of the clan.

But besides being regarded merely as a warlike emblem, the 'Clach na Brataich' was also employed as a charm-stone against sickness. It was, after a short preliminary prayer, dipped in water by the chief, who then with his own hands distributed the water thus qualified to the applicants for it. In this connection it was used by the grandfather of the present chief, in whose possession it now of course remains. For a time it was deposited by him in the museum of the Society of Antiquaries of Scotland for the inspection of the public, but serious warnings were addressed to him as to the fatality which might result.

In form it is a ball of clear rock crystal, in appearance like glass, two inches in diameter, and has been supposed to be a druidical beryl. It may, however, quite as probably be one of those crystal balls which have from time to time been unearthed from ancient graves in the country, and which are said to be the abodes of good or evil spirits, or amulets against sickness or the sword. These symbols were usually carried on the person of the chief, attached to his girdle or suspended from his helmet.

The ancient rite of divination by dream was once regarded as in the last resort a reasonable and proper method of ascertaining the person appropriate to be king. We read in *The Sickbed of Cuchulainn* of a 'bull-feast' being made the occasion of superinducing such a dream.

It is thus that the bull-feast was wont to be made, viz., a white bull was killed and a man partook to his full of its flesh and juice, and slept under that satiety while a spell of truth was chaunted over him by four druids, and in vision there would be divined by him the semblance of the man who would be made king there from his form and description and the manner of work which was performed. The man woke up from his sleep and related his vision.[20]

Lugaidh of the Red Stripes, the pupil of Cuchulainn, who was then lying ill, was so recognized and proclaimed monarch of Ireland.

In the *Sack of Da Derga's Hostel*[21] we read that Conaire was thus elected. Though really begotten by a supernatural bird-man, he was regarded as the son of his predecessor Eterscéle. But this does not seem to have given him any title to succeed. A bull-feast was accordingly given; and the bull-feaster in his sleep at the end of the night beheld a man stark-naked passing along the road of Tara with a stone in his sling. Warned and counselled by his bird relatives, Conaire fulfilled these requirements. He found three kings (doubtless from among the under-kings of Ireland) awaiting him with royal raiment to clothe his nakedness, and a chariot to convey him to Tara. It was a disappointment to the folk of Tara to find that their bull-feast and their spell of truth chanted over the feaster had resulted in the selection of a beardless lad. But he convinced them that he was the true successor, and was admitted to the kingship.

Divination in later times takes various forms, chief of which of old was (*slinneineachd*) the reading of omens in shoulder blades. About forty years ago the shoulder blade of a bear (*math-ghamhuin*) took in belief a foremost place, but as this could not be got, that of a fox or sheep might be used. X.Y., the wife of L.C.Z., who was credited with the gift of stopping blood by a spell, lost one of her young boys. He was missed, and though searched for, he could not be found. G.P., a man notable in the line of finding any dead bodies, failed. She then betook her to a wise man who could divine by reading the omens on the shoulder blades of a bear.[22] He divined and told her to walk to a certain part of the hill which stretched away from her house; he described certain stones near to which the body was to be found. She went thither; found her boy as a heap of bones; she carried them home and had them buried. This falls under the *scapulimantia* of Grimm,[23] and is met with among many races. A kindred rite survives in the reading of one's fate as to marriage in the 'merry thought' or breast-bone of a fowl. One's vision of the future was widened by prognostications of all sorts by the seeing of wraiths and the barking of dogs before funerals, by the phenomena of second sight and of phantom-funerals and death-lights. Special honour was accorded to any traces of the presence of St Brigit on Candlemas Eve. This belief was until recently held in Arisaig. It existed, as we learn from Moore, in the Isle of Man, and Martin[24] writes:

> The mistress and servants of each family take a sheaf of oats and dress it up in woman's apparel, put it in a large basket and lay a wooden club by it, and this they call Briid's bed, and then the mistress and servants cry three times: 'Briid is come, Briid is welcome.' This they do just before going to bed, and when they rise in the morning, they look among the ashes expecting to see the impression of Briid's club there, which if they do they reckon it a true presage of a good crop and a prosperous year, and the contrary they take as an ill omen.

Gregorson Campbell has a section dealing with Premonitions and Divination (*Fiosachd*): for his instances suffice it to refer to his book.[25] He gives prophecies attributed to the Lady of Lawers and to Coinneach Odhar, 'whose name is hardly known in Argyllshire'. Consequently he only devotes a page to him, in which we learn that Kenneth acquired his prophetic gift from a stone found in a raven's nest. The variants of Kenneth's legend are instructive.

The Inverness-shire tradition of Coinneach Odhar takes us back to the birth of the seer. Here we have a story with so strong a resemblance to that of Brian as to show that the tale belongs to a remote period. If I take the Skye tradition there is evidence of interest.

> *We* in Bracadale, Duirinish, never heard that Coinneach Odhar was a Mackenzie, or that his death took place at so recent a date as the seventeenth century, That could not have been. We never heard of the manner of his death. The historian Mackenzie mixed the legend of the original Coinneach with the true fact as to the cruel death of a certain Kenneth who was possessed of clairvoyant faculties and who was buried below the town of Fortrose.

So states Miss Fanny Tolmie, a lady of rare talent and exceptional knowledge of Skye and its traditions. Miss Tolmie's account is as follows:

On a Hallowe'en the people of Boisdale in South Uist were assembling, according to long-established custom, to spend some hours together in mirth and dance. There was a cattle-fold in the neighbourhood which was always watched by night, and on this occasion the duty of guarding it devolved on two young women, who were vexed that they should thus be excluded from participating in the general enjoyment. Casting in their minds how they might find a substitute, they bethought them of an elderly maid who lived in a cottage at no distance from the fold, which in the remote past had been a burying-ground, and probably was of pre-Christian date. The woman acceded kindly to their request, and repaired to her watching station with her distaff in her hand, where she sat beside a fire for a while, spinning peacefully. There were some graves close to where she was sitting, and about midnight she was astonished and awe-stricken to see them moving and heaving and forms emerging from them and passing out of sight in all directions, north, south, east and west. Venturing to approach one of these open graves which seemed larger than the rest, she laid her distaff across the opening, waiting to see the result of this action. Before long the spectres began to return one by one, and every one lay down in his own place while the sod became firm and green over the grave as it had been before.

Last of all arrived the occupant of the largest grave, who seemed to have had a longer way to go, and who, seeing the distaff, exclaimed to the woman: 'Why dost thou hinder me from lying down in peace?' 'First tell me,' she replied, 'who thou art, where thou hast been, and what is to be my fate, and then I will allow thee return once more to thy resting-place.' He answered: 'I was a warrior from Lochlinn and, after having been wrecked and drowned, my body was washed ashore in Boisdale. The corpse of one of my companions, whose name was Til, was found on the west coast of Skye, at a place which has been named after him, Poll' til. It is permitted to us on Hallowe'en to visit our native lands, and I have just been to Lochlinn for an hour. This is what in the fulness of time shall happen to thee: though no longer young, thou shalt bear a son who will be a prophet.' Then raising the distaff, the warrior lay down, and the grave closed over him.

When the elderly woman gave birth to a son, there was great wonder in the land. She named him Coinneach, in addition to which name, because of his sallow complexion, he received the surname of *Odhar*. Coinneach Odhar's name is still well known all over the Highlands and Hebridean Isles, and several districts claim to have given him birth. He received the blue stone of prophecy from the *Maighdeann Shìdhe* or Banshee, with the injunction that he was never to give it to any one. He was once pursued by a wicked person, who wished to wrest from him the precious stone, as he was walking near Loch Ness. Fearful of being overcome, he flung the stone into the lake, crying that a pike (*geadas*) would swallow it, and that in after times it would be found again by a man who would have four and twenty fingers and toes, and two navels, who would also with it receive the prophetic power.

Some prophecies attributed to him in Skye are:

Tribesmen will cross over linns and will leave this isle a black isle of foreigners.

The folks of the white coats, and those of the red coats in Rome will meet in Baileshear.

Six oarsmen will bring every Macleod in the country around Gob-an-t-snoid, beyond Dunvegan Head.

In the battle the ravens will drink their fill from the stone of Ard Uige, and from a stone in Glendale.

St Columba's stone in Snizort churchyard will turn right about.

In Ireland, Brian of the saga appears in *Red Brian Carabine's Prophecy*, which gives the title to a collection of much merit we owe to Mr Michael O Tiománaidhe.[26] He is there pictured as having had his abode at Fál Ruadh, a village in Erris, by the seaside; a decent man who at first did not possess the prophetic gift which was bestowed on him about 1648. At a rent collection he had gone surety for a poor widow and paid on her behalf, whereby he received the divine favour, the woman having taken God to witness that she would pay on such and such a day. 'I like to have another (to give surety) in company with God,' said the lord of the land. Crossing a hill on his way home, what should happen but that Brian fell asleep for he knew not how long. He had a dream, and it was told him in vision that what he would find in the right sleeve of his coat he was to carefully put by, without letting wife nor child nor any one have a sight of it save himself alone. It was a sparkling jewel, which clearly revealed to him the future, both good and evil; a magic stone of prophecy which shone with resplendent lustre. Numerous are the prophecies ascribed him; they are of a nature parallel to those of the Highland Coinneach Odhar, Dun Kenneth. At last his wife's curiosity was aroused, and one day, as she saw him gazing at the magic stone, she came behind him, and what portion of the crystal her eye fell on became black as coal and shone no more. He has the faculty of foreseeing the approach of death in his own case and in that of others. One day, while dictating his visions to his son, a poor woman entered, and she was scornfully rebuked by the busy scribe. 'List to her,' quoth Brian, 'for some of thine own bodily members will perish seven years before thyself.' And true this proved to be, for the son lost a finger which was buried in earth. But when this fore-warning was foretold to Brian's son, he angrily cast the prophetic record into the fire. The first portion had already been thrown into a pool, and thus the written prophecies of Brian perished. Naturally, what survives has come down by word of mouth, and forms the subject of fireside entertainments in West Ireland, in the discourses of William Fleming in Leth-ardan; of Seamus Mac Enri, Inish Bigil; of Seaghan O Conway, Dubh-Thuma; all of which is duly recorded in Michael Timony's narrative. The story of the loss of the written prophecy is similar to a tale told me at Loch Arkaig of how Ossian's works and the history of the Féinne have for the most part perished, having been cast into the fire in his anger by St Patrick. He found them to be mostly lies; but his daughter rescued some!

The legend of Brian the wizard-hermit much resembles in essentials what is told in Highland legend of Coinneach Odhar (Sallow or Dun Kenneth), whose legend does not all fit in with so modern a date as that of the Kenneth on whom Lady Seaforth wreaked her vengeance for his prophecies. It seems to have been taken as fact that a certain unfortunate crystal gazer, possessed of what were held to be clairvoyant faculties, suffered at the hands of the Lady Mackenzie of Seaforth, who is associated with the sad fate of Coinneach Odhar, the Brahan seer, whose prophecies were published in a second edition at Inverness in 1878 by the late Mr Alexander Mackenzie, and reprinted some years ago with a preface by Mr Andrew Lang. The material, however, was collected by the late Mr A.B. MacLennan[27] and forwarded to the editor of the *Celtic Magazine* for insertion. This gives the Ross-shire version. When the old legend got mixed up with a later personality on the Mackenzie of Seaforth's estates, it was natural that his birth should be located at Baile-na-Cille, Uig, Lewis. While his mother one evening was tending cattle in a summer shieling on a ridge called Cnoc-eothail, overlooking the burying ground of Baile-na-Cille (i.e., Kirk-ton), she saw, says the legend, about the still hour of midnight, the whole of the graves in the churchyard opening and a vast multitude of people of every age, from the newly born babe to the gray-haired sage, rising from their graves, and going away in every conceivable direction. In an hour they began to return, and were all soon after back in their graves, which closed upon them as before. But, on scanning the burying-ground more closely, Kenneth's mother observed one grave, near the side, still open. Being a courageous woman, she determined to ascertain the cause of this singular circumstance, so hastening to the grave, and placing her *cuigeal* or 'distaff' athwart its mouth (for she had heard it said that the spirit could not enter the grave again while that instrument was upon it), she watched the result. She had not to wait long, for in a minute or two she noticed a fair lady coming in the direction of the churchyard, rushing through the air from the north. On her arrival, the fair one addressed her thus: 'Lift thy distaff from off my grave, and let me enter my dwelling of the dead.'

'I shall do so,' answered the other, 'when you explain to me what detained you so long after your neighbours.'

'That you shall soon hear,' the ghost replied; 'my journey was much longer than theirs – I had to go all the way to Norway.' She then addressed her:

I am a daughter of the King of Norway, I was drowned while bathing in that country; my body was found on the beach close to where we now stand, and I was interred in this grave. In remembrance of me, and as a small reward for your intrepidity and courage, I shall possess you of a valuable secret – go and find in yonder lake a small round blue stone, which give to your son, Kenneth, who by it shall reveal future events.

She did as requested, found the stone, and gave it to her son, Kenneth. No sooner had he thus received the gift of divination than his fame spread far and wide. Being born on the lands of Seaforth, he was more associated with that family than with any other in the country, and he latterly removed to the neighbourhood of Loch Ussie, on the Brahan estate.[28]

Tradition associated this Loch with his death. For having at a gathering at Brahan Castle, legend says, given expression to some remarks displeasing to Lady Seaforth and others, his punishment was determined on. Having no way of escape, he applied his magic white stone to his eye, uttered the well-known prophetic curse:

I see into the far future, and I read the doom of the race of my oppressor. The long descended line of Seaforth will, ere many generations have passed, end in extinction and in sorrow. I see a chief, the last of his house, both deaf and dumb. He will be the father of four fair sons, all of whom he will follow to the tomb. He will live care-worn and die mourning, knowing that the honours of his line are to be extinguished for ever, and that no future chief of the Mackenzies shall bear rule at Brahan or in Kintail. After lamenting over the last and most promising of his sons, he himself shall sink into the grave, and the remnant of his possessions shall be inherited by a white-coifed (or white-hooded) lassie from the East, and she is to kill her sister. And as a sign by which it may be known that these things are coming to pass, there shall be four great lairds in the days of the last deaf and dumb Seaforth – Gairloch, Chisholm, Grant and Raasay – of whom one shall be bucktoothed, another hair-lipped, another half-witted, and the fourth a stammerer. Chiefs distinguished by these personal marks shall be the allies and neighbours of the last Seaforth; and when he looks round and sees them, he may know that his sons are doomed to death, that his broad lands shall pass away to the stranger, and that his race shall come to an end.

The prediction ended, he threw the white stone into the loch, declaring that the finder thereof would be similarly gifted. Another version has it that he then threw the stone into a cow's foot-mark, which was full of water, declaring that a child would be born with two navels, or, as some say, with four thumbs and six toes, who would in course of time discover it inside a pike, and who would then be gifted with the seer's power.

> As it was the purpose of his pursuers to obtain possession of this wonderful stone, as well as of the prophet's person, search was eagerly made for it in the muddy waters in the footprint, when, lo! it was found that more water was copiously oozing from the boggy ground around, and rapidly forming a considerable lake, that effectually concealed the much-coveted stone. The waters steadily increased, and the result, as the story goes, was the formation of Loch Ussie. The poor prophet was then taken to Chanonry Point, where the stern arm of ecclesiastical authority, with unrelenting severity, burnt him to death in a tar-barrel for witchcraft.[29]

His attainment of the seer's gift is invariably connected with this stone. He got it, says one version, as he was out on the hill cutting peats. His mistress, a farmer's wife, greatly annoyed at his seeing-gift, determined to poison the food which was to be sent to him. It was somewhat late in arriving, and, exhausted, it is said that:

> he lay down on the heath and fell into a heavy slumber. In this position he was suddenly awakened by feeling something cold in his breast, which on examination he found to be a small white stone, with a hole through the centre. He looked through it, when a vision appeared to him, which revealed the treachery and diabolical intention of his mistress. To test the truth of the vision, he gave the dinner intended for himself to his faithful collie; the poor brute writhed and died soon after in the greatest agony.[30]

Another variant is that, resting his head upon a little knoll, he waited the arrival of his wife with his dinner, whereupon he fell asleep. On awaking he felt something hard under his head, and, examining the cause of the uneasiness, discovered a small round stone with a hole through the middle. He picked it up, and looking through it he saw, by the aid of this prophetic stone, that his wife was coming to him with a dinner consisting of sowans and milk, polluted though, unknown to her, in a manner which, as well as several other particulars connected with it, we forbear to mention. But Coinneach found that, though this stone was the means by which a supernatural power had been conferred upon him, it had, as its very first application, deprived him of the sight of that eye with which he looked through it, and he continued ever afterwards *cam*, or blind of an eye.[31] Kenneth's prophecies vary in different parts of the Highlands; some of them may have touches in common with those credited to Thomas the Rhymer, whose legend, however, has elements that go back on native folk belief of the premediaeval age. This finds confirmation in that the death of the Kenneth said to have been burnt at Chanonry is placed under the third Earl of Seaforth, who was born in 1635. But Mr W.M. Mackenzie has found in a Commission against witchcraft, issued in Ross-shire in 1577, a reference to Coinneach Odhar as the head of a school of witchcraft even then.

Coinneach's legend is essentially the same as the Irish one of Red Brian Carabine, but it is in continuous development. In a modern Lewis poem of seventy quatrains, which is in Mr J.N. Macleod's still unpublished collection, there is a different version of the getting of the stone. Coinneach is depicted as on the strand, when a lady appears in the form of a light, and tells her story. After the light turns into a maiden, she declares herself as Gràdhag, daughter of King Swaran of the North. Arna, priest of Odin, was a keen seer, and possessed of a Stone of Virtues, prepared by Odin himself. The king having ordered the priest to be shot with an arrow, the maiden Gràdhag (Dear One) intervened, and saved the priest's life, for which she got the prophetic stone. Then she is pictured as having seen Diarmuid and the Fianna in vision, and seized by a desire to come to Alba, whereupon Swaran determines on invading Eire and on conquering Finn. The lady was shipwrecked on the way, and the stone hidden in the sand at a spot which her wraith points out. Whereupon she changes her human form to a gleam of light, which twinkled thrice, and then vanished. Kenneth dug at the spot and found the jewel, which gold could not buy; such were its virtues.

But Illumination has its widest popular development apart from Stones of Virtue, and under the category of second sight (*an dà shealladh*, i.e., the two sights), which has a literature of its own.[32] Under peculiar psychic conditions the reproductive imagination, working upon memory images, transforms what might remain as 'conjecture' into vision. It takes on the aspect of 'first sight' proper, as when one has a vision of a person absolutely strange to one, and with such vividness that one recognizes what answers to all the foreseen details in actual life afterwards. Parallel to this is the case of the coming of strangers being interpreted from a premonition or warning (*tàrmachduinn*), such as sounds from the opening of presses, or other articles; as also the seeing of forms, which one recognizes afterwards on the arrival of strangers whose 'doubles', it is thought, must have manifested themselves beforehand. This is the so-called phenomenon of apparent double presence. The following incident, of which the scene is in Sutherland, will suffice to illustrate this phantasy or vision proper:

> One evening a crofter was sitting outside his cottage door, when he saw a stranger coming along the high road towards the house. He watched the man for some minutes till, leaving the main road, the traveller took a branch path leading to the crofter's door. The crofter then stepped inside for a moment to inform his wife of the approach of a visitor. On going out again he was more than puzzled to find that the stranger had in the brief interval completely vanished. The house stood, and still stands, on a slight eminence from which an unobstructed view can be had of the immediate neighbourhood. But though the astonished crofter looked on all sides, he could see nothing further of the stranger. None of the villagers whose houses he must have passed had observed him. It is important to note that the crofter there and then gave a full description of the man to his wife and to a brother. In a short time the incident, uncanny though it was, was forgotten. Some months later a child of the same crofter was suddenly taken ill. The doctor, a young practitioner who had but recently come into the district, was sent for, and in the course of the day the father was standing at the door of his cottage waiting impatiently for the doctor's arrival, when, at a bend of the road, appeared the mysterious stranger of several months before. He turned out to be the expected doctor; but in features, dress, and appearance generally he was the exact counterpart of the individual who had formerly presented himself. On inquiry it was ascertained that the doctor had never before been in the neighbourhood, and on the particular day in question had been in the south of Scotland. The crofter, his wife, and brother, most respectable and estimable people, are still hale and hearty, and fond of describing this remarkable incident. (*Chambers's Journal*)

Notes

1 This derivation by Thurneysen may be upheld, but the name may have been extended also to the 'wise men' of the pre-Celtic peoples who brought over their own rites when the incorporation of the various races took place.

2 *Carmina Gadelica*, ii. p. 22, where a specimen of this incantation is given.

3 *Social History of Ireland*, i, p. 386.

4 *Reprint for the Clan Mackay Society*, 1892, p. 88.

5 The Rev. Duncan MacGillivray succeeded in 1817.

6 There is a rite of blessing oneself when making the *frìth* if a woman be seen – she being the omen of some untoward event or other.

7 Gum bu slàn sin oirn-ne is air ar daoine!
   Mas tu chuala cha tu chaoineas.

8 See under *Bird-Soul*.

9 Le d' iarraidh, dosgadh ort!
   Gur e do sheice fhéin a chiad sheic a théid air an sparr.

10 Forbes, *Gaelic Names of Beasts, Birds, Fishes, Insects and Reptiles*, p. 263.

11 *Gaelic Soc. Inv. Trans.* 26, pp. 126 and 42.

12 *Ibid.* p. 265.

13 *Ibid.* pp. 292–3.

14 *Ibid.* 25, p. 127.

15 *Ibid.* 25, p. 130.

16 Chan ann ga mhaoidheadh ort atá mi.

17 Cha deach' R – M – riamh o'n tigh leis an làir aige, gun a chas dheas chur timchioll a ceann an ainm an Athar is crois Chriosda chur air; 's cha robh buitseach no droch spiorad sam bith a b'urrainn thighinn 'na chòir.

18 Comh-dhalaiche; German, *An-gang;* Latin, *primitiae.*

19 *A Brief Account of the Clan Donnachie, with Notes on its History and Traditions.*

20 For the original see Windisch's *Irische Texte*, i, p. 213.

21 *Orgain Brudne Da Dergae*, a text of about the end of the eighth century.

22 Duine còir a leughadh slinneagan a' mhathghamhna.

23 *Teut. Myth.* ed. by Stallybrass, p. 1113.

24 *Western Isles*, p. 119.

25 *Superstitions of the Scottish Highlands*, p. 258.

26 *Targaireacht Bhriain Ruaidh Ui Chearbháin* (Gill & Son, Dublin, 1906).

27 His name is referred to on pages 9, 13, 19, 45, 55, 80 of the 1878 edition; at the foot of page 3, a whole passage is omitted.

28 *Prophecies of the Brahan Seer*, pp. 4–5; cf. 1878 ed.

29 *Ibid.*, pp. 78–9.

30 *Ibid.*, p. 6.

31 *Ibid.* p. 7.

32 *Highland Second-Sight*, ed. by N. Macrae, with Introductory Study by Rev. William Morrison (George Souter, Dingwall).

CHAPTER NINE

The Spells of Women

The Sacred and Magical Role of the Celtic Ninefold Sisterhoods

Caitlin Matthews

NINE IS A COMMON SACRED number throughout the world, since it triples the already sacred number three. Within both insular and continental Celtic tradition, we find the tradition of a threefold goddess and of ninefold nymphs, spirits and priestesses. Let us first examine the threefold female divine pattern, which is the mythic template from which the ninefold aspects arise.

The Threefold

The threefold deities of fate, common to European tradition, appear in many guises: as the Roman Parcae or 'Apportioners', equivalent to the Greek Moirae, daughters of Nyx who, in the Myth of Er,[1] sit about the spindle of necessity on which the thread of life is spun and round which the gifting planetary powers are dispensed. Similarly, there are the Norns of Northern tradition – Urdr (Fate), Verthandi (Being) and Skuld (Necessity) – who tend the World Tree, Yggdrasil, maintaining the life of the universe.

The underlying metaphor of the Fates is of the thread of life with the thread of material. In the processing of thread, we see a progressively more responsible task unfolding: the distaff, the maiden's staff of office, is connected with singing and women's societies, since spinning of flax or wool is a communal activity that must be done before the more solitary and concentrated task of weaving, usually the mature woman's task. The cutting of the cloth and its fitting is associated with the older woman.[2]

The Moirae spin and sing simultaneously, and we discover that the casting of spells and enchantments (literally, en-singings) is the main accusation levelled against women. The work of oracular divining, of enchantment and bespelling are often juxtaposed with a weaving of a more usual nature, as we see in *Taín Bó Cuailgnè*, in which Queen Medbh encounters the seer, Fedelm, a *ban-faith* or seer, who gave Medbh oracular answers while twirling her spindle.[3]

These threefold goddesses oversee the fate of earth's inhabitants and underlie the medieval concept of the Fates and faery-godmothers, who gift the newborn with destined qualities and abilities.[4] Saxo Germanicus tells a story about the Danish king, Fridleif, who took his three-year-old son, Olaf, into the house of the gods to pray to 'three maidens sitting on three seats'. The first two granted him the gifts of charm and generosity, but the third said that he would nonetheless be niggardly in his giving.[5] This description sounds like the Mothers, the Matronae, of both the Rhineland and the Celtic countries, who are depicted as a trio of mature goddesses with cornucopias, bread, fruit and other gifts in many Romano-Celtic dedications.[6]

In the Germanic and Celtic regions of the Rhine, inscriptions to goddesses known as the Gabiae (Givers/Controllers) or Matronae Gabiae (the Gifting/Controlling Mothers) are frequent. A Gaulish inscription to the goddess Garmangabis (Weaver of Fate) also exists and may relate to the Irish goddess, Carman, who is the eponymous founder of the seasonal fair, the Oenach Carmain, in Leinster.[7] The cult of the triple mothers, the Matronae or Matres, was localized to northwestern Europe in countries under Roman occupation. Dedications address them as the 'Mothers of' such-and-such a place, with a variety of locations appropriate to the dedicand's origins, much as modern churches are dedicated to Our Lady of a particular locality.

The Celtic Mothers, in common with the Moirae, Parcae and Norns, are clearly seen as givers of destiny. Although most often depicted as of similar, mature age, some threefold groups show younger and older women. Triple deities are common to Celtic tradition, sharing a common Indo-European derivation, elements of which can be discerned as far abroad as India and Ireland. In Ireland, for example, we find the triplicity of the Morrighan, the triad of catabolic goddesses responsible for victory, battle, and prophecy, known as Morrighan, Badbh and Macha; we may compare the triple goddesses of Irish sovereignty, Eriu, Fodla and Banba; and the triple aspected Brighid, who is the matron of poetry, healing and smithcraft. This last goddess has, as we shall see, direct correlatives with the ninefold sisters of Celtic mythology.

The Ninefold Nymphs

This essay takes its title from an eighth-century Irish lorica or 'breastplate' prayer, which has been called the 'Deer's Cry', a prayer ascribed to St Patrick, which, among other things, invokes divine protection against *fri brichtu ban ocus gobann ocus druad* ('the spells of women, smiths and druids').[8] Why was such earnest prayer required as a protection? We can understand that druids represented the old pagan beliefs and that the magic of smiths was a by-word in Celtic tradition, but what kind of women are being supplicated against here?

This prayer is not alone. The *Amra Columb Cille*, composed by the chief poet known as Dallán Forgaill, of Mag Slécht in Bréifne in Connacht (modern Moynehall, Co. Cavan) some time after St Columba's death in AD597, is an elegiac poem in praise of Columba, composed in the allusive, occluded style of the ancient Gaelic *fili*. Because its composition was prophesied by Columba before his death and because of the saint's promise that all who recite it daily shall see heaven, it was reverentially transcribed and copied by many. The final stanza of this poem is an appeal to God to protect the poet (and reciter) from various dangers, one of which is *rotomsib-sa sech riagu* ('bring me past torments').[9]

These torments are glossed by the anonymous transcriber as 'demons', notably 'the daughters of Oircc, the three daughters of Phorcus who are variously named in heaven, in earth and in hell. In heaven Sthenio [sic], Euryale and Medusa; in earth, Clotho, Lachesis, Atropos; in hell, Alecto, Megaera, Tisiphone'.[10]

The gloss betrays a significant knowledge of classical myths because the children of Oircc or Phorcus (the Old Man of the Sea) by Keto (a primordial sea-creature) are Ladon and Echidna, the three Gorgons (Stheno, Euryale and Medusa) and the three Graiae (Enyo, Pemphredo and Deino) – a family corporately known as the Phorcids.[11] The Gorgons lived in the regions of Night, beyond Okeanos, with the clear-singing Hesperides, a region commonly believed to be in the northwest of Europe. While classical tradition assigns them to an overseas realm, the *Amra* locates them in the celestial pagan equivalent of heaven.

Clotho, Lachesis and Atropos, the three daughters of the goddess Nyx or Night, are together known as the Moirae (Fates). They have the duties of spinning the life-thread, apportioning the fate and of cutting life's thread of each individual. The Orphics believed that they lived in heaven in a cave from which white waters issued. The *Amra* locates them as earthly spirits.

Alecto, Megaera and Tisiphone, the daughters of Gaia, goddess of Earth, are known as the Erinyes (the Angry Ones or Furies) or, euphemistically, as the Eumenides (the Kindly Ones). Alecto (the Neverending), Tisiphone (the Retaliator) and Megaera (Envious Anger) are an infernal triad in both classical and Gaelic traditions.

The glossator of the *Amra* speaks of a ninefold sisterhood of great power, drawing upon classical warrants for his fear, yet such ninefold sisters are found widely within Celtic tradition, and by shrouding their collective identity here by names from other cultures the glossator is, perhaps purposely, inveighing against (and incidentally ignoring) something closer to home.

A tradition of the daughters of Ocean is recorded elsewhere in an early Irish breastplate prayer against the encroachments of age. This invocation draws upon ancient druidic traditions now lost to us:

> I invoke the seven daughters of Ocean
> who weave the threads of the sons of age.
> Three deaths be taken from me,
> three life-times be given me,
> seven waves of surety be granted me.
> No illusions disturb my journey,
> in brilliant lorica without hurt.[12]

Ocean's Daughters become seven rather than ninefold, possibly due to the association of their influence upon the 'seven candles' of vitality instanced in a subsequent stanza:

> I shall not be injured by a bevy of women nor a gang of armed men.
> May the King of the Universe stretch time for me!
> I invoke Senach of the seven aeons,
> fostered by *sidhe* [faery] women on nurturing breasts. May my seven candles never be
>   extinguished![13]

We note again that the reciter is fearful of the 'spells of women', although he implores the aid of Senach, 'the Ancient One' – an unidentified hero from the otherworld – who was himself reared by faery women. We may compare the Norse legend of Heimdall, the watchman of the rainbow Bifrost, who is born of 'nine giant maids, on the edge of earth'. These nine daughters of Aegir, the god of the Sea, may be his foster-mothers and teachers.[14]

Who are these women, to invite such paranoia? The association of otherworldly sisterhoods with powers of harm or healing is particularly relevant to pan-Celtic tradition, which, although fed by classical elements of the Moirae, Parcae and Ocean's daughters, nevertheless betray a consistent three- or ninefold nature from early times down to the Middle Ages. The association of the sea with otherworldly sisterhoods is also borne out by both myth and early testimony.

In two of the *immrama* or otherworldly voyage stories of early Irish tradition, the Island of Women is the goal of both Bran mac Febal and of Maelduin.[15] When King Arthur makes his perilous descent to Annwfn, the British underworld, in the ninth-century poem *Preiddeu Annwn*, he goes in search of a cauldron where 'the breath of nine muses keeps it boiling'.[16] When Arthur is mortally wounded, he is ferried to the Island of Avalon to be healed by the goddess, Morgen, and her eight sisters.[17]

To go beyond the ninth wave in Gaelic tradition was to leave the shores of known land and enter into liminal regions, possibly into the realms of the nine sisters. The tradition of nine sisters as the most ancient rememberers and wise ones can be observed in both classical and Celtic traditions. In a fragment of Hesiod, we read:

The croaking cormorant lives nine generations of ageing men.
The stag (lives) four times the cormorant;
the crow outlives three stags
but the phoenix (outlives) nine crows;
and we, the fair-haired nymphs,
daughters of aegis-bearing Zeus, outlive ten phoenixes.[18]

We may set alongside Hesiod's list, this Scots Gaelic saying collected in the nineteenth century, which enumerates the nine times nine lives of the faery kind. It suggests that, in the latter phases of their myth, the divinity of sisters seems to decline and they become identified as faery-women.

Nine nines sucking the breast,
Nine nines unsteady, weak,
Nine nines on foot, swift,
Nine nines able and strong,
Nine nines strapping, brown,
Nine nines victorious, subduing,
Nine nines bonneted, drab,
Nine nines beardy, grey.
Nine nines on the breast-beating death, And worse to me were these miserable nine
    nines
Than all the other short-lived nine nines that were.[19]

In what manner does this mythic evidence suggest actual native sisterhoods in Celtic countries? Was there real fear behind the protective prayers against the dangers of 'the spells of women?' Were there actual bands of women fulfilling these roles? We know from a variety of Classical sources that such sisterhoods did exist, with both sacred function and magical ability, around the Celtic coastlands of western Europe. Tacitus in his *Annales* (xiv, 30) speaks of women on the Island of Mona facing the attack by Suetonius Paulinus. He says that they ran about the soldiery, dressed in funeral clothing like the Furies, their hair unbound and flourishing brands, while the druids rained down curses on the Romans. Tacitus does not comment on the function of these women nor upon their relationship with druidry.[20]

Although druidesses, *bandruaid*, appear in Irish textual sources, they are not clearly identified as such in other insular or continental traditions, save for two accounts of Gaulish druidesses who predicted the imperial careers of both Diocletian and Aurelian's descendants.[21]

We discern two distinct kinds of magical women from the written evidence: on the one hand, the individual lone women who are seers or oracular poets and prophetesses, such as Veleda and Ganna, mentioned by Tacitus, and the *ban-faithi*, or female seers of Irish tradition, and, on the other hand, groups of women who live together, remotely and frequently on islands.

Pomponius Mela and Strabo both write about Gaulish sisterhoods. Pomponius Mela (in *De Situ Orbis* III, 6, 48) writes of:

> The island of Sein, near the Ossimiens, is known because of the oracle of a Gaulish God; the priestesses of that divinity are nine in number; the Gauls call them 'Senes'; they believe that, animated by a particular spirit, they can by their spells create storms in the air and on the sea, take the appearance of any sort of animals, cure the most serious illnesses, know and foretell the future, but only to those seamen who go over the ocean to see them.[22]

Strabo (in *Geography* IV, 4,6.) reports a similar regime:

> A small island in the ocean not far from the land, lying off the mouth of the Loire; and the women of the Samnitae inhabit it; they are possessed by Dionysus and propitiate the god with initiations and other sacred rites; and no man may land on the island, but the women themselves sail out from it and have intercourse with men and then return. It is their custom once a year to remove the roof from their temple and to roof it again the same day before sunset, each woman carrying part of the burden; but the woman whose load falls from her is torn to pieces by the others, and they carry the pieces around the temple crying out 'euoi' and do not cease until their madness passes away; and it always happens that someone pushes against the woman who is destined to suffer this fate.[23]

We note that both sets of sisters live on islands and are dedicated to a deity of inspiration that gives them oracular and other powers. Strabo's account follows Caesar's, but we know that Caesar roughly equated many Gaulish deities with classical ones and we may safely assume that this Gaulish sisterhood, whose number is not stated, venerated a local deity, not Dionysus. Pomponius Mela enumerates the sisterhood's roles as follows: weather-witching, shapeshifting, healing and foretelling the future. Strabo is less forthcoming, content to dwell salaciously upon their ecstatic, maenadic behaviour and their barbarous rites. We might doubt his report of their Amazonian sexual encounters on the mainland, if it were not for the overwhelming evidence of testimony on this subject.

Celtic myth speaks widely of women being the active instigators of sexual encounters and relationships: Rhiannon loiters at the foot of the Mound of Arberth with the specific intention of winning Pwyll as her husband;[24] Macha walks out of the otherworld and into the household of Crunniuc.[25] In the *immrama* tales a female messenger comes to Bran mac Febal and tells him to find the Island of Women. On arrival, he and his men are paired up with otherworldly women. In the *Immram Maelduin*, Maelduin finds it very hard to escape from the Queen of the Land of Women.[26] To be rapt away by magical women is also the fate of Connla, who is said to be *brechtaib ban mberar* ('taken by the spells of women') in the *Adventures of Connla*.[27]

The vigorous sexuality of those upon the Island of Women is borne out in the Irish story of Ruad, son of Rigdonn (Red, son of Kingly-Gift). While crossing over to Norway with three ships, Ruad's vessels cease to move: on diving to investigate, he discovers three giant women attached to each ship. They bring him to the bottom of the sea where he spends nine nights, lying with each of them. He promises to return to them after leaving Norway but fails to do so. One of the ninefold bears him a child.[28]

We note also that at Cluain Feart (Clonfert) in Ireland, a community of druidesses were also said to be able to raise storms, cure illness and kill enemies by cursing them.[29] These abilities echo those listed by Pomponius Mela and are similar to those mentioned in the *Vita Merlini* where we hear that on the island of Avalon:

> nine sisters rule by a pleasing set of laws those who come to them from our country. She who is first of them is more skilled in the healing art, and excels her sisters in the beauty of her person. Morgen is her name, and she has learned what useful properties all the herbs contain, so that she can cure sick bodies. She also knows an art by which to change her shape, and to cleave the air on new wings like Daedalus; when she wishes she is at Brest, Chartres or Pavia, and when she wills, she slips down from the air onto your shores. And men say that she has taught mathematics to her sisters, Moronoe, Mazoe, Gliten, Glitonea, Cliton, Tyronoe, Thitis, Thetis best know for her cither.[30]

From this myth arises that of the Lady of the Lake who, like the Irish Queen of the Island of Women in the *immrama* stories, oversees her otherworldly entourage in a parallel realm to that of King Arthur's Round Table throughout the Middle Ages.[31]

A conflicting picture results from these sources: of islanded sisterhoods who live fiercely alone, yet can be visited, or who invite visitors to consult them. Yet also there is a consistency: weather-witching, shapeshifting, oracular wisdom and healing are abilities proper to these sisterhoods. Indeed, the number nine incidentally continued to be associated with healing throughout the Middle Ages, as we see in the work of Marcellus of Bordeaux, who wrote of the *novem glandulae sorores*.[32]

What of other ninefolds? The Nine Witches of Gloucester appear in both the *Life of St Samson*[33] and the story of Peredur, in which they become the foster-mothers and trainers in arms of young Peredur, enabling him to overcome otherworldly dangers.[34] This fostering of heroes by such sisterhoods is common in Celtic story. We see the training of Cuchulainn by Scathach, the eponymous goddess of the Island of Skye where he receives his weapon skills; Fionn mac Cumhail is fostered by two druidesses; even the medieval Lancelot receives a truly Celtic fosterage on the island of the Queen of Maidenland, a sea-faery.[35]

The ninefold sisters seem to have a strong interest in educating the young, and they preserve their reputation as inspirers in a muse-like manner in both Geoffrey of Monmouth's account above, and in their depiction as the ninefold guardians of the cauldron of the underworld whose breath not only cools the brew but also imbues it with nine giftings. While not overwhelming, the evidence might support these sisterhoods as colleges of esoteric wisdom, just as the druids and bards had their own seats of learning.

All these accounts might still be set aside by the doubtful as nothing more than myths that borrow from each other or as the Celtic counterparts of such classical figures as the Moirae or the Muses, if it were not for certain key evidence. We are indeed fortunate to have material testimony of 'the spells of women' at first hand in the Larzac fragment, a lead tablet found near the urn of a cremated female body in a necropolis near Millau (the Romano-Gaulish town of Condatomagus) and dated to AD90–110. Discovered in 1983, it gives us direct archaeological evidence of the spells of women. Inscribed in Gaulish, the tablet may be tentatively translated as follows (the square brackets indicate suggested sense or lacunae where the text is fragmentary):

On this [tablet] the spells of women; their special underworld names; the counter-spell of the accomplished seeress, Severa, daughter of Tertiu, maintained by the Goddess Adsagsona in both worlds [of everyday and otherworld] as 'weaver of spells' and 'seeker-out' [lit. 'weapon' of the spirits].

Whether within or without, may those who [have sent forth] to bind by a lying vision spell, be inscribed below [in the underworld]. These are the underworld group of sorceresses:

Banona, daughter of Vlatucia,
Paulla, wife of Potitos,
Vlatucia, mother of Banona,
Iaia, daughter of Adiega,
Potitia, mother of Paulla,
Severa, daughter of Valens, wife of Paullos,
Adiega, mother of Iaia, Potita, wife of Primos, daughter of Abesa.

May the [...] and the endeavour also, O Rufena Casta, wife of [...], and the wish also be deserved. [Against?] Vlatucia and Aucitiena, mother of Potitos, O Vlatucia, mother of Bannonia! May they not strike together, these women in their encircled protection, by Severa's seeking out, by the daughter of Tertiu's spell-craft!

May this curse speed towards them, striking their descendants, pronounces Severa, Tertiu's daughter.

May they not strike in concert, by the souls of the dead whoever [? are entombed ... .] By this mouth [... .]

[...] here within are bound by this mouth; may they not make their magic, by this mouth, may the dead be their judge!

May the mouths of whomever are here inscribed be bound, whether they be spell-maker, diviner or bestower of gifts. They will not strike the seed of this curse's sower: Severa the spell-weaver, the weapon of the underworld. [... .] Whether within or without, the underworld [...] by this mouth [...] may Adsagsona ward off those who [would] strike the descendants [...] may she ward off those who would bind her, all who would injure Severa, Tertiu's daughter, spell-maker, ... bind underworld the ... .

The following verse is written in a different hand:

[...] Aia Cicena [...] keep everlasting faith with these lying bespellers, dweller in the underworld. The dead throw no lots down below, yet are they ancestral witnesses.[36]

The tablet becomes increasingly fragmentary and difficult to translate and the translation above is offered as but one possible interpretation. It follows the standard leaden *defixio* or curse common to this period throughout the classical world, it being the practice to write the curse on lead and throw it into the tomb of one long dead or into water, sometimes with an offering, such as a ring, as was found in this excavation.

From the translation above, we may perceive that Severa, daughter of Tertiu – a spell-maker with a good opinion of her own abilities – is sending a curse against a women's magical group, consisting of eight women, two of whom are named later in the curse with one other. Severa is dedicated to an underworld goddess, Adsagsona, a previously uncited deity of unique and possibly local title, meaning something like 'She Who Seeks Out'. Severa clearly sees herself as the 'weapon of vengeance' in her service. Due to the complexities of the tablet, it is difficult to establish the exact relationship of the curse to those cursing or bespelled. It would seem to suggest that Severa had recently disagreed with her hearth-group, since she is familiar with their initiatic relationships. She is certainly concerned to bind their mouths, possibly against gossip that injures her public reputation.

The interpretation favoured by the collective responsible for the examination of this find is that the relationships of the curse's subjects are not necessarily familial but perhaps initiatory in nature – for example, that Vlatucia is the matron-teacher of Banona, her initiatory 'daughter'. My chart suggests the initiatory relationships in this group:

A				Abesa (deceased)
B	Vlatucia	Potitia	Adiega	Potita
C	Banona	Paulla	Iaia	
D				Severa

Line A represents the elder woman mentioned, who is the initiator/teacher of Potita. Line B represents the matrons of this group, all of whom have initiates. We note that Potita alone has no pupil/initiate; this may be due to her own initiator having died recently. Line C represents the younger women of the group, initiates of the matrons. Line D represents the uninitiated neophyte of the group, a young married woman, Severa, who may be the intended 'daughter' of Potita.

Where fathers and husbands are mentioned, we may speculate that these are relations of former or current initiates of the group; they may, however, be totally unrelated. We note that nine women are specifically mentioned as part of the group; that one of them, Abesa, is no longer living; and that another is not yet initiated. Severa Tertionicnim, the curser, may have been formerly one of the nine herself. Subsequent to the full list of victims, we note that Vlatucia, mother of Banona, is mentioned and also the previously uncited, Aucitiena, mother-in-law of Paulla. The last part of the curse, which is inscribed in another hand, may have been added when the tablet was thrust into the niche of the funerary urn with the iron ring as offering. The urn was inscribed on the base with the word *gemma*. We do not know if the Aia Cicena mentioned in the last stanza was the name of the deceased. We may further speculate that Severa was working on behalf of a rich patroness, Rufena Casta.

The curse certainly does not present a glowing portrait of female co-operation, but rather a high level of malicious back-stabbing. What is remarkable is that the tablet begins with the phrase with which we are already familiar, *bnarcom bricto* ('the spells of women'). We have little idea of the function and activities of the group so roundly cursed here except that the members, like Severa herself, are skilled in the magic of the underworld. Severa exhibits concern that her spell does not rebound upon her own descendants. She wishes to silence the mouths and spells of the group and calls upon both the dead and the goddess, Adsagsona, herself to protect her. Severa is also fearful of the power of the whole group working magic in concert.

In the Larzac fragments we read of women banding together in groups or societies for the purpose of performing magic. Such societies were commonplace around Europe in the centuries that followed, especially as the state religion of Christianity made no provision for active female sacerdotal roles beyond that of cloistered nun. Yet, even here, we find traces of the ninefold sisterhood tradition.

Darerca of Killeavy, founder of the monastery of Killery, near Armagh, was baptized by St Patrick himself and was asked by him to supervise the teaching of female converts. Her first group significantly consisted of nine women.[37] But it is St Brigit's foundation of Kildare that has the most famous reputation. Brigit was fostered in the household of the druid Maithghean according to the *Vita Prima Brigid*;[38] much of her hagiography is directly imported from the mythos of the Irish goddess Brighid. Her foundation at Kildare maintained the holy fire that was continuously invigilated by the sisterhood there. It burned within a sacred thorn-hedge, which men might not cross. Giraldus Cambrensis (Gerald of Wales) reports the foundation as having nineteen sisters (two nines with an abbess) who perpetually watch the sacred fire in rota, one each night. On the twentieth night, the retiring sister builds up the fire and says, 'Brigid, guard your fire,' and the fire is kept in until the next day.[39]

It is interesting to note that the custom of banking up or smooring the fire for the night descends to this day in Irish households. Turf fires are covered with ash, which is arranged in three bosses, and prayers to Brigit are said to guard the fire for the night. The next morning it is easy to raise the fire from the sleeping embers. Although St Brigit's foundation at Kildare was originally a double monastery housing both sexes, the enclosure wherein the eternal flame was kept was always strictly segregated. Giraldus reports that two men tried to gain illegal access. One, knowing that the sisters did not blow on the fire but fanned it with winnowing fans, hopped over the hedge, blew upon the fire, jumped back and began obsessively to blow upon all fires he saw until he became parched, finally dying of drinking too quickly. The other dangled one leg over the hedge in defiance of the male ban, as result of which his leg became withered. We are reminded of the strict segregation of the islanded sisterhood of Strabo's account above.

Brigit's sacred fire continued to burn until the Reformation, when it was extinguished. However, in the last five years there have been many movements to re-institute the tradition at Kildare with some success. These have come from grass roots community level and have been funded by business interests.

It is also apposite to mention here the fact that a perpetual fire was reported at Aquae Sulis, modern Bath in Avon, the site of the only naturally hot springs in Britain. The springs were dedicated to the Celtic goddess, Sul, whom the Romans equated with Minerva. They built a fine temple site there, which Solinus reports as follows:

> Hot baths, finely kept to the use of men, the sovereign of which baths is that of the Goddess Minerva in whose chapel the fire burneth continually, and the coals do never turn into ashes, but as soon as the embers are dead, it is turned into balls of stone.[40]

The strong association of St Brigit with the guardianship of the sacred flame and the domestic hearth undoubtedly draws upon traditions of the Irish goddess, Brighid, her precursor and the mythic template upon which St Brigit's life can be seen to fit. It seems likely that the foundations of both Darerca and Brigit may be modelled on earlier patterns of sisterhood. Brigit, in particular, enjoyed a primacy unknown by women in Christian communities then or since: she is said to have been ordained as bishop and to have used an unorthodox liturgy called the *Ordo Placentinus*, which has not survived. The primacy of Brigit was clearly understood to be a dangerous precedent within the Roman Church, which, despite the recent admission of women to the priesthood within the Anglican and other communions, is still almost universally reluctant to allow women an active role in ministry.

With the spread of Christianity, most pagan practices were expunged, although not thoroughly suppressed or forgotten. Magical sisterhoods may no longer withdraw themselves to practise upon remote islands, but they still met for all that. Women's magical societies continued to meet throughout Europe in rural and urban settings. Such societies were the object of considerable opprobrium and hysterical persecution during the Middle Ages, and throughout this period Inquisitional reports attempt to interpret such societies in the light of a preconceived Christian template, which is now known as 'the witches' sabbath' but which, on the record of extant testimony, reveals an entirely different pattern. The demonization of women's magical meetings, already apparent in some medieval and classical accounts above, became horrific, with accounts of child-sacrifice, intercourse with the devil and intervals for ill-wishing neighbours. But if we look at freely self-confessed activities (rather than those extracted under torture), we find women (with some men) meet together on Thursday evenings to pay homage to a goddess, to divine, to learn herb-lore and healing and to eat, dance and sing.[41]

That such activities were common knowledge in a locality is evident if we look at the attempt to tar Jeanne d'Arc with the brush of witchcraft. When asked at her trial in Rouen in 1430 whether she knew anything about those who 'went or travelled through the air with the fairies', she denied having anything to do with them but knew that it took place on Thursdays'.[42] People are aware of such meetings, but only those within the kinship of interest take part, much as in modern magical societies today.

The feminine spirit to which homage is paid within central western Europe is identified as Diana, or Herodiana (a fusion of Hera with Diana), or a variety of beings, such as Bensozia (*Bona Socia*), Perchta/Bertha and Holda/Holle. The German goddess Holda was believed to fly through the air with women and with the spirits of unbaptized children, but is more often depicted as a benevolent and motherly being with distaff. Each of these beings was generally termed 'Diana' or 'Herodiana' by the Inquisitional clerics as a catch-all title, but names for deities venerated by women in Britain and Scotland include the Queen of Faery, the Gyre Carlin and Nicneven (Daughter of Heaven). These figures were mostly overlooked as goddesses by Inquisitors, who wanted proof of devil-worship, but we can see within these figures remnants of the Mothers. The Mothers are important spirits of place and they continue to survive in women's magical societies.

What then are the roles of the ninefold? From a wide body of evidence we can accumulate the following roles that are traditionally associated with the ninefold sisters, as well as those which may be discerned from the internal evidence of myth and story.

To manifest the spirits through the engendering or fostering of children
To prophesy/divine
To protect from enemies
To teach skills/train in arms
To enchant/shapeshift
To heal
To weather-witch, raise storms etc.
To maintain life/keep the fire
To grant gifts/pronounce destiny.

How long had such sisterhoods endured? Possibly as long as the megaliths of Long Meg and her Daughters in Cumbria or the Merry Maidens in Cornwall – only two of numerous sites in Britain and Europe that eponymously remember the ninefold. And what of the survival of the sisterhoods in the present age?

'The spells of women,' so feared by St Patrick and other clerics, show no sign of abating in the present century. The ninefold sisterhoods of the coasts of northwestern Europe have not ceased to operate. Britain, which has one of the longest coastlines in Europe, still has its complements of women.[43]

Seen as socially subversive and often branded as 'diabolic' by mainstream Christian views, women's magical societies continue to be concerned with the ancient ninefold task of 'life-maintenance' in efficient and gifted ways. These are mostly undramatic, domestic and mutually supportive to the society's members. Activities can also be ritualistic, ecstatic and spiritually enhancing to the group. In my experience, none has partaken in, nor deserved the accusation of, unsocial magical activity that is so often levelled against them. This is not to say that, historically, women's groups did not engage in malign magic, but that it is not customary practice today in a society that is more tolerant of covert spiritual groups.

The concern of groups within which I have worked is not merely for themselves, but for their children, partners, families, jobs and activities, as well as for their community and the wider world. Prayers and blessings for personal and global issues are frequently included as part of women's magical society, usually in the closing moments of the meeting. Songs are sung, deities and ancestors are thanked for their help, candles are extinguished as the spells of women stream out upon the winds for the benefit of the world.

Notes

1 Plato 'The Myth of Er' in *The Republic* (Penguin Books, Harmondsworth, 1957).

2 Elizabeth Barber, *Women's Work* (W.W. Norton, New York, 1994).

3 *Táin Bó Cuailgnè*, trans. by Thomas Kinsella, (Oxford University Press, Oxford, 1972).

4 L Harf-Lancner, *Les Fées au Moyen Age* (Librairie Honoré Champion, Paris, 1984).

5 H.R. Ellis Davidson, *Gods and Myths of Northern Europe* (Penguin Books, Harmondsworth, 1964).

6 Anne Ross, *Pagan Celtic Britain* (Routledge & Kegan Paul, London, 1967).

7 Garrett S. Olmstead, *The Gods of the Celts and the Indo-Europeans* (Beiträge zur Kulturwissenschaft, Innsbruck, 1995).

8 David Greene and Frank O'Connor, *A Golden Treasury of Irish Poetry AD600–1200* (Macmillan, London, 1967), pp. 27–32.

9 Dallan Forgaill, *The Amra Choluim Chilli*, trans. by J. O'Beirne Crowe (Dublin, 1871), p. 3.

10 *Ibid.*

11 C. Kerenyi, *The Gods of the Greeks* (Thames & Hudson, London, 1979).

12 Trans. by Caitlín Matthews; from C. and J. Matthews, *The Little Book of Celtic Wisdom* (Element Books, Shaftesbury, 1994).

13 *Ibid.*

14 Davidson, *op. cit.*, pp. 175, 130.

15 Caitlín Matthews, *The Celtic Book of the Dead* (Thorsons, Wellingborough, 1991).

16 Caitlín Matthews, *Mabon and the Mysteries of Britain: An Exploration of the Mabinogion* (Arkana, London, 1987), p. 107.

17 Geoffrey of Monmouth, *Vita Merlini*, ed. and trans. by J.J. Parry (University of Illinois Press, Illinois, 1925); Nora K. Chadwick *The Druids* (Cardiff, 1966), p. 79.

18 Caitlín and John Matthews, *The Encyclopaedia of Celtic Wisdom* (Element Books, Shaftesbury, 1994).

19 *Carmina Gadelica* trans. by Alexander Carmichael (Scottish Academic Press, Edinburgh, 1972).

20 Nora K. Chadwick, *The Druids* (London, 1962).

21 John T. Koch with John Carey, *The Celtic Heroic Age: Literary Sources for Ancient Celtic Europe and*

Early Ireland and Wales (Malden, Massachusetts, 1995), p. 28.

22 C. and J. Matthews, *op. cit.*, 1994, p. 36.

23 *Ibid.*

24 In *Pwyll, Prince of Dyfed*, see C. Matthews, *op. cit.*, 1987, pp. 20–36.

25 T.P. Cross and C.H. Slover, *Ancient Irish Tales* (Hodges, Figgis & Co., Dublin, 1936), pp. 208–10.

26 C. Matthews, *op. cit.*, 1991, p. 34.

27 P.W. Joyce, *Old Celtic Romances* (Kegan Paul, London, 1879), pp. 106–10.

28 Davidson, *op. cit.*

29 Peter Berresford-Ellis, *Celtic Women* (London, 1995), p. 69.

30 Geoffrey of Monmouth, *op. cit.*

31 C. and J. Matthews, *op. cit.*, 1994, pp. 44–7.

32 Marcellus of Bordeaux, *Corp. Medic* 5, ed. by M. Niedermann (Leipzig, 1916), p. 120.

33 See *Acta Bollandiana* 6, pp. 96–7.

34 See Caitlín Matthews, *Arthur and the Sovereignty of Britain: King and Goddess in the Mabinogion* (Arkana, London, 1989), pp. 161–205, 208.

35 C. and J. Matthews, *op. cit.*, 1994, pp. 91–4.

36 Trans. by Caitlín Matthews; see Michel Lejeune (ed. and coll.), 'Textes Gaulois et Gallo-Romains en Cursive Latine: 3: Le Plomb du Larzac' in *Etudes celtiques*, vol. xxii–iii, 1985–6, pp. 95–117, 10.

37 P. Berresford-Ellis, *op. cit.*, p. 145–6.

38 John Minahane, *The Christian Druids: on the Filid or Philosopher Poets of Ireland* (Sanas Press, Dublin, 1995).

39 Gerald of Wales, *The History and Topography of Ireland*, trans. by John J. O'Meara (Penguin Books, Harmondsworth, 1982), pp. 81–2, 11.

40 Mary Condren, *The Serpent and the Goddess* (San Francisco, 1989), p. 68.

41 Carlo Ginzberg, *Ecstasies: Deciphering the Witches' Sabbath* (London, 1990), pp. 89 ff.

42 *Ibid.*

43 Some of these groups and their practices are examined in the anthropological study by Tanya Luriman, *Persuasions of the Witch's Craft* (Oxford, 1990). The traditional groups in which I have worked refuse the cultural definition of 'witches'.

PART TWO

THE DARK SPEECH: OGHAM AND THE BARDS

THE IMPORTANCE OF LANGUAGE is stressed throughout the traditions of the Celtic bards. Words themselves could be all powerful, as could song, and one of the most important aspects of the bardic training was the learning of a secret language that could enable the initiated poets to converse with each other, if necessary in full view of a hall full of people, without anyone there being any the wiser.

This was done by means of ogham, a linear alphabet found inscribed on stone or wood and apparently devised by the ancient Celts. It has been called 'the secret language of the poets', and in its long and complex history many theories have been advanced to explain its origin and purpose. In the chapters that follow the history of this extraordinary system is examined in detail. But before proceeding to these it may be useful to put the entire subject in context by referring to the descriptions of ogham that can be derived from early texts.

'Early' here means medieval rather than ancient, but we do have an enduring testimony to the age of this system in the shape of the many inscriptions in ogham found carved on menhirs and standing stones throughout England, Scotland and Ireland. The purpose to which these were erected has long been debated. It is assumed, generally, that they were grave markers – 'the stone of …' – indicating where some great chieftain or hero was laid to rest. But there is at least one other possibility: that they were boundary markers, indicating the demarcation between one tribe's lands and another. This would explain the stones with more than one inscription and is in line with the magical association of ogham. A stone with the name of the tribe, its chieftain or clan mark would be as effective as a wire fence today – none would cross it without either permission or evil intent.

Many people have assumed that ogham and runic inscriptions must derive from each other, but this is not so. The former is a Celtic method, the latter a Scandinavian one. Both are concerned with arcane knowledge and are under the patronage of the gods of word-wisdom. Both Odin and Ogmios have reputations for weaving words and gaining wisdom, and it is more than likely that the two systems evolved independently of each other (but see Chapter 10).

The main source of written knowledge about ogham comes from a fourteenth-century Irish manuscript of *The Book of Ballymote*[1] in the Library of the Royal Irish Academy. Contained in this are some eight pages, generally referred to as 'The Ogham Tract' (although its proper name is *Duil Feda*). This has been edited by George Calder with extensive commentaries and is available elsewhere, but certain salient points are worthy of note. The account begins, as one might expect, with the creation of ogham:

What are the place, time, person, and cause of the invention of ogham? [*sic*] Not hard. Its place *Hibernia insula quam nos Scoti habitamus.* In the time of Bres son of Elatha king of Ireland was it invented. Its person Ogma son of Elatha son of Delbaeth brother to Bres, for Bres, Ogma and Delbaeth are the three sons of Elatha son of Delbaeth there. Now Ogma, a man well skilled in speech and in poetry, invented the ogham. The cause of its invention, as a proof of his ingenuity, and that his speech should belong to the learned apart, to the exclusion of rustics and herdsmen. … The father of ogham is Ogma, the mother of ogham is the hand or knife of Ogma. … This moreover is the first thing that was written by Ogham: ⊤ i.e., (the birch) **b** was written, and to convey a warning to Lug son of Ethliu it was written respecting his wife lest she be carried away from him into faeryland, to wit, seven **b**s in one switch of birch: Thy wife will be seven times carried away from thee into faeryland or into another country, unless birch guard her. On that account, moreover, **b**, birch, takes precedence, for it is in birch that ogham was first written.[2]

This tells us several important things. Ogham was intended to be understood by the learned, noble class – i.e., the druids and seers – and not by the common people. Its first use seems to have been to inscribe a warning and to have taken the form of a protective spell – if we are to understand the term 'unless birch guard her' in this way. Also we are told that the alphabet was invented by Ogma, whose rather complex pedigree is given. References to this same figure are found elsewhere, and it is clear from these that he was not a man at all (as in 'The Ogham Tract'), but a god who bore the titles *Cermait* (Honey-mouthed), *Grian-aineach* (Sun-faced) or *Trenfher* (Strong-man, Champion), a son of the great god Dagda. He is usually described as a god of literature and of eloquence, as his alternative epithets suggest, while in Gaul he was called Ogmios and worshipped as a god of light and learning. The classical author Lucian wrote that he was the Celtic Heracles and gives a description of a painting that depicted an ancient figure drawing a group of men chained by their ears to his tongue. Puzzling over this, Lucian found a native Celt at his side who was willing to elucidate:

> We Celts do not agree with you Greeks in thinking that Hermes is Eloquence: we identify Heracles with it, because he is far more powerful than Hermes. And don't be surprised that he is represented as an old man, for eloquence ... is wont to show its full vigour in old age ... . This being so, if old Heracles here drags men after him who are tethered by the ears to his tongue, don't be surprised at that either: you know the kinship between ears and tongue.[3]

Ogmios's title *Trenfher* (Strong-man) suggests an actual identification with Hercules/Heracles, while the latter's Hellenized name means 'the Walker', and if we recall the original meaning of the word 'pedant' is derived from scholar, or 'one who walks up and down', we may see how this may have struck a chord in the minds of the bardic writers. Ogmios is clearly a god of tradition, which binds men together in chains of a kind, and which is shown to derive from the otherworldly realm of the gods. In an inscription found at Richborough, Ogmios is depicted with rays of light coming from around his head and holding the whip of *Sol Invictus* (the Unconquered Sun). He is thus in every way a suitable figure to be credited with the invention of an alphabet which was to be associated with magical activities, with the transmission of secret knowledge and with the writing of poetry.

The ogham alphabet itself consists of various combinations of lines drawn across a vertical or horizontal stave. Each set of five letters has a name, and the letters themselves have names, the most frequent being those of various trees. Thus ogham is sometimes called the Tree Alphabet or Beithe-Luis-Nion after the first three names of the sequence (which occasionally vary from version to version; see below). The complete list, as shown on page 152, has been adapted from several different texts. It will be seen from this that a number of variants exist as to the attribution of a particular tree or bush to a particular letter. In addition, the order has changed throughout its long period of development, so we cannot always be sure of its original form. The variants are thus included here as a point of reference against the various attributes to be found within the followinging chapters.

Doubts, first expressed by Charles Graves as long ago as 1847[4] and more recently explored by Howard Meroney,[5] as to the authenticity of the ogham tree-alphabet, make it clear that we must look again at the whole question of these identifications, which have been accepted quite literally by most commentators since the 1700s. The evidence points to their having been copied and recopied until their *original* meanings became virtually lost or so jumbled as to be virtually indecipherable.

Ogham name	Roman letter	Tree name
Beithe	b	birch
Luis	l	elm/rowan
Fearn	f	alder
Saile	s	willow
Nuin (Nion)	n	ash
(h)Uathe	h	whitethorn/hawthorn
Duir	d	oak
Tinne	t	holly/elderberry
Coll	c	hazel
Quert	q	quicken/aspen/apple
Muinn	m	vine/mulberry
Gort	g	fir/ivy/corn
(n)Getal	ng	broom/fern
Straif	str	willow/brake/blackthorn
Ruis	r	elder
Ailm	a	fir/pine
Ohn	o	furze/ash/gorse
Ur	u	thorn/heather
Edhadh	e	yew/aspen
Ido	i	service tree/yew
Ebadh	eba	elecampane/aspen
Oir	oi	spindle tree
Uilleand	ui	ivy/honeysuckle
Iphin	io	pine/goseberry
Emancoll/phagos	ae	witch hazel/beech

Meroney has reassigned some of the letters, using the poetic glosses that have been attached to several of the printed versions of the alphabet. These appear to have preserved earlier and more accurate glosses to the letters than those contained in the *Auraicept Na N-Eces* or its variants. In these, quite often, the original forms have duplications that suggest that the copyists themselves did not know how to decipher them. (For example, *pin* is glossed as 'a rowan, pine, or gooseberry'.) What appears to have happened is that the *original* glosses for the ogham alphabet (still quite late as against the dating of the alphabet itself) were of a much more ordinary-seeming nature and that these were changed, at some unspecified time (probably between the seventh and ninth centuries) to fit a purely arbitrary system of tree and plant names.

In addition, lists of the various kinds of physically oriented ogham (finger, nose, thigh, foot and so on) also exist and were used in a similar fashion – touching the part of the body in a certain way would indicate to those in the know a word or letter that could be interpreted in this fashion. Still other kinds of ogham listed in 'The Scholar's Primer' include sow ogham, river-pool ogham, fortress ogham, bird ogham, colour ogham, king ogham, water ogham, dog ogham and food ogham.

The poet-druid-seer wishing to make use of the alphabets had thus to be familiar with a vast range of knowledge – not only of the general meaning of the ogham character, but also to the many secret meanings that lay behind it. Thus the letter *n(Getal)* stood not only for *ng*, but also all that *ng* stood for: a tree, a group of letters, a phrase, a part of the body and so on. Interpretation of the signs thus rested on a full spectrum of knowledge in which the relationship of the letter or letters to each other, to the remainder of the inscription and to the context in which they were found had to be taken into account.

R.A.S. Macalister notes that all of the ogham signs could be easily made with the fingers – hence their grouping in fives – and that the five 'extra' letters, which represent the vowel sounds and have often been suggested as late additions, are particularly appropriate for making with the fingers. From this he suggests that the earliest use of ogham was as a sign language and that only later was it adapted for use in the making of inscriptions. He also has some interesting perceptions on the possible origin of the alphabet, which he finds to be very nearly identical with a form of Greek known as the Formello-Cervetti alphabet. This was found inscribed on two vases dating from approximately the sixth century BC, and from this, Calder believes, they were borrowed by Gaulish druids some time in the fifth century and adapted to their own use.

Caesar remarks that the druids used 'Greek letters' to record their communications – although not their orally preserved religious teachings – which seems to bear out this idea. Certainly, there was considerable interaction between the Celts and the Greeks for this curious borrowing to have come about. It establishes a date for ogham of no earlier than 500BC and lends weight to the belief that its original use was as a cryptographic system.

However, the story does not end here. An examination of the *language* of the ogham inscriptions found in Ireland, Britain and Wales shows that they contain archaisms that point to an extremely primitive language still being enshrined in stone long after it had ceased to be spoken. Macalister, who deals with his linguistic evidence at some length, believes that it was Old Goidelic, the primitive language of the Celts, and from this he infers that it continued to be spoken by the druids, who taught it orally in their schools so that they were speaking a language no longer understood by their own people! References to 'the dark speech' found in contemporary literature suggest that this may well have been the case and add not only to the antiquity of ogham but also to the druids themselves. All of this leads Macalister to suggest that a reasonable translation of the word 'ogham' would be 'the language', thus indicating its primary place in Celtic understanding.

As mentioned above, there is a great deal of disagreement about the order that the alphabet should follow and about which tree or shrub belongs to which letter. The earliest lists we possess, and upon which the above listing is based, are those found in 'The Ogham Tract' and the *Auraicept Na N-Eces* ('The Scholar's Primer'), which differ only slightly. In his brilliant exposition of ogham (see Chapter 12), Macalister gives evidence to show that the order changed with phonetic requirements, so that the familiar Beithe-Luis-Nion may well have been the earliest. After this there is a long gap in which various sources repeat the medieval lists more or less verbatim, until the seventeenth-century version by Charles O'Conor, quoted by Edward Ledwich in his eighteenth-century *Antiquities of Ireland.*[6] This was re-defined in Roderic O'Flaherty's *Ogygia,*[7] from whence it was re-defined by the poet and mythographer Robert Graves. He included it in his 'grammar of poetic myth', *The White Goddess,*[8] in which he recognized – correctly it would seem – that it formed the basis for 'a calendar of seasonal tree-magic'. Unfortunately, he made certain amendments to the original order of the trees, in an endeavour to bring the system into line with the overall picture of the tradition he wished to explore.

Plentiful examples are to be found throughout Celtic literature (especially Irish), indicating some of the other uses to which ogham was put. These include the Ulster hero Cuchulainn, who twice left challenges inscribed in ogham before the army of Mabh of Connaught, one on a hoop of birch and a second in the fork of a tree.[9] Again, when Midir abducted Etain, the wife of Art mac Conn, the druid Dalan discovered her hiding place by cutting four wands of yew, on which he wrote ogham inscriptions, thereby discovering the *eochra ecsi* (keys of divination) through which he found that she was being held in the *sidhe* of Breg Leith.[10]

When the Sovereignty of Ireland wished to offer her cup to the hero destined to reign over the land, she asked to whom it should be given and was told that she must listen to the recital of all the sovereigns of Ireland, from Conn to the end of time. The poet Cesarn managed to deliver an incantation (*dichetail*) using ogham inscribed on four yew wands.[11]

Corc, the son of Lugaid, fled after spurning the advances of his step-mother. He arrived at the court of King Feradach and asked for shelter. The king's poet, Gruibne Eces (poet or seer), saw that Corc had ogham written on his shield, requesting that the bearer should be beheaded. But Gruibne liked Corc and instead interpreted the ogham to say that he should marry Feradach's daughter.[12]

After the deaths of the lovers Aillinn and Baile, an apple and a yew sprang from their graves. At the end of seven years the poets, seers and prophets of Ulster cut down the yew tree that was over the grave of Baile and made it into a poet's tablet, 'and they wrote the visions, the espousals, and loves, and courtship's of Ulster upon it'. The same was done with the apple tree growing on Aillinn's grave, and on that were written the courtships, loves and espousals of Leinster. Later, when King Conn of the Hundred Battles was looking at these famous tablets, they sprang together and could not thereafter be separated.

All these instances have to do with magical or divinatory uses of ogham, but in the 'Torchmarc Etain' the woods are described as *eochra écsi* (keys of knowledge). This may refer to a passage from *Senchus Mor* (see Introduction to Part One) concerning a method of judgement known as *crannchur* (casting the woods). According to this, if there was doubt as to the identity of a murderer, thief or adulterer:

> The lots are cast in this manner: three lots are put in, a lot for guiltiness, a lot for innocence, and the lot for the Trinity. This is enough to criminate or acquit them. If it be the lot of the Trinity that came out, it is to be put back each time until another lot comes out.[13]

Despite the Christian gloss, there is an unmistakable ring of truth about this. The fact that three lots are placed within – we may presume a bag – is in line with the Celtic obsession with that number. We may speculate that the method originally involved special woods – perhaps more than three – each of which was sacred to the gods; whichever was pulled forth, would then have become the arbiter in the case, with possible further divinatory methods following.

Apart from these uses, there were numerous other ways in which ogham could be utilized. Whenever a hero was buried, a slip of aspen was placed with him in his tomb with his name written in ogham upon it. There are, besides, accounts of whole libraries of ogham writings inscribed on bark. In another sense ogham was indeed a library – but one that consisted of mnemonics, not unlike the *Welsh Triads*.[14] It was concerned with people, places and things, any number of which could be set against the ogham stave. We may marvel at the complexity of learning necessary to those who used ogham fluently. Depending on the kind of ogham used – and there are no fewer than a hundred listed in 'The Ogham Tract' and 'The Scholar's Primer' – there must have been some kind of code to identify which one was being used. A river, a man or woman, colour, tree, hill or whatever, could be identified and placed in context with local tradition. Thus an ogham might refer to a certain hill, which in turn referred to a legend or tradition concerning that place, and the outcome of that could be applied to the person giving or asking the question. The huge collection of *Dindsenchas* ('Stories of Place')[15] tells literally hundreds of stories connected to the landscape, explaining and amplifying the meaning of the place-name in either riddling or punning form.

In the chapters that follow are grouped a number of primary sources for the study of ogham. E. Ledwick's brilliant essay 'On the Ogham Characters' examines the possible sources for the letters themselves, drawing upon a wide range of sources. G.M. Atkinson sets out the complex structure of the ogham treatises, which remain the primary source for most of what we know of the structure and use to which the alphabet may have been put. This is followed by R.A.S. Macalister's important text on the history of ogham, which draws upon the previous essays and adds a great deal more. Finally in this section is F.C. Diak's little known essay, which takes the less popular view that ogham is nothing more than a reworking of the Latin alphabet. This approach, which has recently found some acceptance among the academic community, suggests a much later point of origin, which in the face of other evidence seems unlikely. The essay is included here to offer a balanced view, despite the fact that it seems less believable than the evidence assembled by the others writers represented below.

In all, this part of the collection sets out to give readers a sufficient grasp of the complexities of ogham to enable them to begin their own researches, to form their own conclusions and, ultimately, to begin working with this mysterious system for themselves.

Notes

1 See George Calder, *Auraicpt Na N-Eces* (John Grant, Edinburgh, 1917).

2 Calder, *op. cit.*

3 Lucian 'Heracles' in *Works*, vol. 1, ed. by A.M. Harmon (Heinemann, London, 1913).

4 C. Graves, 'On the Ogam Beithluisnin' in *The Encyclopedia of Celtic Wisdom*, ed. by John and Caitlín Matthews (Element Books, Shaftsbury, 1994).

5 'Early Irish Letter Names' in *Speculum*, vol. XXIV, 1995–6, pp. 19–43.

6 Edward Ledwich, *Antiquities of Ireland* (John Jones, Dublin, 1804).

7 Roderic O'Flaherty, *Ogygia, or a Chronological Account of Irish Events* (W. MacKenzie, Dublin, 1793).

8 Robert Graves, *The White Goddess* (Faber & Faber, London, 1952).

9 *Táin Bó Cuailgnè,*, trans. by T. Kinsella (Oxford University Press, Oxford, 1970).

10 'Torchmarc Etain' in *Ériu*, vol. 12, 1938, pp. 137–65.

11 T.P. Cross and C.H. Slover *Ancient Irish Tales* (Hodges, Figgis & Co., Dublin, 1936).

12 *The Book of Leinster*, ed. by R.I. Best and M.A. O'Brien (Early Irish Text Society, Dublin, 1954–67).

13 *Senchus Mor*, ed. by W.N. Hancock (Alexander Thom, Dublin, 1895).

14 *Triodd Ynys Prydein*, ed. R. Bromwich (University of Wales Press, Cardiff, 1978).

15 E. Gwynn, *The Metrical Dindsenchas* (Hodges, Figgis & Co., Dublin, 1903–35).

CHAPTER TEN

On the Ogham Characters

Edward Ledwick

THE ORIGIN OF LETTERS among the Celtes is thus delivered by the fabulous Berosus. The great giant Samothes, the brother of Gomer and Tubal, promulged a code of laws for the Celtic nations, taught them the courses of the planets and the nature of sublunary things, gave them the Sagae or Phoenician letters, and led colonies into the Celtic regions 143 years after the deluge, and into Britain 252 years after the same memorable event.

Now for the Irish elements. The celebrated Feniusa Farsa, according to Keating, was the son of Magog, and King of Scythia. Desirous of becoming master of the seventy-two languages created at the confusion of Babel, he sent seventy-two persons to learn them. He established an University at Magh-Seanair near Athens, over which he, Gadel, and Caoith presided. These formed the Greek, Latin and Hebrew letters. Gadel was ordered to digest the Irish into five dialects: the Finian, to be spoken by the militia and soldiery; the poetic and historic, by the senachies and bards; the medical, by physicians, and the common idiom by the vulgar.

Mr O'Conor's account of the Bethluisnion of the Ogma is in the same wild romantic strain.

This [observes he] has not the least resemblance with either the Greek or Roman alphabets. Had our Bards been silent on the original of our letters from a celebrated Phenius or Phoenician, yet the signatures of an early commerce between our predecessors and an oriental lettered people, would appear evident. These letters are arranged in a different order from the alphabet of the Greeks, or abecedarium of the Romans: their ancient virgular figures were peculiar to this western nation alone; and their names partly. Phoenician and partly vernacular, not only shew their Asiatic origin, but their great antiquity in this island.

Mr Pinkerton[1] very justly calls such writers, 'visionaries, who detail superficial dreams to the public, upon no ancient authority, and upon the most silly and irrational ratiocination. Hence, (adds he,) what no foreign antiquary, what no man of sound learning would even imagine, has been seriously advanced, that the Phoenicians settled colonies in the South of Britain, and in Ireland, and that traces of the Phoenician language may be found in the Irish!'

Gower's[2] relation of the progress of the Latin language exactly matches that delivered by O'Conor of the Irish. Gower supposes the Latin invented by the old Tuscan prophetess

Carmens; then reduced to method, prosody &c. by Aristarchus, Donatus and Didymus; adorned with the flowers of eloquence by Tully; enriched by translations from the Chaldee, Arabic and Greek, and especially from St Jerome's version of the Bible. Here both fictions breathe the same spirit and are probably of the same age.

Truth, though clouded, will at length burst the thick envelope of fable. 'What,' says O'Flaherty,[3] 'if I should affirm, that our Phenisius was the Phoenician Cadmus, who depicted the ancient Greek letters, and which resembled the Latin. Nor are the Irish far distant from the Latin.' Here he states an indisputable fact, that the Irish elements are from the Latin, and the Latin from the Greek: but how painful to a liberal mind is the diffidence with which he expresses himself! He had written too large a work, and staked his reputation with his countrymen too deeply, to make the proper application of his learning and abilities to the subject of Irish Antiquities. Like many others, to be consistent he was obliged to be absurd, and to be patriotic, he sacrificed his fame on the altar of national prejudice.

O'Conor, whose dissertations on the ancient History of Ireland, are nothing but scraps translated from Lynch's Cambrensis Eversus and O'Flaherty, grants the letters used by the old Irish, since the reception of Christianity, are evidently[4] borrowed from the first Christian missioners, as more commodious than the old, uncouth and virgular forms imported into Ireland by the Celto-Scythian colony from Spain. What a direct contradiction is this of his former assertion, and how changed his tone from the tumid and bombastic verbosity of his former citation? Sir George Mackenzie and Bishop Stillingfleet had examined the Irish claim to remote history and literature, and found it to be a heap of impertinence and imposture. Father Innes, the two Macphersons, and Mr Whitaker have since totally subverted it. Ashamed of persevering in gross errors, and unable to withstand the conviction flashed on him from every quarter, the Irish antiquary gives up his fables, and reluctantly owns the triumph of learning and criticism.

For the reprobation of these puerile figments no great extent of reading or strength of judgement is requisite: nor should they have farther engaged the reader's attention, did I not imagine the subject has hitherto been totally misunderstood, and of course imperfectly treated. The Irish ground their pretensions to an original alphabet on the traditions of their Bards (who bring their ancestors from the East), and the agreement of these traditions with allowed history. Thus O'Conor compares the accounts in the Leavar Gabhala and Leavar Lecan, two manuscripts which have never seen the light, with the facts given in Newton's chronology. In his way of conducting this matter, he might have parallels equally accurate in Amidis de Gaul or any other romance, as in these Leavars. But what is most extraordinary is, to find in this obscure corner of the Globe literary memorials of unimpeached veracity, not only to supply the defects, but fill up the chasms of sacred and profane history! The genealogies of the Virgin Mary, Joseph and the other holy persons in Scripture are not to be had but in this book of Lecan;[5] and where so likely this book to be preserved as in the island of Saints!

O Fortunatos nimium sua si bona nôrint
Hibernos!

This Book of Lecan was compiled[6] between the years 1380 and 1417, a period, like the rest, of rebellion and domestic confusion. Uneasy under the English yoke, and unable to shake it off, the miserable Seanachies[7] of those times amused themselves and their countrymen with fabulous tales of the antiquity and nobility of their descent; the grandeur and power of their former princes, and the distinguished learning and civility of their ancestors. This invaluable information we are told, was preserved solely by the use of the Irish or Phoenician letters in this isle. The identity of these letters, we see has been much insisted on. But where, it may be asked, did these erudite and perspicacious antiquaries discover the name, figure, order and power of the Phoenician elements, which have escaped the acute eyes of Swinton, Barthelemy, Hottinger and Gebelin? For the Phoenician alphabets of Syria, Crete, Malta, Sicily, Spain and Carthage differ very remotely. The learned M. Dutens thus delivers his sentiments on this point, in his preface to the explication of Mr Duane's Greek and Phoenician Coins.

> Tous ceux qui ont recours aux sources savent fort bien, qu'on nest pas encore arrivé au point de connoître les finesses de la langue Phénicienne, dont, les noms propres exceptés, on scait à peine cinquante mots. Il faut être de bonne foi, & ne pas mettre plus d'ostentation dans l'étude d'une langue, ou d'une science qu'il ne convient de faire. On n'ignore pas, que les savans ne sont pas d'accord entre eux sur la valeur[8] de toutes les lettres de l'aphabet Phénicien, & supposant même qu'ils fussent, après les avoir réduites à la valeur des lettres Hébraïques, ils n'ont pas d'autre moyen d'interpréter les mots que par la signification qu'ils ont dans la langue Hébraïque ou Syriaque, & dans ce cas, on ne peut pas plus dire que ce que l'on apelle la lingue Phénicienne ou Punique soient des langues propres, que l'on ne pourroit le dire du texte Samaritain du Pentateuque, qui ne differe de l'Hébraïque que par les charactères. Et cependant tout en errant dans ce labyrinthe, on voit des Savans en consulter d'autres, qu'ils disent s'y être égarés comme s'ils en tenoient eux-mêmes le fil.

But to obviate every doubt respecting the oriental colonization of Ireland, the Irish language is adduced as proof, 'that the[9] speakers were a civilized and lettered people, which could only be derived from an eastern connection: that the language is masculine and nervous: harmonious in its articulation; copious in its phraseology, and replete with abstract and technical terms; free from anomalies, sterlities and heteroclite redundancies.' We are told, says Mr Pinkerton,[10] of many abstract terms in the old Irish language, as a proof that the people were civilized; yet no such terms are produced, and if they were, how old are they? The use of Latin abstract terms is quite modern. There is not one Irish manuscript extant older than the eleventh century, long after metaphysics and such trifling sort of learning had been successfully studied there. To which I add, that its copiousness arises from its corruption, and so does its harmony; for in the fourth and fifth centuries, and much earlier, it is branded by the ancients[11] with the harshest expressions for its barbarism; and a native writer,[12] about the year 700, calls it a vile tongue. As no genuine specimen of old Celtic has been produced, or possibly can, to warrant the praises bestowed on it, it clearly follows, that to speak it in such panegyrical terms must be to deceive the unlearned reader, while at the same time it betrays the writer's profound ignorance. But to evince how easy it is to indulge in the praise of any tongue, even the most barbarous and unpolished, take the following instance from an admirer of the Gothic.

> Les Goths[13] n'étoient pas une nation si grossière que l'on imagine: ce qu'il prouve par la politesse & par a régularité de leur langue. C'est ce que l'on peut voir, I. par les genres masculin, feminin, & neutre des noms, &c. Ce qu'il y a de plus remarquable dans la langue Gothique, c'est qu'elle ne se sert point due verbe auxiliaire avoir, non plus que les Grécs & les Latins, pour ne point parler des langues orientales, ce qui est une preuve incontestable de sa grande antiquité.

That any nation, particularly the Gothic, wrapt in Cimmerian darkness, should rival the Irish in politeness, regularity and antiquity of language, is enough to stir the bile of the most stoical Hibernian, nor is it less irritating for Rudbeck[14] to make his Gotho-Runic the fountain from whence flowed the Greek and Phoenician letters, whence all the world knows the Irish bethluisnión of the ogma can alone aspire to that distinguished honor; and that the Celtic[15] is the true parent of the Hebrew, Arabic, Persic, Japonese, Mungallic, Greek, Latin, Sclavonian, Oscan, Showiah, Tamzeght, Algonkin and a thousand more. The author of this most eccentric whimsy cannot be serious: if he only meant to banter the unprofitable studies of some Antiquaries, he has succeeded admirably: for

Non potuit melius litem sinire jocosam.

The † aid of etymology is called in to demonstrate the eastern complexion of the Irish tongue, by the Author last cited. If he designed to prove the Celtic to be originally the same as the Hebrew or any other Oriental language, he ought, as a scholar, to have shown their agreement in matter and form;[16] for it is from these, and not from resemblances in sound, the affinity of languages is to be inferred. The Celtic, in its structure, varies from every other tongue. In it,[17] words are declined by changing not the terminations but the initial letters in the oblique cases. Its pronouns alter the beginning of nouns, and its grammar cancels every rule of language. Not to insist on the[18] uncertainty of etymology from the vicious orthography of words by Lexicographers, and the vicious orthoëpy of sounds by the natives themselves, the Irish leavar for liber, litur for litera, and scriptuir for scriptura, abundantly demonstrate, that we had neither letters, writing or books, until received through a Roman intercourse. This Innes has long since observed. The corrupt state of ancient tongues has, at all times, been a fine field for literary trifling, and a rich soil for sciolists and alphabetarians to flourish in. On the whole, the pretensions of the Irish to an eastern origin is a vain and groundless notion, generated in ignorance and mistaken patriotism, disgraceful to the good sense of the nation, and not to be supported by reason, history, or learning.

The part we have now been travelling over is described by Virgil:

Umbrarum hic locus est somni noctisque soparae,
Hic & lucisugae posuêre cubilia blattae.

Something of light and certainty breaks in upon us as we advance in this inquiry. The voice of antiquity is silent as to druidic letters, which are said to have been used in this isle. Caesar[19] says they existed, but that passage has been long suspected as the interpolation of Julius Celsus; who, I believe, had Strabo[20] in view when he inserted it. The want of native British letters is strongly inferred[21] from the legends on the coins of Cunobeline, for if the druids had a peculiar alphabet, or used the Greek letters, as Caesar asserts, superintending religion and learning as they did, and obstinately retentive of their opinions and customs, they assuredly would have put their own and not Roman letters on the coins of their princes. Mabillon[22] is more than doubtful about the existence of the Gaulish letters, nor does he seem to lay much stress on the alphabet collected by Boterue from sepulchral inscriptions. It is above fifteen hundred years ago since Celsus opposed the antiquity of the druids and their wisdom to those of the Jews. What was Origen's answer? I do not know, says the Father,[23] that they have left us any writings. It was incumbent on Celsus then as on our druids now, to support the extraordinary things they have advanced concerning these sages by other arguments than confident assertions.

But the boldest attempt to silence the opposers of ancient Irish literature is the production[24] of an inscription on Callan mountain, in the county of Clare, its date AD295. Here the Gauntlet is thrown down, and the literary world challenged to an investigation of these extraordinary Irish elements. The article in the Archaeologia informs us, that the Irish Seanachies and Antiquaries seriously assert the use of a character called ogham, not used as a cipher but as an uniform alphabet, wherein all matters relating to the state and religion were recorded. But in the next page, the modern bards are charged with inventing oghams, and changing 150 circular scales of Prosodia into right-lined oghams, and imposing them on the world for so many different alphabets. How this author will reconcile the positive accusation of invention and mistake in the writers[25] below cited, with their serious assertion of an uniform alphabet, will require some ingenuity to explain. He confesses he erroneously said, the ogham characters were marked by certain strokes standing perpendicularly on an horizontal master-line, but from ancient manuscripts he found the master-line was drawn perpendicular, and the characters marked by strokes perpendicular to it, on the right and left. Such are the author's words in the Archaeologia. Notwithstanding all the new lights he received, he gives … another manner of writing the ogham, which is with horizontal strokes on each side of a perpendicular line. It appears then, that neither the circular mode of drawing the ogham, nor the horizontal master-line with perpendicular strokes, nor the perpendicular master-line with perpendicular strokes, are right, but the perpendicular line with horizontal strokes. So that here Seanachies contradict manuscripts and manuscripts oppose inscriptions. Does not this jargon approach very near Persius's:

Aegroti veteris meditantis fomnia: Gigni
De nihilo nihil, in nihilum nil posse neverti

I believe the reader will be apt to credit Mr Pinkerton, who affirms this same Celtic has the strange effect to obnubilating the mind, and this he demonstrates, by numerous examples, has been unhappily the case with this writer.

Our author in the Archaeolgia grants, that he has never been able to discover ogham inscriptions on stones, altars or cromlecc, and yet in a former work[26] he asks with strong emphasis – 'shall we doubt the authority of Sir James Ware, shall we disbelieve our eyes, when we behold ogham inscriptions on many remains of antiquity?' In four pages after he says: 'we are sorry it is not in our power to quote any passages of our druidic ogham, such books having not fallen into our hands.' This sort of contradictory writing goes to the subversion of all sober inquiry; it resembles this author's ogham, which, like the characters of the Montcheou Tartars, are legible up and down, backwards and forwards: it is a sort of literary conjuring, where the reader:

Obstupuit, varia confusus imagine rerum.

To rescue therefore a subject thus in danger of being irretrievably lost, we must recur to the old Irish antiquaries, who, after all their vagarees, give the only rational information. Ware is the first, I think, who mentions the ogham, and that in a way not to afford matter of triumph as to its usefulness or antiquity. He describes it as made up of various occult forms, or artificial modes of writing for secrecy. The 150 notes mentioned by Mac Firbis, O'Flaherty calls 'different forms of characters'. These expressions indicate stenographic as well as steganographic notes, referring to some fictitious characters or ciphers.

In 1669, O'Molloy, in his Irish Grammar, enters more fully into this subject, and is literally copied by every writer since. He informs us the ogham was divided into three kinds: I. ogham beith, when bh, or the Irish letter beith being part of the first consonant, is placed instead of the vowel a. This ogham is also called ogham consoine, or the ogham made out of consonants. Here is an example:[27]

a	e	i	o	u
bh.	fc.	ng.	dl.	ft.

The same method may be observed in substituting consonants for dipthongs. Thus:

ae	ia	ua	io	oi
mm.	ll.	bb.	cc.	pp.

The second sort is ogham coll, or the ogham composed out of the letter c: when for all the vowels, dipthongs and tripthongs the letter c is substituted, variously repeated, doubled and turned, as thus:

a	e	i	o	u
c.	cccc.	cccc.	cc.	ccc.
ea	ia	oi	io	ua
ᴜ	ꭒ̥	ꜱ	ꭢ	ꜱꜱ

The third sort is the ogham croabh, or the virgular ogham; it has an horizontal master-line, through which and on each side are perpendicular strokes which stand in the place of vowels, consonants, dipthongs and tripthongs. This is exhibited in the plate, no. 1, as the perpendicular master-line with horizontal strokes is seen in no. 2. and the Callan inscription in no. 3. What is now produced from Molloy is rational and intelligible, nor can there be any doubt but all these cryptographic modes[28] were practised in all the northern countries of Europe: for in the celebrated Icelandic Edda[29] at Upfal is an instance of the ogham consoine, where instead of the vowel, that consonant which followed next in the alphabet is placed. As:

Dfxtfrt scrkptprks bfnfdkth skt pmnkbxs hprks.

Instead of a, e, i, o, u, y, the letters b, f, k, p, x and z were put, so that it reads thus:

Dextera scriptoris benedicta fit omnibus horis.

Von Troil remarks that a similar ogham may be seen in Rabanus Maurus's tract, De usu literarum, written about the middle of the ninth century. Verelius, Wormius, with many existing monuments prove, that the Northerns writ their runes in every possible form; in circles, in angles, from right to left, and vice versa. Wormius[30] enumerates twelve different ways of making runic inscriptions. The German Buchstab[31] or runes were drawn sometime in horizontal, and sometimes in perpendicular lines. Here we have, if not the original of our ogham croabh, a practice exactly similar. In a word, these wonderful Irish oghams were nothing, as we see, but a stenographic and steganographic contrivance, common to the semibarbarians of Europe in the middle of ages, and very probably derived from the Romans.

161

Alphabets & Ogums.

Ogum Croabh		O'Sullivan's Ogum		British Ogum			Bobeloth			Bethluifnion		
Charact.	Power	Character	Pow.	Char.	Pow	Name	Char.	Po.	Name	Charact.	Pow	Name
	B				a	Alap		B	Boibel		B	Beth
	L	+	B		b	Braut		L	Loth		L	Luis
	N	X	L		c	Curi		F	Forann		N	Nion
	T		F		d	Dexu		S	Salra		F	Fearn
	J		S		e	Egin		V	Neiagadon		S	Suil
	H		N		f	Fich		H	Uiria		H	Uath
	D	∧	H		g	Guidir		D	Daibhaith		D	Duir
	T		D		h	Huil		T	Teilmen		T	Tinne
	C		T		i	Iechuit		C	Caoi		C	Coll
	Q		C		k	Kam		Cc	Cailep		M	Muin
	M		M		l	Louber		M	Moiria		G	Gort
	G		G		m	Mum		G	Gath		P	Peth-boc
	Ng		ng		n	Nihn		Ng	Ngoimar		R	Ruis
	Sd		R		o	Or		I	Idra		A	Ailm
	R		A		p	Parth		R	Ruiben		O	On
	Ab		O		q	Quith		A	Acab		U	Ur
	O		U		r	Rat		O	Ose		E	Eadhadh
	Ub		E		t	Traus		U	Ura		I	Idho
	E		I		s	Sung		E	Esu			
	J		ia		u	Uir		I	Jaichim			
			ai		x	Jeil						
			coi		e	Off						
			ua		z	Zeure						
			eg		ae	Auui						
			feo		et	Eftiaul						
			oai		au	Egur						
			oai		au	Aur						
					ei	Eme						
						Kenc						
						Elau						

Callen Inscription. 3

Marcomannic Runes.

Charact.	Po.	Name	Char.	Pos.	Name
	A	Asc		I	His
	B	Byrith		K	Chilch
	C	Chen		L	Lagu
	D	Thorn		M	Man
	E	Ech		N	Not
	F	Fech		O	Othil
	G	Gibu		P	Perc
	H	Hagale			

Publish'd by John Jones Nº 90 Brida Street Dublin.

Mr Macpherson, after ably[32] stating the great improbability of the early use of letters in Ireland, remarks that ogham is a word which has no affinity with any other in the Irish language, and seems therefore to be a cant name imposed upon a species of stenography or cipher, in which the old Irish, like many other nations, write their secrets. This opinion is not quite correct. As to ogham being a cant name and not found in dictionaries, that is partly true and partly false. The word is preserved in the Welsh,[33] where Ogan is augury, divination. Keyzler also tells us,[34] that oga, ogham and ogma are told Celtic words, implying letters written in cipher, and indirectly an occult science. Thus its true import is ascertained.

Innumerable words, in the lapse of time, have been lost in the Irish as well as every other language.

The most polished nations of the world have beheld with astonishment the art, whereby can be comprehended the thoughts, word and actions of men, past and present, and that by the combination of a few letters. The Indians could not conceive how paper marked with black strokes could communicate intelligence, unless it was animated. When Leri[35] wrote down some sentences of the Brazilian language, and the next day repeated them to the natives, they instantly concluded he did it by some magical or supernatural means. The North America Indians thought[36] Carver's book a spirit, when he told them the number of leaves by looking at the figures at the top of the page. The eastern and western runes and oghams were all posterior to the invention of letters, for barbarians, as we have seen, ascribed occult qualities to the former, from discovering the power of the letter. And this is the opinion of Arngrim Jonas,[37] a most skilful northern antiquary, who thinks the northern runer or conjurers had some little common learning, but that they greatly corrupted the alphabetic elements by virgular ciphers and points, which he supposes invented by them, the more to excite admiration of their wisdom and knowledge among a rude people. Letters themselves, says Mallet,[38] were more frequently employed among the Danes for the foolish purpose of working prodigies than to assist the memory, or render words fixed and permanent. And no wonder, when Odin taught, that the art of writing was to be regarded as the art of working all sorts of miracles.

The persons in the North, who thus affected superior skill in learning, in magic, astrology and other branches of ancient lore, were, according to Wormius, styled Runer and Adelruner: so that † rune and ogham are perfectly equivalent in sense, and had the same origin. One singularly remarkable fact here offers itself, which has hitherto escaped notice, and that is, the existence of the word 'run', in the Irish language and dictionaries, signifying a secret or mystery. The word and its meaning must have been adopted from the Northerns, for it could not co-exist in the Teutonic or Gothic and Celtic in similar letters and import, unless we assert these tongues to be the same. As all know they were not, then we must have had it from the Northern invaders of this isle, and to them is to be attributed the loss of the old Celtic name, ogham, for that of Run, introduced by them. O'Brien[39] treating of this word, without any design of doing so, confirms the truth of what is asserted by shewing, that in five dialects of the Teutonic it is preserved, in its original signification.

It is very likely the Northerns had the first notions of these Runes from an eastern connection, when they dwelt on the western side of the Euxine; particularly from the Greeks.[40] To omit the oriental Cabbala,[41] the Greeks had their Ephesian letters, which not only protected[42] from harm, but insured safety and success. The early ages of Christianity were infected with this error, as we learn from Irenaeus, Tertullian and Philastrius; nor were even some of the most learned fathers, as Origen, free from it. There is a passage in Eustathius upon Homer on the power of these Ephesian letters, too long for insertion here, but its spirit is well expressed in these sentences of the Edda.[43] 'Do you,' says Odin, 'know how to engrave runic characters, how to explain them, how to prove their virtue? If we see a man dead, and hanging aloft upon a tree, I engrave runic characters so wonderful, that the man immediately descends and converses with me, &c.' They were believed to have a physical innate quality, which made them noxious, favourable, medicinal and fitted for every wish, action or undertaking.

As soon as the Germans had learned the use of letters from the Romans, their Runer, Adelruner, necromancers or priests adopted the Roman[44] divinatory notes for magic purposes. It would have been very difficult to have determined the figure of these notes, were we not told by Cicero[45] and Suetonius that they resembled old obsolete letters.

Il n'y a rien si vrai, que l'entêtement des scavans septentrionaux pourles Runes: les suedois y tiennent le premier rang; mais Mr Sperling m'a ecrit autrefois qu'il ne les croit pas si anciennes. C'est pourtant une chose assez remarquable, que beaucoup de ces lettres sont semblables a celles qui se trouvent sur les medailles d'Espagne, dont j'a beau coup de copiee tirés du cabinet de Mr de Barry, et sur les piedestaux des statues Etruriennes publies par Bellori, & je n'ai encore trouve personne, quoique j'ay e consulte divers l'taliens qui peut me donner quelque eclaircissement la dessus.

This is part of a letter from Cuper to La Croze. The ancient notes are comprised under three[46] heads: 1. hieroglyphical, where the thing to be understood is expressed by a symbol, as a circle for the sun. Where a cipher or character has the power of many letters, as in the Tyronian notes. Ennius, it is said,[47] invented eleven hundred of the latter, but in reality he took them from Eastern and Grecian archetypes. Tiro and others added many to those of Ennius, and Seneca augmented and digested the whole, and they are to be found at the end of Gruter's inscriptions. In these and in the second sort or Sigla were the Roman laws and proceedings written, which of course became so obscure that Tribonianus, who compiled the Justinian Code, was frequently at a loss to develope their signification. This induced the Emperor in 533 to forbid their use.[48] From their forms they were called[49] puncta, lineae, flexurae, catenationes, signorum capitones and compendiosa aenigmata; terms not easily rendered into English, yet conveying to us an idea of the multiplied modes of ancient brachygraphy and cryptography. Besides these there were notae serviles, pecuariae, juridicae. &c. and many more in common and daily use, all taken from the great body of Tiro's and Seneca's notes. Wherever a Roman station or colony was, there notes were necessary, and we have seen to what purposes they were applied by the surrounding barbarians. In the sixth century, Venantius Fortunatus mentions the old German custom of carving or painting Runes to have been common among the Franks.

Barbara fraxineis pingatur Runa tabellis.

About the year 1500, Trithemius discovered that the ancient Norman and Francic alphabets were mixt with these notes.[50] He met with them in a Davidic Psalter in the Strasburgh library. The Francs had letters[51] before they received Christianity. Here then is an extraordinary authentication of the existence and use of these notes in Germany for more than a thousand years, and this proves that the Northerns (contrary to what is generally believed) were acquainted with the alphabetic elements so early at least as their intercourse with the Romans.

There is no part of literary history more obscure than the formation of alphabets; nor is there any part of it more curious. Writers[52] have contented themselves with deducing the Francic and Saxon from the Latin, and the Runic from the Gothic, which in the improved state of these alphabets is, in some degree true; but they have not accounted for the strange and barbarous characters found in all, nor ascertained the time and cause of their insertions; I presume to offer but a few hints, introductory to an investigation of our Irish elements. The complete elucidation of this subject requires uncommon philological and critical learning, and would very properly have made a part of Mr Astle's ingenious work on the Origin of writing. On the arrival of letters in the North, the various cryptic and stenographic modes of writing practised by the Romans were immediately known. The latter the barbarian priests adopted and studied, and that, in preference to the former, as being better calculated for magical purposes, and to make the vulgar stare. Such was the degradation of Religion in those ages, that it had sunk into inchantment and the grossest superstition; and such the corruption of letters, that they were become Tironian or Runic ciphers. The last particular every diplomatic writer, and every table of alphabets will confirm. During the time of the Gothic power in Italy, the Roman elements suffered a remarkable change.[53] A greater deviation ensued under the Longobards, and in the eighth century Roman letters were only found in the titles of manuscripts. Alphabets were composed of letters and Roman notes, uncouth in their figure, confused in their order, and barbarous in their name. The annexed plate demonstrates this. These alphabets seem to have been a national and even provincial concern. For as each country and tribe was distinguished by some particular ensign, as a Dragon, Raven, &c. so were they by a peculiar alphabet, which, while preserved, was supposed to contribute by its magic and occult qualities to the power and permanence of the state. Let us now attend to the proof.

'It appears,' says a most learned Antiquary,[54] 'that the various foreigners inhabiting Britain, in the Saxon times, framed each an alphabet for themselves. From whence otherwise could spring such a diversity of Letters and Alphabets unknown elsewhere, and greatly surpassing in number those found in the MSS of any other country?' And as evidence he adduces a rubric prefixed to one of these fictitious alphabets, which runs thus: 'Nemninus being upbraided by a Saxon scholar, as if the Britons were ignorant of the rudiments of learning, invented these letters, suddenly forming them from his own conceptions, to wipe away from his nation the imputation of dulness and ignorance.' This was placed before the British ogham in the plate. Neither Langbaine, who I believe first communicated this rubric to Archbishop Usher;[55] nor Hickes,[56] who found it in the Bodleian Library, nor La Croze seem to understand its meaning: the last observes, if it be not a jeu d'esprit, the Britons must have lost all memory of their antiquities, for it suggests, that before this they had not letters. This however is a thoughtless guess, because the Britons had letters at least four centuries before the arrival of the Saxons; and if they had not, this extempore alphabet was not likely to render them general. The rubric records a contest between two literary men, one a Briton, the other an Anglo-Saxon. The latter was well acquainted with stenography and steganography, which in reality required much application and study, and therefore he prized very highly, calling them 'Rudimentum', as the Schoolmen did their Quiddities, the only solid foundation of learning. In these he believed the Briton eminently defective, but by producing an extemporaneous alphabet, the latter showed the Saxon he was mistaken. It was not with ignorance of letters the Briton was upbraided, but of this rudimentum.

That each people had peculiar and appropriated alphabets, I need but cite Arngrim Jonas, who writing to Wormius tells him, there were Greenland, Opland, Greek, and Ira † letur or Irish runes. And from the same work[57] we learn, that the Malrunae were proper to some people and invariably used by them. All the northern alphabets were originally made up of letters and Tironian notes, the latter seem to have been the Malrunae. Wormius[58] has tortured his ingenuity to explain the consonants and vowels in these ciphers, but in vain; as well might he reduce to an alphabet the scrawling of an infant. Used in[59] diabolical exorcisms and conjurations, the zealous Roman missionaries endeavoured to destroy these notes or Runes. Mallet[60] also remarks, that as soon as the Gospel was preached in the North, an intermixture of the Roman letters appeared with the Runic, and that the latter continued to give way till finally abolished. Here he intimates what was nearly the truth, that the Runic like the other barbarous alphabets, was at first almost entirely made up of notes or magic Runes. The Marcomannic Runes,[61] in the plate, have out of fifteen but four letters resembling the Roman. And Wormius declares they agreed with the Runic, in the strangeness of their shape and names. The Norman alphabet in Bede is another instance. The Gothic, improperly ascribed to Ulphilas, has many characters, as given by Johannes Magnus and Bernard in his tables, quite unlike the Greek and Roman, and taken from the notes. The present Runic, without reason said to be derived from the Gothic, exhibits but three or four letters similar to the Greek and Roman. Hickes explicitly declares,[62] the present Anglo-Saxonic elements are not the entire old ones, but a more modern compound of Latin letters; and a very good judge[63] observes, the old Saxon letters resembled the Runic, that is, the notes. Here is a variety of testimonies all uniting in proof of the same fact: that the Northern priests and necromancers, on their acquaintance with the Roman letters, adopted the Roman divinatory and other notes: that these being used in conjurations, and known only to their Runer and Adelruner, acquired the name of Runes: that whole alphabets were formed from them, or with but a few letters scattered through them: that these magical alphabets multiplied in the dark ages, and spread over western and northern Europe, and that such were the ancient Irish elements we shall now see.

The oldest Irish alphabet is said to be the Bobeloth, so called from the names of certain masters,[64] who assisted in forming the Japhetian language. So idle a tale one would not expect to find in a modern Grammar: it is obvious this alphabet was denominated from Bobel, Loth, its two first letters. The other names and the figure of the letters are exactly in the style of the British, Runic, and Marcomannic Runes, as an inspection of the plate will evince. As might be expected, they resemble the Roman notes and Northern Runes. The learned Mr Pinkerton[65] remarks, that the Bobeloth was a contracted mode of writing, well known by the name of Notae Longobardicae. If he had added 'secret' to contracted, he would have been perfectly right; for according to Mabillon, these Longobardic notes were the same as the other northern alphabets before spoken of.

Kinsaolidh, an author of the seventh century, is said[66] to have transcribed and illustrated the Irish Grammar. This notice would have been passed over, but that what it records happened in other countries. Thus the Runic, Anglo-Saxon, Gothic, and other alphabets were gradually purged of their Runes, and in their place Roman letters substituted. The same thing probably happened in Ireland in the seventh age: so that by transcribing and illustrating, I understand the composition of a new alphabet, perhaps the present Bethluisnion, which still preserves strong marks of a barbarous period. The two characters[67] given in the plate as varieties of the letter N; one as H, two as M, one as A, and one as E, being seven, and not to be seen as capitals or currents, as far as I have examined, in the common tables, but all of them in the Roman notes, prove they are the remains of the old ogham or magical alphabet; even were this not the case, its name sufficiently verifies this curious fact: it is called Bethluisnion na Ogma, or the alphabet of magic or mysterious letters; a title expressing the true form of its original ciphers, and the use they were applied to, and such were O'Sullivan's and all other oghams, being derivatives from the Roman notes. At first they were stenographic, then steganographic, then magical, and lastly alphabetic. Every circumstance relative to our letters confirms the truth of what has been advanced. They were called[68] Feadha or Woods, because like the conjuring rods of Tacitus's old Germans and the old tablets of the Franks, these Runes or oghams were carved on them, and these are the genuine virgular characters, noticed by O'Flaherty.

In the Barbarian alphabets the order was not conformable to the Roman, but arbitrary and capricious: nothing less could be expected from the manner of composing them. 'Those,' says Wormius,[69] 'who would accommodate the Runic to the Roman order err egregiously.' Mr Astle[70] cannot be exact as to the time when the order of the Runic letters was confounded: it was in its first formation, and continued so to the reign of Woldemar,[71] AD1185, when the Roman order was established. The Irish Bethluisnion is a living monument of a barbarous age. It begins with B, L, N; but N was anciently the fifth letter: A is its fourteenth, and all the consonants are placed before the vowels, so that in want of order as in every other particular, it entirely agrees with the Runic and other ancient northern alphabets. The rudeness and superstition of the Irish, through every age, invincibly attached them to their Bethluisnion na Ogma, as Runes are, at this day, used in the mountains of Sweden.[72]

We may recollect, that our historical romancers asserted the derivation of our letters from the Phaenicians. The learned Mr Astle[73] speaking of the 'Textus Sancti Cuthberti', written in the seventh century, remarks, that 'it is in capitals, which were used by the Greeks, Etruscans, Romans, Visigoths, Saxons, French, and Germans; and that its alphabet bears strong testimony, that the letters used by our Saxon ancestors are derived from the Phoenician, the Greek, and Etruscan, through the medium of those of the Roman letters.' – If I understand this paragraph, it means that the Saxon alphabet is taken from the Romans, as the latter is from the Phoenician, the Greek and Etruscan, which no one denies, and which Bernard's tables make evident. But, according to Mr Astle, this text of the Gospels is written in letters used by the Greeks, Etruscans, Romans, Visigoths, Saxons, French and Germans. The first question here to be asked is, did all these people use the same alphabet? The answer is direct and positive, that they did not. The Romans had their 'literae unciales, cubitales, grandes and quadratae'. The Franks, besides a mixture of Tironian notes, had their 'literae Francogallicae & Merovingicae', and the Saxons had a very old alphabet and a more recent one. The same may be said of the other people. Where then did Ealfrith the monk, who so beautifully wrote[74] this manuscript for St Cuthbert, find these capital letters of so many nations? The fact is, he neither found them nor fought for them, but he used the Roman notes, which in reality do approximate to the letters of every people, and were originally old obsolete letters, and were adopted by the nations Mr Astle mentions, first as a contracted, then a secret, then a magical mode of writing, and lastly, as alphabetic elements, or mixt with them. Our learned and ingenious author, not aware of this progress, has necessarily expressed himself obscurely, and taken a position not tenable. Here is an additional confirmation of the idea pursued in these pages.

It is probable the use of brachygraphic and cryptographic notes was known in Ireland, at the very time St Cuthbert's text was written, and the numerous capricious alphabets were invented, and this may be inferred from an epistle[75] of Aldhelm to Eahfrid, who was just returned from our isle, after a residence of six years. – It is thus:

Digna fiat fante glingio gurgo fugax fambulo.

The gloss subjoined, which is by no means intelligible, however shews, that it was written in ciphers, each expressing one or more words, as did the Tironian and other notes. It was thrown out by the petulant but ingenious Aldhelm to puzzle Eahfrid, and try the extent of his scholarship and Hibernian education. Perhaps the reader may consider the following instance also in point. Adamnan, an Irishman and Abbat of Hy, in the year 700, composed the life of St Columba, whose successor he was. In the Preface to this performance he says, 'he has cyphered[76] but a few things to avoid tiring the reader'. Though the verb *caraxare* is often used for *scribere*, or *exarare*, yet, from the numerous instances that might be collected, some of which are given below,[77] it is especially applicable to stenographic notes, and the Glossary of Isidore calls the short hand writer, 'Charaxarius'. So that Adamnan talking of the brevity of his work, uses this word with singular propriety.

As to the Callan inscription, which first give rise to this enquiry, the mode of cryptography there used, is the simplest that could be devised, that of strokes on each side of a master-line.

These could never be the 'uncouth virgular characters', spoken of by O'Conor, for uncouth can only be applied to the strange forms of the other oghams, taken from the Roman notes. This was of all the worst calculated to promote literature, or, preserve the memory of events: For it requires fifteen lines or strokes to express the five first letters of the alphabet, or fifty-one, for the eighteen elements of the Irish language. And is this the ogham which we are told,[78] 'the Irish Antiquaries preserved as a piece of the greatest value, and that it was penal for any but the druids, to study or use it'? Indeed it is honouring such reveries too much, to mention them.

Scripta pudet recitare, & nugis addere pondus.

However, as some men of learning think favourably of this inscription, it is necessary to add a few remarks more on the subject.

The inscription in the Archaeologia is:

Beneath lies Conal-Colgac, the long-footed.

It is also read thus:[79] 'Beneath this sepulchral monument is laid Conan the fierce, the nimble-footed.' These different interpretations by the same person look suspicious, but what shall we say, when we are given three other various readings by this writer? This was a fatal step; the Gentleman forgot, that the argument that proves too much, proves nothing: applied to the present case, it must demonstrate to every man of sense, that the different explications are grounded on no certain principles, and made out by different scales of ogham, and by reading it then from right to left, and vice versa. Such childish manoeuvres are really ridiculous, and have justly disgraced our Antiquities.

If two interpretations give the name of Conal, and three confessedly do not, is there not more than an equal chance that the latter is right? And if so, what becomes of the veracity of the Bardic Tale by which this wonderful Sepulchre was discovered? A single erasure or omission of a stroke was sufficient to alter, or bury the meaning in perpetual oblivion. Was accuracy to be expected from rude and barbarous Irish engravers in the third century? Or can it be imagined, that the Callan inscription has stood almost 1500 years in a naked and wild situation, uninjured by the tooth of time, and all the vicissitudes of a variable climate? That the great Atlantic Ocean and its briny atmosphere, have had no influence on this rock, and so far from pulverizing its surface, have rendered it unfit for vegetation? These are wonderful things! Perhaps the venerable druid who performed the funeral rites to the names of Conal-Colgach (and who has not heard of Conal-Colgach?) not only pronounced the 'sit terra levis', but washed the stone with a magic composition of Miseltoe, Samolus and Selago, and in a fine prophetic phrenzy, predicted the amazing discoveries of Irish Antiquaries in the eighteenth century.

Great reason have we then to deplore that easy credulity, which could entertain favourable sentiments of one of the boldest, most artless and groundless figments offered to the learned world, since the days of Annius of Viterbo and Curtius Inghiramus: a figment arising from that too common weakness of mankind, of advancing on every occasion something surprising and marvellous. It was thus (the case is exactly similar) that the fissures[80] on a rock at Deighton, in North America, were taken for Phoenician inscriptions, when even a superficial observer, on viewing them, would instantly pronounce them the effects of frost and of the climate. But an Antiquary would blush at such a vulgar decision: the face of nature and reality of things, stubborn in every other hands, become plastic in his. His ingenuity and literature have not only the magic power of moulding them into any form, but he can fascinate every eye within the sphere of his operations.

The intercourse subsisting between the British Isles naturally introduced[81] a knowledge of the Roman elements into Ireland at an early period. Wanley must therefore be much mistaken when he asserted[82] our Irish letters were communicated to us and the Britons by Augustine, the English Apostle, about the conclusion of the sixth century. Lhuyd shews this opinion to be ill founded so far as regards the Britons: as to the Irish, says he, 'the Roman arms never reached them, so that it is evident, of the three nations, the Britons, the Saxon and Irish, the first had a learned education and civilized manners, and whence should the others have had their letters but from their neighbours? I know the Irish will answer, that Avergin the son of Mil Espaine, who was the first[83] of the nation of the Scots, who arrived in Ireland in the time of Solomon, wrote the same characters which are still in use among them; but every one knows it is impossible to be assured of that, and all learned men agree, that we have no certain knowledge concerning the inhabitants of these islands, nor of the other barbarians of Europe, older than the writings of the Greeks and Romans. This must be granted by the Saxons and Irish, as well as by the Welsh, that some two of them received their alphabet from the third, because each of them not only retains the same letters, but the same pronunciation of them: I say the same letters, because the Saxons did not write any of the letters K, O and X, no more than we; nor do the Irish make use of them to this day. So that either the Britons taught the Saxons and Irish, or the Irish taught the former. If the Irish taught the Britons, then they must have had Latin letters before the coming of the Romans into Britain, which it is impossible to prove. As the Britons had letters before the time of Juvenal and Tacitus, I see no reason to doubt, but that the Irish received their ancient alphabet, first from the Britons, and the Saxons, three of the four ages after, learned them from the Britons and Irish.' Thus far Lhuyd, whose sentiments on every point regarding the ancient literature of these kingdoms merit the greatest attention. The oldest remains of a British alphabet are seen on the coins of Cunobeline, who ruled a part of Britain in the reign of Augustus. Christianity, which was early introduced, extended the use of letters among the provincial Britons: they were necessary for their intercourse with the Romans. But it was to be expected, that the Latin language and letters would have been corrupted in passing through the hands and mouths of rude people. The Spanish poets of Corduba, who composed in Latin, though highly accomplished, had notwithstanding, according to Cicero,[84] something 'pingue atque peregrinum', inelegant and foreign to an Italian ear, and which detracted from their excellence. The same was observed of all the municipal schools.[85] The Roman soldiery in Britain were mostly of German Latinized cities, and the auxiliaries, German and French, consequently the purity of the Latin tongue and the shape of its letters were soon changed: barbarism was perceived in the enunciation of the one and in the form of the other. Through this medium the Roman divinatory and other notes, and the notion of their magic powers were communicated to the Britons.

But the corrupt Roman elements, which the Irish adopted, were inadequate to a notation of the sounds of their language. O'Molloy, our oldest grammarian,[86] allows but seventeen letters, excluding h, k, q, w, x, y and z: O'Conor reckons eighteen, taking in h; p he says is not found in the more ancient glossaries. Lhuyd makes them eighteen, with thirteen dipthongs, five tripthongs and five vowels, so that there are forty-one sounds expressed by but eighteen letters. This number of sounds must not appear incredible, for the present Russian has forty-one,[87] the Sanscrit fifty, the Malabarian and Cashmirian many more; ours arose from the corruption of the Celtic by the swarms of barbarians who over-ran the country at different times; for in the island of St Kilda, remote from human intercourse, the simple sounds of the Celtic were but few, and the natives[88] did not use the letters D, G and R.

Confusion and uncertainty in writing and pronouncing the Irish, unavoidably resulted from this want of notation. Thus b, e, d, f, g, m, p, r and f, with h, or a point added, totally changed their sounds, and they became other consonants. The pronunciation of the dipthongs and tripthongs are quite unintelligible from their notations, and can only be learned by the ear;[89] and O'Conor confesses, the compounds gn, oi and to have no equivalent sound in any language he knew. The remarks of a judicious grammarian and lexicographer[90] are to the present purpose, and not undeserving the reader's notice.

> The French language has seventeen vowels, though there is a notation but for five: there are twenty-one consonants, but a notation only for eighteen, and there are four consonants, ch, gn, ill, and y, of which the alphabet gives no manner of knowledge. Both vowels and consonants are represented different ways: some can not be represented for want of proper simple characters, but by several letters. Now each of the letters which make up these diverse combinations has not the sound or articulation which it has when pronounced by itself; and those letters blended together, represent a sound which has no affinity with those which each of them represents singly. If therefore a teacher makes his pupils name each of the letters which make up these combinations, he will make them pronounce false sounds. As the present French alphabet does not contain all the sounds and articulations of the language, nor all the ways of representing them, a more rational and easy method must be thought of to facilitate a knowledge of them. Spelling words will never give them the sounds, they must be pronounced after a master.

The fact is therefore, as might be expected, that the speech of the Irish became a fluctuating jargon, full of strange dialects; it had no analogy in its sounds; its anomalous verbs[91] are so variously formed as to depend entirely on the practice of writers; there are no rules[92] for its cases; it possesses neither alphabetical sounds, words for ideas, orthography, or syntax. The essay on the colonization of Ireland will satisfactorily account for these particulars. The Welsh is[93] equally disfigured, mutilated and corrupted.

To confirm what is advanced, Lombard, titular Archbishop of Armagh in 1632, shews[94] how widely the dialects of the four provinces differed, and that Leinster was defective in just phraseology and pronunciation: and O'Conor[95] informs us, that it is little more than an hundred years since the schools wherein the Irish language had been taught in its purity have failed; and yet anomalies and solecisms have multiplied, and the growing ignorance in the true orthoëpy has already thrown many words out of their radical structure. 'Did we read a passage,' adds he, 'of classical Irish to the common people of Ireland, the greater part would be absolutely unintelligible to them.' The interval between the time Lombard and O'Conor writ, was more than a century, and yet the latter talks of Irish being taught in its purity at time the former declared it to be corrupted. Almost a century before Lombard's age, Stanihurst in Hollinshead writes thus, 'the true Irish differeth so much from that they commonlie speak, that scarce one in five hundreth can either rede, write, or understonde it; therefore it is preserved among certeine of their poets and antiquaries.' So that as soon as the language came to be examined by scholars and grammarians they found it a jargon not reducible in orthography, orthoëpy, or syntax to any standard. This is the language which the very eccentric author of the *Collectanea de rebua Hibernicis* asserts to be the parent of every other on the globe.

170

O tribus Anticyris
Caput infanabile!

'I shall not determine,' says Leibnitz,[96] 'whether the Anglo-Saxons brought their letters into England, or whether they learned them from the Britons.' That the Saxons and Irish had their original elements from those of the Romans, is the opinion of the best antiquaries; and so similar were they, that formerly they were indifferently called Saxon or Irish. The reason for ascribing the Anglo-Saxon alphabet to the Irish was, their having converted, according to Bede, almost the whole nation, and communicating to them together the light[97] of the gospel and of letters. In the Bodleian library[98] is Mac Reguil's, or Regol's gospels in Irish, of the seventh century, and Fareman's and Oen's copy of St Jerome's translation of the gospels, with an interlineary Dano-Saxon version of the tenth century. In the same library is Ovid's Art of Love in Latin, but in Irish characters. In the front or title-page is Christ painted, and at his feet St Dunstan, with inscriptions, all executed by St Dunstan himself. Now it is well known that this saint was an Anglo-Saxon,[99] born in Somersetshire and educated at Glastonbury; so that these Irish letters must have been Anglo-Saxon. Doctor Langbaine, in a letter[100] to Archbishop Usher, says: 'what characters the ancient Britons used, whether that which the Saxons after, as your Lordship if I remember well is of opinion: or the same with your ancient Irish, which I conceive to be not much different from the Saxon, to which the monument of Corcenn,[101] both as to form of some letters and the ligatures of them seem to come nearer than to the Saxon, I dare not take upon me to determine.' If then we can rely on those excellent judges, Uther Langbaine, Hickes and Astle, there can be no doubt of the almost perfect identity of the Anglo-Saxon and Irish elements about the year 830.

To conclude, I am very sensible how much I stand in need of the learned diplomatic reader's indulgence for the hints advanced in this Essay; if they urge a farther investigation of the subject, I shall think my labour fully compensated.

Non quisquam fruitur veris odoribus,
Hyblaeos latebris nec spoliat favos;
Si fronti caveat, si timeat rubos.
                                    Claudian

Notes

1 *History of Scotland*, V. 2. p. 31. He treats some Irish Antiquaries and their compositions with critical severity.

2 Warton's *Hist. of English Poetry*, V. 2. p. 24.

3 Ogyg. p. 221; Innes, p. 448.

4 Ogyg. vindicated. p. 242.

5 Lhuyd, *Archaeol. Brit.*, p. 435.

6 Ogyg. vind. p. 141. This seems doubtful, the specimens of Irish from it are too modern for so early a date.

7 The wretched Aodhgan or Egan, in 1575, could find no place to shelter him, while making remarks on the Brehon laws, but the mill of Dunadaigne. Collect. No. 10. p. 123. Cox. V. 1. p. 346, for the state of the country.

8 To the same purpose one of the first Orientalists of the last century, speaking of some Punic coins says: 'Priores duos Punicos esse libentur darem, si Puncae literature vestigia extarent. Needum ab

aliis, meo judicio, offensum perspicue satis est cujusmodi veterum Paenorum elementa. Hottinger. Cipp. Heb, p. 183.

9 Irish Grammar, p. 2. Edit. 1781.

10 Supra, p. 19.

11 Irenaei adv haeres. lib. 1. Non esse sastidio rudem hunc & incultum transalpini sermonis horrorem. Pacat. Panegyr sermonis Celtici squamam. Sid. Apollin. l. 3. cp. 3.

12 Adamnan, apud Usser. Syllog. p. 42.

13 Bibliothêque Chos. par le Clerc. T. 28. p. 307.

14 Atlant. c. 38.

15 Collectanea reb. Hib. and Irish Grammar, sup. passim.

† Scis enim quam proclive sit quidvis ex quavis lingua exculpere, si genio indulgeamus, Goropii & Rudbeckii & ejus exemplo, qui nuper de origine Hungarorum scripsit. Primus in Belgica, alter in Suecica, tertius en Hungarica vetera deorum vocabul nullo negotio invenit. Leibnitz. Oper. T. 8. p. 138.

16 Wotton, de conf. Ling. apud Chamberlayne, p. 46.

17 Mallet, V. 1. pref. p. 42. Pinkerton's Diff. p. 123, and Scotland pass.

18 Mr Pinkerton can scarcely keep his temper when speaking of our absurd and ridiculous Irish etymologies; he considers them as instances of the grossest insults ever offered to the sense and reason of mankind. Scotland sup. V. 2. iuido.

19 Caesaris hic locus est & alii apud eundem de Graecorum literarum usu, suo tempore apud Gallos, longe suspectus superioria aetatis viris summis. Burton. Hid. Graec. ling. p. 19. Hotoman. Franco-Gall. c. 2. Lips. Elect. l. 2. c. 7. Eayle. Article César.

20 Caesar's words are: publicis privatisque rationibus Graecis literis utuntur. Lib. 6.

21 By Whitaker, sup. pp. 37–373 Astle's Origin of Writing, p. 56.

22 De re Diplom. l. I. c. ii. Leibnitz is of the same opinion. Tom. 8. p. 195. Edit, Dutens.

23 Contra Cels. l. 3.

24 Inserted in the Archaeologia, V. 7. p. 276.

25 The writers here disguised under the name of modern bards are, I apprehend, Mac Firbis and O'Flaherty. Let the reader judge. Ex his aliquas inter antiquitatam monumenta apud se (Mac Firbis) supersuisse, ut ei diversas characterum formulas, quas ter quinquagenas a Fenicii usque aetate numero, & croabb ogham, i.e., virgeas characteres nomine recenset, non ita pridem ad me scripsit Dualdus Firbisius O'Flah. Ogyg. p. 233. Ogyg. vind. p. 9.

26 Irish Grammar, p. 7.

27 Harris's Ware, p. 19.

28 The ancients disposed letters variously for secrecy and amusement. For the seytale of the Greeks see Schol. Thucyd. lib. 1. Plutarch in Lyfand A. Gell. l. 17. c. 9. For Roman contrivances, see Suet. in Aug. c. 88, in J. Caes. c. 56. Dio. 1 39 Morhoff, Polyhist. T. 1. p. 624. Salmuth in Pancipol. tit. 14.

29 Von Troil's Letters on Iceland, p. 299.

30 Literat. Run. p. 138, 139.

31 Pelloutier, Hist. des Celtes. T. I. p. 402. Mallet, V. I. p. 363.

32 Introduction. Indes, 1. p. 445. Astle. p. 122.

33 Rowland's Mona Antiqua. p. 238. 5d Edition.

34 Antiq. septent. select. p. 38.

35 Navig. in Braz. c. 16. Benzoin. hist. nov. Orbis.

36 Travels, p. 241.

37 Existimo verisimile esse magos illos literature aliqua usos, & quidem vulgari, majori ex parte, sed virgulis & pundis suo marte excogitatis corrupta. Worm. Lit. Run. p. 34.

38 Supra V. I. p. 216. The Chamans of Siberia, and the Hottentot priests are equally addicted to magic conjurations. See Gmelin and Sparman's travels.

† Cum litera inter barbaros initio arcanae essent, arcanarum notarum appellatio literia mansit, etiam cum publicae esse coepêre. Leibnitz. apud Chamberl. p. 28.

39 Irish Dic. voce Run.

40 Clarke on Saxon Coins, p. 53.

41 Holm de script. apud Crenii Analect. p. 422.

42 Hug. de orig. scribend. p. 315. Ed. Trotz.

43 Mallet and Wormius supra. Barthol. p. 649. Loccen. p. 83.

44 Virgam fructiferae arbori decisam, in surculos amputant, cosque Notis quibusdam discretos, &c. Tacit. Germ. Sed manendum, tum isra aut populina fors aut abiegiua est tua. Plaut. Cas. Ac, 2. Taubman. in loco. For the employment of the Adelruni. Worm. Faft. Dan. 1. I. p. 124.

45 In robore insculptas priscarum literarum notas. Cic de divin. 1. 2. c. 41. Nactns puerilem iconculam eju aeneam vetecrem ferreis ac fere jam exolescentibus literis inscriptam. Suet. in Oct. c. 7.

46 Astle, supra sub fin.

47 Isidor. Orig. 1. I. c. 21.

48 Cod. rit. 17. leg. I.

49 Lips epist. ad Belg. cent. I. ep. 27.

50 Trithem. de Polygraph. p. 599.

51 Hickes Thesaur, Franco. Theotise.

52 Bernard's tables improved by Morton.

53 Mabillon, supra.

54 La Croze. Vindic. Vet. p. 89.

55 Uther's letters by Parr, p. 551.

56 Catalog. Lib. septent. p. 149.

57 Literat. Run. pp. 37–40. Ut literas confingerent, quasi proprias genris fuae. La Croze, supra, p. 89. † The Ira Letur, or Irish ogham characters did not differ greatly from the other runic ones. Worm. Literat Run. 1. Rowlands never saw the Ira Letur, and does not know whether they were the same as the Bethlussnion. Mona Artiq. p. 110. They were all the same.

58 Worm. supra. p. 40.

59 Nicholson's Irish Hist. Library, Preface.

60 Supra, p. 378.

61 Rab. Maurus says, they were used in incantations and divinations. De invent, liter. Tam quoad figuram, quam quoad nomina cum nostraibus convenire. Worm, supra, p. 47.

62 Alphabetum Anglo-Saxonicum non est integrum illud vetus, cujus multi defideran:ur characters. Gram. Anglo-Sax. p. 2.

63 Walker on Saxon Coins, apud Camden.

64 Irish Grammar, p. 14. Harris's Ware, p. 21.

65 Scotland, V. 2, p. 17.

66 Irish Grammar, p. 13.

67 O'Conor's Diff. p. 37.

68 O'Conor, supra. O'Flahert. Ogyg. p. 233. The Runic Biarkan was the same.

69 A scopo & instituto majorum nostrorum longissime exorbitate video, Sup. p. 86, 87.

70 Origin of writing, p. 89.

71 Illas (Runas) a principio nec omnes eadem qua nune alphabeteria schcemata praeferunt forma extitisse dixit, nec serie collocatas cadem. Vulgarium ordinem numerumque a Voldemare ad formulam alphabeti Romani institutum esse aiebat. Worm. sup. p. 42.

72 Mallet, supra, p. 378.

73 Supra, p. 97.

74 Strutt's Chronicle, V. I. p. 346.

75 Usser. Syllog. p. 41.

76 Pauca sint caraxata, Usser, Syllog. p. 42.

77 Ubi est susus in hanc lucem, mirabile dictu totum ejus corpusculum invenitur charaxatum, quasi crucicularum stigmatibus.

    Charaxat ambas ungulis scribentibus,

    Genas, cruentis et fecat faciem notis.

                (Prudent.)

Barth. Advers. 1. 13, 18, 1. 45, 19. Turneb Advers. 1. 14. c. 24.

78 Irish Grammar, supra, p. 8.

79 Transactions Royal Irish Academy, V. I. p. 9.

80 Archaeologia, V. 8. p. 290.

81 Ware, chap. I. Whitaker thinks it one or two centuries before St Patrick. Sup. V. I. p. 373.

82 Apud Lhayd's letter to the Welsh in Malcolm's tracts, p. 6.

83 This is from despicable Irish romance, for Europe was then thinly inhabited by wandering tribes of barbarians. Solomon lived above a thousand years before our era.

84 Poetis Cordubae natis, pingue quiddam sonantibus atque peregrinum. Cic. pro Archia. Hoc est. says Cellarius, aliquid solocci vel Graecis vel Latinis carminibus miscerent Difs. Academ, p. 367. Cicero probably means something more.

85 Auson. grat. act. p. 256.

86 Habet literas in rigor septendecim. Gram. p. 5.

87 Astle, p. 20.

88 Malcolm's tracts, p. 35.

89 Qualiter dipthongi vel tripthongi apud Hibernos debeat pronunciari res est scitu difficilis: hoc opus, hic labor, meo judicio, vix ullus perfecte discet qualiter essserantur, nisi attente auscultet peritum in hac lingua eas proaunciaotum. O'Molloy, Sup. p. 47.

90 Chambaud's elements of the French lang. preface.

91 Verborum alia variantur valde apud Hibernos, velut heteroclita & diversimode, ita ut universalis regula pro in nequit dari, adeoque insistendum fit auctoribus ubique probatis. O'Molloy, p. 125.

92 Nec extant regulae, sed usus & auctoritas pro hujusmodi declinationebus. O'Molloy, p. 120.

93 Lhuyd, At I Kymry. Bernard epist, ad Hickes. Pinkerton, p. 122.

94 De regno Hib. p. 7.

95 Ogyg, vind, p. 20.

96 An Angli vel Saxones fuas literas in Britanniam fecum attulerint, an a Britannis didicerint, non dixerim. Leibnitz, apud Chamberlayne. Orat. Domin.

97 Nihil hactenus invenire potui, quod ante fidem a Saxonibus susceptam literis istis exaratum fit. Sheringham, de orig. Angl. p. 293. Bulland. Acta fanct. 17 mart. p. 517.

98 Hickes, catal. Septent, p. 149. Astle, p. 99.

99 Cave, Hist. Liter. V. I. p. 409.

100 Parr's letters, p. 551.

101 He was prince of Powis in Wales. The inscription is in the abbey of Langholen in Denbighshire, and is of year 830. Lhuyd, pp. 226–9.

CHAPTER ELEVEN

The Ancient Ogham Treatises

G.M. Atkinson

WITH THE KIND PERMISSION of the Council of the Royal Irish Academy, in September 1872, I made a tracing of the different forms of ogham character contained in the manuscript known as the Book of Ballymote, now preserved in their library.

This volume, though defective in a few places, consists of 251 leaves of large folio vellum (10½ by 13½in), transcribed by different persons, but chiefly by Solomon O'Droma and Manus O'Duigenann; and it is stated at folio 62b, that it was written at Ballymote (in the county of Sligo), in the house of Tomaltach ôg MacDonough, lord of Corann, in that county, at the time that Torlough ôg, the son of Hugh O'Conor, was king of Connacht; and Charles O'Conor, of Belanagar, has inserted in it the date 1391, as the precise year in which this part of the book was executed. It is a compilation collected from various sources, and may be held to represent to a great extent several other manuscripts. It begins with a copy of the ancient Leabhar Gabhála, or Book of Invasions of Erinn, imperfect, and differing in a few details from others of the same subject. This is followed by a series of ancient chronological, historical, and genealogical pieces in prose and verse. Then come the pedigrees of Irish saints, and of the great families of the Milesian race, with the various minor tribes and families; accounts of the kings, and tragical death of the beautiful Lady Luaidet, &c., &c. Some of these pieces are doubtless mixed up with what must be regarded as mythological stories, and to these may be traced many of the characteristic popular customs and superstitions still remaining among the native Irish. It contains, also, an ancient grammar and prosody, richly illustrated with specimens of ancient Irish verification; and a treatise on the ogham alphabets of the ancient Irish, with illustrations. Photo-lithographs of these, taken from my tracings (Plates I, II, III and IV, including on Plate IV the very characteristic interlaced initial letter of the succeeding treatise, the Uraicecht-na n-Eiges, or Precepts of the Poets), accompany this paper. The manuscript ends with the adventures of Aeneas after the destruction of Troy. In the manuscript treatise on the ogham (fol. 167bb), the invention of the ogham character is ascribed to Ogma, son of Elathan, a member of the Tuatha De Danann colony.

Ogham inscriptions are constantly referred to in the oldest Irish historical tales, as engraved on the tombs and monuments of pagan kings and chieftains (see the 'Irish Grammar' by J. O'Donovan, and 'MS. Materials of Irish History', by E. O'Curry); and from these tales it would appear that such inscriptions contained simply the names of the persons interred. Thus, in the story in Leabhar na h-Uidhré, as to the identifying of the grave of king Fothadh Airgtheach, in the third century, it is stated that his headstone exhibited in ogham characters the inscription:

Fothadh Airgthech here.

Also, in a very ancient poem, beginning Ogum ilba, lia uar leact, 'Ogham on the stone, the stone over the monument', preserved in the 'Book of Leinster', p. 28 b, a stone placed over a monument, with an ogham inscription, situated on the site of a battle fought in the third century, is thus alluded to:

That Ogum which is on the stone,
Around which many were slain;
If Finn of the many battles lived,
Long would the Ogum be remembered.

In the tale of Deirdre, published in the 'Transactions of the Gaelic Society of Dublin', pp. 127, 128, the sepulchral monument of Naisi and Deirdre is thus spoken of:

Their stone was raised over their monument, their ogham names were written, and their ceremony of lamentation was performed.

In the ancient tale of the *Taín Bó Cuailgnè* (which we find in a part of the Leabhar na h-Uidhré, a manuscript as old as 1106), Cuchulainn wrote or cut an ogham in hoops or wands, which he placed in such positions as would be found by Queene Maeve and her army; these, when discovered, were carried to Fergus and other Ultonian champions, in the camp of the Queen, to read and explain, which they were always able to do. Frequent mention also is made of Fergus reading the ogham writings, and using their characters; and we have the pretended revelation of it at his grave to Scanchan's pupil in the one version, as well as the recovery of it, according to another account, at a great meeting of poets and ecclesiastics said to have taken place at his grave. This compilation, in a complete form, is not now known. It was taken to Italy, probably, by the *Saoi*, and it may yet turn up in some neglected corner of the great libraries there.

As regards the material in which, or upon which, the ante-Christian Gaedhels wrote, besides stone, we find it mentioned under four different names: Staves of the poets; Tablet staves; Tables of the poets; and The Wand of the poet.

In the tale of Bailé Mac Buain, we learn a story of Bailé 'The sweet spoken', favourite lover of Aillinn, after recording their tragical death and burial, we are informed that an apple and a yew tree sprang up over their graves. At the end of seven years the poets, and prophets, and seers of Ulster cut down the yew tree which was over the grave of Bailé, and made it into a poets' tablet, 'and they wrote the visions, and espousals, and loves, and the courtships of Ulster in it'. The same was done to the apple tree over the grave of Aillinu, and the courtships, loves etc, of Leinster were written in it. (This shows a good growth in such a short time – but seven is the mystic number.) At the time when Art, the son of Conn of the Hundred Battles, was monarch of Erinn (AD166), on the great periodical feast of *Samhuin*, or November eve, the poets and professors of all arts gathered together with their tablets.

These two tablets were brought to Art, and, as he was looking at them, they suddenly closed together, and it was found impossible to separate them. 'The value of the story (observes O'Curry) is the evidence it supplies of the existence in Art's time of ancient written books, so old that the leaves could not be separated.' The anachronisms with regard to the trees and tablets are remarkable.

In the tale of the exile of the sons of Duil Dermait (*circa* AD1) we have a talismanic influence ascribed to an *Oghuim* inscribed by Cuchulainn on a little spear; and in the Book of Leinster (fol. 206), in the story of Corc, son of Lughaidh, king of Munster, who was driven into exile by his father about A.D. 400, and was recognized by Gruibné, King Feradach of Scotland's poet, who, while examining his shield, detected an *Oghuim* inscription on it. The fatal purport of this Corc was ignorant of, nor could he read the *Oghuim*.

The verses quoted from Mac Lonan (chief poet of Erinn, who died AD 918), are curious:

Cormac of Cashel with his champions,
Munster is his, may he long enjoy it;
Around the King of Raith Bicli are cultivated,
The letters and the trees.

The 'letters' are taken to signify our present Gaedhelic alphabet and writings; the trees, the ogham letters. Cormac, in his 'Glossary', often speaks of the ogham writing as having been in use among the older pagan as well as the latter Christian Gaedhils: he explains the word *Fe* to mean a pole or rod, with which bodies and graves were measured, and in which the people 'wrote in *Oghuim* whatever was hateful or detestable relating to them, and left it in the cemetery'.

O'Curry thinks the *Taibhli Fileadh* (Tablets of the Poets) had the form of a fan, which, when closed, took the shape of a staff, and was serviceable as such to the poet and historian. A very ancient article in the Brehon Laws accords the privilege to the order of a poet, *Tabhall-Lorg*, or Tablet-staff – these squared, headless staves of the Gaedhils, on the angles and lines of which they wrote or carved in the *Buthe Luis Nin*, that is, Birch-Alder Letter, and for this kind of writing neither pen nor ink was required; all the materials requisite were a square staff in hand and knife in the pocket.

The late Mr John Windele (to whose zeal, with that of the late Rev. Matthew Horgan, P.P. of Blarney, is due the revival of ogham learning) had a stick inscribed with ogham characters; but, as well as my memory serves, it was modern. All the inscriptions known (with the exceptions of that on the Clarendon silver brooch, now in the Royal Irish Academy Museum, Lord Londesborough's amulet, the two lines in the Harleian manuscript, and the writing in the 'Annals of Inisfallen', a manuscript in the Bodleian Library), are found on stone. Careful research will, I trust, yet reveal some of the inscriptions on timber.[1] We have a family likeness in the Rune sticks, Clog-Almanacs, and Exchequer tallies. King Charles I's cypher, which he used in correspondence with the Earl of Glamorgan, 1646, may be considered the last effort. I hope to have the pleasure of submitting it, with the others, in a future communication. The very primitive style found on all the inscribed ogham stones up to the present time corroborates the facts recorded in the manuscripts from which I quote; and I understand from Mr R.R. Brash, that in his book on the ogham-inscribed monuments (soon to be published) he will give above one hundred and fifty similarly written examples.

My tracing only gives the last of the written forms of ogham, and the figured or illustrated portion of the manuscript treatise on this subject in the Book of Ballymote. Engagements in

Dublin very much limited my time and research; but being anxious to obtain further information, I consulted several manuscripts and works in the library of the British Museum, and was fortunate in finding (among others) a manuscript which purports to be a translation of the treatise on the ogham in the 'Book of Ballymote', by J. McQuige, and from his 'History and Explanation of the Irish Oghams, in two letters to the late Dr A. Clarke', given in the ancient form of question and answer. I make the following abridgment in order to fill up omissions and correct the portions I have traced from the 'Book of Ballymote':

The Irish Oghams

From whence, what time, and what person, and from what cause, did the ogham spring? Answer. The place is (Hibernia Insola quam nos Scoti habitamus) Hybernia's Ile, which we Scots inhabit; in the time of Breass, the son of Elathan, then king of all Ireland. The person was Ogma, the son of Elathan, the son of Dealbadh, brother to Breas, for Breas, Ogma and Dealbadh were three sons of Elathan, who was the son of Dealbath.

Ogma, being a man much skilled in dialects and in poetry, it was he invented the ogham, its object being for signs of secret speech only known to the learned, and designed to be kept from the vulgar and poor of the nation.

Where were the names and figures of the ogham found? Who were the mother and the father of the ogham? What was the first name written in ogham characters? What tree was it written in? Why was it written? What was written? and from whom came the art of numbering and forming books regularly in ogham? It is called ogham from Ogma, the inventor. The derivation is ogham, from Ghuaim, i.e., the guaim, or wisdom through which the bards were enabled to compose [there is a seeming confusion here]; for by its branches the Irish bards sounded their verses. The father of ogham was Ogma, and the mother of the ogham was the hand or knife of Ogma. *Soim* was the first thing written in ogham, thus: ₥₊⊥⌐₹ [I did not see or trace this word in the manuscript Book of Ballymote; and I understand from a gentleman connected with the Royal Irish Academy (Mr Mac Sweeney), who has since kindly searched for me, that it is not to be found figured. There is an erasure of this word in McQuige's manuscript; and from the way it was written it appears to me possible to read it *Mage*.] In a birch was it written, and given to Lug, the son of Etlem, with an explanation multiplying branches, which ran as from the roots, viz.: seven slips in one sheaf slip, ²⊤·⊤·⊤·⊤·⊤·⊤·⊤ᶜ thus, and gave them folded, entitled male and female; another name, man or woman, of the birch; for of the birch they first wrote oghams.

How many and what are the divisions of ogham? Four; B, her five; II, her five; M, her five, and A, her five.

How many sciences in the ogham are taught, and what are they? Answer: Three: VIII royal or gentle trees; VIII kiln trees; and VIII spiral trees. The VIII royal trees are, the elm, oak, hazel, vine, ivy, blackthorn, broom, spine; and the VIII kiln are the birch, the quicken, willow, ash, whitethorn, fig, apple, and cork; and the spiral are all from green trees.

How many kinds of ogham are there? Answer: 150, Figuras eorum et potestates per ordinem nunciabimus [the Latin is given as written]. First, the branches of the trees are they from whence come the names of the branches in ogham, per alios & alios nominantur.

Question. By whom and from whence are the veins and beams in the ogham tree named? Answer: *Per alios*. It came from the school of Phenius, a man of Sidon, viz.: schools of philosophy under Phenius through the world, teaching the tongues (he thus employed), in number 25. Noble youths (or 25 noble schools through the world).

About this time, in Asia reigned
Accomplished Neil, great Pheneis' son:
Three score and ten men he retained
In forming tongues from Babilon.

From whence come the figures and names in the explanation of B, L and N in ogham?
Answer: From the branches and limbs of the oak tree: they formed ideas which they expressed
in sounds, i.e., as the stalk of the bush is the noblest part; from them they formed the seven
chief figures as vowels, thus:

>−+−#−##−###−####−✕−◇−<
a e i o u ea oi

and they formed three others, which they added to these as helpers, formed on different sides
of the line

ui ia ae
>−✕−ᴖ−⬛

per alios, the branches of the wood give figures for the branches and veins in ogham, chief of
all. The tribe of B, from birch, and the daughter, i.e., the ash of the wood, is chief; and of
them the first alphabet was formed; of L, viz. L, from *luis*, the quicken tree of the wood; F,
from *fearn*, alder, good for shields; S, from *sail*, a willow from the wood; N, in ogham, from
nin, the ash, for spears; H, in Og, from *uath*, whitethorn, a crooked tree, or a bush, because
of her thorns; D, from *dur*, the oak of fate from the wood; T, from *tine*, cypress, or from the
elder tree; C, in Og, from *coll*, the hazel of the wood; Q, in Og of *quert*, apple, aspen or
mountain ash; M, from *mediu*, (muin), the vine branching finely; G, from *gort*, viz., ivy
towering; NG, from *getal*, or gilcach, a reed; ST or Z, from *draighean*, blackthorn; R, Graif,
not explained; A, from *ailm*, fir; O, from *on*, the broom, furze; U, from *up*, heath; E, from
edadh, aspen trembling; I, from *ida*, or *ioda*, or *ioga*, the yew tree (Heb. *jod*); EA, *eabhadh*,
ye aspin; OI, *oir*, ye spine (spindle tree); UI, *uilleann*, honeysuckle; IO, ye gooseberry (ifin),
AE the witch hazel (amhancholl); Pine, og, i.e., the divine pine from the wood, from whence
are drawn four *ifins*, or vineyards, per alios, the name of that branch. The figure resembles
the hurdle of wrought twigs, or like a bier.

The letters in ogham are situated with regard to one principal stem or ridge (druim) line,
under, over, or through which they are drawn. This line serves only as a rule, and not for any
letter. Its upper side is called the left, and under, the right hand. All the characters which serve
for consonants, vowels, diphthongs and triphthongs, are drawn in connection with it. This
line is drawn from the left hand to the right. Of the small notes or signs, one ✕ is put for the
diphthongs and triphthongs beginning with the vowel *e*, though only signed with *ea*. This ◇
on the said ruling line imports *oi*. This hook ᴖ on the line, right side, imports all diphthongs
and triphthongs beginning with the vowel *u*, though marked only with *ua*. The four lines
crossing each other under the line, thus ⧻ signify all diphthongs and triphthongs beginning
with *i*, though marked only with *ia*. The eight lines ⬛ on the left or upper side of the line
signifies all diphthongs and triphthongs beginning with the vowel *a*, though marked only with
ao. The small line drawn under and parallel with the main line signifies P [this is a recent
contrivance: *P* is an aspirated *b*], all which may be seen thus in one view:

179

b l f s n h d t c q m gng$^{st}_{x}$ r a o u e i

ea oi ui ia ao P

This form is called the *ogham craobh*, from the characters of it resembling (craob) branches of trees. There is also the *ogham coll*, the letter C being substituted in various ways … ; and the *ogham beith*, so called when *bh* or letter *beith* is placed instead of the vowel *a*. It is also called *ogham congoine*, or ogham of consonants, for in this method of writing you change vowels into consonants. [Of the diphthongs, none but the first, up to the present time, has been found engraved on the stone monuments in Ireland. The stone at Bressay, Shetland, figured in Stuart's 'Sculptured Stones of Scotland', Plate XCV, perhaps contains another.]

The Painted or Spotted Ogham of Many Beauties, by McMain

B This division, set forth by a head of hair, which a tuft of the birch tree resembles; and it is called *moraind* (moran), for the multitude of its lines and branches. This letter begins it, hanging under the line. [Then follow the names and explanations of the other letters, finishing] with AE, the king's *motein*, or way, a breastplate in danger, i.e., rods wrought in a hurdle as a shield, or laid on beams for a bridge. *Emon*, AE in ogham, is taken thus formed . End of the scheme of Moran McMain.

Rules for Understanding the Bush Ogham in All its Parts

According to Elodhain, B stands alone right drawn to my right hand; L has two fair strokes well drawn with command; F has its three; (S) four of equal length; N, with her five, abides with mighty strength, and so on to the end of the diphthongs AO, in this form.

Oghaim coll. C Oghaim, taken from *H*.18, a manuscript in Trinity College.

c – One c in *A* begins this *Oghaim fine.*
cc – Two c's, right joined in *O*, you may combine in human speech set out with taste and shoe.
ccc – Three c's well formed give *U* in equal rowe.
cccc – Four c's make *E* fair seen by learning's eye.
ccccc – Five c's produce the ancient vowel *I.*
∪ C on its back *EA*, produces sure, nor do we err from ancient strictures, sure.
ƆC Two C's thus placed, the Irish Ifin (O)gain.
∩∩ Two C's a groove, *UA* in power retain.
Ɔ One C thus placed, *AO* in order takes,
∩ One C turned upside down *OI* bespeaks.

Thus it lay in the Book of Ballymote:

a	o	u	e	i		ea	o	ua	oi	ao
c	cc	ccc	cccc	ccccc		∪	ƆC	∩∩	Ɔ	∩

The Ogham of Consonants

BH, constitute A.

DL, invariably O.

FT rightly form U.

SC, make E.

NG, bravely make I.

MM, from their backs give EA.

LL, of two Ls make IA.

BB, two Bs produce UA.

PP, in ogham IO.

GG, as the directed.

The amharcholl, i.e. AO, all seen in this scale.

a	o	u	e	i	ea	ia	ua	ao	oi
bh	dh	ft	st	ng	mm	ll	pp	bb	gg

Here begins M'Inoch's declarative ogham [and after going through the letters and his descriptions (which I omit) we come to the] Muc og in ro aicine bedi ro pig.

The (Muc i.e.) colour ogham. The letters are placed and expressed by colour: B, finn, white; L, liat, grey; F, loc, black; S, cron, brown; N, feglar green.

Lin og, the names of places, pools of water, are given to their initials: B, Banba, or Ireland; L, Luimneach, Limerick; F, Febhal; S, Sinaind; N, Nearcnid – words signified by their initials.

['Lín is a deep part of a river, made deeper by the action of the tide. Banba is perhaps intended for Berba, the River Barrow. Liumneach was the name of the River Shannon at the place where the city of Limerick stands. Febhal is the River Foyle, which flows into the Lough Foyle. Sinaind is the Shannon. – E.B.']

Din og, hill ogham, terms connected with a hill: B, Bruidher; L, Lifi; F, Femi; S, Scolach; N, Nemhthend, &c.

En og, bird ogham, the ancient names of birds: B, Besan; L, Lachu; F, Fail; S, Insegh; N, Neascu, &c.

Dat og, colour ogham, the names given to character: B, Ban; L, Liath; F, Flann; S, Sodath; N, Necht.

Ceall og, battle ogham, the names of instruments, &c.: B, Beanchor, a horn; L, Leath, a city; F, Fearnae, a mast; S, Saighear, a spear; N, Nacndruim.

Daen og, human ogham, a man or champion for the division of B: thus, a man, two men, three men, &c,; the softer sex, a woman, or the clergy, for the division of H, viz., a woman, two women, three, four, and five women; a young man for the division of M, viz., a youth, two youths, &c.; a son or slave for the division of A, viz., a son, two sons, three, &c.; one on A, two on O, 3 on U and so on.

† Daen og, poetic ogham, a poem on the division of B, as one for B, two for L, three for F, and so on, through all *Caillchu' la*, i.e. *Caillethumhall*, an old woman; *a tale* for the division of II in the same manner; the good son through the division of M; the same way Beaga, little ones, through A, as one for A, two for O, three for U, and so on.

† Og tinida, ogham of countries: B, Biail; a hatchet; L, Loman; a banner; F, Feba; S, Srathar; N, Naise, H, Huartan; D, Dabach; T, Tal; C, Cair; Q, Quil.

† Rig og, kingly ogham, state names applied: B, Brian; L, Labhraid; F, Filann, &c., names of kings given by the king, applied to the branches.

† Og Uscedc, water ogham [glas is green, but glaise, is a rivulet, and must be the word

intended here, E. B.]; green through the division of B, for B, one green; two for L, three for F, four for S, five for N; waterish through the division of H, one water for H, two for D, three for T, four for C, five waters for Q [a very bad liquor].

Aman, Amhan, a river, through the division of M, one river for M, two &c; Tipra, a wall, through the division of A, one for A, &c.

Con og, hound ogham, a coller'd hound for B; B, one hound; L, two hounds; F, three hounds; S, four hounds; N, five hounds; a greyhound for H, one g-h, &c.; a hound boy through M; a lapdog through A's division, for A one lapdog, two lapdogs, three lapdogs, four lapdogs, five lapdogs.

† Dam og, ox ogham, names of males given: a bull for division B, one bull, two bulls, three, four, five bulls; an ox for division H, one ox, two oxen, three, four and five oxen; a year-old for division M; the bull of the herd through A.

Bo og, cow ogham, the female names given: one milks cow B, two milks cows, &c.; a stripper for H, one stripper, &c.; a fatling through the division of M, one fatling, &c.; a cow with calf through the division of A, A one cow with calf, two cows with calves, &c.

† Caec og, blinding or (puzzling) ogham, the divisions taking its figures from Man; the division of *B* is on the right side; that of *H* on the left; of *M* on the right, and that of *A* on the left.

† Lorc og, deceiving ogham, transposing the parts as above.

Mac og, son, og, or ogham of a pregnant womb, denominated from a woman bearing children, and naming its branches from them, whether males or females; the figures are called either after a son or daughter, as produced by the pregnancy.

† Coir og, foot ogham, the fingers of the hand give figures for the branches and characters around the shin; formed right side through the division of B, right across through the division of A; one finger through M, first branch of the division; second on the next, and so on; five for the fifth branch, ending the division.

† Spon og, nose ogham, the fingers of the hand around the nose, viz., *Similiter*, to the right and left, and right straight across.

† Bar og, .i. a hand ogham, viz, Manus aliam percutit lignorum. [This form of ogham line is given on Plate I, between the illustrations from MS. Brit. Mus. Add 4783, and line No. 4 from the MS. Book of Ballymote.]

† Haom og, saint ogham, the initials of the saint's names it is which forms the letter. B, Brenaid; L, Laisreann; F, Finden; S, Sinchell; N, Neasan; H, Hadamnan; D, Donnan; T, Tigheanach; C, Cronan; Q, Qeran; M, Manchan; G, Guirgu; Ng, Ngeman; Cr, Crannan; R, Ruadhanachd; A, An; O, Oena; U, Ultan; E, Eruan; I, Ite.

† Dan og, the science ogham. Sciences whose names begin with the power or character called by them, as B-Bruthmhnacht; L-Lumnacht; F-Filiacht; S-Sairsi; N-Nothaircetal.

† Biad og, meat ogham, as Bairghean, Leumhnach, Sic usum in finem.

† Luss og, the herb ogham. The initials of herbs give names to the characters B-Braishech, &c.

† Cend amuine .i., the head from the neck. But as Plate I contains the latter part of the explanation of *Cend a muine*, and the treatise is continued on Plates II and III to the conclusion on Plates IV, I omit the remainder of M'Quiges' History, and have much pleasure in presenting the following valuable translation and explanation of the accompanying plates and illustrations, kindly prepared for me by the Rev. R. Smiddy, P.P., Aghada, author of 'The Druids' Ancient Churches, and Round Towers of Ireland', and the Rev. E. Barry, Aghada, for publication in this journal. It was at the instigation of these gentlemen that I completed the tracings. The

amount of labour bestowed (although one of love to them) will, I feel sure, be duly appreciated by the members of the Association, particularly when I mention that, notwithstanding all the trouble they have taken, their only regret is that I did not, by tracing the entire treatise, enable them to complete the work. All errors are to be attributed to my ignorance in transcribing. Taking up the history, the first portion translated is the line before referred to, just over illustration No. 4, Plate I. … Dochli co fian ceart tarsna, bas ogam iodon, Manus aliam percutit lignorum. From the left oblique quite across, the palm of the hand ogham, that is the hand strikes another (alium) of the trees (that is, of the ogham letters).

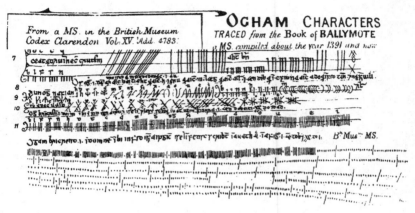

Plate I Ogham Characters

1a, 2a, 3a, are the diphthongs ea, ui, ae; 4a an index mark.

ᴅᴀɪʙ ᴀɪᴘᴇᴅᴀɪʙ ＋ ＃ ＃＃ ＃＃ ×◇ ≪ ᴀᴢᴜꝛ ꝛᴏ ᴄʜᴜɪʟʟ.

certain letters   a o u e i ea oi and there fitted.

5a. ᴀn ʟᴇᴢʜ ᴘᴀɪʟᴇ ×◇▦, apart ea ia ae, other letters.

Agur ogam nairsmech ainm ele in ogaim sea ut est ▦▦▦, and ogham *Nairismeach* is another name of this ogham, as-*qule*, that is *certle* 'a ball of yarn'.

Cenn fo muine don co tarsna int ogam semut iodon, tairifin, for fid in derid in anma a tosach do seribed, iar na fedaib i dilsib ut est; ＋＋▦▦ iodon mael, r, iodon, ruis.

Head under neck, then, the inscription is contrary-wise before you; that is instead of[2] the final letter of the name to write its initial letter over again, after the letters proper [to the name], as M. A. E. R., that is *mael* R, that is *ruis* [the elder tree = the name of the letter R].

Nathair im ceann iodon in fid toisech in anma do seribenn in medon na craibi agus int ainm do scribad co direach uada co dered na craibi agus a soribad fri trosc co tosach na craibi conid inann ni bir I tosach agus an deredh na craibi iodon dered in anma issed bis a cectar de ut est in hac figura. Ceallach coimdes a air legind sis agus suas agus is as a medon ap legtar int ainm ar is ann ita in fid tosach in aninna.

A serpent [coiled] around [its] head; that is, to write the first letter of the name in the middle of the line [or series], and to write the name from it in direct order to the end of the line, and in reversed order to the beginning of the line; so that it is the same thing that is written at the beginning and at the end of the line, that is, the end of the name is what is on either [extremity] of it, as in this figure *Cellach*. With equal correctness it is to be read down and up, and it is from the middle the name is read, for the first letter of the name is there.

(See No. 1 and a) ut est.

h c a l l c C e l l a c h

No. 2 and b. Aradach finn ann so sis, Fionn's ladder-ogham here below.

No. 3 and c. Aicme bethi, the group of B, the group of H, the group of M, the group of A, otherwise, BLFSN. HDTCQu. MG, so the rest (i.e., Ng str. R.); AO, so the rest (i.e., U, E. 1.); the out group as an end.

No. 4 and d.

Luth ogam ann so,
The sinew ogham here.

Aicme huatha,	muine,	ailme,
group of H,	of M,	of A.

foraicme so,
This is an out group.

No. 5 and c.

Tre dhruimnech so,
The three-ridged [ogham] this.

The H group,	the M group.

No. 5$_2$ and f.

Tre lurgach find,
The three-staff [ogham] of Fionn.

No. 6 and 7.

Lad ogam,	aicme H,
A canal ogham	the group of H.
aicme, b	aicme, m,
the group of B,	aicme, M,
aicme, ailme,	
the group of A.	

No. 8. Ceatar druimnech Cruteni.

The four-ridged [ogham] of Crutine.

Aliter bethi	map seo uili.
otherwise B [group].	All like this.

Dro ised coig ar in fid dedenach idon aicme uile,
so that there are (5) for the last letter of every group.

Or ogam iodon, dam ar aicmi beithi elit ar aicme h, iarnu ar aicme m. laeg ar aicmi ailme iodon aen dib ar mced fid na aicmi ado ar m fid tanaiste agus mar rin uile.

A faun-ogham, that is (dam) a buck, for the B group; a doe (elit) for the H group; a faun (iarnu) for the M group; a sucking calf (laeg) for the A group; that is, one of them for the first letter of the group, two of them for the second, and thus all; so that there are five of them for the last letter of every group.

No. 9. Run Ogam na fian[?]

The secret ogham of the Fianna.
aroile.
[so] the rest.

No. 10. Ebadach ilaind.

The aspen, or character × [ogham] of Ilann [ebad, the aspen tree being the name of × – the diphthong ea]. [This × character is misplaced on the Run ogham line No. 9].

No. 11. Ogam bricrenn iodon in doimni in bi in fid isin aipgitin ise lin flere scripbtan in a uath ut in figura iddon aen do beithi fiche do idad.[3] ┼ ╫ ╫╫ ╫╫╫ ╫╫╫╫

The ogham of *Bricriu*, that is, the distance of a letter from the top of the alphabet, corresponds with the number of strokes [scores] that are written to form that single letter, as in the figure; that is, one for the letter B, twenty for the letter I.

Plate II Ogham Characters

No. 1. Ogam uird int ord bis fria fedaib in aibgitin, idon, in fid is toseachu araile in aipgitin ise ir torecu scribthar ac denam anma dgdencha he isin ainm idon bran B.L.D.R.A.A.I. labraid.

The ogham of order – the order letters have in the alphabet, that is, the letter which precedes the rest in the alphabet, is sooner written in forming the name [and the letter which comes later in the alphabet] is later in the name, as in this figure:

B N R A   B L D R A A I

╕┰ ▥ ╫╫╫ ┼ (that is Bran)   ╕┰ ┰┰ ╨╫╫╫ ┼ ┼╫╫╫ Labraid.

Ogam ar a mbi aen idon aen flers for craib do scribad la gach fid, ut est in hac figura B ┰┰, L ┰┰, aroile H ╨, D ╨╨, aroile ╫, M ╫╫, s aroile A ┼, O ╫╫

The ogham, with an additional one, that is, with every letter to write one stroke more than it has in the ogham alphabet [*craobh*], as in this figure [so], the rest do. do.

No. 2. Ogam adlen fid, the ogham a letter elopes. Gleselgi idon, da ainm do gébionn idon cach tri na cele dib idon tosach in cet anma do scribad dingi a leth agus tosach in anma ele in a diaid agus dered in ced anma in a diaid agus dered in anma ele postea agus ita anmanna a ndentar sin anna tosaigh sin agus derid inunn ainm ataid ism da craib ann.

The struggle of the chase, that is, to link two names, i.e., both entangled together; that is, to write the beginning of the first name to the extent of half of it; and the beginning of the second name after it; and the end of the first name after that; and the end of the second name after all; and thus, in both series, the names that are formed in the beginnings and in the endings are the same name.

Fethnat segnat aliter. Gleselgi; otherwise, the struggle of the chase.

No. 3. Crad cride eces.

Torment of a learned man's heart? [so] the rest, i.e. g Ng. St. [so] the rest, i.e., o-u-é.

Arm ogam idon, gai ar aicmi bethi. Sciath ar aicmi h. Claidiom ar aicmi m. Calgadeg[4] ar aicmi a aen dib ar cet fid gibe aicme a da ar in tanaire.

The arms-ogham; that is, a dart [gai] for the group commencing with B; a shield [sciath] for the H group; a broad-sword [claidim] for the M group; a good or red-pointed sword [colg] for the A group; that is, one of them instead of the first letter, whatever be the group; two of them for the second.

No. 4. Ogam acomaltach idon in fid is nera don fid do scribad i maille fris gan troisc

aroile aroile aroile aroile.

The bonded ogham; that is, together with a letter to write the letter next to it to the right; [so] the rest, F, S, N; [so] the rest, T, C, Qu; [so] the rest, do.

Ogam eannach idon da fid munna ap in fid idon da bethi ar bethi.

Unison ogham, that is, to write the same letter twice instead of once; that is, two Bs for B, and [so] the rest.

No. 5. Do foraicmib agus deachuib in ogaim annso airncaig brogmoir las na biat a deich agus a foraicmi agus a forbethi afur aroile.

Of the out groups and syllables of the ogham here: For neaig brogmoir? which have their syllables and out groups and their strange B and the rest.

Sigla, bacht, lacht, flacht, secht, necht, huath, drong, tect, caecht, quar, maei, gaeth, ngael, sturrecht, rect, ang, ong, ung, eng, ing.

Nos. 6, 7, 8. Various other syllabic characters not in the order of the alphabet follow.

No. 9.[5] ioon, that is,

beichi	leam = Elm	penn	rail	nenoaic = Nettle?
bechi	luir	pehn	rail	nin
Birch	Mountain ash	Alder	Willow	Ash
B	L	F	S	N
⊤	⊤⊤	⊤⊤⊤	⊤⊤⊤⊤	⊤⊤⊤⊤⊤
rse = Hawthorn	oain	cnom = Elder	collo	quilleann = Holly
huache	oan	cinoi	coll	quenc
Hawthorn	Oak	Unknown	Hazel	Apple-tree
H	D	T	C	Q
⊥	⊥⊥	⊥⊥⊥	⊥⊥⊥⊥	⊥⊥⊥⊥⊥
mioin	siur = Mistletoe	sileach = Broom	onoision = Blackthorn	perun
			rail onons	naic
muin	sonc	ngeoal	rcpaiph	nuir
Vine	Ivy	Reed	Blackthorn	Elder
M	G	NG	STR	R
+	#	##	###	####

αbαll = Apple	ꝼeꝫuꝩ	uıꝳꝛeαnn = Ash	eꝺen = Ivy	ıubαꝳ = Yew
αılm	onn	uꝩ	eꝺαꝺ	ıꝺαꝺ
Fir	Furze	Heath	Aspen	Yew
A	O	U	E	I
+	++	+++	++++	+++++

	eα	oı	uı	ıα	αe
	✳	⊖	⊠	⊡	▦

Saitheach fochrom, clu comboil dodaing foluaich lucht asmbin brec oc finnglais derg [gloss, inidoth findi agus aroile] oc find inaelsem [gloss, ar dath findi agus aroile] fuirind [derg maesech leitel bran, cruithean fororc an so sis, dodaing brec.

A vessel curved underneath, a dismal habitation, worthless people [?] speckled, of a light-green colour, red [of the colour of whiteness, and the rest]; light doe colour, red doe colour, half-white or greyish-white, black, variegated. Foreign swine: here below, darkish-speckled.

No. 10. Muc ogaim findliath loch cron forglas cedoth finni cedoth leithi agus aroile.

Swine ogham, or ogham of the colours of swine. White – any shade of fairness; gray – any shade of grayness; black, brown, ultra-gray, and the rest.

No. 11. Ogam ro merc Breas idon Bres mac Elathan idon ba ges do dul sech gan a legadh no lad iaram int ogamso in a ucht ic tecd a cat muige tuireg ro mebaid iaram in cath fairsin gen ro bai ac legad in agaim iriro apgitinr inogaimsea idon scribthar in fid iarsrin lin litir bis isin amm in duine.

The ogham which Breas composed: that is, Breas, son of Elatha. It was a druidical prohibition for him to go past without reading it; then he put this ogham in his breast when coming into the battle of Moytura. Afterwards he lost the battle, not having been reading the ogham. Here is the alphabet of this ogham: the letter or ogham character is written after the number of letters in the name of the person, see line No. 11; *Bethe, Luis, Fern, Sail, Nin, Huath, Dur, Tinne, Coll* and the rest.

No. 12. Ogam deginach, idon in litir deghinach don ainm do scribad ar son in feda idon, edad ap bethi sail ap luis nin ap fernn luis ap sail nin ar nin agus aroile.

The final ogham: that is to write the last letter of the name [of a character] instead of the character; that is, E [the final letter of Bethe] for B; S [the last letter of Luis] for L; Nn for F [not written]; L for S, N for N, and so the rest.

No. 13. Cenn ar nuaill, iodon, in fid dedinach do gach aicme scribad ar in fidh toisech agus in fid toisech do cach aicme ar in fid ndedinach idon nin air bethi agus bethi ap nin agus gach fid ar a cele isin aicmi uili agus gach ni dimpod inti fen uile fri trosc.

The head howling [at being degraded to the last place]; that is, to write the last letter of every group instead of the first letter, and the first letter of every group instead of the last letter; that is, N for B, and B for N, and every letter throughout the group for another, and to reverse the position of everything in the entire group itself.

No. 14. Ogam an abairtear cetran idon ceatora feada nama labairtean ann idon duir agus tinni, luis fern idon duir ar bethi aicme uile tinni ar uath aicme uile luis ar muin aicme uile fern ar nailm aicme uile idon duir ar bethi da duir ar luis agus mar sin uile.

The ogham called the company of four: that is, only four letters are pronounced in it, that is D and T, L and F; that is, D instead of all the B group; T instead of all the H group; L for M's entire group; and F for A's entire group; that is a D for B, two Ds for L, and so all: see illustration No. 14.

No. 15. Ogam buaidhir foranna, idon, in cetna sid do gach aicm ap bethi, aicme uile in fid tanaise do gach aicme ar uath aicme uile in tres fid do gach aicme ar muin aicme uile agus aroile.

The ogham of extraordinary disturbance: that is the first letter of every group in place of the entire B group; the second letter of every group in place of the entire H group; the third letter of every group in place of the entire M group, and so the rest.

No. 16. Ogam rin fri derca idon fraech fri trosc idon aicme ailme fri trosc ar aicme bethi idon idad ar bethi agus bethi ar idad, aicme muine ar aicme uath idon ruis ar uath agus uath ar ruis agus aroile aicme beithi ar aicme ailme fri trorc agus aicme uath ar aicme muine fri trose.

The ogham, 'point towards the pit', heath, the direction of its growth reversed; that is the A group reversed in place of the B group, that is I for B and B for I; the M group reversed in place of the H group, that is R for H and H for R, and so the rest; the B group reversed in place of the A group, and the II group reversed in place of the M group.

Fraech fri trosc fa lios.

The heath with the direction of its growth reversed, drooping from the rampart.

No. 17. Ogam maignech idon inaigin iter gach da fid idon cocrich nama don fidh fen.

The enclosed ogham: that is, an enclosure between every two letters, that is merely a boundary to the letter itself.

Drec mon, the great trout [from the spots].

No. 18. Ogam comergda idon gach dara fid daicmib bethi agus huath do scribad comergda gach dara fid daicmib muine agus ailme in cedna.

Mixed ogham: that is, to write every second letter from the group of B and H mixed together, and in the same way to write the letters of the groups of M and A alternately.

Ogam inarbach idon aicme h re aicme b agus aicme ailme re aicme muine.

The ogham of banishment: that is, the group of H before the group of B, and the A group before the M group.

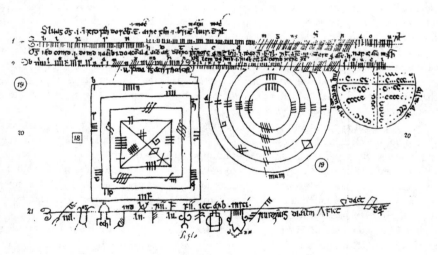

Plate III Ogham Characters

No. 1. Sluag Ogam idon in fid ren do scribad, ter [gl. idon, inatri] ain efen idon bethi ter [gl. inatri] luis ter [gl. inatri] agus aroile.

The multitude ogham: that is, instead a letter to write the letter itself three times; that is B three times, L three times, and so the rest (the gloss gives an equivalent in Irish for the Latin ter).

No. 2. Ogam ind co ind, idon da ind na craibi do acomal idon aicme ailme do merc fri trors an aicme bethi idon idhad iter bethi agus luis agus aroile aicme m do merc ar aicme h na foraicmi mar sin.

The ogham 'end to end': that is, to bring together both ends of the ogham alphabet; or to mix the reversed group of A with the B group, that is I between B and L, and so the rest; and to mix the (reversed) group of M with the II group; the out groups in like manner.

Ogam lem da reib, idon riab etir gach da fid in cert ogam.

The ogham with its two streaks: that is, a line between every two letters of the standard ogham.

No. 3. Ogam reramach ar is amedon inonn ar is ann forbaitearp agus is ar a leth aeginaigh leghthar prius ar is ann bis aicmi bethi agus huatha ar irin a medon ata forba na ceitre naicme.

'Stationary ogham', for its middle is the same, for it is there it is completed, and it is from its latter half it is first read, for the B and H groups are there; for the conclusion of the four groups are in its middle.

Gort fo lid, ar na bet da fid for aen lit idon tri feda etin gach da fid d'aieme bethi.

'The garden under colour', for there are not two letters [in succession] of one colour; that is, three letters between every two letters of the B group.

No. 4. Coll ar guta, idon aicme b agus aicme h agus aicme m gan comerengudh agus coll ar aicme ailme a uile idon coll agus da coll agus tricuill agus cethri cuill agus coig cuill.

'The letter of C in place of the vowels:' that is, not to disturb the B, H and M groups, and to put C for the entire A group, that is a C, two Cs, three Cs, four Cs, five Cs.

Brec og beo, the lively little trout (comp. bpec mor, Plate II No. 17a).

No. 5. Ceand imreasan, the head strife.

No. 5. Ogam dedach, the toothed ogham.

No. 6. Ceand debta, the head dispute.

No. 7. Insintheach, the inwardly prolonged.

No. 7. Didruin, the ridgeless or lineless.

No. 8. Ogam foasac, the ogham of stops.

No. 8 Ogam negladae idon in cuiged fid fodailt. Negligent ogham, that is, the fifth letter cut off.

No. 9. Ogam ebadach idon ebad etif gach da fid.

The aspen ogham: that is, an ✗ between every two letters [Ebhadh being the name of ✗, the ogham equivalent of the diphthong ea].

No. 10. Ogam foneara idon in fid bain in fid ap a gualaind do buain i maille fris gan fognam fain.

The ogham bearing the next: that is, to take together with a letter the letter that touches it on the shoulder without affecting its power.

No. 11. In diupartach ann so idon diupairt gach aicme ar aile imon cet fid ise cet fid na haicme tanaise ut est.

The encroaching ogham here: every group encroaches on another as to the first letter, the first letter it is of the succeeding group – As example. Taeb ogam tlachtga idon d'aen taeb uile na regasa sis. See line L, Plate IV. The side ogham of Tlachtga: that is, on one side are all the letters here below.

No. 12. [Not named.] Ogam tromcheann, the ogham heavyhead [M and N, Plate IV also].

Ogam Epimoin, the ogham of Erimon; agus aroile, and so the rest.

No. 13. Snaiti snimach, the twining thread [Line O, Plate IV also].

Ogam fordunta, the ogham enclosed in front.

Plate IV Ogham Characters

No. 14. Nathair fria fraech, the adder in the heath.

Bac Ogam, hinge [or staple] ogham; B group, H group, M group, &c.

No. 15. [Not named.] Ogam ceangalti, bound ogham.

Ogam tregdae, the ogham of piercing.

No. 16. [Not named.] Ogam sgeamach, wall-fern like ogham.[6]

Loch Ogam, the lake ogham.

No. 17. Fiaclach find agus isar cumsi nach scribthear acht da fid do gach aicme.

Fionn's tooth-like ogham. It is for brevity that only two letters are written of every group.

Ogam airenach, the shield ogham; agus aroile and so the rest.

No. 18. Triaig sruth fercertne idon coig feda in gach snaithi.

The triple stream of Fercertine: that is, five letters on every thread.

No. 19. Fege Finn, Fionn's window.

No. 20. Roth Ogam Roigm Rorcadha ig reo, the wheel ogham of Roighne Roscadhach.

Beithi idon aicm uile	Huath aicme uile.
B, that is the whole group.	All the H group.
Muin aicme uile	Ailm aicme uile
All the M group.	All the A group.[7]

No. 21. Lul, &c., are syllabic characters.

Nos. 1, 2, 3, 4. Forsheda, extra characters (these are syllabic characters).

Fian Ogam, oblique ogham, B, agus aroile, and so the rest.

No. 5.   Fean R,   A(leph),   B(eth),   G(imel),   D(aleth),

Ile,   V(au),   Z(ayin),   H(eth),   T(eth),   I(od),   C(aph),

L(amed),   M(em),   N(un),   *Samech*,   *Ain*,   *Phe*,   *Sade*,   *Coph*,

R(esh),   S(in),   *Tau.*

No. 6. Aibgitir Egipteach ann so. The Egyptian alphabet here.[9]

No. 7. Apgitir afraicda, the African alphabet. This is a variation of the preceding alphabet, and is a mixture of Latin, Runic, and other elements.

No. 8. Traig sruth fercertni, the foot stream of Fercertne.

Ronere nemnig nuaill bretaigh dianagá indan ni raigea ro rlumm dirig dian iúdscib gá itrlún ogam an aichnid i ceartaib comairci ar is crano fo loch lerceartach lll. nog, mlarda dorada fri huair urstrudain.

Monere, venemous, clamorously censorious, impetuous ...

Ogam anaichnid, ogham of the pleader in just questions of protection ...

Ogam neathrach idon barc fri beithi-aicme uile, long fri huath idon aicme uile ho fri muin aicme uile Curach fri ailm aicme uile aen dib ar in cet fid a do ar in fid tanaise Coroiseda coig in fid deginach se cip na naicme.

The ship ogham: that is, a (barc) bark for the whole B group; (long = Longa navis), a full-rigged ship for the whole group of II; (No = navis), a ship for the whole group of M; (cupach = carina), a leathern boat for the whole group of A; one of them for the first letter, two of them for the second letter, so that five stand for the last letter of whatever group it be.

No. 9. Suag Ogam, the rope ogham.

Ogam cuidectach ⎬⊤ᵣ bacllaid, laicera.

⊤⊤

The company ogham, herdsmen, heroines, fianna, senada, noeim, ar sin uile,[10] fenians,

⊤⊤⊤   ⊤⊤⊤⊤·

⊤⊤⊤

ancients, saints and so all

No. 10 and P. (Not named.) See note, Plate III No. 16.

No. 11 and 2. Ogam lochlanach ann so, the Scandinavian ogham here. The inhabitants of the coasts of Norway and shores of the Baltic Sea were called Lochlandach, Lochlandaig, i.e. Lake Landish, Lakelanders.

No. 12. F A T O R G H N I A S D B M L E, found at Greenmount.

No. 13. Gall ogam, foreign ogham. [Gall meant originally an inhabitant of Gaul, afterwards any foreigner. In the eleventh century a Dane was a Gaul; in the sixteenth century an Englishman was often so styled]. Anmand na feadh sa, the names of these letters: Fea, Ar, T[n]urs, Or, Raid, Cann, Hagal, Naun, Isar, Sol, Diur, B-gann, Mann, Lagor, Eis. [This is not the usual order of the Icelandic Futhorc.]

End of the oghams, commencement of the Precepts. In the name of God. Amen ... And a good thing in my opinion.

Names of Persons Mentioned in the Plates

Fionn

Of the many Fionns mentioned in Irish history the most celebrated was Fionn Mac Cumhall, who was the son-in-law of the famous Cormac Mac Art, monarch of Ireland, and the general of his standing army, known as the Fianna Erenn. According to the 'Annals of Tighernach', Fionn McCumhall was slain in the year AD284.

Cruitine

A poet, of whom an anecdote is told at considerable length in the Glossary of Cormac M'Cuilennan, Bishop and King of Cashel, who was slain in the year 903.

Iollann

An ancient Irish tale, in which the name of King Arthur occurs, is entitled Echtra Iollainn, 'The Adventures of Iollann.'

Bricriu

This is a story of the first century of the Christian era, entitled, Fledh Bricriu, 'The Feast of Bricriu.'

Breass Mac Elathan

The son of Elatha, king of the Fomorians. He accompanied the Tuatha de Danann on their invasion of Ireland, and helped them to subdue the Firbolg at the battle of Moytura, near Cong. In return, the Tuatha de Danann elected him king when their previous king, Nuada, resigned the throne, in consequence of having lost one of his hands in the battle of Moytura. After a reign of seven years, however, Breass was deposed to make room for Nuada, to whose wrist a hand of silver was now fitted. Breass retired to the court of his father, but after a time he returned to Ireland with a Fomorian army, and gave battle to the Tuatha de Danann at Moytura of the Fomorians, where he was defeated and slain.

Fercertne

Chief *file*, that is, poet and philosopher, at the court of Conor Mac Nessa, king of Ulster, at the beginning of the Christian era. This Fercertne was the original author of the Uraicechet-na n-Eiges, or 'Precepts of the Poets', a treatise that was enlarged about the year 628 by Cennfaeladh, son of Ailill. It is a copy of this work, as remodelled by Cennfaeladh, that immediately succeeds the tract on the oghams in the 'Book of Ballymote.' (The initial letter is given, Plate IV.)

Roighne Roscadach

The author of many ancient law maxims was one of the sons of Ugaine Mor, monarch of Ireland 633BC, or, according to O'Flaherty, 330BC.

Ogma Grian Aineach

Ogma of the sun-like face, the inventor of the ogham characters, was a brother of Breass Mac Elathan, king of the Tuatha de Danann. The mother of Breass and Ogma was a princess of the Tuatha de Danann. Their father, Elatha, was king of the Fomarach, or Scandinavian vikings.

Thachtga

A daughter of Mogh Ruith, archdruid of Ireland in the first century of the Christian era.

1. Ogham means an inscription (making sense) written or engraved in the characters invented by Oghma Grian Aineach.

2. Drum (a ridge) means the angle line on which, in the case of stones and staves, the inscription rests; hence it further means any line used to support ogham characters.

3. Craobh (a wide-spreading branch) is such a line furnished with ogham characters, in alphabetical or any other order, making sense or not making sense.

4. Fleasc (a rod or switch) means a single stroke or score on, under, or across the craobh, or stem-line.

5. Fidh (a tree) means an ogham letter, or rather the ogham equivalent for a letter – *litir* always meaning a Latin character, and *fidh* an ogham character. A *fidh* ordinarily consists of from one to five similar flesc or strokes.

As the ogham characters, taken in general, are called *feadha*, or trees, so, taken in particular, each character takes the name of some tree, the initial letter of whose name corresponds with the alphabetical power of the character.

Aicme (a sect, &c.) means a group of five letters all formed of *flesc*, or strokes, that rest similarly on the stemline, that is, all branching off to the left, or all branching off to the right, or all cutting the stem-line obliquely, or all cutting it perpendicularly, &c.

An Ogam craobh, that is, the ogham branch, means, *par excellence*, the ogham alphabet.

Ceart ogham (the right ogham) appears to have been the ogham alphabet as arranged by Ogma himself. All the other ogham alphabets are variations of it. Of these, the most important are as it were written in cipher.

An explanation of the arrangement of the letters of the ogham alphabet is suggested as follows:

It is not easy to discover on what principle Ogma grouped BLFSN together at the head of his alphabet. M, G, Ng, Str, R, seem to have been the last group completed, as *str*, at least, seems a stop-gap imported into the alphabet to complete the group, which fittingly ends with R, which brings up the rear, as being the last letter of *iar*, which means after.

The vowels A, O, U, E and I, are rightly a group to themselves. A has the first place almost as much by natural right as by custom. O and U immediately follow A, because in the Irish language they give, like A, a thick sound to the consonants they immediately follow. O has the middle place between A and U; because the sound of O is intermediate between the sound of A and the sound of U. E and I are side by side, because alike they give a slender sound to whatever consonants they immediately follow. Of the two, E is the nearer to A, because the sound of E is intermediate between the sound of A and the sound of I. The arrangement, then, of these five vowels in the ogham alphabet is the most philosophical and the most in accordance with the genius of the Irish language, consistently with allowing A to retain the first place.

It was most congruous to group the five letters, H, D, T, C, Q, thus together, to express the powers of a group of characters formed respectively of one, two, three, four, and five strokes, as those five letters are the initial letters of the cardinal numbers one, two, three, four, and five in the Irish language. H, whose ogham character is one stroke in the written language, is at least the occasional initial of aon or h-aon, one; while in the spoken language in the county of Cork, and it may be elsewhere, it is its constant initial, thus, *haon*. D, whose ogham character is composed of two strokes, is the initial of *do*, two.

T, whose ogham character is composed of three strokes, is the initial of tri, three. C, whose ogham character is composed of four strokes, is the initial of ceathan, four. Q, whose ogham character is composed of five strokes, is equivalent to cu, the initial of cuig, five. In the ninth century cuig, though sometimes written cuic, was usually written coic[, a form of which the co departs a little more from Qu than does the cu of cuic or cuig. But even this coic is held by Zeuss to have been but a modification of a more ancient Celtic *cinc* or *cuinc*, which latter form, resembling so much the Latin *quinque*, indicates that in tracing back we approach, rather than depart from, the Qu type as that of the original initial of the fifth cardinal of the Irish language.

It is an open question whether the Irish-speaking inhabitants of Cork county have in *haon* preserved an original radical H, or have corruptly prefixed H to *aon*. Should the latter view be adopted, it will seem at first sight an overstraining to make the initial of aon or oin be H, rather than A or O. But though for a thousand years H may not have been the radical and necessary initial letter of any word nath, the very name of H, still in all the stages of the Irish language throughout that period, H has been the adventitious and occasional initial letter of all words commencing with vowels, and of aon, or oin, equally with the rest. Now, having to confer on the ogham character[11] the power of the initial letter of Haon or H, om, Oghma would have in any case to reject its radical initial vowel, whether A or O, as having already a place in the vowel group of his alphabet, and would have to accept its accidental initial H, which should somehow find a place in the alphabet. But though in the written language of the last thousand years H does not appear as a radical initial, the case may have been different in Oghma's time, perhaps, three thousand years ago. This is the more probable, as H is a radical in the Welsh, Anglo-Saxon and Latin languages – the three languages which have the closest analogy to the Irish. In this way the word uath itself, the tree name of H, yields some faint reason to think that H was once a radical initial in the Irish language, for the analogy between uath and the English word haw, in hawthorn, favours the notion that at some remote period H was the first letter of uath, as it is of haw, if indeed uath and haw be the same word in origin as they are in meaning.

If, then, two or three thousand years ago, H was in any instance a radical initial, we may assume that it was so in the case of aon or oin, then haon or hoin. For this we may plead not only the present usage of the county Cork, and its past usage for at least one hundred years, but also the analogy of the Greek ἕν, and an approach to a like analogy in the English word – one at least in pronunciation.

The word uath, already so often mentioned, yields a singular confirmation of the connection now sought to be established between the cardinal number haon and the ogham character for the letter H. Uath means, first, the hawthorn tree; second, it is the name of the ogham character for the letter H; third, it is, as a numeral substantive, meaning a unit – anything single. Its derivative, uathath, or uathadh, is the grammatical term of the Irish language for the singular number. Now there is no apparent reason why the idea of unity should attach itself to uath, a single stroke above the line, and not equally attach itself to Bethe, a single stroke below the line, or to Muin, a single stroke obliquely across the line; or to Ailm, a single stroke at right angles to the line; except the reason, which our hypothesis supplies, namely, that uath is not merely the name of a character formed of one stroke, but is precisely the name of that particular character so formed, whose power could only be that of the initial letter of haon. For our hypothesis is that Ogma conferred the powers of the initial letters of the first five cardinal numbers upon the group of ogham characters formed above the line, and thus gave the power of H, which must have been the initial of haon to the character formed of one stroke above the line. His next step was to attach to each character the name of a tree, whose initial letter was that which the character represented. In this way uath, at that time huath, as having an initial H, became the name of the character whose power is H. Haon therefore gave that character its power of H, and its power of H procured it its name of huath. Huath being thus connected with haon, acquired in time the meaning of haon, in addition to its other meanings.

To fill up Plates Nos. I and IV, I traced, for purposes of comparison, some of the ogham characters preserved in a manuscript now in the library of the British Museum, Codex Clarendon, Vol. XV. Add. 4783. This vol., fol. 3, contains a short list of different forms of ogham, written on vellum, including all that are marked thus †, in the before mentioned history, as well as illustrations substantially the same as those in the Book of Ballymote. Below the Finit, given on Plate IV, an erasure of some old writing was effected, and about the year 1550 over it was written 'Anonymi Tractatus de varijs apud veteres Hibernicos occulto scribendi formulis seu artificijs (Hibernicé ogoib)[ogum].' This manuscript vol. was presented to the British Museum by the late Rev. Dr Milles, Dean of Exeter, President of the Society of Antiquaries of London, and was in the library of Henry Earl of Clarendon, who obtained it from Sir James Ware; and there is a possibility of its being a portion of that ancient writing of the Gael, inscribed with ogham characters to the number of 150, known to have been once in the possession of Duald Mac Firbiss.

Mac Curtin, in his English-Irish Dictionary, pub. Paris, 1732, p. 713, chapter xiv, on Irish Grammar, 'of the antient character call'd Ogam, and of the abbreviations call'd nodaige', informs us that the 'Irish antiquaries preserved this ogham as a piece of the greatest value in all antiquity, and it was penal for any one to study or use it but one of the sworn antiquaries. In those characters the antiquaries wrote the evil acts of their monarchs and great personages, male and female, so that it may not be known to the vulgar or common multitude, only to the learned; and for the better understanding of these characters it is necessary to get and keep by heart certain verses in the Irish language'. I find these verses also are given in a manuscript. in the British Museum (Egerton, 134). Mac Curtin, I believe, copied from a manuscript in the library of Trinity College, Dublin, H. 18., a rather modern work; and I find a reference to a fine manuscript octavo volume on vellum, relating to the subject of ogham writing, also in that library, but which I regret not having yet seen.

The subject of ogham writing since the Callen stone, in 1785, was brought under the notice of antiquaries, has considerably advanced, notwithstanding the ridicule heaped upon it. Even Petrie, in 1845 (see the 'Ecclesiastical Architecture of Ireland', p. 83), wrote: 'I utterly deny that the lines on the stone at Ardmore are a literal inscription of any kind.' This may be excusable in Ledwich, who saw everything with jaundiced eyes. But the latest curiosity (published in the 'Journal of the Anthropological Institution', Vol. II. p. 201) ascribes all the ogham inscriptions to cow-boys' calculations.

The 'Journal' of this Association from its first volume, contains many excellent papers on the subject.

There can be no question (as the Lord Bishop of Limerick has shown in papers published by the Royal Irish Academy, 1849) that the ogham, in the form we find it, is the work of a grammarian, and very likely to have its counterpart in the Runic writings further borne out by the discovery, by the late E. O'Curry, in Trinity College Library, of a fragment of vellum manuscript, used as a fly-leaf, containing a short poem furnishing rules for the construction of a Runic ogham, which, though imperfect and indistinct in parts, contains in the last lines an account of the introduction of this form of ogham:

Hither was brought, in the sword-sheath of Lochlan's king,
The ogham across the sea. It was his own hand that cut it.[12]

The references in the old manuscripts quoted nearly all record pagan practices in Christian times. It is most difficult to judge the age of ogham writings by the state (from decay and mutilation) of the existing monuments; and of those, the greater number are found close to the sea coast of the south of Ireland – a rather significant fact. The rude construction of such places as the chambers near Dunloe Castle and at Dromloghan may belong to the pre-historic age, or be constructed yesterday by people in a primitive state. Their utility is still an enigma. The Christian age of the ogham-inscribed stones is very doubtful. On the Trabeg stone, repeatedly offered as evidence, the arm of the inscribed cross cuts off a portion of the ogham score, proving distinctly the ogham was first inscribed. On the stone figured in the 'Catalogue of Antiquities', in the Museum of the Royal Irish Academy, by Sir W. R. Wilde, p. 136, there are two Thor's crosses, omitted in the illustration; and the builders of some of the earliest Christian churches had no respect for such monuments, and used them as common building stones in the constructions.

The illustrations which accompany this paper show the method was dead at the time the originals were compiled; and, as Professor G. Stephens, of Copenhagen, in a letter to me, remarks, 'The lists are more traditional than for practical use; accordingly, they are all more or less cryptic for secret writing,' and this is exactly what is recorded. I have placed figures before each line, and numbered the plates, which will, I trust, facilitate reference. They tell their own tale much better than I could hope to do. I have endeavoured to render them as nearly in fac-simile as possible, even to the repetition of the vowels in line 3, Plate III. (I find it so in the Brit. Mus. MS. also, the last group should be lettered N. S. F. L. B.), but they fall far short of the originals. Still, they will, I trust, afford the Members facility for corrections, and help to advance their study of this subject.

Notes

1 I am informed by the Rev. James Graves that he has seen in the collection of Mr Browne, Manager of the National Bank at Roscrea, some ogham-inscribed wooden objects found in the cranog of Strokestown.

2 This translation is in keeping with the figure which omits L; for might otherwise be translated beyond. In either case the text requires the example to end not in R but in M. The emphatic words idon puir, that is R, probably express the surprise of the writer who transcribed the Book of Ballymote at finding R instead of M in the text which he copied.

3 A little poem is given in this character, but the vellum is so discoloured that it is impossible to make it all out correctly.

4 Calgadeg, seemingly an error for calg-noec, which, according to O'Curry was an 'Ivory-hilted small sword'.

5 The fifth line gives the ogham character; the fourth its corresponding Latin letter; the third, Dr O'Donovan's translation of the tree-names of the characters; the second those tree-names, and the top line gives a gloss on those names. The gloss on 'coll' and perhaps on 'muin', is merely a repetition. In the case of B, F, S, D, R and I, it gives a more modern form of their names. For huath, straiph, and perhaps onn, which are obsolete, it substitutes in explanation more modern names which have the same meaning, though not the same initials, as the obsolete names.

In the case of L, N, I, Q, G, Ng, A, U, and perhaps E, for the obsolete names of trees commencing with these letters, it substitutes names of trees which have the same initials, but far different meanings, assuming that Dr O'Donovan's translation is correct.

6 Forms of characters very like this and No. 10, Plate IV, are given among the examples of 'Ancient Alphabets', by Ahmab bin Abubekr bin Wahshih, pp. 38 and 46; translated into English by Joseph Hammer, 1806; similar characters, with other descriptions and illustrations of oghams, are also figured by Joh. T. Liljegren, in 'Run-Lara', Plate II, published at Stockholm, 1832.

7 In this figure the characteristic characters of every group appear to be those along the vertical diameter, if so, one to five upside-down Cs represent the B group of letters; one to five Cs on their backs represent the H group; one to five Cs represent the M group, and one to five inverted Cs represent the A group. The semicircle or letter C attached to the top of a wheel revolving from left to right, will, in its mid-descent, be concave beneath; at the bottom it will be concave to the left; in mid-ascent it will be concave above, and at the top it will be concave to the right, as at first. The four classes of characters that make up the wheel ogham are produced from one by the revolution of a wheel, hence its name. See Ogham Coll., M'Curtin.

8 This alphabet is a copy of the Hebrew alphabet; for, first, the order of these letters is that of the Hebrew letters; second, their number would be the same only that 'He' is here omitted; thirdly, the names of these letters, where given in full, viz., Samech, Ain, Phe, &c, are the corresponding Hebrew names; lastly, in shape most of these letters differ but little from the modern Hebrew

letters, and a few, such as H(eth) and T(au), are identical with them. The Vaw here given resembles the Phoenician Vaw, and Beth and Phe resemble the old more than the modern Hebrew letters; on the other hand, the H(eth) and Tau of this alphabet are peculiar to the modern Hebrew. On the whole, then, we may take this alphabet to be a careless transcript of the modern Hebrew alphabet.

9 This alphabet has no connection whatever with the hieroglyphic, the hieratic, or the demotic systems of writing, the three in use among the ancient Egyptians, nor has it anything in common with the Coptic of the later Egyptians. Its order is that of the Latin alphabet, with a character for str and one apparently for et appended. It contains the Latin letters A, C, D, F, G, H, R, N and S, but transposed, and so changed in signification. In addition to these it contains Runic A and M, and some other characters greatly resembling oghams.

10 Ap ru unle. This, I think, should be (m)an pm uile, in the same way all; or rather it should be, t map rm uile, that is, agur map rin uile, and so all. Compare Plate I, line os, ogham No. 8.

11 The form haon is given in the 'Irish Dictionary' published in 1768 by the Right Rev. Dr O'Brien, Bishop of Cloyne, a native of the county of Cork.

12 See No. 17, 1858, of this 'Journal'. The Rev. D.H. Haigh figures No. 5, and describes at p. 193 this curious alphabet, ascribing it to the Franks.

CHAPTER TWELVE

Ogham

R.A.S. Macalister

I. The Testimony of Caesar

GAIUS IULIUS CAESAR, THE ARCH-DESTROYER of Celtic civilization on the Continent of Europe, is nevertheless the writer of antiquity who has preserved for us more valuable details about that civilization than all the rest put together. Every study of Celtic Religion begins with a passage from *De Bello Gallico*, wherein the chief gods worshipped by the Gauls are enumerated; an important passage, though requiring some caution in making use of it. Every study of Celtic Literature begins with another passage from the same history (Book VI, chaps. xiii, xiv) wherein the author speaks of the druids; and from this rule our present investigation is not exempt. These chapters have been quoted so often, that it might be supposed that every possible minim of juice had been squeezed from them long before this: yet we shall find it profitable to remind ourselves of what Caesar has to tell us, on the subject with which they deal.

Two classes of people, he says, among the Gauls, are held in especial honour – druids and *equites*. The druids are concerned with matters of religion, and with the conduct of public and private sacrifices. A great number of youths go to them for teaching; and they – presumably the druids, not the youths, but the sentence is ambiguously worded – are held in high honour. They decide almost all judicial cases, public and private, criminal and civil – questions of inheritance or of territorial boundaries, for example. Anyone who refuses to accept their decision is punished by excommunication from the sacrifices. This is the heaviest of all their penalties, for he who is put under such a ban is made the object of a drastic boycott – thus we may render Caesar's words, though naturally he could not anticipate the transcendencies of modern civilization so far as to use this particular terminology.

One of the druids holds chief authority. When he dies, his successor is elected by vote, if there be no one marked out for the vacant office by supereminence in dignity. Sometimes, however, competition for the office becomes so hot, that they contend for it by force of arms. At a certain season of the year they assemble in a sacred place in the land of the Carnutes, regarded as being the central point of Gaul [and in modern times believed to be the site of Chartres Cathedral]. Hither comes everyone who may have any dispute, in order to have it decided.

It is supposed that their teaching was discovered in Britannia, and carried thence to Gallia; even yet those who wish to understand it in greatest perfection journey to Britannia for instruction. As druids are exempt from military and fiscal services, these privileges attract many students, who go of their own accord, or are sent by their parents. It is said that they learn by heart a great number of verses, and that some spend as much as twenty years in this discipline. They do not consider it right (*fas*) to commit these verses to script, though in almost all public or private matters they make use of Greek letters. I suppose, adds Caesar parenthetically, that this is either because they desire to guard against the vulgar becoming acquainted with their mysteries, or because they are afraid of weakening their students' power of memory, seeing that much of this power is lost by trusting to written notes. He concludes with a few vague notions about the subjects of the druidic teaching – the immortality of the soul the stars and their motions, the world, the size of lands, natural philosophy, and the nature of the gods. On these matters, we read, the druids hold disputations and impart instruction to youths.

Thus far Caesar, who next proceeds to tell us about the other honourable class, the *equites*. There we need not follow him; in the two chapters which we have paraphrased he has given us sufficient food for thought. He has introduced us to a caste of functionaries, semi-religious, semi-judicial; who preside over ritual ceremonies and courts of law; who are held in high honour and enjoy high privileges; who are expert in the traditional theology of their people, in natural philosophy as it was understood at the time, in astronomy, and in all such matters; who endeavour by disputations to enlarge the knowledge which they possess; and who impart that knowledge to schools full of pupils. These pupils come for instruction, often from a distance and even from beyond the sea; for though there are schools in Gaul, those which are most frequented are in Britain, where, it was believed, the doctrines of the druids were first formulated.

Instruction in the schools is conveyed in the form of verses, dictated to the pupils and by them committed to memory; for a religious tabu – such is the implication of the word *fas* – forbids both teacher and taught to commit them to writing. And in this drudgery many pupils spend as much as twenty years.

Let us consider what this implies. Suppose that the pupils were allowed two months' annual holiday, which is probably liberal: in other words, let us for arithmetical convenience keep them at school, 300 working days in a solar year. Then, if they learn no more than ten lines of poetry in the day, they will have acquired a total of 3000 by the end of the year, and in twenty years they will be masters of 60,000 lines. This is considerably more than twice the united lengths of the two Homeric epics. Even if they learnt only one single line *per diem*, they would have assimilated matter roughly equal in amount to the first ten books of the *Iliad*: if they enlarged their daily task to thirty-five or forty lines, they would in the end possess, stored in memory, matter equal in extent to the prodigious *Mahabharata*.

As we have no information upon the average rate of work, we can come to no definite conclusion as to the magnitude of the literary material imparted to the students. But on any theory, if we accept the premises, we must conclude that it was of very considerable bulk. And there is no obvious reason why we should not accept the premises. Caesar had ample opportunity for learning these three superficial facts, which were probably common knowledge – that the druids taught screeds of verse to their pupils; that these verses were never written; and that the instruction often lasted twenty years. It is unlikely that he had any information as to the contents of the poems, or their literary quality: they may have been impressive hymns or epics; they may have been mere mnemonic doggerel. The carefully guarded secrets of a druidic freemasonry would not have been communicated to Caesar, a hostile alien: it is significant that when he begins to tell us what the teachers taught, he drops into hazy and obvious generalities. ...

No other source of information in antiquity supplements Caesar's testimony with details of any value. Diogenes Laertius, in a passage undeservedly quoted at least as frequently as Caesar's chapters, says something about the druids teaching their followers 'to worship the gods, to do no evil, and to exercise courage'.[1]

Canon MacCulloch, whose very useful book on *The Religion of the Ancient Celts* treats Caesar's testimony with more than a spice of scepticism, says (p. 304), 'If the druids taught religious and moral maxims secretly, these were probably no more than an extension' of the three excellent precepts just quoted. But surely the pupils must have been very dull if they found it necessary to spend twenty years in assimilating such rudimentary morality, however extended: and it is not obvious that any body of initiates would suffer harm in prestige or otherwise by committing to writing these copybook platitudes. If those who repeat the quotation from Timaeus would take the trouble to refer to the original passage, they would find that it is the most casual of *obiter dicta*, devoid of all authority, and professing to do no more than to express current notions about the Celtic druids and the Indian gymnosophists. It is just as worthless as contemporary notions about Freemasonry among those who (like the present writer) are not in the secrets of the craft, and so cannot by any possibility know what they are talking about. Incidentally, we must describe it as a mere fatuity to imagine a Celtic 'triad' as underlying the threefold maxim stated by Timaeus.

Let us therefore return to Caesar; let us now consider for a moment the prohibition of writing. Caesar's speculations as to the reason for this are not convincing, though they possess a very real secondary value. It is certainly true that, other things being equal, a memory which has never known the crutch of pen and paper is stronger than one which relies upon these supports. But, apart from the moral conditions imposed by competitive examinations, the external memory of a notebook is superior to the memory which is the gift of nature. The former is permanent, and is always available for reference: the latter is liable to fluctuations due to ill-health, advancing age, and so forth. Regard for the student's power of memory was not a sufficient reason for the total prohibition of writing. The alternative suggestion, that its purpose was to guard against the vulgar becoming acquainted with the mysteries, is much more to the point: in all ages the medicine-man has surrounded himself with an aura of occultism, which establishes and safeguards his powers and his prestige. We learn, in passing, from Caesar's theory that if the druidic teaching had been written down, and if the writings had fallen into the hands of the vulgar, the vulgar could have read them. Writing was no learned monopoly: Caesar implies that it had to be prohibited by those interested in maintaining the secrets of their order, just because it was cultivated with some freedom for secular purposes.

If, in these modern times, we can improve upon Caesar's guesses, it is because we know of analogies with which he was not acquainted. Writing is a secular art, used for profane purposes: those who have inherited religious faiths and formulae from an unlettered ancestry have an instinct that this novelty profanes sacred texts. Religion is conservative. Candles seem more suitable than electric lights as illuminants for churches. Solomon must build his temple without the touch of iron,[2] then newly brought into use – a metal against which, even yet, supernatural beings are alleged to feel repugnance.

The first enthusiasts for Islam were reluctant to write down the revelations of which their prophet had been the medium – did not he himself make a proud boast of illiteracy? They fixed them with pen and ink only when they discovered that within a single generation wars were thinning out the human repositories of the tradition, and moreover that the treachery of human memory was introducing intolerable variants into the divine words. To this day, according to strict orthodox views, the book dictated piecemeal by Muhammad must be multiplied by hand, or, at most, by lithography: the secular mechanism of the printing-press is unworthy of a duty so exalted. To this day, translation of the book into any language other than its native Arabic is looked upon, to say the least, with disfavour. To this day many – even Turks, to whom Arabic is a foreign language – burden themselves with the tremendous task of committing the whole of its interminable monotony to memory.

India presents a yet closer analogy. We hesitate before citing the august canon of the *Rig-veda* in connection with Caesar's druids. We recall only too vividly such cautionary tales as the tragedy of the frog who sought to emulate the ox. Before pursuing the analogy, we must safeguard ourselves by disclaiming any knowledge, or any theory, as to the literary value of the druidic traditions. They may have soared with Homer or with Pindar: they may have grovelled with the incredible people whose inspirations adorn the provincial press. In any case this question is irrelevant, so long as the druids themselves were satisfied with their inheritance. Comforting ourselves with this assurance, let us examine the Indian parallel a little further.

In the *Rig-veda* we have a *corpus* of lyric poetry, the work of a succession of sages, roughly equal in quantity of matter to the Homeric epics, and essentially religious in character. Its composition extended over several centuries, some time in the latter half of the second millennium B.C.; and for nearly a thousand years it was transmitted by oral tradition only, although for much of that time writing in one form or another was freely practised. These hymns 'are largely mythological ... [they] enable us to see the process of personification by which natural phenomena developed into gods ... one poet ... wonders where the stars go by day. ... The unvarying regularity of sun and moon, and the unfailing recurrence of the dawn, however, suggested to these ancient singers the idea of the unchanging order that prevails in Nature.'[3] This is not unlike Caesar's statements, for what they may be worth, as to the subjects of druidic teaching.

Indeed, the analogy – a frog-and-ox analogy if you will – is so complete that it cannot be ignored. The druids must have had a canon of traditional hymns, at once the instruments and the subjects of instruction; and must have preserved them in memory because they were too sacred to be committed to the Greek letters used for secular purposes. We shall have something more to say about these Greek letters presently.

This Indian analogy now leads us a step further. Human language changes with changing generations, even in these latter days, when the printing-press exercises a steadying influence. On the other hand, the iron discipline of a sacred tradition resists all such linguistic innovations. I remember hearing a minister of religion, during the European War, in an extemporaneous prayer, offering a petition 'for those who ascend into the heights of the air, or descend to the depths of the sea'. Evidently he shrank from the utterance, in an act of worship, of such modern words as 'aeroplanes' and 'submarines'! Language, on the popular lips, is in a state of constant flux, and before many generations have passed, it parts company with the stereotyped language of hymn or of ritual. What meaning does an English bumpkin, in his heart, attach to such phrases as 'trumpets and shawms', 'to lie in the hell like sheep', or 'to grin like a dog' which he encounters periodically in the Church recitation of the Psalter? What would a Roman guttersnipe have made of the Litany of the Arval Brothers? With these and similar analogies before us, we may doubt whether a Gaulish youth, packed off by provident parents to a British school that he might acquire knowledge which in years to come would exempt him from military service and taxation, could have understood without a commentary the very first lines that his new preceptors caused him to recite.

It was so in India. The Vedic literature of necessity accumulated around itself a vast body of explanatory material, as advancing time increased its obscurities. Ultimately, the language of the Vedas had become so completely divorced from any current vernacular, that it became in itself a subject for special study; and thus the mountainous erudition of the Indian grammarians gradually came into being.

Likewise, the students in the druidic schools would have found their hymns more or less unintelligible; just as an Englishman without preparatory study finds an Anglo-Saxon document or even Chaucer unintelligible. This helps us to understand why the curriculum extended over so long a time. The pupils were not like Sunday-school scholars, learning off by heart easy and popular hymns. Rather were they like French schoolboys, whose master makes them learn odes of Horace off by heart: we say 'French' because it makes the analogy closer, seeing that French and Latin are essentially one language at different stages of evolution. It is no illegitimate straining of the imagination to reconstruct the process of the teaching in such a way as this. The master first repeated a line, or a quatrain, or whatever was regarded as the unit of verse. The students repeated it after him till they were perfect in pronunciation and intonation. The master then analysed it, explaining its grammatical structure word by word, and setting forth its meaning and the truths, or supposed truths, which it was intended to convey. When he was satisfied that the pupils had assimilated his teaching, he proceeded to the next section of the composition. In this slow, laborious way we may suppose the sacred canon to have been passed from generation to generation.

Grammar, therefore, must in some form have been an important subject of study in the schools; and when the pupils left, they possessed, among their other acquisitions, a mastery of what was virtually a new language. Scholars of the Middle Ages had Latin for a second language. Latin franked them over the whole world of learning: in Latin they could discuss high problems in theology, science, and what not, undeterred by the risk of giving away injudicious secrets to unlettered eavesdroppers. So a druid, fresh from his schooling, wheresoever in the Celtic world he might find himself, could shew, among his other credentials, a mastery of an ancient speech, known only to those of his own order. And to everyone who has a secret to keep, be he the most exalted ambassador or the most disreputable gangster, a secret language in one form or another – an official cryptographic code or an arbitrary and irresponsible *argot* – is as necessary as the elementary needs of the body.

II. The Testimony of Irish Literature

Though Caesar is speaking more particularly of the druids of Continental Gaul, he makes it clear that the educational system which he describes was current over a wider area. He points, indeed, to Britain as the original source of the teaching, and as the centre where it was still to be acquired in its fullest perfection.

Statements like this must not be forced to carry more weight than they can bear. The most that we can derive from Caesar is, that in his time it was believed that Britain was the region in which the doctrine originated. How far was that belief justified in fact? Popular beliefs are so frequently wrong, that they must always be corroborated by some responsible authority before they can be accepted.

On the other hand, we may admit that the teaching might well be less contaminated on an island, protected by its marine bulwark from foreign influence, than in the open area of a continent. This, however, does not imply a concession of the claim of Britain to having originated the druidic doctrine: and when we look to see if Britain has any corroboration of Caesar's statements to offer, we meet with disappointment. The scanty and obscure literature of early Wales tells us little or nothing to the point, and the field is confused by the antics of 'neo-druidism'. Tacitus and Dio Cassius tell us something about the sacred groves of Mona, and the worship of an otherwise unknown goddess Andrasta, but these matters, interesting though they may be in themselves, are here of no special importance.

Caesar makes no mention of Ireland in this connection. The omission may, however, be apparent rather than real. In his condensed description – which was never meant, and should not be taken, for an exhaustive treatise – it may be that 'Britannia' includes 'Hibernia'. If it appears that the testimony of Irish literature follows along lines parallel to those of Caesar, we may reasonably infer that this was actually the case, and that the druids in Ireland taught in the same way as their brethren on the Continent, and belonged to the same philosophical freemasonry.

We must, however, bear in mind that neither the later Roman authors, nor the Christian editors through whom we have received the surviving fragments of Irish literature, had any temptation to accord fair treatment to the druids. In Gaul, druidism was the chief unifying force: without its influence, the divided, often mutually hostile peoples of Gaul would have yielded much more easily to Roman arms. In Northern Europe, druidism was the chief obstacle to the extension of Christianity. In both cases, therefore, what we know about the druids has been transmitted by their enemies.

By a fortunate chance, however, the two hostilities have taken different forms, which cancel each other out. The Romans held up their hands in a horror pestilentially Pecksniffian, which ignored the ghastly orgies of the Colosseum, as they spoke of the monstrosities of druidic human sacrifices. After all, these sacrifices were little more than sanctified judicial executions, for the victims were usually criminals; and though disgustingly cruel, they were humanity itself in comparison with the hell-begotten abomination of Roman crucifixion. But the Romans admit, notwithstanding, that the druids were reverend personages, held in honour by their own people. When we turn to the Irish writers, we find little or nothing about druidic sacrifices, human or otherwise: but they delight in putting the druids into awkward or undignified positions, or in representing them as mere jugglers or buffoons – reminding us of Aristophanes and his outrageous caricature of Socrates. Thus the two adverse testimonies are in flat contradiction each of the other; yet they converge, almost against their will, in a corroboration of the truth of what we are told of the more honourable sides of the druidic functions.

We are not writing a book on the druids, and we therefore make no exhaustive analysis of the references to the druidic order to be found in the extant fragments of Irish literature. For our present purpose it will be sufficient to set one or two passages side by side with each statement of Caesar, so as to shew the similarity between them.

The druids were held in especial honour. This is the case in the Irish documents, though to recognize the fact we have often to 'read between the lines'. The writers do not tell us this in so many words: but they permit us to see lay-folk (kings and commoners alike) paying regard to the druids. They are the power behind the thrones of the former: they dominate the minds and the lives of the latter. Throughout the sagas of the Ultonian cycle, for example, the druid Cathub 'pulls the strings'. He is the adviser of the great king, Conchobor mac Nessa; to his decisions the king himself submits. In like manner the druids of Loiguire mac Neill, the king of Ireland at the time of St Patrick, direct and advise their master in his dealings with the new teacher.

As an interesting illustration of the form in which these and similar traditions have come down to us, take the following, from the life of St Senan.[4] Before the saint was born, his mother, a peasant woman, entered an assembly in which was a druid. The druid rose, to do her reverence. Forthwith the whole assembly rose, 'for great was the honour which they had for the druid at that time'. But the story goes on to say that when the druid had thus paid respect to a peasant, they ridiculed him; whereupon he explained that his respect was offered, not to the mother, but to the great saint whose birth was to be expected. Sift out from this story what is obviously unhistorical: the druid's foresight, and his reverence for a future champion of a rival creed – and what remains? An understanding between author and reader that an assembly would not remain seated while a druid stood, 'for great the honour which they had for the druid'. Our good hagiographer has tried to 'dis-harm' this damaging admission by telling us of the assembly's laughter at the druid's supposed *faux pas*. But even here he confesses more than he imagines: he makes a tacit admission that it would have seemed impossibly absurd for a druid to condescend to perform an act of courtesy to a peasant woman.

The druids were concerned with matters of religion, and with the conduct of public and private sacrifices. This testimony is confirmed, for Gaul, by Diodorus Siculus (v, 31): but so little has been allowed to survive in Irish literature bearing upon the pre-Christian religion, that we cannot point to any description of a ritual act of worship in which the druids take part. In the arts of magic and divination they are adepts: they interpret omens, reveal hidden truths, utter spells, and perform sundry miracles. They are, in fact, the medicine-men of the communities which they serve; as such, we need not hesitate to assume that the duties involved in the performance of religious celebrations would be committed to their charge.

A great number of youths go to them for teaching. We may quote here the famous story of the interview between St Patrick and the daughters of king Loiguire: it is told in the *Vita Tripartita Patricii*, and is of considerable antiquity. We need not trouble ourselves here with the details of the colloquy, but we note that these maidens were at the time under instruction, at the hands of the druids of the royal seat at Cruachu. If girls were sent for instruction to druids – which must have been unusual – we may infer that boys would likewise enjoy that privilege. In the life of St Ciaran, from the same hagiological collection as that which we have already quoted,[5] there is a variant of the Senan story which contains the same ideas – a druid, appearing to pay honour where it was not due, and getting himself laughed at. In this case the druid heard the noise of a carriage, and told the boys who attended upon him to see who was travelling in it, 'for that is the sound of a carriage bearing a king'. The 'king' was the unborn saint: the boys saw no one but the peasant mother, and ridiculed their master. Once more we may expunge as obviously unhistorical the druid's prophecy, his expression of obeisance, and the mockery of which he is made the victim. He was attended by a number of lads – presumably his pupils. He had to ask them who was in the carriage, therefore presumably he was blind, and must have imparted his teaching by oral instruction.

The druids decided judicial cases. Here at first sight we encounter a discrepancy. The Irish texts seem rather conspicuously to avoid putting a *drui* or 'druid' in the place of a judge or legal advocate. These functionaries are usually called *brethem* 'judge' or *file* [dissyllable], a word which for want of a better equivalent we must translate 'poet', though in doing so we must empty the English word of most, if not all, of its natural associations. 'Weaver of spells' is, perhaps, a more accurate equivalent: the *file* was much more magical than literary in his duties. The chief poet (*ardfhile*) of a king was no mere poet laureate. He was a personage who was believed to possess supernatural powers, which it was his business to exercise on behalf of the king whom he nominally served. We say *nominally* served, for we often are uncertain which is to be regarded as master and which as man.

But this was the function, or one of the functions, of the druids. The druids were not likely to tolerate rival magicians at the royal court, so we must infer that the druid and the *file* were different aspects of one and the same official.

Let us take a peep at a law case which was transacted at the court of the great Ultonian king, Conchobor mac Nessa, who is said to have reigned just before the beginning of the Christian era. It is described in a glossarial note inserted in the law tract called *Senchus Mor*.[6] We read that down to this time the privileges of judgement had been the monopoly of the *file*-class. It fell out that two sages went to law in the matter of the right to possession of the robe of office of another, by name Adna, who had shortly before solved the riddle of existence. The two claimants were Fer Chertne and Neide, the latter being son of the late Adna. And as they respectively pleaded their cause they spoke 'in a dark tongue', so that the chieftains standing by were unable to understand them.

'These people', they complained, 'keep their judgements and their knowledge to themselves. We know not the meaning of what they say.'

'That is only too true,' said the king, 'and an end must be put to such a state of matters. Henceforth every man must have a fair share of justice; the *file*-people must not have any more than what is due to them.' That king Conchobor so much as conceived the possibility of breaking the *file* monopoly marks him out as a great man.[7]

In these disputing *file*-people we must see the druids, secret language and all. In this respect also the evidence of Caesar is valid for Ireland as for Gaul. The Christian writers were unwilling to represent the chief exponents of a hostile paganism as sitting in the seat of justice, especially as St Patrick himself did not hesitate to retain the services of a *file*, Dubthach maccu Lugair by name, when he was faced with legal trouble.[8] We, however, need not share their qualms. We have found our druid-judges, and we have heard them speaking in a language which even kings and chieftains could not understand.

A man who refused to accept their decisions was punished by excommunication. As we are told so little about the normal religious rituals of paganism in extant Irish literature, we cannot expect to find evidence of any such rite of exclusion therefrom. But the consequences of offending a druid are always represented as being of the direst. Examples of this might be multiplied almost indefinitely; as one single illustration, we may recall how the Ultonian king Mongan hardly dared to maintain the accuracy of his own version of an historical incident, against that set forth by his own court *file*, although he had first-hand knowledge that his version was correct.[9] Perhaps we may look in this direction to explain the remarkable phenomenon of 'blotches on the face' and similar disfigurements, appearing after an offender has been cursed, bespelled, or satirized by a druid.[10] As we recall the many strange instances on record of the influence of mind upon matter, we hesitate to assert the impossibility of the curse of a man, to whom superhuman powers are attributed, producing physical effects of the kind upon a superstitious layman. But it is more probable that the expression is to be understood metaphorically. One blighted with such a curse became in the eyes of his fellows a moral leper, a *katharma*, to be shunned as though he were infected with physical disease.

One of the druids held chief authority – as Dubthach maccu Lugair, mentioned above, is described as 'chief *file* of Ireland'. *When he died there was often a contention for the vacant seat* – we have just been reading what looks like the report of such a contention. No doubt Fer Chertne and Neide would have been quite ready to go to war to settle their dispute, just as no less a person than Colum Cille, the apostle of Scotland, is said to have gone to war because the king of Ireland decided an arbitration against him.

At a certain season of the year they assembled at a sacred place, supposed to be the central point of Gaul. The great assemblies of Ireland, held at various seasons of the agricultural year at places of established sanctity, were among the most important elements in the religious and secular life of ancient Ireland. They were held for ritual purposes, doubtless to ensure fertility in the fields and cattle-byres; and at the same time were used as convenient occasions for the promulgation of laws, the settlement of judicial cases, and the conduct of horse-races and literary and musical contests. One of these assembly places was the Hill of Uisnech, in the modern county of Westmeath, which was believed to be the exact central point of Ireland.

We repeat, that we are not writing a book on the druids. We have contented ourselves with setting down, more or less at random, a number of illustrations which, when read in connection with Caesar's chapters, lead us to the conclusion that the druids in Ireland differed in no essential respect from those of Gaul. They were alike members of one and the same organization, whose influence was not confined to any one region. This being so, we may infer that they possessed the same literary heritage. From Caesar's evidence, we have drawn the conclusion that the druids in Gaul must have had at their service, in the language in which this literary heritage was composed, a means of communication known to no one, however exalted, outside their own circle of initiation: though we have no means of ascertaining what this language was, and indeed find no means of verifying our conclusion in Classical literature. This verification we found, when, unseen spectators from a century then far in the distant future, we took our place in an Ultonian court in or about the first century BC, and watched the indignant perplexity of the king and his courtiers. Their druids had discovered, and were making a practical exposition of, the great maxim which has made and unmade more empires, and upset more applecarts, than any other: Language was given to Man, to the end that he might conceal his thoughts!

III. What was the Druids' Language and of what Nature was the Traditional Literature?

In or about the year 560 a dyspeptic British monk, by name Gildas, writing in the safe retreat of a French monastery, produced a pamphlet called *De excidio Britanniae liber querulus*, which has had the unmerited good fortune to be the earliest extant native authority on British history. In this book he made a vitriolic attack upon the contemporary rulers of his country, whose crimes, he told them, had brought the Saxons upon them as instruments of divine vengeance. Among the princes at whom he rudely protrudes his tongue was Voteporius, or Voteporix, king of the Demetae, the people who lived in what is now Pembrokeshire: and the only thing of real importance which we learn from Gildas about him is, that he was alive, and advancing in years, when the book was written about the middle of the sixth century AD.

Towards the end of the nineteenth century the tombstone of this ruler was discovered, at a place called Llanfallteg, on the border-line of the modern counties of Pembroke and Carmarthen. The stone bears two inscriptions: one in Latin, VOTEPORIGIS DEMETORVM PROTICTORIS, giving the king's name in its Brythonic form; and the other in ogham letters, translating it into Goidelic for the benefit of the Irish colonists who continued to speak their ancestral language, VOTECORIGAS.

The names in ancient Celtic inscriptions are almost invariably in the genitive case, some such words as 'grave', 'stone' or the like being understood to complete the sense. In this name, the genitive of the ogham form is expressed by the external suffix -AS. Before the extant beginning of written literary Irish, as we have it in glosses of a century or two later, this termination had shed, first its -S, and then its -A, in colloquial speech. But if the Llanfallteg inscription truly represents the colloquial speech of its own epoch, these changes could hardly have had time to take place and to become completely established, when the glosses began to be written – for the latter represent a literary tradition that was already old and stereotyped, where the grammatical conventions of the ogham inscriptions are absolutely lost. Moreover, if the inscription were as old as the -AS genitive would suggest, the writer would hardly have made the mistake of representing the Brythonic P by C. He should have written the very different letter Q, which is never confused with C except in late and degenerate examples of ogham writing. We find only one conclusion open to us. 'VOTECORIGAS' is a piece of what the lamented H.W. Fowler called literary 'Wardour-street'. The writer of the inscription had endeavoured, with incomplete success, to write the name in a form older than the time to which the known date of Voteporius obliges us to assign his monument.

We chose this inscription as a text, because it can be dated with sufficient exactness from external evidence. There are many others which do not possess this special advantage, but which shew something of the same characteristics. These are scattered throughout Ireland, being found in greatest abundance in the southern counties; they also appear in the parts of Wales where Irish colonists settled. They are certainly in some form of the Gaelic language: but linguistically they are quite irreconcilable with the oldest extant monuments of Irish literary composition, which date back at least as far as the sixth century. In orthography, in the accidence of substantives (we have no material for saying anything about the verbs), they reveal a stage of the language, centuries removed, philologically speaking, from that of the earliest manuscript literature, although historically they are not separated from the manuscripts by any great stretch of time; the latest inscriptions, in fact, overlap with the earliest manuscripts.

The inscriptions make use of letters – Q, V, Ng – unknown to the manuscripts. They have a wealth of inflexional desinences, evanescent or altogether lost in the Irish of the oldest manuscript sources. It is hardly an exaggeration to say that the linguistic gulf which separates the manuscripts from the inscriptions is as great as that which separates a page of *La Chanson de Roland* from a page of classical Latin.

These differences are not much more than a matter of orthographical tradition. The English word *bought* is no longer pronounced with a rough guttural (boxt), as it still is in some parts of Scotland: but the *gh* remains in its spelling as a record of the time when it was actually so pronounced. The Goidels, for whose benefit the king's name was written as *Votecorigas* on his monument, are not likely to have *spoken* the syllable '-as', when they had occasion to mention his name in the genitive case. Their ancestors at some time then remote in the past would have done so: but the case-endings had been first slurred and then dropped, as speakers found that they could understand each other perfectly without them. When we find in one district, or even in one cemetery, stones, apparently not differing greatly in date, bearing an ancestral name rendered here *Dovinias*, and there *Dovinia*, it is reasonable to infer that the *s* had ceased to be of practical importance. It could be retained or omitted according to the taste and fancy, or the energy, of the engraver, or to the space available on the stone. It was a mere fossil of speech, like *gh* in *bought* – a word often spelt *bot* in bill-heads, and in that form ugly, but intelligible. If the *s* had retained its ancient importance as a sign of the genitive case, it would have been carefully inserted where-ever a name to which it belonged was to be expressed in genitive relationship.

We are thus introduced to a language which, in comparison with that of the oldest manuscript Irish, was highly flexional, and had a well-established and more or less stereotyped orthographical tradition totally different from the manuscript tradition. At the time when the inscriptions were cut, this inflexional language, as a spoken tongue, was dead; the peculiar forms used in the inscriptions are archaistic survivals. The archaisms are not always philologically accurate. Sometimes names are declined with wrong case-endings: we have already seen a phonetic confusion between C and Q, which would never have happened in the time of the living language. The tradition is no longer healthy, and is rapidly heading for dissolution.

On the other hand, such complicated forms of declension could not have been maintained at all, even with the imperfections and inaccuracies which it is possible to detect, unless some literary tradition had been in existence, to transport them from the ancient and forgotten speakers who used them in their daily conversation, to the inscription-writers who used them merely because 'it was the thing to do'. 'Bought' would be written in some such way as *bawt* if English were only now beginning to be written for the first time: the inscription-cutters would never have known or cared anything about these case-endings, much less written them, if their inscriptions had represented the first effort ever made at writing down the Gaelic language. It is absolutely necessary to postulate an extensive *literary* tradition, accompanied with elucidatory grammatical study, if we are to explain the phenomena of the inscriptions.

But this is just what we have been seeking: and now we begin to suspect that in the language of these inscriptions we catch the last echoes of the language of the druidic literature and of druidic instruction. *This* is the secret language which perplexed the court of Conchobor: there is no need to look for any other. The language of the traditional druidic literature was Old Goidelic – which, as has already been hinted, bears much the same relation to the earliest Irish of the manuscripts as Latin does to mediaeval Italian or French.

Very slight differences in a spoken language are enough to cause a measure of perplexity such as Conchobor suffered. It is not easy (*experto crede*) for one who has grown up amid the English of the Irish Pale to understand instantaneously the English of the Cambridgeshire peasant. The difference between the literary affectations of the learned poet-judges, and the colloquial conventions of the illiterate chieftains, need not have been much greater than the difference between the French of the simple-minded Monsieur de Pourceaugnac in Molière's lively comedy, and that of the physicians who persecuted him, to produce the mysteries which irritated the Ultonian court. I once knew a family of children who had contrived a private language of arbitrarily modified English words, which they spoke fluently, to the complete bewilderment of their elders.

This, then, is the conclusion at which we arrive. The ancient inscriptions of Ireland and of Wales represent the end of a literary tradition, absolutely different from the tradition which, for us, is inaugurated by the earliest extant Celtic glosses and other literary fragments. These two traditions overlap, but do not intermingle. The one descended from a remote past of the language; the colloquial speech, contemporary with its scanty extant records, had parted company with it. The other is a development of that colloquial. It is rooted in no literary antiquity: its beginnings are merely explanatory notes, designed to help students, whose vernacular was colloquial Irish, to understand words and sentences in Latin texts. The Church has introduced a new literature: for the moment, Latin is the only admissible literary language. Druidism is waning, but it is still a force to be reckoned with: its literature, with its pagan associations, is to be discouraged; and the archaic language which is its vehicle, must perish. But, as it disappears, a few 'die-hards' write it upon the tombstones of their friends.[11]

The inscriptions of which we have been speaking are written in a peculiar alphabet, to which is given the name 'ogham' (in Old-Irish spelling *ogum, ogom*), a word of uncertain etymology and meaning. This alphabet consists of groups of strokes, from one to five in number, arranged in various positions about a central stem-line: and five other characters, a little more complicated, which, in the mediaeval manuscripts where we find the alphabet set forth, are interpreted as diphthongs, but which more often than otherwise have a consonantal value in the inscriptions. The alphabet, as usually written, is as follows:

B L V S N H D T C Q M G Ng Z R A O U E I

Ea Oi Ia Ui Ae

The third letter is always called F in the Irish manuscripts which give us particulars of the alphabet; but for philological reasons, here irrelevant, the old value of V must be restored. In the inscriptions the sign Ea must have a guttural value, which it is convenient to express by K; Ia, in the few cases where we find it in practical use, is *always* to be interpreted as P. Ae is used only once, in a scribble on the margin of a manuscript; and there the context shews that it must be interpreted SC, CS or X.

The reader has only to jot down a few sentences in this alphabet to convince himself that it can never have been used for any extended literary purpose. The short inscriptions which we possess are the longest documents which could in reason be expressed by these laborious and clumsy letters – their very monotony would deaden all literary inspiration! – and even such inscriptions often extend along the whole length of a tall pillar-stone. But the ogham letters are quite suitable for spelling out words and sentences by means of finger-signs. The number of the groups of scores, from one to five, irresistibly suggests the hand and its fingers. All these letters, including the group of complex characters at the end of the row, can be made with one hand or with both, held in various attitudes, and with as many fingers outstretched as may be required.

Evidently this is a convenient device for secret communication. I have some knowledge of the common 'deaf-and-dumb' manual alphabet, but I am without skill or practice in its use; and it would be impossible for me *ex improviso* to follow a rapid conversation between two expert deaf-mutes. Two druids communicating by finger-signs such as these, in the presence of an illiterate or semi-illiterate audience, could 'conceal their thoughts' in perfect security; they could even secretly contradict what they were saying openly, by word of mouth! There seems to be no reasonable explanation for the invention, and continued existence, of an alphabet so childishly unpractical, other than that it was originally intended as a manual sign-alphabet, and that its use as a script was secondary and adventitious.

'Childishly unpractical', certainly. But when we examine it critically we see that its construction is very far from childish. There is learning behind it. Its inventor knows the difference between vowels and consonants – indeed, it is the only European alphabet which resembles that wonderful monument of phonetic analysis, the Devanagari script, in keeping those groups of sound-symbols apart. Moreover, the vowels are arranged in a phonetic order of tone-colour, as in this diagram:

A
O   E
U   I

Again, the consonants shew some rudiments of classification. They are divided into groups, of which one is headed by the labial B, another by its corresponding nasal M. The rest of the B group, L, V, S, N, is composed of continuative or vowel-consonant sounds; the next group, headed by the spirant H, contains stop consonants – the dentals D, T side by side, the guttural C and the closely related labio-velar Q side by side. The M group contains the sonant guttural G and its nasal Ng side by side, and also Z, R: these two likewise have some superficial relationship, for in certain circumstances, at least in modern Irish, the letter R has a Z colour in its pronunciation. There can be no doubt that the ogham alphabet is the contrivance of a grammarian, or, at least, of a phonetician.

But not even a grammarian could invent a manual sign-alphabet unless he were already able to spell. Like all other cryptographic systems, ogham must be founded upon some pre-existing alphabet. Endeavouring to identify this, it is natural to think first of the alphabet with which Imperial Rome endowed the world; and it is usually assumed that this was the foundation of the ogham cypher. The presence of Q in the ogham favours the assumption: but there are some very troublesome difficulties in the way. Our grammarian must have made a selection from the Roman letters: what principle did he follow in doing so? Why did he burden himself with Z and H, which are never used in any inscription (except in some late adaptations of the ogham script to the alien Pictish language, found in the region of the Picts in Scotland)? Why did he trouble to differentiate between U and V? or to introduce a sign for Ng? Why did he leave F and P out of his scheme, which, though rare, were sometimes wanted? These questions at least suggest the possibility that we may have to look elsewhere for the origin of the alphabet.

Let us recall Caesar's statement that they – the druids – in secular matters make use of *Greek* letters: and let us remember also that 'Greek letters' is a vague expression, covering a long period in time, and a considerable range of epigraphic evolution. We have to bear this in mind when reading Caesar, in other passages beside that set at the head of this chapter. Army lists were found in the Helvetian camp written in Greek letters (*B. G.* I, 29): the druids habitually used Greek letters: yet Caesar, writing a despatch from the land of the Nervii, used Greek letters to guard against its being read if it were intercepted (V, 48). It is admittedly possible that Caesar wrote to his correspondent in some pre-arranged cypher involving the use of Greek letters, though naturally he would not share the secret of its construction with his readers: but even though the Nervii may have been an especially barbarous community, who forbade the entry of foreigners, the proceeding seems hazardous. Experience teaches us all that, disregarding the demands of courtesy, it is unwise to discuss secrets in an out-of-the-way tongue, trusting to luck that none of the bystanders will understand it: there was every chance that some one would be hanging about the Nervian headquarters who could undertake to spell the letter out.

The extant epigraphic evidence indicates that Gaulish inscriptions from the South of France are written in Greek letters, because the Gauls in that region learnt to write from the Greek colony at Massilia,[12] those from Northern Gaul are in Roman characters, except on coins, some of which carry the Greek alphabet further north than the lapidary inscriptions. A few Gaulish inscriptions from northern Italy are in the script which the Gauls there learnt from the Etruscans. There is no *a priori* impossibility in maintaining that it was the Greek alphabet rather than the Roman which afforded the foundation upon which the ogham script was constructed.

The alphabet of the ordinary grammars will not serve, however, if only because it does not possess a Q. But the Greek alphabet once included that letter: and if we examine the varieties of the Greek alphabet which contain a Q, we shall discover with surprise – it certainly surprised me – that there is one which in its selection of letters is to all intents and purposes identical with the ogham alphabet.

This version of the Greek alphabet is scratched upon two vases, found respectively at Formello near Veii, and at Cervetri, the ancient Caere. They are assigned to about the middle of the sixth century BC. Facsimiles are accessible in various textbooks, such as Roberts's *Introduction to Greek Epigraphy*, vol. I, p. 17. The letters upon the vases are reversed (according to modern European practice), and the script proceeds from right to left: it will be sufficient to represent them here conventionally:

А В Г Δ Ε Φ Z Η Θ Ι Κ Λ ? Ν Ξ Ο Π Μ Ϙ Ρ Σ Τ Υ + Φ Χ

a b g d e v z h t^c I k l m n x o p š q r s t u x' p^c k^c

The letter H denotes the *spiritus asper*, not the vowel η. All students of the history of the Greek alphabet know that the parent Phoenician alphabet bequeathed to its Greek progeny an *embarras* of sibilant riches, and that the five letters Z,≡, M, Σ, and + were far more than were needed to express the sibilants of Greek. The last of these early disappeared altogether, though it lingers in the Formello-Cervetri alphabet. M (=*sh*) persisted for a little longer, but it ultimately ceased to exercise any phonetic function; in the form ⋟ it maintained a foothold, but as a numerical sign only.

Let us expunge the evanescent + from the Formello-Cervetri alphabet: we should find it gone if we could discover a similar graffito of the fifth century. Let us imagine a druidic scholar of that later time adapting the twenty-five signs that remain as instruments for the expression of his own language. We are not to suppose for a moment that the prohibition of writing, in connection with the sacred oral literature, implied a total exclusion of the art in other connections. Caesar, in fact, states the exact contrary: 'in all other matters they make use of Greek characters.'

Our scholar takes the alphabet as it stands, with one modification – a modification for which there are plenty of precedents. It often happens that when one community borrows a script from another, it gives new values to letters that would otherwise be of no service. The Greeks did so, in adapting the Phoenician alphabet to their own use: finding a new use, as vowels, for some signs which originally represented consonants peculiar to the Semitic languages. Our druid had no use for M (*sh*): but he felt the want of a symbol for ꜫ,[13] and adapted for the purpose this otherwise useless character. The expedient was presumably suggested by the external resemblance of the letter to ΝΓ, or the Greek convention ΓΓ.

Let the reader now copy out the Greek alphabet as set forth above, omitting +, writing *c* for *k*, and substituting ꜫ for *š* as the equivalent for M. Let him then turn back to the ogham alphabet on an earlier page, and take each letter in order, striking out the corresponding Greek letter in his copy. After he has gone through the first four ogham letter-groups, he will find that in each alphabet he is left with five letters. He will also not fail to notice that these letters have a close similarity in outward form; this has been shewn above, by writing the Greek letters above the ogham signs to which each corresponds.

The *Ea* sign is identical with X. The *Oi* sign, plus the section of the stem-line which its loop encloses, is identical with Θ. The equation of the *Ia* sign to Π is especially interesting. Let the reader make an imitation of the Greek letter Π by stretching the thumbs in a line, apposited at the tips, and protruding the first two fingers of each hand at right angles to that line. He will find that the slightest pressure on the thumb-tips will cause the fingers to fall into the cross position of the ogham letter. This will not happen if the index fingers only are stretched out: but we may suppose that the fingers were doubled to prevent the correspondent from reading the symbol as D or L. The *Ui* sign resembles φ written cursively (φ). The *Ae* sign should be a cross of 3+3 lines: it has been made into 4+4 simply on account of the physical difficulty of keeping three consecutive fingers out-stretched and doubling up the others.

Thus, all of the peculiar letters which form the fifth ogham group are merely equivalents, as nearly as can be conveniently represented by the fingers, of the residual letters of the Caere-Formello alphabet. A mathematician might possibly be able to calculate the chance against the exact coincidence of these two alphabets being altogether fortuitous: probably it would be a figure as far on the way to infinity as any non-mathematician could desire.

This comparison leads us to the further inference that in the so-called ogham diphthongs, the consonantal value, for which we have no manuscript authority but which we can infer from the ancient inscriptions, was primary; the vocalic value, which monopolizes the mediaeval manuscript alphabets, was secondary. The Greek values of these letters would be of little use to Celtic writers. The sound of ☰, on the few occasions when it had to be used, could be represented by ΚΣ just as conveniently as by the clumsy sign in the Formello alphabet. The sound of *p* (Π) is eschewed in Goidelic: that it appears in Brythonic, as a development of the Indo-European *q*, is beside the point, for the ogham script is not associated with the Brythonic branch of the Celtic tongues. The three characters ΘΦΧ, when the druids took over the alphabet, were still true aspirates (t', i.e. *t+h* as in *pothook*, and so for the rest), not the fricatives which they became in later times (as *th* in *moth* etc). As such, they were of no use either to Celts or to Latins, and if used at all by the Celts they must have dropped the aspirate and become mere doublets of T, P, K. In the inscriptions X is indistinguishable in its use from C (=K);[14] the other two 'aspirates' are never used at all as consonantal signs, except possibly in some of the Scottish Pictish inscriptions.

When the 'druids' first borrowed this Greek alphabet, they did not necessarily disturb the original order of its letters. But a body of teachers, whose duty it is to secure the preservation of an oral literature, must pay close attention to phonetics. The Indian grammarians did so, and the Devanagari script is the monument of their industry in this department of study. The Jewish Massoretes did so, and the huge elaboration of vowel, accent, and tone-marks in the Hebrew Bible testifies to their zeal for exactitude in reproducing traditional pronunciation. The less elaborate, but still punctilious notation superimposed upon the fundamentally consonantal script of Arabic, especially in the rendering of sacred texts, is analogous both in intention and in achievement.

To return once more to our 'bought' analogy. We pronounce it *bawt* in current speech. But if we attached a religious importance to maintaining the pronunciation of words in the English Bible exactly as it was in the days of Wycliffe or of some other early translator, we should be obliged, in such sacred connections, to say *boxt*; and we should be compelled to invent a special symbol for the guttural sound, which English has discarded, and to train our theological students in pronouncing it. To preserve a traditional literature against the inroads of linguistic evolution calls for a study of phonetics no less than of accidence and syntax: and this involves a phonetic classification of the symbols by which the sounds are expressed.

We need not suppose that the analysis of the sounds of this traditional druidic language, and the adaptation to them of the Greek sound-symbols, was all the work of one man, or even of one century. Whatever may have been the steps of approximation, the final form of the letter-order seems to have been as follows:

Consonants	continuatives	ΛNF
	sibilants	ΣΖΡ
	gutturals and velar	ΓΜ(=ng)ΚϘ
	dentals	ΔΤ
	labials	Βμ
	spirant	Η
Vowels		ΑΕΙΟΥ
Superfluous letters		⊞ΘΦΧΠ

Obviously this is not a perfectly scientific arrangement, but it is creditable: and we now proceed to shew that such an arrangement must be at the basis of the alphabetic order of the ogham cypher. The inventor had to find symbols for fifteen consonants, five vowels, and the five superfluous letters: the five fingers, coupled with these groups of fives, would suggest a symmetrical arrangement – five rows with five letters in each. He had already the two bottom rows before him, in the table printed above: to head the other three rows he took the three letters which precede them, thus:

B	*	*	*	*
μ	*	*	*	*
H	*	*	*	*
A	E	I	O	Y
⊞	Θ	Φ	X	Π

and filled in the gaps with the remaining consonants in order, just as they come in the foregoing scheme:

B	Λ	N	F	Σ
μ	Z	P	Γ	M
H	K	Ϙ	Δ	T
A	E	I	O	Y
⊞	Θ	Φ	X	Π

This was the first approximation to the alphabet, and it lasted long enough to establish for it the native name B-L-N (in Irish, *beith-luis-nion*), which it maintained in spite of subsequent changes.

An improver altered the vowel-order from the traditional alphabetic to a stricter phonetic arrangement. With it he shifted all the consonant groups. It looks as though the alphabet had been conceived of vertically rather than horizontally – associating together letters with the same number of scores, rather than those with scores in the same position. The effect of this change (which did not affect the otiose superfluous letters) was as follows:

B	F	Σ	Λ	N
μ	Γ	M	Z	P
H	Δ	T	K	Ϙ
A	O	Y	E	I
⊞	Θ	Φ	X	Π

A further shift brought the consonant group with long scores to a position next to the vowel group with long scores – reversing the μ and the H groups in the above table. This accentuated the inconvenience of trying to distinguish between these two long-score groups when represented by finger-signs: an inconvenience at least sometimes evaded by giving to the superfluous consonants the sense of the vowel just above. And it will be noticed that the figures have a chance resemblance to one another in their Greek forms. ⊞ is something like A; Θ like O; Φ like Y; X (especially when it is written in the form ψ, as it actually is at Cervetri) is like E, and Π like I. Thus it comes about that these letters are provided with vowel or diphthong values in the manuscript tradition, and their true, but unnecessary, consonant values are forgotten.

Finally, and after Caesar's time, the druids abandoned the Greek for the dominant Roman letters. All bilingual-ogham inscriptions are accompanied by Roman, never by Greek letters, and no trace suggesting the continuance of Greek letters appears to have survived. This induced a slight shift in the B group. F (*digamma*) was now represented by V, as was also the vowel V; it was convenient to have the now identical letters represented by signs which used the same number of digits. This had the further advantage of bringing the related sounds S and Z into the same relative position, each in its own group. About the same time, probably, the extra characters, which had become alternate vowel-signs, were rearranged into a symmetrical order. The cross characters, like the linear characters, are placed in the order of the number of fingers required to make them, two, four, and eight: and then the two loop characters are alternated with them. This is the proper order, as the tract on ogham in *The Book of Ballymote* makes clear: following an old mistake, which goes back at least as far as the time of General Vallancey, printed books often transpose Ia and Ui. In this laborious way the alphabet seems to have finally attained to the order of letters set out at the beginning of the present discussion.

All the foregoing argument may seem fantastic, over-elaborate, and far-fetched to the reader. But it explains, better than any other theory that I can hit upon, certain facts that call for explanation; and it explains them completely. These facts are:

1. The letters of the ogham alphabet are exactly the same selection as the letters of the Formello-Cervetri alphabet, allowing for the early disappearance of + and giving a new value to the otherwise useless M. No other alphabet can have been used as a basis without forcing us to assume an arbitrary selection of letters, which does not actually correspond to the needs of the ogham writers.

2. Five letters of the Formello-Cervetri alphabet proved by experience to be superfluous; but being in the alphabet they were allowed to remain there. The ogham symbols representing them are as close as may be to a manual reproduction of the original forms of those letters.

3. The ogham alphabet certainly betrays the work of an inventor with some skill in phonetics. Its Irish name indicates that for some time after its first invention its first three letters were B-L-N. The separation of the vowels and consonants, the arrangement of the vowels in a phonetic order, and the vertical or horizontal juxtapositions of letters having cognate sound values *cannot* be accidental.

4. The ogham alphabet is associated in its inscriptions with an archaic form of the Gaelic language artificially preserved, and appears to be based on a form of the Greek alphabet. According to Caesar's testimony, and to legitimate deductions that can be drawn from it, the druids had an archaic language, artificially preserved; and they made use of Greek characters.

These are facts, not theories; and the explanation given above, which may now be summarized, fits them exactly.

1. An early form of the Greek alphabet, current in some parts of Italy, was borrowed by the druids in Southern Gaul for the purpose of writing (though not of writing their sacred texts), probably some time in the fifth century BC.

2. The letters of this alphabet were rearranged on a phonetic basis, to assist students in learning to pronounce the sacred texts with the necessary exactitude.

3. The alphabet called ogham was invented on the basis of this phonetic rearrangement, for the *sole* purpose of secret communication by means of manual signs. It was never intended to be written: its use as a script probably began in short private messages, nicked on slips of wood and sent from a druid to some colleague at a distance – the nicks representing the outstretched fingers. It is to be noticed that this involved the restoration of the original vowel-

signs. The new vowels, based on the superfluous consonants, were convenient to frame with the fingers, but troublesome to nick upon wood. They are rare in the inscriptions.

We must not confuse the druidic adaptation of the old Formello-Cervetri Greek alphabet with the later adaptation, to which reference has been made already, of the ordinary Greek alphabet by dwellers in the region of Massilia. This was a perfectly independent process, and the two alphabets were quite distinct, though both of them could be described as Greek. The Formello-Cervetri alphabets are written, as we have seen, in a reversed form, and run from right to left. It is conceivable that this is why Caesar felt safe in writing his secret correspondence in Greek characters; these, being penned in the ordinary way, from left to right, would look like *Spiegelschrift* to a native scholar who happened to get hold of them; and Latin, written in Greek letters which seemed to be turned the wrong way, might have been quite a sufficient puzzle. We need not infer from the use of Greek letters that the druids were skilled in the Greek language. The druid Diviciacus seems to have known no language but his native Gaulish, and Caesar had to communicate with him through an interpreter. On the other hand, the scholarly Celt who, appropriately enough, instructed Lucian[15] in the nature and attributes of the god Ogmios, was not only acquainted with Greek but had some familiarity with Greek literature.

Our conclusion is that the druidic language was archaic Goidelic. It is in archaic Goidelic that the ogham writers of Ireland endeavour to express themselves: and there is no reason to endow the druids with more sacred or secret languages than one.

'Ogham,' says the treatise on the subject which we find in *The Book of Ballymote*, 'was put together by Ogma Sun-face, son of Bres, son of Elada.' This conducts us into august company. Whatever the author of the treatise may have supposed, there is no shadow of a doubt that Ogma was originally a god. He was one of the Tuatha De Danann, the numerous pagan gods of the Goidelic people, whose complicated *theogonia*, euhemerized into a bald string of genealogies, is made into an 'invasion' of Ireland in the history of the country concocted and taught in the native schools. It scarcely admits of doubt that Ogma is to be equated with Ogmios, the god of eloquence, whose gospel the learned Celt preached into the unresponsive ears of Lucian; and what Lucian tells us – and it does not read like one of that ingenious scoffer's fabrications – is enough to shew that he was a god of the first rank of importance.

But what did Ogmios or Ogma invent? Surely it did not require the intervention of a god to invent the puerile ogham *alphabet*! But a *language* – that might well have been the gift of a god to his particular votaries. The druids or their students may have speculated on how this difficult speech, which they acquired with so much toil, and which was so exclusively their special possession, came into existence. It would have required more philology than we can credit to them, to have realized that it was merely an obsolete form of the common talk of the *profanum vulgus*. That a god had endowed them therewith would be the most easily evolved of aetiological myths; and it would have the advantage of increasing the reverence in which they held it, and the care with which they preserved it. We suggest that 'ogham' (however we may choose to spell it) originally meant *the language*. 'A stone written in ogham' meant an inscription in *the language*. But as the language was expressed, on such stones, in a script-adaptation of the finger-signs, the expression first became ambiguous (just as the Devanagari character may be loosely called 'the Sanskrit alphabet') and finally veered toward the significance of 'a stone written in the finger-script'. So the word ogham became a name, not for the Proto-Goidelic cultivated by the druids, but for the secret alphabet which first began to be written down, just when it, and the language, and, indeed, the druids themselves, were passing off the stage.

The literature of the ogham language, as a whole, is lost for ever. But we possess a poetical composition which may very well be one of its hymns: and we have some hints as to its contents and its limitations.

The poetical composition is a wild spell, said, in the tale of the landing of the 'Children of Mil', who, for the synthetic historians of early Christian Ireland, represent the latest incomers, to have been chanted by their chief bard, Amorgen, as he set his foot on the soil of Ireland. That some such spell should have been uttered on such an occasion is only to be expected. To set foot in a strange country was indeed a terrifying experience. Its unknown and savage inhabitants, human and animal, would be formidable enough; but worst of all were its unknown gods. The foreigners with whom the king of Assyria colonized the ravaged city of Samaria were devoured by lions because, they believed, 'they knew not the manner of the god of the land'[16] and they were assuredly not the only strangers who attributed misfortunes which befell them to a like cause. Spells and enchantments to avert the terrors that awaited them were an absolute necessity, if an invasion was to have propitious consequences. We need not have any doubt that Amorgen actually sang such spells, in the old story which the historians worked up into a literary form. But we may very reasonably question whether the chant which they have put into his mouth was the spell which he actually sang. It is quite inappropriate to the situation: and a garbled version of it appears in Welsh literature, in a totally different context. The story in which it there occurs is a late hotch-potch of tattered shreds and patches, professing to narrate the mystical early history of the bard Taliesin. In the course of the story the child bard is made to utter a poem, narrating his transformations in previous existences: and this poem is obviously a translation into Welsh of as much of the song of Amorgen as the compiler could remember.

What, then, is this song of Amorgen? It is a hymn, setting forth a pantheistic conception of a Universe where Godhead is everywhere and omnipotent. This interpretation has been challenged: but it still seems to me to cover the sense of the poem better than any other. What we have is, of course, only a translation, possibly an expurgated translation, into the colloquial Irish of the Christian historians, out of the druidic 'ogham' speech: doubtless it has lost something in the process, but it is still not without a measure of sublimity. Of this, we feel, the Christian writers were conscious; amid all the wreckage of druidic tradition, they were unwilling to let it go; and to avoid all risk of the charge of disseminating paganism, they forced it into the incongruous association where we now find it. God speaketh: and this is what He saith:

I am wind in the sea,
I am wave of the billows,
I am sound of the sea:
I am an ox of seven fights,
I am a vulture on a cliff,
I am a tear of the sun [= a dewdrop],
I am fair among flowers,
I am a boar,
I am a salmon in a pool,
I am a lake in a plain,
I am a word of knowledge,
I am the point of the spear that fighteth,
I am the god who formeth fire for a head [= giver of inspiration],

Who maketh clear the ruggedness of a mountain?
Who telleth beforehand the ages of the moon?
Who telleth where the sun shall set?
Who bringeth the cattle from the house of Tethra?
   [Tethra = the ocean; the reference is to the stars rising from the sea]
On whom do the cattle of Tethra smile?
What man, what god formeth weapons,
Singeth spells ... . [Is it not I ?]

The last line or two are very obscure and corrupt, and need not here detain us. As we read a poem like this, we cannot but feel that it is a very suitable preface to the hymnary of a philosophical school: and, like the opening chapter of the Koran, or like the Apostles' Creed in Christendom, such a composition might well have been used, not merely in the studies of druidic pupils, but in the liturgies of public religious functions – such functions as that from which recalcitrants were excommunicated. Knowledge of its contents would thus make its way outside the druidic schools: was it of this hymn, or of what he had been told of the contents of this hymn, that Caesar was thinking, when he wrote that the druids taught of the stars and their motions, the world, the size of lands, natural philosophy, and the nature of the gods?

But the canon was not confined to philosophical hymns. There was an historical canon as well. A list is preserved of the stories which historians were expected to know, and to be able to recite when called upon, at feasts, assemblies, and what not. Some of these stories are still extant, in more or less late prose versions; many are totally lost; of a number of others, the general lines can be recovered from chance allusions. They were 350 in number; 250 'principal stories' and 100 'subordinate stories'; and they were classed under the headings of destructions, cattle-raids, courtships, battles, tragical deaths, voyages etc.

The list of stories, which might not be diminished – for a complete knowledge of the whole was a necessary qualification for the historian – and to which, apparently, no addition was permissible, was not, like the catalogue of a seaside circulating library, an index to the amusing fiction available. Otherwise there would be no point in its rigidity. Though, as we have it, the list, and the use made of the list, have undergone modifications due to the incidence of Christianity, it is the end of a tradition, going back into far older times. It is a summary of the historical section of the druidic canon.

The hostility of the Roman emperors brought druidism to an end on the Continent. Whether or not their teaching was more perfectly preserved in Britannia (and Hibernia?), we may be certain that the cutting-off of the supply of Continental students was a heavy blow to the schools: and the growth of Christianity effected in no long time a complete breach in the tradition. For a time there appears to have been a sort of working compromise between the disciples of Christ and those of Ogmios. We have even memorials in the ogham character of a bishop, a presbyter, and a deacon, as well as of other persons whose Latinized names – Sagittarius, Marianus, Amatus – suggest that they were Christian ecclesiastics. But, quite apart from the impossibility of a permanent pact between Christianity and paganism, the druidic system was doomed by the democratic appeal which the new religion made.

In Ireland, for example, Christianity gave an opportunity to the servile classes: aborigines whose masters, first Celtic-speakers and then Teutons, had reduced them to vassalage. These, the hewers of wood and drawers of water, had no share in druidic learning, such as it was. But they had a very considerable share in the shaping of the then colloquial dialect of the Irish language, and in making complete the already wide breach between the spoken tongue and the traditional 'ogham' literary language. For when conquerors force upon a people a language which these do not speak by nature, the conquered will inevitably mould it to the phonetics and idiom of their own tradition. Servants, to whom the new language is foreign, will impart their contaminations to children under their charge; and thus the blunders of the unlearned will filter into the upper strata of society. This is what has happened to English as spoken in Ireland: it has assumed an Irish intonation, phonesis,[17] and syntax, even on the lips of persons of education. It is what is happening now, by a curious turn of the wheel, to the artificially revived 'Irish' of the present generation. The spelling has been 'simplified' to make it easy for people who originally learnt to spell on an English basis; and speeches and writings are riddled with adaptations of English words and idioms. Very probably certain of the peculiarities which the Irish language displays are due to its coexistence for some time with another, older speech, spoken by the *majority* of the population; ultimately, however, ousted, because Irish was the language of the classes that held the monopoly of domination.

To these unlettered aboriginal folk the monasteries opened their doors – or some of them at least: there were exceptions. These people had to be taught, and means of writing the colloquial language had to be improvised, rather than naturally developed. The traditional spelling of the older language was utterly unsuitable to the new, so far had the two travelled apart. No doubt the ecclesiastical authorities did not, at first, contemplate the literary use of any language but Latin; but gradually the familiar vernacular made its way. Good stories were either translated out of Latin, or were modernized out of the old Goidelic tradition; thus step by step, a new Christian Irish literature came into being, and the older language, the heritage of the druids, fell into oblivion. It is to the time of overlap, in which the druidic learning was gradually coming to an end, that most or all of the extant ogham inscriptions are to be assigned. 'We're giving up Romani very fast,' said a strolling knife-grinder, of whom we shall hear later: 'its a-gettin' to be too blown.' In his own idiom he was echoing a complaint that we might have heard from an ancient druid. 'There is no use talking our secret language, making our secret signs, if our pupils change their religion, and so emancipate themselves from the vows of secrecy which safeguarded our monopoly' would have been the substance of the druidic complaint. 'Our symbol-alphabet is useless now, as a secret: let us keep it as a magic benediction for those who die in our faith and obedience.'

But the language did not wholly die. There is a strange story to the effect that Colum Cille, who was a man of literary enterprise, came on a visit to the dwelling of a scholar named Longarad. Longarad hid his books, so that Colum Cille could not see them; whereupon the indignant saint uttered an imprecation against them, putting upon them the curse that never again should they be of any use to anyone.[18] And the biographer adds that the curse was fulfilled: 'for the books are still extant, but no man reads them'. Why was Longarad so churlish? What was wrong with the books? When a hagiographer dips his hand into the lucky-bag of folklore, to find miracles with which to trick out the lives of his heroes, that is one thing, and we take his statements in the spirit in which they are offered. But when he assures us in so many words, 'These books are even now in existence, but they cannot be read', that is quite another matter. We are bound to accept what he tells us, unless we can prove that some contemporary weighed it in the balance and found it wanting. The story becomes crystal-clear if we suppose these books to have been relics of the ancient learning and of the ancient language. Longarad had a pardonable pride in possessing them – a pride, however, tempered with uneasiness. Was it quite right to own these pagan things? Would Colum Cille approve of them? Might he not perhaps order them to be destroyed? No bookman would take the risk! So he kept his books, and they endured for a season after their owner had joined the druids in the world of shadows. And those who pored unintelligently over their mysteries consoled themselves for their want of comprehension by fashioning this myth of a saintly curse.

Even then, if they had got hold of the right man, they might have learned what was in the books. The tradition of the language still lived on; the last we hear of it is so late as the year 1328. The so-called *Annals of Clonmacnois* tells us that in that year there died a certain 'Morish O'Gibellan, master of art, one exceedingly well learned in the ould & new law, siuill and canon, a cunning and skilfull philosopher, an excellent poet in Irish, & an excellent eloquent & exact speaker of the speech which in Irish is called ogham, in sume, one that was well seen in many other good sciences: he was a Cannon and singer in Twayme, Olfin, Aghaconary, Killalye, Ednagh Downe [Tuam, Elphin, Achonry, Killala, Annaghdown] and Clonfert: he was officiall and common Judg of the whole Dioceses, & ended his dayes this yeare.'

In estimating the eulogy of this Admirable Crichton, we must make some allowances. The original text of the *Annals of Clonmacnois* is lost, and the book is known to us only by a manuscript translation, in a queer Pepys-like style, made in 1627. The manuscript of the Irish text was in many places injured and barely decipherable, and we know not the translator's qualifications for the task which he undertook. His work does not read like what a translation of any other volume of Irish annals would be, and we suspect that it is a free paraphrase rather than a literal rendering. The Irish text was compiled some time after 1408, the date of the last entry, and therefore something over eighty years after O'Gibellan's death. We have no information as to the authority here followed by the compiler, or as to the qualification of that authority to adjudicate upon O'Gibellan's death, but say nothing about this special accomplishment. Certainly a man of such diverse interests might have thought it worth his while to acquire some knowledge of the ancient speech; and he might have had access to books, like Longarad's, to help him in studying it. But this story of a fluent speaker of 'ogham' in the fourteenth century reminds us only too vividly of the meeting between Lamartine, on his Syrian travels, and a worthy who claimed to be the only person in the world able to converse in ancient Phoenician. When Lamartine very naturally asked where, in the circumstances, he could find a partner for his colloquies, he drew himself up impressively, and replied: '*Monsieur, j'en fais des monologues!*'

It is convenient to speak here in terms of Ireland, where the 'Celtic' tradition has been most perfectly preserved; but it should not be forgotten that 'Celticism' is there an altogether exotic growth. The "Irish" language is, in Ireland, the monument of the most savage and bloodthirsty invasion which that country ever suffered – the raid of the brachycephalic horde who swooped on her in the middle Bronze Age, coming doubtless out of the land now called England, and impelled by a lust for the gold-fields. They had few virtues: later, but still contemporary, authority (Strabo) describes them, with some reserve, as cannibals. Like other cannibals, in Central Africa and in the Southern Seas, they were excellent workers in metal. In the second La Tène period they were subdued by an iron-using immigration, also questing gold: the ethnological evidence that this new people, who established a dominant aristocracy, was of Teutonic blood, is absolutely unshakable. Their use of native women, however, had the result, normal in such cases, of preventing their Teutonic tongue from ousting the Celtic, which had already 'dug itself in'.

Claudius (AD41–54) issued decrees expelling druids from the Roman Empire. Ireland, now reduced to some sort of order by its Teutonic masters, could have afforded them an asylum. This combination of Celticized Teutonic patrons, and cultured refugees who could not but have absorbed some veneer of Roman civilization, is just what is wanted to account for the literary and juristic efflorescence which subsequent centuries witnessed in Ireland. Quite possibly all Irish tales about druids, dating from before the decrees of Claudius, are backward projections of conditions actually produced in the country after, and as a consequence of, those decrees.

Notes

1 *Vit. Phil.* introd. § 5.
2 I Kings vi. 7.
3 A.A. Macdonell, *A History of Sanskrit Literature* (London, 1900), p. 67.
4 Whitley Stokes, *Lives of Saints from the Book of Lismore*, ed. Stokes, line 1875.
5 *Ibid.*, line 4013.
6 *Ancient Laws of Ireland* (Rolls Series), vol. i, p. 18 f.
7 Some tenth-century charlatan who knew this story has endeavoured to reconstruct the dispute, in a composition called *Immacallam in da Thuarad* ('The Colloquy of the Two Sages'). The text will be found, accompanied with the tentative translation which alone is possible, but which is quite sufficient to set forth the nature of this production, in *Revue celtique*, vol. xxvi, pp. 4 ff. The disputants are shewn to us, seeking to confound each other with obscure allusive kennings and other literary vices; but (except for some otherwise unknown words) there is not much in the composition bearing on the question of a secret language. Most of it is mere childish affectation; and the influence of Christianity, which it quite evidently displays, sufficiently proves its spuriousness.
8 *Ancient Laws of Ireland*, vol. i, p. 6.
9 See the story in Meyer and Nutt, *The Voyage of Bran*, vol. i, pp. 45–52.
10 Here again examples might be multiplied: the story told in O'Curry, *Manners and Customs of the Ancient Irish*, vol. ii, p. 217, is as good as any.
11 For further details on the subject of the foregoing paragraphs, consult E. MacNeill, 'Notes on the Distribution, History, Grammar, and Import of the Irish Ogham Inscriptions', *Proceedings*, Royal Irish Academy, vol. xxvii, section C, p. 329. *Idem.* 'Archaisms in the Ogham Inscriptions', *ibid.* vol. xxxix, section C, p. 33.
12 On the use of Greek by the Massiliotes, see Strabo IV, i, 5.
13 As it is convenient to represent a single sound or a single letter by a single equivalent character, we shall in future represent the ogham Ng by the usual phonetic convention נ.
14 On Gaulish coins the name PICTILOS is sometimes written PIXTILOS and also, apparently by a misinterpretation of the C, PISTILLUS. See Blanchet, *Traité des monnaies Gauloises*, vol. I, p. 135.
15 Lucian, *Heracles*, I ff.
16 II Kings xvii. 26.
17 Perhaps I should apologize for this word, which dropped unconsciously from my pen. I find it branded as 'not naturalized' in the *Oxford Dictionary*. But it is not without its usefulness, and I venture to let it remain.
18 *Martyrology of Oengus*, ed. by Whitley Stokes (Henry Bradshaw Society), p. 198.

CHAPTER THIRTEEN

The Origins of the Ogham Alphabet

F.C. Diak

I T IS MATTER OF COMMON AGREEMENT that the ogham alphabet, used in some of the Celtic inscriptions of Ireland, Wales and England, and Scotland, is nothing but a re-writing of letters of the Latin alphabet in a different series of signs. That is to say, the inventor of it already knew the Latin alphabet and for some reason desired to represent the letters of it by an altogether different pictorial system. Two questions naturally suggest themselves and seem to require an answer. (1) For what reason was the inventor not content with the Latin alphabet as he learnt it? Whence came the impulse to change it? (2) Why did he devise the particular signs that he did, thereby producing a cumbrous, impracticable script, which instead of being an improvement was a retrogression in every way on the original? Surely some better system could have been invented if there was no special reason in favour of this one.

It is possible, I think, to point to facts that supply an answer to both these questions. From certain extant remains we seem justified in supposing that the Celts of Britain and Ireland already practised a form of writing in prehistoric times; not alphabetic writing indeed, but some arrangement of signs by which words were visibly represented. Pictorially it bears a close resemblance to the alphabetic ogham of the Celtic inscriptions; and the suggestion is that, once the Latin alphabet became known among them, the superiority of the alphabetic system of writing was recognized, and that it was the idea of turning their native script into an improved alphabetic form that led to the creation of the ogham alphabet[1]. Some reluctance to abandon their native system, with all its age-long, native associations, in favour of a foreign novelty was natural, and it was probably that motive that was at work. The ogham alphabet may thus be regarded as in some measure a sentimental *tour de force*. The attempt, however, though theoretically successful, was practically a failure owing to the enormous number of scores required and to other imperfections, and the new alphabet ultimately failed to maintain itself in ordinary currency. To distinguish alphabetic ogham from the old script out of which, according to this theory, it sprang, the latter may be called *proto-ogham*.

My acquaintance with this proto-ogham on stones began some years ago when I happened to find a rather striking stone in the parish of Rayne, Aberdeenshire, at Irelandbrae ... , the inscriptions on which seemed to indicate, without much difficulty, the model from which alphabetic ogham might be derived.[2] Since then a great quantity of the same material has gradually come under notice in various parts of Scotland. At Milngavie, near Glasgow, an uncultivated rough piece of ground contains a large number, and the area has as yet been only cursorily examined. Examples occur at Yarrow, Selkirkshire, and, by report, in the Island of Gigha, Argyle. In the parishes of Banchory-Devenick and Maryculter, Kincardineshire, there are many, and one has been casually noted in the parish of Strachan. The editor of *Scottish Gaelic Studies* has found specimens in Nairn, Inverness and Ross: and Mrs Macdonald, who has kindly made a rather particular examination of the neighbourhood of their home, has been able to contribute a large number to the list (parishes of Peterculter, Drumoak and Echt). A stone at Drumfours, Cushnie, Aberdeenshire, was noted by the late James Ritchie[3] for its cupmarks and for what he supposed might be 'the remains of an ogham inscription'. At the same site there are other smaller stones, not noted by him, containing similar inscriptions.

Already therefore a very large number of stones bearing these oghamic-like inscribings has come to light. They are of all sizes and shapes, mostly natural boulders, from the massive block of several hundredweights down to stones small enough to be easily lifted. How many specimens are at present known I am not in a position to say. For one thing, a certain number are so badly weathered that the markings may be counted doubtful: with others again, which from their position have evidently been removed from tilled land, the possibility of scorings by the plough has to be taken into account. But even with full allowance made for this doubtful margin, it can be said that there are many more than a hundred inscribed stones awaiting classification and study.

That being so, it may be thought strange that they should not have been noticed by archaeologists before, as they have been in Ireland. Perhaps the chief reason is that, in Scotland, as far as is yet known, these inscriptions seem to occur very rarely on pillar stones (only one of these is recorded up to now), and it is these prominent monoliths that have attracted attention. And besides that, these scorings on rude boulders would be apt to be disregarded even when noticed, as conveying nothing to the observer. But however this may be, the existence of this archaeological material in great abundance is certain.

What is now wanted is of course to see the whole series made available for students in good photographs or drawings. At present, that undertaking has hardly been begun .... . In a general way it can be said that they consist of arrangements of rectilinear scores more or less parallel. Sometimes they are arranged along an edge in the stone, but by no means always. In others, again, the parallel lines are cut across by a straight line at right angels, and in some the scores are slightly waved rather than rectilinear. Instead of being parallel, two straight lines sometimes meet to form an acute angle. It is useless, however, to pursue these details without illustrations. One of the features which must be regarded as highly significant, and which is soon noticed as one becomes acquainted with the stones, is their similarity over the whole of Scotland; a stone at Milugavie, for example, immediately reminds one of another, perhaps in Inverness, and similarly within any narrower area. It is plain that it is not random scorings that we have to do with, but systematic work. As already mentioned, it occurs on all sizes of stones, but the character of the script remains the same. In a few examples there are also cup-marks present ..., a fact that points to high antiquity.

There is nothing to suggest that all this mass of inscribed stones is exclusively sepulchral. The Irelandbrae block, for example, is to all appearance an altar stone. It is of reddish granite, from 20 to 23in high, 41in in extreme width, and 24in in the other direction. The scorings on the main face are about 10in long on the average, and deeply cut, but there are others on the left-hand face, which a proper photograph would show ... . They are in a different technique, being much shallower and narrower, but equally clear to the eye. This association on the same stone of the two kinds is to be seen in other examples, and evidently occurs in

Ireland, as will be pointed out immediately. The impression that is forced on the mind after one has become familiar with the inscriptions from many examples, is that it is impossible to regard them as mere symbols, but that they must be representations of words. On what principle the representation is effected is the problem to be studied once the material is all set out together. Are the graphic signs symbols of whole words? Probably not, but rather of syllables. They are not, I think, symbols of the elementary sounds of which syllables are composed: that is to say, the writing is not alphabetic. If it were, there would be, I think, regularity of recurrence of particular signs, which seems to be absent. As to whether the key to the system will ever be discovered it is too soon to express any opinion; perhaps not, unless some example should turn up containing a rendering in the Latin alphabet or in alphabetic ogham as well.

This proto-ogham is apparently well-known in Ireland, where archaeologists, putting the cart before the horse or affiliating the father on the child, call it 'imitation' or 'sham' ogham. In an account of the tall Gormlee monolith[4] it is stated that 'there are imitation ogham markings on the northeast corner, and very faint similar marks on the northwest corner.' Here there seems to be the same double technique of deep and shallow that I have just mentioned in connection with the Irelandbrae stone. In a recent book[5] reference is made to the class of monuments in Ireland bearing what the author calls 'pseudo-oghams', and they are stated to be numerous. The script in the one illustration which he gives, a pillar stone at Hawkinstown, Co. Meath, can be readily paralleled, in general appearance and arrangement, in the Scottish material. The writer dismisses these oghamic-looking inscriptions in a word: 'undoubtedly,' he says, they are 'spurious imitations of ogham'. This theory of sham oghams does not appear to be quite so axiomatic as the writer supposes. For what reason should such be written at all. The answer offered is that when the survivors of a deceased person, wishing to have an ogham inscription over his friend, were too poor or too greedy to pay the 'literary specialist' to write one, they cut something on the stone which looked like one, but was only casual scratches.[6] The supposed sentiments of these survivors are rather curious. These people began by taking the trouble to erect an imposing monument over the friend whom they wished to honour, and whose name they ought to have recorded, and ended by equipping him with some meaningless gibberish. But the reasonable view is that everything is genuine enough about these monuments if only we understood the writing, and that the writing belongs to a widely diffused system, as the Scottish material shows.

It occurs also in Wales. In *Archaeologia Cambrensis.* vol. XI., 1880, p. 296, there is a short article on 'The supposed ogham stone at St Florence,' with an illustration, which shows the already familiar sort of scorings. There is this particular point of interest here that the inscription occurs 'on the face of the base of a cross'. This would seem to indicate, what we might have theoretically conjectured, that the older script did not immediately die out when alphabetic ogham came into existence, but survived for a time.

As is well known, the orthography of ogham presents the unexplained peculiarity that consonants are often written double which are not historically double. It seems probable that the origin of this abnormality lies within the proto-ogham system, and also that the rearrangement in ogham of the order of the letters of the Latin alphabet may derive in some way from the same source.

By way of postscript I add a remark on some recent discoveries in the so-called Pictish prehistoric village that is being excavated at Skara Brae, in the Orkneys. In *The Times* of 3 September 1928, Professor Childe has the following: 'Its upper edge (i.e., of a great stone slab) was carved with markings too regular and deep to be accidental. We had previously found a stone carved with a geometrical pattern in one of the "street." and a former excavation had brought to light a rune. But the new marks are neither merely ornamental, nor do they belong to the ordinary runic alphabets. They must be assigned provisionally to an unknown script.' One cannot help wondering if the 'rune', which Professor Childe admits throws the archaeological chronology of the village into difficulties, is really one, and is not rather simply a piece of this proto-ogham, and similarly whether the 'unknown script' does not belong to the same category.

Notes

1 This expresses no opinion as to where it was that this took place. It may have been among the Goidels of Britain or among those of Ireland. But wherever it was, the inventors know the Latin alphabet.

2 *Proceedings Soc. of. Ant. of Scotland*, XI., Fifth Series, p. 269.

3 *Proceedings Soc. of. Ant. of Scotland*, IV., Fifth Series, p. 90.

4 *Journal Roy. Soc. of Antiq. of Ireland*, 1916, p. 60.

5 R.A.S. Macalister, *Archaeology of Ireland*, (1928), p. 224.

6 The author implies that before an (alphabetic) ogham inscription could be written a literary specialist was required, the reason for this being that the Irish inscriptions in the ogham alphabet are not written in the contemporary language of the country, but in an older form known only to the literary specialist. Thus, for example, when he was writing on a stone *Dalagni magi Dali* '(the stone of) Dalagnos son of Dalos', the ordinary non-literary person of the time was saying *Dáláin maie Dáil*. When a proof of this theory is offered it will be curious to see what the Celtic historical grammarian has to say of it. It will be time enough to introduce the 'literary specialist' into the discussion of ogham when that proof is given and accepted. Till then the Irish inscriptions are to be regarded as genuine examples of the speech of their time; from which it follows that there was no difficulty whatever in writing an ogham inscription, since the alphabet is simple and easily learnt, and as easily cut on a stone. The great number of existing inscriptions proves diffused knowledge of the alphabet: why inscribe stones at all unless there is a considerable public that understands? Necessity for recourse to 'sham' ogham as an explanation is indicated by nothing in the situation of things, and to label this proto-ogham script by that name is uncritical, not to say fantastic.

PART THREE

POETRY AND PROPHECY: VISIONS OF THE DREAM

B Y THEIR NATURE, MOST PROPHETIC or visionary statements are made orally, emerging from an individual situation and at a specific time. With time however, certain prophetic statements, the significance of which extended further than the individual, evolved into a literature of sorts. In part this was due to political events, when an oppressed people – as the Celts were from the middle of the sixth century onwards – sought solace and hope in the prophetic statements of an earlier time.

Thus, with the passing of Arthur *c.*655, which seemed to signal an end to organized resistance of the Britons against their Saxon invaders, the need for a prophesied 'better future', became pronounced. In reality, other chieftains, like Owein Gwynedd, continued to carry out sporadic raids on the enemy, and enclaves of native resistance existed across the country. Added to this was the belief, which came into operation within months of his passing, that Arthur would one day return from the otherworld to lead his people to victory.

This situation created the need for a continuing bardic tradition, above all for the art of prophecy. Famous bards, such as Taliesin, Myrddin and, to a lesser extent, Myrddin's sister Gwendydd, all prophesied the return of Arthur, and in later times these prophecies were taken up, elaborated and added to, giving rise to a body of vaticinatory literature – much of it forged – which began to be applied to later political events.

As Margaret Griffiths pointed out in her important study of early Welsh prophetic literature, from which the opening chapter follows in this section:

> During this period between the sixth and twelfth centuries, when the Britons were losing their lands and being gradually pushed westward till eventually they were confined to Wales, vaticination played an extremely important part in spurring on the hopes of the people from time to time.

In fact, the Britons in Wales never ceased to fight the Saeson (English), and to hope for the appearance of a deliverer – whether in the shape of Arthur, Owein or Cadwaladyr, or of countless lesser figures. The prophetic literature of the period 600–1500 abounds in references to the strength of the Britons, to their expected triumphs and to battles they have fought or will fight. To such an extent was this recognized, and with what effect, is shown in a statute of Edward I against: 'westours, Bards, Rhymers and others, idlers and vagabonds … lest by their invectives and lies they lead the people to mischief and burden the common people with their impositions.' Henry IV was later even more specific in his condemnation of wandering minstrels, who by their '*divinations* and lies were the cause of insurrection and rebellion in Wales' (my italics).[1]

These factors played no small part in the way the ancient texts were handled and the treatment they received at the hands of 'English' scribes, and it is for this reason (among others) that we have to treat the material that has come down to us with particular sensitivity and an awareness of the circumstances in which much of it came into being.

In the selection that follows will be found a selection of prophetic works reflecting the many aspects of culture and belief among the Celts from the ninth to the eighteenth centuries. Following Margaret Griffiths's detailed exploration of the subject of early vaticination in Wales will be found a new version of one of the earliest and most famous prophetic poems relating to the future of the Britons. This is found in the fourteenth-century *Book of Taliesin* and is known as *Armes Prydein Fawr* ('The Great Prophecy of Britain'). It is generally supposed to have been written in the ninth century, and Sir Ifor Williams, the poem's editor, established that in its present form it was written about AD930 and that it deals with historical events relating to the reign of King Athelstan. References to the English are clear, and a kind of pan-Celtic alliance between the Scots of Dalriada, the Irish Gaeltacht and possibly the Danes settled around Dublin is described in terms specific enough to add to the evidence. Many of the same details appear in the later text known as the *Vita Merlini* ('Life of Merlin'), written by the cleric Geoffrey of Monmouth *c*.1150. A number of references indicate that Geoffrey knew the *Armes Prydein* and borrowed from it for Merlin's prophecies – as he may well have done from other prophetic works in the *Book of Taliesin*. A selection from both the *Vita* and the *Prophecies of Merlin*, compiled by Geoffrey, follow here, illustrating not only the continuity of themes, but the way in which the prophetic and visionary tests were manipulated by the writers who inherited them.

The *Vita* is indeed a fascinating document, recording as it does a very different version of the life of the famous magician of Arthurian fame. Here Merlin is a prince in his own right, driven mad by the death of his family in battle, rescued and restored by Taliesin and finally retiring to his 'observatory', a magical building with seventy-seven windows built for him by his sister Ganeida. The section included here concerns a visit made to Merlin by Taliesin, during which the two seers exchange words on everything from the nature of weather to the creation of the universe and define the extent of their knowledge, derived from earlier sources.

Merlin had become famous by the time Geoffrey collected his prophecies into a book, which later still became part of the longer *History of the Kings of Britain*. The book of Merlin's prophecies makes for fascinating reading. At least two of the prophecies, one apparently describing a Thames Barrier built to protect the city of London from rising tides and the 'poisoning' of the hot springs at Bath, have been seen to be true, many hundreds of years after the time in which Merlin is supposed to have lived.

It is nowadays generally accepted that Geoffrey borrowed a good deal of his material from various sources dating from various periods, which he then placed in the mouth of Merlin, and this indicates that the material in the *Armes* could also have been of an early date – one that Geoffrey saw, quite rightly, as belonging to his account of Arthurian Britain.

Searching for a shorter version of the *Armes*, Professor Williams came across another poem in the *Book of Taliesin*, which despite the lateness of the manuscript shows clear signs of being an earlier version of the *Armes*. Called 'The Lesser Prophecy of Britain', it is an excellent example of the kind of visionary statement to which we have been referring:

My awen foretells the coming of a multitude
Possessed of wealth and peace;
Of a generous sovereign, and eloquent
    princes –
But after this tranquillity, commotion in
    every place.
The seven sons of Beli will arise.
Caswallawn, Lludd, and Custennyn.
They will crack the heart of Prydein.
The country in uproar as far as Blathaon:
Exhausted warriors, tired mounts,
A country ravaged to its borders.
The Cymry will loose all their bounty,
And their servants seek new masters.

Lleminawg will come,
An ambitious man,
To subdue Mona,
To ruin Gwynedd.
From its borders to its heartland,
Its beginning to its end,
He will take its pledges.
Furious his face,
Submitting to no one,
Cymry or Saeson.
Another will come from concealment
Bringing universal slaughter:
How extensive his armies,
A triumph to the Britons!
(translated by John Matthews)

Following these examples come three very different kinds of visionary statement. The first, the poems of Suibhne Geilt, are drawn from a much longer work (published in a full version in *The Encyclopaedia of Celtic Wisdom* by Caitlín and John Matthews) are attributed to the sixth-century king of Dalriardan Ireland, who incurs the wrath of St Ronan and finds himself adopting the nature and abilities of a bird. This terrible curse causes him to dissociate himself from his normal environment and seek out wild and unfrequented places away from the dwellings of men. While he is in this state he encounters many strange beings, including the Hag of the Mill, who seems to be connected in some way to the initiation of seer-poets and shamans. Suibhne's dialogue with her is full of prophetic references, as are his many other wild and visionary statements. In the end he is rescued from his madness by another saint, Molling, who is kinder to him. The whole story includes themes that turn up later on in accounts of Merlin's life, including Geoffrey of Monmouth's version.

This is followed by the strange and wonderful 'Vision of MacConglinne', again taken from a much longer work, which can be read in its entirety in Kuno Meyer's edition from which this extract comes. It is unusual, even unique, in being the only extended work of its kind from this period (it dates from around the middle of the twelfth century) that is essentially a satire of the purest kind. Indeed, as one of its editors has said: 'we find nothing quite so preposterous again until we come to Rabelais' (Cross and Slover).

The story concerns 'a demon of gluttony', which lived in the throat of Cathal mac Finguine, a king of Munster from an earlier, semi-mythological time. This demon had been enchanted into him by the druid of Fergal mac Maelduin, whose sister Cathal wished to marry but who was in contention with him for the kingship of Ireland. It caused him to eat at least five times as much as any man, to the point where his store houses were becoming empty. The vision described by MacConglinne, the king's bard, draws entirely upon the imagery of food, and when he describes it he lures the demon from Cathal, whence it can be safely disposed of. In the process, we are treated to some of the wildest (and funniest) flights of fancy in the history of bardic literature.

This is followed in turn by a later text, deriving from sixteenth- or possibly seventeenth-century Scotland, concerning the Brahan Seer, Coinneach Odhar, who was believed to have been born on the Isle of Lewis, although he is such a shadowy figure that it is impossible to say with any certainty. He became famous for a number of prophecies concerning the depopulation of the Highlands, the end of crofting and the building of the Caledonian Canal. Most dramatically, however, he foretold the doom of the Seaforth Mackenzies, the family that brought about his horrifying death. Odhar's prophecies remained in oral tradition and were collected by Alexander Mackenzie in 1887. So many of the seer's words have come true that he may be accounted as one of the greatest and certainly most accurate prophets of any period or place.

Finally, as a coda to the entire collection, comes Lewis Spence's chapter on Prophecy and Divination, which reviews many of the themes and texts presented above and draws attention to the druidic connections possessed by many of them. This makes a fitting conclusion to this assembly of writings on the subject of seership, which is still, as stated in the Introduction, as alive and relevant today as it was in the past.

Note

1 Margaret Griffiths, in *Early Vaticination in Welsh with English Parallels* (Cardiff, 1932).

CHAPTER FOURTEEN

Vaticination in Wales Prior to the Twelfth Century

Margaret Griffiths

NFORTUNATELY, THE EARLIEST Welsh manuscripts containing any vaticinatory material are later than the twelfth century, so that we are confronted at the outset with a serious difficulty in attempting to study the early development of vatication in Wales. Many of the manuscripts, however, which date after the twelfth century, undoubtedly contain much older material, and are probably copies of earlier manuscripts, so that we might expect to find in them some references to the customs and practices of pagan Britons, for it is to these practices we must turn, to find the original of Welsh vatication. As a matter of fact, such references are very meagre and scanty, and if we had to depend on them alone, we should not be able to build up any adequate conception of the beliefs of our pagan ancestors.

We have therefore to rely upon outside authorities. We know that when the Romans came to Britain the island was inhabited by Brythonic and Goidelic Celts, together with a remnant of older inhabitants of the island, generally called Iberians. We know, too, that the Romans found in Britain a class of men called druids, whose practices must have impressed themselves deeply on the Roman mind before they would have given any account of them. The sacrifice of human victims, the belief in the transmigration of souls and the skilful use of the terrors of religion are all recorded by the classical writers.[1] It has been suggested that these practices and beliefs represent non-Aryan beliefs which were taken over by the Celts from the race which they found in Britain on their arrival.[2]

From the classical accounts of druidism we gather that the druid held an important position in the life of the tribe. He had certain duties to perform, one of which was the education of the young, and he was expected to give the secular chief the full benefit of his magical powers. Though we know comparatively little of the druid, the fact that he was a wizard or magician stands out quite clearly. Sir John Rhys writes: 'one may sum up the impressions of ancient authors as to the druids by describing them as magicians who were medicine men, priests and teachers of the young.'[3]

Another source from which we may form some conception of the British druid is that of Irish literature, which provides many tales describing ancient customs. This literature, as it has come down, all belongs to Christian times, and is therefore frequently coloured with Christian sentiments, but there are also many passages purely pagan in character. The druidic system in Ireland must have differed to some extent from that of Britain or Gaul, but as the three sprang originally from the same sources they must have had a great deal in common. The druids were all magicians and combined in themselves all the learned professions, 'they were not only druids but judges, historians, poets and even physicians'.[4] The greatness of their reputation as magicians may be judged from the fact that the general Irish word for sorcery or magic is 'druidecht', which meant 'druidism', and is still a word in use. Joyce in his 'Social History' has given an excellent account of the Irish druids drawn solely from the literature of Ireland. From this account we see that the druid was a prophet, and with the aid of his magic practised the art of divination. In this capacity he was frequently consulted by the chief of the tribe and was expected to forecast the result of military expeditions etc. 'The druids forecasted partly by observation of natural objects or occurrences and partly by certain artificial rites.'[5] Joyce gives a description of the various types of divination used by them.[6] They observed the movements of clouds, and the popularity of this method may be judged from the fact that in Irish the word *neladoir*, cloud diviner, is generally used for an astrologer or diviner. A simple kind of astrology, too, seems to have been practised by the Celtic druids. They scanned the stars and the moon for the determination of propitious days to begin any undertaking. The belief in lucky and unlucky days is common to almost all races, but amongst the Celts, it seems to have been allied to a kind of primitive astrology. Thus a druid, when consulted by St Columkille as to when his son should begin his lessons, scanned the heavens before giving his answer. Wedel[7] who claims that the astrology of western Europe is an importation from Greece and Rome, though he admits that these Celtic references are puzzling, does not think that astrology was practised by the Celts. It seems only fair, however, from such references to conclude that the Celts had developed an astrological science – primitive though it may be – of their own.

Amongst other methods practised by the Irish druids was divination by means of birds, especially from the cries of birds. As we have seen, this method was common amongst many nations and was especially popular in the Mediterranean area. In Ireland, the raven and the wren seem to have been the favourites and in an old life of St Moling, the name for a wren, *drean*, is fancifully derived from *drui en*, 'druid of birds'. It is interesting to notice that in Welsh the name for 'wren' is 'dryw', while 'drywon' is used for prophets or seers. The 'brân' or raven must have been used for divinatory purposes in Wales as we see from the folk song, 'Un frân ddu, daw anlwc eto'. Probably, the druids professed to be able to understand the language of birds, just as did the ancient seers of Greece. In the Welsh vaticinatory poems called the 'Afallenneu' and 'Hoianeu',[8] which probably contain very old material though their present form is late, Myrddin, before he delivers his vaticinations, frequently tells his companion, a little pig, to listen to the sound of the birds. It seems that he obtained his knowledge of the future by listening to the birds:

> Oian ap*ar*chellan pir puyllutte hun
> Andaude adar clywir eu hymevtun
> Teernet dros mor adav dyv llun.
> (*Black Book of Carmarthen*, p. 49, ll. 11–14)

In the 'Hoianeu' water birds and sea birds seem to be the favourites:

> Andaude leis adar duffyr dyar leissev.
> (*B.B.C.*, p. 56, ll. 9–10)

Andaude leis adar mor maur eu dias.
(B.B.C., p. 62, ll. 1–2)

Divination by means of a rod and by means of a wheel seem to have been practised amongst Irish druids; and sneezing and clapping of the hands also seem to have been treated in some way as omens. There is no evidence amongst the Irish of human sacrifice such as was supposed to have been practised by the Gauls. Animals, however, were undoubtedly sacrificed as part of the ceremony of divination, and probably movements of the animal's body, and the direction of the smoke and flames, played an important part.

Other rites practised by the people – not necessarily by druids – in pagan times are described by Joyce.[9] One of these involved amongst other rites the eating of an animal's flesh, after which the person fell asleep, and obtained foreknowledge of future events during his sleep. With this we may compare the practise of sleeping on the skin of an animal, as seen in the Welsh tale 'Breuddwyd Rhonabwy'. Similar rites were practised by the Greeks and Romans.

Gods were worshipped in pagan times and idols were probably erected to them. Some pillar stones, which were probably idols or oracle stones originally, still exist, and there is a vivid tradition that some of these stones responded to questions. As a Welsh parallel exists in the Llech-lavar mentioned by Giraldus, this tradition must go back to a period before the separation of these two Celtic branches.

Joyce also describes certain ordeals which are common to most peoples, but these are not so much methods of divining the future, as of discovering whether a person is innocent or guilty.

From the classical and Irish accounts, therefore, we are able to form a conception of the position, the beliefs and practices of the druids. Their influence depended on their power as magicians, and as diviners they held an important position, for in that capacity they were consulted by the chiefs of the tribes before any important undertaking.

With the coming of Christianity, the place of the druids was filled by the saints, who took over many of their practices. 'Celtic Christianity was the dilution of Christianity with paganism, a mixture in which paganism largely predominated.'[10] This is true of Christianity generally. In order to win the people over to them, the saints had to beat the druids at their own game, so that we frequently find accounts of contests between Christian saints and pagan druids. The saint denounced the pagan practices of divination, but he himself could not only prophesy, but by means of incantations and curses, could even control future events.[11]

In considering the lives of the saints which have come down to us, we must remember that none of them are contemporary. Most of them are compositions of the eleventh or twelfth centuries, and are altered and embellished to enhance the glory of the saint according to the ideals of those centuries. Beneath all the embellishments, however, we are able to discern the essentially pagan customs of the saint glossed over with a thin veneer of Christianity. Thus when St Beuno cursed a man, we are told that the man died, and most of the saints had only to express a wish to make it come to pass. The life of St David provides an example of a contest between saint and pagan – for that is what the quarrel between Dewi and Boya really represents. Boya's wife is supposed to have sacrificed to her gods and Boya, too, in some manner, had foreknowledge of future events, for as soon as he saw the smoke from Dewi's fire, he knew that the man who kindled the fire would possess all the land as far as the smoke spread.[12]

The foreknowledge of the saints, however, differed from that of the druids in that it was supposed to have been derived from God himself through the medium of visions, of angels etc. Most of them were warned by angels of the date of their forthcoming death, while St Aydan was informed through a vision that Dewi was to be poisoned by his disciples.[13]

231

Many of these details are undoubtedly late additions, but it is almost certain that the saints who, to hold their own against the druids, would have to be able to foretell future events, saw visions which they believed to have come directly from God. That they were consulted by kings as to the future is seen from an early life of St Columba, written by Adamnan, the ninth abbot of Iona, late in the seventh century. In this there is an anecdote 'de rege Roderico filio Tothail qui in Petra Cloithe regnavit', who sent to ask St Columba whether he would be killed by his enemies. The saint told him that he would die in his house on a feather bed, and this, according to Adamnan, was fulfilled.[14]

We see then, that in function the saints did not differ appreciably from the old pagan druids. Willis Bund sums up the position of the saint when he says:

> Probably his power and influence to a great extent rested on the success of his predictions or interpretations of the Divine will … The priest or rather the family of priests were the magicians on whom the king or chief relied for obtaining supernatural aid when required.[15]

From this examination of the druids and early Christian saints, we have obtained some idea of the position and development of vaticination in Britain in the earliest times. We may further supplement this from an examination of some of the folklore and superstitions current in Wales, which undoubtedly represent the beliefs and customs of our ancestors.

The oldest records of Celtic folklore are to be found in the old Welsh tales the 'Pedair Cainc y Mabinogi', and the oldest Arthurian legends. Though these in their present written form may not be earlier than the thirteenth century, it is universally agreed that the material contained in them comes down from a period of remote antiquity. They deal with men who appear to be semi-gods in their magical power. The kings seem to be those who excel in this power, and one gets the impression that the magic is handed down; for example, Mathonwy teaches Gwydion as his successor. Knowledge of the future is of course part of this magical power, and not only knowledge of the future but of all things. In the Old Arthurian legend 'Kulhwch ac Olwen', Arthur is the chief of a band of followers who are really nothing but magicians. Sgilti Ysgawndroet does not need to ask the way for he always knows it, while Gwrhyr Gwalstawt Ieithoedd understands all languages, even that of the birds. Branwen, in the second of the Pedair Cainc, teaches a starling to speak. From the Welsh tales, however, we learn practically nothing of divinatory practices, for these superhuman heroes have no need of a formal art. It is generally agreed that they represent the ancient pagan gods, and when once we realize this, it is no longer surprising to find that they are all-powerful.

More light is thrown upon the art of divination by the superstitions which still persist in Wales. Many of these are attached to Hollantide Eve and to New Year's Eve. Amongst the Celts great significance was attached to the Winter Calends, while amongst the Romans the Calends of January occupied a more important place, so that in Britain after the Roman occupation superstitions clustered around both the Winter and January Calends. Certain rites, for example, are still performed so that a maiden may find out who is her husband-to-be. She must eat a salt herring and retire backwards to bed, when she will see in a dream her future husband handing her a cup of water. This is reminiscent of the pagan Irish method of finding out who is to be king by eating of the flesh of a red pig before falling asleep. There are many variations of this superstition.[16] Other methods practised on New Year's Eve and at Hollantide are to find out who is to die during the year, by observing piles of salt on plates, or footmarks in ashes. Similar beliefs are found in Manx folklore, and probably the superstitions are developments of ancient pagan rites, the significance of which has been lost.

232

On these nights, too, it is believed that one may see people who are doomed to die during the year knocking at the church porch, or hear a voice inside the church announcing their names. Similar forecasts of death are announced by the appearance of phantom funerals, corpse candles and the sound of 'cwn annwn'.[17] The screech of an owl, the howling of a dog, are evil omens, and a blackbird or crow flying over the house is said to bring bad luck. A bird beating against a window or flying into the room is also supposed to foretell death.

Examples of similar superstitions might be multiplied almost indefinitely. A different method of foretelling the future was practised at sacred wells. This, as we have already seen, is common in many countries. In pagan times, springs and wells, together with other natural phenomena were undoubtedly worshipped by the Celts. They believed that a deity dwelt in the well – this belief has come down in the numerous legends of wells and lakes being inhabited by fairy beings. Wells might also be venerated because druids had died near them, but with the conversion to Christianity all this was changed, and they became associated with saints, and were frequently named after them. The water was supposed to have healing power, and for this reason pilgrimages to sacred wells were frequent. They were used also for divinatory purposes, and Rhys says that certain wells were considered to be oracular.[18] The devotee at a well in Llanbedrog had to kneel and avow his faith in the water first, and then he threw some objects, such as pieces of bread or pins, into the well, and foretold what was going to happen from the movements of the objects. In an old poem in the Black Book, 'Seithenhin sawde allan',[19] a maiden seems to be connected with the well, and is cursed because she has somehow let the waters overflow. Rhys quotes Irish parallels where the overflowing of the waters is due to neglect to replace a covering over the well, or to keep the stone door shut.[20] Possibly there may have been maidens or priestesses to look after the wells in a period long before the coming of Christianity.

As we have seen, the ancient Irish divined from the cries of birds, and there is evidence in Welsh superstitions that the flight of birds was used for the same purpose. There is, however, no evidence for the existence of a complicated science of such augury as existed amongst the Greeks and Romans.

Necromancy[21] too, probably flourished amongst the Britons, for Welsh superstitions provide many examples of the belief in ghosts bringing information to human beings. An interesting tract throwing light on such beliefs, as they existed in the seventeenth century, is 'Dau Gymro yn Taring Oddi-cartref' to be found in Stephen Hughes's edition of 'Cannwyll y Cymry'. In the course of a discussion between two Welshmen far from home, mention is made of 'a welsom ac a glywsom ynghylch consurwyr rheib-wyr dewiniaid a'r fath'.[22] Gronw holds that such people obtain their power from intercourse with the devil. Tudyr is surprised, for, as he says:

nis gwrthwynebir gyda ni dynnu plant rhwng deudan, neu trwy fwa, neu i troi ar eingion y gof, neu i gosod ymmhinneu hoppran y felin, na llawer o gastie eraill o'r fath; ac am ddewin, planedydd, brudiwr, daroganwr a'r fath heini (hynny) y maent hwy mewn mawr barch a chymmeriad gyda'r gwyr goreu boneddigion ac iangwyr trwy'r holl wlad ... ie mae rhai a dwfyr ac a deiliach, neu wrth daflu cnau yn tân nos galan-gaya a ddywed i chwi pwy a fydd marw y flwyddyn honno.[23]

These practices current in the seventeenth century were not sudden growths; they were the remains of pagan beliefs which persisted in spite of the fact that they were denounced by Christianity as practices of the devil.

Dream divination, which is common to all nations, must have been practised by our pagan ancestors, to judge from the present widespread belief that dreams are intimations of the future. Many other methods such as the divination from sneezing, itching etc, and from such portents as earthquakes and storms, still persist, and these too are common to all races.

To sum up, from this evidence drawn from classical and Irish sources, from the lives of the saints and from Welsh folklore, we see that vaticination was an important factor in the life of our ancestors, that divination in a variety of different ways was practised by them, and that in the early period it was closely allied to magic. Later the true significance of the magical rite was forgotten, so that they degenerated into mere formalism.

As we have already stated, there is no Welsh vaticinatory material which has come down to us in a written form earlier than the twelfth century, but there are some references in Latin records written by Welshmen. Gildas in this respect is disappointing. He himself speaks as a prophet foretelling disaster for the British on account of their sins. He mentions these sins, but the practice of divination is not one of them. He does, however, mention that the Saxons came 'with omens and divinations. In these it was foretold, there being a prophecy firmly relied upon among them, that they should occupy the entire country to which the bows of their ships were turned for three hundred years'.[24] From this we see that vaticination was esteemed amongst the Saxons at the time when they came to Britain.

Nennius is a little more fruitful for our purpose. The 'Historia Brittonum' attributed to him in the form we now have it, was probably put together about AD800, though parts of it may be older. As we should expect therefore it deals with the struggle of the Britons against the Saxons and prophesies the ultimate triumph of the Britons. This is important as containing the germ of subsequent Welsh prophecies, and as forming the background for Geoffrey of Monmouth's prophecies of Merlin. According to the story in Nennius, Vortigern, a king of the Britons, was advised by his wise men to build and defend a fortress in Snowdon against the Saxons. He ordered this to be done, but the building material constantly disappeared during the night. The wise men, on being consulted, said that it was necessary to sprinkle on the foundation the blood of a boy without a father. After much searching they found such a boy playing ball in Glewysing. He is brought before the king, but on learning for what purpose he has been summoned, begins questioning the wise men, and confounds them. He then explains that under the foundations there is a pool and in it two vases. In them are two serpents sleeping, one white, one red. The king commends his men to dig under the foundations, and they find that the boy had spoken the truth. The serpents begin to struggle with each other, and after a great deal of fighting, the red one triumphs. The boy explains the meaning of this.

> The pool is the emblem of the world ... the two serpents are two dragons; the red serpent is your dragon, but the white serpent is the dragon of the people who occupy several provinces and districts of Britain, even almost from sea to sea; at length, however, our people shall rise and drive away the Saxon race from beyond the sea, whence they originally came.[25]

After this explanation the boy claims the citadel and reveals his name, Ambrose.

This prophecy is the first expression we have of the hope of final triumph for the Britons, a hope which continued to flourish throughout the centuries in the face of tremendous difficulties. The story of the wonderful boy without a father whose blood was to be sprinkled on the foundations, which forms a background for the prophecy, was probably an old Celtic tradition which was applied by Nennius or some previous redactor to Ambrosius. Irish parallels of the sprinkling of blood on foundations to give them stability exist,[26] so that the belief must be a very old one, and it seems that it is still current in India.

Prophecies in which dragons represent nations exist in other countries – Hebrew prophecy and the later Jewish and Christian apocalypses are full of such symbolism.

It is in Nennius, too, that we have the first record of Arthur; he is a 'dux bellorum', which probably represents a military office similar to those established in Britain during the latter years of the Roman occupation. He distinguished himself so greatly in the battles against the Saxons, that after his death all kinds of fabulous exploits and legends became attached to his name. It was said that he was not really dead, and that he would return again to lead the Britons to victory. This belief is obviously a product of a period of unrest and of national emergency, when the Britons found it difficult to hold their own against the Saxons.

> Compelled to yield their country, the Welsh avenged themselves on the Saxons by creating in the person of Arthur, not only a phantom of glory which towered above every warrior, but a political saviour who, like the Barbarossa of German popular superstition, was only temporarily hid, and would one day re-appear and reassert the national independence.[27]

It has been thought that Geoffrey of Monmouth first invested Arthur with the legendary glory which is now always associated with him, and that the belief in the return of Arthur was Geoffrey's own invention. We can see, however, that already in the time of Nennius legend was busy with his name, for in that account of twelve victorious battles fought by him, it is said that in the engagement of Badon Hill 'nine hundred and forty fell by his hand alone.' In the Mirabilia, which were appended to the 'Historia Brittonum' by Nennius or some earlier scribe, we find an account of Arthur's wonderful dog and a reference to the hunting of the magic boar, Porcum Troit, the story of which is to be found in the tale of 'Kulhwch ac Olwen'. There is in Nennius, however, no mention of the legend of the return of Arthur. Gildas and Bede do not mention Arthur, while the 'Annales Cambriae' have only scanty references to him, and no mention of the legend of his return.

Possibly, therefore, the belief in Arthur's return did not become popular for some centuries after his death, though we know that various legends were beginning to focus around his name from an early date. There is, however, definite evidence that this belief was circulated freely in Brittany, Cornwall and Wales before Geoffrey of Monmouth's time. This evidence has been gathered together by Mr Lewis Jones in his book on the Arthurian legend.[28] He gives the anecdote taken from Migne's 'Patrologia' 156 col. 983, of a tumult at Bodmin in 1113, caused by the fact that a monk of Laon denied that Arthur still lived. Later in the same century Alanus de Insulis testifies to the fact that the Bretons so firmly believed in Arthur's return that no one dared deny it on pain of death.

Two chronicles also record the currency of such traditions, which must have been very popular and widespread before serious historians would mention them in their works. William of Malmesbury, in the first chapter of his 'History of the Kings of Britain', completed in 1125, refers to the victories of Arthur and adds:

> This is the Arthur of whom the idle tales of the Britons rave even unto this day, a man worthy to be celebrated not in the foolish dreams of deceitful fables, but in truthful histories. For he long sustained the declining fortunes of the native land, and roused the uncrushed spirit of his people to war.[29]

Later on he refers to the grave of Gawain, and then adds: 'The grave of Arthur is nowhere to be seen, hence ancient songs fable that he is still to come.'[30] Here is positive evidence that before Geoffrey of Monmouth's time the bards of old sang of the return of Arthur, but none of these songs have come down to us. The only reference to the legend we have is a stanza in 'Englynion y Beddau', probably a very old composition, contained in the Black Book of Carmarthen:

> Bet y march, bet y gwythur,
> bet y gugaun cletyfrut.
> Anoeth bid bet y arthur.
>
> (*B.B.C.*, p. 67, ll. 12–13)

The last line is capable of more than one translation, but in all possible translations there is the same general idea that Arthur has no grave. Another chronicler, Henry of Huntingdon, is interesting not so much for his History as for a letter which he wrote to a friend from the Abbey of Bec, where he had seen an early version of Geoffrey's 'Historia' in 1139. He gives an abstract of the book in his letter, but his account of the passing of Arthur is much fuller and more highly coloured than Geoffrey's, and he says that 'his kinsmen the Britons deny that he is dead, and do even yet solemnly await his coming'.[31] Henry added to Geoffrey's account either from his own knowledge, or quite probably from tales current amongst the Bretons at the time, which he could have heard from Robert of Torigni at the Abbey of Bec.

Here then is definite evidence that a belief in Arthur's return existed long before Geoffrey's time. When exactly the legend originated it is impossible to say, but it is the natural product of the long struggle between Britons and Saxons. The popular growth of the legend on a large scale amongst 'the Celtic fringe' probably took place in a period from the ninth to the twelfth century. Similar legends in Welsh become attached to Cadwaladr and Owain as we shall see later, and parallels exist in the history of other countries. The hope of the coming of the Messiah, expressed by many of the Hebrew prophets of the Old Testament belongs to the same type, though there is a difference, for it was not the return of an old hero that was expected. In Portugal, Dom Sebastian was expected to return to restore the glories of the land and Cid Roderigo was expected to do the same for Castile.[32]

In Wales the legend of the return of Arthur took more than one form. One of these is mirrored in Geoffrey of Monmouth's 'Historia', and in the 'Vita Merlini' attributed to him. In the 'Historia', Book XI, Ch. 2, after an account of the battles against Mordred and his end, comes the following: 'Even the renowned King Arthur himself was wounded deadly, and was borne thence unto the isle of Avalon for the healing of his wounds.'[33] A fuller account is given in the Vita Merlini. Taliesin, in a discourse attributed to him, on the island of Britain, mentions:

> the island of apples which men call 'The Fortunate Isle', which gets its name from the fact that it produces all things of itself.[34] ... Thither after the battle of Camlan we took the wounded Arthur, guided by Barinthus to whom the waters and the stars of heaven were well known. With him steering the ship we arrived there with the prince, and Morgen received us with fitting honour, and in her chamber she placed the king on a golden bed and with her own hand she uncovered his honourable wound and gazed at it for a long time. At length she said that health could be restored to him if he stayed with her for a long time and made use of her healing art. Rejoicing, therefore, we entrusted the king to her and returning spread our sails to the favouring winds.[35]

Later when Merlin depicted the misery which the Welsh were to suffer at the hands of the Saxons, Taliesin exclaimed: 'Then the people should send some one to tell the chief to come back in a swift ship if he has recovered his strength, that he may drive off the enemy with his accustomed vigor and re-establish the citizens in their former peace.'[36]

Geoffrey's account is coloured by his knowledge of classical literature, but the tradition he records is in its essentials purely Celtic. The story of the fairy Morgen and her sisters is Celtic in origin, and Miss Paton in her Studies in Fairy Mythology[37] quotes a passage from Pomponius Mela which seems to reflect Celtic tradition. According to this account there lived nine virgin sisters on an island in the British sea, who had magic power, and who could change their forms and cure those deemed incurable. This closely resembles the account of the Fortunate Isle with its fairy inhabitants. The Celtic fairyland was generally believed to be across the sea or beneath the ground so that it was natural, when once the legend grew that Arthur was not dead, that the people should believe that he had only gone across the sea to fairyland to be cured of his wounds.

There is, however, another form of the legend in Welsh tradition. According to this, Arthur and his knights are sleeping in a cave below the ground, waiting for the day when they will be called to lead their country once more to victory. A Glamorgan form of this legend is recorded in Y Brython.[38] A Welshman goes to London taking with him a stick cut from a hazel tree. On London Bridge he meets an Englishman who asks him where he obtained the stick. After some argument and adventures the two find the hazel tree, and digging, find beneath it a large cave in which are sleeping thousands of mighty warriors with their armour spread around them. One of them is mightier than all the rest. In the centre of the cave is a huge bell with two watchmen sleeping near it. The Welshman is told that the knights are Arthur and his followers who will arise when the bell is rung. After the Welshman has helped himself to some of the treasure lying about the cave, they prepare to go out, but on the way the heavily laden Welshman inadvertently touches the bell, which clangs through the cave. One of the watchmen immediately awakes and asks, 'A yw hi yn ddydd?' Whereupon the Welshman who had been warned what to do immediately answers, 'Nac ydyw, cwsg di'; and the watchman sleeps again. Sometime later, however, the Welshman visits the cave again, and again touches the bell, but this time forgets the answer. No one knows what he suffered, but from that day forward he never enjoyed health and could never again find the cave.

There are obviously many later additions in this tradition, such as the mention of London Bridge which was very popular in English stories, and the moral which is hinted at towards the close, but in its essentials the tradition is undoubtedly a very old one. The existence of caves all over Wales either called Ogof Arthur or somehow connected with his name[39] proves this, and also testifies to the fact that the legend was widespread. In north, south, east, and west there are caves where it is claimed that Arthur and his knights sleep their long sleep.

In most of the different versions of the tradition there is treasure in the cave where Arthur sleeps, and Rhys therefore suggests that originally the legend was not connected with Arthur at all, – that it was purely a legend of hidden treasure. Such legends are very old, and in some cases the safe keeping of treasure is the reason for the presence of an armed host. Such a legend as this could easily become attached to Arthur. The treasure would then sink into the background and the knights form a bodyguard for Arthur, ready to sally forth at the destined hour.

On the other hand Arthur may have taken the place of some sleeping divinity, who was watched over by guardians, just as in the account given by Plutarch of an island in Britain, a god whom he identifies with Cronus is watched over by Briareus.[40] In such a legend there is no treasure, but neither is there in some of the Welsh legends. Rhys draws attention also to an Irish parallel in the story of Garry Geerlaug (probably a corruption of a Scandinavian name) who sleeps in an enchanted fort surrounded by his warriors ready to wake up in a time of need.[41]

In some of the traditional cave legends we find that Owain and not Arthur is the sleeping warrior. As we shall see later on the return of a traditional Owain was expected by the Welsh bards, and he was from time to time identified with various persons. Owain Lawgoch who died in 1378 was one of these, and it is probable that he is the hero who superseded Arthur in some forms of the cave legends, especially in South Wales.[42] He is the sleeping warrior in the tale told in one of the numbers of *Y Brython* as one of the stories of the old folk of Troed yr Aur in Cardigan;[43] both Arthur and Owain are associated with Ogof Llanciau Eryri, a cave supposed to be in the Snowdon district. It is unnecessary to suppose that various legends gradually clustered around Owain's name as in the case of Arthur. What happened was that the popularity of Owain Lawgoch in the fourteenth century became greater than that of Arthur, so that in some cases he stepped into Arthur's place in the traditional legends.

It is strange that none of the old poems mentioned by William of Malmesbury as fabling the return of Arthur have come down to us, for we have evidence that the influence of this tradition must have been tremendous. In 1170 the English king Henry II even went as far as to cause two bodies to be disinterred at Glastonbury, in order to shatter the Welsh belief in the return of Arthur. These bodies were supposed to be those of Arthur and Gwenhwyfar. An account of their disinterment is given in some of the Welsh manuscripts. The oldest I have found occurs in a Llanstephan manuscript[44] written according to Dr Gwenogvryn Evans about 1400. This is said to be taken from 'dau gabidwl gwedy eu hyspyssu on llyfyr ni yr hwnn a elwir drych yr eglwys', and is really a translation from Giraldus Cambrensis' *Speculum Ecclesiae*, Cap. VIII, IX and X[45] with additions by the scribe.

The Welsh version opens with a description of the finding of the grave as in the *Speculum*, but gives details not found in the latter; such as the division of the grave into thirds. Arthur's body occupying two, and Gwenhwyfar's one third; the enormous size of Arthur's bones; his many wounds etc. Such details must have been well known for they occur in another account of the opening of the grave found in Ranulph Higden's Polychronicon,[46] written late in the thirteenth century.

After giving these details the Welsh version follows Giraldus closely, giving first the incident of the finding of Gwenhwyfar's golden hair which is given also by Higden, and which provides Giraldus with an excellent opportunity of moralizing.

Ac ymplith yrei hynny (the bones) ykaffat pleth owallt melyn, tec oed edrych arnaw. ac ar ybleth honno ydodes manach or vanachlawc yolwc arydathoed ygyt ar niver wrth agori ybed. ac yd arganuu ymblaen pawb. abryssyaw a oruc ac ysglyyeit ybleth. ac val ykymerth yny law aedangos a phawp ynedrych ac ynryuedu ythecket yndeissyfyeit yggwyd pawp ydifflannawd oe law. ac nyt heb wyrtheu ydamchweinyawd hyny. ac ydangosset ynhonneit ybawp ... vot pop peth bydawl yndaruodedic ac ynsathredic ac ynbennaf oll ypetheu teckaf oedrych arnunt.[47]

This is the end of the tenth chapter in the *Speculum Ecclesiae*, and before beginning to translate the next chapter the Welsh scribe has added a few words about Arthur's devotion to Mary.

Giraldus opens the third chapter by giving his reason for describing the grave, which the scribe duly translates.

A chanys gnottaei dywedut llawer obetheu petrus amdiwed Arthur. Ac ynenwedic chwedylydyon ybrytanyeit aymryssonant ac a gadarnhaant etto y vot ef ynvyw, yny vwynt wrthladedic a diffodedic adifflanedic ychwedleu geu hynny a cherdet ywirioned racdi amhynny yn amlwc ohynn allan y paryssam nidodi yma petheu prouedic or wirioned diamheu.[48]

This is followed by a curious attempt to explain away the legendary Morgen who was to heal Arthur's wounds, as an old woman who took Arthur's body to Glastonbury to be buried:

yduc hen wreicda a margan oed y henw ygorff hyt yn yns avallach y lle aelwir yrawrhonn glastynbri. Athrannoeth gwedy yvarw yperis ywreicda honno ygladu yny vynwent gyssegredic val ydywetpwyt uchot. Sef ygnotaei tord ynys prydein ae chwedylydon dechymygu panyw margan dwywes o annwfyn ae rygudyssei ef yn ynys auallach (quod dea quaedam phantastica, scilicet et Morganis dicta, corpus Arthuri in insulam detulit Avalloniam) y iachau oe welioed. A phan veynt iach yd ymchoelei drachefyn at ybrytanyeit oe hamdiffyn megys y gnotaei. Ac am hynny etto ymaent mal yny adolwyn ef ac yn aros ydyuodyat rac llaw megys yr Idewon am grist onyt bot yn vwy yd ydys yn twyllaw yr Idewon o ynvydrwyd ac anfydlonder ac andedwytyt.[49]

There is, too, an ingenious explanation of how Ynys Afallach got its name Ynys Wydrin or Glastonbury 'o achaws auon aoed yny damgylchny a lliw glas gwydrawl ar y dwfyr. Ac wrth hynny y gelwis y saesson hi gwedy ygoresgyn glastynbri Kanys glas yn saesnec yw gwydyr ygkymraec' ('Glasenim Anglice vel Saxonice vitrum sonat').[50]

The abbot of Glastonbury was aided in finding the grave by 'hen lyfreu ac ystoryeu' as well as by Henry who had heard of the deeds of the Britons from 'hen dynyon a beirdd a chyuarwydeit'.

Then Giraldus gives a full account of the finding of the bones together with the leaden cross, which the Welsh scribe glibly translates, though he had previously given a similar description at the beginning. The bodies had been hurriedly interred in a coffin of oak fifteen feet below the ground 'rac ofyn ysaesson awrthladyssei ef ynvynych ac adeholassei or ynys'; while the cross, which was found seven feet below the ground, was put there later in a time of peace by a monk.

The tenth chapter describes how Henry caused the bodies to be honourably interred in a marble tomb 'megys ygwedei ac ydylyit y seilyawdyr penaduraf ylle hwnnw'.[51]

This account is extremely interesting because it reveals that the Welsh belief in the return of Arthur was considered a menace by Henry II, who spared no effort to destroy it; and also as an attempt on Giraldus' part to explain away some of the legends as mere perversions of simple fact. Possibly this attempt is due to the influence of Henry, for if he could go as far as disinterring two bodies to prove that Arthur was actually dead, then it is almost certain that he would employ Welshmen to circulate the story of the finding of Arthur's grave amongst their countrymen, and to attempt to destroy their belief in his return.

Other versions of the Welsh translation of Giraldus occur in later manuscripts[52] but as they are all alike in essentials there is no need to describe them here.

To this period of early struggle against the Saxons also belongs the legend of the return of Cadwaladr, but as this legend is reflected in Welsh poems which occur in manuscripts later than the twelfth century, we will defer a discussion of it until those poems come under consideration.

In this survey of Welsh vaticinatory material prior to the twelfth century we must mention Myrddin and Taliesin, who were reputed to be bards and prophets of the sixth century. However, as the vaticinatory material attributed to them is all spurious, and not to be found in manuscripts earlier than the twelfth century, it will be more convenient to defer an examination of this material also until that period comes under discussion.

During this period between the sixth and twelfth centuries when the Britons were losing their land and being gradually pushed westward till eventually they were confined to Wales, vaticination played an extremely important part in spurring on the hopes of the people from time to time. It is in this period that Welsh vaticination took on its most characteristic form – the expectation of a deliverer who was to be one of the old heroes returned again to lead the people. As we draw near the twelfth century, in a period of the revival and spread of learning, we should expect to find Welsh vaticination influenced by the literary prophecies of Europe and this, to some extent, is the case.

As we have seen, the most popular European prophecies in the Middle Ages were those attributed to the Sibyl. The 'Prophecy of Sibyl Tiburtina' was known throughout Europe and in each country local prophecies were attributed to the Sibyl in order to give them authority. Wales was no exception in this matter, and we have a Welsh version of the 'Prophecy of Sibyl Tiburtina' in several manuscripts. One of the oldest is that in Llyfr Gwyn Rhydderch.[53] The prophecy opens with an account of the parentage of the Sibyl and her double name, 'Tiburtina' in Greek, 'Albunea' in Latin. She explains the dream of the nine suns which one hundred Romans had dreamed the same night. The nine suns represent 'ykenedloed adelont racllaw', which she proceeds to describe. In the fourth Christ will arise, and here we have a long description of his birth, life and death. After this the prophecy chiefly relates to the succession of Western Emperors whose names are indicated by initials. Then Antichrist arises and the king of Rome gives up his crown in Jerusalem; Antichrist rules for a short time but is finally overthrown just before the Judgement, which is heralded by a series of awful signs. Of the Emperors mentioned, those which seem to be historical end with the three Os, which stand for the three Othos (936–1002); H for Henry II (1002–1024); C for Conrad II (1024–1029), and 'brenin arall o genedyl salic' whom Ward[54] identifies as Henry III (1029–1056), though in the Welsh version his name is said to begin with R, and in his time there will be many evils. After him come B, A, and then several Bs.

This prophecy of Sibyl Tiburtina was very popular in England also, as may be seen from the number of versions in Latin preserved in manuscripts at the British Museum.[55] Several versions have been printed all of which have been taken from the Cotton Titus DIII version, or one similar to it. One of these printed by Migne[56] is attributed to Bede, but it cannot have been composed before the eleventh century. A comparison of this with the Welsh version brings to light certain minor differences. The Latin version begins with an account of ten sibyls of whom Sibyl Tiburtina is the tenth, whereas the Welsh version begins immediately with a description of Sibyl Tiburtina. The account of the miracles of Christ is fuller in the Latin, the Welsh version contenting itself with the statement 'yr hwnn a wna llawer o wyrtheu'. The initials of the Kings are not quite the same. After the three Os, H, C, and 'alius salicus,' the Latin version has F and (Frederick Barbarossa and Henry VI, 1190–1198) followed by several Hs. There is, however, a Latin version[57] which has B and A followed by several Bs as in the Welsh, and this and the Welsh represent a form earlier than the other Latin versions in which the initials have been altered to suit the course of events.

All the Latin versions have the opening account of the ten Sibyls, and in all of them the signs at the end are written in the form of twenty-seven hexameters translated from the first twenty-seven hexameters of a Greek acrostic which is to be found in Eusebius and in the eighth book of Oracula Sibyllina; and the lines in their present form are quoted by St Augustine[58]. The Welsh version of the signs is a free translation in prose of these lines as the following comparison will illustrate:

Dejiciet colles, valles extollet ab imo:
Non erit in rebus hominum sublime vel altum,
Jam aequantur campis montes et caerula ponti.[59]

is rendered in Welsh: 'yna ygostygir y lleoed uchel. Ac ydrycheuir yglynnyeu. ny byd nac uchel nac issel ar ydaear nywneler yngynwastatet.'[60] There are several copies of this prophecy in Welsh manuscripts. One occurs in the Red Book of Hergest[61] which follows the White Book version closely. Peniarth MSS 14, a manuscript dating from the middle of the thirteenth century, has a different version lacking the beginning. The initials are practically identical except for a slight difference in some of the early ones preceding the Othos, and the 'alius salicus' is called B and not R as in the White Book. This version follows the Latin more closely on the whole than the White Book version and a late copy of it is to be found in Peniarth MS 58, p. 113 (sixteenth century)[62]

None of the Welsh or Latin versions occur in manuscripts older than the thirteenth century, but we have seen that the Welsh versions are translations of a form which must have been composed at least as early as the middle of the eleventh century. Apart from these translations of the 'prophecy of Sibyl Tiburtina', the influence of the Sibylline prophecies upon the Welsh does not seem to have been very great. There are passages in Welsh prophecies describing the evils to come which resemble the passage describing the reign of 'alius salicus', when brother will kill brother and the son the father; when morals will be loose and the clergy profligate and neglectful. This, however, need not be a case of borrowing, for such material is common to most predictions and is found in the oldest Hebrew prophecies.

The Sibyl is mentioned by name fairly frequently in Welsh prophecies, but usually in prose prophecies, which, as we shall see, are mostly translations or copies of English prophecies. Geoffrey of Monmouth mentions the songs of the Sibyl in the twelfth book of his *Historia*, which was written early in the twelfth century, but he does not make use of the Sibylline prophecies, nor do they seem to have had much influence upon his prophecies of Merlin. In the explanations of the terms used in the 'brudiau' the Sibyl is mentioned as one of the prophets. In Welsh prophetic poems she is also referred to occasionally. In 'Cyfoesi Merddin a Gwenddydd', Stanza 59, there is a reference to 'Chwipleian chwedleu'[63] and it is now generally supposed that the 'chwipleian' is the Sibyl. She is associated with Myrddin also in the Afallenneu:

Disgogan hwimleian hwetil adiwit.
(*B.B.C.*, p. 51, l. 9)

and is referred to twice in the Hôianeu:

Rimdyuueid huimleian chuetyl enryuet.
(*B.B.C.*, p. 55, l. 7)

Rymdywod huimleian chuetil amechrin.
(*B.B.C.*, p. 55, ll. 13–14)

Here we have a point of contact between two streams of tradition, the native tradition of Mydrddin as a famous prophet and bard, and the continental tradition of the Sibyl as a great seer.

As we have seen, at the close of the 'Prophecy of Sibyl Tiburtina', there was a passage describing the signs which will accompany the coming of the day of judgement. Religious poems predicting and describing the approaching end were very popular amongst the monks, and a poem with this as its theme occurs in the Book of Taliesin, called 'Yrymes detbrawt'.[64] The term 'arymes' (*yrymes*) is explained by Mr Ifor Williams[65] as coming from a root *med-*. He compares 'arymes' or 'armes', for both forms are found, with the Irish *ardmes* (airdmes) 'considering', 'calculating' or 'cloudgazing', and this is the meaning implied in the Welsh which he translates as 'soothsaying' or 'prophecy'. He postulates the form *are-mbhi-med-t*, which would give 'armes' or 'erymes'. He then gives examples of *armes* with this meaning and shows how later, because poems of the 'arymes' type dealt with trouble and disaster, the word developed a secondary meaning 'loss' or 'sorrow'.

The poem opens with the usual prayer to God and then proceeds to describe the coming of the day of judgement which will come with terror accompanied by various signs. The elements will act as messengers on that day, and there will be confusion amongst sea and stars. Trumpets will sound and fire and floods occur on the earth, which will be as a level plain. Storms will be frequent, and the heavens will fall to earth. Then the Trinity comes to judgement, reminding the wicked of the opposition Christ met with on earth, and appealing to them to touch the marks of suffering on his body.

> Tafaw ti vyndeu troet mor tru eu hadoet ...
> Tauaw dyr cethron ymywn vyg callon ...

They are refused forgiveness, and judgement is passed on them.

> Ac awch bi wynnyeith gwerth awch ynuyt areith.
> Kayator ydyleith arnawch y vffernlleith.[/ex]

This poem has a simple dignity and poetic feeling unusual in the medieval religious poems.

As for the time of its composition, it occurs in a manuscript which belongs to the fourteenth century but which, as we shall endeavour to show later, contains a number of prophetic poems written long before the twelfth century. It is quite probable that this poem belongs to the period preceding the year 1000 which was awaited in fear and trembling as the year of the millennium, when all things would come to an end.

Other Welsh manuscripts reflect the popularity of prophecies of the approaching end. These signs became crystallized into a definite number fifteen, which are found, though not always in the same order, in most of the versions. These signs like those in 'Arymes detbrawt', and in the Sibyl Tiburtina prophecy, go back to the time of the early apocalypse of St John.[66] They are frequently associated with the Antichrist legend, and that of the Last King of Rome, just as they are in the Sibyl Tiburtina, and many of the old apocalypses, though here the signs are not definitely numbered as fifteen.

Some of the Welsh versions are of this type, as that in a Llanstephan manuscript[67] of the fifteenth century, which describes the evils which will occur in the reign of Antichrist who will appear in 1403. He will be defeated and the day of judgement comes heralded by the fifteen signs.

Then comes a description of the judgement and the separation of the good and evil. This is obviously a late form of the prophecy, but the legends are really much earlier. In the same manuscript there is ... a version of the approaching end which is applied to the time of Edward III and the French wars. The sixth age will last until AD1355 when Antichrist will arise and in his time there will be wars on all sides of France. This is probably a translation of an English prophecy circulated during the time of Edward III.

The fifteen signs occur on the fifteen days before the day of judgement, and may be summarized this:

1. Rising of the sea as a wall.
2. Sinking of the sea from sight.
3. Return of the sea to its normal level (this is sometimes omitted).
4. Fish and inhabitants of the sea come to the surface and make a great noise.
5. Burning of the sea.
6. Trees and plants will be full of dew like blood.
7. Falling of buildings.
8. Stones and rocks smite each other.
9. Trembling of the earth.
10. Hills and valleys become one level plain.
11. Men come out of their hiding places in caves and shall be as madmen.
12. Falling of the stars and the 'signs' of the heavens.
13. Rising of the dead.
14. Death of the living.
15. Burning of the world.

This is the usual order[68] though there are slight variations in the many versions found in Welsh manuscripts.[69] Llanstephan MSS 24 for example, ends with the blowing of trumpets as the fifteenth sign. The White Book of Rhydderch has a version in verse, in which the order differs considerably from the usual type.[70] This version is attributed to Bishop Morud and is headed: 'Llyma yir arwydon a vydant yn pymthec niewarnawt kyn dydbrawt. a gauas morud esgob olyureu sein Jeronym. amorud esgob agant yr eglynyon.' This version is also found in the Myvyrian Archaeology[71] where it is attributed to Llywelyn Fardd.

The poem opens with a description of the fifteenth day before the judgement when the sea will rise:

Gwyn gwarandaw dy synnwyr a draetha y llyureu mor llwyr
gwrtheu goleu guelhitor dyrcheuit mor hyt awyr

and continues with the signs concerning the sea, and the rising of the fish to the surface. Then all creatures will tremble, there will be fire; the stars fall; war will come; hill and valley will be levelled etc. On the seventh day stones will split, on the sixth blood will drip from the trees:

Seithuettyd, dyd darogan mein mwyhaf oll a hollan ...
Arwydon chwero chwechuettyd y daw guaet or guellt ar gwyd.

Then the earth will tremble and animals flee to the wild places; people will await the judgement with fear, and on the last day:

… dybyd oll poploed plant adaf o bell
amut a drut a drythyll yn llwyr yn y llaun dyall.

The fifteen signs were not only popular amongst the Welsh, but 'formed a subject of extreme interest in the Middle Ages and were consigned to prose and verse in almost every language'.[72] English versions are numerous, and many have been printed[73] which closely resemble the Welsh versions. The majority of the versions, in Welsh and English, are said to be taken from St Jerome, though occasionally as in the English version printed by Furnivall[74] this is changed to 'Seint Ieremie'. Mr Furnivall also quotes a statement[75] that 'no copy of the original is to be found in the Benedictine edition of Jerome's Works'. Probably the 'signs' became crystallized into fifteen at a fairly early period, and from the resemblance between the different versions it is probable that they come from one ultimate source.

Another type of Welsh vaticination which shows European influence is astrology. As we have already seen, a primitive kind of astrology existed amongst the pagan Celts, and this formed an excellent basis on which the more complicated systems developed in Greece and Rome and in the science of the Moors could be grafted. We have seen, too, that during the eleventh and twelfth centuries astrology was gradually establishing itself throughout Europe, and that by the thirteenth century the interest in it was very keen. In Welsh manuscripts we have reflected the ancient belief in lucky and unlucky days. In the Red Book of Talgarth[76] written about 1400, there is an entry of this type.

Hyspys yw bot yny vlwydyn pedwar diwarnawt ardec arhugeint. a phwybynnac adigwydo ymywn clefyt gorweidyawc yn un ordydyeu hynny. ny chyfyt vyth. A phwybynnac aaner yn un or dydyeu hynny ny byd hir hoedlawc.

Then comes an enumeration of the unlucky days in each month. Parallels exist in Anglo-Saxon manuscripts and have been printed and translated in the Saxon Leechdoms.[77] There is an enumeration of days unlucky for blood-letting.[78] In the same way certain days are lucky for dreams. 'Y dydd kyntaf or lloer o gwely vreuddwyd llewenydd a arwyddocka,'[79] and there is a close parallel in Old English. 'On the first night of the moon's age whatever you dream turns out joy etc.'[80] An interpretation of dreams 'herwyd danyel broffwyt' is given in some Welsh manuscripts:

Gwelet adar drwy dy hun.Ennill aarwydockaa
Dwyn arueu drwy dy hun.enryded aarwydockaa
Colli adar drwy dyhun.collet aarwydockaa …
Gwelet eryr yn dyuot yr ty.anghyfeillach aarwydoca
Gwelet eryr neu golomen arnaw.enryded arwydoka …
Gwneuthur llauuryeu mawr terwysc aarwydokaa …[81]

In the Saxon Leechdoms is printed 'A Book of Dreams by the Prophet Daniel. In dreams to see fowls that quarrel, betokens some dispute. In dreams to catch fowls, betokens profit. To see fowls snatch something from the dreamer, betokens harm. … To seem to bear weapons in dreams, betokens cause for weariness etc.'[82] However the English version continues quite differently from the Welsh and is very much longer. Another English version is printed, p. 169, and the opening words: 'If a man dreams that he sees an eagle settle on his head that betokeneth much honour,' has a parallel in the Welsh as we have seen, but apart from this the two versions are not alike.

Another group of prophecies consists of meteorological predictions according to the day on which New Year's Day or Christmas day falls.

'O syrth duu kalan ar duu sul: da vyd ygaeaf. a gunnuyn guynnauc. Ahaf sych aguinllanneu ynfynnu. ar deueit yn lluydau.'[83] With this we may compare the English version.[84] 'If the mass day of midwinter fall on a sunday, then there shall be a good winter, and a windy spring, and a dry summer, and good vineyards, and sheep shall thrive.'

Other similar prophecies which occur in Welsh and English, are those which predict events according to the nature of Christmas day and the eleven days immediately following. 'Os duu nadolic yguelir yrheul. llauenhau auna guas-sanaethuyr duu. Os yreildyd yguelir eur ac aryant a vyd amyl.'[85]

And again: 'Nos nadolic or byd guynt. yny vluydyn honno ycollir y brenhined ar esgyb. Os yr eilnos ybyd guynt. drut uyd y guin … os ydeudecvet nos. ymyun lluyd y kollir llauer.'[86] Or according to the first month: 'Mis Ionaur orbyd trysteu. guynt maur ac amyl ffruyyhreu. ac ymladeu avyd yny vluydyn honno. Mis chuefraur orbyd trysteu. maruolyaeth avyd ynvwyaf ar y kyfoethogyon.'[87]

English parallels occur: 'On the first day of the Lord's birth festivals, if the sun shine, there shall be much joy among men and abundance. If the sun shines on the second day, then gold shall be easy to get among the English.'[88]

And again: 'Here is told about the birth day of our Lord about the Christmas twelve nights. If the wind occurs on the first night men in holy orders shall die … If there be wind on the twelfth night, then there shall be some great battle on earth.'[89]

And again: 'In the present year if it thunders on a Sunday then that betokeneth a great bloodshed. If on the next day, Monday, that storm betokeneth that a royal child shall be put to death.'[90]

Other predictions take into account the influence of the moon on different days.

Y dyd kyntaf oloer enidyd. pob gueith or auneler cryno vyd … Pobpeth orawelych druy dyhun ynllewenyd y try. Orgenir mab arderchauc vyd. ac astut achall allyth-yraul. ac ymyun dufyr vyd y berigyl. or dieingk ynteu hir vyd yoes. Os merch aenir hi avyd diweir. ahygar athec. a rangkvodus gan wyr. Puy byn(n)ac aglefycho hir y byd claf … Yr eil dyd orlloer pob peth or awnelych. cryno vyd. Prynu agwerthu. ysgynnu myun llong. mynet yhynt. heu hateu.[91]

The prediction continues for the first ten days. A similar version occurs in English:

The first moon of the lunar month is useful for all purposes. A child born on it will be illustrious, clever, wise, booklearned; endangered on water; from which if he escapes he will be long in life. A maiden then born will be pure, chaste, mild, handsome, acceptable to men, of a right discrimination … He who takes to his bed on that day will be long ill … The second day is useful for all purposes: to buy, to sell, to go aboard ship.[92]

The predictions continue for thirty days.

These examples, taken from Welsh manuscripts,[93] with English parallels, are sufficient to show that a mass of material existed in Wales and England dealing with lucky days, with meteorological forecasts, and miscellaneous predictions for each day of the lunar month; and we can conclude from the close resemblance between the parallel passages that they must have come from the same source. Wedel says that these predictions, primitive as they are, 'belong to the learned literature of the day and trace their origin to foreign and not to native sources,'[94] and that they are translations from Latin or Greek originals.

According to Cockayne the books dealing with the interpretation of dreams owe their origin to the numerous books on dream divination amongst the Mediterranean races.[95] And of astrology he says that in the centuries immediately following the Christian era, some forger issued books under the name of Hermes (the supposed author of the Egyptian sacred books) containing:

> astronomical forecasts of diseases, setting forth the evil influence of malignant stars upon the unborn; telling how the right eye is under the sun, the left under the moon, the hearing under Saturn, – so that if any of these planets be in a bad aspect at conception or birth, the man will suffer some debility in the corresponding part of his body.[96]

It was not, however, till the thirteenth century that astrology really established itself in the northwest of Europe, though Greek and Arabian science was filtering through in the twelfth century. During the Crusades men came into contact with the astrological science of the Moors, a complicated jumble of classical and Arabian systems. The pure 'judicial' astrology of Ptolemy dealing only with the prediction of the future according to the configuration of the stars at birth was associated with necromance, with the belief in lucky days, and with complicated rules for discovering a thief; or propitious moments to begin undertakings.[97]

The astrology which filtered through to the West was therefore a complicated system and it was found very difficult to reconcile it with Christianity, which strongly denounced intercourse with demons.[98] As early as the first part of the twelfth century we meet with a reference to astrology in Wales in Geoffrey of Monmouth's 'Historia Regum Britanniae'. The close of his seventh book which gives the prophecies of Merlin, takes the form of astrological allusions. They are however very obscure and vague and consist chiefly of classical reminiscences. 'Most of Geoffrey's allusions are only vaguely astrological. Such phrases as the "amber of Mercury" and "Stilbon of Arcady" may mean "anything or nothing" … The most definite astrological allusions occur in his references to the "malignity of Saturn" and the "houses of the planets".'[99] These allusions, however, prove that astrology was known as early as the beginning of the twelfth century.

In the earliest Welsh manuscripts there are very few references to astrology. The earliest Welsh tales, 'Pedeir Ceinc y Mabinogi', and the Arthurian legends contain no trace of it, but in later forms of these legends astrology plays an important part. A Welsh manuscript dating from the middle of the thirteenth century[100] gives an account of the universe according to the Ptolemaic system. This includes an account of the seven planets, and in this there is occasionally a little material of a predictive nature, such as, 'O byd coch y lleuat en betwared megys lliw eur gwynnyeu, a darogan. Os eny chyrrieu y byd manneu duon dechreu y mis a dengys e uot en glawauc,' and in the account of Saturn there is a reference to the making of images, a practice which was indulged in by the Greeks and Romans. The idea behind the practice was that the melting of a waxen image of a person would bring about his downfall. Images were also made in connection with medicine and they had to be made at certain times when the 'signs' were propitious. This is the reference in the Welsh manuscript: 'aphuybennac adineuei delw o euyd yn dechreu sadwrn ef abrouit dywedut o honei val den.'[101]

In an account of the heavens, a weather prediction occurs. 'O chocha y furuaven y pyrnawn arwyd eglurder drannoeth … Os e bore y cocha dryckin a arwydha.' This type of prediction has come down in the familiar 'Red in the morning shepherd's warning, red in the night shepherd's delight.'

There is given, too, a detailed account of the signs of the zodiac and how they were formed, but no rules for prophesying from them. Other later manuscripts, however, contain what is called the 'Book of Fate' or the 'Book of Nature,' and this foretells the character of a person, and events which will happen to him, according to the sign under which he is born.

> Dyma llyfyr a elw(ir llyfyr Natur)ieth eraill ai geilw llyfyr y dynghedfen. pa fab bynag aner ne ferch o fewn y deuddeg arwydd ai kaffo darllened y llyfyr hwn i ysbysu iddo ef a ddichon ddatkan iddo i gerdded ai ddamwain ai hoedl.[102]

It then gives a brief account of the influence of the planets, some for good some for evil, followed by the actual prediction.

> Y mab aner dan arwydd yr myharen syf yw hyny o haner mawrth i haner ebrill ymdrawr mawr fydd ag ni fydd kywaethoc fyth na thlawd iawn ... ag ef a orfydd ar i holl wrthnebwyr ag ef a gaiff y gore arnunt agwellwell fydd iddo yn i yfiyngtud noc yni henaint, ... etc.[103]
>
> ... Ar mab a aner dan yr arwydd a elwir y krank sef yw hyny o haner myhevin i haner gorffenaf man(n)oc vydd i gorff o glwyf naturiol a elwyr yrriuwnt a chymhedrol o vaint vydd i gorff a chwanoc vydd i wragedd ac aniwair vydd ond (r)wydd a hayl a chlodvawr vydd ac ond odid kylvyddgar vydd ... ar verch a aner dan yr un arwydd nidta iddi oherwydd natur kans hi a ddyly vod yn vlin ac yn llavurus ac yn ddrwc i hanwyde. ar vyr enyd a byan i dervydd ond oherwydd natur hi a ddyly vod yn lladrones a hi a ddyly vod yn valch ynddi ehun ... a herwydd natur hi a ddiaink o bob peric1. a gwra a gaiff a fflant lawer a vydd iddi ac oddiurth y gwr i kaiff lywenydd a dayoni ac oi lx mlwydd allan i dechre i fferygle etc.[104]

Such tracts as this must have been common in the Middle Ages when astrology had become popular, and are most probably translations of some Latin work.

Later Welsh manuscripts contain many treatises on the elements, the firmament, signs of the zodiac, planets etc, and their influence for good or evil on mankind. Elaborate calculations were made to find out propitious times for certain undertakings or for 'letting blood' and administering medicine etc. For example, 'Pen fo y lleuad yn benna ar y pysc ne ar y krank ne ar y Sarff: ai bod hwynt dan y sygyn honno ar lleuad dan guddedigeth y ddauar, arwyddion da fydd y rrai hyny i roi Meddeginiaeth redegog.'[105] Peniarth MS 172 is a manuscript of Astrology, Palmistry and Interpretation of Dreams, and contains most detailed instructions for predictions by these various methods. It includes a supposed book of Aristotle written for King Alexander.

All these, however, are foreign importations into Welsh, and most of them are translations, taken ultimately from Latin and Greek sources, probably executed during the thirteenth and fourteenth centuries or later, when the interest in astrology was very keen.

It will not be out of place here to glance back over the early history of vaticination in Wales. We see that it developed along the same lines as in other countries. First there was a primitive kind of divination closely associated with magic, gradually degenerating, as time went by, into a formal art, and being condemned by the upholders of Christianity. It is impossible now to say of what diverse elements the primitive art was composed. We know that Celtic and Iberian practices must have intermingled, and during the Roman occupation there must have been to some extent an influx of Mediterranean customs and practices, so that the superstitions which have come down to the present day contain traces of the beliefs of more than one race.

As amongst other nations, vaticination in Wales from the earliest times was frequently used for political purposes, and the struggle against the Saxons resulted in the production of a special type of prophecy of the return of a popular hero, a prophecy which has parallels in other countries. This type became exceedingly popular and had a potent influence right down to the time of the Tudors. Religious prophecies of the end of the world and the day of judgement were produced also in the centuries prior to the twelfth, influenced by the Apocalyptic literature of Europe. Other points of contact between the native tradition and continental vaticination are to be found in the occasional Sibylline prophecies, and the astrological predictions which became so popular after the twelfth century.

Notes

1 See Lloyd, *History of Wales*,. Vol. I, pp. 43–6.
2 *Ibid.*, p. 44, and O.M. Edwards, *Wales*, p. 14.
3 Rhys, *Celtic Heathendon*, p. 222.
4 Joyce, *Social History of Ancient Ireland*, p. 222.
5 *Ibid.*, p. 229.
6 *Ibid.*, pp. 229–34.
7 Wedel, *Mediaeval Attitude towards Astrology*, p. 43.
8 *The Black Book of Carmarthen* (reprod. Evans), p. 48–63.
9 *Social History*, Vol. I, pp. 240–310.
10 Willis Bund, *The Celtic Church of Wales*, p. 17.
11 Baring Gould and Fisher, *Lives of British Saints*, Vol. II, pp. 285–322.
12 *Life of St David* etc, ed. by J. Morris-Jones, pp. 11–12.
13 *Ibid.* p. 14.
14 Ifor Williams, 'Review of Gwenogvryn Evans's "Taliesin"', *Y Beirniad*, Vol. VI, pp. 132–3.
15 *Celtic Church of Wales*, pp. 85–6.
16 Rhys, *Celtic Folklore*, Vol. I, p. 320.
17 Howells, *Cambrian Superstitions*, p. 52.
18 *Celtic Folklore*, p. 364.
19 *B.B.C.*, p. 106.
20 *Celtic Folklore*, pp. 394 *et seq.*
21 It is interesting to note that the Welsh term 'nigromawns' is probably from the old French 'nigromaunce'.
22 See Stephen Hughes's translation, 'of … things spoken and acted by an Unclean Spirit at Mascon', in Hughes's edition of Rhys Prichard's *Cannwyll y Cymry* (London, 1681), p. 457.
23 *Ibid.*, p. 464.
24 Hugh Williams (ed.), Gildas, Cymmrodorion Record Ser., p. 55.
25 Giles's trans., *The History of the Britons* by Nennius, p. 24.
26 Joyce, *op. cit.*, pp. 284–5.
27 Dunlop, *History of Fiction*, Vol. 1, p. 136.
28 W. Lewis Jones, *King Arthur in History and Legend*. See also L.A. Paton, *Introd. to Hist. of Kings of Britain* (Everyman Series), p. vii–xiv.
29 W. Lewis Jones's trans., *op. cit.*, p. 32.
30 *Ibid.*, p. 33.
31 *Ibid.*, p. 34.

32 Rhys, *Celtic Folklore*, Vol. II, p. 482.
33 *Histories of the Kings of Britain*, p. 200.
34 J.J. Parry (trans.), *The Vita Merlini*, p. 83.
35 *Ibid.*, p. 85.
36 *Ibid.*, p. 87.
37 *Ibid.*, p. 122, note 48.
38 *Y Brython*, Medi 3, 1858, p. 162.
39 See Rhys, *Celtic Folklore*, pp. 457 *et seq.*
40 *Ibid.*, pp. 493–4.
41 *Ibid.*, p. 483.
42 Rhys, *Welsh cave legends and the story of Owain Lawgoch*, trans. of Cymmrod., 1899–1900.
43 *Y Brython*, Medi 10, 1858, p. 179.
44 Llanst. 4, folios 505a–509.
45 Brewer (ed.), *Giraldi Cambrensis opera*, Vol. IV, p. 47–51.
46 Lumby (ed.), *Polychronicon*, Vol. VIII, pp. 60–64.
47 Llanst. 4 f. 506a, 'Speculum Ecclesiae', Rolls Series, Vol IV, pp. 47–8.
48 Fol. 506b; cf. *Speculum*, p. 48.
49 Fol. 507a; cf. *Speculum*, p. 49.
50 Fol. 507b; cf. *Speculum*, p. 49.
51 Folio 509; cf. *Speculum*, p. 50–1.
52 For example, p. 147, p. 163; see Evans' Cat. of Welsh MSS, under 'Diwedd Arthur'.
53 P. 5, f. xii, l. 30-f. xiv., l. 38.
54 Ward, *Cat. of Romances in Brit. Mus.*, Vol. I. p. 190.
55 *Ibid.*, pp. 190–95.
56 Migne, *Patrologia*, Tom. 90, col. 1181.
57 Egerton, 810; see Ward, p. 191.
58 Ward, *op. cit.*, p. 190.
59 Migne's version, *Patrologia*, Tom. XC, col. 1186.
60 Pen. 5, f. XIVa.
61 For copy of this see Llanst. 148, p. 114.
62 For other later copies see Evans' *Catalogues* under 'Sibli ddoeth'.
63 Evans, *Poetry of Red Book*, col. 580, l. 10.
64 Evans, *Facsimile and Text of Taliesin*, p. 10.
65 *Bulletin*, Board of Celtic Studies, Vol. 1, pp. 35–6.
66 *Revelations*, chap. vi.
67 Llanst. MS 2, p. 212; also Llanst. MS 34, p. 12 *et seq.*
68 As in Llanst. MS 27, f. 161a.
69 Llanst. MS 24, f. 98; Llanst. MS 28, p. 140; Llanst. MS 34, pp. 16–18; Llanst. MS 117, p. 100 (re-numbered 199b). All differ slightly in the order of the signs. For other versions see Evans' *Cat.*, under 'Arwydd' and 'Pymtheg'.
70 P. 5. ff. XIb–XIIa. See also *Myv. Arch.*
71 See Denbigh ed. 1870, p. 250.
72 Wright, *Chester Plays*, Vol. 2, pp. 218 *et seq.*
73 See Furnivall, *Adam Davy's Dreams*, pp. 91 *et seq.*
74 *Ibid.*, p. 92.
75 *Ibid.*, p. 91.
76 Llanst. MS 27, f. 160.
77 Cockayne, *Leechdoms, Wortcunning, and Starcraft*, Rolls Series, Vol. 3, p. 150, *et seq.*
78 Llanst. 27, pp. 157–8.
79 P. 26 (*c*.1456), p. 71.
80 *Saxon Leechdoms*, transl., III, p. 155, see also p. 159, taken from a MS *c*.1120.
81 Llanst. MS 27, ff. 153b–156b; cf. P. 26, p. 71; P. 172, p. 253.

82 *Saxon Leechdoms*, III, p. 199.

83 P. 12, p. 124, detached portion of White Book; Llanst. MS 27, f. 160a.

84 *Saxon Leechdoms*, III, p. 163.

85 Llanst. MS 27, f. 158a.

86 *Ibid.*, f. 158a.

87 *Ibid.*, f. 158b.

88 *Saxon Leechdoms*, III, pp. 165–6.

89 *Ibid.*, III, p. 165.

90 *Ibid.*, III, p. 167.

91 Llanst. MS 27, f. 157a.

92 *Saxon Leechdoms*, III, p. 185.

93 I have taken the examples where possible from the earliest manuscripts containing them. For other later versions see Evans's *Catalogues* under 'Dreams', 'Astrology'.

94 *Med. Attitude towards Astrology*, p. 45.

95 *Saxon Leechdoms*, Vol. 3, Introd., p. x.

96 *Ibid,* p. xiii.

97 Wedel, *Med. Attitude towards Astrology*, p. 12 *et seq.*

98 *Ibid.*

99 *Op. cit.*, footnote 4, pp. 47–48.

100 P. 17, p. 17 *et seq.*

101 *Ibid.*, p. 21.

102 P. 86, p. 187.

103 P. 86, p. 189 (sixteenth century).

104 P. 27, pt. ii, p. 4 (late fifteenth century).

105 P. 77, p. 311 (late sixteenth century).

CHAPTER FIFTEEN

Armes Prydein

('Prophecy of Britain')

Attributed to Myrddin

newly translated by John Matthews

ASCRIBED TO MYRDDYIN, THE WELSH MERLIN, this is one of the most famous prophetic poems to have survived. In fact, it was written as much as 300 years after the period when the great bard and seer is believed to have lived and refers to events that took place around AD930. Many of the internal references are, therefore, in protest at the taxes imposed by the Saxons on the Cymry (Welsh) of Caer Geri (Cirencester) in the Anglo-Saxon kingdom of Wessex. Several of the characters mentioned in the poem may well be historical figures, including Cynan and Cadwaladr, who are known heroes of the Celtic struggle against the invaders. The Gwretheryn mentioned more than once is Vortigern, a fifth-century ruler who is accused of having brought the Saxons into Britain in the first place. Several of the place-names that are mentioned can be traced to actual sites, including Caer Wynt (Winchester), Dyfed and Glywysing (southwestern and southeastern kingdoms in Wales), Manau (probably Edinburgh) and Llydaw (Brittany). Dyfed is in the southwest coastal area of Wales, and Gwawl is on the Roman Wall near Carlisle. Gweryd is probably somewhere in the area of the Firth of Forth. Prydein is one of the old names for Britain. Although there is probably a good deal of hindsight in the 'prophetic' aspect of the poem, it is powerful work with a grimly realistic view of warfare.

Hosts will come.
We shall possess riches
Prosperity and peace;
Generous rulers, benevolent lords;
And, after disruption, the region settled.
Fierce men, wrathful, mighty
Bold in combat, angry, powerful,
As far as Caer Weir will rout their foes.
Celebration follows devastation,
Agreement between Prydein and
    Dublin;
Ireland, Mon, Scotland, Cornwall
At one in their endeavour.

Britons shall have triumph,
Long since foretold;
Noble rulers, Northmen too,
Shall embark on an assault.

Myrddin tells us how
An assembly at Aber Peryddon
Will bring the High King's stewards
(They will moan of death)
To gather taxes
The Cymry will not pay.
Mary's Mabon, sovereign Word,
Unbroken by Saxon battery!

Down with Gwrtheyrn's pariahs!
Foreign foes will go into exile,
No welcome anywhere, no land given –
Rivers will be strange to them
    everywhere!
Hengist and Horsa bought Thanet
With deceit and guile; since then
They have grown ever stronger.
Secret slayings, drunkenness, terror,
Have given them power;
Now destitution reigns
From many deaths, and women's tears
Sow desolation on the land.
We yearn to be free of savage rulers,
Sorrowing at a world upturned;
Thanet's thieves may rule us,
Our lands laid waste –
God's word prohibiting blows –
But we pray they may retreat
Before our lands are overrun.

Mabon of Mary, unbroken
The Cymry remain – nobles, princes,
Warriors – all cry out one-voiced,
Single-hearted, of one mind.
Not from pride, but shunning disgrace,
They avoid parley – preying
To God and Dwi – send home the
    Saxon,
Who shamefully ravished the land.
Cymry and Saxon will meet,
Both sides struggling for supremacy,
Fierce warbands testing their strength,
While on the hills battle-cries are heard
And the clash of blades.
On Wye's banks ring out;
Banners deserted through savage
    assault.
Food for wolves the Saxons,
Cymric lords gathering their forces,
Attacking vanguard and rear.
Saxons will kneel in blood,
Bleeding men on every side;
Many will flee through the forest
Like foxes in the streets,
Banished forever from Britain's land
Driven to the sea in terror and dismay.

Caer Geri's stewards will groan,
Uttering their fear in holt and hide,
To Aber Peryddon with ill-luck
To gather fatal taxes.
Attacking with eighteen thousand,
Only eight thousand will return
With blood-soaked shirts –
A sorry tale to tell their wives.
Cymry from the south
Contend without care their taxes.
Sharp blades cut cleanly,
Paying no doctor's fee.
Great war-bands come
As the Cymry arise and give battle.
Unavoidable death has been evoked;
Never again will the Saxons
Gather such evil taxes.

In forest, field, hill and dale
A candle will lighten the darkness.
Cynan will lead the assault,
As the Saxons, groaning, cry: 'Ah, God!'
And Cadwaladr, mighty pillar,
Gathers his stern lords,
Driving them to beds of earth
With bloody faces.
In the end, the Saxons will rush,
Furiously into Caer Wynt.
Blessed are the Cymry who invoke
The Trinity to give them freedom.
Let neither Dyfed nor Glywysing
    tremble:
The high king's stewards will fail,
And Saxon warriors, though savage,
Won't get drunk at our expense.
With orphaned sons, stiff and cold,
The foe will flee to Lego's banks.

The *awen* foretells: the day will come
When Wessex will have one mind,
One voice, a single thought.
With Angles, fleeing daily, outcast, lost,
We will rush into battle like bears,
Taking dreadful toll of the enemy.
Spear-play will be seen, much
    bloodshed,
Heads split open, brains scattered,

Wives widowed, steeds left riderless,
Terrible groans after the charge.
Death's messengers gather
Where corpses stand in ranks.
Vengeance for endless taxes,
Proud envoys, deceitful foes.
The Cymry must be hardened,
Trained, united, sworn
Companions in the field.

Compelled to wage war,
The Cyrmy will muster,
Under Dewi's banner,
Dublin's clansmen fighting at our sides.
Demanding first what the Saxon's want,
What right they have to ancient lands,
And whence they come and why.
Since Gwrtheyrn's time they have sought
To trample us under foot – no rights
Have they to do so – great wrongs
Have they done to us,
Breaking Dewi's laws.
The Cymry will be certain
To let no Saxon walk away;
We'll punish them for all they did
With death their payment now.
Paid will be all debts,
Four hundred and four years after
   Christ.

Great warriors, bright-haired, battle-
seasoned,
Will come from Ireland to our aid;
From Lego a fleet of ships will come,
Baneful in battle, rending all before
   them;
From Alclud will come reckless men
To drive the Saxons out of Prydain;
From Llydaw a mighty army,
Warlike warriors who spare not their
   foes.
On every side Saxons will fall,
Their day ended, their stolen lands
   forsworn.
Death, brought hither on warrior's
   blades,
Will pay for the thieving courtiers.

May a hedge be their only haven,
May the sea be their council,
And may blood be their companion.
Cynan and Cadwaladr, leaders of the
   war-band,
Will be praised forever, grace be theirs;
Powerful lords prudent in council,
Crushing the Saxons in the sight of
   God.
Two generous men, gives of land and
   cattle,
Two mighty heroes, bulwarks of
   Prydain,
Bears undaunted by force of battle.

Seers foretell the Saxons will depart.
From Manaw to Llydaw our lands will
   stretch;
From Dyfew to Thanet, will be ours;
From Gwawl to Gweryd, right to the sea
Our sway over Yrechwydd.
The Saxons won't return:
The Irish will rejoin their comrades,
The Cymry will rise a mighty force,
Ale-filled war-bands and soldiers in
   swarms,
God's kings who protected their flocks,
Wessex men in every ship,
Cynan bonding with his comrades.
Soon every man will shout for joy,
That the Saxons are gone –
Only corpses facing the heroes
As far as Sandwich.
Driving out the foreigners,
One after another to the sea,
The Cymry will be one people
From now till doomsday,
Seeking neither druid nor Bard.
None but I foretell this island's future.
Prey to the Lord who made heaven and
   earth:
Let Dewi be our leader,
In Caer Gelli – for God's sake:
Who dies not, hides not, nor ever fails,
Who withers never, bends not, but
   endures.

CHAPTER SIXTEEN

Vita Merlini

Geoffrey of Monmouth

translated by J.J. Parry

MEANWHILE TALIESIN HAD COME to see Merlin the prophet who had sent for him to find out what wind or rainstorm was coming up, for both together were drawing near and the clouds were thickening. He drew the following illustrations under the guidance of Minerva his associate.

'Out of nothing the Creator of the world produced four [elements] that they might be the prior cause as well as the material for creating all things when they were joined together in harmony: the heaven which He adorned with stars and which stands on high and embraces everything like the shell surrounding a nut; then He made the air, fit for forming sounds, through the medium of which day and night present the stars; the sea which girds the land in four circles, and with its mighty refluence so strikes the air as to generate the winds which are said to be four in number; as a foundation He placed the earth, standing by its own strength and not lightly moved, which is divided into five parts, whereof the middle one is not habitable because of the heat and the two furthest are shunned because of their cold. To the last two He gave a moderate temperature and these are inhabited by men and birds and herds of wild beasts. He added clouds to the sky so that they might furnish sudden showers to make the fruits of the trees and of the ground grow with their gentle sprinkling. With the help of the sun these are filled like water skins from the rivers by a hidden law, and then, rising through the upper air, they pour out the water they have taken up, driven by the force of the winds. From them come rain-storms, snow, and round hail when the cold damp wind breathes out its blasts which, penetrating the clouds, drive out the streams just as they make them. Each of the winds takes to itself a nature of its own from its proximity to the zone where it is born. Beyond the firmament in which He fixed the shining stars He placed the ethereal heaven and gave it as a habitation to troops of angels whom the worthy contemplation and marvellous sweetness of God refresh throughout the ages. This also He adorned with stars and the shining sun, laying down the law, by which the star should run within fixed limits through the part of heaven entrusted to it. He afterwards placed beneath this the airy heavens, shining with the lunar body, which throughout their high places abound in troops of spirits who sympathize or rejoice with us as things go well or ill. They are accustomed to carry the prayers of men through the air and to beseech God to have mercy on them, and to bring back intimations of God's will, either in dreams or by voice or by other signs, through doing which they become wise. The space beyond the moon abounds in evil demons, who are skilled to cheat and deceive and tempt us; often they assume a body made of air and appear to us and many things often follow. They even hold intercourse with women and make them pregnant, generating in an unholy manner. So therefore He made the heavens to be inhabited by three orders of spirits that each one might look out for something and renew the world from the renewed seed of things.

'The sea too He distinguished by various forms that from itself it might produce the forms of things, generating throughout the ages. Indeed, part of it burns and part freezes and the third part, getting a moderate temperature from the other two, ministers to our needs. That part which burns surrounds a gulf and fierce people, and its divers streams, flowing back, separate this from the orb of earth, increasing fire from fire. Thither descend those who transgress the laws and reject God; whither their perverse will leads them they go, eager to destroy what is forbidden to them. There stands the stern-eyed judge holding his equal balance and giving to each one his merits and his deserts. The second part, which freezes, rolls about the foreshorn sands which it is the first to generate from the near-by vapor when it is mingled with the rays of Venus's star. This star, the Arabs say, makes shining gems when it passes through the Fishes while its waters look back at the flames. These gems by their virtues benefit the people who wear them, and make many well and keep them so. These too the Maker distinguished by their kinds (as He did all things), that we might discern from their forms and from their colors of what kinds they are and of what manifest virtues. The third form of the sea which circles our orb furnishes us many good things owing to its proximity. For it nourishes fishes and produces salt in abundance, and bears back and forth ships carrying our commerce, by the profits of which the poor man becomes suddenly rich. It makes fertile the neighboring soil and feeds the birds who, they say, are generated from it along with the fishes and, although unlike, are moved by the laws of nature. The sea is dominated by them more than by the fishes, and they fly lightly up from it through space and seek the lofty regions. But its moisture drives the fishes beneath the waves and keeps them there, and does not permit them to live when they get out into the dry light. These too the Maker distinguished according to their species and to the different ones gave each his nature, whence through the ages they were to become admirable and healthful to the sick.

'For men say that the barbel restrains the heat of passion but makes blind those who eat it often. The thymallus, which has its name from the flower thyme, smells so that it betrays the fish that often eats of it until all the fishes in the river smell like itself. They say that the muraenas, contrary to all laws, are all of the feminine sex, yet they copulate and reproduce and multiply their offspring from a different kind of seed. For often snakes come together along the shore where they are, and they make the sound of pleasing hissing and, calling out the muraenas, join with them according to custom. It is also remarkable that the remora, half a foot long, holds fast the ship to which it adheres at sea just as though it were fast aground, and does not permit the vessel to move until it lets go; because of this power it is to be feared. And that which they call the swordfish because it does injury with its sharp beak, people often fear to approach with a ship when it is swimming, for if it is captured it at once makes a hole in the vessel, cuts it in pieces, and sinks it suddenly in a whirlpool. The serra makes itself feared by ships because of its crest; it fixes to them as it swims underneath, cuts them to pieces and throws the pieces into the waves, wherefore its crest is to be feared like a sword. And the water dragon, which men say has poison under its wings, is to be feared by those who capture it; whenever it strikes it does harm by pouring out its poison. The torpedo is said to have another kind of destruction, for if any one touches it when it is alive, straightway his arms and his feet grow torpid and so do his other members and they lose their functions just as though they were dead, so harmful is the emanation of its body.

'To those and the other fishes God gave the sea, and He added to it many realms among the waves, which men inhabit and which are renowned because of the fertility which the earth produces there from its fruitful soil. Of these Britain is said to be the foremost and best, producing in its fruitfulness every single thing. For it bears crops which throughout the year give the noble gifts of fragrance for the use of man, and it has woods and glades with honey dripping in them, and lofty mountains and broad green fields, fountains and rivers, fishes and cattle and wild beasts, fruit trees, gems, precious metals, and whatever creative nature is in the habit of furnishing. Besides all these it has fountains healthful because of their hot waters which nourish the sick and provide pleasing baths, which quickly send people away cured with their sickness driven out. So Bladud established them when he held the scepter of the kingdom, and he gave them the name of his consort Alaron. These are of value to many sick because of the healing of their water, but most of all to women, as often the water has demonstrated. Near to this island lies Thanet which abounds in many things but lacks the death-dealing serpent, and if any of its earth is drunk mixed with wine it takes away poison. Our ocean also divides the Orkneys from us. These are divided into thirty-three islands by the sundering flood; twenty lack cultivation and the others are cultivated. Thule receives its name "furthest" from the sun, because of the solstice which the summer sun makes there, turning its rays and shining no further, and taking away the day, so that always throughout the long night the air is full of shadows, and making a bridge congealed by the benumbing cold, which prevents the passage of ships.

'The most outstanding island after our own is said to be Ireland with its happy fertility. It is larger and produces no bees, and no birds except rarely, and it does not permit snakes to breed in it. Whence it happens that if earth or a stone is carried away from there and added to any other place it drives away snakes and bees. The island of Gades lies next to Herculean Gades, and there grows there a tree from whose bark a gum drips out of which gems are made, breaking all laws. The Hesperides are said to contains a watchful dragon who, men say, guards the golden apples under the leaves. The Gorgades are inhabited by women with goats' bodies who are said to surpass hares in the swiftness of their running. Argyre and Chryse bear, it is said, gold and silver just as Corinth does common stones. Ceylon blooms pleasantly because of its fruitful soil, for it produces two crops in a single year; twice it is summer, twice spring, twice men gather grapes and other fruits, and it is also most pleasing because of its shining gems. Tiles produces flowers and fruits in an eternal spring, green throughout the seasons.

'The island of apples which men call "The Fortunate Isle" gets its name from the fact because it produces all things of itself; the fields there have no need of the ploughs of the farmers and all cultivation is lacking except what nature provides. Of its own accord it produces grain and grapes, and apple trees grow in its woods from the close-clipped grass. The ground of its own accord produces everything instead of merely grass, and people live there a hundred years or more. There nine sisters rule by a pleasing set of laws those who come to them from our country. She who is first of them is more skilled in the healing art, and excels her sisters in the beauty of her person. Morgen is her name, and she has learned what useful properties all the herbs contain, so that she can cure sick bodies. She also knows an art by which to change her shape, and to cleave the air on new wings like Daedalus; when she wishes she is at Brest, Chartres, or Pavia, and when she wills she slips down from the air onto your shores. And men say that she has taught mathematics to her sisters, Moronoe, Mazoe, Gliten, Glitonea, Gliton, Tyronoe, Thitis, Thitis best known for her cither. Thither after the battle of Camlan we took the wounded Arthur, guided by Barinthus to whom the waters and the stars of heaven were well known. With him steering the ship we arrived there with the prince, and Morgen received us with fitting honor, and in her chamber she placed the king on a golden bed and with her own hand she uncovered his honorable wound and gazed at it for a long time. At length she said that health could be restored to him if he stayed with her for a long time and made use of her healing art. Rejoicing, therefore, we entrusted the king to her and returning spread our sails to the favoring winds.'

Merlin said in answer: 'Dear friend, since that time how much the kingdom has endured from the violated oath, so that what it once was it no longer is! For by an evil fate the nobles are roused up and turned against each other's vitals, and they upset everything so that the abundance of riches has fled from the country and all goodness has departed, and the desolated citizens leave their walls empty. Upon them shall come the Saxon people, fierce in war, who shall again cruelly overthrow us and our cities, and shall violate God's law and his temples. For He shall certainly permit this destruction to come upon us because of our crimes that He may correct the foolish.'

Merlin had scarcely finished when Taliesin exclaimed, 'Then the people should send some one to tell the chief to come back in a swift ship if he has recovered his strength, that he may drive off the enemy with his accustomed vigor and reestablish the citizens in their former peace.'

'No,' said Merlin, 'not thus shall this people depart when once they have fixed their claws on our shores. For at first they shall enslave our kingdom and our people and our cities, and shall dominate them with their forces for many years. Nevertheless three from among our people shall resist with much courage and shall kill many, and in the end shall overcome them. But they shall not continue thus, for it is the will of the highest Judge that the Britons shall through weakness lose their noble kingdom for a long time, until Conan shall come in his chariot from Brittany, and Cadwalader the venerated leader of the Welsh, who shall join together Scots and Cumbrians, Cornishmen and men of Brittany in a firm league, and shall return to their people their lost crown, expelling the enemy and renewing the times of Brutus, and shall deal with the cities in accordance with their consecrated laws. And the kings shall begin again to conquer remote peoples and to subjugate their own realms to themselves in mighty conflict.' 'No one shall then be alive of those who are now living,' said Taliesin, 'nor do I think that any one has seen so many savage battles between fellow citizens as you have.' 'That is so,' said Merlin, 'for I have lived a long time, seeing many of them, both of our own people among themselves and of the barbarians who disturb everything.

'And I remember the crime when Constans was betrayed and the small brothers Uther and Ambrosius fled across the water. At once wars began in the kingdom which now lacked a leader, for Vortigern of Gwent, the consul, was leading his troops against all the nations so that he might have the leadership of them, and was inflicting a wretched death upon the harmless peasants. At length with sudden violence he seized the crown after putting to death many of the nobles and he subdued the whole kingdom to himself. But those who were allied to the brothers by blood relationship, offended at this, began to set fire to all the cities of the ill-fated prince and to perturb his kingdom with savage soldiery, and they would not withstand the rebellious people, he prepared to invite to the war men from far away with whose aid he might be able to meet his enemies. Soon there came from divers parts of the world warlike bands whom he received with honor. The Saxon people, in fact, arriving in their curved keels had come to serve him with their helmeted soldiery. They were led by two courageous brothers, Horsus and Hengist, who afterwards with wicked treachery harmed the people and the cities. For after this, by serving the king with industry, they won him over to themselves, and seeing the people moved by a quarrel that touched them closely they were able to subjugate the king; then turning their ferocious arms upon the people they broke faith and killed the princes by a premeditated fraud while they were sitting with them after calling them together to make peace and a treaty with them, and the prince they drove over the top of the snowy mountain. These are the things I had begun to prophesy to him would happen to the kingdom. Next roaming abroad they set fire to the houses of the nation, and strove to make everything subject to themselves. But when Vortimer saw how great was the peril of his country, and saw his father expelled from the hall of Brutus, he took the crown, with the assent of the people, and attacked the savage tribes that were crushing them, and by many battles forced these to return to Thanet where the fleet was that had brought them. But in their flight fell the warrior Horsus and many others, slain by our men. The king followed them and, taking his stand before Thanet besieged it by land and sea, but without success, for the enemy suddenly got possession of their fleet and with violence broke out and, led over the sea, they regained their own country in haste. Therefore, since he had conquered the enemy in victorious war, Vortimer became a ruler to be respected in the world, and he treated his kingdom with just restraint. But Hengist's sister, Rowena, seeing with indignation these successes, and protected by deceit, mixed poison, becoming on her brother's account a malignant step-mother, and she gave it to Vortimer to drink, and killed him by the draught. At once she sent across the water to her brother to tell him to come back with so many and such great multitudes that he would be able to conquer the warlike natives. This therefore he did, for he came with such force against our army that he took booty from everybody until he was loaded with it, and he thoroughly destroyed by fire the houses throughout the country.

'While these things were happening Uther and Ambrosius were in Breton territory with King Biducus and they had already girded on their swords and were proved fit for war, and had associated with themselves troops from all directions so that they might seek their native land and put to flight the people who were busy wasting their patrimony. So they gave their boats to the wind and the sea, and landed for the protection of their subjects; they drove Vortigern through the regions of Wales and shut him up in his tower and burned both him and it. Then they turned their swords upon the Angles and many times when they met them they defeated them, and on the other hand they were often defeated by them. At length in a hand to hand conflict our men with great effort attacked the enemy and defeated them decisively, and killed Hengist, and by the will of Christ they triumphed.

'After these things had been done, the kingdom and its crown were with the approval of clergy and laity given to Ambrosius, and he ruled justly in all things, but after the space of four years had elapsed he was betrayed by his doctor and died from drinking poison. His younger brother Uther succeeded him, and at first was unable to maintain his kingdom in peace, for the perfidious people, accustomed by now to return, came and laid waste everything with their usual phalanx. Uther fought them in savage battles and drove them conquered across the water with returning oars. Soon he put aside strife and re-established peace and begat a son who afterwards was so eminent that he was second to none in uprightness. Arthur was his name and he held the kingdom for many years after the death of his father Uther, and this he did with great grief and labor, and with the slaughter of many men in many wars. For while the aforesaid chief lay ill, from Anglia came a faithless people who with the sword subdued all the country and the regions across the Humber. Arthur was a boy and on account of his youth he was not able to defeat such a force. Therefore after seeking the advice of clergy and laity he sent to Hoel, King of Brittany, and asked him to come to his aid with a swift fleet, for they were united by ties of blood and friendship, so that each was bound to relieve the distresses of the other. Hoel therefore quickly collected for the war fierce men from every side and came to us with many thousands, and joining with Arthur he attacked the enemy often, and drove them back and made a terrible slaughter. With his help Arthur was secure and strong among all the troops when he attacked the enemy whom at length he conquered and forced to return to their own country, and he quieted his own kingdom by the moderation of his laws.

'Soon after this struggle he changed the scene of the war, and subdued the Scots and Irish and all these warlike countries by means of the forces he had brought. He also subjugated the Norwegians far away across the broad seas, and the Danes whom he had visited with his hated fleet. He conquered the people of the Gauls after killing Frollo to whom the Roman power had given the care of that country; the Romans, too, who were seeking to make war on his country, he fought against and conquered, and killed the Procurator Hiberius Lucius who was then a colleague of Legnis the general, and who by the command of the Senate had come to bring the territories of the Gauls under their power. Meanwhile the faithless and foolish custodian Modred had commenced to subdue our kingdom to himself, and was making unlawful love to the king's wife. For the king, desiring, as men say, to go across the water to attack the enemy, had entrusted the queen and the kingdom to him. But when the report of such a great evil came to his ears, he put aside his interest in the wars and, returning home, landed with many thousand men and fought with his nephew and drove him flying across the water. There the traitor, after collecting Saxons from all sides, began to battle with his lord, but he fell, betrayed by the unholy people confiding in whom he had undertaken such big things. How great was the slaughter of men and the grief of women whose sons fell in that battle! After it the king, mortally wounded, left his kingdom and, sailing across the water with you as you have related, came to the court of the maidens. Each of the two sons of Modred, desiring to conquer the kingdom for himself, began to wage war and each in turn slew those who were near of kin to him. Then Duke Constantine, nephew of the king, rose up fiercely against them and ravaged the people and the cities, and after having killed both of them by a cruel death ruled over the people and assumed the crown. But he did not continue in peace since Conan his relative waged dire war on him and ravaged everything and killed the king and seized for himself those lands which he now governs weakly and without a plan.'

CHAPTER SEVENTEEN

The Prophecies of Merlin

compiled by Geoffrey of Monmouth

BOOK VII
Concerning the Prophecies of Merlin

Chapter I – Geoffrey of Monmouth's preface to Merlin's prophecy

I had not got thus far in my history, when the subject of public discourse happening to be concerning Merlin, I was obliged to publish his prophecies at the request of my acquaintance, but especially of Alexander, bishop of Lincoln, a prelate of the greatest piety and wisdom. There was not any person, either among the clergy or laity, that was attended with such a train of knights and noblemen, whom his settled piety and great munificence engaged in his service. Out of a desire, therefore, to gratify him, I translated these prophecies, and sent them to him with the following letter.

Chapter II – Geoffrey's letter to Alexander, bishop of Lincoln

The regard which I owe to your great worth, most noble prelate, has obliged me to undertake the translation of Merlin's prophecies out of British into Latin, before I had made an end of the history which I had begun concerning the acts of the British kings. For my design was to have finished that first, and afterwards to have taken this work in hand; lest by being engaged on both at once, I should be less capable of attending with any exactness to either. Notwithstanding, since the deference which is paid to your penetrating judgement will screen me from censure, I have employed my rude pen, and in a coarse style present you with a translation out of a language with which you are unacquainted. At the same time, I cannot but wonder at your recommending this matter to one of my low genius, when you might have caused so many men of greater learning, and a richer vein of intellect, to undertake it; who, with their sublime strains, would much more agreeably have entertained you. Besides, without any disparagement to all the philosophers in Britain, I must take the liberty to say, that you yourself, if the business of your high station would give you leisure, are capable of furnishing us with loftier productions of this kind than any man living. However, since it was your pleasure that Geoffrey of Monmouth should be employed in this prophecy, he hopes you will favourably accept of his performance, and vouchsafe to give a finer turn to whatever you shall find unpolished, or otherwise faulty in it.

Chapter III – The prophecy of Merlin

As Vortigern, king of the Britons, was sitting upon the bank of the drained pond, the two dragons, one of which was white, the other red, came forth, and, approaching one another, began a terrible fight, and cast forth fire with their breath. But the white dragon had the advantage, and made the other fly to the end of the lake. And he, for grief at his flight, renewed the assault upon his pursuer, and forced him to retire. After this battle of the dragons, the king commanded Ambrose Merlin to tell him what it portended. Upon which he, bursting into tears, delivered what his prophetical spirit suggested to him, as follows:[1]

'Woe to the red dragon, for his banishment hasteneth on. His lurking holes shall be siezed by the white dragon, which signifies the Saxons whom you invited over; but the red denotes the British nation, which shall be oppressed by the white. Therefore shall its mountains be levelled as the valleys, and the rivers of the valleys shall run with blood. The exercise of religion shall be destroyed, and churches be laid open to ruin. At last the oppressed shall prevail, and oppose the cruelty of foreigners. For a boar of Cornwall shall give his assistance, and trample their necks under his feet. The islands of the ocean shall be subject to his power, and he shall possess the forests of Gaul. The house of Romulus shall dread his courage, and his end shall be doubtful. He shall be celebrated in the mouths of the people; and his exploits shall be food to those that relate them. Six of his posterity shall sway the sceptre, but after them shall arise a German worm. He shall be advanced by a sea-wolf, whom the woods of Africa shall accompany. Religion shall be again abolished, and there shall be a translation of the metropolitan sees. The dignity of London shall adorn Dorobernia, and the seventh pastor of York shall be resorted to in the kingdom of Armorica. Menevia shall put on the pall of the City of Legions, and a preacher of Ireland shall be dumb on account of an infant growing in the womb. It shall rain a shower of blood, and a raging famine shall afflict mankind. When these things happen, the red one shall be grieved; but when his fatigue is over, shall grow strong. Then shall misfortunes hasten upon the white one, and the buildings of his gardens shall be pulled down. Seven that sway the sceptre shall be killed, one of whom shall become a saint. The wombs of mothers shall be ripped up, and infants be abortive. There shall be a most grievous punishment of men, that the natives may be restored. He that shall do these things shall put on the brazen man, and upon a brazen horse shall for a long time guard the gates of London. After this, shall the red dragon return to his proper manners, and turn his rage upon himself. Therefore shall the revenge of the Thunderer show itself, for every field shall disappoint the husbandmen. Mortality shall snatch away the people, and make a desolation over all countries. The remainder shall quit their native soil, and make foreign plantations. A blessed king shall prepare a fleet, and shall be reckoned the twelfth in the court among the saints. There shall be a miserable desolation of the kingdom, and the floors of the harvests shall return to the fruitful forests. The white dragon shall rise again, and invite over a daughter of Germany. Our gardens shall be again replenished with foreign seed, and the red one shall pine away at the end of the pond. After that, shall the German worm be crowned, and the brazen prince buried. He has his bounds assigned him, which he shall not be able to pass. For a hundred and fifty years he shall continue in trouble and subjection, but shall bear sway three hundred. Then shall the north wind rise against him, and shall snatch away the flowers which the west wind produced. There shall be gilding in the temples, nor shall the edge of the sword cease. The German dragon shall hardly get to his holes, because the revenge of his treason shall overtake him. At last he shall flourish for a little time, but the decimation of Neustria shall hurt him. For a people in wood and in iron coats shall come, and revenge upon him his wickedness. They shall restore the ancient inhabitants to their dwellings, and there shall be

261

an open destruction of foreigners. The seed of the white dragon shall be swept out of our gardens, and the remainder of his generation shall be decimated. They shall bear the yoke of slavery, and wound their mother with spades and ploughs. After this shall succeed two dragons, whereof one shall be killed with the sting of envy, but the other shall return under the shadow of a name. Then shall succeed a lion of justice, at whose roar the Gallican towers and the island dragons shall tremble. In those days gold shall be squeezed from the lily and the nettle, and silver shall flow from the hoofs of bellowing cattle. The frizzled shall put on various fleeces, and the outward habit denote the inward parts. The feet of barkers shall be cut off; wild beasts shall enjoy peace; mankind shall be grieved at their punishment; the form of commerce shall be divided; the half shall be round. The ravenousness of kites shall be destroyed, and the teeth of wolves blunted. The lion's whelps shall be transformed into sea-fishes; and an eagle shall build her nest upon Mount Aravius. Venedotia shall grow red with the blood of mothers, and the house of Corineus kill six brethren. The island shall be wet with night tears; so that all shall be provoked to all things. Woe to thee, Neustria, because the lion's brain shall be poured upon thee; and he shall be banished with shattered limbs from his native soil. Posterity shall endeavour to fly above the highest places; but the favour of new comers shall be exalted. Piety shall hurt the possessor of things got by impiety, till he shall have put on his Father: therefore, being armed with the teeth of a boar, he shall ascend above the tops of mountains, and the shadow of him that wears a helmet. Albania shall be enraged, and, assembling her neighbours, shall be employed in shedding blood. There shall be put into her jaws a bridle that shall be made on the coast of Armorica. The eagle of the broken covenant shall gild it over, and rejoice in her third nest. The roaring whelps shall watch, and, leaving the woods, shall hunt within the walls of cities. They shall make no small slaughter of those that oppose them, and shall cut off the tongues of bulls. They shall load the necks of roaring lions with chains, and restore the times of their ancestors. Then from the first to the fourth, from the fourth to the third, from the third to the second, the thumb shall roll in oil. The sixth shall overturn the walls of Ireland, and change the woods into a plain. He shall reduce several parts to one, and be crowned with the head of a lion. His beginning shall lay open to wandering affection, but his end shall carry him up to the blessed, who are above. For he shall restore the seats of saints in their countries, and settle pastors in convenient places. Two cities he shall invest with two palls, and shall bestow virgin-presents upon virgins. He shall merit by this the favour of the Thunderer, and shall be placed among the saints. From him shall proceed a lynx penetrating all things, who shall be bent upon the ruin of his own nation; for, through him, Neustria shall lose both islands, and be deprived of its ancient dignity. Then shall the natives return back to the island; for there shall arise a dissension among foreigners. Also a hoary old man, sitting upon a snow-white horse, shall turn the course of the river Periron, and shall measure out a mill upon it with a white rod. Cadwallader shall call upon Conan, and take Albania into alliance. Then shall there be a slaughter of foreigners; then shall the rivers run with blood. Then shall break forth the fountains of Armorica, and they shall be crowned with the diadem of Brutus. Cambria shall be filled with joy; and the oaks of Cornwall shall flourish. The island shall be called by the name of Brutus: and the name given it by foreigners shall be abolished. From Conan shall proceed a warlike boar, that shall exercise the sharpness of his tusks within the Gallic woods. For he shall cut down all the larger oaks, and shall be a defence to the smaller. The Arabians and Africans shall dread him; for he shall pursue his furious course to the farther part of Spain. There shall succeed the goat of the Venereal castle, having golden horns and a silver beard, who shall breathe such a cloud out of his nostrils, as shall darken the whole surface of the island. There shall be peace in his time; and corn shall abound by reason of the fruitfulness of the soil. Women shall become serpents in their gait, and all their motions shall be full of pride. The camp of Venus shall be restored; nor shall the arrows of Cupid cease to wound. The fountain of a river shall be turned into blood; and two kings shall fight a duel at Stafford for a lioness. Luxury shall overspread the whole ground; and fornication not cease to debauch mankind. All these things shall three ages see; till the buried kings shall be exposed to public view in the city of London. Famine shall again return; mortality shall return; and the inhabitants shall grieve for the destruction of their cities. Then shall come the board of commerce, who shall recall the scattered flocks to the pasture they had lost. His breast shall be food to the hungry, and his tongue drink to the thirsty. Out or his mouth shall flow rivers, that shall water the parched jaws of men. After this shall be produced a tree upon the Tower of London, which, having no more than three branches, shall overshadow the surface of the whole island with the breadth of its leaves. Its adversary, the north wind, shall come upon it, and with its noxious blast shall snatch away the third branch; but the two remaining ones shall possess its place, till they shall destroy one another by the multitude of their leaves; and then shall it obtain the place of those two, and shall give sustenance to birds of foreign nations. It shall be esteemed hurtful to native fowls; for they shall not be able to fly freely for fear of its shadow. There shall succeed the ass of wickedness, swift against the goldsmiths, but slow against the ravenousness of wolves. In those days the oaks of the forests shall burn, and acorns grow upon the branches of teil trees. The Seven sea shall discharge itself through seven mouths, and the river Uske burn seven months. Fishes shall die with the heat thereof; and of them shall be engendered serpents. The baths of Badon shall grow cold, and their salubrious waters engender death. London shall mourn for the death of twenty thousand; and the river Thames shall be turned into blood. The monks in their cowls shall be forced to marry, and their cry shall be heard upon the mountains of the Alps.'

Chapter IV – The continuation of the prophecy

Three springs shall break forth in the city of Winchester, whose rivulets shall divide the island into three parts. Whoever shall drink of the first, shall enjoy long life, and shall never be afflicted with sickness. He that shall drink of the second, shall die of hunger, and paleness and horror shall sit in his countenance. He that shall drink of the third, shall be surprised with sudden death, neither shall his body be capable of burial. Those that are willing to escape so great a surfeit, will endeavour to hide it with several coverings, but whatever bulk shall be laid upon it, shall receive the form of another body. For earth shall be turned into stones; stones into water; wood into ashes; ashes into water, if cast over it. Also a damsel shall be sent from the city of the forest of Canute to administer a cure, who, after she shall have practised all her arts, shall dry up the noxious fountains only with her breath. Afterwards, as soon as she shall have refreshed herself with the wholesome liqour, she shall bear in her right hand the wood of Caledon, and in her left the forts of the walls of London. Wherever she shall go, she shall make sulphureous steps, which will smoke with a double flame. That smoke shall rouse up the city of Ruteni, and shall make food for the inhabitants of the deep. She shall overflow with rueful tears, and shall fill the island with her dreadful cry. She shall be killed by a hart with ten branches, four of which shall bear golden diadems; but the other six shall be turned into buffalo's horns, whose hideous sound shall astonish the three islands, of Britain. The Daneian wood shall be stirred up, and breaking forth into a human voice, shall cry: Come, O Cambria, and join Cornwall to thy side, and say to Winchester, the earth shall swallow thee up. Translate the seat of thy pastor to the place where ships come to harbour, and the rest of the members will follow the head. For the day hasteneth, in which thy citizens shall perish on account of the guilt of perjury. The whiteness of wool has been hurtful to thee, and the variety of its tinctures. Woe to the perjured nation, for whose sake the renowned city shall come to ruin. The ships shall rejoice at so great an augmentation, and one shall be made out of two. It shall be rebuilt by Eric, loaden with apples, to the smell whereof the birds of several woods shall flock together. He shall add to it a vast palace, and wall it round with six hundred towers. Therefore shall London envy it, and triply increase her walls. The river Thames shall encompass it round, and the fame of the work shall pass beyond the Alps. Eric shall hide his apples within it, and shall make subterraneous passages. At that time shall the stoues speak, and the sea towards the Gallic coast be contracted into a narrow space. On each bank shall one man hear another, and the soil of the island shall be enlarged. The secrets of the deep shall be revealed, and Gaul shall tremble for fear. After these things shall come forth a hern from the forest of Calaterium, which shall fly round the island for two years together. With her nocturnal cry she shall call together the winged kind, and assemble to her all sorts of fowls. They shall invade the tillage of husbandmen, and devour all the grain of the harvests. Then shall follow a famine upon the people, and a grievous mortality upon the famine. But when this calamity shall be over, a detestable bird shall go to the valley of Galabes, and shall raise it to be a high mountain. Upon the top thereof it shall also plant an oak, and build its nest in its branches. Three eggs shall be produced in the nest, from whence shall come forth a fox, a wolf, and a bear. The fox shall devour her mother, and bear the head of an ass. In this monstrous form shall she frighten her brothers, and make them fly into Neustria. But they shall stir up the tusky boar, and returning in a fleet shall encounter with the fox; who at the beginning of the fight shall feign herself dead, and move the boar to compassion. Then shall the boar approach her carcass, and standing over her, shall breathe upon her face and eyes. But she, not forgetting her cunning, shall bite his left foot, and pluck it off from his body. Then shall she leap upon him, and snatch away his right ear and tail, and hide herself in the caverns of the mountains. Therefore shall the deluded boar require the wolf and bear to restore him his members; who, as soon as they shall enter into the cause, shall promise two feet of the fox, together with the ear and tail, and of these they shall make up the members of a hog. With this he shall be satisfied, and expect the promised restitution. In the meantime shall the fox descend from the mountains, and change herself into a wolf, and under pretence of holding a conference with the boar, she shall go to him and craftily devour him. After that she shall transform herself into a boar, and feigning a loss of some members, shall wait for her brothers; but as soon as they are come, she shall suddenly kill them with her tusks, and shall be crowned with the head of a lion. In her days shall a serpent be brought forth, which shall be a destroyer of mankind. With its length it shall encompass London, and devour all that pass by it. The mountain ox shall take the head of a wolf, and whiten his teeth in the Severn. He shall gather to him the flocks of Albania and Cambria, which shall drink the river Thames dry. The ass shall call the goat with the long beard, and shall borrow his shape. Therefore shall the mountain ox be incensed, and having called the wolf, shall become a horned bull against them. In the exercise of his cruelty he shall devour their flesh and bones, but shall be burned upon the top of Urian. The ashes of his funeral-pile shall be turned into swans, that shall swim on dry ground as on a river. They shall devour fishes in fishes, and swallow up men in men. But when old age shall come upon them, they shall become sea-wolves, and practise their frauds in the deep. They shall drown ships, and collect no small quantity of silver. The Thames shall again flow, and assembling together the rivers, shall pass beyond the bounds of its channel. It shall cover the adjacent cities, and overturn the mountains that oppose its course. Being full of deceit and wickedness, it shall make use of the fountain Galabes. Hence shall arise factions provoking the Venedotians to

war. The oaks of the forest shall meet together, and encounter the rocks of the Gewisseans.
A raven shall attend with the kites, and devour the carcasses of the slain. An owl shall build
her nest upon the walls of Gloucester, and in her nest shall be brought forth an ass. The serpent
of Malvernia shall bring him up, and put him upon many fraudulent practices. Having taken
the crown, he shall ascend on high, and frighten the people of the country with his hideous
braying. In his days shall the Pachaian mountains tremble, and the provinces be deprived of
their woods. For there shall come a worm with a fiery breath, and with the vapour it sends
forth shall burn up the trees. Out of it shall proceed seven lions deformed with the heads of
goats. With the stench of their nostrils they shall corrupt women, and make wives turn
common prostitutes. The father shall not know his own son, because they shall grow wanton
like brute breasts. Then shall come the giant of wickedness, and terrify all with the sharpness
of his eyes. Against him shall arise the dragon of Worcester, and shall endeavour to banish
him. But in the engagement the dragon shall be worsted, and oppressed by the wickedness
of the conqueror. For he shall mount upon the dragon, and putting off his garment shall sit
upon him naked. The dragon shall bear him up on high, and beat his naked rider with his
tail erected. Upon this the giant rousing up his whole strength, shall break his jaws with his
sword. At least the dragon shall fold itself up under its tail, and die of poison. After him shall
succeed the boar of Totness, and oppress the people with grievous tyranny. Gloucester shall
send forth a lion, and shall disturb him in his cruelty, in several battles. He shall trample him
under his feet, and terrify him with open jaws. At last the lion shall quarrel with the kingdom,
and get upon the backs of the nobility. A bull shall come into the quarrel, and strike the lion
with his right foot. He shall drive him through all the inns in the kingdom, but shall break
his horns against the walls of Oxford. The fox of Kaerdubalem shall take revenge on the lion,
and destroy him entirely with her teeth. She shall be encompassed by the adder of Lincoln,
who with a horrible hiss shall give notice of his presence to a multitude of dragons. Then shall
the dragons encounter, and tear one another to pieces. The winged shall oppress that which
wants wings, and fasten its claws into the poisonous cheeks. Others shall come into the
quarrel, and kill one another. A fifth shall succeed those that are slain, and by various stratagems
shall destroy the rest. He shall get upon the back of one with his sword, and sever his head
from his body. Then throwing off his garment, he shall get upon another, and put his right
and left hand upon his tail. Thus being naked shall he overcome him, whom when clothed
he was not able to deal with. The rest he shall gall in their flight, and drive them round the
kingdom. Upon this shall come a roaring lion dreadful for his monstrous cruelty. Fifteen parts
shall he reduce to one, and shall alone possess the people. The giant of the snow-white colour
shall shine, and cause the white people to flourish. Pleasures shall effeminate the princes, and
they shall suddenly be changed into beasts. Among them shall arise a lion swelled with human
gore. Under him shall a reaper be placed in the standing corn, who, while he is reaping, shall
be oppressed by him. A charioteer of York shall appease them, and having banished his lord,
shall mount upon the chariot which he shall drive. With his sword unsheathed shall he
threaten the East, and fill the tracks of his wheels with blood. Afterwards he shall become a
sea-fish, who, being roused up with the hissing of a serpent, shall engender with him. From
hence shall be produced three thundering bulls, who having eaten up their pastures shall be
turned into trees. The first shall carry a whip of vipers, and turn his back upon the next. He
shall endeavour to snatch away the whip, but shall be taken by the last. They shall turn away
their faces from one another, till they have thrown away the poisoned cup. To him shall
succeed a husbandman of Albania, at whose back shall be a serpent. He shall be employed in
ploughing the ground, that the country may become white with corn. The serpent shall

endeavour to diffuse his poison, in order to blast the harvest. A grievous mortality shall sweep away the people, and the walls of cities shall be made desolate. There shall be given for a remedy the city of Claudius, which shall interpose the nurse of the scourger. For she shall bear a dose of medicine, and in a short time the island shall be restored. Then shall two successively sway the sceptre, whom a horned dragon shall serve. One shall come in armour, and shall ride upon a flying serpent. He shall sit upon his back with his naked body, and cast his right hand upon his tail. With his cry shall the seas be moved, and he shall strike terror into the second. The second therefore shall enter into confederacy with the lion; but a quarrel happening, they shall encounter one another. They shall distress one another, but the courage of the beast shall gain the advantage. Then shall come one with a drum, and appease the rage of the lion. Therefore shall the people of the kingdom be at peace, and provoke the lion to a dose of physic. In his established seat he shall adjust the weights, but shall stretch out his hands into Albania. For which reason the northern provinces shall be grieved, and open the gates of the temples. The sign-bearing wolf shall lead his troops, and surround Cornwall with his tail. He shall be opposed by a soldier in a chariot, who shall transform that people into a boar. The boar shall therefore ravage the provinces, but shall hide his head in the depth of Severn. A man shall embrace a lion in wine, and the dazzling brightness of gold shall blind the eyes of beholders. Silver shall whiten in the circumference, and torment several wine presses. Men shall be drunk with wine, and, regardless of heaven, shall be intent upon the earth. From them shall the stars turn away their faces, and confound their usual course. Corn will wither at their malign aspects; and there shall fall no dew from heaven. The roots and branches will change their places, and the novelty of the thing shall pass for a miracle. The brightness of the sun shall fade at the amber of Mercury, and horror shall seize the beholders. Stilbon of Arcadia shall change his shield; the helmet of Mars shall call Venus. The helmet of Mars shall make a shadow; and the rage of Mercury pass his bounds. Iron Orion shall unsheath his sword: the marine Phoebus shall torment the clouds; Jupiter shall go out of his lawful paths; and Venus forsake her stated lines. The malignity of the star Saturn shall fall down in rain, and slay mankind with a crooked sickle. The twelve houses of the star shall lament the irregular excursions of their guests; and Gemini omit their usual embraces, and call the urn to the fountains. The scales of Libra shall hang obliquely, till Aries puts his crooked horns under them. The tail of Scorpio shall produce lightning, and Cancer quarrel with the Sun. Virgo shall mount upon the back of Sagittarius, and darken her virgin flowers. The chariot of the Moon shall disorder the zodiac, and the Pleiades break forth into weeping. No offices of Janus shall hereafter return, but his gate being shut shall lie hid in the chinks of Ariadne. The seas shall rise up in the twinkling of an eye, and the dust of the ancients shall be restored. The winds shall fight together with a dreadful blast, and their sound shall reach the stars.

Note

1 The prophecy which follows has been commented on by various writers, who have taken the trouble to point out the events in English history which answer to the various predictions which it contains. Such labour seems to be altogether superfluous in the present day: the prophecy may be allowed to remain as an illustration of the absurd credulity of former times.

CHAPTER EIGHTEEN

The Poems of Suibhne Geilt

translated by J.G. O'Keefe

A year to last night
have I been among the gloom of branches,
between flood and ebb,
without covering around me.

Without a pillow beneath my head,
among the fair children of men;
there is peril to us, O God,
without sword, without spear.

Without the company of women;
save brooklime of warrior-bands –
a pure fresh meal –
watercress is our desire.

Without a foray with a king,
I am alone in my home,
without glorious reavings,
without friends, without music.

Without sleep, alas!
let the truth be told,
without aid for a long time,
hard is my lot.

Without a house right full,
without the converse of generous men,
without the title of king,
without drink, without food.

Alas that I have been parted here
from my mighty, armed host,
a bitter madman in the glen,
bereft of sense and reason.

Without being on a kingly circuit,
but rushing along every path;
that is the great madness,
O King of Heaven of saints.

Without accomplished musicians,
without the converse of women,
without bestowing treasures;
it has caused my death, O revered Christ.

Though I be as I am tonight,
there was a time
when my strength was not feeble
over a land that was not bad.

On splendid steeds,
in life without sorrow,
in my auspicious kingship
I was a good, great king.

After that, to be as I am
through selling Thee, O revered Christ!
a poor wretch am I, without power,
in the Glen of bright Bolcan.

The hawthorn that is not soft-topped
has subdued me, has pierced me;
the brown thorn-bush
has nigh caused my death.

The battle of Congal with fame,
to us it was doubly piteous;
on Tuesday was the rout;
more numerous were our dead than our living.

A-wandering in truth,
though I was noble and gentle,
I have been sad and wretched
a year to last night.

* * *

Cold is the snow tonight,
lasting now is my poverty,
there is no strength in me for fight,
famine has wounded me, madman as I
    am.

All men see that I am not shapely,
bare of thread is my tattered garment,
Suibhne of Ros Earcain is my name,
the crazy madman am I.

I rest not when night comes,
my foot frequents no trodden way,
I bide not here for long,
the bonds of terror come upon me.

My goal lies beyond the teeming main,
voyaging the prow-abounding sea;
fear has laid hold of my poor strength,
I am the crazy one of Glen Bolcain.

Frosty wind tearing me,
already snow has wounded me,
the storm bearing me to death
from the branches of each tree.

Grey branches have wounded me,
they have torn my hands;
the briars have not left
the making of a girdle for my feet.

There is a palsy on my hands,
everywhere there is cause of confusion,
from Sliabh Mis to Sliabh Cuillenn,
from Sliabh Cuillenn to Cuailgne.

Sad forever is my cry
on the summit of Cruachan Aighle,
from Glen Bolcain to Islay,
from Cenn Tire to Boirche.

Small is my portion when day comes,
it comes not as a new day's right (?),
a tuft of watercress of Cluain Cille
with Cell Cua's cuckoo flower.

He who is at Ros Earcach,
neither trouble nor evil shall come to
    him;
that which makes me strengthless
is being in snow in nakedness.

* * *

The man by the wall snores,
slumber like that I dare not;
for seven years from the Tuesday at Magh
    Rath
I have not slept a wink.

O God of Heaven! would that I had not
    gone
to the fierce battle!
thereafter Suibhne Geilt was my name,
alone in the top of the ivy.

Watercress of the well of Druim Cirb
is my meal at terce;
on my face may be recognized its hue,
'tis true I am Suibhne Geilt.

For certain am I Suibhne Geilt,
one who sleeps under shelter of a rag,
about Sliabh Liag if …
these men pursue me.

When I was Suibhne the sage,
I used to dwell in a lonely shieling,
on sedgy land, on a morass, on a
    mountain-side;
I have bartered my home for a far-off
    land.

I give thanks to the King above
with whom great harshness is not usual;
'tis the extent of my injustice
that has changed my guise.

Cold, cold for me is it
since my body lives not in the ivy-bushes,
much rain comes upon it
and much thunder.

Though I live from hill to hill
in the mountain above the yew glen;
in the place where Congal Claon was left
alas that I was not left there on my back!

Frequent is my groan,
far from my churchyard is my gaping
    house;
I am no champion but a needy madman,
God has thrust me in rags, without sense.

'Tis great folly
for me to come out of Glen Bolcain,
there are many apple-trees in Glen
    Bolcain
for ... of my head.

Green watercress
and a draft of pure water,
I fare on them, I smile not,
not so the man by the wall.

In summer amid the herons of Cuailgne,
among packs of wolves when winter
    comes,
at other times under the crown of a wood;
not so the man by the wall.

Happy Glen Bolcain, fronting the wind,
around which madmen of the glen call,
woe is me! I sleep not there;
more wretched am I than the man by the
    wall.

* * *

Suibhne:
At ease art thou, bright Eorann,
at the bedside with thy lover;
not so with me here,
long have I been restless.

Once thou didst utter, O great Eorann,
a saying pleasing and light,
that thou wouldst not survive
parted one day from Suibhne.

Today, it is readily manifest,
thou thinkest little of thy old friend;
warm for thee on the down of a pleasant
    bed,
cold for me abroad till morn.

Eorann:
Welcome to thee, thou guileless mad one!
thou art most welcome of the men of the
    earth;

though at ease am I, my body is wasted
since the day I heard of thy ruin.

Suibhne:
More welcome to thee is the king's son
who takes thee to feast without sorrow;
he is thy chosen wooer;
you seek not your old friend.

Eorann:
Though the king's son were to lead me
to blithe banqueting-halls,
I had liefer sleep in a tree's narrow
    hollow
beside thee, my husband, could I do so.

If my choice were given me
of the men of Erin and Alba,
I had liefer bide sinless with thee
on water and on watercress.

Suibhne:
No path for a beloved lady
is that of Suibhne here on the track of
    care;
cold are my beds at Ard Abhla,
my cold dwellings are not few.

More meet for thee to bestow love and
    affection
on the man with whom thou art alone
than on an uncouth and famished
    madman,
horrible, fearful, stark-naked.

Eorann:
O toiling madman, 'tis my grief
that thou art uncomely and dejected;
I sorrow that thy skin has lost its colour,
briars and thorns rending thee.

Suibhne:
I blame thee not for it,
thou gentle, radiant woman;
Christ, Son of Mary – great bondage –
He has caused my feebleness.

Eorann:
I would fain that we were together,
and that feathers might grow on our
    bodies;

in light and darkness I would wander
with thee each day and night.

Suibhne:
One night I was in pleasant Boirche,
I have reached lovely Tuath Inbhir,
I have wandered throughout Magh Fail,
I have happened on Cell Ui Suanaigh.

* * *

Loingseachan:
O Suibhne from lofty Sliabh na nEach,
thou of the rough blade wert given to
     wounding;
for Christ's sake, who hath put thee in
     bondage,
grant converse with thy foster-brother.

Hearken to me if thou hearest me,
O splendid king, O great prince,
so that I may relate gently
to thee tidings of thy good land.

There is life for none in thy land after
     thee;
it is to tell of it that I have come;
dead is thy renowned brother there,
dead thy father and thy mother.

Suibhne:
If my gentle mother be dead,
harder is it for me to go to my land;
'tis long since she has loved my body;
she has ceased to pity me.

Foolish the counsel of each wild youth
whose elders live not;
like unto a branch bowed under nuts;
whoso is brotherless has a gaping side.

Loingseachan:
There is another calamity there
which is bewailed by the men of Erin,
though uncouth be thy side and thy
     foot,
dead is thy fair wife of grief for thee.

Suibhne:
For a household to be without a wife
is rowing a rudderless boat,

'tis a garb of feathers to the skin,
'tis kindling a single fire.

Loingseachan:
I have heard a fearful and loud tale
around which was a clear, fierce wail,
'tis a fist round smoke, however,
thou art without sister, O Suibhne,

Suibhne:
A proverb this, bitter the ... –
it has no delight for me –
the mild sun rests on every ditch,
a sister loves though she be not loved.

Loingseachan:
Calves are not let to cows
amongst us in cold Araidhe
since thy gentle daughter, who has loved
     thee died,
likewise thy sister's son.

Suibhne:
My sister's son and my hound,
they would not forsake me for wealth,
'tis adding loss to sorrow;
the heart's needle is an only daughter.

Loingseachan:
There is another famous story –
loth am I to tell it –
meetly are the men of the Arada
bewailing thy only son.

Suibhne:
That is the renowned drop (?)
which brings a man to the ground,
that his little son who used to say 'daddy'
should be without life.

It has called me to thee from the tree,
scarce have I caused enmity,
I cannot bear up against the blow
since I heard the tidings of my only son.

Loingseachan:
Since thou hast come, O splendid warrior,
within Loingseachan's hands,
all thy folk are alive,
O scion of Eochu Salbuidhe.

Be still, let thy sense come,
in the east is thy house, not in the west,
far from thy land thou hast come hither,
this is the truth, O Suibhne.

More delightful deemest thou to be
    amongst deer
in woods and forests
than sleeping in thy stronghold in the east
on a bed of down.

Better deemest thou to be on a holly-
    branch
beside the swift mill's pond
than to be in choice company
with young fellows about thee.

If thou wert to sleep in the bosom of hills
to the soft strings of lutes,
more sweet wouldst thou deem under the
    oak-wood
the belling of the brown stag of the herd.

Thou art fleeter than the wind across the
    valley,
thou art the famous madman of Erin,
brilliant in thy beauty, come hither,
O Suibhne, thou wast a noble champion.

* * *

Suibhne:
O hag of yonder mill,
why shouldst thou set me astray?
is it not deceitful of thee that, through
    women,
I should be betrayed and lured?

The hag:
'Tis not I who betrayed thee,
O Suibhne, though fair thy fame,
but the miracles of Ronan from Heaven
which drove thee to madness among
    madmen.

Suibhne:
Were it myself, and would it were I,
that were king of Dal Araidhe
it were a reason for a blow across a chin;
thou shalt not have a feast, O hag.

Longing for my little home
has come on my senses —
the flocks in the plain,
the deer on the mountain.

Thou oak, bushy, leafy,
thou art high beyond trees;
O hazlet, little branching one,
O fragrance of hazel-nuts,

O alder, thou art not hostile,
delightful is thy hue,
thou art not rending and prickling
in the gap wherein thou art.

O little blackthorn, little thorny one;
O little black sloe-tree;
O watercress, little green-topped one,
from the brink of the ousel (?) spring.

O *minen* of the pathway,
thou art sweet beyond herbs,
O little green one, very green one,
O herb on which grows the strawberry.

O apple-tree, little apple-tree,
much art thou shaken;
O quicken, little berried one,
delightful is thy bloom.

O briar, little arched one,
thou grantest no fair terms,
thou ceasest not to tear me,
till thou hast thy fill of blood.

O yew-tree, little yew-tree,
in churchyards thou art conspicuous;
O ivy, little ivy,
thou art familiar in the dusky wood.

O holly, little sheltering one,
thou door against the wind;
O ash-tree, thou baleful one,
hand-weapon of a warrior.

O birch, smooth and blessed,
thou melodious, proud one,
delightful each entwining branch
in the top of thy crown.

The aspen a-trembling;
by turns I hear
its leaves a-racing –
meseems 'tis the foray!

My aversion in woods –
I conceal it not from anyone –
is the leafy stirk of an oak
swaying evermore. (?)

Ill-hap by which I outraged
the honour of Ronan Finn,
his miracles have troubled me,
his little bells from the church.

Ill-omened I found
the armour of upright Congai,
his sheltering, bright tunic
with selvages of gold.

It was a saying of each one
of the valiant, active host:
'Let not escape from you through the
     narrow copse
the man of the goodly tunic.'

'Wound, kill, slaughter,
let all of you take advantage of him;
put him, though it is great guilt,
on spit and on spike.'

The horsemen pursuing me
across round Magh Cobha,
no cast from them reaches
me through my back.

Going through the ivy-trees –
I conceal it not, O warrior –
like good cast of a spear
I went with the wind.

O little fawn, O little long-legged one,
I was able to catch thee
riding upon thee
from one peak to another.

From Carn Cornan of the contests
to the summit of Sliabh Niadh,
from the summit of Sliabh Uillinne
I reach Crota Cliach.

From Crota Cliach of assemblies
to Carn Liffi of Leinster,
I arrive before eventide
in bitter Benn Gulbain.

My night before the battle of Congal,
I deemed it fortunate,
before I restlessly
wandered over the mountain-peaks.

Glen Bolcain, my constant abode,
'twas a boon to me,
many a night have I attempted
a stern race against the peak.

If I were to wander alone
the mountains of the brown world,
better would I deem the site of a single
     hut
in the Glen of mighty Bolcan.

Good its water pure-green,
good its clean, fierce wind,
good its cress-green watercress,
best its tall brooklime.

Good its enduring ivy-trees,
good its bright, cheerful sallow,
good its yewy yews,
best its melodious birch.

If thou shouldst come, O Loingseachan,
to me in every guise,
each night to talk to me,
perchance I would not tarry for thee.

I would not have tarried to speak to thee
were it not for the tale which has
     wounded me –
father, mother, daughter, son,
brother, strong wife dead.

If thou shouldst come to speak to me,
no better would I deem it;
I would wander before morn
the mountains of Boirche of peaks.

By the mill of the little floury one (?)
thy folk has been ground, (?)
O wretched one, O weary one,
O swift Loingseachan.

O hag of this mill,
why dost thou take advantage of me?
I hear thee revile me
even when thou art out on the mountain.

O hag, O round-headed one, (?)
wilt thou go on a steed?

The hag:
I would go, O fool-head (?)
if no one were to see me.

O Suibhne, if I go,
may my leap be successful.

Suibhne:
If thou shouldst come, O hag,
mayst thou not dismount full of sense!(?)

The hag:
I sooth, not just is what thou sayest,
thou son of Colman Cas;
is not my riding better
without falling back?

Suibhne:
Just, in sooth, is what I say,
O hag without sense;
a demon is ruining thee,
thou hast ruined thyself.

The hag:
Dost thou not deem my arts better,
thou noble, slender madman,
that I should be following thee
from the tops of the mountains?

Suibhne:
A proud ivy-bush
which grows through a twisted tree –
if I were right on its summit,
I would fear to come out.

I flee before the skylarks –
'tis a stern, great race –
I leap over the stumps
on the tops of the mountains.

When the proud turtle-dove
rises for us,
quickly do I overtake it
since my feathers have grown.

The silly, foolish woodcock
when it rises for me
methinks 'tis a bitter foe,
the blackbird (too) that gives the cry of
alarm.

Every time I would bound
till I was on the ground
so that I might see the little fox
below a-gnawing the bones.

Beyond every wolf(?) among the ivy-trees
swiftly would he get the advantage of me,
so nimbly would I leap
till I was on the mountain-peak.

Little foxes yelping
to me and from me,
wolves at their rending,
I flee at their sound.

They have striven to reach me,
coming in their swift course,
so that I fled before them
to the tops of the mountains.

My transgression has come against me
whatsoever way I flee;
'tis manifest to me from the pity shown
me
that I am a sheep without a fold.

The old tree of Cell Lughaidhe
wherein I sleep a sound sleep;
more delightful in the time of Congal
was the fair of plenteous Line.

There will come the starry frost
which will fall on every pool;
I am wretched, straying
exposed to it on the mountain-peak.

The herons a-calling
in chilly Glenn Aighle,
swift flocks of birds
coming and going.

I love not the merry prattle
that men and women make:
sweeter to me is the warbling
of the blackbirds in the quarter in which
it is.

I love not the trumpeting
I hear at early morn:
sweeter to me the squeal
of the badgers in Benna Broc.

I love not the horn-blowing
so boldly I hear:
sweeter to me the belling of a stag
of twice twenty peaks.

There is the material of a plough-team
from glen to glen:
each stag at rest
on the summit of the peaks.

Though many are my stags
from glen to glen,
not often is a ploughman's hand
closing round their horns. (?)

The stag of lofty Sliabh Eibhlinne,
the stag of sharp Sliabh Fuaid,
the stag of Ealla, the stag of Orrery,
the fierce stag of Loch Lein.

The stag of Seimhne, Larne's stag,
the stag of Line of the mantles,
the stag of Cuailgne, the stag of
    Conachail,
the stag of Bairenn of two peaks.

O mother of this herd,
thy coat has become grey,
there is no stag after thee
without two score antler-points.

Greater than the material for a little cloak
thy head has turned grey;
if I were on each little point,
there would be a pointlet on every point.

Thou stag that comest lowing
to me across the glen,
pleasant is the place for seats
on the top of thy antler-points.

I am Suibhne, a poor suppliant,
swiftly do I race across the glen;
that is not my lawful name,
rather is it Fer benn.

The springs I found best:
the well of Leithead Lan,

the well most beautiful and cool,
the fountain of Dun Mail.

Though many are my wanderings,
my raiment today is scanty;
I myself keep my watch
on the top of the mountains.

O tall, russet fern,
thy mantle has been made red;
there is no bed for an outlaw
in the branches of thy crests.

At ever-angelic Tech Moling,
at puissant Toidhen in the south,
'tis there my eternal resting-place will be,
I shall fall by a [spear]-point.

The curse of Ronan Finn
has thrown me in thy company,
O little stag, little bleating one,
O melodious little clamourer.

* * *

O woman who pluckest the watercress
and takest the water,
thou wouldst not be without something
    tonight
even though thou didst not take my
    portion.

Alas, O woman!
thou wilt not go the way that I shall go;
I abroad in the tree-tops,
thou yonder in a friend's house.

Alas, O woman!
cold is the wind that has come to me;
nor mother nor son has pity on me,
no cloak is on my breast.

If thou but knewest, O woman,
how Suibhne here is:
he does not get friendship from anyone,
nor does anyone get his friendship.

I go not to a gathering
among warriors of my country,
no safeguard is granted me,
my thought is not on kingship

I go not as a guest
to the house of any man's son in Erin,
more often am I straying madly
on the pointed mountain-peaks.

None cometh to make music to me
for a while before going to rest,
no pity do I get
from tribesman or kinsman.

When I was Suibhne indeed
and used to go on steeds –
when that comes to my memory
alas that I was detained in life!

I am Suibhne, noble leader (?),
cold and joyless is my abode,
though I be tonight on wild peaks,
O woman who pluckest my watercress.

My mead is my cold water,
my kine are my cresses,
my friends are my trees,
though I am without mantle or smock.

Cold is the night tonight,
though I am poor as regards watercress,
I have heard the cry of the wild-goose
over bare Imlech Iobhair.

I am without mantle or smock,
the evil hour has long clung to me (?),
I flee at the cry of the heron
as though it were a blow that struck me.

I reach firm Dairbre
in the wondrous days of Spring,
and before night I flee
westward to Benn Boirche.

If thou art learned, O fair, crabbed one,
my field ...
there is one to whom the burden thou
     takest
is a grievous matter, O hag.

It is cold they are
at the brink of a clear, pebbly spring –
a bright quaff of pure water
and the watercress you pluck.

My meal is the watercress you pluck,
the meal of a noble, emaciated madman;

cold wind springs around my loins
from the peaks of each mountain.

Chilly is the wind of morn,
It comes between me and my smock,
I am unable to speak to thee,
O woman who pluckest the watercress.

The woman:
Leave my portion to the Lord,
be not harsh to me;
the more wilt thou attain supremacy,
and take a blessing, O Suibhne.

Suibhne:
Let us make a bargain just and fitting
though I am on the top of the yew;
take thou my smock and my tatters,
leave the little bunch of cress.

There is scarce one by whom I am beloved,
I have no house on earth;
since thou takest from me my watercress
my sins to be on thy soul!

Mayest thou not reach him whom thou
     has loved,
the worse for him whom thou hast
     followed;
thou hast left one in poverty
because of the bunch thou hast plucked.

May a raid of the blue-coated Norsemen
     take thee!
thine has not been a fortunate meeting for
     me,
mayest thou get from the Lord the blame
for cutting my portion of watercress.

O woman, if there should come to thee
Loingseachan whose delight is sport,
do thou give him on my behalf
half the watercress thou pluckest.'

* * *

Gloomy this life,
to be without a soft bed,
abode of cold frost,
roughness of wind-driven snow.

Cold, icy wind,
faint shadow of a feeble sun,
shelter of a single tree,
on the summit of a table-land.

Enduring the rain-storm,
stepping over deer-paths, (?)
faring through greensward
on a morn of grey frost.

The bellowing of the stags
throughout the wood,
the climb to the deer-pass,
the voice of white seas.

Yea, O great Lord,
great this weakness,
more grievous this black sorrow,
Suibhne the slender-groined.

Racing over many-hued gaps
of Boirche of hut couches,
the sough of the winter night,
footing it in hailstones.

Lying on a wet bed
on the slopes of Loch Erne,
mind on early departure,
morn of early rising.

Racing over the wave-tops
of Dun Sobairce,
ear to the billows
of Dun Rodairce.

Running from this great wave
to the wave of the rushing Barrow,
sleeping on a hard couch
of fair Dun Cermna.

From fair Dun Cermna
to flowery Benn Boirne,
ear against a stone pillow
of rough Cruachan Oighle.

Restless my wandering
in the plain of the Boroma,
from Benn Iughoine
to Benn Boghaine.

There has come to me
one who has laid hands on me,

she has brought no peace to me,
the woman who has dishonoured me.

She has taken my portion
on account of my sins,
wretched the work –
my watercress has been eaten.

Watercress I pluck,
food in a fair bunch,
four round handfuls
of fair Glen Bolcain.

A meal I seek –
pleasant the bogberry,
a drink of water here
from the well of Ronan Finn.

Bent are my nails,
feeble my loins,
pierced my feet,
bare my thighs.

There will overtake me
a warrior-band stubbornly,
far from Ulster,
faring in Alba.

After this journey –
sad is my secret song –
to be in the hard company
of Carraig Alastair.

Carraig Alastair,
abode of sea-gulls,
sad, O Creator,
chilly for its guests.

Carraig Alastair,
bell-shaped rock,
sufficient were it half the height,
nose to the main.

Sad our meeting;
a couple of cranes hard-shanked –
I hard and ragged,
she hard-beaked.

Wet these beds
wherein is my dwelling,
little did I think
it was a rock of holiness.

Bad was it for Congal Claon
that he arrived at the battle;
like an outer yoke
he has earned a curse.

When I fled
from the battle of Magh Rath
before my undoing,
I deserved not harshness.

Sad this expedition;
would that I had not come!
far from my home
is the country I have reached.

Loingseachan will come,
sad his journeys;
though he follow me,
it will not be easy.

Far-stretching woods
are the rampart of this circuit –
the land to which I have come –
not a deed of sadness.

The black lake of fortressed Boirche
greatly has it perturbed me;
the vastness of its depths,
the strength of its wave-crests.

Better found I
pleasant woods,
choice places of wooded Meath,
the vastness of Ossory.

Ulaidh in harvest-time
about quivering Loch Cuan,
a summer visit
to the race of enduring Eoghan.

A journey at Lammastide
to Taillten of fountains,
fishing in springtime
the meandering Shannon.

* * *

Cold tonight is Benn Boirche,
'tis the abode of a blighted man;
no place is it for food or milk,
nor in storm and endless snow.

Cold is my bed at night
on the summit of Benn Boirche;
I am weak, no raiment covers me
on a sharp-branching holly-tree.

When cold has gripped me in the ice
I move sharply against it,
I give fire to the glinting wind
blowing over the plain of Laoghaire's
    Leinster.

Glen Bolcain of the clear spring,
it is my dwelling to abide in;
when Samhuin comes, when summer
    goes,
it is my dwelling where I abide.

Headless I left Oilill,
and right glad was I thereat;
by me also there fell
five sons of the king of Magh Mairge.

Wheresoever I might wander west and east
throughout Glanamhrach's glens
the biting snowstorm is in my face,
for shelter of the chilly madman of Erin.

That is my beloved glen,
my land of foregathering,
my royal fortress that has fallen to my
    share,
my shelter against storm.

For my sustenance at night
I have all that my hands glean
in dark oak-woods
of herbs and plenteous fruit.

I love the precious bog-berries,
they are sweeter than …
brooklime, sea-weed, they are my desire,
the *lus bian* and the watercress.

Apples, berries, beautiful hazel-nuts,
blackberries, acorns from the oak-tree,
raspberries, they are the due of generosity,
haws of the prickly-sharp hawthorn.

wood-sorrels, goodly wild garlic,
and clean-topped cress,
together they drive hunger from me,
mountain acorns, *melle* root.

I in a green land that is not a glen,
O Christ, may I never reach it!
it is not my due to be there;
but though I am cold, it also is cold.

* * *

I am in great grief tonight,
the pure wind has pierced my body;
wounded are my feet, my cheek is wan,
O great God! it is my due.

Last night I was in Benn Boirche,
the rain of chilly Aughty beat on me;
tonight my limbs are racked
in the fork of a tree in pleasant Gaille.

I have borne many a fight without
    cowardice
since feathers have grown on my body;
each night and each day
more and more do I endure ill.

Frost and foul storm have wrung my
    heart,
snow has beaten on me on Sliabh mic Sin;
tonight the wind has wounded me,
without the heather of happy Glen
    Bolcain.

Unsettled is my faring through each land,
it has befallen me that I am without sense
    or reason,
from Magh Line to Magh Li,
from Magh Li to the impetuous Liffey.

I pass over the wooded brow of Sliabh
    Fuaid,
in my flight I reach Rathmor,
across Magh Aoi, across bright Magh
    Luirg,
I reach the border of fair Cruachan.

From Sliabh Cua – no easy expedition –
I reach pleasant Glais Gaille;
from Glais Gaille, though a long step,
I arrive at sweet Sliabh Breagh to the east.

Wretched is the life of one homeless,
sad is the life, O fair Christ!
a meal of fresh, green-tufted watercress,
a drink of cold water from a clear stream.

Stumbling from withered tree-tops,
faring through furze – deed without
    falsehood –
shunning mankind, keeping company
    with wolves,
racing with the red stag over the field.

Sleeping of nights without covering in a
    wood
in the top of a thick, bushy tree,
without hearing voice or speech;
O Son of God, great is the misery!

* * *

Mournful am I tonight,
I am sad and wretched, my side is naked,
if folk but knew me
I have cause for lament.

Frost, ice, snow, and storm,
forever scourging me,
I without fire, without house,
on the summit of Sliabh Eidhneach.

I have a mansion and a good wife,
everyone would say that I was a prince;
'tis He who is Lord and King
has wrought my downfall.

Wherefore did God rescue me from the
    battle
that no one was found there to slay me,
rather than that I should go step by step
with the hag of the mill?

The hag of the mill at her house,
Christ's curse on her soul!
woe whosoever has trusted the hag!
woe to whom she has given his dog's
    portion!

Loingseachan was on my track
throughout every wilderness in Erin,
until he lured me from the tree
what time he related my son's death.

He carried me into the great house
wherein the host was feasting,
and bound me behind in the house (?)
face to face with my first love.

The people of the house without reproach
playing games and laughing;
I and my folk in the house
leaping and jumping.

Were it not for the hag of the house,
I would not have gone again into
 madness;
she besought me by Christ of Heaven
to leap for her a little while.

I leaped a leap or two
for the sake of the Heavenly Father
 Himself;
the hag at her house said
that even so could she herself leap.

Once more I leaped out
over the top of the fortress;
swifter than smoke through a house
was the flight of the hag.

We wandered through all Erin,
from Teach Duinn to Traigh Ruire,
from Traigh Ruire to Benna Brain,
but the hag I did not elude.

Through plain and bog and hillside
I escaped not from the slattern
until she leaped with me the famous leap
to the summit of Dun Sobairce.

Thereafter I leaped down the *dun*,
nor did I step back,
I went out into the sea,
yonder I left the hag.

There came then to the strand
the devil's crew to meet her,
and they bore away her body;
woe to the land of Erin in which it was
 buried!

* * *

Suibhne:
Though thou hast wounded me in the
 hedge,
I have not done thee ill;
I would not trust in thine own wife
for the earth and its fruits.

Alas for him who has come for a while
 from home
to thee, O Moling Luachair,
the wound thy herd has dealt me
stays me from wandering through the
 woods.

Moling:
The curse of Christ who hath created
 everyone
on thee, said Moling to his herd,
sorry is the deed thou hast done
through envy in thine heart.

Since thou hast done a dread deed,
said Moling to his herd,
thou wilt get in return for it
a short span of life and hell.

Suibhne:
Though thou mayest avenge it,
O Moling, I shall be no more;
no relief for me is it,
your treachery has compassed me.

Moling:
Thou shalt get an *eric* for it,
said Moling Luachair, I avow;
thou shalt be in Heaven as long as I shall be
by the will of the great Lord, O Suibhne.

Mongan:
It will be well with thee, O slender
 Suibhne,
thou in Heaven, said the herd,
not so with me here,
without Heaven, without my life's span.

Mongan:
Speak to me if thou hearest,
who art thou in truth, man?

Suibhne:
Suibhne Geilt without reproach am I,
O herd of Moling Luachair.

Mongan:
If I but knew, O slender Suibhne,
O man, if I could have recognized thee,
I would not have thrust a spear against
 thy skin
though I had seen thee harm me.

Suibhne:
East or west I have not done
harm to one on the world's ridge
since Christ has brought me from my
    valiant land
in madness throughout Erin.

Mongan:
The daughter of my father and my
    mother
related – 'twas no trifle to me –
how she found thee in yonder hedge
with my own wife at morn.

Suibhne:
It was not right of thee to credit that
until thou hadst learnt its certainty,
alas that thou shouldst come hither to slay
    me
until thine eyes had seen!

Though I should be from hedge to hedge,
its harm were a trifle to thee,
though a woman should give me to
    drink
a little milk as alms.

Mongan:
If I but knew what comes of it,
from wounding thee through breast and
    heart,
till Doom my hand would not wound
    thee,
O Suibhne of Glen Bolcain.

Suibhne:
There was a time when I deemed more
    melodious
than the quiet converse of people,

the cooing of the turtle-dove
flitting about a pool.

There was a time when I deemed more
    melodious
than the sound of a little bell beside me
the warbling of the blackbird to the
    mountain
and the belling of the stag in a storm.

There was a time when I deemed more
    melodious
than the voice of a beautiful woman
    beside me,
to hear at dawn
the cry of the mountain-grouse.

There was a time when I deemed more
    melodious
the yelping of the wolves
than the voice of a cleric within
a-baaing and a-bleating.

Though goodly you deem in taverns
your ale-feasts with honour,
I had liefer drink a quaff of water in theft
from the palm of my hand out of a well.

Though yonder in your church you deem
    melodious
the soft converse of your students,
more melodious to me is the splendid
    chant
of the hounds of Glen Bolcain.

Though goodly ye deem the salt meat and
    the fresh
that are eaten in banqueting-houses,
I had liefer eat a tuft of fresh watercress
in some place without sorrow.

CHAPTER NINETEEN

The Vision of MacConglinne

translated by Kuno Meyer

AS I LAY LAST NIGHT in my beautiful canopied bed, with its gilded posts, with its bronze rails, I heard something, viz., a voice coming towards me; but I answered it not. That was natural; such was the comfort of my bed, the case of my body, and the soundness of my slumber. Whereupon it said again: 'Beware, beware, MacConglinne, lest the gravy drown thee!'

At early morn on the morrow I arose, and went to the well to wash my hands, when I saw a mighty phantom approaching me. 'Well, there,' said he to me. 'Well, indeed,' said I to him. 'Well, now, wretch,' said the phantom, 'it was I that gave thee warning last night, lest the gravy should drown thee. But, verily, 'twas

Warning to one fey,
Mocking a beggar,
Dropping a stone on a tree,
Whispering to the deaf,
A legacy to a glum man,
Putting a charm in a hurdle,
A withe about sand or gravel,
Striking an oak with fists,
Sucking honey from roots of yew,
Looking for butter in a dog's kennel,
Dining on the husks of pepper,
Seeking wool on a goat,
An arrow at a pillar,
Keeping a mare from breaking wind,
Keeping a loose woman from lust,
Water on the bottom of a sieve,
Trusting a mad (?) bitch,
Salt on rushes,
A settlement after marriage,
A secret to a silly woman,
(Looking for) sense in an oaf,
Exalting slaves,

Ale to infants,
Competing (?) with a king,
A body without a head,
A head without a body,
A nun as bell-ringer,
A veteran in a bishop's chair,
A people without a king,
Rowing a boat without a rudder,
Corn in a basket full of holes,
Milk on a hide,
Housekeeping without a woman,
Berries on a hide,
Warning visions to sinners,
Reproof to the face,
Restoration without restitution,
Putting seed in bad land,
Property to a bad woman,
Serving a bad lord,
An unequal contract,
Uneven measure,
Going against a verdict,
To outrage the gospel,

Instructing Antichrist,

to instruct thee, MacConglinne, regarding thy appetite.'

'I declare by my God's Doom,' said I, 'the reproof is hard and severe.'

'How is that?' asked the phantom.

'Not hard to say,' I answered. 'I know not whence thou comest, nor whither thou goest, nor whence thou art thyself, to question thee, or tell thee again.'

'That is easily known,' said the phantom. 'I am Fluxy son of Elcab the Fearless, from the Fairy knoll of Eating.'

'If thou art he,' I said, 'I fancy thou hast great news, and tidings of food and eating. Hast any?'

'I have indeed,' said the phantom; 'but though I have, 'twould be no luck for a friend who had no power of eating to come up with it.'

'How is that?' I asked.

'Indeed, it is not hard to tell,' said the phantom.

'Even so: unless he had a very broad four-edged belly, five hands in diameter, in which could be fitted thrice nine eatings, and seven drinkings (with the drink of nine in each of them), and of seven chewings, and nine digestions – a dinner of a hundred being in each of those eatings, drinkings, swallowings, and digestions respectively.'

'Since I have not that belly,' answered I, 'give me thy counsel, for thou hast made me greedy.'

'I will indeed give thee counsel,' said the phantom. 'Go,' said he, 'to the hermitage from which I have come, even to the hermitage of the Wizard Doctor, where thy appetite for all kinds of food, which thy gullet and thy heart can desire, will find a cure; where thy teeth will be polished by the many wonderful manifold viands of which we have spoken; where thy melancholy will be attacked; where thy senses will be startled; where thy lips will be gratified with choice drink and choice morsels, with eating and putting away every sort of soft, savoury, tender-sweet food acceptable to thy body, and not injurious to thy soul – if only thou gettest to the Wizard Doctor, and to sharp-lipped Beenat, daughter of Baetan the monstrous Eater, the wife of the Wizard Doctor.

'The day thou wilt arrive at the fort will be the day on which his pavilion of fat will be raised about him, on its fair round wheat plains, with the two Loins, the Gullet, and the worthy Son of Fat-kettle, with their mantles of ... about them. It will be a happy day for thee when thou shalt come unto the fort, O MacConglinne,' said the phantom; 'the more so as that will be the day, on which the chieftains of the Tribe of Food will be summoned to the fort.'

'And what are their names?' asked MacConglinne.

'Not hard to tell,' said the phantom; 'they are Little Sloey, son of Smooth-juicy-bacon; Cakey, son of Hung Beef; and Hollow-sides, son of Gullet, and Milkikin, son of Lactulus, and Wristy-hand, son of Leather-head, and young Mul-Lard, son of Flitch of Old-Bacon.'

'And what is thy own name, if we may ask?'

'Not hard to tell,' said the phantom.

Wheatlet, son of Milklet,
Son of juicy Bacon,
    Is mine own name.
Honeyed Butter-roll
Is the man's name
    That bears my bag.

Haunch of Mutton
Is my dog's name,
    Of lovely leaps.
Lard, my wife,
Sweetly smiles
    Across the kale-top.

Cheese-curds, my daughter,
Goes round the spit,
 Fair is her fame.
Corned Beef, my son,
Whose mantle shines
 Over a big tail.

Savour of Savours
Is the name of my wife's maid:
Morning-early
Across New-milk Lake she went.

Beef-lard, my steed,
An excellent stallion,
 That increases studs;
A guard against toil
Is the saddle of cheese
 On his back.

When a cheese-steed is sent after him
 Rapid his course,
Fat ... is on his ribs,
 Exceeding all shapes.

A large necklace of delicious cheese-
 curds
 Around his back,
His halter and his traces all
 Of fresh butter.

His bridle with its reins of fat
 In every place.
The horsecloth of tripe with its ... ,
 Tripes are his hoofs.
Egg-horn is my bridle-boy.
...
Before going to a meeting with death.
...
My pottage tunic around myself
 Everywhere,
... of tripe with its ... .
 Of uncooked food.

'Off with thee now to those delicious prodigious viands, O MacConglinne,' said the phantom,

many wonderful provisions,
pieces of every palatable food,
brown red-yellow dishes,
full without fault,
perpetual joints of corned beef,
smooth savoury lard,
and heavy flitches of boar.

'Off with thee now to the suets and cheeses!' said the phantom.

'I will certainly go,' said MacConglinne, 'and do thou put a gospel around me.'

'It shall be given,' said the phantom; 'even a gospel of four-cornered even dry cheese, and I will put my own paternoster around thee, and neither greed nor hunger can visit him around whom it is put.' And he said:

'May smooth juicy bacon protect thee, O MacConglinne!' said the phantom.

'May hard yellow-skinned cream protect thee, O MacConglinne!

'May the caldron full of pottage protect thee, O MacConglinne!'

'By my God's doom, in the presence of the Creator,' said MacConglinne, 'I wish I could get to that fortress, that I might consume my fill of those old strained delicious liquors, and of those wonderful enormous viands.'

'If thou really *so* wishest,' said the phantom, 'thou shalt have them. Go as I tell thee; but only, if thou goest, do not go astray.'

'How is that?' said MacCouglinne.

'Not hard to tell,' said the phantom. 'Thou must place thyself under the protection and safeguard of the mighty peerless warriors, the chiefs of the Tribes of Food, lest the gravy destroy thee.'

'How, then,' said MacGonglinne, 'which of the chiefs of the Tribes of Food are the most puissant safeguards against the heavy waves of gravy?'

'Not hard to tell,' said the phantom. 'The Suets and the Cheeses.'

'Thereupon then I advanced,' said MacConglinne, 'erect, with exultant head, with stout steps. The wind that comes across that country – it is not by me I wish to go, but into my mouth. And no wonder; so heavy was the disease, so scant the cure, so great the longing for the remedy. I advanced vehemently, furiously, impatiently, eagerly, greedily, softly, gliding, like a young fox approaching a shepherd, or as a clown to violate a queen, or a royston-crow to carrion, or a deer to the cropping of a field of winter-rye in the month of June. However, I lifted my shirt above my buttocks, and I thought that neither fly, nor gadfly, nor gnat could stick to my hinder part, in its speed and agility, as I went through plains and woods and wastes towards that lake and fort.

'Then in the harbour of the lake before me I saw a juicy little coracle of beef-fat, with its coating of tallow, with its thwarts of curds, with its prow of lard, with its stern of butter, with its thole-pins of marrow, with its oars of flitches of old boar in it.

'Indeed, she was a sound craft in which we embarked. Then we rowed across the wide expanse of New-Milk Lake, through seas of broth, past river-mouths of mead, over swelling boisterous waves of butter-milk, by perpetual pools of gravy, past woods dewy with meat-juice, past springs of savoury lard, by islands of cheeses, by hard rocks of rich tallow, by headlands of old curds, along strands of dry cheese; until we reached the firm, level beach between Butter-mount and Milk-Lake and Curd-point at the mouth of the pass to the country of O'Early-eating, in front of the hermitage of the Wizard Doctor. Every oar we plied in New-milk Lake would send its sea-sand of cheese curds to the surface.'

It was then MacConglinne said, at the top of his voice: 'Ha, ha, ha! these are not the seas that I would not take!'

Then the Wizard Doctor spoke to his people: 'A troublesome party approaches you tonight, my friends,' said the Wizard Doctor, 'viz., Aniér MacConglinne of the men of Munster, a youngster of deep lore, entertaining and delightful. And he must be well served; for he is melancholy, passionate, impetuous, violent and impatient; and he is eager, fond of eating early; and he is voracious, niggardly, greedy; and yet he is mild and gentle, … easily moved to laughter. And he is a man great in thanksgivings and in upbraidings. And no wonder; for he has wit both to censure and to praise the hearth of a well-appointed, gentle, fine, mirthful house with a mead-hall.'

Marvellous, indeed, was the hermitage in which I then found myself. Around it were seven score hundred smooth stakes of old bacon, and instead of the thorns above the top of every long stake was fried juicy lard of choice well-fed boar, in expectation of a battle against the tribes of Butter-pat and Cheese that were on Newmilk Lake, warring against the Wizard Doctor.

There was a gate of tallow to it, whereon was a bolt of sausage.

'I raised myself up then out of my boat,' said MacConglinne, 'and betook myself to the outer door of the entrance porch of the fortress, and seizing a branchy cudgel that lay directly on my right hand outside the porch of the fortress, I dealt a blow with it at the tallow door, on which was the sausage lock, and drove it before me along the outer porch of the fortress, until I reached the splendid inner chief residence of the enormous fort. And I fixed my ten pointed purple-bright nails in its smooth old-bacon door, which had a lock of cheese, flung it behind me, and passed through.

'Then I saw the doorkeeper. Fair was the shape of that man; and his name was Bacon-lad, son of Butter-lad, son of Lard; with his smooth sandals of old bacon on his soles, and leggings of potmeat encircling his shins, with his tunic of corned beef, and his girdle of salmon skin around him, with his hood of flummery about him, with a seven-filleted crown of butter on his head (in each fillet of which was the produce of seven ridges of pare leeks); with his seven badges of tripe about his neck, and seven bosses of boiled lard on the point of every badge of them; his steed of bacon under him, with its four legs of custard, with its four hoofs of coarse oaten bread under it, with its ears of curds, with its two eyes of honey in its head, with its streams of old cream in its two nostrils, and a flux of bragget streaming down behind, with its tail of dulse, from which seven handfuls were pulled every ordinary day; with its smooth saddle of glorious choice lard upon it, with its face-band of the side of a heifer around its head, with its neck-band of old-wether spleen around its neck, with its little bell of cheese suspended from the neck-band, with its tongue of thick compact metal hanging down from the bell; and a whip in that rider's hand, the cords whereof were twenty-nine fair puddings of white-fat cows, and the substance of every juicy drop that fell to the ground from the end of each of these puddings would, with half a cake, be a surfeit for a priest; with his slender boiled stick of *bundrish* in his hand, and every juicy drop that trickled from the end of it, when he turned it downwards, would contain the full of seven vats.

'Open the hermitage to us,' said MacConglinne.

'Come in, wretch!' answered the doorkeeper.

'On going in, then, said MacConglinne, I saw on my left hand the servants of the Wizard Doctor with their hairy cloaks of … with their hairy rags of soft custard, with their shovels of dry bread in their hands, carrying the tallowy offal that was on the lake-bridge of custard, from the porch of the great house to the outer porch of the fortress.

'On my right hand I then beheld the Wizard Doctor, with his two gloves of full-fat rump-steak on his hands, setting in order the house, which was hung all round with tripe from roof to floor.

'Then I went into the kitchen, and there I saw the Wizard Doctor's son, with his fishing-hook of lard in his hand, with its line made of fine brawn of a deer, viz., the marrow of its leg, with its thirty-hand rod of tripe attached to the line below, and he angling in a lake of lard. Now he would bring a flitch of old bacon, and now a weasand of corned beef from the lake of lard mixed with honey, on to a bank of curds that was near him in the kitchen. And in that lake it is that the Wizard Doctor's son was drowned, for whom the celebrated clegy was made:

The son of Eoghan of lasting fame, etc.

'Afterwards I went into the great house. As I set my foot across the threshold into the house, I saw something, viz., a pure white bed-tick of butter, on which I sat; but I sank in it to the tips of my two ears. The eight strongest men that were in the king's house had hard work to pull me out by the top of the crown of my head.

'Then I was taken to the place where the Wizard Doctor himself was.

'Pray for me!' said I to him.

'In the name of cheese!' said he to me. 'Evil is the limp look of thy face,' said the Wizard Doctor. 'Alas! it is the look of disease. Thy hands are yellow, thy lips are spotted, thine eyes are grey. Thy sinews have relaxed, they have risen over thy brow and over thy flesh, and over thy joints and nails. The three hags have attacked thee, even scarcity and death and famine, with sharp beaks of hunger. An eye that sains not has regarded thee. A plague of heavy disease has visited thee. No wonder, truly; for thine is not the look of a full-suckled milk-fed calf, tended by the hands of a good cook. Thou hast not the corslet look of well-nourished blood, but that of a youth badly reared under the vapours of bad feeding.'

'Very natural that,' said MacConglinne. 'Such is the heaviness of my ailment, the scarcity of cure, the longing for the remedy.'

'Tell me thy disease, my man,' said the Wizard Doctor.

'I will tell thee,' said MacConglinne, 'what it is that shrivels me up and what makes me low-spirited, inactive, even love of good cheer, hatred of bad cheer, desire of eating early, the gnawing of my many fancies, the gnawing of flesh, the consumption of white-meats, greed and hunger. The thirst and voracity which I feel in consuming my food, so that what I eat gives neither satiety nor substance; inhospitality and niggardliness, refusal and uncharitableness regarding what is my own, so that I am a burden to myself, and dear to none. Hunger, with its four-and-twenty subdivisions in addition thereto, sadness, niggardliness, anxiety to be welcomed before everybody to all kinds of food, and the injurious effect to me of every food.

'My wish would be, that the various numerous wonderful viands of the world were before my gorge, that I might gratify my desires, and satisfy my greed. But alas! great is the misfortune to one like me, who cannot obtain any of these.'

'On my word,' said the Great Doctor, 'the disease is grievous. Woe to him on whom it has fallen, and not long will it be endured. But as thou hast come to me to my hermitage and to my fort at this time, thou shalt take home with thee a medicine to cure thy disease, and shalt be for ever healed therefrom.'

'What is that?' asked MacConglinne.

'Not hard to tell,' answered the Great Doctor. 'If thou goest home tonight, go to the well to wash thy hands, rub thy teeth with thy fists, and comb every straight rib of thy hair in order. Warm thyself afterwards before a glowing red fire of straight red oak, or of octagonal ash that grows near a hill-side where little sparrows leave their droppings; on a dry hearth, very high, very low, that its embers may warm thee, that its blaze may not burn thee, that its smoke may not touch thee. Let a hairy calf-skin be placed under thee to the northeast before the fire, thy side resting exactly against a rail of alder. And let an active, white-handed, sensible, joyous woman wait upon thee, who must be of good repute, of good discourse, red-lipped, womanly, eloquent, of a good kin, wearing a necklace, and a cloak, and a brooch, with a black edge between the two peaks of her cloak, that sorrow may not come upon her; with the three nurses of her dignity upon her, with three dimples of love and delight in her countenance, without an expression of harshness in her forehead, who shall have a joyous, comely appearance, a purple five-folded cloak about her, a red-gold brooch in her cloak, a fair broad face, a good blue eye in her head, two blue-black brows of the colour of the black chafer over those eyes, ruddy even checks, red thin lips, white clear teeth in her head as though they were pearls, soft tender white fore-arms, two smooth snowy sides, beauteous shapely thighs, straight well-proportioned calves, thin white-skinned feet, long slender fingers, long pale-red nails. So that the gait and movements of the maiden may be graceful and quick, so that her gentle talk and address may be melodious as strings, soft and sweet; so that, from her crown to her sole, there may be neither fault, nor stain, nor blemish, on which a sharp watchful observer may hit.

'Let this maiden give thee thy thrice nine morsels, O MacConglinne, each morsel of which shall be as big as a heath-fowl's egg. These morsels thou must put in thy mouth with a swinging jerk, and thine eyes must whirl about in thy skull whilst thou art eating them.'

'The eight kinds of grain thou must not spare, O MacConglinne, wheresoever they are offered thee, viz., rye, wild-oats, beare, buck-wheat, wheat, barley, *fidbach*, oats. Take eight cakes of each fair grain of these, and eight condiments with every cake, and eight sauces with each condiment; and let each morsel thou puttest in thy mouth be as big as a heron's egg. Away now to the smooth panikins of cheese-curds, O MacConglinne,

'to fresh pigs,
to loins of fat,
to boiled mutton,
to the choice easily discussed thing for which the hosts contend – the gullet of salted beef;
to the dainty of the nobles, to mead;
to the cure of chest-disease – old bacon;
to the appetite of pottage – stale curds;
to the fancy of an unmarried woman – new milk;
to a queen's mash – carrots;
to the danger awaiting a guest – ale;
to the sustenance of Lent – the cock of a hen;
to a broken head – butter-roll;
to hand-upon-all – dry bread;
to the pregnant thing of a hearth – cheese;
to the bubble-burster – new ale;
to the priests' fancy – juicy kale;
to the treasure that is smoothest and sweetest of all food – white porridge;
to the anchor … – broth;
to the double-looped twins – sheep's tripe;
to the dues of a wall – sides (of bacon);
to the bird of a cross – salt;
to the entry of a gathering – sweet apples;
to the pearls of a household – hens' eggs;
to the glance of nakedness – kernels.'

When he had reckoned me up those many viands, he ordered me my drop of drink. 'A tiny little measure for thee, MacConglinne, not too large, only as much as twenty men will drink, on the top of those viands: of very thick milk, of milk not too thick, of milk of long thickness, of milk of medium thickness, of yellow bubbling milk, the swallowing of which needs chewing, of the milk that makes the snoring bleat of a ram as it rushes down the gorge, so that the first draught says to the last draught: "I vow, thou mangy cur, before the Creator, if thou comest down, I'll go up, for there is no room for the doghood of the pair of us in this treasure-house."

'Whatever disease may seize thee from it, MacConglinne, 'tis I that Will cure thee, excepting one disease, I mean the disease of sages and of gentlemen, the best of all diseases, the disease that is worth perpetual health – loose bowels.'

CHAPTER TWENTY

The Prophecies of the Brahan Seer

Alexander Mackenzie

Seaforth's Doom

KENNETH, THE THIRD EARL, had occasion to visit Paris on some business after the Restoration of King Charles II, and after having secured his liberty. He left the Countess at Brahan Castle unattended by her lord, and, as she thought, forgotten, while he was enjoying the dissipations and amusements of the French capital, which seemed to have many attractions for him, for he prolonged his stay far beyond his original intention.

Brahan Castle was founded in the fourteenth century and rebuilt entirely during the reign of James VI who gave grants of additional land in the Brahan district, and other portions to the south and west of Dingwall, to Mackenzie of Kintail on his appointment as Commissioner in charge of portions of the royal properties in Ross-shire. Brahan Castle was the scene of stirring activities and romantic episodes in the religious struggles and Jacobite risings. It was for a time occupied by government troops – a garrison 'planted upon Seafort's nose' – and it was here, after the Disarming Act, that the Mackenzie clan laid down their weapons. On the day appointed, over eight hundred clansmen who acknowledged Seaforth as chief filed before General Wade and laid down their arms at Brahan Castle. The heads of families including the Earl of Cromartie and Sir Colin Mackenzie of Coul, entered into an agreement to transfer their loyalty from Prince Charles Edward and the Stuarts to King George and the Hanoverians. The main body of clansmen, their weapons attached to the backs of their Highland ponies, marched in fours up to the steps of the Castle entrance, where Wade and his officers received them. Refreshment was served so that they could drink a loyal toast. In the following year Seaforth received the King's Pardon. The Castle was demolished soon after the Second World War, and the ground where it once stood is now a great green spread of grass.

Lady Seaforth had become very uneasy concerning his prolonged absence, more especially as she received no letters from him for several months. Her anxiety became too strong for her power of endurance, and led her to have recourse to the services of the local prophet. She accordingly sent messages to Strathpeffer, summoning Coinneach to her presence, to obtain from him, if possible, some tidings of her absent lord. Coinneach, as we have seen, was already celebrated, far and wide, throughout the whole Highlands, for his great powers of divination, and his relations with the invisible world.

Obeying the orders of Lady Seaforth, Kenneth arrived at the Castle, and presented himself to the Countess, who required him to give her information concerning her absent lord.

Coinneach asked where Seaforth was supposed to be, and said that he thought he would be able to find him if he was still alive. He applied the divination stone to his eyes, and laughed loudly, saying to the Countess, 'Fear not for your lord, he is safe and sound, well and hearty, merry and happy.' Being now satisfied that her husband's life was safe, she wished Kenneth to describe his appearance; to tell where he was now engaged, and all his surroundings. 'Be satisfied,' he said, 'ask no questions, let it suffice you to know that your lord is well and merry.' 'But,' demanded the lady, 'where is he? with whom is he? and is he making any preparations for coming home?' 'Your lord,' replied the Seer, 'is in a magnificent room, in very fine company, and far too agreeably employed at present to think of leaving Paris.' The Countess, finding that her lord was well and happy, began to fret that she had no share in his happiness and amusements, and to feel even the pangs of jealousy and wounded pride. She thought there was something in the Seer's looks and expression which seemed to justify such feelings. He spoke sneeringly and maliciously of her husband's occupations, as much as to say, that he could tell a disagreeable tale if he would. The lady tried entreaties, bribes and threats to induce Coinneach to give a true account of her husband, as he had seen him, to tell who was with him, and all about him. Kenneth pulled himself together, and proceeded to say – 'As you will know that which will make you unhappy, I must tell you the truth. My lord seems to have little thought of you, or of his children, or of his Highland home. I saw him in a gay-gilded room, grandly decked out in velvets, with silks and cloth of gold, and on his knees before a fair lady, his arm round her waist, and her hand pressed to his lips.' At this unexpected and painful disclosure, the rage of the lady knew no bounds. It was natural and well merited, but its object was a mistake. All the anger which ought to have been directed against her husband, and which should have been concentrated in her breast, to be poured out upon him after his return, was spent upon poor Coinneach Odhar. She felt the more keenly, that the disclosures of her husband's infidelity had not been made to herself in private, but in the presence of the principal retainers of her house, so that the Earl's moral character was blasted, and her own charms slighted, before the whole clan; and her husband's desertion of her for a French lady was certain to become the public scandal of all the North of Scotland. She formed a sudden resolution with equal presence of mind and cruelty. She determined to discredit the revelations of the Seer, and to denounce him as a vile slanderer of her husband's character. She trusted that the signal vengeance she was about to inflict upon him as a liar and defamer would impress the minds, not only of her own clan, but of all the inhabitants of the counties of Ross and Inverness, with a sense of her thorough disbelief in the scandalous story, to which she nevertheless secretly attached full credit. Turning to the Seer, she said, 'You have spoken evil of dignities, you have defamed a mighty chief in the midst of his vassals, you have abused my hospitality and outraged my feelings, you have sullied the good name of my lord in the halls of his ancestors, and you shall suffer the most signal vengeance I can inflict – you shall suffer the death.'

Coinneach was filled with astonishment and dismay at this fatal result of his art. He had expected far other rewards from his art of divination. However, he could not at first believe the rage of the Countess to be serious; at all events, he expected that it would soon evaporate, and that, in the course of a few hours, he would be allowed to depart in peace. He even so far understood her feelings that he thought she was making a parade of anger in order to discredit the report of her lord's shame before the clan; and he expected that when this object was served, he might at length be dismissed without personal injury. But the decision of the Countess was no less violently conceived than it was promptly executed. The doom of Coinneach was sealed. No time was to be allowed for remorseful compunction. No preparation was permitted to the wretched man. No opportunity was given for intercession in his favour. The miserable Seer was led out for immediate execution.

Such a stretch of feudal oppression, at a time so little remote as the reign of Charles II, may appear strange. A castle may be pointed out, however, viz, Menzies Castle, much less remote from the seat of authority, and the Courts of Law, than Brahan, where, half a century later, an odious vassal was starved to death by order of the wife of the chief, the sister of the great and patriotic Duke of Argyll! …

When Coinneach found that no mercy was to be expected either from the vindictive lady or her subservient vassals, he resigned himself to his fate. He drew forth his white stone, so long the instrument of his supernatural intelligence, and once more applying it to his eyes, said – 'I see into the far future, and I read the doom of the race of my oppressor. The long-descended line of Seaforth will, ere many generations have passed, end in extinction and sorrow. I see a chief, the last of his house, both deaf and dumb. He will be the father of four fair sons, all of whom he will follow to the tomb. He will live careworn and die mourning, knowing that the honours of his line are to be extinguished for ever, and that no future chief of the Mackenzies shall bear rule at Brahan or in Kintail. After lamenting over the last and most promising of his sons, he himself shall sink into the grave, and the remnant of his possessions shall be inherited by a white-coifed (or white-hooded) lassie from the East, and she is to kill her sister. And as a sign by which it may be known that these things are coming to pass, there shall be four great lairds in the days of the last deaf and dumb Seaforth – Gairloch, Chisholm, Grant and Raasay – of whom one shall be buck-toothed, another hare-lipped, another half-witted and the fourth a stammerer. Chiefs distinguished by these personal marks shall be the allies and neighbours of the last Seaforth; and when he looks around him and sees them, he may know that his sons are doomed to death, that his broad lands shall pass away to the stranger, and that his race shall come to an end.'

When the seer had ended this prediction, he threw his white stone into a small loch, and declared that whoever should find that stone would be similarly gifted. Then submitting to his fate, he was at once executed, and this wild and fearful doom ended his strange and uncanny life.

Sir Bernard Burke, to whose *Vicissitudes of Families* we are mainly indebted for this part of the Prophecies, says: With regard to the four Highland lairds, who were to be buck-toothed, hare-lipped, half-witted and a stammerer – Mackenzie, Baronet of Gairloch; Chisholm of Chisholm; Grant, Baronet of Grant; and Macleod of Raasay – I am uncertain which was which. Suffice it to say, that the four lairds were marked by the above-mentioned distinguishing personal peculiarities, and all four were the contemporaries of the last of the Seaforths.

We believe Sir Hector Mackenzie of Gairloch was the buck-toothed laird (*an Tighearna Storach*); the Chisholm, the hare-lipped; Grant, the half-witted; and Raasay, the stammerer, all of whom were contemporaries of the last Lord Seaforth.

In the Wardlaw Manuscript, the Rev. James Fraser writes:

Another prediction of some alteration upon the famelies when black-kneed Seaforth, black-spotted Lord Lovat, squint-eyed Mackintosh and a Chisholm blind of an eye; and these four are just now contemporary: and though much stress should not be laid upon such prophesies, yet they ought not to be vilified or contemnd; and seeing these things were observed before they came, we can do no less than remark then when they fall out, as now they doe. And I remember to heare a very old man, Eneas M'kdonell in Craigscorry, relate this prediction to Sir James Fraser, tutor of Lovat, anno 1648; and as I heard the observe then with my eares, so I now see it with my eyes. God Almighty turn all to the best!

With regard to the black-spotted Lovat, Fraser gives a full acount of his birth:

My Lord Lovat ... got a sudden call from south ... . He left his lady big with child, in continuall feare. It pleased God she was safely brought to bed of a sone, September 28, being Michaelmas eve; and the child being tender by his mother's former indisposition he was presently christened Hugh. ... The midwife, Janet Fraser, daughter of Donald, son of Robbie, an honest widow in Finask, told myselfe instantly, 'Take well about your young cheefe, the Master of Lovat, for his mother will never bear another.' He was born with a large black spot uppon his upper right lip. When Kathrin M'kenzie, Mistress of Kingily, one of the godmothers, got him in her lap, and spying the mark, she said to the midwife 'Berwom E Berwom E (*Beir uam e, beir uam e*, Take him from me) take him, away with him, he will do no good,' and alas future events proved it true. His mother, my Lady Lovat, whither by apprehension or naturall contingent hysterick fit, was like to passe; but beside the skillfull midwife, Doctor George Mackenzie was domestick, and Jean Turnbull, her own maid, had good preactices of such maladies, which made us fear the lesse. Now is our old prediction confirmed of four considerably chiftens in the North born with signall marks, of which the Master of Lovat is one. ... All four are so, and whither for good or evil to raise or ruin their famelies, they are signally marked and remarked.

Elizabeth Grant of Rothiemurchus, in her *Memoirs of a Highland Lady*, writes of the year 1815:

My last year's friend, the new member for Ross-shire, Mr Mackenzie of Applecross, was at this Meeting, more agreeable than ever, but looking extremely ill. ... He was a plain man, and he had a buck tooth to which someone had called attention, and it was soon the only topic spoken of, for an old prophecy ran that whenever a mad Lovat, a childless —, and an Applecross with a buck tooth met, there would be an end of Seaforth. The buck tooth all could see, the mad Lovat was equally conspicuous, and though Mrs— had two handsome sons born after several years of childless wedlock, nobody ever thought of fathering them on her husband. In the beginning of this year Seaforth, the Chief of the Mackenzies, boasted of two promising sons; both were gone, died within a few months of each other. The Chieftainship went to another branch, but the lands and the old Castle of Brahan would descend after Lord Seaforth's death to his daughter Lady Hood – an end of *Cabarfeidh*. This made everyone melancholy, and the deaths of course kept many away from the Meeting. ...

Mr Macintyre supplies the following account of the Seaforth prophecy and the Seer's death, as related at this day, in the Black Isle:

Coinneach's supernatural power was at length the cause which led to his untimely and cruel death. At a time when there was a convivial gathering in Brahan Castle, a large concourse of local aristocratic guests was present. As the youthful portion were amusing themselves in the beautiful grounds or park surrounding the castle, and displaying their noble forms and features as they thought to full advantage, a party remarked in Coinneach Odhar's hearing, that such a gathering of gentlemen's children could rarely be seen. The Seer answered with a sneer, 'that he saw more in the company of the children of footmen and grooms than of the children of gentlemen', (*Is mo th' ann do chlann ghillean-buird agus do chlann ghillean-stabuil no th'ann do chlann dhaoin' waisle*), a remark which soon came to the ears of Lady Seaforth and the other ladies present, who were so much offended and provoked at this base insinuation as to the paternity of the Brahan guests, that they determined at once to have condign punishment on the once respected Seer. He was forthwith ordered to be seized; and, after eluding the search of his infuriated pursuers for some time, was at last apprehended. Seeing he had no way of escape, he once more applied the magic stone to his eye, and uttered the well-known prophetic curse [already given] against the Brahan family, and then threw the stone into a cow's footmark, which was full of water, declaring that a child would be born with two navels, or as some say, with four thumbs and six toes, who would in course of time discover it inside a pike, and who then would be gifted with Coinneach's prophetic power. As it was the purpose of his pursuers to obtain possession of this wonderful stone, as well as of the prophet's person, search was eagerly made for it in the muddy waters in the footprint, when, lo! it was found that more water was copiously oozing from the boggy ground around, and rapidly forming a considerably lake, that effectually concealed the much-coveted stone. The waters steadily increased, and the result, as the story goes, was the formation of Loch Ussie (Oozie). The poor prophet was then taken to Chanonry Point, where the stern arm of ecclesiastical authority, with unrelenting severity, burnt him to death in a tar-barrel for witchcraft.

It is currently reported that a person answering to the foregoing description was actually born in the neighbourhood of Conon, near Loch Ussie, and is still living. Of this I have been credibly informed by a person who saw him several times at the Muir of Ord markets.

We see from the public prints, our correspondent humorously continues, that the Magistrates and Police Commissioners of Dingwall contemplate to bring a supply of water for *Baile-'Chail* from Loch Ussie. Might we humbly suggest with such a view in prospect, as some comfort to the burdened ratepayers, that there may be, to say the least, a probability in the course of such an undertaking of recovering the mystic stone, so long compelled to hide its prophetic light in the depths of Loch Ussie, and so present the world with the novel sight of having not only an individual gifted with second sight, but also a Corporation; and, further, what would be a greater terror to evil-doers, a magistracy capable, in the widest sense of the word, of discerning between right and wrong, good and evil, and thus compelling the lieges in the surrounding towns and villages to exclaim involuntarily – *O si sic omnes!* They might go the length even of lending it out, and giving you the use of it occasionally in Inverness.

When Coinneach Odhar was being led to the stake, fast bound with cords, Lady Seaforth exultingly declared that, having had so much unhallowed intercourse with the unseen world, he would never go to Heaven. But the Seer, looking round upon her with an eye from which his impending fate had not banished the ray of joyful hope of rest in a future state, gravely answered:

I will go to Heaven, but *you* never shall; and this will be a sign whereby you can determine whether my condition after death is one of everlasting happiness or of eternal misery; a raven and a dove, swiftly flying in opposite directions will meet, and for a second hover over my ashes, on which they will instantly alight. If the raven be foremost, you have spoken truly; but if the dove, then my hope is well-founded.

This prophecy was also attributed to Michael Scot or Scott, the thirteenth-century philosopher who may possibly have been born in Balwearie, Fife, but was more probably a Borderer. He was a remarkable scholar who studied Arabic, astrology and alchemy at Oxford, travelled to Paris, Padua and Toledo to study theology, chemistry and medicine. He served the Emperor Frederick II as royal astrologer and physician, and published among other works a collection of his predictions. In Scotland he was known as Auld Michael, a notorious necromancer who wrote a mighty book of spells which included a recipe for flight, and which was buried with him. His death was said to have been due to supping a broth of breme, a sow in heat, but in Italy legend has it that he was killed by a falling stone.

And, accordingly, tradition relates that after the cruel sentence of his hard-hearted enemies had been executed upon the Brahan Seer, and his ashes lay scattered among the smouldering embers of the faggot, his last prophecy was most literally fulfilled; for those messengers, emblematically denoting – the one sorrow, the other joy – came speeding to the fatal spot, when the dove, with characteristic flight, closely followed by the raven, darted downwards and was first to alight on the dust of the departed Coinneach Odhar; thus completely disproving the positive and uncharitable assertion of the proud and vindictive Lady of Brahan, to the wonder and consternation of all the beholders.

Mr Maclennan describes the cause of Coinneach's doom in almost identical terms; the only difference being, that while the former has the young ladies amusing themselves on the green outside, the latter describes them having a grand dance in the great hall of the Castle. The following is his account of the prophet's end:

In terms of her expressed resolution, Lady Seaforth, some days after this magnificent entertainment, caused the Seer to be seized, bound hand and foot, and carried forthwith to the Ness of Chanonry, where, despite his pitiful looks and lamentable cries, he was inhumanly thrown, head foremost, into a barrel of burning tar, the inside of which was thickly studded with sharp and long spikes driven in from the outside. On the very day upon which Coinneach was sent away from the castle to meet his cruel fate, Lord Seaforth arrived, and was immediately informed of his Lady's resolution, and that Coinneach was already well on his way to the Chanonry, where he was to be burned that very day, under clerical supervision and approval. My lord, knowing well the vindictive and cruel nature of his Countess, believed the story to be only too true. He waited neither for food nor refreshment; called neither for groom nor for servant, but hastened immediately to the stable, saddled his favourite steed with his own hands, for lairds were not so proud in those days, and set off at full speed, hoping to reach Chanonry Point before the diabolical intention of her ladyship and her religious (!) advisers should be carried into effect. Never before nor since did Seaforth ride so furiously as he did on that day. He was soon at Fortrose, when he observe a dense smoke rising higher and higher from the promontory below. He felt his whole frame giving way, and a cold sweat came over his body, for he felt that the foul deed was, or was about to be, perpetrated. He pulled himself together, however, and with fresh energy and redoubled vigour, spurred his steed, which had already been driven almost beyond its powers of endurance, to reach the fatal spot to save the Seer's life. Within a few paces of where the smoke was rising the poor brute could endure the strain no longer; it fell down under him and died on the spot. Still determined, if possible, to arrive in time, he rushed forward on foot, crying out at the height of his voice to those congregated at the spot, to save their victim. It was, however, too late, for whether Seaforth's cries were heard or not, the victim of his lady's rage and vindictive nature had been thrown into the burning barrel a few moments before his intended deliverer had reached the fatal spot.

The time when this happened is not so very remote as to lead us to suppose that tradition could so grossly blunder as to record such a horrible and barbarous murder by a lady so widely and well known as Lady Seaforth was, had it not taken place.

It is too much to suppose that if the Seer had been allowed to die a peaceful and natural death, that such a story as this would have ever originated, be carried down and believed in from generation to generation, and be so well authenticated in many quarters as it now is. It may be stated that a large stone slab, now covered under the sand, lies a few yards east from the road leading from Fortrose to Fort George Ferry, and about 250 yards northwest from the lighthouse, which is still pointed out as marking the spot where this inhuman tragedy was consummated, under the eyes and with the full approval of the highest dignitaries of the Church.

A stone commemorating the legend of the Brahan Seer and his burning at Chanonry Point was erected by Fortrose Town Council and Academy near the Lighthouse in 1969. Half-way between the Light-house and the Golf Clubhouse, on a ridge in the rough, there stands another much older stone. This is said to mark the spot where the last witch was burned, but it is not known who this was, or when. An ancient title deed to one of the original crofts near the neck of the Ness recorded the site of 'Coinneach Odhar's stone', but this has been removed in the recent development of the area.

Some ten years ago the local lighthouse-keeper was approached by a woman in distress who asked if she could bury something in front of the Seer's commemorative stone. She believed her family was still under the influence of Coinneach Odhar's curse and hoped to alleviate it. The keeper told her to do as she pleased, and next day he noticed that a neat rectangle of turf had been cut out and replaced. Such is the power of the Brahan Seer in the Highlands to this day.

Having thus disposed of the Seer himself, we next proceed to give in detail the fulfilment of the prophecies regarding the family of his cruel murderer. And we regret to say that the family of Seaforth will, in this connection, fall to be disposed of finally and for ever, and in the manner which Coinneach had unquestionably predicted. As already remarked, in due time the Earl returned to his home, after the fascinations of Paris had paled, and when he felt disposed to exchange frivolous or vicious enjoyment abroad for the exercise of despotic authority in the society of a jealous Countess at home. He was gathered to his fathers in 1678, and was succeeded by his eldest son, the fourth Earl. It is not our purpose to relate here the vicissitudes of the family which are unconnected with the curse of Coinneach Odhar, further than by giving a brief outline, though they are sufficiently remarkable to supply a strange chapter of domestic history.

The fourth Earl married a daughter of the illustrious family of Herbert, Marquis of Powis, and he himself was created a Marquis by the abdicated King of St Germains, while his wife's brother was created a Duke. His son, the fifth Earl, having engaged in the rebellion of 1715, forfeited his estate and titles to the Crown; but in 1726 his lands were restored to him, and he, and his son after him, lived in wealth and honour as great Highland chiefs. The latter, who was by courtesy styled Lord Fortrose, represented his native county of Ross in several Parliaments about the middle of last century. In 1766, the honours of the peerage were restored to his son, who was created Viscount Fortrose, and in 1771, Earl of Seaforth; but those titles, which were Irish, did not last long, and became extinct at his death in 1781. None of these vicissitudes were foretold in the Seer's prophecy; and, in spite of them all, the family continued to prosper. That ruin which the unsuccessful rising in 1715 had brought upon many other great houses, was retrieved in the case of Seaforth, by the exercise of sovereign favour; and restored possessions and renewed honours preserved the grandeur of the race. But on the death of the last Earl, his second cousin, descended from a younger son of the third Earl and his vindictive Countess, inherited the family estates and the chiefdom of the Mackenzies, which he held for two short years, but never actually enjoyed, being slain at sea by the Mahrattas, at Gheriah, in the south of India, in 1783, after a gallant resistance. He was succeeded by his brother, in whom, as the last of his race, the Seer's prophecy was accomplished.

Francis Humberston Mackenzie was a very remarkable man. He was born in 1754, and although deaf, and latterly dumb, he was, by the force of his natural abilities and the favour of fortune, able to fill an important position in the world. ...

It would have been already observed that the 'Last of the Seaforths' was born in full possession of all his faculties, and that he only became deaf from the effects of a severe attack of scarlet fever, while a boy in school, which we have previously noticed in connection with his remarkable dream. He continued to speak a little, and it was only towards the close of his life, and particularly during the last two years, that he was unable to articulate – or perhaps, unwilling to make the attempt, on finding himself the last male of his line. He may be said to have, prior to this, fairly recovered the use of speech, for he was able to converse pretty distinctly; but he was so totally deaf, that all communications were made to him by signs or in writing. Yet he raised a regiment at the beginning of the great European war; he was created a British peer in 1797, as Baron Seaforth of Kintail; in 1800 he went out to Barbados as Governor, and afterwards to Demerara and Berbice; and in 1808 he was made a Lieutenant-General. These were singular incidents in the life of a deaf and dumb man. He married a very amiable and excellent woman, Mary Proby, the daughter of a dignitary of the Church, and niece of the first Lord Carysfort, by whom he had a fine family of four sons and six daughters. When he considered his own position – deaf, and formerly dumb; when he saw his four sons, three of them rising to man's estate; and when he looked around him, and observed the peculiar marks set upon the persons of the four contemporary great Highland lairds, all in strict accordance with Coinneach's prophecy – he must have felt ill at ease, unless he was able, with the incredulous indifference of a man of the world, to spurn the idea from him as an old wife's superstition.

However, fatal conviction was forced upon him, and on all those who remembered the family tradition, by the lamentable events which filled his house with mourning. One after another his three promising sons (the fourth died young) were cut off by death. The last, who was the most distinguished of them all, for the finest qualities both of head and heart, was stricken by a sore and lingering disease, and had gone, with a part of the family, for his health, to the south of England. Lord Seaforth remained in the north, at Brahan Castle. A daily bulletin was sent to him from the sick chamber of his beloved son. One morning, the accounts being rather more favourable, the household began to rejoice, and a friend in the neighbourhood, who was visiting the chief, came down after breakfast full of the good news, and gladly imparted it to the old family piper, whom he met in front of the Castle. The aged retainer shook his head and sighed – 'Na, na,' said he, 'he'll never recover. It's decreed that Seaforth must outlive all his four sons.' This he said in allusion to the Seer's prophecy; thus his words were understood by the family; and thus members of the family have again and again repeated the strange tale. The words of the old piper proved too true. A few more posts brought to Seaforth the tidings of the death of the last of his four sons.

At length, on 11 January 1815, Lord Seaforth died, the last of his race. His modern title became extinct. The chiefdom of the Mackenzies, divested of its rank and honour, passed away to a very remote collateral, who succeeded to no portion of the property, and the great Seaforth estates were inherited by a white-hooded lassie from the East. Lord Seaforth's eldest surviving daughter, the Honourable Mary Frederica Elizabeth Mackenzie, had married, in 1804, Admiral Sir Samuel Hood, Bart, KB, who was Admiral of the West India station while

Seaforth himself was Governor in those islands. Sir Samuel afterwards had the chief command in the Indian seas, whither his lady accompanied him, and spent several years with him in different parts of the East Indies. He died while holding that high command, very nearly at the same time as Lord Seaforth, so that his youthful wife was a recent widow at the time, and returned home from India in her widow's weeds, to take possession of her paternal inheritance. She was thus literally a white-coifed or white-hooded lassie (that is, a young woman in widow's weeds, and a Hood by name) from the East. After some years of widowhood, Lady Hood Mackenzie married a second time, Mr Stewart, a grandson of the sixth Earl of Galloway, who assumed the name of Mackenzie, and established himself on his lady's extensive estates in the North. Thus, the possessions of Seaforth may be truly said to have passed from the male line of the ancient house of Mackenzie. And still more strikingly was this fulfilled, as regarded a large portion of these estates, when Mr and Mrs Stewart Mackenzie sold the great Island of Lewis to Sir James Matheson.

After many years of happiness and prosperity, a frightful accident threw the family into mourning. Mrs Stewart Mackenzie was one day driving her younger sister, the Hon Caroline Mackenzie, in a pony carriage, among the woods in the vicinity of Brahan Castle. Suddenly, the ponies took fright, and started off at a furious pace. Mrs Stewart Mackenzie was quite unable to check them, and both she and her sister were thrown out of the carriage much bruised and hurt. She happily soon recovered from the accident, but the injury which her sister sustained proved fatal, and, after lingering for some time in a hopeless state, she died, to the inexpressible grief of all the members of her family. As Mrs Stewart Mackenzie was driving the carriage at the time of the accident, she may be said to have been the innocent cause of her sister's death, and thus to have fulfilled the last portion of Coinnearch's prophecy which has yet been accomplished.

A monument commemorating this sad accident may be seen on the A835 road between Maryburgh and Contin. The Latin inscription reads as follows:

Hic fato ut fertur praedicto abrepta est Francis Baron de Seaforth filia Carolina Mackenzie cujus soror eusdem pericli particeps domus suae redintegrandae spes ultima super fuit. MDCCCXXIII (At this point, according to the prophecy uttered, Caroline Mackenzie daughter of Francis, Baron Seaforth, was snatched from life; her sister who shared the same hazard was the last surviving hope of restoration of his house. 1823)

The inscription is important for it shows that the prediction was known before the accident.

The monument, smothered in undergrowth since the recent upgrading of the road which runs through the Brahan estate, is badly in need of massive restoration.

Thus we have seen that the last chief of Seaforth was deaf and dumb; that he had four sons; that he survived them all; that the four great Highland lairds who were his contemporaries were all distinguished by the peculiar personal marks the Seer predicted; that his estates were inherited by a white-coifed or white-hooded lassie from the East; that his great possessions passed into the hands of other races; and that his eldest daughter and heiress was so unfortunate as to be the innocent cause of her sister's death. In this very remarkable instance of family fate, the prophecy was not found out after the events occurred; it had been current for generations in the Highlands, and its tardy fulfilment was marked curiously and anxiously by an entire clan and a whole county. Seaforth was respected and beloved far and near, and strangers, as well as friends and clansmen, mourned along with him the sorrows of his later years. The gradual development of the doom was watched with sympathy and grief, and the fate of

Seaforth has been, during the last half-century of his life, regarded as one of the most curious instances of that second sight for which the inhabitants of the Highlands of Scotland have been so long celebrated. Mr Stewart Mackenzie, the accomplished husband of the heiress of Seaforth, after being for many years a distinguished member of the House of Commons and a Privy Councillor, held several high appointments in the Colonial Dominions of the British Crown. He was successively Governor of Ceylon and Lord High Commissioner of the Ionian Islands, and died, universally beloved and lamented, in the year 1843.

Lockhart in his *Life of Scott*, in reference to the Seaforth prediction, says: 'Mr Morrit can testify thus far – that he heard the prophecy quoted in the Highlands at a time when Lord Seaforth had two sons alive, and in good health, and that it certainly was not made after the event'; and he goes on to tell us that Scott and Sir Humphrey Davy were most certainly convinced of its truth, as also many others who had watched the latter days of Seaforth in the light of those wonderful predictions.

The late Duncan Davisdon of Tulloch, Lord-Lieutenant of the County of Ross, on reading our second edition, wrote to the author, under date of 21 May 1878, as follows: 'Many of these prophecies I heard of *upwards of 70 years ago, and when many of them were not fulfilled*, such as the late Lord Seaforth surviving his sons, and Mrs Stewart-Mackenzie's accident, near Brahan, by which Miss Caroline Mackenzie was killed.' Tulloch was, he said, during the latter years of Lord Seaforth, a regular visitor at Brahan Castle, and often heard the predictions referred to among members of the family. The letter is in our possession, and it was published, during Tulloch's life, and by his special permission, in Mackenzie's *History of the Mackenzies*, p 267.

An attempt was recently made to sell the remaining possessions of the family, but fortunately, for the present, this attempt has been defeated by the interposition of the Marchioness of Tweeddale and Mrs Colonel Stanley, daughters of the present nominal possessor of the property. At the time a leading article appeared in the *Edinburgh Daily Review* giving an outline of the family history of the Seaforths. After describing how the fifth Earl, with the fidelity characteristic of his house, 'true as the dial to the sun', embraced the losing side in 'the Fifteen'; fought at the head of his clan at Sheriffmuir; how in 1719 he, along with the Marquis of Tullibardine, and the Earl Marischal, made a final attempt to bring the 'auld Stewarts back again'; how he was dangerously wounded in an encounter with the Government forces at Glenshiel, and compelled to abandon the vain enterprise; how he was carried on board a vessel by his clansmen, conveyed to the Western Isles, and ultimately to France; how he was attainted by Parliament, and his estates forfeited to the Crown; how all the efforts of the Government failed to penetrate into Kintail, or to collect any rent from his faithful Macraes, whom the Seaforths had so often led victorious from many a bloody conflict, from the battle of Largs down to the Jacobite Rebellions of 1715 and 1719; and how the rents of that part of the estates were regularly collected and remitted to their exiled chief in France, with a devotion and faithfulness only to be equalled by their own countrymen when their beloved 'bonnie Prince Charlie' was a wanderer, helpless and forlorn, at the mercy of his enemies, and with a reward of £30,000 at the disposal of many a poverty-stricken and starving Highlander, who would not betray his lawful Prince for all the gold in England; the article continues:

But their (the Seaforth's) downfall came at last, and the failure of the male line of this great historical family was attended with circumstances as singular as they were painful. Francis, Lord Seaforth, the last Baron of Kintail, was, says Sir Walter Scott, 'a nobleman of extraordinary talents, who must have made for himself a lasting reputation, had not his political exertions been checked by painful natural infirmity'. Though deaf from his sixteenth year, and inflicted also with a partial impediment of speech, he was distinguished for his attainments as well as for his intellectual activity. He took a lively interest in all questions of art and science, especially in natural history, and displayed at once his liberality and his love of art by his munificence to Sir Thomas Lawrence, in the youthful traits and struggles of that great artist, and by his patronage of other artists. Before his elevation to the peerage, Lord Seaforth represented Ross-shire in Parliament for a number of years, and was afterwards Lord-Lieutenant of the county. During the revolutionary war with France, he raised a splendid regiment of Ross-shire Highlanders (the 78th, the second which had been raised among his clan), of which he was appointed Lieutenant-Colonel Commandant, and he ultimately attained the rank of Lieutenant-General in the Army. He held for six years the office of Governor of Barbados, and, by his firmness and even-handed justice, he succeeded in putting an end to the practice of slave-killing, which at that time was not unfrequent in the Island, and was deemed by the planters a venial offence, to be punished only by a small fine.

Lord Seaforth was the happy father of three (four) sons and six daughters, all of high promise; and it seemed as if he were destined to raise the illustrious house of which he was the head, to a height of honour and power greater than it had ever yet attained. But the closing years of this nobleman were darkened by calamities of the severest kind. The mismanagement of his estates in the West Indies involved him in inextricable embarrassments, and compelled him to dispose of a part of his Kintail estates – 'the giftland' of the family, as it was termed – a step which his tenantry and clansmen in vain endeavoured to avert, by offering to buy in the land for him, that it might not pass from the family. He had previously been bereaved of two of his sons, and about the time that Kintail was sold, his only remaining son, a young man of talent and eloquence, the representative in Parliament of his native county, suddenly died. The broken-hearted father lingered on for a few months, his fine intellect enfeebled by paralysis, and yet, as Sir Walter Scott says, 'not so entirely obscured but that he perceived his deprivation as in a glass, darkly'. Sometimes he was anxious and fretful because he did not see his son; sometimes he expostulated and complained that his boy had been allowed to die without his seeing him; and sometimes, in a less clouded state of intellect, he was sensible of his loss in its full extent. The last *Cabarfeidh* followed his son to the grave in January 1815, and then –

Of the line of Fitzgerald remained not a male,
To bear the proud name of the Chiefs of Kintail.

The most remarkable circumstance connected with this sorrowful tale, is the undoubted fact that, centuries ago, a Seer of the Clan Mackenzie, known as Kenneth Oag (Odhar), predicted that when there should be a deaf and dumb *Cabarfeidh* (Staghead, the Celtic designation of the chief of the clan, taken from the family crest), the 'gift-land' of their territory (Kintail) would be sold, and the male line become extinct. This prophecy was well known in the north long before its fulfilment, and was certainly not made after the event. 'It connected,' says Lockhart, 'the fall of the house of Seaforth not only with the appearance of a deaf *Cabarfeidh*, but with the contemporaneous appearance of various physical misfortunes in several other great Highland chiefs, all of which are said to have actually occurred within the memory of the generation that has not yet passed away.'

On the death of his lordship, his estates, with all their burdens and responsibilities, devolved on his eldest daughter, Lady Hood, whose second husband was James Stewart

Mackenzie, a member of the Galloway family, and whose son has just been prevented from selling all that remains of the Seaforth estates. 'Our friend, Lady Hood,' wrote Sir Walter Scott to Mr Morritt, 'will now be *Caberfeidh* herself. She has the spirit of a chieftainness in every drop of her blood, but there are few situations in which the cleverest women are so apt to be imposed upon as in the management of landed property, more especially of a Highland estate. I do fear the accomplishment of the prophecy that, when there should be a deaf *Caberfeidh*, the house was to fall.'

The writer concludes thus:

Scott's apprehensions proved only too well founded. One section after another of the estates had to be sold. The remaining portion of Kintail, the sunny braes of Ross, the church lands of Chanonry, the barony of Pluscarden, and the Island of Lews – a principality itself – were disposed of one after the other, till now nothing remains of the vast estates of this illustrious house except Brahan Castle, and a mere remnant of their ancient patrimony (and that in the hands of trustees), which the non-resident, nominal owner has just been prevented from alienating. *Sic transit.*

The 14,000-acre estate of Kintail is now owned by the National Trust for Scotland. The present owner of Brahan, Andrew Matheson, is a relative of the old Seaforth family and manages the Brahan estate.

Leaving these extraordinary prophecies with the reader, to believe, disbelieve, or explain away on any principle or theory which may satisfy his reason, his credulity, or scepticism, we conclude with the following:

Lament for 'The Last of the Seaforths'
By Sir Walter Scott

In vain the bright course of thy talents to wrong
Fate deadn'd thine ear and imprison'd thy tongue,
For brighter o'er all her obstructions arose
The glow of the genius they could not oppose;
And who, in the land of the Saxon, or Gael,
Might match with Mackenzie, High Chief of Kintail?
Thy sons rose around thee in light and in love,
All a father could hope, all a friend could approve;
What 'vails it the tale of thy sorrows to tell?
In the spring time of youth and of promise they fell!
Of the line of MacKenneth remains not a male,
To bear the proud name of the Chief of Kintail.
And thou, gentle Dame, who must bear, to thy grief,
For thy clan and thy country the cares of a Chief,
Whom brief rolling moons in six changes have left,
Of thy husband and father and brethren bereft;
To thine ear of affection, how sad is the hail
That salutes thee – the heir of the line of Kintail!
Na'm biodh an t' earball na bu ruighne biodh mo sgialachd na b' fhaïde.

299

CHAPTER TWENTY ONE

Prophecy and Divination

Lewis Spence

T HE GREAT ART OF FORETELLING AND PREVISION in all its branches was as second nature
to the Celtic peoples, who, from the earliest recorded times in their history, almost
until the present, have been regarded by their neighbours as prophets and diviners *par
excellence*. It is noticeable that in Celtic vaticination there is little or no resort to outside
agencies, no recourse to heighten 'with euphrasy and rue the visual nerve', or to employ
narcotic draughts to quicken the native gift of prophetic sight, as in Oriental Magic. In this
chapter I shall divide the evidence for Celtic prevision into its necromantic, prophetic and
divinatory aspects, leaving the question of second sight for a separate and later chapter.

The term necromancy, strictly speaking, signifies divination by the aid of the spirits of the
dead, but it is frequently applied to divination through spirits of any kind. It is in the latter
sense almost exclusively that I will employ it here, as the raising of the spirits of the dead by
Celtic magicians seems to have been a matter of rare occurrence only. By far the most celebrated
and usual method of employing the necromantic faculty was by what is known as *taghairm*,
a word which signifies 'an echo' – that is, a response as from a distance, a spiritual reply. Perhaps
it may most fittingly be Englished as 'the spirit call'.

The awful and mysterious – and frequently repellent – rites of *taghairm* were certainly not of
one particular kind, but appear to have been multiform. In its modern form it appears to have
been confined exclusively to Scotland. The less obnoxious examples of it were associated with the
wrapping of the seer in the hide of a newly slaughtered bull, much after the manner in which the
priests of Egypt and those of the Jews and the Babylonians donned the fleece of a ram when engaged
in certain magical or divinatory acts. Thus attired, he stretched himself beside a waterfall, or at
the foot of some wild precipice reputed to be haunted by spirits, and awaited their coming.
Whatever the seer desired to know, the fate of a family or the outcome of a battle, was duly
communicated to him by agencies who may have been demons or nature-spirits.

Martin, in his *Description of the Western Isles*, provides a startling picture of this mystical
proceeding. The seer, he tells us, who was frequently chosen by lot, was left by his companions
beside some stream which marked the boundaries of two villages. When he had closed his
eyes, four of the company laid hold of him and, rocking him to and fro, struck his hips forcibly
against the bank of the rivulet. One of them then exclaimed as though in question, 'What
have you there?' to which another replied: 'A log of birchwood.' The intention seems to have

been to delude the spirits into the belief that the seer was one of these logs or rude images which fairies and other spirits were in the habit of placing in children's cradles when they kidnapped the infants, or which they employed as magical substitutes for grown-up persons whom they had spirited away.

This part of the rite must indeed have been a relic of more ancient and primitive practice. The first speaker then cried: 'Let his invisible friends appear from all quarters and relieve him by giving an answer to our questions.' At this a swarm of diminutive spirits rose from the sea some distance away, replied to the man's queries more or less satisfactorily, and as suddenly disappeared. The seer was then liberated and the company returned home, bearing with them the appropriate, if ambiguously oracular, rejoinder of the spirit host.

'Mr Alexander Cooper,' adds Martin, 'present minister of North Uist, told me that one John Erach, in the Isle of Lewis, assured him it was his fate to have been led by his curiosity with some who consulted this oracle and that he was a night within the hide as above mentioned; during which time he felt and heard such terrible things that he could not express them.' The impression was ineradicable, and 'he would not for a thousand worlds be concerned in a like performance'. A second method, says Martin, was to leave the seer in the hide at a remote place throughout the night, and it was obviously this to which the case just alluded to applies. That this description of *taghairm* was practised in Wales is clear from a statement in the tale known as 'The Vision of Rhonabwy', in which Rhonabwy, a warrior of Powys, beheld a vision of the Court of King Arthur while sleeping on the skin of a yellow heifer, as we read in the *Mabinogion*.

Still a third and much more cruel and barbarous magical device went by the name of *taghairm*. This was known in tradition as 'giving his supper to the devil', and at least three instances of it are recorded in Highland lore. The most celebrated case is that in which one Lachlan Oer and a companion, Allan, the son of Hector, shut themselves up in a barn near the Sound of Mull, and, impaling black cats on spits, roasted them alive by a blazing fire. Other cats entered the building, setting up an infernal caterwauling, which well-nigh daunted the men, but they remained inexorable until a greater cat of ferocious appearance entered and remonstrated with them, threatening them that if they did not desist from their horrid employment they would never see the face of the Trinity. Lachlan struck the hideous animal on the head with the hilt of his sword, whereupon the devil, for he it was, assumed his appropriate shape and asked the pair what it was they wanted of him. They replied that they craved prosperity and a long life to enjoy it. This was granted, and it is said that Lachlan, for his part, never relented of the dreadful act, even upon his deathbed.

Although it might seem that these two rites of *taghairm* differ in their origin, the underlying intention is the same in both cases – to compel supernatural beings to rescue one or more of their kind or species who are in the power of mortals by agreeing to some bargain which will be to the lasting benefit of those mortals. Those who bore the man wrapped up in a bull-hide, as related in the first instance, pretended that he was a fairy changeling whom they were maltreating by striking his body against the river bank, and they then called upon 'his invisible friends' to rescue him. In the case in which cats were tortured the same idea prevails, except that the cat – believed to be a diabolical creature – was actually maltreated in the hope that its satanic master would come to its aid. The other description of *taghairm*, described by Martin, was obviously of a different nature. In carrying it out, the seer was wrapped up in a bull-hide in the hope that the spirits of the deserted locality where he was placed would be tempted to approach him by the odour proceeding from the hide, and that he would learn of some coming event from their conversation.

It is said that Cameron of Lochiel received at a *taghairm* a small silver shoe, which, if placed on the foot of a newborn son of his family, would endow the child with courage and fortitude. One baby, however, had, at his birth, a foot too large for the shoe, a defect inherited from his mother, who was not of Cameron origin. His lack of the magically bestowed courage was apparent at the battle of Sheriffmuir, where he fled before the enemy.

Another divinatory rite in which the bull figured – in this case a white bull – was associated with the election of an Irish king and was known as *imbas forosnai*, or 'divination by holding the cheeks'. The flesh of a white bull was partaken of by a man; who then went to sleep, holding his cheeks in his hands, four druids chanting over him 'to render his witness truthful'. He then saw in a vision the person who should be elected king and what he was doing at the moment. Probably hypnotic influence entered into the rite. Sometimes a piece of pig's, dog's or cat's flesh was chewed instead, and then offered to an idol of the god in cases where the divination had no connection with royalty. Canon MacCulloch alludes to this method of divination in his *Religion of the Ancient Celts* (p. 248).

Giraldus Cambrensis, in the sixteenth chapter of his *Itinerary Through Wales*, alludes to a certain class of persons there whom he calls Awenydhyon, or people inspired. When consulted as to the future, they were in the habit of roaring violently, seeming to become possessed of a spirit. They did not deliver the answer to any question put them in a rational or connected manner, and the gist of their replies usually had to be disentangled from incoherent speeches. That these were the remaining practitioners of a druidic tradition can scarcely be questioned when the resemblance of their procedure to the rite of *imbas forosnai* is considered.

Prophecy may be defined as ecstatic utterance concerning future events delivered under great spiritual and mental stress. It has no artificial or outward aids, as has divination or auspices, and, if truly inspired, is usually regarded as divine utterance voiced through a human mouthpiece. In Celtic lore the druids are generally associated with the prophetic afflatus. It was an Irish druid who revealed to the Fomorian god Balor that he would meet his death at the hands of his grandson. Determined to render the prediction vain, Balor imprisoned his daughter Ethnea in an impregnable tower built on the summit of an almost inaccessible rock at the eastern extremity of Tory Island, at the same time directing a company of twelve matrons to guard her. But the hero Mackineely, by the aid of another druid, gained access to her and she gave birth to three sons, whom Balor cast into a whirlpool. One of them escaped, however, and later slew the darksome god, as had been predicted.

When the Tuatha Dé Danann were challenged by the Milesians to yield the soil of Ireland to them they consulted the bard Amairgen, who predicted that the Milesians would temporarily abandon the island to the Tuatha Dé so far as 'the distance of nine waves' – a typically oracular saying, for, after taking ship, the Milesians landed again elsewhere!

In his *General History of Ireland* Keating relates that in an ancient book known as *The Etymology of Names* he discovered a passage which narrated how a certain druid, who had the gift of prophecy, foretold to Daire, an Irish monarch, that he should have a son whose name should be Lugaidh, and that, to give the prophecy the fullest force, he must call all his sons by that name. The druid had added that this particular son should sit upon the throne of Ireland. When his sons arrived at man's estate, King Daire enquired of the prophet which of them should succeed to the throne. The druid advised him to take all five of the young men to Tailtenn, at which place a meeting of the nobility was to be held, when a fawn would appear before the gathering. This animal was to be pursued by the five lads, and that one who overtook and killed it should be his father's heir. The advice was accepted, the fawn was duly chased, a magic mist enveloped it, but the genuine Lugaidh succeeded in running it to earth and dispatching it.

On another occasion, by the prophecy of a druid, three brothers of the family of Colla, says Keating, were saved from execution. They had rebelled against the King of Ulster, but when the druid Dubhchomair predicted that the crown of Ireland would not descend to the dynasty which then enjoyed it, should they be slain, their lives were preserved. Later they fled to Scotland, but learning that, should they die by order of the Irish monarch their heirs should succeed to the throne, they returned to Ireland, gave battle to the royal forces, were victorious, and divided the land between them. It would seem, therefore, that the prophecy does not appear to have been accurately forecast or fulfilled.

But the most outstanding topic in Celtic prophecy is that of the Lia Fail, the ancient coronation stone of the Irish Kings, a prophetic stone indeed, and, as its importance demands, we must make a very real endeavour to come to conclusions concerning the origin of this ancient relic, the legend of which is bound up with the destinies of the British race. … The Tuatha Dé Danann, it is said, conveyed it from the mythical isle of Fal (Destiny) or from the 'city of Falias' to Ireland, where it became the test-seat of the Kings of Ireland, crying out when the genuine heir to the crown of Eire placed his feet upon it.

Now we find that a stone of a similar kind existed at Scone, the later metropolis of the old Celtic Kings of Scotland. 'Legend,' says William Skene, 'has much to tell of how it was brought from the East to Scotland, but history knows of it only at Scone.' The great majority of Britons still credit the ancient tradition that the Coronation Stone at Westminster Abbey is ultimately of Irish origin, that it is actually the 'Lia Fail', or Stone of Destiny, spoken of in Irish legend which was brought to these shores by the conquering Irish Scots from the Hill of Tara. Are there any grounds for assuming the credibility of this time-honoured notion?

There are not. The Coronation Stone, as we know it, can most definitely be proved to have been situated in the royal Scottish demesne at Scone in the thirteenth century, being housed, in all probability, at the Abbey there, and not in the open, as some authorities have stated, until it was removed by Edward I to Westminster in the year 1296. In all likelihood it had been at Scone from much earlier times. But what is the basis for the belief in its transportation from Ireland?

The very earliest Scottish 'edition' of the legend of the Stone known to us is the statement of Baldred Bisset, one of the Scots Commissioners sent to Rome in 1301 to plead the cause of Scottish independence before the Pope. In quite a few words he tells us that the Stone was brought to Ireland by the Princess Scota, 'the daughter of Pharaoh'. Later she came to Scotland, carrying the relic with her, conquered the Picts and gave the country its present name. The Scottish Government of the time did not, however, substantiate Baldred's story, and in a separate report made no mention of it or of the Stone whatsoever, although in a famous communication to Rome, dated from Arbroath in 1321, and outlining the reasons for the separate existence of Scotland as a nation, it received passing mention.

If we follow the course of the legend, we find the next allusion to it in an English manuscript, the *Scalachronica*, written about 1355, which, relates that one Simon Breac, a son of the King of Spain, sailed to Ireland, taking with him a stone on which the monarchs of Spain were accustomed to be crowned. This, of course, is merely a version of the Irish myth as given in the *Book of Invasions*. The royal seat, we are informed, was later carried to Scone by a certain chieftain, Fergus, son of Ferchar.

The Scottish historian Fordun, writing a little later, associated this account with that which refers to the Princess Scota, whom he made the ancestress of Simon Breac. But he adds an alternative tale that the Stone was fished up out of the sea off the coast of Ireland by the anchor of one of Simon's ships. Fergus, son of Farquhar, he states, later brought the stone from

Ireland to Scotland. Andrew of Wyntoun, writing about 1424, accepted this version, but preferred to assume a more historical and much later Fergus as he who brought the Stone to Scottish soil. This chieftain, he assures us, set up the relic in Iona. Blind Harry, the Minstrel, a Scottish poet, followed this account in part and averred that the Stone was brought to Scone from Iona by King Malcolm Canmore.

In the somewhat mendacious history of Hector Boece we have the legend in its latest and fullest form. The Egyptian Princess Scota and her husband Gathelus, he tells us, fled to Portugal after the disaster to the Egyptians in the Red Sea and reigned in that country. Their descendant, Simon Breac, brought the Stone to Ireland, whence it was carried to Dunstaffnage in Argyll by Fergus, son of Ferchar, the first King of the Scots to reign in Scotland. Later, the second Fergus placed it in Iona, but Kenneth MacAlpine, after he had conquered the Picts, brought it to Scone. The story is so explanatory in its circumstances as to render its hypothetical character apparent.

The belief that the Stone had once been situated at Dunstaffnage Castle rests upon the authority of Boece alone. In the nineteenth century, McCulloch, in his *Western Isles of Scotland*, remarked that the Coronation Stone bore a strong resemblance to that which crowned the doorway of Dunstaffnage Castle. Almost at once a rumour arose that it had actually been removed from that building, and the very space from which it had been taken was solemnly pointed out!

But long before McCulloch's day a popular notion seems to have been in circulation that a missing stone at Dunstaffnage was none other than the famous Lia Fail, or Stone of Destiny, which, said the Irish 'Leabhar Gabhala' or *Book of Invasions*, had been brought from 'the city of Falias' to Ireland by way of Scotland. The stone was associated with a prophecy which averred that wherever it was situated 'the Scottish race should rulers be'. This, all Scotland devoutly believed, was the stone which had been carried from Ireland to Argyll and thence to Scone. But Irish antiquaries have proved conclusively that the stone believed to be identified with the Lia Fail, and which was situated on the Hill of Tara, *is still there*.

Petrie, in his *Antiquities of Tara Hill*, says that in 1798 it stood near the hill known as 'the Mound of Hostages', when 'it was removed to its present position in the Rath near the Forradh, to mark the grave of the rebels slain in the insurrection of that year'. That this stone still remains there is indeed common knowledge among Irish antiquaries. It is a pillar, and by no means an easily portable one, and does not at all resemble the Coronation Stone at Westminster. Petrie quotes a tenth-century Irish poem which reveals that the Lia Fail remained in Ireland. Indeed, Skene has made it particularly plain in his monograph on the Stone that it had no association with its Irish equivalent, which, he assures us, never left Ireland, and was there in the eleventh century.

The Scottish Stone, now at Westminster, was not situated in Argyll during the early times of the Scots dynasty there, the ancient historians of that province, Adamnan and Cumine, making no mention of it in their accounts of contemporary coronations. The tale that it was carried from Dunstaffnage to Scone is frankly mythical, a mere political legend, devised to give it an antiquity to which it can lay no claim.

Geologists who have examined the Stone are in substantial agreement that it was quarried at or near Scone. The late Professor Geikie wrote: 'I do not see any evidence in the Stone itself why it may not have been taken from the neighbourhood of Scone; indeed, it perfectly resembles the sandstone of that district.' Professor A.C. Ramsay arrived at much the same conclusion, though he indicated that it might have come from any part of Scotland where red sandstone abounds.

The even more absurd story that it was the stone on which Jacob pillowed his head while sojourning in the desert was the invention of one Rishanger, an English chronicler of the thirteenth century. St Columba's pillow of stone at Iona, mentioned by Adamnan and Cumine, has also been confused with the Coronation Stone, but the former writer states most distinctly that the stone associated with the saint was placed on his grave.

The Celtic peoples almost invariably employed stones of the kind in connection with the ceremonies of a royal inauguration, and I cannot doubt that when the Scottish monarchy first selected Scone as its capital in the ninth century it had such a stone quarried in the neighbourhood for that specific purpose. But where did the stories of its Irish and Egyptian origin spring from? The first was evidently a garbled version of the Hibernian myth respecting the Lia Fail applied to the Scottish Stone, the *sedes*, or throne-seat of a dynasty originally hailing from Ireland. The latter story may be a distant recollection of the myth of the divine kingship, which had its rise in ancient Egypt. If the whole cult and circumstances, ritual and legend, of the divine king could make its way from Egypt to Ireland, as I have, I think, made plain that it did in the twelfth chapter of this book, I see no reason why the story of the Princess Scota, obviously a myth intended to explain its introduction, could not have accompanied it. Indeed, such myths, explanatory not only of the divine kingship but of many other institutions, invariably accompany the cultus which they seek to elucidate, as the whole history of mythic development reveals.

But Edward I of England, that highly romantic and superstitious monarch, had at least the best of occult reasons for carrying off the stone from Scone to Westminster, for he believed it to be the habitation of an oracular spirit which advised the Scots both politically and in a military sense. This is clear enough from the terms of a poem in doggerel Latin which is to be found in the Bodleian Library, and a rough translation of which avers that:

In Egypt, Moses preached to the people saying
That Scota, the fairy maiden, who is the stone,
Told of the strange manner in which the land should be conquered.

These words seem to imply that the spirit of Scota inhabited the stone and prophesied therefrom, and parallels the tradition in the Irish *Book of Invasions* that such royal monuments were haunted by a 'demon', who exclaimed in recognition when the rightful monarch of Ireland took his seat upon it. So that we find Scota, the mythic representative of the divine kingship in its Celtic form, acting as the Egeria, or advisory and prophetic nymph, to her royal descendants and employing the stone of hereditary regality as her shrine. It follows that if the Scottish royal stone, which is known as the Coronation Stone, is not the genuine Lia Fail, she must have been thought of as inhabiting it in a complimentary sense only, as an Irish *banshee* might have been inherited by a younger branch of a family betaking itself to Scotland. And I think, as I have mentioned in my remarks on the subject of the *banshee*, to be found elsewhere in this book, the royal family of Scotland were favoured by the patronage of a spirit of that class. The whole legend is mnemonic of the ancient belief that the royal race of Ireland, and thus of Scotland and consequently of Britain, were, in their successive kings, the avatars or reincarnations of the Celtic sun-gods. It follows that, according to this belief, our present King George VI is, in the mythical sense at least, as certainly the living representative of the Celtic solar deity as the Emperor of Japan is of the sun-goddess Ama-Terasu. I may add that I have devoted so much space to this topic for the excellent reason that so much confusion prevails concerning it – a confusion which, as it affects the authenticity of the most ancient royal and prophetic relic in our islands, should surely be dispelled.

The occult science of augury or divination does not appear to have taken any form among the Celts unknown to the arcane practice of other races. Among the Celtic races we observe divination, or forecasting the future, by means of omens and auspices, through the media of the flight and motions of birds, by the casting of bones, or omen-sticks, the movements and direction taken by animals, by dreams and crystal-gazing, almost precisely as we find these several methods employed by many other races. Yet there were one or two forms of divining which may have been either exclusively of Celtic provenance or more particularly in use among the Celtic tribes, and these I will indicate when dealing with their circumstances.

Diodorus Siculus expressly states that the druids predicted the future from the flight of birds. Diodorus was a Sicilian Greek and a contemporary of Julius Caesar and Augustus, and if he did not penetrate to Britain, he is known to have exercised the greatest care in sifting his information. Indeed, his statement is fortified by quite a number of instances of omens drawn from bird-flight which appear in Scottish and Irish folktales. In a well-known Gaelic poem attributed to St Columba, the saint is made to say that he pays no heed to 'the voices of birds', which seems to imply that the druids to whom he alludes in these strophes, divined the future from bird-song, or flight, as did the augurs of ancient Rome. We have no 'official' statement of the manner in which the druids divined coming events by this means, but it seems probable that they effected it in a manner similar to that practised by the Roman augurs – that is, by marking out a given space and judging from the species of birds, lucky or otherwise, which alighted there or passed over it the nature of their flight and their cries, whether such and such a question was answered in the affirmative or negative. It is remarked that it was from Pictish settlers in Ireland that the Irish derived 'every spell, every charm, every augury by sneezing, voices of birds, and every omen'. The Irish would seem to have domesticated the wren and the raven for the purposes of divination. If a raven cried from above the bed in a house a distinguished grey-haired guest would visit it. If it called *bach*, the visitor would be a monk; if *gradh, gradh*, twice, it would be one of the clergy. If it called from the northeast end of the dwelling, robbers would raid the place; if it called from the door, strangers or soldiers. If it spoke with 'a small voice', chirping *err, err*, sickness would come upon the inhabitants. Each sound, position and movement of the tame bird had its own significance. The subject has been closely examined by Mr R.I. Best, the translator of D'Arbois de Jubainville's work on the Irish Mythological cycle, in *Ériu*, the journal of Irish studies (Vol. VIII.)

'I heard the cuckoo while fasting, and I knew the year would not go well with me,' exclaimed a Scottish Gael. It is unlucky in the Scottish Highlands to hear the first cuckoo of the season ere one has broken bread. When the minister of the parish of Dornoch, in 1816, was ill, a large cormorant settled on the steeple of the parish church, and the minister's death a few days later was regarded as a fulfilment of the fatal omen. When, thirty-five years later, a similar appearance occurred and the incumbent also died, the people regarded their predictions as amply justified. 'Raven-knowledge' or wisdom was also a well-known portent in the Highlands, and especially in the remote isle of St Kilda. It is referred to in a poem entitled 'The Massacre of the Rosses', and is amply documented by Toland in his *History of the Druids*. When at the village of Finglass, near Dublin, in 1697, he tells us, he struck up an acquaintance with two gentlemen 'of the old Irish stock', who were on private business, and says that these were assured that the affair they were concerned in would proceed fortunately because of the appearance on the road of a raven which had some white feathers in its plumage. They refused to stir until they saw in which direction the bird would fly, and when it disappeared southwards their certainty regarding the success of their mission was confirmed. They assured the Celtic sage that a raven so marked, and flying on the right hand of any person, croaking the while, 'was an infallible presage of good luck', and he, for his part, recalled that Pompeius Trogus, a Roman historian of the first century, had laid it down that 'the Gauls excel all others in the skill of augury'. Cicero, however, was of opinion that druidic predictions were as much grounded on conjecture as on the accepted rules of augury. He was probably thinking of the hard-and-fast Roman code as contained in the *Libri Augurales*, or 'Book of Auguries'.

A belief seems to have lingered in Lancashire that the cuckoo was able to predict how long one was to live – a reminiscence, perhaps, of Celtic augury by bird-call. In the northeast of Scotland a crow alighting on the roof of a house indicated that death was hovering over it. If rooks flew up and down in a tumbling fashion it was held to be ominous of windy conditions. To meet a magpie in the morning, in the same area, was unlucky. To scratch a magpie's tongue and insert in the wound a drop of blood from a human tongue was thought to endow the bird with human speech. A dove flying round a person's head was considered a sign of approaching mortality. Leyden remarks how unlucky this bird is in Scottish eyes.

In Wales the eagle was a bird of divination. 'The descendants of a person who had eaten eagle's flesh to the ninth generation possessed the gift of second sight.' In the time of Henry I, Gruffyd ap Rhys ap Tudor, the rightful Prince of Wales, according to native genealogies, was informed by Milo, Earl of Hereford, when they were riding past Llangorse Lake in Brecknockshire, that a tradition existed which averred that if the natural Prince of Wales commanded the waterfowl upon this lake to sing they would obey him. The Norman, who bore the minor title of Lord of Brecknock, himself tried the experiment, but without result. Gruffydd, dismounting from his horse, prayed earnestly that the Lord would justify his claim to the principality of Wales by causing the birds to sing, whereupon they rose into the air and chorused vociferously. When the incident was reported to the King he generously admitted the Welsh prince's hereditary claim, though he was careful to take no steps to enforce it.

The wren is also a bird of augury, as the Latin *Life of St Moliny* avers. 'The Pseudo-Cormac Glossary,' says George Henderson, 'explains it as *drui-en*, a druid bird.' In Welsh the wren's name is *dryw*, an etymological resemblance of significance. O'Curry remarks that the druids divined the course of events from the chirping of tame wrens. Duncan Campbell, in his *Memoirs*, mentions that 'some will defer going abroad, tho' called by business of the greatest consequence if, happening to look out of the window, they see a single crow'. It will, of course, be understood that here I am concerned only with such beliefs as may properly be regarded as Celtic in origin and ominous in their nature, and not with the British folklore of birds in general, although I cannot claim that the above enumeration of such instances is in any way exhaustive.

Omens from the habits or movements of animals were certainly drawn by the Celts. Before going into battle against the Romans, Boadicea, the courageous Queen of the Iceni, a British tribe dwelling in Norfolk and Suffolk, drew a hare from her bosom, 'and,' says Cassius Dio, 'since it ran on what they considered the auspicious side the whole multitude shouted with pleasure', seeing victory within their grasp. 'The hare,' says Rhys, 'was regarded as an animal sacred to the Celtic Zeus or to his associate.' Superstitions still cling to the hare in Wales. Sir Laurence Gomme thought that the above occurrence was an instance of the totemic animal serving as an omen to its clansmen. The head of a black bull was ominous of evil throughout Scotland – wherefore is unknown – but the appearance of such a trophy at the 'Black Dinner' given to Earl Douglas and his brother at Edinburgh Castle by the supporters of James II was the signal for the massacre of the unhappy guests.

In Celtic Devonshire, if a swarm of bees alights on a dead tree it is believed that there will be a death in the owner's house within the year. A strange swarm settling in one's garden implies an access of prosperity. Divination by worms was also formerly practised in Scotland. If a certain worm in a medicinal spring on the top of a hill in the parish of Strathdon were found alive it augured the survival of a patient, and in a well at Ardnacloich, in Appin, the questing invalid, 'if he bee to dye, shall find a dead worm therein, or a quick one, if health be to follow'. A witch, arraigned for sorcery, was charged with having described a circle in a field and making a hole in the midst of it, from which issued a great worm, followed by a smaller one, and a third, which died because it could not crawl out of the circle as the others had done. She informed those who had sought her advice that the first worm represented the head of the household, who should live, that the second and smaller worm was an infant, still unborn to his wife, and that it should survive, and that the last stood for the woman herself, who should die – 'all of which came to pass'.

I see nothing unreasonable in the theory that these ominous beliefs concerning birds, animals and insects represent the survivals or reminiscences of an older druidic system of augury, from which they have descended. They are in no wise associated as regards their origin with witchcraft, or later arcane practice, which appears to have merely adopted them, and they seem to me to be associated with a much more definite and well-digested system of augury than any which the looser and less intelligent sorcery of a medieval peasantry could have devised. Indeed, the evidence for the existence of such a divinatory system in druidic times is much too strong to admit of the theory of a more modern origin.

Omens were frequently drawn from the direction taken by the smoke and flames of sacred fires and from the appearance of the clouds. The Irish *file* or druid bard discovered auspices by the practice of what was known as the *teinm laegha*, or the 'analysis of song'. He composed verses and sang them over any person or object respecting which he sought information, or placed his magical staff over a man or woman to secure the arcane information he sought respecting them. The Irish diviners forecast the appropriate time for building a house by the stars. If an Irish druid wished to get on the track of stolen goods, he sang an incantation through his half-open fist, using it as a trumpet. If this did not serve, he went to sleep and traced the stolen property through a dream, or trance. What was known as 'illumination by rhymes' was brought about in a heavy sleep by a professional seer, who, after roaring violently, became lucid and gave the information required.

It was in a dream, too, that the beautiful Eachtach, the favourite of Art, son of Conn of the Hundred Battles, beheld a terrible vision, in which she saw her head slashed from her shoulders and a tree growing out of her neck, whose branches overspread the whole kingdom of Ireland, as Keating tells us. But the sea rose and destroyed the tree, and when a second sprang up in its place it, too, was blasted by a west wind and perished. This dream Art interpreted as signifying that he himself would be slain in an impending battle, and that their son, still unborn, should sit upon the throne of Ireland, but would die from a fish-bone sticking in his throat. The second tree symbolized this prince's son, who would perish in strife with the Fianna Eirionn, or Militia of Ireland, who would rise in arms against him and who were represented by the western tempest. All these happenings came to pass, as the lady's dream foretold.

What was known in the Scottish Highlands as *slinneineachd*, and in occult practice generally as *scapulimancy*, or divining by means of the shoulder blades of animals, was formerly engaged in by certain people as a definite profession. Important events were foretold in the life of the owner of a slaughtered animal from the marks on its shoulder or blade bones. The right blade bone of a black pig or sheep was considered the most suitable for this purpose. It was thoroughly boiled so that not a particle of flesh adhered to it, but great care had to be exercised to ensure that it was not scratched or marked in any way. The bone was then divided into areas corresponding to the natural features of the district in which the divination was to be made. 'Certain marks indicated a crowd of people, met at a funeral, fight, sale etc.' The largest hole or indentation symbolized the grave of the beast's owner, and from its position the problem of whether he should survive the current year, or otherwise, was resolved. If it lay near the side of the bone, the omen was fatal, but if in its centre, prosperity was indicated.

A celebrated bone-reader in Barra, says J.G. Campbell, was present at the festivities connected with the completion of the Castle of the MacNeills and was pressed to divine its fate. He foretold that it would become an abode of thrushes, and that this would happen 'when the Rattle stone was found', when people worked at gathering seaweed in a village then far from the sea, and when deer swam across to Barra from Uist. 'All this happened and the castle is now in ruins.' On the night of the treacherous massacre of Glencoe, a party of MacDonalds were amusing themselves by examining the shoulder blade of a beast that had been slaughtered to provide food for the Government troops who had been billeted upon them, and who subsequently attacked them. Suddenly one of them exclaimed, 'There is a shedding of blood in the glen,' and sensing that treason of some kind was afoot, they made a hasty departure and were among the few who escaped from butchery on that terrible night, when Highlander slew Highlander without mercy. Numerous references to divination by shoulder blade are made in the Old Testament, and the right shoulder of a sacrificed animal was the especial perquisite of the priest. On one occasion Samuel set before Saul 'the shoulder and that which was upon it', to elucidate a divinatory act (Samuel ix, 24). Dalyell states that 'the humbler class of Scottish seers' turned towards the east 'when divining futurity from the lines, shades or transparence disclosed by its inequalities'. And MacLeod ('Theophilus Insulanus'), in his book *On the Second Sight*, alludes to it as 'another kind of divination, whereby, on looking into the shoulder blade of a sheep, goat etc, as in a book, some skilful in that occult science pretend to read future events'.

John of Salisbury speaks of this practice as being common in England in the twelfth century, and Giraldus Cambrensis writes of it as a familiar proceeding in the Wales of the early thirteenth century. He mentions that the bone usually employed was the right shoulder blade of a ram, boiled, not roasted, and he provides specific instances in which this method was resorted to. That it was also customarily an Irish usage is clear from an allusion by Camden. The practice had, indeed, a wide acceptance among peoples in many parts of the world.

What were known as *coelbreni*, or 'omen-sticks', were, it is alleged, employed by the druids for casting lots. As the sticks fell, so the diviner interpreted the fates. On All Saints Eve (31 October), in Wales, it was formerly customary to build a great fire known as *coel coeth*, and when it was almost extinguished, to mark a white stone for each member of the household and throw the same into the ashes. In the morning these were sought for, and if any were missing, the person who cast it in, it was believed, 'would not see another All Saints Eve'. This custom was also maintained in Scotland on the same date.

That divination by crystal-gazing was familiar to the Celtic peoples is evident. When prophesying to Queen Maeve of Ulster before the Cattle Raid of Cooley concerning its probable results, the mystic maiden Fedelm appears to have gazed into a glass or crystal, 'seeing all red'. To eat of a roasted egg for three Sundays in succession and then with unwashed hands to wash one's eyes was regarded in the Highlands as imparting mystical knowledge of all things. To divine the presence of the distemper known as *esane*, ascribed to fairy influence (probably the 'fairy stroke'), Irish necromancers put some burning coals into a cup of clear water and called upon the elves from the four parts of the compass.

A strange method of divination practised in the North of Scotland was 'the swimming of names in water'. It was resorted to in cases of theft, in order to discover the guilty person. The names of those suspected were written upon slips of paper and cast into water, and that which sank was regarded as belonging to the miscreant. In the same area, the seat of a disease was divined by taking three stones representing the head, the heart and the body, and placing them overnight in the hot ashes of the hearth. In the morning they were dropped into a basin of water, and that which made the loudest sound when it came in contact with the water revealed the part chiefly affected.

In Scotland dumb people were frequently regarded as diviners and even as necromancers. Dalyell cites several such cases in his *Darker Superstitions of Scotland*. 'Jonka Dyneis, being questioned after a vision, "could not give answer, bot stude as if bereft of hir senssis"', and after a vision, or some spectral illusion, one Elspeth Reoch 'had na power of hir toung, nor could not speik'. Penance was imposed on several persons for consulting a dumb woman regarding a theft, while a man was fined for letting a house to Margaret Rannald and her two dumb daughters. For being acquainted with 'the signs' of a dumb woman, two people in Edinburgh were cited to appear before the Kirk Session there in the year 1596. Dumb folk alleged to be sorcerers appear to have abounded in the Scotland of the sixteenth century, and it is plain from the circumstances of their trials that quite a fair proportion of these merely simulated speechlessness. The mere fact that a sorcerer was dumb appears to have attracted scores of people to seek his advice. In any case the dumb were thought to possess second sight and an uncanny prescience of future events. Probably the strange sounds they emitted and the curious gestures they made heightened the popular belief in their arcane or diabolic associations.

Gregor, in his *Folk-lore of the North-East of Scotland*, tells of a weird method of divination by which it was thought possible to discover whether a case of illness would end in death. Two holes were dug, one being described as 'the living grave' and the other as 'the dead grave'. The sick person was laid between them, without being told which was which. If he turned with the face to the 'living grave' he would recover; if the reverse happened he would perish. For engaging in this practice a woman named Marjorie Pulmer, who had an ailing child, was debarred from the Sacrament by the Presbytery of Cullen, in Banffshire, in the year 1649.

Elsewhere in this book I have dealt with the subject of human sacrifice by the druids and the divinatory methods resorted to by them on such occasions. They also appear to have used for the purpose of divining a species of frame, known as *peithynen*, or 'the Elucidator'. This object has sometimes been described as 'the druids' wheel'. Sir John Daniel (who illustrates the apparatus on page 136 of his book) says of this machine: 'The Elucidator consisted of several staves called faith-sticks or lots, on which the judicial maxims were cut, and which, being put into a frame, were turned at pleasure, so that each staff or bar, when formed with three flat sides, represented a triplet; when squared or made with four flat sides, a stanza (in verse). The frame itself was an oblong, with right angles.'

It has been said that the druids also divined from the appearance of the roots of trees and from the howling of dogs, as from the manner in which smoke arose from a fire. Divination by sticks is alluded to frequently in the mystic Welsh poems. Thus Taliesin exclaims:

I am Taliesin,
Chief of the Bards of the West,
I am acquainted with every sprig
In the cave of the Arch-diviner

and Llywarch Hen alludes very freely to the 'Elucidator' in one of his poems. Davies also informs us that the druids of Ireland employed 'an alphabet of their own which, in all its essential points, agrees to that of the Bards in Britain'. It was, he says, 'a magical alphabet', and was used by them in their divinations. There were, however, three such alphabets in Ireland, he adds, and these have been described by O'Flaherty in his *Ogygia*, and by the present writer in his work *The Mysteries of Britain*.

The Scottish expression 'fey', used of a person who appears to be fated or doomed, or raised to a pitch of supernatural excitement, is usually associated with a condition of mind in which the sufferer becomes ecstatic or prophetic. It appears to be derived from the Old English 'fay', signifying 'enchanted'. Those who were afflicted with it, says Kirk, were supposed to have been wounded by fairy weapons, or were 'fairy-struck', 'which makes them do somewhat verie unlike their former Practice'. Dalyell says that the persons who lost their white stones in the Bealltainn fire were regarded as fey, or 'devoted'. But the term appears to have also had a magical meaning in Old Irish. According to Cormac's *Glossary* the *Fé*, or magic wand, was so called, while the expression *Fá* seems to have been associated with the Lia Fail, or Stone of Royal Destiny, and with the spell of Fith-Fath (pronounced Fee-Fa).

I must not conclude this chapter without some remarks upon the weird women whom Shakespeare introduced into the greatest of his tragedies. Do the 'witches' in *Macbeth* actually reflect the Celtic idea of prophetic sibyls? Are they merely ordinary Highland sorceresses, or a memory of Caledonian druidesses? The question is not unimportant, as the very frequent presentation of the great work alluded to may well inspire erroneous ideas concerning the nature of Celtic sibylline characteristics in the minds of thousands.

The whole passage, so far as criticism is concerned, has produced an extraordinary tangle of Gordian knots. Nor is this surprising, for when the man of letters approaches mythical or occult problems he is, as a rule, much in the same category with the blacksmith who claims to be an authority upon motor engines. Neither the old criticism nor the new has uttered anything definitive concerning the weird sisters who so sedulously haunted the Celtic monarch nor have the oracles of folklore been other than equivocal regarding them.

The early nineteenth century saw in Shakespeare's weird women 'typical Scotch witches', and the prints which illustrated its contemporary theatre displayed them as attired in voluminous swathings of tartan. Critics wrangled as to whether they were terrestrial or spiritual in origin, but as the main facts concerning witchcraft were still obscure, the conclusions they arrived at were more or less negative. Indeed, Shakespeare himself left the question of their actual affinities very much an open one. In one scene he gave them the prophetic character of Norns or Fates, while in the next they appear as very ordinary Elizabethan witches who might have haunted the purlieus of Wapping or the Burgh. In the first of these capacities they foretell events and unroll the flying scroll of visionary prophecy in a manner no self-respecting British witch would ever have thought of doing, while in the second they definitely reveal themselves as the creatures of literary reflection, the hag-shapes of a popular belief in sorcery.

That Shakespeare made his fatal trio speak their lines in the Sibylline metre of accepted magical utterance seems to show that he must have gone to ancient Rome or to Scandinavia for hints as to the speech of the sisterhood of sorcery, even though the language he puts into the mouths of his crones is by no means exclusively classical or Scanian. The opening scene has been strangely neglected by generations of critics, although it strikes the keynote of the tragedy to come. It gives the impression that the weird women have been flying over the field of battle, where King Duncan is contending with the Norsemen, much as the Scandinavian Valkyries or the Morrigans of Irish myth were wont to hover above the plains of conflict. Yet

311

this rather obvious clue remains so far unnoticed both by critic and theatrical producer. In the same breath, however, in which the witches chant of battle, they call upon their familiars Paddock and Grimalkin, as any beldame from Suffolk or Essex might have done, for the familiar was certainly not a ubiquitous figure in British witchcraft, being confined almost entirely to the southeast of England and nearly unknown to Scotland.

It is in the third scene of Act I, however, that the weird sisters appear in what most critics believe to be their truly Jacobean or Elizabethan guise as genuine English witches. Yet in this passage practically every expression they employ, every allusion they make, if we except the First Witch's lines descriptive of her meeting with the 'rump-fed ronyon' munching her chestnuts, proves the opposite. Even here the local colour disappears, for the allusion to the witch sailing in a sieve is Scythian, and has only two definitely British analogies, the best known of which is that of the North Berwick and Edinburgh covens who had conspired to shipwreck James VI on his return from his honeymoon at Oslo. These are said to have put to sea for that purpose in their 'riddles or cives'. Had Shakespeare read *Newes from Scotland*, the description of a contemporary English journalist of that dingily picturesque incident? The raising of winds mentioned in this scene is more in keeping with the witches' character as Scottish beldames of the more ancient world, derived as it is from Finnish magical practice current in the Orkneys and the Western Isles.

The sisters predict the destinies of Macbeth and Banquo as might the Greek Moirai or the Norns of Scandinavia. I cannot recall a single instance in the history of native English or Scottish witchcraft racy of prophecy in the grand manner. But that prophecy was practised by druidesses we have already seen. It is when we find them calling themselves the 'weird sisters', however, that we receive the first clue to their actual character and position.

For the expression 'weird' carries us back to the Scandinavian Norns. That it was in common use in the older Scotland as a word expressive of prophetic foresight is clear from several instances, as, for example, that in Gawain Douglas's translation of Vergil, and in the *Complaynt of Scotland*, where, among the titles of popular tales, some now entirely lost to us so far as their content is concerned, is to be found that of 'The Thrie Weird Systers', which, in all likelihood, had reference to the occult passages in the history of Macbeth, and may have been taken from a more ancient Celtic or Norse original. The three Scandinavian Norns were Urdhr, Verdandi and Skuld, the Present, the Past and the Future, and the name of the first was used to describe generically all three of them as dispensers of destiny. From this is derived the word 'weird' as implying the prophetic quality, which came in time, and by popular acceptance, to describe the uncanny or the occult.

The Norns were thought of as prophetic concerning the destiny of children at their birth, but they were also gifted with powers to predict the future at any period of life, as the 'Nornagests Saga' makes plain when it tells us that they 'travelled about the land, foretelling their fate to men'. In like manner the old Roman Fatae, or Fates, became in the Romance-speaking lands of France, Spain and Italy the Fée, the Fatua and the Hada, travelling sisters who foretold men's futures from the cradle to the grave. In the older Scotland a similar trio of supernatural spaewives seem to have 'dreed their weird' to all and sundry. Indeed, Norns, Fates and the Greek Moirai would appear to have had a common origin in a primitive Pan-European mythology.

It is, however, in the cavern scene, where they are discovered at their nefarious rites with the bubbling cauldron, that the three sisters depart more than ever from British witch-practice. For the cauldron is Scythian, Scandinavian, Finnish, and still more remotely Hellenic in its folklore symbolism. Nor do the ingredients of the seething pot, as 'listed' by Shakespeare, bear any resemblance to the components of any known system of witchcraft or sorcery, with the exception of the toad and the 'witches' mummy', the desiccated corpse-flesh familiar to Scottish witch-lore and known to some English witches of Shakespeare's time. But the cauldron, as we have seen, is also Celtic, though in the Celtic version of it its components were not of a deadly nature.

The phantasmagoria revealed to Macbeth in this scene, the crowned figures and blood-boltered babes, are also utterly alien to the humilities of British native sorcery, and are reminiscent of the more highly coloured necromantic spectacles of mediaeval and classical magic. These visions were, of course, designed out of compliment to James VI and I, the new King of Great Britain, and were prophetic, in the poetic sense, of a presumed illustrious survival of his house, as well, perhaps, as sympathetic to his notorious personal interest in witchcraft – though the revelation of a glorious descent through the agency of those very arcane forces which the royal James had so persistently sought to destroy appears as scarcely tactful in the circumstances!

Shakespeare's witches are therefore a mingling of the Elizabethan English witch, of the Scandinavian Norns and the classical Fates, while the ritual they employ is mainly Scythian, Finnish or Scandinavian. That the weird sisters in the lost Scottish legend concerning them – that alluded to in the *Complaynt of Scotland* – were a later conception of the three Scandinavian Norns is scarcely to be doubted, and that the idea of these prophetesses was imported from Norway to the north of Scotland, which, in Macbeth's time, was occupied by people of Scandinavian origin, seems highly probable. That these circumstances were reflected in Holinshed's *Chronicle*, from which Shakespeare certainly derived the plot of *Macbeth*, and that links between Holinshed's account and an older Celtic-Scandinavian narrative are visible in more than one of the more venerable Scottish historians, is scarcely to be gainsaid. Of course it is just possible that the weird sisters may have been derived from the Irish *Badbhs*, or *Morrigans*, the Valkyrie women of Irish myth. In a word, Shakespeare's witches are not 'Scotch', as most authorities have believed them to be. But that they possess certain druidic traits – the gift of prevision and the use of a cauldron seemingly associated with the gift of prophecy – cannot be denied.

Further Reading

The following is but a small selection from the huge literature on the visionary and prophetic traditions, particularly as they relate to the history of the Celts. Many of these titles were useful in the compilation of this collection and are especially valuable for a study of the heritage of seership.

Aneirin, *Y Gododdin: Britain's Oldest Heroic Poem* (ed. and trans. by A.O.H. Jarman), The Welsh Classics, Dyfed, 1988

Atkinson, G.M., 'The Ancient Ogham Treatises' in *Journal of the Royal Historical and Archaeological Association of Ireland*, 4th series, vol. 3, 1874–5, Dublin, 1876

Bergin, Osborn, 'Irish Bardic Poetry', a lecture delivered before the National Literary Society, Dublin, 15 April 1912, in *Journal of the Ivernian Society*, vol. v, 1912–13, pp. 153–66; reprinted Dolmen Press, Port Laoise, 1970

Best, R.I., 'Prognostication from the Raven and the Wren', *Eriu*, vol. viii, 1916, pp. 120–26; see pp. 123–5

Bonwick, J., *Irish Druids and Irish Religions*, Dorset Press, Marlborough, 1986

Brennan, M., *The Boyne Valley Vision*, Dolmen Press, Port Laoise, 1980

Bromwich, Rachel (ed. and trans.), *Triodd Ynys Prydein* ('The Welsh Triads'), University of Wales Press, Cardiff, 1961 (2nd ed., 1978)

Caldecott, M., *Taliesin and Avagddu*, Bran's Head, Frome, Somerset, 1983

Campbell, John G., 'Augury, Dream and Prophecy' in *Superstitions of the Highlands and Islands of Scotland*, James Maclehose & Son, Glasgow, 1900

Carney, James, *Medieval Irish Lyrics with The Irish Bardic Poet*, Dolmen Press, Port Laoise, 1985

Chadwick, Nora K., 'Imbas Forosnai' in *Scottish Gaelic Studies*, vol. 4, 1934–5, pp. 97–135

Chadwick, Nora K., 'Dreams in Early European Literature' in *Celtic Studies* (ed. by J. Carney and D. Greene), Routledge & Kegan Paul, London, 1968, p. 38

Cross, T.P. and Slover, C.H., *Ancient Irish Tales*, Hodges, Figgis & Co., Dublin, 1936; Harrap, London, 1937

Davidson, H.R. Ellis (ed.), *The Seer in Celtic and Other Traditions*, John Donald, Edinburgh, 1989

Diak, F.C., 'The Origins of the Ogham Alphabet' in *Scottish Gaelic Studies*, vol. 3, 1934

Dillon, Myles, *The Cycles of the Kings*, Oxford University Press, Oxford, 1946

Ellis, P.B., *A Dictionary of Irish Mythology*, Constable, London, 1987

Ettlinger, E., 'Omens and Celtic Warfare' in *Man*, vol. xliii, no. 4, 1943, pp. 11–17; see pp. 11–12

Ettlinger, E., 'Precognitive Dreams in Celtic Legend' in *Folklore*, vol. lix, 1948, pp. 97–117

Evans, J.G., *Poems from the Book of Taliesin*, Tremvan Llanbedrog, 1915

Flower, R., *The Irish Tradition*, Clarendon Press, Oxford, 1953

Ford, Patrick K. (ed. and trans.), *The Mabinogion and Other Medieval Welsh Tales*, University of California Press, Berkeley, 1977

Ford, Patrick K., 'The Well of Nechtan and "La Gloire Luminesse"' in *Myth in Indo-European Antiquity* (ed. by G.J. Larson), University of California Press, Berkeley, 1974, pp. 67–74

Gantz, Jeffrey, *Early Irish Myths and Sagas*, Penguin Books, Harmondsworth, 1981

Geoffrey of Monmouth, 'The Prophecies of Merlin' in *Six Old English Chronicles* (ed. and trans. by J.A. Giles), G. Bell, London, 1910

Geoffrey of Monmouth, *Vita Merlini* (trans. by J.J. Parry), University of Illinois Press, Urbana, 1925

Geoffrey of Monmouth, *Life of Merlin* (ed. and trans. by B. Clarke), University of Wales Press, Cardiff, 1973

Gerald of Wales, *The Journey Through Wales/ The Description of Wales* (trans. by Lewis Thorpe), Penguin Books, Harmondsworth, 1978

Gerald of Wales, *The Historical Works* (ed. and trans. by T. Wright), Bohn's Antiquarian Library, London, 1863

Glass, Justine, *The Story of Fulfilled Prophecy*, Cassell, London, 1969

Gose Jr, E.B., *The World of the Irish Wonder Tale*, University of Toronto Press, Toronto, 1985

Graves, Robert, *The White Goddess*, Faber & Faber, London, 1952

Green, Miranda, *The Gods of the Celts*, Alan Sutton, Gloucester, 1986

Green, Miranda, *Symbol and Image in Celtic Religious Art*, Routledge, London, 1989

Griffiths, Margaret, 'Vaticination in Wales Prior to the Twelfth Century' in *Early Vaticination in Welsh with English Parallels*, University of Wales Press, Cardiff, 1932

Guest, Lady Charlotte (ed. and trans.), *The Mabinogion*, J.M. Dent, London, 1906; David Nutt, London, 1910; Ballantyne Press, London, 1910

Gwynn, Edward (ed. and trans.), *The Metrical Dindsenchas* (parts 1–5), Hodges, Figgis & Co., Dublin, 1903–35

Hartland, Ernest S. 'The Voice of the Stone of Destiny' in *Folklore*, vol. xiv, 1908

Henderson, George, 'Illumination' in *Survivals in Belief among the Celts*, J. Maclehose & Son, Glasgow, 1911

Hersh, J., 'Ancient Celtic Incubation' in *Sundance Community Dream Journal*, vol. iii, winter 1979, pp. 81–90

Hull, Eleanor, 'The Silver Bough in Irish Legend' in *Folklore*, vol. xix, 1908, pp. 431–45

Humphreys, E., *The Taliesin Tradition*, Black Raven Press, 1983

Jackson, Kenneth Hurstone, *A Celtic Miscellany*, Routledge & Kegan Paul, London, 1951

Jones, Gwyn and Jones, Thomas (trans.), *The Mabinogion*, J.M. Dent, London, 1948

Jones, O., Williams, Edward and Pughe, William Owen (eds.), *The Myvyrian Arhcaiology of Wales*, Thomas Gere, Denbigh, 1870

Jones, T.G., *Welsh Folk-lore and Folk-custom*, Methuen, London, 1930

Joyce, P.W., *A Social History of Ancient Ireland* (2 vols.), Longman, Green & Co., London, 1903

Jubainville, Henri d'Arbois de, *The Irish Mythological Cycle* (trans. by Richard Irvine), O'Donoghue & Co., Dublin, 1903; (trans. by R.I. Best), Hodges, Figgis & Co., Dublin, 1903

Kinsella, Thomas (trans.), *Taín Bó Cuailgnè*, ('The Cattle Raid of Cooley'), Oxford University Press, Oxford, 1970

Knott, E., and Murphy, G., *Early Irish Literature*, Routledge & Kegan Paul, London, 1966

Krippner, S., 'Dreams and Shamanism' in *Shamanism* (compiled by S. Nicholson), Theosophical Publishing House, London, 1987

Ledwick, Edward, 'On the Ogham Characters' in *Antiquities of Ireland*, John Jones, Dublin, 1804

Lloyd, John Edward, *A History of Wales* (2 vols.), Longman, Green & Co., London, 1911

Lofmark, C., *Bards and Heroes*, Llanerch Enterprises, Llanerch, 1989

Loomis, R.S., *Wales and the Arthurian Legend*, University of Wales Press, Cardiff, 1956

Macalister, R.A. Stewart, 'Ogham' in *The Secret Languages of Ireland*, Cambridge University Press, 1937; Amorica Books Co., St Helier, Jersey, 1976

Mackenzie, Alexander, *The Prophecies of the Brahan Seer*, Edinburgh, 1899; Constable, London, 1998

Mackenzie, Donald A., *Scottish Folk-lore and Folk Life*, Blackie & Son, Glasgow, 1935

McNeill, F.M., *The Silver Bough* (vol. 1), Canongate Publishing, Edinburgh, 1989

Mallory, J.P., *In Search of the Indo-Europeans*, Thames & Hudson, London, 1989

Matthews, Caitlín, *Mabon and the Mysteries of Britain*, Arkana, Harmondsworth, 1986

Matthews, Caitlín, *Arthur and the Sovereignty of Britain*, Arkana, Harmondsworth, 1989

Matthews, Caitlín, *Elements of the Celtic Tradition*, Element Books, Shaftesbury, 1989

Matthews, Caitlín, *The Celtic Book of the Dead*, Thorsons, Wellingborough, 1991; St Martin's Press, New York, 1992

Matthews, Caitlín, *A Celtic Yearbook*, Godsfield Press, Alresford, 1995

Matthews, Caitlín, *A Celtic Devotional*, Godsfield Press, Alresford, 1996

Matthews, John, 'Auguries, Dreams and Incubatory Sleep' in *Psychology and the Spiritual Traditions* (ed. by R.J. Stewart), Element Books, Shaftesbury, 1990

Matthews, John, *A Celtic Reader*, Aquarian Press, Wellingborough, 1991

Matthews, John, *Song of Taliesin: Stories and Poems from the Books of Broceliande*, Aquarian Press, Wellingborough, 1991

Matthews, John, *Taliesin: Shamanism and the Bardic Mysteries in Britain and Ireland*, HarperCollins, London, 1991

Matthews, John (ed.), *The World Atlas of Divination*, Headline Books, London, 1992

Matthews, John, *The Celtic Shaman's Pack*, Element Books, Shaftesbury, 1992

Matthews, John (ed.), *The Druid Source Book*, Cassell, London, 1996

Matthews, John (ed.), *The Bardic Source Book*, Cassell, London, 1998

Matthews, John and Caitlín, *The Western Way* (2 vols.), Arkana, London, 1985–6

Matthews, John and Caitlín *The Aquarian Guide to British and Irish Mythology*, Aquarian Press, Wellingborough, 1988

Matthews, John and Caitlín, *The Little Book of Celtic Wisdom*, Element Books, Shaftesbury, 1993

Matthews, John and Caitlín, *The Encyclopedia of Celtic Wisdom: A Celtic Shaman's Sourcebook*, Element Books, Shaftesbury, 1994

Meyer, Kuno (trans.), 'The Vision of MacConglinne' in *Aislinge Meic Conglinne*, David Nutt, London, 1892

Meyer, Kuno, *The Voyage of Brân, Son of Febal* (2 vols.), David Nutt, London, 1895

Meyer, Kuno, *Fianaigecht*, Hodges, Figgis & Co, Dublin, 1910

Minahane, John, *The Christian Druids*, Sanas Press, Dublin 1993

Morris, J., *The Matter of Wales*, Oxford University Press, Oxford, 1984

Murphy, Gerard, *Early Irish Lyrics*, Oxford University Press, Oxford, 1956

Nagy, J.F., 'Otter, Salmon and Eel in Traditional Gaelic Narrative' in *The Celtic Review*, vol. 20–23, 1985–8, pp. 123–44

O'Curry, Eugene, *Manners and Customs of the Ancient Irish* (3 vols.), Williams & Norgate, 1873

O'Driscoll, Robert (ed.), *The Celtic Consciousness*, Canongate Publishing, Edinburgh; Dolmen Press, Port Laoise, 1982

O'Grady, S. (ed. and trans.), *Silva Gadelica* (2 vols.), Williams & Norgate, 1892

O'hOgain, Daithi, *The Hero in Irish Folk History*, Gill & Macmillan, Dublin, 1985

O'hOgain, Daithi, *Fionn mac Cumhail: Images of the Gaelic Hero*, Gill & Macmillan, Dublin 1988

O'Keefe, J.G. (trans.), 'The Poems of Suibhne Geilt' in *The Adventures of Suibhne Geilt*, David Nutt, London, 1913

O'Rahilly, Thomas F., *Early Irish History and Mythology*, Institute for Advanced Studies, Dublin, 1946

Parry, Thomas, *A History of Welsh Literature* (trans. by H. Idris Bell), Clarendon Press, Oxford, 1955

Pennar, M., *The Black Book of Carmarthen*, Llanerch Enterprises, Llanerch, 1989

Pennar, M. (trans.), *Taliesin Poems*, Llanerch Enterprises, Llanerch, 1989

Rees, Alwyn and Brinley, *Celtic Heritage*, Thames & Hudson, London, 1961

Rhys, John, *Lectures on the Origin and Growth of Religion as Illustrated by Celtic Heathendom*, Williams & Norgate, London, 1888

Rhys, J., *Celtic Folklore, Welsh and Manx* (2 vols.), Wildwood House, London, 1980

Scott, Robert D., 'The Thumb of Knowledge' in *Legends of Finn, Sigurd and Taliesin*, Columbia University, New York, 1930

Sjoestedt, M.L., *Gods and Heroes of the Celts*, Turtle Island Foundation, Berkeley, California, 1982

Skene, W.F. (ed. and trans.), *The Four Ancient Books of Wales* (2 vols.), Edmonston & Douglas, Edinburgh, 1869; AMS Press, New York, 1984–5

Spence, Lewis, 'Prophecy and Divination' in *The Magic Arts in Celtic Britain*, Rider & Co., London, 1946

Stephens, M. (ed.), *The Oxford Companion to the Literature of Wales*, Oxford University Press, Oxford; Irish Academic Press, Dublin, 1986

Stewart, R.J., *Celtic Gods, Celtic Goddesses*, Cassell, London, 1990

Stewart R.J. and Williamson, Robin, *Celtic Bards, Celtic Druids*, Cassell, London, 1996

Wentz, W.Y. Evans, *The Fairy Faith in Celtic Countries*, Lemma Publishing Co., New York, 1973; Colin Smythe, Gerrards Cross, Buckinghamshire, 1977

Williams, G., *An Introduction to Welsh Poetry*, Faber & Faber, London, 1953

Williams, I., *Lectures on Early Welsh Poetry*, Institute for Advanced Studies, Dublin, 1970

Williams, I., *The Beginnings of Welsh Poetry* (ed. by Rachel Bromwich), University of Wales Press, Cardiff, 1980

Williamson, Robin, *The Craneskin Bag: Celtic Stores and Poems*, Canongate Publishing, Edinburgh, 1979

Index

318